A PLUME BOOK

THE SOURCE FIELD INVESTIGATIONS

DAVID WILCOCK is a lecturer, filmmaker, and researcher of ancient civilizations, consciousness science, and new paradigms of matter and energy. He lives in California.

Praise for *The Source Field Investigations*

"A magnificent case . . . that a Golden Age is indeed within our grasp."
—from the foreword by Graham Hancock,
author of *Fingerprints of the Gods*

"We are not alone in the universe. And we have David Wilcock to prove it—and to guide us to this golden prophecy."   —James V. Hart

"The author writes a narrative as fast-paced and scintillating as a sci-fi novel."   —*Kirkus Reviews*

"Read this book."   —*Omega New Age Directory*

"David Wilcock is a dedicated and passionate investigator determined to understand this chapter in our collective history."
—*New Dawn* magazine

"Full of amazing ideas, philosophical notions, and alternative science . . . This is an important book."   —*Red Dirt Report*

THE
SOURCE FIELD
INVESTIGATIONS

The Hidden Science and Lost Civilizations

Behind the 2012 Prophecies

DAVID WILCOCK

A PLUME BOOK

PLUME
Published by the Penguin Group
Penguin Group (USA) Inc., 375 Hudson Street, New York, New York 10014, U.S.A. • Penguin Group
(Canada), 90 Eglinton Avenue East, Suite 700, Toronto, Ontario, Canada M4P 2Y3 (a division of Pearson
Penguin Canada Inc.) • Penguin Books Ltd., 80 Strand, London WC2R 0RL, England • Penguin Ireland,
25 St. Stephen's Green, Dublin 2, Ireland (a division of Penguin Books Ltd.) • Penguin Group (Australia),
250 Camberwell Road, Camberwell, Victoria 3124, Australia (a division of Pearson Australia Group Pty.
Ltd.) • Penguin Books India Pvt. Ltd., 11 Community Centre, Panchsheel Park, New Delhi – 110 017,
India • Penguin Group (NZ), 67 Apollo Drive, Rosedale, Auckland 0632, New Zealand (a division of
Pearson New Zealand Ltd.) • Penguin Books (South Africa) (Pty.) Ltd., 24 Sturdee Avenue, Rosebank,
Johannesburg 2196, South Africa

Penguin Books Ltd., Registered Offices: 80 Strand, London WC2R 0RL, England

Published by Plume, a member of Penguin Group (USA) Inc. Previously published in a Dutton edition.

First Plume Printing, August 2012
10   9   8   7   6   5

Copyright © David Wilcock, 2011
All rights reserved

Ⓟ REGISTERED TRADEMARK—MARCA REGISTRADA

The Library of Congress has catalogued the Dutton edition as follows:

Wilcock, David, 1973-
   The source field investigations : the hidden science and lost civilizations behind the
2012 prophecies / David Wilcock.
      p.   cm.
   Includes bibliographical references and index.
   ISBN 978-0-525-95204-6 (hc.)
   ISBN 978-0-452-29797-5 (pbk.)
   1. Force and energy—Miscellanea.   2. Cosmology—Miscellanea.   3. Two thousand
twelve, A.D.   I. Title.
   BF1999.W5582   2011
   001.9—dc23   2011016585

Printed in the United States of America

This book is dedicated to you, the One Infinite Creator—the author of space, time, matter, energy, biology and consciousness—now reading these words in your temporary human form.

Contents

PART TWO: TIME AND SPACE

List of Figures

Foreword

by James V. Hart

Allow me to take you back in time, before David Wilcock welcomes you to the future. It is one A.M. on Monday, September 28, 2009: exactly 3 years, 84 days, 10 hours, 11 minutes and 11 seconds before the world ends on December 21, 2012. I am in my barn in Pound Ridge, New York, writing what I think is the best screenplay I have ever been involved with since I was fortunate enough to have written the original screenplay for the motion picture *Contact*, having worked with the late, great man of the universe, Carl Sagan. And then I receive an e-mail from my writing partner in California, Amanda Welles. She directs me to a YouTube site and there I have my first encounter with David Wilcock: seer, scientist, philosopher, dream reader. And he is quoting and citing passages from two of the films I have written, *Contact* and *The Last Mimzy*, as if their filmic content were the equivalent of a cinematic Rosetta stone—unlocking the secrets of the universe. I was impressed that this young, gangly sage, part oracle and part stand-up cosmic comedian, found so much meaning in one of the greater film experiences I'd had as a writer—*Contact*, and one of my lesser—*The Last Mimzy*.

So I introduced myself to David and thus began a most fortuitous journey—for myself and my collaborator, Amanda Welles—that continues into the haze of 2012 and the clarity beyond.

I don't know about you, but I know where I am going to be on January 1, 2013; and it won't be buried under volcanic ash and mud from a tsunami, or crushed by a ten-mile-high tidal wave. Not this believer. I will be wherever David Wilcock is—celebrating the genesis of a new Golden Age, and enjoying every precious second of it. If you want doom and gloom, and a replay of the tortured end to humankind's existence, there is plenty of that at the multiplex. Read no further if you are hopeless, do not believe in the power of consciousness, and think that $#.+ happens and there is nothing we as a species can do about it. Stop right here if you truly believe we are alone in the universe. As I wrote in the film *Contact*, based on Carl Sagan's brilliant novel, regarding whether or not the universe is populated with intelligent life: "If we are alone, seems like an awful waste of space."

But I am here to tell you: We are *not* alone in this universe. And we have David Wilcock to prove it—and to guide us to this golden prophecy.

From that very first encounter with David Wilcock, watching him in *2012 Enigma* on YouTube at one A.M. in the morning, I understood with great clarity that here, finally, was a mind that was taking the time to connect the dots between the human species and the rest of the cosmos— to ready us to finally become Citizens of the Galaxy.

This was Carl Sagan's wish as well. The time I spent with this generous, visionary man of science prepared me for this big adventure with David Wilcock. Sagan did not believe in UFOs and little green men, but he did believe in the abundance of life in the universe, and our potential to join the collective cosmos of that life if we would only open ourselves to the possibility—and stop destroying one another with our warring religions, small gods, and hateful, divisive dogmas and political insanities. David Wilcock has added Carl Sagan's hope for the human race to his synthesis of the cosmos and our place in it.

As I write this introduction to David's seminal work on our collective future in the post-2012 world we will evolve into, I am filled with that same awe and childish wonder at what is going to happen next. What is waiting for us as a species—to embrace and to invigorate. It ain't going to happen if we just sit and wait. We have to understand now what our role is in this great opportunity that begins on December 21, 2012.

A line comes to mind that I wrote ten years ago, for a new animated epic that is now in production at Fox for release in 2013. The line sums up the truth that I firmly believe David Wilcock is bringing from the universe to the human species. . . .

"One heart beats for all. . . . All hearts beat for one."

Thank you, David Wilcock, for putting hope back on the table. Pay attention, humans. And keep your karma dry.

J. V. Hart
Pound Ridge, New York
2009

Introduction

by Graham Hancock

I was researching my book *Fingerprints of the Gods* in the early 1990s when I first became aware of the so-called Mayan prophecy that the world will come to an end on December 21, 2012.

It's since become obvious—thank goodness—that there is more than one way to read the "prophecy."

Some still favor gloom and doom but growing numbers have found good reasons to interpret 2012 not so much as a specific date but as *an epoch* that has already begun—a period of thirty, fifty, even a hundred years in which, though there may be trials and tribulations, a bright new future will dawn for humanity—allowing us to manifest a higher state of consciousness and realize our full potential.

David Wilcock is a leading thinker amongst the latter group—and he makes a magnificent case in the pages that follow that a golden age is indeed within our grasp and can be brought into manifestation if only we choose to make it so. Skeptics react to such unorthodox notions with savage attacks on those who put them forward, and David must expect a firestorm of criticism as the influence of this book spreads. Indeed, if the establishment behaves true to form, then just about everything he says here is going to be combed through for mistakes and weakness by teams of very clever people. Whatever they find—and no author ever wrote a book without making at least some mistakes—will be used to suggest that everything else in the book is wrong as well.

Do not be discouraged. There is a tremendous amount of good science here, much of it new to Western readers because it is the work of Russian scientists. David has done a great service in bringing all this material together in one place for the first time. In some cases the implications of the Russian research are so radical that it has already been outlawed or disregarded by the mainstream.

Keep an open mind, especially where the establishment says "NO," accept David's invitation to dig deeper into the facts, and pretty soon you will find that things are beginning to connect before your eyes into an entirely new pattern that you might never have considered before.

It's not my purpose to comment on all the extraordinary concepts in this big book of ideas, but here are three David puts forward, all closely interlinked, that particularly stand out for me:

1. The visible, material realm—the collective experience that we all agree to call the "real world"—is an emanation into three-dimensional space of an invisible parallel universe. We cannot claim a full understanding of the "real world" without taking account of the hidden realm that it emerges out of.

2. Precisely because it is an emanation—and therefore in some senses like an illusion or a hologram—the "real world" is not a fixed and firm, immutable construct that can be changed only by direct physical or mechanical action. Sometimes it behaves more like a lucid dream that can be changed by the power of thought and imagination.

3. "Thoughts" are therefore "things" and we should be aware that our thoughts can manifest tangible effects in the "real world."

In one sense these are very modern, twenty-first-century ideas that David is exploring here—ideas at the cutting edge of disciplines such as quantum physics and consciousness research. But what draws me to all of them are the ways in which they also resonate deeply with ancient wisdom traditions, reminding us that the truth is always true and indivisible, wherever—and whenever—it is expressed.

For example, the notion that the "real world" is an emanation or manifestation of a hidden realm is central to the ancient Egyptian idea of the nature of reality expressed in documents as old as the *Pyramid Texts* (circa 2200 B.C.). The same idea is reworked and restated through the various recensions of the *Coffin Texts*, the *Book of What Is in the Duat*, and the *Book of the Dead*, and finally trickles down into the Gnostic and Hermetic texts that began to be compiled in Greek and Latin around the time of Christ—and had a profound influence on mystical Christianity.

The essence of this ancient idea can be summed up in the simple and beautiful Hermetic dictum "As Above So Below"—which is to say that the pattern of things here on earth in the "real world" (the "sensible Kosmos" as it is known in the Hermetic texts) can only be understood properly when you realize that it manifests the workings of a higher, unseen domain:

> "If you consider the whole you will learn that in truth the sensible Kosmos itself, with all things that are therein, is woven like a garment by that higher Kosmos."[1]

> Or put another way, there exists a Kosmos that is "imperceptible to sense. This sensible Kosmos [i.e., the "real world"] has been made in the image of that other Kosmos and reproduces eternity in a copy."[2]

I can see no difference between the Hermetic Kosmos "imperceptible to sense"—which weaves the visible Kosmos like a garment—and David's concept of the Source Field, undetected as yet by our conventional scientific instruments, but shaping and defining every aspect of our reality.

What the Hermetic texts say about the cyclical nature of time and its interpenetration with matter also gels nicely with the latest science on the subject brought together by David in these pages. After you've finished *The Source Field Investigations,* come back here and reread the three passages from the Hermetica set out below and I guarantee you will see what I mean:

> The Kosmos is that in which time is contained; and it is by the progress and movement of time that life is maintained in the Kosmos. The process of time is regulated by a fixed order; and Time in its ordered course renews all things in the Kosmos by Alteration.[3]

> The Kosmos revolves with an everlasting movement. That movement has had no beginning, and will have no end; it manifests itself and disappears by turns in the several parts of the Kosmos, and that in such fashion that again and again in the checkered course of time it manifests itself anew in those same parts in which it disappeared before. Such is the nature of circular movement; all points in the circle are so linked together, that you can find no place at which the movement can begin; for it is evident that all points in the line of movement both precede and follow one another forever, and it is in this manner that time revolves.[4]

> If you suppose the present time to be separate from the past time, and the future from the present, you will find yourself in a difficulty. For it is impossible for the present to come into being unless the past has also come into being (and for the future to come into being unless the present has); for the present issues from the past and the future from the present. And inasmuch as the past joins onto the present, and the present to the future, they are made one by their continuity. They are therefore not separate from one another.[5]

David's very useful and interesting notion that the "real world" may actually be a form of lucid dream, subject to change by acts of will or imagination, is also prefigured in the Hermetic writings—which go so far as to state that "Illusion is a thing wrought by the working of Reality."[6]

Even the human bodies that we inhabit are, in the Hermetic view, unreal:

> You must understand that that which always exists, and
> that alone, is real. But man is not a thing that always exists
> and therefore man is not real, but is only an appearance. . . .[7]

In these realms of appearances, thoughts may indeed become things and we must take care with the thoughts we put out there. It's difficult with twenty-four-hour rolling news showing us the worst aspects of humanity; if too many of us focus for too long on doom and destruction, if too many of us continue to dwell on negative emotions like hatred and envy, if too many of us fail to express love and gratitude and remain unwilling to seek forgiveness, then it will not be long before we turn our lucid dream into hell on earth.

It doesn't have to be that way.

A fundamental message of this book, and of many ancient wisdom teachings, is that we are cocreators of our own reality and that the golden age is therefore just around the corner, all the time, for all of us. To embrace it we must set aside the negative patterns and reference frames of the past, let go of rigid habits of thought that serve us no longer, and be willing to accept a permanent shake-up in our outlook on just about everything.

It's proof of how difficult it is to do any of this that the golden age has been so long coming. Yet if David is right, the hidden Source Field generating the lucid dream that we call reality can be expected to make its presence and its influence felt with great power and persistence in the coming years—and to have profound effects on human consciousness.

Perhaps the epoch of 2012 really does mark a crossroads in our story. And perhaps the time has come for us to pay close attention to the Kosmos—both seen and unseen—which does not idly send us signs and wonders, or speak to us through dreams and visions, but which ungrudgingly favors our welfare and seeks always to set us on the right track.

Graham Hancock
Author, *Fingerprints of the Gods*
www.grahamhancock.com

PART ONE

THE MIND
AND THE BODY

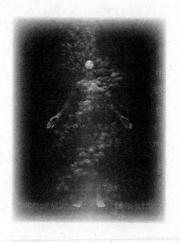

A Future Beyond Our Wildest Dreams

S ince the dawn of self-awareness on earth, we have been inexorably driven to ask the "big questions": Who am I? Where did I come from? How did I get here—and where am I going? Various teachers have come along who claimed to have the answers—and the differences of opinion on these overwhelmingly profound concepts have led to many of the greatest sorrows and atrocities in recorded history. Nonetheless, consistent themes emerge in almost all spiritual traditions—including the idea that the Universe is not made of "dead" and inert matter, but is rather a living, conscious Being. This superintelligence, we are told, has woven the strands of space, time, energy, matter, biology and consciousness together in Its own image. Despite the vastness of the Universe, we all apparently have a personal connection to this majestic Identity—and we will live on long past the death of our physical bodies.

Most spiritual teachings also say we will eventually reunite with this "Oneness"—and even when we walk in complete ignorance of these greater realities, a hidden spiritual curriculum is influencing our lives—and will eventually guide us back Home. We also consistently hear that benevolent super-beings, such as Jesus, Buddha, Krishna and others, have directly intervened in earth's history to help show us the way to this greater Truth. As Graham Hancock, Zecharia Sitchin and others have reported, many of the oldest cultures speak of "gods" who gave them practical assistance—written language, mathematics, astronomy, agriculture, animal husbandry, ethics, law and architecture—including massive stone edifices, built out of impossibly heavy multiton blocks, which apparently served some useful purpose. Despite the immense difficulty in duplicating these feats even with today's technology, these "megalithic" structures appear all over the world.

In our own "modern" era, the awe-inspiring origins of major world religions and spiritual traditions are usually written off as mythology and superstition. Due to the seemingly irresolvable differences between these various philosophical systems, and our ever-increasing desire for information that is provable, Science has replaced Religion as the ultimate arbiter of Truth in many people's minds—and this formerly majestic, wonderful view of a Divine Cosmos has been dismissed. The Universe has become a giant collection of dead, empty "stuff." Our minds, thoughts and emotions—not to mention all the richness and diversity of species on this planet—are now seen to be the result of sheer coincidence and happenstance in an otherwise unthinking, unfeeling, infinitely cold, and depressing void. We have nothing to live for, nothing to look forward to after we die—and even the need for ethics or morality at all becomes a subject of healthy philosophical debate. If we know we can't escape death, and all we have is this one chance to exist, then why not devote our lives to the pursuit of as much pleasure as we can find? Why not throw ourselves fully and completely into a hedonistic lust for money, power and privilege, and hope we can then pass on these same benefits to our children, who are created from our own bodies?

The more we think we know, the more lonely our lives seem to be. The magic has been stripped away. We have no special abilities or mystical powers. We have nothing to look forward to after we die. We have no one else in the Universe to meet. And before we ever even get the chance to travel out into space on any sustainable basis, we may all perish in a planetary catastrophe—either by our own weapons of mass destruction, or by natural causes we apparently have no ability to control or prevent. A seemingly endless lineup of big-budget disaster movies entertains audiences by threatening the earth with total annihilation. You may now be listening to the "profits of doom" a little more carefully—and might indeed be wondering if, in fact, all is well.

If you have seen my YouTube documentary that was the genesis for this book entitled *The 2012 Enigma*,[1] my Web site, Divine Cosmos,[2] or some of my television appearances, you probably know I do not believe our future is depressing, terrifying or cataclysmic. Instead, I feel our destinies on earth are being carefully and meticulously guided by a hidden intelligence—a living energy field the entire Universe is built from. Many great researchers have independently discovered this unseen Universal force and given it their own names, without there ever being a single, unifying standard. Since this force may well be the source of all space, time, matter, energy, biology and consciousness in the Universe, the simplest all-inclusive term I use is the Source Field.

This is not a book of philosophy, speculation or wishful thinking—it is a vast synthesis of investigations into the Source Field. I am standing on the shoulders of giants in writing this book, as the overwhelming majority of these findings was developed by Ph.D.s from accredited universities, who ended up discovering things that often put them at odds with their colleagues, employers and much of the mainstream world. There are also many examples in which a scientist or research institute made one specific breakthrough that was released into the mainstream press—but the media did not see or understand how well it tied in with so many other related discoveries. In Russia, however, there has been a consistent, focused effort to investigate the Source Field since at least the 1950s—but until the fall of the Soviet Union in 1991, the vast majority of all these revelations were classified for national security. Over ten thousand papers investigating the Source Field were published by 1996 alone,[3] with more than half of them from Russia. The implications of what they found are so staggering that I suspect you will be stunned by how much we already know about this unseen force—which influences absolutely everything we see, hear, do and believe.

It has taken me over thirty years of dedicated research to assemble this grand collection of data—and particularly since 1993, I have spent as many waking hours as possible in pursuit of this radical rethinking of science. After I became self-employed in the summer of 1998, I began working fourteen hours a day, seven days a week researching and investigating the Source Field phenomena. After Brian Tart, the president of

Dutton Books, contacted me and offered to publish this research, it took me almost two years of focused, concentrated effort to develop this book. When I finally started combining the very best of everything I had found into one single vision, a seemingly endless parade of stunning new connections emerged. If these breakthroughs become common knowledge and are developed into working technologies—and/or if existing technologies that use these principles are declassified and released to the public—we could end up in a world that rivals or exceeds our finest visionary science fiction films and novels.

As I bring you on a guided tour into the deeper mysteries of space, time, energy, matter, biology and consciousness, we will also explore subjects as fascinating as antigravity, dematerialization, teleportation, the parallel reality where time is three-dimensional, quantum geometry, natural "vortex points" on the earth where ships and planes disappear, real-world examples of time travel, the Maya calendar as a tool for calculating when these "portals" will open, and an analysis of how our galaxy is driving all the different cycles we experience—for our own physical, biological and spiritual evolution. The potential technological applications of this science are incredible. Furthermore, we may see a fundamental change in the nature of space and time itself as we fully cross over into this new zone of energy in the galaxy you will learn about.

The Source Field is the key to unlock all of these mysteries, and ultimately understand the big questions: who are we, where did we come from, how did we get here, and where are we going. Our journey into the Source Field Investigations begins in the next chapter by exploring the work of Dr. Cleve Backster—a pioneer who helped us understand the true nature of Mind. We no longer need to remain ignorant about the structure, identity and purpose of Consciousness. It is not merely a biological phenomenon—it is written into the energy of the Universe itself.

David Wilcock, January 2011

CHAPTER ONE

The Backster Effect, Free Energy and the Consequences

C ould all space, time, energy, matter, biological life and consciousness in the Universe be the product of a Source Field? Is it possible that the ancient spiritual teachings and philosophies are correct when they say "As Above, So Below"? What if everything we see in the visible universe is ultimately a crystallization of a vast Mind—which has a singular identity and awareness? Might we be living in amnesia—going through experiences that will eventually guide us through a full awakening into the vastness of this infinite consciousness?

The Source Field Investigations must begin with compelling evidence that consciousness is not strictly trapped within our own brain and nervous system. We would need to see tangible proof that our thoughts are constantly interacting with our environment—and having an effect upon our surroundings. If our concept of a Source Field is correct, then Mind would become an energetic phenomenon that is not confined to biological life-forms, but can pass between them—through allegedly "empty space."

A variety of scientists and scholars in the Western world have made discoveries that reveal the existence of the Source Field—including controversial figures like Wilhelm Reich, who was a protégé of Dr. Sigmund Freud, the father of psychology. Here, our Source Field Investigations will begin with Dr. Cleve Backster—who summarized his fascinating life's work in his recent book *Primary Perception*.[1]

The Stunning Power of Hypnosis

While attending Rutgers University prep school, Backster was fascinated to hear his friend describe a hypnosis technique he'd just learned from his professor. Backster decided to try to hypnotize his roommate with this technique, who soon fell into a very deep trance. Backster then told him, "Now, I want you to open your eyes, but you're not going to wake up. I want you to go down the hall and get permission for late lights."[2] In this prep school, the students could not have their lights on past ten P.M. without special permission. Under hypnosis, Backster's roommate then opened his eyes, got up, walked down the hall and got permission for late lights from the professor on duty. He signed the log and returned to the room. When Backster brought his roommate back out of hypnosis, he didn't even realize anything had happened to him: "See? It doesn't work. This so-called hypnosis is a bunch of baloney."[3] When they walked down to the on-duty professor, he confirmed that Backster's roommate had just come and asked permission a few minutes earlier—but the roommate couldn't believe it was real. He was then shocked to discover his own signature in the late lights log.

Backster began researching hypnosis—reading as many books as he could find on the subject, which were not that many in the late 1930s—and performed additional successful experiments. After the devastating attack on Pearl Harbor in 1941, Backster joined the military ROTC program at Texas A & M University—and there he began making frequent demonstrations of hypnosis to larger audiences. Typically about a third of his audience went into some stage of trance—and he picked the deepest subjects for more intensive work. One man was told he would not be able to see Backster in the room for the next thirty minutes after he woke up. Indeed, once this subject was brought out of hypnosis, he could not see Backster at all. Just to test how far this would go, Backster picked up a cigarette and blew out some smoke, although he was not a smoker. This man saw the cigarette and the smoke levitating in the air, but he could not see anyone holding it—and he became very alarmed. He wanted to leave the room, but the audience compelled him to stay. After the thirty minutes, Backster again reappeared to him; he followed his posthypnotic commands perfectly, with no conscious memory of what he had been told to do.[4]

My own introduction into the powers of hypnosis came after I had a dramatic out-of-body experience. When I was only five years old, I woke up one night and found myself floating about three feet over my own body. That little boy in the bed was breathing normally—but if he was "me," then who the heck was I? This quickly started to scare me—and as soon as I panicked, I snapped back into my body. For the next two years, I wished I could have another chance to explore this bold, new frontier—but nothing happened. When I finally asked my mother how I could learn more about this, she took me down into the basement and suggested I read some books she had on ESP—extrasensory perception. The first one I read was Harold Sherman's *How to Make ESP Work for You.*[5] Sherman said that when you hypnotize someone, you can get them to have an out-of-body experience like I had—with apparently stunning results.

> The deeper the state of trance, the more activated become the Extra Sensory faculties of the subject. Under these conditions, he can be instructed to leave the body and to visit a certain person or place, and to report on what he sees and hears.

Hypnotism and Astral Projection

Dr. Thomas Garrett, a therapeutic hypnotist who pioneered in the treatment of shell-shocked soldiers in the First World War, told me of an outstanding experience he had had with one of his private patients. The young man, son of a famous Broadway playwright, came to Dr. Garrett emotionally upset over a broken romance. He submitted to hypnotism and told Dr. Garrett that he and his former fiancée, who was a student at Wellesley, had had a falling-out over some trivial matter and she had returned his ring.

Dr. Garrett, on impulse, told the hypnotized young man he could visit the woman he loved and see if he could determine how she now felt about him. Dr. Garrett explained he had the power to leave his physical body, in his astral form, and travel direct to Wellesley, to the sorority house where the young lady was residing. There was a moment of silence. Then the entranced subject announced that he was standing in the hall outside the girl's closed door.

"Don't let that stop you," said Dr. Garrett. "You can pass right through the door. Go on in and tell me what she is doing."

After another moment, the young man said: "She is at her desk, writing a letter."

"That's fine," said Dr. Garrett. "Look over her shoulder and read to me what she is writing."

Almost instantly the face of the sleeping subject took on a surprised and delighted expression. "Why, she's writing to me."

"What is she saying?" demanded Dr. Garrett, picking up a pencil.

The young man then read to Dr. Garrett several word-for-word paragraphs, to the effect that his sweetheart was sorry for her part in the lovers' quarrel, was asking forgiveness, and expressing the hope for a reconciliation. The young man became so excited that he tried to embrace the girl and the reaction on his physical body was such that Dr. Garrett quickly brought him back from his astral adventure and woke him up, with the suggestion that he would remember all that had transpired.

Late the following day, this young man received a special delivery letter from his sweetheart—the very letter he had either astrally or telepathically perceived. Dr. Garrett has this letter in his files, together with the notations he had made, as reported by his entranced subject. There were only a few words of variation between the two.[6]

An even more fantastic-sounding hypnosis story can be found in Michael Talbot's epic work *The Holographic Universe*—one of the best collections of Source Field investigations ever committed to the printed page. Talbot witnessed his father's friend Tom being hypnotized in the early 1970s by a professional. The hypnotist told Tom his daughter, Laura, would be invisible to him when he came out of trance. He then had Laura stand directly in front of her father. Tom apparently saw right through her body as he woke up and gazed around the room—and also could not hear her giggling. The hypnotist then pulled a watch out of his pocket and quickly pushed it into the small of Laura's back, keeping it concealed in his hand so no one could have seen what it was—and asked Tom if he could see what he was holding.

> Tom leaned forward as if staring directly through Laura's stomach and said it was a watch. The hypnotist nodded and asked if Tom could read the watch's inscription. Tom squinted as if struggling to make out the writing and recited both the name of the watch's owner (which happened to be a person unknown to any of us in the room) and the message. The hypnotist then revealed that the object was indeed a watch, and passed it around the room so that everyone could see that Tom had read its inscription correctly. When I talked to Tom afterward, he said his daughter had been absolutely invisible to him. All he had seen was the hypnotist standing and holding a watch cupped in the palm of his hand. Had the hypnotist let him leave without telling him what was going on, he never would have known he wasn't perceiving normal consensus reality.[7]

I read this back in 1995, and it made a huge impression upon me. Tom's hypnotized mind could see right through his daughter as if she didn't even exist—and he could read detailed written inscriptions from a pocket watch. If true, this challenges everything we think we know about solid matter—and suggests there is a part of our minds with vastly greater capabilities than most of us are ever aware of. What we think we see may be nothing more than the product of a collective decision we're all making to see it that way—a form of mass hypnosis. Remember—we can walk, talk and interact with the world under hypnosis, travel out of body and make accurate observations, and may or may not have any conscious memory of what we did after we are brought out of trance. We can also be given posthypnotic suggestion to act, think or behave a certain way after we wake up. These suggestions are apparently powerful enough to make a human being utterly invisible to us while we're in an otherwise normal state of consciousness. When we discover that ordinary people can be hypnotized like this, we typically write it off as the work of the "subconscious mind"—but we still don't understand what, exactly, this is . . . or why it works. The subconscious seems to automatically obey hypnotic commands—generally without question—as if it were quite accustomed to hearing orders and acting upon them.

After his university training, Cleve Backster eventually joined the U.S. Counter-Intelligence Corps, and lectured on the potential danger of foreign powers using hypnosis to extract classified information from overseas government personnel. Backster took a huge risk to demonstrate the seriousness of this subject to a high-ranking military officer. With her permission, Backster hypnotized the secretary of the commanding general of the Counter-Intelligence Corps. While under hypnosis, he asked her to remove a highly classified document from the general's locked file cabinet—and she willingly obeyed. Backster told her she would not remember what she had done when she awoke—and sure enough, she had no idea she had just leaked very sensitive information when he brought her back.

> That night I secured the document in my locked file and the next day presented it to the General. I explained to him that I might be risking a court martial, but hoped instead to expedite further consideration of the importance of my research. Rather than a court martial, on December 17, 1947, I received a very favorable letter of recommendation from the General, stating that my research was "of high importance to military intelligence." Then positive things started to happen.[8]

Early Pioneer of the Polygraph

After giving ten days of hypnosis and sodium pentothal "truth serum" demonstrations at the Walter Reed Hospital in Washington, D.C., Backster began working for the Central Intelligence Agency as of April 27, 1948. Shortly after joining the CIA, Backster studied with Leonarde Keeler—a pioneer in the use of the polygraph.

"In addition to other classified activities, I was a key member of a CIA team that was prepared to travel to any foreign location to analyze the possible use of unusual interrogation tactics, including my original areas of concern, mainly hypno-interrogation and narco-interrogation. . . . Back in Washington, D.C., the polygraph operation I had established was becoming popular for the screening of applicants for employment at the CIA and for some general screening of key CIA personnel. The ever-increasing schedule of rather routine polygraph examinations started to interfere with my more creative interests in research."[9]

Shortly after Leonarde Keeler's death, circa 1951, Backster left the CIA—to serve as director of the Keeler Polygraph Institute in Chicago. This was the only classroom-type school teaching the use of the polygraph at the time. Backster went on to start his own polygraph consultant business, working with several government agencies, in Washington, D.C.—and then expanded into a second office in Baltimore, Maryland. By 1958, Backster had freed up the time to begin intensive polygraph research, and he developed the first standardized system for numerical evaluation of polygraph charts—which is still being used today. He moved to New York City in 1959 and continued to operate a commercial polygraph business. Seven years later, Backster struck gold.

> In February 1966 an event occurred that was about to expand the entire focus of my research through a kind of paradigm shift in my own awareness. At the time of its occurrence I had been involved in the use of the polygraph on humans for eighteen years.[10]

Backster's secretary purchased a rubber plant and a dracaena cane plant from a store that was going out of business. This was the first time Backster had ever owned any plants. On February 2, 1966, Backster had worked through the night in his lab, and finally took a coffee break at seven A.M. In those weary hours, Backster got an idea—he would try to connect his new dracaena plant to the polygraph and see what happened. Much to his surprise, the plant did not have a smooth, flat pattern of electrical activity—it was surprisingly jagged and alive, changing moment to moment. Then, as Backster kept watching in amazement, it got a whole lot more interesting.

> About one minute into the chart recording, the tracing exhibited a short-term change in contour—similar to a reaction pattern typical of a human subject who might have been briefly experiencing the fear of detection.[11]

In simple language, the plant's electrical activity looked just like the graph from a person who was starting to tell a lie. Backster knew that if you want to catch someone lying, you first have to confront them about whatever they might be hiding. If your questions then cause them to feel threatened and anxious, the electrical activity in their skin gets much stronger. Backster wanted to see if he could get a humanlike response out of his new plant by threatening its well-being somehow.

> An example of what we do with a human taking a polygraph test is ask a question such as, "Did you fire that shot [that was] fatal to John Smith?" If they did commit the crime, that question threatens their well-being and produces a reaction that shows up on the chart.[12]

Backster tried dipping one of the leaves into a cup of hot coffee. Nothing. He tapped one of the leaves with his pen. There was hardly any response.

> Then, after about fourteen minutes of elapsed chart time, I had this thought: As the ultimate plant threat, I would get a

match and burn the plant's electroded leaf. At that time, the plant was about fifteen feet away from where I was standing. . . . The only new thing that occurred was this thought.[13]

What happened next would change the history of science forever—and the impact still has not reached our common, public awareness.

> The very moment the imagery of burning that leaf entered my mind, the polygraph recording pen moved rapidly to the top of the chart! No words were spoken, no touching the plant, no lighting of matches, just my clear intention to burn the leaf. The plant recording showed dramatic excitation. To me this was a powerful, high-quality observation. . . . I must state that, on February 2, 1966, at 13 minutes, 55 seconds into that chart recording, my whole consciousness changed. I then thought, "Gee, it's as though this plant read my mind!"[14]

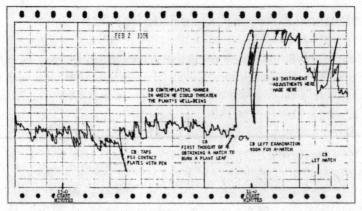

Dr. Cleve Backster's graph of his dracaena cane plant having an electrical reaction right as he thought of burning one of its leaves.

As the plant continued to have what would be considered an enormous, panicked reaction, Backster then went and got matches from his secretary's desk.

When I returned, the plant was still showing highly visible reactions. . . . I made a feeble pass at [a] leaf with a lighted match, but by then I was not really into harming the plant. I thought the best thing for me to do was to remove the threat, and see if the plant would calm down. After returning the matches to my secretary's desk, the tracing [finally] returned to the calmness displayed prior to the original decision to burn the electroded leaf.[15]

As of nine A.M., Backster's associate Bob Henson came to work—and was fascinated when he heard about what Backster had just done. When Henson repeated the experiment and threatened the plant himself, the same reaction occurred. Backster now felt sympathy for the plant and did not let Hanson actually burn any of the leaves. In fact, Backster never again did an experiment that involved burning or threatening to burn plants.

A Personal Experience of the Backster Effect

In 2006, I called Backster's research laboratory in San Diego to ask if he wanted to participate in a film shoot to dramatize this event in a modern classroom setting. Until I was actually on the phone with him, I did not realize that I had called on February 2, 2006—forty years to the day from when he first made this discovery in 1966. Backster agreed to do my movie. A few months later we brought him up to Los Angeles and spent a healthy chunk of investor capital for a professional Hollywood-level shoot.

In this key scene, Backster is invited to a college classroom to discuss his original experiment—while he has a live plant connected to his polygraph. One rebellious student in the audience gets excited and impatient, and wants to re-create the Backster Effect for himself. The kid jumps out of his seat with a lighter in his hand and runs toward the plant to burn it—but my character holds him back. The plant still "screams" from the fear of being burned—thus proving to the entire class that the Backster Effect really works.

This was how I had written the scene. I had a significant amount of investor dollars on the line, and Backster had promised to work as an actor and follow the script. To my horror, he refused to "pretend" that the plant was having a terrified reaction each time I held the kid back. We did take after take, but Backster simply wouldn't act out his part. Unless he saw the graph actually go wild, like he witnessed in his original discovery forty years earlier, he obviously wasn't going to have any kind of authentic reaction on camera. I then realized the only way I could save my film was to use the Backster Effect myself.

Up until then, we were only acting. There were no strong emotions going around. The kid didn't really want to burn the plant, and I knew he wasn't really going to try to push past me. The plant "knew" it wasn't in any real danger—so as a result, its graph stayed nice and smooth. I knew I had to do something—and fast. The next time we did the scene, I sent that plant the blackest, darkest thoughts I could possibly conjure up—right when I confronted the kid. I really felt it deep down in my core. I absolutely hated that plant. I wanted to tear it to pieces. Burn it to a crisp. Right at that exact moment, the polygraph needle went completely nuts—just like a person screaming in terror. With the cameras still rolling, Backster said, *"Wow, we've got quite a reaction here!"* I saved the shoot—and proved, for myself, that the Backster Effect really works.

I then told the plant I was sorry, and sent genuine feelings of love to it, in case it could somehow hear me or feel me. The graph calmed right back down. Backster let me save the graph paper from this stunning event—and I still have it in the box with all the bills we racked up from that day of shooting. The script went through many more changes and we never ended up using our promo footage professionally, but I was very happy to get my own chance to experience the Backster Effect with the man himself—and really know, deep down inside, that it works. I also will never forget the day I was speaking to my landlady and her ten-year-old daughter about Backster's amazing discovery. Her daughter suddenly ran outside and started rolling around in the grass, in total ecstasy, saying, "You can hear me! You can hear me!"

They're Always Listening

After his initial discovery in 1966, Backster found out that once you start taking care of a plant, it seemingly tracks your thoughts and feelings.

> During plant monitoring sessions, when I left the lab to run an errand, I found that the moment I decided to return to where that plant was, the plant often showed a fairly significant reaction—especially when my decision to return was made in a spontaneous manner.[16]

Backster used synchronized watches to prove that the plant was responding at the exact moment he made the decision. In another case, Backster set up a plant experiment in New York and traveled to Clifton, New Jersey, with his associate Bob Henson, who was unaware that his wife had set up a surprise party for their wedding anniversary. Backster noticed several strong reactions in the plant as they went through various phases of their trip—including the time they approached Port Authority, the time they boarded the bus for Clifton, the time the bus entered the Lincoln Tunnel, and the time they made the final part of the trip out to Clifton. Right at the moment they entered the house and everyone yelled, "SURPRISE!" the plant definitely felt it. Backster said, "There was a big reaction from the plant at that exact time."[17]

Backster began leaving plants connected to his polygraph without trying to do anything—just observing their reactions and then trying to figure out what might have caused them. One day he found a very strong reaction—and eventually realized it happened right as he poured a pot of boiling water into the sink in his lab. I've been in Backster's lab myself and know how disgusting those sinks can get. Later tests revealed that his sink was loaded with bacteria—"somewhat similar to the cantina scene from *Star Wars*"[18]—and when the bacteria suddenly died from the scalding hot water, the plant perceived a threat to *its own* well-being—and "screamed."

Backster later designed an experiment to try to standardize this effect.

He tried to think of the most expendable living creature he could find—and he chose brine shrimp, which are commonly used as fish food. He invented a machine that would dump the shrimp into boiling water at a random time. The plants did indeed react, strongly, as the shrimp died—but only if the experiment was done at night, when no human beings were around in the lab. Otherwise, the plants seemed to "lose interest" in the shrimp; the energy fields from an average person were much stronger. Skeptics later attempted to repeat this experiment—but they did not follow Backster's protocols.

> As best we could determine, the people trying to replicate really didn't understand how to automate human consciousness out of an experiment. They thought you could go to the other side of a wall and watch the experiment unfold through closed-circuit television. That wall meant nothing as far as the plant-to-human attunement was concerned.[19]

This study was given a brief column-and-a-half write-up in *Electro-Technology Magazine*—and a stunning 4,950 scientists wrote Backster to request more information.[20]

Then, on November 3, 1969, Backster demonstrated this effect at Yale University Linguistics School. An ivy leaf was plucked and connected to the polygraph: "I then asked if they had any insects around that could be utilized for hopefully stimulating a plant reaction." The students captured a spider—which is actually an arachnid, as Backster points out. They put the spider on a table and had one guy surround it with his hands so it couldn't escape. The ivy leaf did not react during this time.

> But, when he took his hands away, as the spider became conscious that it was able to run, you'd see a huge chart reaction just prior to its attempt to escape. This sequence was repeated several times.[21]

Backster soon appeared on numerous television shows to demonstrate this effect, including ones hosted by Johnny Carson, Art Linkletter,

Merv Griffin and David Frost.[22] Frost asked Backster if his plant was male or female. Backster and his plant both had an amusing response to this rather personal question.

> I suggested he go over and lift up a leaf and take a peek. Before he even approached the plant, [it] . . . showed a wild reaction, evoking a very amused reaction from the studio audience.[23]

Backster's results were replicated by Russian scientist V. N. Pushkin in 1972, using EEG instrumentation. People under hypnosis were brought into a powerful state of emotional stimulation, and a nearby geranium would have a strong reaction each time this occurred.[24] Despite all these intriguing results, the scientific community was predictably severe in its criticism. Dr. Otto Solbrig of Harvard University's biology department was not amused.

> [This is a] waste of time. This work is not going to advance science very much. We know enough already about plants— so that when someone comes up with something like this, we say it's quackery. You might say we are prejudiced. Maybe we are.

Yale professor Arthur Galtson was a little more polite—but still not supportive.

> I don't say Backster's phenomena are impossible. I just say there are enough other things of more value to work on. . . . It's attractive to think that plants are listening to you or that they respond to prayer, but there's nothing in it. There's no nervous system in a plant. There are no means by which sensation can be transferred.[25]

Others, like Stanford Research Institute's Dr. Hal Puthoff, were more encouraging.

I don't regard Backster's work as quackery. The way he conducts his experiments is pretty good. It's not the sloppy thing that most people believe who think the work's no good.[26]

All of Nature Is in a Constant "Conversation"

Backster also connected yogurt bacteria, ordinary chicken eggs from his refrigerator and even live human cells to his polygraph—and continued to get stunning results. Consistently, what he found was that every living thing is intimately attuned to its environment. When any stress, suffering or death occurs, all the life-forms in the surrounding area have an immediate electrical response—as if they all share the pain.

Backster first got the idea to wire up chicken eggs when a philodendron plant had a strong reaction—right as he cracked one open for breakfast.[27] Even though he used conventional, non-fertilized eggs from the grocery store, Backster's electroded eggs displayed unexpected behavior—including patterns similar to a heartbeat on an EEG, and complex "cycles within cycles" on an EKG.[28] One of Backster's electroded eggs had a sudden shock when he picked up his Siamese cat, Sam, and startled him out of a deep sleep. Even more impressive is the graph of an electroded egg "screaming" each time its former neighbors are dropped into boiling water, one by one. This egg was kept inside a lead-lined box that screened out all electromagnetic fields. That meant this effect could not be due to any radio waves, microwaves or other electromagnetic frequencies.[29]

Backster clearly understood the importance of shielding out electromagnetic fields in an experiment like this.

At the suggestion of several scientists, and the physicists in particular, I later attempted to shield the smaller electroded plants from electromagnetic interference by using a copper screen cage [also known as a Faraday cage]. . . . The plants behaved as if the screen cage enclosure did not exist. Much

later I had the opportunity to confirm this using [a] state-of-
the-art shielded room. . . . I felt certain [the information passing between plants, bacteria, insects, animals and humans]
was not within the known electromagnetic frequencies, AM,
FM or any form of signal which could be shielded by ordinary means. Distance seemed to impose no limitation. I
made observations that suggested that this signal could traverse dozens, even hundreds of miles. It seemed that the signal may not even fall within the electromagnetic spectrum. If
not, this would certainly have profound implications.[30]

This is one of many such investigations that proved the Source Field
is almost certainly not electromagnetic (EM). Every scientist knows EM
waves cannot penetrate through lead-lined enclosures, copper-screened
Faraday cages and/or shielded rooms.

Backster's experiments with human cells made his discovery far more
personal. In these experiments, Backster would obtain living cells from
someone's mouth by having him swish a little water around and spit it
into a test tube. This tube was then whirled in a centrifuge, bringing the
living white blood cells to the top, which Backster extracted with an
eyedropper. The cells were then placed into a tiny one-milliliter test tube
and electroded with very thin gold wires.[31] These living samples could
survive this way for "ten to twelve hours,"[32] giving high-quality reactions
the entire time.

My favorite example of Backster's work with human cells was performed with NASA astronaut Dr. Brian O'Leary in 1988, who served on
the faculties of Cornell University, California Institute of Technology,
University of California and Princeton University. O'Leary brought an
ex–lady friend along to the lab and apparently they had a strong
argument—which "provided ample opportunity for him to witness firsthand extremely high quality chart reactions."[33] O'Leary then left for the
San Diego airport so he could fly back to Phoenix, Arizona—some three
hundred miles away. He synchronized watches with Backster, and his
cells were monitored in the lab the entire time.

It was previously agreed that [Dr. O'Leary] would keep an accurate log of events which might have caused him momentary anxiety. These included missing a turn on the freeway while returning his rental car to the airport, nearly missing his flight because of the long line at the ticket counter, his flight's departure and landing in Phoenix, his son's failure to meet him on time at the airport, and a number of other logged events. Later when comparisons were made by transferring the logged events to the appropriate portions of the chart recording, there was a good correlation between chart reactions and nearly all of the perceived anxieties. His chart became very quiet after he returned home and retired for the evening.[34]

I discussed this experiment with Dr. O'Leary over a private dinner in Zurich, Switzerland, while we were both speaking at a conference—and he confirmed to me how amazed he was by it. His own mind was broadcasting waves of information that were being picked up by his living cells in a lab three hundred miles away. The effect works just as well if the cells are kept in shielded rooms, again proving the signals are not being transmitted by electromagnetic energy. There is something "out there," some energy field, that allows our thoughts to propagate through space—even over vast distances. The implications of this are stunning—particularly when you start to consider how it seems that every living thing in nature is listening to everything else. We are definitely not excluded from this process.

I've lectured on this subject a number of times, and invariably the audience groans when they find out that vegetables, fruits, yogurt, eggs and the living cells in raw meat are all "screaming" when they are cooked and/or eaten. Even hard-core vegan/vegetarian/raw foodists who consider themselves to be on a "cruelty-free" diet are now faced with the fact that the food they eat must go through measurable distress—at least from a human's perspective. Even if you do not cook your vegetables, your digestive activity still has a "burning" effect. Backster did tell me that if you "pray" over your food, by sending it positive, loving thoughts, it then seems to accept its role in helping you stay alive—and these severe reactions no longer occur on the graph paper.[35] Many cultures and spiritual traditions encourage us to "thank our food." With Backster's research we now see that this seemingly unimportant behavior—from a scientific standpoint—has a definite purpose in our new model.

Free Energy—and the Consequences

At this same Zurich conference, Dr. Brian O'Leary revealed a wealth of information suggesting "free energy" devices have been invented, again and again, but are invariably suppressed by corporate power brokers. According to the Institute for New Energy, as of 1997, "the U.S. Patent Office has classified over 3,000 patent devices or applications under the secrecy order, Title 35, U.S. Code (1952) Sections 181-188."[36] The Federation of American Scientists revealed that by the end of Fiscal Year 2010, this number had ballooned to 5,135 inventions—and included "review and possible restriction" on any solar cell with greater than twenty percent efficiency, or any power system that is more than seventy to eighty percent efficient at converting energy.[37] According to Dr. O'Leary, some researchers are bought off and their discoveries put on a shelf. Others are threatened into submission, while others die under strange circumstances. Dr. O'Leary then brought me up onstage for a panel discussion, and he mentioned how Dr. Stefan Marinov—"the head of the European free energy movement"—allegedly jumped to his death from the tenth story of the library building at the University of Graz in Austria. Marinov flew out of the window backward, as if he had been shoved. And according to Dr. O'Leary, "He left no suicide note, and he was one of the most positive, highly spirited persons I've ever met."[38] O'Leary also mentioned Dr. Eugene Mallove, arguably the world's leading figure in alternative energy research, during this same time.

Overwhelmed with emotion, I actually burst into tears onstage in front of this four-hundred-person audience while I discussed my own personal experience with Dr. Mallove. I'm sure you could have measured a huge electrical surge in the plants that were around me onstage when this happened. Dr. Mallove started out as the head science writer for Massachusetts Institute of Technology's own journal. Mallove claimed he was ordered to suppress research into cold fusion—during which they had gotten positive results suggesting free energy was being generated from the reaction.[39] From there, he quit his job and went on to start *Infinite Energy Magazine*[40]—and became arguably the top coordinator, publisher and liaison for alternative-energy inventors worldwide.

On May 15, 2004, I was a featured guest on an episode of *Coast to Coast*, the largest nighttime talk-radio program in the United States, with Art Bell and Richard Hoagland.[41] I found out a few days before airtime that Dr. Mallove was going to come on as our surprise special guest. We were about to make a stunning announcement: Hoagland and Mallove were going to visit Washington, D.C., the following week, and bring along a working, tabletop free-energy device. This device apparently would begin spinning by simply being stared at and did not use any conventional power source. I wasn't sure how it worked but it sounded fascinating—and I knew such things were theoretically possible from the Source Field investigations I had been doing already. Hoagland had lined up meetings with various senators and congressmen to demonstrate the device—and push for these breakthroughs to be released to the public for study and commercial application.

Less than twenty-four hours before we were about to go live on the air, Dr. Mallove was bludgeoned to death outside his parents' home.[42] I found it quite suspicious that this happened right before the announcement to the public of Dr. Mallove's secret device—and of his imminent political mission to Capitol Hill.

Certain groups do appear to have a serious, vested interest in suppressing the Source Field Investigations. I am aware that any discussion of these issues invariably gets you labeled as a "paranoid nutcase," but the events surrounding the death of Dr. Mallove have made it much more personal for me.

Regardless of the skepticism, sarcasm, ridicule, humiliation, and threats that may be associated with the Source Field investigations, there is real truth to be found—hard science you need to know, today, to help make a brighter future for everyone. And best of all, these discoveries are very positive—ultimately proving that most people's idea of a loving God is, in fact, alive and well.

CHAPTER TWO

Consciousness, Eternity and Universal Mind

We are on a quest to discover if a Source Field really does exist—and our investigation is starting to uncover surprising information. Dr. Cleve Backster's research gives the compelling suggestion that all living things—bacteria, plants, insects, animals, birds, fish and humans—are in some form of constant communication with one another. This communication involves the use of a field that is not supposed to exist—because it cannot be found in the conventional electromagnetic spectrum of visible light, radio waves, infrared, microwaves, X-rays, and others. Furthermore, Backster is only one of a variety of hypnosis researchers who have discovered that we can become completely unaware of signals in our environment if we are simply told, while in trance, that we will not be able to see or hear them. If all living things are sharing a constant, psychic attunement with one another, perhaps our minds deliberately screen out most of this information for our own sanity.

In Mexico, there lived a remarkable female healer known as Pachita—born Barbara Guerrero—who was a practitioner of psychic healing. Pachita discovered in childhood that she had a profound healing ability, and practiced it on animals while she worked as a high-wire acrobat for the circus. She later fought alongside Pancho Villa as a teenager, sang in cabarets and sold lottery tickets before recovering her abilities as a thirty-year-old housewife. For the next forty-seven years, she strictly avoided publicity as she practiced her skills, and helped many different people with seemingly incurable medical problems. Only in late 1977 did she become open to the idea of her talents being scientifically studied—and asked Dr. Andrija Puharich to investigate her psychic healing powers with a team of specialists from the United States.[1]

Carla Rueckert wrote firsthand of her healing treatment from Pachita in *The Law of One, Book I.*

> In late 1977 and early 1978 we accompanied Dr. Andrija Puharich and his research associates to Mexico City to investigate a Mexican psychic surgeon, a seventy-eight-year-old woman called Pachita, who had been practicing for a great many years. . . . Pachita used a very dull knife with a five-inch blade. She passed it around amongst the entire research group watching to see our reactions, especially mine, since I was the guinea pig. Since her "operations" took place with me lying on my stomach I cannot give a firsthand account of what occurred, but Don informs me that the knife seemed to disappear four inches into my back and was then moved rapidly across the spine. This was repeated several times. Pachita was, she said, working on my kidneys. Again we made no attempt to conserve "evidence" as we knew that it would come to nothing. Many have attempted to research psychic surgery by analysis of its products, and have found either inconclusive results or null results, indicting that psychic surgery is a fraud.[2]

I was definitely curious about what this actually felt like, so that was the first thing I asked Carla when I interviewed her. Apparently the procedure did cause her very significant pain. She also said there was some blood, even though the wounds miraculously closed up as soon as Pachita withdrew the knife. I am aware this sounds crazy, but it was all witnessed by a room full of trained scientific observers.

Dr. Puharich also received a treatment from Pachita for progressive hearing loss in both ears due to otosclerosis—excess spongy bone growth.

Pachita apparently stuck the tip of her blade right into each of his ear-drums for about forty seconds each—causing him extreme pain—but the wounds then immediately closed up, and there was minimal bleeding and no additional pain. Though this knife trauma should have caused him permanent hearing loss, by any conventional medical understanding, he was stunned by the healing results he then achieved.

> My head was ringing with loud noises. . . . I estimated them to be at the level of a New York subway train, or about 90 decibels above hearing threshold. The noise was so loud that I could not discern speech of those around me, but I had no fear that I might be going deaf as a result of the procedure. Pachita gave me a tincture (contents unknown) and told me to put one drop in each ear daily. The head noises decreased about 10 decibels each day, and by the eighth day, post operative, the noises had ceased. My hearing, however, had become so keen that telephone conversations were painful, and I had to hold the earpiece away from my head to a comfortable distance. This hyperacusia lasted for about two weeks. One month post-operative I had normal pure tone hearing in both ears.[3]

If Pachita was actually just a hypnotist, somehow inducing mass hallucinations, then apparently her treatments were still quite effective. Carla Rueckert described only the first of two operations she had from Pachita. The second operation was explained by Dr. Andrija Puharich in H. G. M. Herman's book—in far more detail.

> Twelve days after the aforementioned operation, Pachita was ready to perform the second operation. She had been able to obtain a human kidney from a post mortem examination. It was brought to her placed in an unsterile jar, suspended in ordinary water, and was stored in a kitchen refrigerator. On the day of the operation, Pachita lifted the kidney out of the jar with her bloody hands. She then sliced it in two longitudinally,

stating that she was going to transplant each half separately. Next she plunged the knife deeply into one side of the back, twisted the knife around, and asked me to drop one kidney half into the hole. I was utterly surprised to find that the kidney in my hand was literally "sucked" into the body of the patient. When I palpated the spot where the kidney had been "sucked" in, I found that the tissue had closed immediately, there was no hole in the skin. It was awesome! In this manner both halves of the kidney were transplanted. The entire operation lasted 92 seconds. One hour afterwards the patient was able to stand. She slept well, and was urinating normally some 14 hours later. After three days she boarded a plane and flew home to the United States.[4]

Said the book's author, "Andrija was convinced that Pachita's 'instant surgery' was completely genuine, and that no fraud of any kind was possible under his and his colleagues' scientific observation and documentation."[5]

Mexican Neuroscientist Enters the Twilight Zone

Whether or not these were actual surgical procedures, Pachita's work also had a huge impact on Dr. Jacobo Grinberg-Zylberbaum—arguably Mexico's most controversial neuroscientist. In 1977, Grinberg took a teaching job at the National Autonomous University of Mexico (UNAM) in Mexico City—and produced a wealth of hard scientific data on the physiology of learning and memory, visual perception and physiological psychology. That same year, Grinberg met Pachita—who completely transformed everything he thought he knew about biology, psychology and medicine. Sam Quinones described the effect Pachita had on Grinberg in a 1997 article.

According to Grinberg, [Pachita] performed successful surgery without anesthesia, using a mountain knife. She replaced diseased organs with others that appeared out of thin air. . . . Grinberg spent several months watching Pachita's operations and talking and traveling with her. He admitted that his descriptions of her operations sounded like ravings, but he insisted he'd seen them.[6]

According to this same article, Grinberg ultimately wrote seven volumes on the shamans of Mexico, and had gone deeply into this type of research by the mid-1980s. Puzzled by the feats he believed he had observed Pachita performing, he theorized that there must be a "neuronal field," as he called it, created within the brain, which in turn interacts with what he called the "pre-space structure"—a field that all space, time, matter, energy, biological life and consciousness emanates from— i.e., the Source Field. Here is how Grinberg explained it in his own words—which are admittedly technical.

> The pre-space structure is a holographic, non-local lattice that has . . . the attribute of consciousness. The neuronal field [created by the brain] distorts this lattice, and activates a partial interpretation of it that is perceived as an image. Only when the brain-mind system is free from interpretations, do the neuronal field and the pre-space structure become identical. In this situation, the perception of reality is unitary, without ego and with a lack of any duality. In this situation, pure consciousness and a feeling of an all-embracing unity and luminosity is [sic] perceived. All the systems that spiritual leaders have developed . . . have had the goal of arriving at this direct perception of the pure pre-space structure. . . . The science of consciousness that I would like to develop is a science that will try to understand, study and research the above-mentioned ideas."[7]

Obviously, if such feats as Pachita's are even possible, very few people possess such abilities. In order to awaken the world to what our true potential might be, Grinberg knew he would need to start with something very simple and repeatable. His earliest experiments in this category began in 1987. Two people, usually a male-female couple, would sit and meditate together for twenty minutes—to form a close bond with each other. They were then separated into two different rooms, each of which was shielded from any and all electromagnetic fields. Both participants' brainwaves would begin to noticeably synchronize, even while they were apart—and Grinberg could measure it on their EEG readouts. He also found that both hemispheres within each person's brain would show the same patterns—which normally only happens in deep meditation. Furthermore, the person who had the most coherent, well-organized brain waves seemed to always "win"—exerting a greater influence upon the other.[8]

In 1994, Grinberg came up with an even more compelling way to demonstrate this effect. Most of the experiment was the same—two people meditated together for twenty minutes and then went into separate, shielded rooms. Now, however, he flashed bright lights in one participant's eyes—causing them to experience sudden shocks. Each time he ran the experiment, one hundred different flashes of light were given at random. Twenty-five percent of the time when he flashed the light in one person's eyes, the other person had a very similar brainwave "shock"—at the exact same time. Grinberg's control subjects did not show any such connections. This was a stunning discovery—and the results were published in the prestigious, peer-reviewed journal *Physics Essays*.[9] A revolution in science seemed to be well under way—the Source Field was finally going mainstream, in a rigorous, clinically verifiable fashion—taking Backster's breakthroughs to the next level.

This is when disaster struck. Shortly after the publication of his paper in 1994, Grinberg disappeared. He still has never been found—and there is even a Facebook page dedicated to tracking him down after all these years.[10] His wife was seen a few times after his disappearance, the last time being in mid-1995, and her behavior indicated that she was extremely distressed about whatever had happened.[11] Some people interpret this as a sign that she may have murdered her husband, but it is also possible that she was threatened that the same fate would happen to her if she didn't disappear for good. We will probably never know what happened—but we can safely add Grinberg-Zylberbaum to the list of Source Field investigators who may have met with lethal threats as a result of their groundbreaking work. That certainly doesn't stop us from putting all the pieces together in this investigation.

Rigorous Laboratory Proof of Consciousness Transfer

Thankfully, other scientists have performed similar experiments, further validating Backster's initial results, without disappearing or being threatened. Dr. Charles Tart, from Berkeley, set up a bizarre experiment where he gave himself painful electrical shocks, automatically—and then attempted to "send" his pain to another person who was the "receiver." This person was wired up to measure heart rate, blood volume and other physiological signals. Tart found that the receiver's body did indeed respond to the shocks—through things such as an increase in heart rate and a decrease in blood volume—but the receiver had no conscious knowledge of when Dr. Tart was sending them.[12]

Probably the greatest modern pioneer in these sorts of experiments is Dr. William Braud. According to Lynne McTaggart in *The Field,* Dr. Braud began by performing an experiment in the late 1960s in which he attempted to transmit his thoughts to one of his students—while the student was under hypnosis. When Dr. Braud pricked his hand, the student felt pain. When he put his hand over a candle flame, the student felt heat. When he stared at a picture of a boat, the student made comments about a boat. When Braud stepped into the sun, the student mentioned sunlight. Distance did not seem to matter; even when Braud was many miles away, it worked just as well.[13] This certainly suggests that the Backster Effect is just the beginning—we share much more information with one another than just the shocks from our nervous system. As the years went by, Dr. Braud sought ways to study this effect under controlled laboratory conditions—and he has now published more than 250 articles in professional psychology journals, and written numerous book chapters.[14][15]

Braud's first rigorous laboratory experiment involved knife fish, which emit electrical signals that change whenever they move from one position to another. These electrical signals can be used to precisely determine the fish's position, and can be picked up by electrodes attached to the side of the tank. Braud's participants were consistently able to change the position of the fish by their conscious intent alone. Similarly, Braud found that participants could increase the speed that Mongolian gerbils ran on their activity wheels, with all other factors being ruled out. Braud also designed an experiment in which he put human red blood cells in a test tube—along with a saline solution that had enough salt in it to kill the cells. His participants were able to focus their minds and protect these cells from bursting open. This was easily verified by measuring how much light could pass through the solution. The more the cells broke down, the more transparent the solution became—so less light was a sign of healthier cells.[16]

From there, Braud moved on to human beings. Have you ever felt someone staring at you, only to turn around and find out you were right? Braud wanted to see if he could study this effect in the lab, and confirm that it really works. He put one person in a private room with a small video camera, wired him up to the polygraph and told him to relax. In a neighboring room, he could see the participant's face on his television monitor. A second participant was then told to stare intently at this person on the monitor and try to get his attention—but only when a computerized random-number generator told them to. Sure enough, when the first person was being stared at, his skin revealed significant electrical spikes. This occurred an average of 59 percent of the time he was being stared at—as opposed to the 50 percent that would be expected by random chance.[17] This might not sound like much, but a 9-percent increase above chance is considered highly substantial.

Dr. Braud then changed the experiment. He had his participants meet each other first—and stare intently into each other's eyes while they talked. He encouraged them to get comfortable with each other. Now, when the person was stared at by his new friend, he noticeably relaxed—on a measurable electrical level.[18] This is solid proof that people can be staring at us, sending us their pain, transmitting thoughts—and even though our bodies may react to these signals on a physical level, we usually don't have any conscious awareness of what's going on. The same thing might be happening when the phone rings and we think we know who it is—only to find out we were right. When the caller visualizes our face, we feel something—and if our mind is quiet enough, we might get a mental image of who it is. Rupert Sheldrake, one of the most renowned Source Field investigators in modern times, also has proven "the sense of being stared at" is indeed genuine—in multiple, published experiments.[19]

The Outer Limits of Shared Consciousness

Minor anxiety disorders, like nervousness and the inability to concentrate, also were measurably improved in Dr. Braud's studies. In an experiment from 1983, Dr. Braud and an anthropologist named Marilyn Schlitz studied a group of highly nervous people along with a group of calmer people. The nervousness of each group, in this case, could be directly measured by the amount of electrical activity on their skin. In some cases, the groups were given common relaxation techniques and instructed to calm themselves down. In other cases, Braud and Schlitz tried to calm them down by simply concentrating on them from another room. The originally calm group showed very little change by practicing the exercises or being "remote influenced," but the nervous group became much calmer—in both cases. Surprisingly, Braud and Schlitz's remote influencing effects upon the nervous group worked almost as well as any relaxation exercises they did for themselves.[20] Similarly, when Braud and Schlitz remotely concentrated on someone in an attempt to help him focus his attention, the subject had an immediate improvement. The people whose minds were the most apt to wander gained the strongest benefits from this process.[21]

Thankfully, Braud also found out that we are not helpless against these remote influences—we can shield the ones we don't want.[22] If you visualize a protective shield, a safe, a barrier or a screen—whatever you feel comfortable with—you can indeed stop these influences from affecting you.[23] The remote influencers did not know which participants were trying to block their thoughts, but the people who did try to shield themselves were successful.[24] Other evidence suggests a positive attitude in life is your best protection, as we will see—the highest "coherence" wins.

Sperry Andrews put together a proposal for a series of ninety-second television spots that would demonstrate these "collective consciousness" experiments to the world—for an initial investment of $711,000 dollars.

> The Human Connection Project contends that a signifi-
> cant number of people will share a greater sense of belonging
> together after watching extensive media announcements and
> presentations that illustrate this subject. Out of this height-
> ened sense of connection to a larger whole, it is predicted that
> a new level of shared intelligence, compassion, and creativity
> will begin to emerge among people.[25]

In this proposal, Andrews mentions some startling facts. More than five hundred different scientific studies have proven that human consciousness can affect biological as well as electronic systems[26]—and we will learn more about the electronic experiments later on. Schlitz and Honorton explored thirty-nine different studies during which people successfully shared thoughts and experiences—while they were physically separated from one another. The overall probability that these effects were caused by chance alone was less than one part in a trillion.[27] In some studies, ordinary people detected events that had not even happened yet in linear time.[28] [29] In an extremely comprehensive paper on the Source Field from 2004, Robert Kenny revealed that the Institute of HeartMath developed Grinberg's original discoveries about brain-to-brain entrainment much further:

> Even when participants were in separate rooms, their heart
> and brain waves became synchronized or entrained, when
> they had close living or working relationships, or when they
> felt appreciation, care, empathy, or love toward each other. . . .
> When people were able to internally entrain their own

personal heart and brain waves [through meditation and other related techniques], they caused the heart and brain waves of other individuals to entrain with theirs. Entrainment appears to increase attention, to produce feelings of calm and deep connection, and to facilitate tele-prehension of each other's sensations, emotions, images, thoughts and intuitions.[30]

There is no turning back. These discoveries are undeniable facts. Our mind-to-mind connection, sharing our thoughts and experiences, has now been proven—at odds of more than a trillion to one against chance. Skeptics continue to boldly proclaim that "there is no evidence," but perhaps a better phrase to use is "there is no publicity." No one has taken Sperry Andrews's offer to produce these groundbreaking, civilization-defining TV spots. Hardly any of this information appears in newspapers, magazines, TV shows or movies. In 2006, Britain's premier science forum featured research from Rupert Sheldrake suggesting that some people know who is calling them before they answer the telephone—and this prompted a furious reaction among participating scientists. Dr. Peter Fenwick also presented his conclusions that consciousness survives after clinical death, and Deborah Delanoy discussed research similar to William Braud's—showing we can influence someone else's body by thinking about him or her. Oxford Professor of Chemistry Peter Atkins said, "Work in this field is a complete waste of time . . . there is absolutely no reason to suppose that telepathy is anything more than a charlatan's fantasy."[31]

Just as this book was in its final edits in January 2011, great controversy again arose because *The Journal of Personality and Social Psychology*, a highly respected science journal, decided to publish the research of Dr. Daryl J. Bem—an emeritus professor at Cornell University. What makes this research so controversial is it contains some of the most stunning proof ever revealed that human consciousness has direct access to events in the future.

In one case, Dr. Bem wanted to see if people would "remember" words that they didn't actually study until after they had already been tested on these words. This experiment began with the participants being given a test in which they had to memorize certain vocabulary words. After they took the test, Dr. Bem randomly chose some of the specified vocabulary words and had the participants study them closely: learn their definitions, practice with them and become comfortable with them. The words they studied in the future (after the test) became the words they memorized the most easily in the past (during the test). Another experiment proved that the emotional shock of seeing an erotic picture would actually travel backwards in time. In this case, a computer screen showed two "curtains." The participant was told that one of the curtains would have a picture behind it, and he was asked to guess which curtain. The picture was chosen, at random, only after the participant made a guess—which the computer program had no access to. Dr. Bem found that when the computer selected an erotic picture, the participants were more likely to guess which curtain it would appear behind—an average of 53 percent of the time. Photographs that were neutral or negative did not have this effect.[32]

Naturally, this turns everything we think we know about science and physics on its end—so many scientists are obviously "mortified" about it, and believe it is "pure craziness."[33] Science should be about discovering the truth, and that requires an open mind. Dr. Bem's research is very sound—it just reveals new things about ourselves, and about reality, that most people do not already know. The data is there—but up until very recently, the publicity has been lacking. Hopefully the publication of Dr. Bem's paper will help start a new trend.

Obviously, some of the problem is that we are constantly being bombarded with new information, and it is increasingly difficult to sort through all of it. However, this research is obviously far more important than the latest news about which celebrity got drunk, angry, naked or arrested, or photographed in some embarrassing way. It does appear, however, that these same celebrities can get addicted to being stared at—as we now know there is a very real energy high they get from all the attention.

The Backster Effect occurs within each and every cell, as we saw in his studies with the white blood cells from a human mouth. However, many ancient traditions adamantly insisted there is a master gland in the human body that is responsible for pulling in thoughts and images from the Source Field, and sending our own thoughts back out. In the next chapter, we will pursue this intriguing investigation—and see if modern science can shed any new light on this ancient mystery.

CHAPTER THREE

The Pineal Gland and the Third Eye

Many different ancient traditions say there is a physical gland, nestled deep within the center of the brain, where telepathic thought transmissions and visual images are received. This tiny pinecone-shaped gland is known as the epiphysis or pineal gland, and is about the size of a pea. In fact, the word "pineal" comes from the Latin *pinea,* which means "pinecone." Ancient cultures all over the world were fascinated by the pinecone and pineal-gland-shaped images, and consistently used them in their highest forms of spiritual artwork. Pythagoras, Plato, Iamblichus, Descartes and others wrote of this gland with great reverence. It has been called the seat of the soul. Obviously, if this "third eye" is receiving direct impressions from the Source Field, we have not yet identified how such a mechanism might work—but that doesn't necessarily mean the ancients were wrong.

The pineal gland is not technically a part of the brain; it is not protected by the blood-brain barrier.[1] It exists in the approximate geometric center of the brain's mass, has a hollow interior filled with a watery fluid, and receives more blood flow than any other

The pineal gland, a pea-sized endocrine gland located in the geometric center of the brain that fascinated many ancient cultures. Notice the pinecone shape.

part of the body except the kidneys. Since it is not protected by the blood-brain barrier, the fluid inside the pineal gland gathers an increasing amount of mineral deposits, or "brain sand," over time—which have optical and chemical properties similar to the enamel on your teeth.[2] This calcification appears as a bonelike mass in the center of your brain on an X-ray or MRI. Doctors use this hard, white cluster to tell if you have a brain tumor. If the white dot appears to be pushed off to one side in your scan, they know a tumor has changed the shape of your brain.

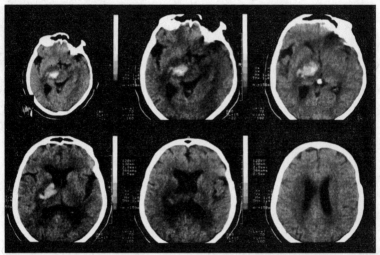

X-ray images showing tumor in left ventricle of the brain. Calcified pineal gland appears in the top-right image as a round white mass, slightly offset by the tumor.

As I detailed in my online documentary *The 2012 Enigma,*[3] pinecones are prominently featured in sacred art and architecture from all over the world—in an apparent homage to the pineal gland. This is a truly astonishing phenomenon that has never been adequately explained. A Christian article entitled "Pagans Love Pine Cones and Use Them in Their Art" has many pictures that prove the point[4]:

- A bronze sculpture of a hand from the mystery cult of Dionysus in the late Roman Empire has a pinecone on the thumb, amidst other strange symbols;

- A Mexican god holds pinecones and a fir tree in a sculpture;
- A staff of the Egyptian sun god Osiris from a museum in Turino, Italy, has two "kundalini serpents" that entwine together and face a pinecone on the top;
- The Assyrian/Babylonian winged god Tammuz is pictured holding a pinecone;
- The Greek god Dionysus carries a staff with a pinecone on top, symbolizing fertility;
- Bacchus, the Roman god of drunkenness and revelry, also carries a pinecone staff;
- The Catholic pope carries a staff with a pinecone directly above where his hand is positioned—and the staff then extends up into a stylized tree trunk;
- Many Roman Catholic candle holders, ornaments, sacred decorations and architectural samples feature the pinecone as a key design element;
- The largest pinecone sculpture in the world is prominently featured in Vatican Square—in the Court of the Pinecone.

We'll come back to these startling Catholic examples in a minute. In *The 2012 Enigma,* I also pointed out that King Tut's golden burial mask features a *uraeus,* or "kundalini serpent," emerging from the general area of the pineal gland in his forehead. Statues of Buddha often feature a prominent third eye between his eyebrows as a raised, circular area. Buddha's hair appears to be stylized in the shape of a pineal

Pope Benedict XVI holding papal staff with carved pinecone—apparently symbolizing his ability to contact higher intelligence via the pineal gland.

gland as well. Almost all Hindu gods and goddesses are pictured with a *bindi*, or third eye, between their eyebrows. Many Hindus still wear such a symbol to this day. The Hindu god Shiva's hair also looks like a stylized pineal gland—and the "kundalini serpents" wrap around his neck.[5]

After I released *The 2012 Enigma,* I found a sculpture of the Meso-american god Quetzalcoatl emerging from the mouth of a serpent—and the body of the serpent is coiled into the exact shape of the pineal gland. In this same sculpture, Quetzalcoatl wears a necklace made out of pine-cones.[6][7] Better yet, the pinecones appear to have energetic waves stream-ing into them from the bottom. The mouth of the serpent frames Quetzalcoatl's face just like we would see in a modern astronaut's helmet. Also, if you look at pictures of the Temple of Quetzalcoatl, the "Plumed Serpent," at Teotihuacan, you can easily see multiple images of pinecones carved alongside the serpent heads.[8]

Statue of Quetzalcoatl emerging from serpent's mouth and wearing a wreath of pinecone-shaped objects. The entire statue is shaped like the pineal gland.

Sacred Stones

Ancient cultures also used sacred stones to symbolize the pineal gland. The Sumerian version was called the "Primitive Mountain"—and it was believed to be the first piece of land to emerge from the primordial sea during the foundation of Heaven and earth. This may represent how the pineal gland is allegedly the first place in the body that is contacted by the waters of Spirit—the nonphysical realms of the afterlife. In

Babylonian culture, this same mountain became a symbol for the *axis mundi*—the axis the world turns on, and/or the central navel of the earth. This was the place where the gods came and went—and it was illustrated with the king standing directly on top of the mountain. A physical stone was also erected to mark this most sacred location—and it determined all the parallels and meridians, as well as the cardinal points of the compass.[9]

The Egyptians had the same myth of a stone marking the center of the world, which they called the Benben—and the king Atum stood upon it during his act of creation. Some forms of the Benben are shaped exactly like the pineal gland. The capstone of a pyramid, as well as the pyramid structure itself, is also believed to represent the Benben stone.[10] This obviously gives incredible new context to the Great Seal of the United States. Here we have a single eye in a triangle, floating on top of a pyramid. In light of the pyramid/Benben/third-eye relationship, the symbolic connection between the Great Seal and the pineal gland is undeniable—and we will discuss this mysterious symbol in chapter 7. In early illustrations of the Great Seal of the United States, the bird on the front side was not an eagle—it was deliberately illustrated as a phoenix.

The Egyptians drew the Benben stone with a bird flanking it on either side—called the Bennu bird.[11] This bird may be depicted as a

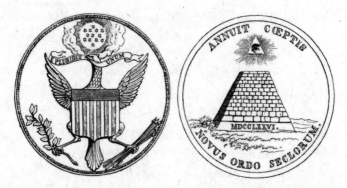

Early concept art for Great Seal of the United States, c. 1776–1782. The bird is a stylized phoenix, and bears no resemblance to an eagle.

hawk, eagle, heron or yellow wagtail, depending upon which Egyptian source you study—but in Greek mythology the Bennu bird is known as the phoenix.[12] This mythical creature experiences death by fire, followed by a spontaneous rebirth from the ashes—clearly associating the Bennu bird with a profound spiritual awakening and transformation. The words *Benben* and *Bennu* are both derived from the root syllable *Bn*, which means "ascension" or "to rise" in Egyptian.[13] Two serpents may also be pictured with the Benben stone, at times, and they appear equivalent to the "kundalini serpents" in Hinduism—illustrating the flow of energetic currents moving up the spine and on into the pineal gland.

It is also fascinating to note that in Egyptian mythology, the Bennu's cry is believed to have started the great cycles of time. These cycles were said to have been appointed by a Divine intelligence—and Horus, the Bennu bird, became the Egyptian deity associated with the division of time.[14] There is a strong possibility that the main unit of time represented by the Bennu's cry is the Precession of the Equinoxes—a 25,920-year cycle that appears as a slow wobble in the earth's axis. This strongly implied association between the Bennu and the 25,920-year cycle may be a prophecy that humanity will experience a phoenix-like transmutation effect at the end of this cycle—and we will explore other prophetic traditions that support this concept as well. (Our investigation into the precession begins in chapter 6.) The Egyptian Book of the Dead features instructions on how the spiritual seeker may transform himself or herself into a Bennu bird or phoenix, symbolically speaking—and the results of this practice, if successfully achieved, are very interesting:

> I have flown up like the primeval ones . . . I appear in glory with the strides of the gods. . . . As for him who knows this pure spell, it means going out into the day after death and being transformed at will. . . . And nothing evil shall have power over him.[15]

In Hinduism the Shiva lingam is a stone shaped exactly like the pineal gland—and is mythologically associated with the center of the world, from which the god Shiva first burst through in a fiery spectacle.[16] Again we remember the pineal gland is in the geometric center of the brain, and was believed to be the first point of contact for telepathic information exchange—not unlike the idea of a god bursting through to communicate a message. Let's not forget that Shiva is also drawn with the fully opened third eye, the kundalini serpents around his neck and his hair stylized to look like a pineal gland.

In Greece we have the omphalos stone, which was housed at the Oracle at Delphi and is also shaped exactly like the pineal gland. This was believed to be a stone in which the god Apollo resided—and through it, the oracles could communicate with him and harness the power of prophecy. Some omphalos stones are clearly pictured with the "kundalini serpent" wrapping around them. The word *omphalos* means "the center of the earth" and "navel" in Greek, and this area was again the main geographic reference point for the entire Hellenic empire.[17]

In the Roman empire this same stone was known as the *baetyl*, a

Greek coins with eagle/phoenix and omphalos stone with Tree of Life emerging from it (top) and winged god and pyramid-shaped baetyl with capstone (bottom).

Phoenician word that was later written as Beth-el[18]—and was apparently
the word root for Bethlehem, the birthplace of Jesus, who became the
"chief cornerstone" of the Christian world. The baetyl stone was directly
associated with oracles and prophecy. A surprising number of Greek and
Roman coins prominently feature the omphalos or baetyl stone on one
side, sometimes guarded by a hawk—as one ancient depiction of the
Bennu bird—or a serpent. Some of these coins feature the "Tree of Life,"
another symbol of the *axis mundi,* growing directly out of the stone—or
adjacent to it.

Other Roman coins feature a triangular baetyl—specifically an isos-
celes triangle with a narrow base and two longer sides of equal length.
This triangle looks halfway between a pyramid and an obelisk in shape,
and is curiously similar to the pyramid we see on the U.S. dollar bill,
although steeper. Even more interestingly, some of these Roman coins
have the top part of the triangle cut off by a horizontal line, which forms
the equivalent of a small capstone.[19] If you think about a Roman coin
with a baetyl on one side and a hawk or eagle on the other, you're now
much closer to the Great Seal of the United States, with a pyramid on
one side and the eagle on the other—and this does not appear to be a
coincidence.

Many of these Roman baetyl coins feature the image of a winged
angel on the opposite side. The design of this angel is very similar to that
of winged Babylonian gods, such as Tammuz, who were pictured holding
a pinecone in one hand and pointing it as if it possessed mystical powers.

Greek coins with god Apollo sitting on omphalos stone, stylized to look like a
pinecone.

One coin from Syria, circa 246–227 B.C., features the god Apollo sitting on the omphalos stone—which is very clearly stylized to look like a pinecone in this case. Two other Greek coins show Apollo sitting on an omphalos that is even more blatantly stylized as a pinecone.[20]

Given this history, and the widespread use of the omphalos and baetyl on Greek and Roman coins, we can understand why the Romans placed a giant bronze statue of a pinecone in the center of Saint Peter's in the Vatican, and built a pinecone into the pope's staff. The pope is supposed to be God's anointed messenger, and in the ancient traditions, this requires an "awakened" pineal gland. A quick Google Images search proves the staff I show in *The 2012 Enigma* is not the only one with a pinecone in it that the pope carries.

The gigantic bronze pinecone at the Vatican is much taller than a human being, and is surrounded by Egyptian symbols. This statue fixed the Vatican as the center of the Roman Catholic world—the *axis mundi*—in accordance with the ancient tradition. Two lions guard the statue at its base—sitting on pedestals that are inscribed with Egyptian hieroglyphics. The statue itself is flanked with two birds that almost certainly represent the Egyptian Bennu/phoenix, but none of this is

explained. Behind the looming pinecone statue lies an open Egyptian-style sarcophagus, similar to what is found in the King's Chamber of the Great Pyramid. Elsewhere in the Vatican we find Egyptian obelisks—with Christian symbols apologetically included on their tops.

View behind Vatican pinecone, showing open Egyptian sarcophagus with protective Plexiglas cover to stop people from lying in it.

This massive bronze pinecone is found in the Court of the Pigna, or Court of the Pinecone—at the northern end of the great Renaissance Belvedere Courtyard in Saint Peter's. To the south, we find Pope Pius VII's Braccio Nuovo. Eastward we see the Chiaromoni Gallery. Pope Innocent VIII's palazzetto is to the north, and Pope Sixtus V's Apostolic

The Vatican Court of the Pinecone, showing giant pinecone statue (right) and bronze "sphere within sphere" sculpture (left), stylized much like an eye.

Library galleries are to the west. This huge pinecone was cast in the first or second century A.D., by Publius Cincius Salvius—who inscribed his name on the base. Near the end of the eighth century, it was moved directly into the center of the entrance hall in the medieval Saint Peter's. It wasn't dismantled and moved into its current position until 1608.[21]

Obviously, the early Church fathers felt the pinecone was an extremely important symbol if they placed it so prominently in the Vatican. Further clues may be found in the Bible—where Jesus said, "The light of the body is the eye: if therefore thine eye be single, thy whole body shall be filled with light." (Matthew 6:22)[22] The Court of the Pinecone also has an enigmatic "sphere within sphere" sculpture at the center. Various images seem to be conveyed, including the shell of an egg cracking open, the possible idea of two planets colliding together, and the concept of hidden gears and machinery being exposed under the surface of the spheres. The two spheres are offset from each other by ninety degrees, and various physics models have suggested we must make an angular turn like this—what they call an "orthogonal rotation"—to enter into higher dimensions. Intriguingly, this sculpture also looks like a stylized eye—which fits with the idea of the pinecone representing the pineal gland or "third eye."

Close-up view of peculiar bronze sculpture in Vatican Court of the Pinecone, suggesting a cracked egg and hidden machinery underneath.

Islamic tradition is also built around a sacred stone—the Ka'aba—that is the central object of devotion for the pilgrimage to the holy land of Mecca. It also is the *axis mundi* of the Islamic world, since every Muslim in the world prays toward this location. A small area of the stone is exposed for the pilgrims to kiss, and this area is surrounded by a polished metallic brace that looks just like a vertical, stylized third eye. The Ka'aba may therefore be another representation of the pineal gland, in further accordance with the ancient tradition. Ireland also has cult stones dating back to around 200 B.C. that fit the pattern—and the Turoe Stone in County Galway looks just like the omphalos, Benben, shiva lingam and baetyl, with stylized, firelike waves of energy carved across its surface.[23]

The Written Legends

The written history of the pineal gland as our possible gateway to the Source Field, where it is discussed without any veiled symbolism, begins with the work of Pythagoras and Plato—as the occultist Helena Blavatsky explained. When she brings up "the Mysteries," she is referring to an allegedly hidden tradition of secrets that have been handed down from ancient Egypt and other civilizations in the distant past. Apparently there are "mystery schools" that have continued teaching these ancient traditions through to the present day.

> The key to the whole Pythagorean system, irrespective of the particular science to which it is applied, is the general formula of unity in multiplicity, the idea of the One evolving and pervading the many. . . . Pythagoras called it the Science of Numbers. Pythagoras taught that this science—the chief of all in occultism—was revealed to men by "celestial deities," those godlike men who were the Divine Instructors of the Third Race. It was first taught to the Greeks by Orpheus, and for centuries made known only to the "chosen few" in the Mysteries. . . .

In his *Life of Pythagoras,* Iamblichus repeats the statement of Plato that the study of the science of Numbers tends to awaken that organ in the brain that the ancients described as the "eye of wisdom"—the organ now known to physiology as the pineal gland. Speaking of the mathematical disciplines, Plato says in *The Republic* (Book VII), "the soul through these disciplines has an organ purified and enlightened, an organ better worth saving than ten thousand corporeal eyes, since truth becomes visible through this alone."[24]

According to the prolific and controversial Masonic scholar Manly Palmer Hall, Freemasonry traces itself back to these same Egyptian mystery schools. He also claims the biggest secret of Freemasonry is the regeneration of the human being into a Divine state—through the awakening of the pineal gland. Each of the thirty-three degrees of Masonry correspond to one of the vertebrae in the human spine—as the kundalini fire rises up to merge with the pineal gland.

> The exact science of human regeneration is the Lost Key of Masonry, for when the Spirit Fire is lifted up through the thirty-three degrees, or segments of the spinal column, and enters into the domed chamber of the human skull, it finally passes into the pituitary body (Isis), where it invokes Ra (the pineal gland) and demands the Sacred Name. Operative Masonry, in the fullest meaning of that term, signifies the process by which the Eye of Horus is opened.
>
> E. A. Wallis Budge has noted that in some of the papyri illustrating the entrance of the souls of the dead into the judgment hall of Osiris, the deceased person has a pinecone attached to the crown of his head. The Greek mystics also carried a symbolic staff, the upper end being in the form of a pinecone, which was called the thyrsus of Bacchus. . . . In the human brain there is a tiny gland called the pineal body, which is the sacred eye of the ancients, and corresponds to the third eye of the Cyclops. Little is known concerning the function of the pineal body, which Descartes suggested (more wisely than he knew) might be the abode of the spirit of man. As its name signifies, the pineal gland is the sacred pinecone in man—the eye single, which cannot be opened until CHiram (the Spirit Fire) is raised through the sacred seals [or chakras,] which are called the Seven Churches in Asia."[25]

Hall gave additional information into this deep Masonic secret in another book, *The Occult Anatomy of Man.*

> The Hindus teach that the pineal gland is the third eye, called the Eye of Dangma. It is called by the Buddhists the all-seeing eye, and is spoken of in Christianity as the eye single. . . . The pineal gland is supposed to secrete an oil, which is called resin, the life of the pine tree. This word [*resin*] is supposed to be involved in the origin of the Rosicrucians, who were working with the secretions of the pineal gland and seeking to open the eye single; for it is said in scripture: "The light of the body is the eye: if therefore thine eye be single thy whole body shall be filled with light." . . .
>
> [The pineal gland] is a spiritual organ which is later destined to be what it once was, namely a connecting link between the human and the divine. The vibrating finger on the end of this gland is the rod of Jesse and the scepter of the high priest. Certain exercises as given in the Eastern and Western mystery schools cause this little finger to vibrate, resulting in a buzzing, droning sound in the brain. This is sometimes very distressing, especially when the individual who experiences this phenomena, in all too many cases, knows nothing about the experiences through which he is passing."[26]

It appears the Freemasons and other secret societies may have also referred to the awakened pineal gland as the Philosopher's Stone. Manly Palmer Hall's description is but one of many that make this strong suggestion—when you consider the context.

> The Philosopher's Stone is an ancient symbol of the perfected and regenerated man whose divine nature shines forth. . . . As the rough diamond is dull and lifeless when first removed from the black carbon, so the spiritual nature of

man in its "fallen" state reveals little, if any, of its inherent luminosity. . . . He who possesses the Philosopher's Stone possesses Truth, the greatest of all treasures, and is therefore rich beyond the calculation of man; he is immortal because Reason takes no account of death and he is healed of Ignorance—the most loathsome of all diseases.[27]

Rudolf Steiner, a well-known scholar of the esoteric mystery schools, argued that the legend of the Holy Grail—a chalice filled with the "waters of life" or "elixir of immortality"—is yet another symbolic reference to the pineal gland.[28] The bowl of the Grail chalice is shaped like a pineal gland in most historic illustrations—but upside down compared to everything else we've been discussing so far. A recent Steiner compilation entitled *The Mysteries of the Holy Grail* establishes detailed connections between the Grail legends and the pineal gland.

The [Holy] Grail is also located within each of us, in the castle of the skull, and can nourish our subtlest perceptions in a way that dispels all but the most refined material influence. . . . Steiner is referring here to the pineal gland in the brain. . . .[29]

The legends of the "Cosmic Egg," "World Egg" and particularly the "Orphic Egg" also appear to be pineal gland references. The Orphic Egg is pictured with a serpent wrapped around it, and the shape of an egg is similar to the shape of the pineal gland. Manly Palmer Hall again gives insight into the meaning of this ancient symbol, hinting at a connection with the pineal gland—when you consider his other statements as well.

The ancient symbol of the Orphic Mysteries was the serpent-entwined egg, which signified Cosmos as encircled by the fiery Creative Spirit. The egg also represents the soul of the philosopher; the serpent, the Mysteries. At the time of initiation the shell is broken and man emerges from the embryonic state of physical existence wherein he had remained through the fetal period of philosophic regeneration.[30]

Hall also believed the unicorn was another mythical symbol of the awakened pineal gland:

> The single horn of the unicorn may represent the pineal gland, or third eye, which is the spiritual cognition center in the brain. The unicorn was adopted by the Mysteries as a symbol of the illumined spiritual nature of the initiate. . . .[31]

According to the *Stanford Encyclopedia of Philosophy,* René Descartes believed that human beings were composed of two main ingredients—a body and a soul—and the pineal gland was the junction point between them. In Descartes's view, the pineal gland is "involved in sensation, imagination, memory and the causation of bodily movements." Though much of what Descartes said does not line up with modern understandings of the brain, some of his thoughts may have come directly from the ancient mystery schools.

> The part of the body in which the soul directly exercises its functions is not the heart at all, or the whole of the brain. It is rather the innermost part of the brain, which is a certain very small gland situated in the middle of the brain's substance. . . . A low-pressure image of the sensory stimulus [from the soul] appears on the surface of the pineal gland.[32]

Descartes's idea of visual images appearing on the surface of the pineal gland may be far more accurate than most people realize—as we are about to discover. This suggests that he did not think of this concept himself, but might have leaked ancient secrets he had been entrusted with—mixing them in with his own ideas as well.

The Edgar Cayce Readings also spoke about the pineal gland on a variety of occasions—and agreed that this was a literal eye in the center of the brain stem, and that it was the anchor point where the soul joins with the body.[33]

Medical Investigations of the Third Eye

According to Dr. Richard Cox in USC's *Health & Medicine* journal, Descartes "perceived the mind as some sort of out-of-body experience expressed through the pineal gland."[34] Cox reveals some surprising facts about the pineal gland.

> Under the skin in the skull of a lizard lies a light-responsive "third eye" which is the evolutionary equivalent of the bone-encased, hormone-secreting pineal gland in the human brain. The human pineal is denied access to light directly, but like the lizard's "third eye," it shows enhanced release of its hormone, melatonin, during the night. . . . Dissected, the reptile's pineal looks much like an eye, with the same shape and tissue. The pineal . . . uniquely remains the major source of circulating melatonin, [which tells us] when to go to sleep at night and when to get up in the morning. . . . The presence of light reduces the pineal gland's secretion of melatonin, and darkness stimulates production. Since daylight and darkness affect the gland's production of the hormone, the pineal functions as a kind of internal timepiece.[35]

It is certainly strange that a reptile's pineal gland has the same shape and tissue as a normal eye—considering the ancients literally believed the pineal gland was a third eye within the human body, performing a similar biological function. The more I researched this subject, the more I found clues the ancients may have indeed known something that has since been lost. An article in *Science News* by Julie Ann Miller began to reveal the biological connection between the pineal gland and the retina of the eye.

The retina and the pineal gland are the organs primarily responsible for the body's recognition and sophisticated processing of external light. Until recently these two organs in mammals seemed to have little else in common and were consequently studied by separate groups of scientists. But a new alliance of researchers is now exploring striking similarities that are speeding research efforts in both fields. . . . Once the groups of scientists began working together, they discovered surprising similarities between the two organs.[36]

An article in *Science Daily* featured startling statements from Dr. David Klein, the chief scientist in the National Institute of Child Health and Human Development's Section on Neuroendocrinology. Many sub-mammal species already detect light with their pineal glands—as a third eye.

Dr. Klein noted that the photoreceptor cells of the retina strongly resemble the cells of the pineal gland, and that the pineal cells of sub-mammals (such as fish, frogs and birds) detect light."[37]

An even more surprising suggestion can be found in a 1986 paper by A. F. Weichmann, in the professional science journal *Experimental Eye Research*.

It is apparent that several relationships exist between the pineal gland and retina. The similarities in development and morphology have been obvious for many years. A recent resurgence of interest in this field has led to a further understanding of many functional similarities between these two organs. . . . Although the mammalian pineal gland is considered to be only indirectly photosensitive, the presence of proteins in the pineal which are normally involved in phototransduction [light sensing] in the retina, raises the possibility that direct photic events may occur in the mammalian pineal gland. This possibility awaits further study.[38]

Weichmann is openly speculating that "direct photic events"—flashes of photons of light—may be somehow occurring in the pineal gland by an unknown mechanism. Due to the similarity of the pineal gland and the retina in the eye, the cells within your pineal gland may be detecting photons and sending them to your brain—by a process called photo-transduction.

R. N. Lolley and associates also noticed the similarities between the light-sensing activities of the retina and the pineal gland—in a paper from the peer-reviewed science journal *Neurochemical Research*. Recent breakthroughs in understanding how the retina actually works have made this connection much clearer than it would have been before.

> As the mechanisms of phototransduction in retinal photo-receptor cells have become more clear, it has equally become apparent that pinealocytes [pineal gland cells] have . . . a selective group of retinal proteins that are involved in the phototransduction cascade. How the pinealocytes utilize these proteins and whether [they] participate in signal trans-duction in the pineal is still unknown. . . . The pinealocytes and retinal photoreceptors seem to possess a similar repertoire of activities. . . .[39]

No one has proven that the area inside the pineal gland is com-pletely dark. Trace amounts of photons may be appearing by an unknown mechanism, as Descartes appears to have suggested. The pineal gland does appear to be set up for signal transduction, just like the retina of the eye, where it picks up visual images and sends them to the brain. Another group of scientists studying the pineal gland in chickens also concluded that "the pineal gland may contain a rodlike phototransduc-tion cascade."[40]

Piezoluminescence

Why would the body go to all this trouble to make a third eye, with the same tissues and light-sensing mechanisms as the retina, if there was nothing for us to see in there? What are we really seeing when we dream, have an out-of-body experience or get sudden images flashing into our minds? And why were ancient cultures all over the world so obsessed with this gland as the center of our psychic vision? In a 2002 study published in the *Bioelectromagnetics* journal, S. S. Baconnier and associates may have found the answer—without even realizing it. They dissected twenty different human pineal glands and found one hundred to three hundred microcrystals per cubic millimeter that were floating inside—largely composed of a common mineral called calcite. Each of these crystals were between two and twenty micrometers in length, basically hexagonal in shape, and were very similar to other crystals we find in the inner ear called otoconia. These inner-ear crystals are known to be *piezoelectric*—which means they expand and contract in the presence of electromagnetic fields.[41] The hairs inside the inner ear detect sounds when the otoconia bump against them—as they move around from the vibrations picked up by the eardrum.

Piezoelectric crystals can be used to tune in to radio stations without any electricity. The electromagnetic waves that are jittering all around us make these crystals expand and contract constantly. These movements can then be detected and amplified to make sound.[42] Microphones also have piezoelectric crystals that pick up sound vibrations and turn them directly into electrical current. Some, if not many, piezoelectric crystals also give off varying amounts of light—in a process known as piezoluminescence.[43] This can be seen in a handheld lighter; when you push the button down, a spark of light comes out—which is caused by compressing a piezoelectric crystal inside. Through a process called *piezochromism*, some piezoelectric crystals release different-colored photons from the same crystal, depending upon the signal they receive. So far, these piezoelectric color changes have only been spotted in crystals under high pressure. According to the *Royal Society of Chemistry* in the United Kingdom, these piezoelectric color changes "have been observed in a few systems, but have not been exploited in any commercial way."[44] So far, no one has needed to make a microscopic computer monitor or video projection system, for example.

Baconnier's calcite crystals may not be the only potential source of light in the pineal gland. Some scientists, such as Dr. Rick Strassman, suggest the pineal gland may also secrete a psychoactive chemical called DMT—though this has not yet been proven, due to how fast it breaks down. DMT also appears to release light by piezoluminescence, as we will see. Dr. Laurance Johnston discussed the controversial idea that the pineal gland creates DMT, which is chemically similar to melatonin and serotonin—two chemicals that appear naturally in the pineal gland and appear to be synthesized by it.

> DMT is structurally similar to melatonin. The biochemical precursor to both molecules is serotonin, a key neurotransmitter whose pathways are involved in mood and targeted in the treatment of psychiatric disorders. DMT also structurally resembles other psychedelic drugs, such as LSD and psilocybin, and is the active agent in ayahuasca brew Amazon shamans use to provoke out-of-body experiences. . . .
>
> Trace amounts of DMT have been found in humans, particularly in the lungs, but also in the brain. Strassman emphasizes that the pineal gland is theoretically more capable than virtually any other tissue to produce DMT, including possessing prerequisite biochemical precursors and transforming enzymes. However, we do not yet know for certain whether DMT is made by the pineal.[45]

DMT may very well be the "resin" that Manly Palmer Hall said the ancient mystery schools were looking for. However, I am definitely not an advocate of taking psychedelic drugs, as they can be very dangerous and upsetting. There are spiritual practices that achieve similar effects in a positive way, and I'd rather use what I already have—naturally and safely. However, I was fascinated to discover that Nick Sand, the son of a prominent scientist on the Manhattan Project, found that DMT had enormous piezoluminescence—and apparently color-shooting piezochromism as well.

> Sand was . . . the first underground chemist on record to have synthesized DMT. Sand and a lab colleague were the first people to notice that DMT exhibits piezoluminescence: when hardened DMT that had collected in a tray was being chipped out with a hammer and screwdriver in a brightly lit room, the blows emitted massive amounts of colored light.[46]

Since the pineal gland is not protected by the blood-brain barrier, flooding the bloodstream with DMT may load up the pineal gland with piezoelectric microcrystals. This in turn may cause the third eye to pull in many more photons—which might be emerging directly out of the Source Field, thanks to principles we have not yet discussed. (DNA also appears to be pulling in photons by a similar process, as we will see.) Baconnier's groundbreaking pineal gland studies helped set the stage for this speculative idea of how the third eye could actually be "seeing" photons of light.

> If piezoelectricity were to exist [in the pineal calcite microcrystals], an electromechanical coupling mechanism to external electromagnetic fields may be possible.[47]

> These crystals could be responsible for an electromechanical biological transduction mechanism in the pineal gland, due to their structure and piezoelectric properties.[48]

For this same reason, Baconnier expresses deep concern about our use of cellular phones and other microwave-emitting devices—as they may couple directly with these piezoelectric crystals in the pineal gland and change how they function. This could interrupt our synthesis of melatonin—with negative health consequences.

Health Consequences of Pineal Gland Calcification

The more we find out about the pineal gland, the more important it becomes in human health.

> Until relatively recently, the pineal gland was considered a vestigial organ lacking function, i.e., the brain's appendix. Then scientists showed it produced melatonin, a hormone that profoundly affects us. The pineal gland converts the amino acid tryptophan into serotonin (a neurotransmitter) and, in turn, melatonin. The melatonin then is released into the bloodstream and cerebrospinal fluid where it is transported throughout the body. The release is closely correlated to our sleep-wake cycle. . . . Researchers have actually found magnetite clusters near the pineal gland. Like homing pigeons, humans have residual ability to orient to geomagnetic directional cues, an ability lost with pineal dysfunction. . . .
>
> Because the gland accumulates fluoride, it contains the body's highest fluoride concentration. Research shows that this accumulation depresses melatonin synthesis with adverse consequences such as accelerating puberty onset . . .
>
> Because pineal dysfunction and, in turn, low melatonin secretion are correlated with MS [multiple sclerosis] symptoms, pineal failure may predispose one to MS. For example, Dr. Reuven Sandyk (New York) has stated, "Dysfunction of the pineal gland can explain a far broader range of biological phenomena associated with MS, and therefore the pineal gland should be considered the pivotal mover of the disease." . . . Sandyk suggests that MS severity may be related to the degree of pineal failure. . . .
>
> Clearly, MS is associated with pineal calcification. For example, one study showed 100 percent of individuals with

MS who were consecutively admitted to a hospital had pineal calcification compared to only 43 percent for similar-aged controls with other neurological disorders. In addition, groups that have a low MS incidence (e.g., African Americans, Japanese) also have less pineal calcification.[49]

Fluoride—such as you get in tap water and commercial toothpaste—is very likely a no-no if you want a healthy pineal gland. Fluoride apparently passes directly into the pineal gland through the bloodstream, where it then attaches itself to the tiny crystals that are already floating around inside and covers them with hard mineral deposits—creating the white, bonelike lumps we see in X-ray images. This may damage the pineal gland's ability to synthesize the chemicals we need.

> Fluoride may affect the enzymatic conversion of tryptophan to melatonin . . . Fluoride may also affect the synthesis of melatonin precursors (e.g., serotonin), or other pineal products (e.g., 5-methoxytryptamine). . . . In conclusion, the human pineal gland contains the highest concentration of fluoride in the body. . . . Whether or not fluoride interferes with pineal function in humans requires further investigation.[50]

As your pineal gland fills up with brain sand, or calcification, such as from fluoride, you may well be losing your ability to produce melatonin—and that's definitely not a good thing. One study in the *Journal of Pineal Research* revealed how many problems could be caused by pineal calcification and malfunction—including depression, anxiety, eating disorders, schizophrenia and other forms of mental illness.

> Collectively, these findings suggest that melatonin probably is significantly associated with the regulation of memory, cognition, and also involved in emotional processes. . . . These findings emphasize a specific role for melatonin in mechanisms of consciousness, memory, and stress, [and] are

also consistent with reported studies that indicate melatonin alterations in psychopathology mainly in patients with depression, schizophrenia, anxiety disorders, eating disorders and also in other mental disorders. . . .

For example, in many studies decreased melatonin levels in patients with depressive disorder were reported. . . . Typical melatonin alterations have also been found in schizophrenia and suggest that diminished melatonin secretion may be associated with the pathophysiology of a subgroup of schizophrenic patients. . . . [C]haracteristic alterations in rhythm of melatonin secretion have been found in various mental disorders. . . .[51]

I learned in 1995 that emotions like happiness don't just happen automatically because you want them to—they are controlled by chemicals in the brain. If your brain doesn't have enough serotonin, you will be chemically incapable of feeling happiness—even if you have many things in your life that should otherwise make you feel good. I had no idea how important the pineal gland was in manufacturing serotonin— and therefore in how happy we will feel—until I did the research for this book.

Nicholas Giarmin, a professor of pharmacology, and Daniel Freedman, a professor of psychiatry, confirmed that the human brain manufactures serotonin at various sites in the brain. For example, in the Thalamus, they discovered 61 nanograms of serotonin per gram of tissue; in the Hippocampus, 56 ng.; in the Central Gray Section of the Midbrain, they found 482 ng. But in the Pineal Gland, they found 3140 ng. of serotonin per gram of tissue. The Pineal Gland was unmistakably the richest site of serotonin in the brain. This discovery implicates the Pineal Gland as an important site of serotonergic [serotonin-forming] activity.[52]

These same scientists also found even more connections between the pineal gland, its serotonin levels and various mental disorders.

An absolutely shocking discovery was the correlation between high serotonin levels in the Pineal Gland and certain mental disorders! . . . The average amount of serotonin found in the Pineal Glands of normal persons is about 3.14 to 3.52 micrograms per gram of tissue. One schizophrenic was found to have a Pineal Gland containing 10 micrograms of serotonin, around 3 times higher, while another patient, a sufferer from delirium tremens, had a Pineal Gland containing 22.82 micrograms of serotonin, around 10 times higher then the average amount![53]

This same study also established a direct connection between serotonin levels in the pineal gland and tremors, such as tardive dyskinesia, Parkinson's disease and even epileptic seizures. They found several studies showing "significant differences between the severity of dystonic movements [tremors] in patients with no Pineal Gland calcification and those with pathologically enlarged Pineal Gland calcification."[54]

Many health professionals have discussed the problems with calcification in the body. In the worst-case scenario it can even create painful conditions like gout, in which your feet and toes have so much calcification that they form crystals that hurt when they break. The most important key to eliminating calcification is a healthy diet. If you drink lots of purified water, you help your liver and kidneys flush out all these toxins. Eating a diet of fresh, organic raw foods insures you won't have pesticides and preservatives accumulating in your body and creating mineral deposits.

Dr. Weston Price found that many traditional, undisturbed cultures had much higher bone density from eating their native foods. Their teeth stayed beautifully straight, without any need for orthodontics, and they hardly ever got cavities—without even brushing. As soon as processed Western foods were introduced into their diets, such as refined sugar, white flour, nonorganic dairy and factory-farmed meats, their teeth became crooked and started to rot out of their heads. Thankfully, by going back to a pure, natural diet, rich in traditional foods—including organic animal products—we can actually reverse these problems and decalcify the pineal gland.

Dr. Price identified a compound he called Activator X, which is also now known as vitamin K2, in these traditional foods—which seemed to be the key ingredient. If you're a vegetarian, you can get it from organic butter oil—harvested from cattle who feed only on fresh, organic, rapidly growing grass. Meat eaters can take fermented cod liver oil or ratfish liver oil, which is even better. Price also recommended combining land and sea—butter oil and fermented fish liver oil—for even stronger results. Activator X is also found in organic grass-fed eggs and meat products. In his book *Nutrition and Physical Degeneration,* Dr. Price reveals controversial photographs of people who apparently reversed tooth decay and regrew enamel once they restored Activator X into their diets. Arterial plaque—the great killer in heart attacks and strokes— could also be cleaned out, and pineal function greatly improved by decreasing its calcification.[55]

As we look over the information in this chapter, there are compelling avenues for new research. I want to make it clear that I do not consider the Source Field to be some abstract, metaphysical idea. I agree with many Russian scientists who have concluded that the Source Field is directly measurable—as a spinning current within gravity. It appears that the more you screen out the influence of electromagnetic energy fields, the more sensitive you become to the information within the Source Field—perhaps through the pineal gland, as the ancient traditions suggest.

Considering all the information we have surveyed in these last three chapters, the obvious question we now must ask ourselves is this: What is consciousness? Where is the mind getting its orders from—in what may be a hidden, ongoing form of posthypnotic suggestion from some other aspect of ourselves? Are thoughts happening in the brain, where they then generate an energy wave that can move through the Source Field? Or, are we actually using the Source Field to think—and even share a collective mind with all others as well?

CHAPTER FOUR

Thinking with the Field—in the Great Cycles of Life

Ancient cultures all over the world were fascinated with pineal gland symbolism. Many different spiritual teachings—including secret mystery-school traditions—believed the pineal gland acts as a literal third eye in the brain. Recent scientific breakthroughs have determined that there are substantial, biological similarities between the retina and the pineal gland. Piezoelectric microcrystals may be transmitting photons that can be picked up by the retina-like tissue in the pineal gland—where they are then sent to the brain and descrambled into visual images. This may be responsible for what we call the "mind's eye"—such as when we suddenly see a mental image of our friend right before he or she calls us.

Clearly, more research is necessary to fully understand how the pineal gland actually works, but we already have some intriguing clues. Either way, in chapters 1 and 2 we found compelling scientific proof that all of Nature is in constant telepathic communication—through a field that is clearly not electromagnetic. When we combine Dr. William Braud's extensive research with Backster's breakthroughs, everything we think we know about being living, conscious humans must change. No longer can we see ourselves as separate from our environment; we are fundamentally intertwined with those around us. Whatever we think, they think—and whatever we feel, they feel. Exactly how far can this mind-sharing effect go? Does it only work from one person to another? Does this knowledge have any practical value, or is it just another piece of "weird science"?

At this point, we may need to consider a shift in perspective. Let's start by asking ourselves this question: What, exactly, is Mind? Even when we discuss the pineal gland, we are still prone to think of the mind as something that exists within each person—where one mind then sends messages to another mind like a two-way radio. However, what if we're actually all sharing the same mind, to some degree—and that mind is far more energetic in nature than we've been led to believe?

Let's go back to Backster and really think about what he discovered. If the mind is an energetic field, then bacteria could be sharing the same mind as plants. Plants could share the same mind as eggs. Eggs could share the same mind as animals. And all living things may share the same mind with us. When Backster wanted to burn a leaf, the plant responded. When Backster started watering a plant, it tracked his movements. Backster once told me his plants always "screamed" when one man came into the lab—and this man turned out to mow lawns for a living. When two people meditate together and then go their separate ways, a jolting flash of light in one person's eyes will create an identical brainwave shock in the other person—25 percent of the time. The Institute of HeartMath showed that when we live together, work together or have an affinity for each other, we begin synchronizing brainwaves, heartbeat patterns and other vital signs. Dr. William Braud found that a nervous person could be calmed down by "remote influencing." A distracted person could have better concentration and an immediate improvement in mental focus—simply by having someone else do the thinking for them at a distance.

Thoughts Occurring Directly in the Source Field

A September 2010 article in *Wired* magazine featured a discussion between Kevin Kelly and Steven Johnson on what they called "the hive mind." A surprising number of human innovations appear in different people's minds simultaneously—as if we're all using the same energy field to think with. As new ideas are introduced into that energy field, they suddenly become available to everyone.

> Steven Johnson: . . . Calculus, the electrical battery, the telephone, the steam engine, the radio—all these ground-breaking innovations were hit upon by multiple inventors working in parallel with no knowledge of one another. . . .
>
> Kevin Kelly: It's amazing that the myth of the lone genius has persisted for so long, since simultaneous invention has always been the norm, not the exception. Anthropologists have shown that the same inventions tended to crop up in prehistory at roughly similar times, in roughly the same order, among cultures on different continents that couldn't possibly have contacted one another. . . . Gregor Mendel's ideas about genetics, for example: He formulated them in 1865, but they were ignored for 35 years because they were too advanced. Nobody could incorporate them. Then, when the collective mind was ready and his idea was only one hop away, three different scientists independently rediscovered his work within roughly a year of one another.[1]

An article in *The New Yorker* by Malcolm Gladwell reveals that this phenomenon is far more prevalent than most people think. As of 1922, fully 148 different major scientific discoveries had been documented as occurring nearly simultaneously.

> This phenomenon of simultaneous discovery—what science historians call "multiples"—turns out to be extremely common. One of the first comprehensive lists of multiples was put together by William Ogburn and Dorothy Thomas, in 1922, and they found a hundred and forty-eight major scientific discoveries that fit the multiple pattern. Newton and Leibniz both discovered calculus. Charles Darwin and Alfred Russel Wallace both discovered evolution. Three mathematicians "invented" decimal fractions. Oxygen was discovered

by Joseph Priestley, in Wiltshire, in 1774, and by Carl Wilhelm Scheele, in Uppsala, a year earlier. Color photography was invented at the same time by Charles Cros and by Louis Ducos du Hauron, in France. Logarithms were invented by John Napier and Henry Briggs in Britain, and by Joost Bürgi in Switzerland. "There were four independent discoveries of sunspots, all in 1611; namely, by Galileo in Italy, Scheiner in Germany, Fabricius in Holland and Harriott in England," Ogburn and Thomas note, and they continue:

"The law of the conservation of energy, so significant in science and philosophy, was formulated four times independently in 1847, by Joule, Thomson, Colding and Helmholz. They had been anticipated by Robert Mayer in 1842. There seem to have been at least six different inventors of the thermometer and no less than nine claimants of the invention of the telescope. Typewriting machines were invented simultaneously in England and in America by several individuals in these countries. The steamboat is claimed as the "exclusive" discovery of Fulton, Jouffroy, Rumsey, Stevens and Symmington."[2]

Dr. Erwin Laszlo commented on how often this effect appears in history.

The great breakthroughs of classical Hebrew, Greek, Chinese and Indian culture occurred almost at the same time [750 to 399 B.C.] . . . among people who were not likely to have been in actual communication.[3]

In Dr. Rupert Sheldrake's classic *The Presence of the Past,* a variety of experiments support the idea that we are all accessing a common databank of information when we try to think about something—such as to solve a particular puzzle or problem—just like these inventors were doing. In one case, Sheldrake gave a difficult hidden-figure puzzle to random groups of people and timed how long it took them to solve it.

Then the solution was revealed to two million viewers in a British television broadcast. Everyone watched as the hidden face of a Cossack emerged from the background—including his handlebar mustache. When Sheldrake then gave the puzzle to new groups in Europe, Africa and America who had not seen the original puzzle nor the British TV show with the answer, they nonetheless solved it much faster.[4]

Dr. Paul Pearsall's fascinating work with organ transplants is another example of shared thoughts—though in this case there is a clear biological component involved. Dr. Pearsall has authored more than two hundred professional articles and eighteen best-selling books on this fascinating subject, and the entire article—with all the incredible specifics— is free to read on Pearsall's Web site.[5]

> According to this study of patients who have received transplanted organs, particularly hearts, it is not uncommon for memories, behaviors, preferences and habits associated with the donor to be transferred to the recipient. . . . A total sample of 74 transplant recipients (23 of which were heart transplants) . . . showed various degrees of changes that paralleled the personalities of their donors.[6]

Thoughts are apparently being stored within individual organs before they appear in the recipient's mind. The Source Field has spoken once again.

The *Co-Intelligence Institute* gives a thorough summary of experiments Sheldrake has either run himself or compiled in his impressive works on this concept of the shared mind. All of these breakthroughs suggest we are using the Source Field to think—at least to some degree.

> In one experiment, British biologist Rupert Sheldrake took three short, similar Japanese rhymes—one a meaningless jumble of disconnected Japanese words, the second a newly composed verse and the third a traditional rhyme known by millions of Japanese. Neither Sheldrake nor the English schoolchildren he got to memorize these verses knew

which was which, nor did they know any Japanese. The most easily learned rhyme turned out to be the one well-known to Japanese.[7]

Experiment 1: In the 1920s Harvard University psychologist William McDougall did experiments for 15 years in which rats learned to escape from a tank. The first generation of rats averaged 200 mistakes before they learned the right way out; the last generation 20 mistakes. . . .

Experiment 2: In later efforts to duplicate McDougall's experiments in Australia, similar rats made fewer mistakes right from the start. Later generations of rats did better even when they were not descendents of the earlier rats. . . .

Experiment 3: In the 1920s in Southampton, England, a bird called the blue tit discovered it could tear the tops of milk bottles on doorsteps and drink the cream. Soon this skill showed up in blue tits over a hundred miles away, which is odd in that they seldom fly further than 15 miles. . . . [The habit] spread faster and faster until by 1947 it was universal throughout Britain[,] . . . Holland, Sweden and Denmark. German occupation cut off milk deliveries in Holland for eight years—five years longer than the life of a blue tit. Then, in 1948 the milk started to be delivered. Within months blue tits all over Holland were drinking cream. . . .

Experiment 4: In the early sixties psychiatrists Dr. Milan Ryzl of Prague and Dr. Vladimir L. Raikov of Moscow hypnotized subjects into believing they were living incarnations of historical personages. Such subjects would develop talents associated with their alter egos. A subject told she was the artist Raphael took only a month to develop drawing skills up to the standard of a good graphic designer. . . .

[Experiment 5 is Sheldrake's hidden-figure puzzle, already discussed.]

Experiment 6: Psychologist Dr. Arden Mahlberg of Madison, Wisconsin, created a variation of Morse code that should have been no harder to learn than the standard variety. Subjects learned the real code much faster than his invented one, not knowing which was which.

Experiment 7: Gary Schwartz, Yale professor of psychology, selected 24 common 3-letter words in Hebrew and 24 rare ones, all from the Old Testament, all in Hebrew script. For each word, he created a scrambled version (as, in English, one might do by scrambling "dog" to spell "odg"). . . . [Among participants with no knowledge of Hebrew,] not only was the confidence [in the accuracy of their guesses] significantly higher with the real words than with the false words (regardless of subjects, words, or experiments), but the common words got higher confidence scores than the rarer words. . . .[8]

Schwartz's experiment was also covered in Combs, Holland and Robertson's *Synchronicity: Through the Eyes of Science, Myth and the Trickster* in 2000. The phrase "morphic fields" is Sheldrake's own term for thought forms that build up within the Source Field.

Schwartz found, as Sheldrake's theory would predict, that students rated the real words with considerably greater confidence than the ones that had been scrambled (though they did not accurately guess their meaning). Moreover, he found that confidence ratings were about twice as high for the words that occur frequently in the Old Testament compared with those that occur only rarely. The idea here is that the real words had, in fact, been learned by countless persons throughout history, forming strong morphic fields; the most frequently occurring words had, of course, been seen and read the greatest number of times. . . . Similar experiments have been carried out using Persian words and even Morse code.[9]

Richard Linklater's 2001 film *Waking Life* features a scene in which two characters discuss this phenomenon—and one of them mentions a study where crossword puzzles become easier to solve once they have been published and worked on by large numbers of people.[10] A graduate student named Monica England conducted this research for her thesis at the University of Nottingham, and summarized the results in the August 1991 *Noetic Sciences Bulletin*—but it was never published in a traditional academic journal. Sheldrake wrote about it in words that are no longer found on his Web site, but were originally published in a *Journal of Memetics* discussion forum post—on the memorable day of September 11, 2001.

> The crossword puzzles she used were from the London *Evening Standard*, not *The New York Times*, and in the experiments she tested groups of subjects before and after the crossword puzzles were published in the *Evening Standard* on Feb 15th 1990. Each group of subjects also did a control crossword which had been published ten days earlier in the *Evening Standard*. . . . She found that . . . the subjects performed better after the crossword had been published in London, relative to scores before publication. This difference was significant at the 5 percent level, using the one-tailed t test. . . . The reason Monica England thought of doing this experiment in the first place is that there is a folklore among people who do crosswords, especially difficult ones like those in *The Times* or the *Daily Telegraph*, that these crosswords are easier to solve if they're done the next day or in the evening rather than on the morning of the day they are published, suggesting a possible influence from others who have done them.[11]

Remote Viewing: Venturing Directly Into the Field

If we actually do use the Source Field to think, at least to some degree, then why couldn't we venture directly out into it—rather than having our awareness trapped within our own bodies? Harold Sherman, the author of *How to Make ESP Work for You*, was one of the early test subjects brought in by the military, and its contractors, to develop the science of remote viewing[12]—which theoretically allows us to access any point in the Source Field. Their results suggest that everything in the Universe is ultimately One Mind—as the consciousness of the viewer can project into any remote location and experience it as a part of his own awareness. In my opinion, some of the best books on remote viewing are David Morehouse's *Psychic Warrior*—and you may want to get the first edition from 1996[13]—and the works of Joe McMoneagle.[14] A good remote viewer can make detailed sketches of a remote location that are almost perfect—with nothing more than random numbers called "coordinates" that were assigned to the target. The person acting as their guide also does not know what these coordinates correspond to either. Joe McMoneagle has located three different missing persons in sessions filmed for Japanese television—leading the crews right to the door of where these people were, while he sat at his home in Virginia. The cameras then filmed their tearful reunions.[15]

Jahn and Dunne trained forty-eight ordinary people in an early type of remote viewing, where one person would visit a randomly chosen location from five to six thousand miles away and the viewer would attempt to gain information about what that person was seeing. In 336 rigorous trials, almost two-thirds of the viewers' observations appeared to be significantly accurate—at odds of a billion to one against chance. When the sender and receiver were bonded emotionally or by familial relationship, their results improved dramatically.[16] A distinguished government panel of skeptical scientists and two Nobel laureates studied twenty-three years of experimental data in remote viewing—and concluded the research was flawless.[17] Another team, headed by noted skeptic Dr. Ray Hyman, concluded the results were much too strong to be written off as random chance or coincidence.[18] Screened rooms were used to prove electromagnetic waves could not be responsible for transferring the information to the viewer's conscious mind.[19] Remote viewers also were able to see events that had not yet happened in linear time, even when those events were chosen at random—after they had already been correctly viewed in a secure location.[20,21] This suggests the mind is not confined to linear time at all, in the greater sense—and we will have much more to say about this in Part Two.

Do we create measurable energetic traces when we go out and remote-view a particular area? In 1980, Drs. Karlis Osis and Donna McCormick performed a remarkable experiment to see if they could find out. A gifted psychic named Alex Tanous was asked to remote-view a specific target. Several different scattered pieces were used to form an image, but only when they were viewed from one location. Tanous had no idea what the target looked like, and it was changed at various times. In the exact location where the pieces all lined up, Osis and McCormick hung two metallic plates side by side on strain gauges, which can detect very subtle movements. When Tanous was describing the target accurately, the plates jiggled around much more than usual. Their greatest movement occurred immediately after Tanous began viewing the image. There was no obvious visible light in the area as Tanous did the viewing—only the slight but measurable movement of the plates.[22]

Two years later, the People's Republic of China expanded this investigation even further. The Chinese scientists asked remote viewers with "exceptional vision" to view complex characters from their own alphabet as targets. These characters were placed in a room where no visible light could possibly enter. Very sensitive light-detecting devices were also positioned inside the room. During the times the viewers properly described the target, the number of photons in the room surged tremendously—from one hundred to one thousand times above the normal background levels of "virtual photons." This could amount to as many as fifteen thousand individual photons that were released during any one event.[23] [24] A group of American scientists led by Dr. G. Scott Hubbard attempted to replicate this experiment in 1986. They used a very high-quality photomultiplier tube for sensing light and a 35-millimeter slide of a scene as the target. Their results were excellent. During the times the viewers correctly described the target, pulses of photons consistently appeared—at a level much higher than random chance. However, their strongest pulses were only twenty to forty times larger than the background noise level, unlike the Chinese results of one hundred to one thousand times above normal.[25] This may be because the participants in the Chinese experiments were found by an open, systematic, nationwide sweep for the most talented intuitives.

In 1907, as published in the *American Medicine* journal, Dr. Duncan MacDougall found that his patients suddenly lost a little over one ounce of weight directly after their physical death. In these studies, the patients were kept on beds within a metallic basin that would catch any bodily fluids. The air they exhaled from their lungs upon death did not weigh anywhere near one ounce—nonetheless, the weight loss remained consistent in every case.[26] In 1975, Dr. Hereward Carrington and associates found that the average person would lose two and a quarter ounces of weight while they were having an out-of-body experience. When they returned to the body, the missing mass immediately returned.[27]

It appears there is an "energetic" component of our bodies that may be withdrawing from each and every cell, and projecting to other locations—either at death, when remote viewing or when having an out-of-body experience. As we sit inside an electrically shielded room, we can create photons in a remote location we are viewing—even if no visible light can get into that area, as we saw in the Chinese experiments. This gives us a compelling insight into how light may actually be appearing inside the pineal gland. A surprisingly high number of people who have out-of-body or near-death experiences see a silver cord that attaches their astral body to their physical body. In the majority of cases the cord appears to be attached to the exact location of the pineal gland, and emerges either from the front or the back of the head.[28] It may very well be that we all have an *energetic duplicate* of our physical body that is constantly traveling outside ourselves, as in remote viewing, and reporting back what it sees to the pineal gland—through the silver cord. Ecclesiastes 12:6 seems to refer to this energetic cord: "Remember him—before the silver cord is severed, or the golden bowl is broken."[29]

Experiences After Death

A surprising number of people experience a continuing consciousness when they are clinically dead—again suggesting that some part of our thinking mind is strictly energetic, and does not need a physical body at all. In order for a person to be considered clinically dead, the heart has to stop beating, the lungs stop breathing and there is no measurable brain wave activity due to the lack of oxygen. By any conventional medical account, our minds should no longer function—or even exist. However, a variety of people report having vivid near-death experiences (NDEs) during this time. According to Dr. Sam Parnia and his associates at the University of Southampton, many studies have concluded that being clinically brain dead does not interrupt the continuity of our thinking minds—in a surprising number of cases.

> A number of recent scientific studies carried out by independent researchers have demonstrated that 10–20 percent of people who go through cardiac arrest and clinical death report lucid, well structured thought processes, reasoning, memories and sometimes detailed recall of events during their encounter with death.[30]

The largest hospital-based study of NDEs was led by Dr. Pim van Lommel, a cardiologist in the Netherlands. Dr. Van Lommel heard his first NDE report in 1969, where a patient reported a tunnel, a light, beautiful colors and wonderful music. Dr. Raymond Moody's groundbreaking description of NDEs did not appear until seven years later, in 1976, and Dr. Van Lommel's interest wasn't piqued again until 1986—when he read a more detailed account of an NDE that occurred during a six-minute period of clinical death.

> After reading [this] book I started to interview my patients who had survived a cardiac arrest. To my great surprise, within two years about fifty patients told me about their NDE. . . . So, in 1988 we started a prospective study of 344 consecutive survivors of cardiac arrest in ten Dutch hospitals with the aim of investigating the frequency, the cause and the content of an NDE. . . . Results: 62 patients (18%) reported some recollection of the time of clinical death . . . In the core group 23 patients (7%) reported a deep or very deep experience. . . .

In our study about 50% of the patients with an NDE reported awareness of being dead, or had positive emotions, 30% reported moving through a tunnel, had an observation of a celestial landscape, or had a meeting with deceased relatives. About 25% of the patients with an NDE had an out-of-body experience, had communication with "the light," or observed colours, 13% experienced a life review, and 8% experienced a border. . . . Patients with an NDE did not show any fear of death, they strongly believed in an afterlife, and their insight in what is important in life had changed: love and compassion for oneself, for others, and for nature. They now understood the cosmic law that everything one does to others will ultimately be returned to oneself: hatred and violence as well as love and compassion. Remarkably, there was often evidence of increased intuitive feelings.[31]

For further information, the Web site Near-Death.com has an excellent list of fifty-one different proofs that support the reality of NDEs.[32] At the very top of the page they mention the groundbreaking studies of Dr. Kenneth Ring, who investigated cases where people reported accurate observations of real events—sometimes far away from the location of their physical bodies—while they were clinically dead. They saw the events taking place and also overheard the conversations, in some cases, and their reports were later verified as being stunningly correct. In other examples, the clinically dead person appears in a ghostlike form to a loved one—and both people end up reporting the same experience once the patient has been resuscitated.[33]

Where do we go and what happens to us after we die? In his wonderful books *Journey of Souls* and *Destiny of Souls,* Dr. Michael Newton reports his detailed investigations into this fascinating subject. Dr. Newton conducted thousands of deep hypnotic regressions, where he would bring people back through the events of their lives, eventually return them into the womb and then further regress them into the "life between lives"—and he found remarkable consistency in the reports.

In the introduction to *Journey of Souls,* I explained my background as a traditional hypnotherapist and how skeptical I had been about the use of hypnosis for metaphysical regression. In 1947, at age fifteen, I placed my first subject in hypnosis, so I was definitely old school and not a New Ager. Thus, when I unintentionally opened the gateway to the spirit world with a client, I was stunned. . . . After more years of quiet research, I was able to construct a working model of spirit world structure. . . . I also found that it did not matter if a person was an atheist, deeply religious, or believed in any philosophical persuasion in between—once they were in the proper superconscious state of hypnosis, all were consistent in their reports. . . . I built up a high volume of cases. . . . While these years of specialized research into the spirit world rolled on, I worked practically in seclusion. . . . I even stayed out of metaphysical bookstores because I wanted absolute freedom from outside bias.[34]

Newton's first book, *Journey of Souls,* is organized sequentially, in terms of time and location, to walk us through all ten stages from initial death to final reincarnation: Death and Departure, The Gateway to the Spirit World, Homecoming, Orientation, Transition, Placement, Life Selection, Choosing a New Body, Preparation and Embarkation, and Rebirth.[35] I highly recommend these books, as the number of commonalities Dr. Newton points out among his participants, and the depth of inspiration their accounts provide, is quite profound. Dr. Newton also found that souls displayed visible colors that were relative to their level of advancement—falling neatly in line with the spectrum we see in the rainbow.

I found that typically, pure white denotes a younger soul and with advancement soul energy becomes more dense, moving into orange, yellow, green and finally the blue ranges. In addition to these center core auras, there are subtle mixtures of halo colors within every group that relate to the character aspects of each soul. For want of a better system, I have classified soul development as moving from a level I beginner through various learning stages to that of a master at level VI. These greatly advanced souls are seen as having a deep indigo color. I have no doubt even higher levels exist, but my knowledge of them is restricted because I only receive reports from people who are still incarnating . . . it is my subjects who use "level" to describe where they are on the ladder of learning. . . . While in a superconscious state during deep hypnosis, my subjects tell me that in the spirit world no soul is looked down upon as having less value than any other soul. We are all in a process of transformation to something greater than our current state of enlightenment. . . .

There certainly is structure in the spirit world, but it exists within a sublime matrix of compassion, harmony, ethics and morality far beyond what we practice on earth. . . . There is a value system here of overwhelming kindness, tolerance, patience and absolute love. . . . Advanced subjects talk about the time of conjunction when they will join the "Most Sacred Ones." In this sphere of dense purple light there is an all-knowing Presence.[36]

Dr. Linda Backman received training from Dr. Michael Newton and since 1993 has conducted her own research into the "life between lives." Her work serves as a valuable source of independent, professionally obtained data that corroborates the results Newton gained in his own practice—although she focuses on the more highly advanced souls. One of her main conclusions is that these people often take on very difficult lives as a way of dramatically increasing their own rate of spiritual growth.[37]

Reincarnation

Have we lived before? Is there any proof that we return to a new body, in another lifetime, after we die? In this case we have very reliable and extensive scientific data. Dr. Ian Stevenson, a professor of psychiatry at the University of Virginia School of Medicine, spent more than forty years tracking down over three thousand children who experienced specific, detailed memories of their alleged "past lives." Many of these children were able to tell Dr. Stevenson what their names used to be, as well as who their alleged friends and family were. They often revealed how and where they died, along with many other astonishingly specific details that could easily be proven or disproven by investigation. Personality and behavioral quirks carried over from one apparent lifetime to another, and the children bore a surprising facial resemblance to whomever they said they had been before.[38]

Over and over again, Dr. Stevenson found the names the children gave were correct. The surviving relatives could be tracked down. Their faces looked similar to their suspected past lives, and the specific details all checked out. One Lebanese girl was able to remember the names and precise interrelationships of twenty-five different people she claimed to have known before, without ever having had any contact with them, or anyone who knew them, in her current life. Respected academics like Dr. Jim Tucker, medical director of the Child and Family Psychiatric Clinic at the University of Virginia, have said that "reincarnation is the most likely explanation for the strongest cases."[39]

Dr. Tucker is considered the worthy successor to Dr. Ian Stevenson, and has continued his research, including many new cases, with a focus on documentable evidence such as specific details that can be verified from the children's memories. Or matching birthmarks. (Our new bodies often have visible birthmarks in areas where our alleged former selves were mortally wounded.) And facial recognition software—allowing Dr. Tucker to prove that they do both look the same.[40] Since these cultures believed in reincarnation, the children did not receive any "hypnotic suggestions" telling them to overlook or dismiss any memories they may have had.

Skeptics can and do write off such accounts as anecdotal and unverifiable in nature, but Dr. Ian Stevenson's forty-plus years of scientific research provided solid proof that reincarnation is real—just as the adherents of Hinduism, Buddhism and even Orthodox Judaism have often believed. The implications are stunning, and absolutely central to our main theme in this book—it means you can look yourself in the eye, standing in front of a mirror, and say "I will always exist," with a deep inner knowing that this is true. Without the hidden fear of non-existence hanging over your head, you will soon lead a much happier life. If you are willing to try out certain practices, you can have personal experiences that will confirm this greater truth for you—and which may ultimately cause you to wonder if we are all living in a "global lucid dream."

CHAPTER FIVE

Are We Living in a Lucid Dream?

Bacteria, plants, insects, eggs, animals and humans all appear to be sharing the same Mind—thanks to a non-electromagnetic energy field. We now know that if you have trouble concentrating, and someone else in a remote location tries to help you think, then soon you will be able to focus much better. Scientific breakthroughs all over the world consistently seem to happen in parallel. Organ transplant recipients may pick up thoughts, behaviors and habits from their donors. Humans and animals appear to draw from a common databank of information—which in our case includes written words in foreign languages, Morse code and crossword puzzle solutions. Remote viewers can make detailed observations of distant locations, and create measurable signals of their presence in those areas—including surges of visible photons. Our bodies lose small but measurable amounts of weight when we die or have an out-of-body experience.

An energetic conduit seems to exist between our astral body and our physical body—the silver cord—and it may be sending visible images from distant locations directly into our pineal gland, not unlike a fiber-optic cable. Floating piezoluminescent crystals in the pineal gland may then release these images in a three-dimensional matrix of light. The retinal tissue in the pineal gland might be capturing these photons and sending them to the brain, where they are unscrambled into visual images if they remain stable enough. Ancient mystery schools and religions seemed singularly obsessed with pineal gland symbolism—and believed that awakening this gland was the ultimate key to spiritual advancement. Many people continue to be able to observe their environment and think normal thoughts while they are clinically dead, showing no brain waves whatsoever. Some people have appeared in a ghostly form to their loved ones while having a near-death experience, and both people report the same sequence of events afterward. Dr. Michael Newton found remarkable consistency in reports from the afterlife among thousands of people he had hypnotized into a superconscious state. Dr. Ian Stevenson identified over three thousand children who gave specific, detailed and accurate memories of past lives—and even looked like the people they claimed to have been before.

There does appear to be a parallel reality out there that we all have access to—at least on some level. Is there any way you can travel into this alternate world and experience this unbound awareness for yourself—without actually dying? Are you already doing this every night when you dream? Is there a way you can bring your conscious awareness with you and become lucid—so you have full control over your experience? I believe there is—because I've done it myself. Certain techniques do allow you to recognize you are dreaming while it is actually happening, "wake up" in the dream, and take conscious control of your experience. After having had enough of these experiences personally, I can't help but wonder if the real world behaves more like a lucid dream than we ever imagined—thanks to how interconnected we are in the Source Field.

This adventure started when I was still a high school student, and I read *Lucid Dreaming*[1] and *Exploring the World of Lucid Dreaming*[2] by Dr. Stephen LaBerge—from Stanford University's Sleep Research Center. Dr. LaBerge was able to scientifically prove that you can be fully conscious in a dream, while being physiologically asleep and dreaming at the same time. Dr. LaBerge also works with Dr. William Braud, who performed many experiments proving our mind-to-mind connections—as we already discussed in chapter 2.

In 1952, Dr. Eugene Aserinsky found that in the lighter stages of sleep, we all experience rapid eye movement, or REM. If we get awakened from this state, we usually report having just experienced a vivid dream.

By 1973, Dr. Montague Ullman and Dr. Stanley Krippner published ten years of pioneering experiments in dream telepathy at the Maimonides Medical Center in New York City, with more than one hundred participants. In these groundbreaking studies, ordinary people could concentrate on specific images while awake, and send them to people who were dreaming. The dreamers then experienced symbols and events in their dreams that were obviously similar to the senders' message.[3]

Drawing upon the experience of over nine hundred lucid dreams of his own, Dr. LaBerge developed exercises that would allow you to wake up, or become lucid, while you were dreaming in his lab. Once you achieved the lucid dreaming state, you would signal Dr. LaBerge by repeatedly moving your eyes back and forth—since the rest of your body could not move due to sleep paralysis. By signaling LaBerge with your eyes, counting to ten and signaling again, he was able to confirm that your physical time and dream time are just about the same. LaBerge also reported on cases where people seem to share the same dream—although this has not been investigated as rigorously as dream telepathy.

> Accounts of "mutual dreaming" (dreams apparently shared by two or more people) raise the possibility that the dream world may be in some cases just as objectively real as the physical world. This is because the primary criterion of "objectivity" is that an experience is shared by more than one person, which is supposedly true of mutual dreams. In that case, what would happen to the traditional dichotomy between dreams and reality?[4]

In his book *Lucid Dreaming: Gateway to the Inner Self,* Robert Waggoner gives a variety of compelling examples in which people shared the same dream environment, and reported the same experiences, in isolation, after they woke up. This again implies that dreams are not merely psychological artifacts, but are occurring in a parallel reality, of sorts—where more than one person can have experiences and interactions with others at the same time.[5] This idea was popularized in Christopher Nolan's highly successful 2010 film *Inception.*

The key to Dr. LaBerge's technique, which he called Mnemonic Induction of Lucid Dreaming, or MILD, was that after you wake up naturally from a dream—which might be in the middle of the night—you say, internally, "Next time I'm dreaming, I want to remember to recognize that I'm dreaming" as you fall back asleep. At the same time, you review the dream in your mind, but then change the ending, by imagining yourself becoming lucid—realizing that you're actually living, walking and breathing in a dream. LaBerge also said the best way to tell if you were, in fact, dreaming was to simply look at something, look away from it and then look back again. In dreams, the "before" and the "after" view will always be different enough that you can easily spot the changes.

I did not succeed right away when I began practicing Dr. LaBerge's techniques, but I kept on trying . . . and eventually struck gold. In a lucid dream you can fly, levitate objects, walk through walls, and manifest anything you want to see or experience—even change your entire environment with the snap of a finger. I remember one time I was in a department store, and I levitated a whole series of big gray plastic garbage cans and started orbiting them around each other like a little solar system. Everyone in the store stood there in awe. Some were even moved to tears. The experience is so fantastic and awe-inspiring that if you haven't actually done it yet, there really are no words to describe it. However, Dr. LaBerge cites a great quote from Hugh Calloway's report of a lucid dream he had in 1902, at age sixteen, which began his research into consciousness.

Then the solution flashed upon me: though this glorious summer morning seemed as real as real could be, I was dreaming. With the realization of this fact, the quality of the dream changed in a manner very difficult to convey to one who has not had this experience. Instantly, the vividness of life increased a hundred-fold. Never had sea and sky and trees shone with such glamorous beauty; even the commonplace houses seemed alive and mystically beautiful. Never had I felt so absolutely well, so clear-brained, so inexpressibly free. The sensation was exquisite beyond words, but it lasted only a few minutes and I awoke.[6]

Indeed, many of Dr. LaBerge's own participants ended up concluding that they had "never really been awake before." This may be what will happen to you when you experience a direct awareness of the Source Field, and your greater identity within it, for the first time in your conscious, waking life. And of course, no drugs or occult rituals are required to do this—just a consistent effort to practice Dr. LaBerge's technique.

In one particularly fantastic lucid dream, I was soaring high over the treetops, gliding through impossibly vibrant colors in the sky and connecting with a gorgeous woman who kept appearing along the way. I desperately wanted to write down everything that was happening to me, as I knew I would probably forget most of it otherwise. So, I took a break, landed on solid ground, and manifested a pen in my right hand and a notebook in my left. In my dreaming trance, I somehow hoped, or believed, that I could bring the notebook back through with me, and it would show up there next to me in bed. I frantically scribbled down what was going on. Eventually I went back and read my notes—but they were all in French. I had studied French in high school, but I was nowhere near good enough to have written anything like this. And yet, I absolutely knew that everything was written properly. I could read it back, out loud, and I knew exactly what I was saying. My thoughts still felt the same, but now they were coming out in French. I could speak to anyone in French, at any speed—and I knew it would be perfect. It was very, very strange. When I woke up, the papers were gone, of course, and my French was no better than usual. But what if, I wondered? What if I could somehow bring that new ability back "through the veil" of dreaming?

In 2007, an eighteen-year-old Czech motorcycle racer named Matěj Kůs got knocked out in an accident. Before the crash, he only knew the most basic phrases in English, but after he woke up, he was speaking perfect, fluent English with the paramedics. Peter Waite, the promoter for the Berwick Bandits, his racing team, was quite surprised.

I couldn't believe what I was hearing. It was in a really clear English accent, no dialect or anything. Whatever happened in the crash must have rearranged things in his head. Before his crash, Matěj's use of the English language was broken, to put it mildly. . . . Yet, here we were at the ambulance door listening to Matěj talking to the medical staff in perfect English. [He] didn't have a clue who or where he was when he came round. He didn't even know he was Czech.[7]

Sadly, Kůs quickly lost the new ability, and could not remember anything that happened during the accident, nor for the next two days afterward—just as if he had been in a hypnotic trance. This was not the only case, however. On April 12, 2010, the U.K. *Telegraph* featured the story of a Croatian girl who awoke from a coma speaking fluent German, even though she'd only just started studying it in school—and she no longer could speak her own native Croatian. Psychiatrist Dr. Mijo Milas explained his view on this intriguing phenomenon:

> In earlier times this would have been referred to as a miracle; we prefer to think that there must be a logical explanation—it's just that we haven't found it yet. There are references to cases where people who have been seriously ill and perhaps in a coma have woken up being able to speak other languages—sometimes even the Biblical languages such as that spoken in old Babylon or Egypt.[8]

In a lucid dream, out-of-body experience, remote viewing session, hypnotic trance, coma or near-death experience, our thinking minds may be using the Source Field much more than when we are conscious. This appears to give us much greater access to the information stored within the Source Field—including the ability to speak various languages. Many people don't realize that Edgar Cayce, while in a hypnotic trance, could give people funny little sayings or even have complete conversations with them in their own language—despite being unable to speak anything but English in his waking mind. He is estimated to have spoken over twenty-four different languages while in trance.[9]

Dr. LaBerge believes that every landscape, every object, every character and every situation in the dream represents some aspect of yourself. A dream is a message from your subconscious mind and/or "astral self," and the language is symbolism. In a dream, you are presented with various problems from your waking life, but they often appear in disguise. If someone is abusing you in your waking life, they may become a monster in your dream, as one example. Everything in the dream is symbolic, and every symbol is some part of who you are—or some situation that is happening to you in your waking life. The basic aspects of this symbolic language are commonly understood among dream researchers.[10] Nothing is more frustrating than watching people share dreams in which the earth is being destroyed, and then treat it as a prophecy of real events that are about to happen in the world—rather than a reflection of some massive change that is about to happen, or has already been happening, in their own lives.

So when you run into terrifying, threatening and aggressive characters in a dream, don't think of it as a nightmare. You can train yourself to recognize that such frightening situations must be dreams, and then use them as triggers to become lucid. Dr. LaBerge says those evil characters ultimately represent some aspect of yourself that you have not forgiven and accepted. If you learn the art of lucid dreaming, you can quickly turn your worst nightmares into the greatest triumphs. Dr. LaBerge shared his own experience of how you do this:

> I dreamed that I was in the middle of a classroom riot; a furious mob was raging about, throwing chairs and trading punches. A huge, repulsive barbarian with a pockmarked face, the Goliath among them, had me hopelessly locked in an iron grip. . . . At this point, I recognized I was dreaming, and remembering what I had learned from handling similar situations previously, I immediately stopped struggling. . . . I was absolutely certain about the proper course of action. I knew only love could truly resolve my inner conflict, and I

tried to feel loving as I stood face to face with my ogre. At first I failed utterly, feeling only revulsion and disgust. He was simply too ugly to love: that was my visceral reaction. But I tried to ignore the image and seek love within my own heart. Finding it, I looked my ogre in the eyes, trusting my intuition to supply the right things to say. Beautiful words of acceptance flowed out of me, and as they did, he melted into me. As for the riot, it had vanished without a trace. The dream was over, and I awoke feeling wonderfully calm.[11]

As LaBerge and others have said, the dreamer often experiences blinding white light as the villainous character merges back into them—and he or she awakens in tears. I have had multiple experiences like this, and was very deeply moved.

Nearly every day, I hear a story that people are becoming more aware . . . more attuned to the consciousness of the world and its effects. I believe this is no accident: It appears that our thinking minds are being energetically transformed by outside forces that are affecting our entire solar system, as we will explore in later chapters. And this raises an intriguing question: Is it possible that the rules of the dream world could also apply to the physical world? If we all share a collective consciousness, are there practical things we can do to improve the world, by nothing more than the power of our own thoughts? Could we improve the lives of others by improving ourselves? Can we change the dream when we change our own minds? There is rigorous evidence that we have much more power to improve the overall health of the people on earth than we ever believed.

Heal the World by Healing Yourself

Over a two-year period, groups of about seven thousand people gathered three different times—and during these meetings, they were able to reduce all acts of terrorism, worldwide, by a phenomenal 72 percent. Obviously, the tactical value of such a winning strategy would be of massive importance to national security. Were these people diplomats, politicians or military planners plotting out the next offensive? Were they peace activists, diving down into the trenches and rescuing people in a hail of gunfire? Were they protestors, gathering in front of government buildings and demanding change? What exactly did they do?

The answer may well change everything we think we know about the way the Universe really works. These people got together and meditated—with thoughts of love and peace. Bear in mind that this was a scientific study, published and accepted in the *Journal of Offender Rehabilitation*. They ruled out cycles, trends, weather, weekends, holidays and all other variables—the 72 percent reduction in terrorism had to be caused by them meditating, and nothing else.[12] In another example, violent crime in Washington, D.C., was decreased by up to 23.6 percent over a two-month period in the summer of 1993, as the number of participants rose from eight hundred to four thousand—despite the fact that violent crime had been increasing before they met. As soon as their meetings ended, the crime level started going back up again.[13] The likelihood that this effect could have been caused by a "chance variation in crime levels" was less than two parts per billion, and all other factors—including temperature, precipitation, weekends, and police and community anticrime activities—were ruled out.[14]

As of 1993, fifty different scientific studies had rigorously proven that this effect really works—over the preceding thirty years. They were published in mainstream peer-reviewed journals and showed the meditators had created improvements in health and quality of life, as well as decreases in accidents, crime, war and other such factors.[15] I propose that this effect works because we're all sharing the same mind, to some degree. There appears to be a balance between private thoughts and information we acquire directly from the Source Field. Let's not forget the Institute of HeartMath's experiments, in which those people with the greatest coherence affected the brain wave patterns and biorhythms of others who were close to them. If seven thousand people can reduce worldwide terrorism by 72 percent, this suggests the Source Field is significantly biased in favor of positive emotions rather than negative ones.

Therefore, any time someone tries to tell you it's hopeless, that "we're all going to die," that some dream or prophecy said we have no ability to control the outcome of our future here on earth, I highly recommend you don't fall into the trap of indulging in such faceless fear. We can scientifically prove that by simply focusing on a positive attitude in your own life, you are helping to reduce war, terrorism, suffering and death. There is also compelling evidence from Russia that severe weather, earthquakes, volcanic activity and the like can also be reduced by the effects of consciousness, as we will see.

Dr. LaBerge thought the ogre attacking him in his dream was really someone else: the villain, the enemy, the other. However, once he became lucid, he realized the ogre was just a mirror of himself—and love was the key to solving the problem. Now we know that simple meditations on love and peace can actually change the behavior of people out in the world—ordinary folks living their lives, apparently making free will decisions. These are people we will never see, never meet, never know. When even a small number of us move into a state the meditators called "Pure Consciousness," there is less death, less terrorism and less warfare. According to Saint John of the Cross, from sixteenth-century Spain, "a little of this pure love is more precious to God and the soul and more beneficial to the Church, even though it seems one is doing nothing, than all these other works put together."[16] By "works" he means anything we normally would do in our attempts to help the world. In a book called *The Cloud of Unknowing*, a revered English priest in the fourteenth century referred to this same state as "Pure Contemplation," and said, "The whole of mankind is wonderfully helped by what you are doing, in ways you do not understand. . . . It is more profitable to your friends, natural and spiritual, dead or alive . . . [and] without it all the rest is virtually worthless."[17]

Now that we see how strongly a small group of people can affect everyone's behavior on a mass scale, the idea that the real world is like a lucid dream or a hologram doesn't seem so crazy-sounding after all. What if the rules of the dream world actually do apply to the physical world? If so, then all these global disasters may actually be symbolic reflections of our own inner distress: our fear, pain, sorrow and anger. After years of my own meditation, I finally concluded on a deep level that our sadness comes from a very convincing illusion: the seemingly inescapable truth that we feel alone.

The evidence I have already presented here suggests that we all have a soul—constantly watching over us, while also enjoying its own experiences, thoughts and travels. I believe any one of us can reach out to this greater aspect of our own being, and develop the ability to gain reliable spiritual guidance—to understand the greater plan and Purpose we may have chosen to fulfill before we ever came here. We might also avoid a great deal of needless suffering in the process. However, when we resist our Purpose, we only encounter more and more pain, difficulty and seemingly random bad luck. According to Edgar Cayce, the noteworthy psychic reader who practiced in the early twentieth century, ignorance does not grant us an exemption from the great spiritual laws—and this includes the Law of Karma[18]—in which whatever we measure out to others will be measured back to us. If we sufficiently violate someone's free will, we may require another lifetime to balance ourselves out—by enduring similar hardships. Cayce also said we can eliminate this entire cycle of karma by practicing true forgiveness and acceptance—both of ourselves and of others. That, ultimately, appears to be the core Purpose we are all here to achieve. And if it were easy, we wouldn't require multiple incarnations to figure it out.

I realize the label "God" for some people is emotionally charged—although you may now be thinking differently about such a "foolish notion" after reading these last few chapters. Either way, the Cayce Readings used this word to discuss the universal intelligence that we have been investigating in this book. Cayce's Readings, which allegedly came from a greater part of his own being that spoke while he was under hypnosis, said all the disturbances in the world today—wars, terrorism, government corruption, natural disasters, earthquakes—were all part of a big Story that we are being told. It's a story about our Selves, and our relationship to the Universe.

> For, as ye do unto others, ye do to thy Maker. And when those activities . . . dishonor thy fellow man, ye dishonor thy God—and it brings all of those forms of disturbance that

exist in the world today. . . . When there has been in the earth those groups that have sufficiently desired and sought peace, peace will begin. It must be within self.[19]

The Cayce Readings spoke of God as a universal loving intelligence that does not discriminate against anyone—nor should we: "More wars, more bloodshed have been shed over the racial and religious differences than over any other problem. These, too, must go the way of all others; and man must learn . . . whether they be called of this or that sect or schism or ism or cult, the Lord is ONE."[20] According to the Cayce Readings, you don't need to get a group of seven thousand people together in order to be effective. The reality of our greater shared mind is powerful enough that even ten souls can do an amazing amount of good for the planet.

Man's answer to everything has been POWER—Power of money, Power of position, Power of wealth, Power of this, that or the other. This has NEVER been GOD'S way, will never be God's way. Rather little by little, line upon line, here a little, there a little, each thinking rather of the other fellow. . . . [This is what] has kept the world in the various ways of being intact. Where there were ten, even, many a city, many a nation has been kept from destruction.[21]

Dr. Hew Len, a Hawaiian psychiatrist,[22] discovered a similar technique that could substantially increase health and happiness in the psychiatric ward he managed. It didn't start out very well: "That ward where they kept the criminally insane was dangerous. Psychologists quit on a monthly basis. The staff called in sick a lot or simply quit. People would walk through that ward with their backs against the wall, afraid of being attacked by patients."[23] Dr. Len's job allowed him to be completely isolated from the ward—he reviewed patients' case files to prescribe medication and/or treatment plans with the staff. Nonetheless, by simply holding each patient's file in his hand and practicing the "Ho'oponopono" technique we are about to discover, he got results.

After a few months, patients that had to be shackled were being allowed to walk freely. . . . Others who had to be heavily medicated were getting off their medications. And those who had no chance of ever being released were being freed. . . . Not only that . . . but the staff began to enjoy coming to work. Absenteeism and turnover disappeared. We ended up with more staff than we needed because patients were being released, and all the staff was showing up to work. Today, that ward is closed.[24]

What exactly was Dr. Len doing while he reviewed each patient's file? He simply took on their pains and problems as if they were his own, and worked on healing those issues within himself: "I just kept saying 'I'm sorry' and 'I love you' over and over again."[25] Dr. Len was practicing his own variation of a Hawaiian spiritual practice called Ho'oponopono.[26] Dr. Len recommends going inside, to wherever you feel hurt by a particular person or issue, and then saying each of these four statements with as much feeling as possible—thinking through the real reasons why you genuinely feel this way: "I love you. I am sorry. Please forgive me. Thank you."[27] That's all it takes. You heal the other person by healing yourself—and this apparently works because in the greater sense, you are both sharing the same Mind.

Proof, Belief and Hope

I've encountered some very sarcastic people in my life. They don't want to hear about spirituality. They don't care about religion. They see a Higher Purpose as nothing more than ignorant nonsense. They use Science as a weapon against anyone who believes there is a loving Purpose to the universe—that we are more than just "meat computers" who struggle for a while on the earth before our Awareness fades into a black nothingness.

At the other extreme, I have met religious fundamentalists—including Christians and occultists—who can be just as aggressive, and just as certain that they must be right. As soon as they hear the word *god*, or any of a number of other words, they feel like they automatically know exactly what that means—and there's no point in arguing with them. It's as if everybody were in a big horse race, and we all want our lucky number to take home the big prize. Religious folks may even try to use the scientific breakthroughs in this book as proof that their small group of chosen or elect will soar up into the heavens—while the rest of us burn in eternal hellfire. Dr. David B. Barrett spent forty years, and enlisted the help of 444 specialists, to discover that there are over ten thousand different religions in the world—of which 150 have at least one million followers. Dr. Barrett went and visited most of these 238 nations and territories in person. He found that within Christianity alone, there are an incredible 38,830 denominations.[28] So, with almost fifty thousand groups in competition—38,830 splinters of Christianity, combined with ten thousand other world religions—how many of them honestly believe that unless you see things their way, you might as well kiss your butt good-bye?

Imagine how quickly Christianity would have failed if Bible scholars could quote Jesus as saying, "Love thy neighbor as thyself . . . as long as he's a Christian. Otherwise, go ahead and kill him. You'll be doing us both a favor, believe me."

I have a strong feeling that as the Source Field investigations become increasingly mainstream—no longer suppressed by ignorance, threats or worse—the positive effects will rapidly increase. We don't have to wish that our leaders and politicians will obey the campaign promises we voted for in the first place. We don't need to sit by and wait for a Messiah, or Divine Intervention, in the hopes that we will be rescued from some terrible fate that is outside our control. Cayce's interpretation of the Book of Revelation confirmed that the Earth Changes are not merely random events—they are a "real world" story of our struggle to love and respect each other. In reading 281-16, Cayce's source said, "The visions, the experiences, the names, the churches, the places, the dragons, the cities [in the Book of Revelation] all are but emblems of those forces that may war within the individual in its journey through the material."[29]

And what about the dreaded anti-Christ that so many Christians and conspiracy theorists shout from the rooftops about?

> (Q) In what form does the anti-Christ come, spoken of in Revelation?
> (A) In the spirit of that opposed to the spirit of truth. The fruits of the spirit of the Christ are love, joy, obedience, long-suffering, brotherly love, kindness. Against such there is no law. The spirit of hate, the anti-Christ, is contention, strife, fault-finding, lovers of self, lovers of praise. Those are the anti-Christ, and take possession of groups, masses, and show themselves even in the lives of men.[30]

The Cayce Readings also gave dramatic new insight into the devastating events of the Tribulation that many people—Christians or otherwise—are expecting. The existing catastrophes we are already experiencing now—the earthquakes, volcanoes, tsunamis, hurricanes, tornadoes—are said to be a collective mirror of what each of us is going through. This again demonstrates the principle of a shared consciousness.

> The great tribulation and periods of tribulation, as given, are the experiences of every soul, every entity. They arise from influences created by man through activity in the sphere of any sojourn.

I think hope is a good thing, as it leads us into knowing, through direct experience, that all is well. And if we feel that everything is not well, then we can do something about it. Within this book is information that unites the 38,830 religious sects beautifully, and shows that each of them have the truth in some form . . . including their most magnificent prophecies of a Golden Age that will soon arrive in our future.

CHAPTER SIX

A Precession of Prophecies

Was there an advanced ancient civilization on earth, much older than we normally believe could be possible? Did these ancestors deliberately create a wide variety of myths and spiritual teachings, worldwide, about the pineal gland? Could these cultures, or their forgotten creators, manipulate giant blocks of stone to build massive pyramids in two totally separate cultures—namely, the Mayan and the Egyptians? Did the people of these cultures enjoy direct contact with "gods"—human extraterrestrials who may have been far older, and far more advanced, than they were? Did these "ancient astronauts" understand that there was a Source Field we were all a part of—and in fact were using to think? And lastly, are there enough surviving traces of these ancient cultures left behind so we can figure out what happened—to understand who these people were, and what they might have known?

The earth almost certainly went through a catastrophe around the last Ice Age, some twelve thousand to thirteen thousand years ago. If there was an advanced civilization on earth before then, as many ancient astronaut theorists suggest, this Great Flood seems to have largely destroyed it. Rand and Rose Flem-Ath tied together a whole host of unique references worldwide, with impeccable research, to arrive at this conclusion.

From all corners of the earth, the same story is told. The sun deviates from its regular path. The sky falls. The earth is wrenched and torn by earthquakes. And finally a great wave of water engulfs the globe. Survivors of such a calamity would go to any lengths to prevent it from happening again. They lived in an age of magic. It was natural and necessary to construct elaborate devices to pacify the sun-god (or goddess) or monitor its path.[1]

Thanks to the best-selling *Fingerprints of the Gods* by Graham Hancock, the scholarly work of Giorgio de Santillana and Hertha von Dechend is now central to any investigation of these ancient prophecies. Why? Their magnum opus *Hamlet's Mill* tied together an incredible number of different ancient legends around the world—and found that they all had common roots. Author Colin Wilson stated it clearly.

In effect, Santillana is presenting a rich tapestry of legends of the Eskimoes, Icelanders, Norsemen, American Indians, Finns, Hawaiians, Japanese, Chinese, Hindus, Persians, Romans, ancient Greeks, ancient Hindus, ancient Egyptians, and dozens of other nations, and asking: how did these strange similarities develop unless [all these] myths have some common origin? And this origin, he is inclined to believe, lies in astronomy.[2]

What could possibly have caused all these different cultures around the world to end up with the same exact information—about astronomy? And what did all these different worldwide legends want us to know? The answer is deceptively simple: The myths encoded a long-term cycle in the earth's orbit, which takes some twenty-five thousand years to complete. The prophecies also tell us these periods of great difficulty give way to what they often call a Golden Age. One classic example is the Norse legend of the Ragnarok. This is admittedly one of the most doom-and-gloom-sounding prophecies out there—but it does have a happy ending, as Bulfinch described in 1855:

It was a firm belief of the northern nations that a time would come when all the visible creation, the gods of Valhalla and Niffleheim, the inhabitants of Jotunheim, Alfheim, and Midgard, together with their habitations, would be destroyed. . . . The earth itself will be frightened and begin to tremble, the sea leave its basin, the heavens tear asunder, and men perish in great numbers. . . . The whole universe is burned up. The sun becomes dim, the earth sinks into the ocean, the stars fall from heaven, and time is no more. After this Alfadur (the Almighty) will cause a new heaven and a new earth to arise out of the sea. The new earth filled with abundant supplies will spontaneously produce its fruits without labour or care. Wickedness and misery will no more be known, but the gods and men will live happily together.[3]

Let's consider the evidence we've examined so far. I do not believe these are literal prophecies, but they may be telling us a story about our future—using dreamlike symbolism. We have powerful clues that the basic energy of the Universe is conscious, and we all "think with the field," to some degree. Could there be long cycles of time in which the character, quality and even *intelligence* of the Source Field change for everyone here on earth? Could these cycles drive our entire planet through a mass evolution—so we don't all keep reincarnating again and again, learning the same lessons, for millennia? Many scholars agree this great twenty-five-thousand-year cycle ends in 2012, or thereabouts—which makes this a very cutting-edge and relevant discussion in today's world.

Understanding the Precession

The best way to understand this twenty-five-thousand-year cycle is to imagine the earth as if it were a spinning top. Let's say you have a top that is spinning clockwise at a fast speed. At first it stands up straight, but then it starts tracing circles in the opposite direction—counterclockwise—as it slows down. Now imagine the earth is the top. Imagine you can see the earth's axis, as if it were a solid bar running through the North and South Poles. Over the course of about 25,920 years, the earth's axis makes a nice, slow circle in the opposite direction from the earth's normal rotation—like the circles the top starts making as it winds down. Some ancient myths compare the earth's axis to a long spoon in a pot of soup. The slow circular path of the earth's axis is the stirring of the pot. (This visual only works if you keep the bottom of the spoon in one place as you make circles with it.) This slow movement of the earth's axis causes the position of the stars in the night sky, during the equinox, to shift by one degree every seventy-two years. If you built your church or temple to line up with a certain star during every spring equinox, as many cultures, from the Druids at Stonehenge to Anasazis in Arizona, did, you'd be pretty unhappy when the stars started drifting away. By the time your grandchildren started growing up, your building would already be noticeably out of alignment.

In Western astrology, this master cycle is divided up into twelve "Ages of the Zodiac." Though the earth changes its speed slightly over time as it moves through this cycle, most astrologers round it off to 50 arc seconds per year. This creates twelve ideal Ages of the Zodiac at 2,160 years each, adding up to a total of 25,920 years.[4] If you calculate the cycle based on our current speed of 50.3 arc seconds per year, it would come out to 25,675 years—but since it fluctuates, most modern astronomers round it off at about 25,800.[5] The technical name for this cycle is the precession of the equinoxes. The word *precession* essentially means "movement."

Remember that Santillana and Von Dechend's book is called *Hamlet's Mill*? The Hamlet story is one of many ancient myths that describe the *axis mundi*—the earth's own axis—getting disrupted in its orbital path. The earth's axis is often described, in metaphor, as the axle of a mill for grinding corn. In order to build a mill, you have a horizontal wooden rod that runs through the center of a heavy stone wheel. The wooden rod is connected to a central, vertical axle. A strong worker then grabs the rod and starts pushing it around in circles. As the heavy stone wheel moves along, it grinds the corn underneath it.

Many myths set up a scene like this and then have the axle break. This is believed to represent the earth shifting on its axis. The myths then

Stone mill for grinding corn. This imagery was used in various ancient myths worldwide to describe a slow wobble in the Earth's axis lasting 25,920 years.

feature scenes where destructive Earth Changes seem to occur. Dr. Susan Lea, the Physics and Astronomy Department Chair at San Francisco State University, explains the deeper context behind this story—which is much older than the works of William Shakespeare.

> . . . the Hamlet myth is cosmological, and describes the precession of the equinoxes. By the time Shakespeare adapted the story to his purposes, its origin and meaning had lapsed into obscurity. . . . The mill is explained in the Indian Bhagavata Purana. ". . . the exalted seat of Vishnu, round which the starry spheres forever wander, like the upright axle of the corn mill." According to Santillana and Von Dechend, all these myths aim to explain precession: the mill represents the rotation of the celestial sphere; the mill axle is the polar axis and the theme of the breaking of the mill represents the precession. . . . Each age ends with a catastrophic event,

frequently involving a flood or water in some way. This is where the Hamlet tragedy fits in.[6]

Entire books could be written just on this one subject, and some already have been. One common symbol in these myths is the earth's axis—or the *axis mundi*.

Let's not forget that in chapter 3, we saw how the *axis mundi* was often symbolized by a stone—such as the Primitive Mountain, Shiva lingam, Benben, omphalos or baetyl—and this symbol was

25,920 YEARS

directly associated with the pineal gland. Let's also not forget that the Romans also used tall pyramid shapes to represent the baetyl on their coins. What we did not discuss in chapter 3, however, is that many of the Roman baetyl coins have a vertical axis running right through the center of the pyramid-shaped stone.

Precession of the equinoxes—a 25,920-year wobble in the Earth's axis.

Although this sacred stone is presumed to be solid . . . there is something mysterious going on inside. It is as if the outside skin has been rendered open to reveal some sort of structure. Four of the five coins show a pole or strut. . . . The mundane answer to this pole could be, and most likely is, the *axis mundi*. These coins may be telling us something con-

nected with the baetyl in a mystical way. . . . All of these
coins also have the angel on them.[7]

This suggests a curious, ongoing fascination in the top levels of the
Roman empire with the movement of the earth's axis, pyramids and the
pineal gland. If the Romans inherited a greater, worldwide secret about
the 25,920-year cycle, then they may well have believed there would be
direct effects upon human consciousness at the end of the cycle. Let's not
forget that in the Egyptian mythologies, the Benben stone is surrounded
by two Bennu birds. The Bennu is the phoenix—a bird that undergoes
a radical transformation. The Egyptians also taught that the Bennu's cry
was responsible for creating great cycles of time that were ordained by
Divine intelligence. We also saw teachings in the Egyptian Book of the
Dead on how the seeker could achieve his or her own phoenix-like
transformation—and when this happened, they could levitate, perform
miracles and glow with bright light. The mystery schools and the major
religions all seem to agree on the importance of the pineal gland in this
spiritual awakening process.

Many authors want to sound the alarm about what they feel is imminent doom associated with this cycle—and its apparent due date of 2012.
Some of the people I've spoken to who worked in various classified projects would agree with them. There is compelling evidence that significant Earth Changes do occur at the end of each of these cycles, but
remember—we are already seeing those changes now.

The Final Destruction

According to Santillana, these ancient legends from all over the world
describe the conditions on the earth getting worse and worse as we head
toward the end of the cycle—much like the flaming death of the phoenix
before it is reborn. These prophecies forecast a wide variety of problems
in government and society—wars, famines, diseases and corruption, not
to mention catastrophic Earth Changes—but the myths say they then

usher in a stunning new Golden Age. Again, using our analogy of the lucid dream, it's as if these events show us a worldwide reflection of who we are, and how asleep we have become—so we can be inspired to change our lives for the positive. If there is an intelligence throughout the Universe, and intelligent beings visited us who already knew about the Source Field, it seems quite ridiculous to consider that they would give us these prophecies just to tell us we were all going to die on a certain date—and that there was nothing we could do about it.

Our next set of prophecies come from the Mahabharata, a Hindu sacred scripture. They sound remarkably relevant to our own recent history, including Earth Changes, widespread corruption and moral decline—despite the fact that they may have been written some five thousand years ago. The numbers and symbolism in these legends fit Santillana's theory perfectly—the writers did seem to be aware of the twenty-five-thousand-year precession cycle. The Mahabharata describes humanity's entrance into the final age of hell on earth, or Kali Yuga, before we again return to the Golden Age that will follow. Again, bear in mind what the Cayce Readings said about prophecies of physical catastrophes—they are metaphors of the changes we are all going through. The Cayce Readings also said the Book of Revelation frequently described objects in groups of seven to symbolize the seven "chakras" or energy systems in the body. Here in this Hindu text, we apparently see the same symbolism being used—in the form of "seven blazing suns" that appear at the end of the age.

> In the Kali age, the Brahmanas [spiritual leaders] . . . abstain from prayers and meditation. . . . The course of the world looketh contrary, and indeed, these are the signs that foreshadow the Universal Destruction.
> And, O lord of men, numerous Mleccha kings then rule over the earth! And those sinful monarchs, addicted to false speech, govern their subjects on principles that are false. . . . And, O tiger among men, the merchants and traders then full of guile, sell large quantities of articles with false weights and measures. And they that are virtuous do not prosper; while

they that are sinful prosper exceedingly. And virtue loseth her strength while sin becometh all powerful. . . .

And, O king, girls of seven or eight years of age do then conceive, while boys of ten or twelve years beget offspring. . . . And women given to impropriety of conduct and marked by evil manners, deceive even the best of husbands. . . .

O king, toward the end of those thousands of years constituting the four Yugas and when the lives of men become so short, a drought occurs extending for many years. And then, O lord of the earth, men and creatures endued with small strength and vitality, becoming hungry, die by thousands.

And then, O lord of men, seven blazing Suns, appearing in the firmament, drink up all the waters of the earth that are in rivers or seas . . . the fire called Samvartaka, impelled by the winds, appeareth on the earth that hath already been dried to cinders by the seven Suns. And then that fire, penetrating through the earth and making its appearance in the nether regions also, begetteth great terror in the hearts of the gods. . . . And, O lord of the earth, consuming the nether regions as also everything upon this earth, that fire destroyeth all things in a moment."[8]

I do not think these prophecies of a final destruction are literal—the "seven blazing suns" appear to symbolize a sudden spiritual awakening that occurs throughout humanity. Right after everything on earth is allegedly "destroyed in a moment" by this incredible fire, the story mysteriously continues—and everyone is still alive. A savior figure now arrives, with supernatural abilities, who defeats the bad guys and helps the planet transform. Symbolism again appears to be at work here. There are dreamlike myths like this all over the world, and the Hindu prophecy seems surprisingly similar to how our world appears today. The fiery catastrophe we just read about appears to be another metaphorical symbol of worldwide changes that sweep through our society at lightning speed—toppling our castles of sand, which we built in ignorance, and eliminating the old ways of doing things. Cayce described a very similar set of metaphors in his decoding of the Book of Revelation.

The Coming of the Golden Age

One could argue that things in society have always been this challenging, and the authors are just pining away for a spiritual ideal that was never reached. Nonetheless, the Hindu myths begin with the Golden Age, which is literally Paradise on earth, and then gradually work their way down to the Kali Yuga—over many thousands of years. All Santillana's myths, worldwide, indicate that things get worse and worse, and then we get major Earth Changes—which we are now seeing. Some of the myths end in a flood. The Hindu myths end in a fire. The rules of logic suggest that if "all things were destroyed in a moment" at the end of every 25,000-year cycle, then no life on earth could ever have survived for very long—so obviously we can't take this prophecy literally. Similarly, the Bible begins with Adam and Eve, in the book of Genesis—allegedly the first people to live on earth—and ends with a major catastrophe in the Book of Revelation. That's not the end in the Bible either—the Tribulation leads directly to a New Heaven and New Earth; a resplendent, glorious Golden Age.

Just as we see in the Bible, the Hindu prophecy doesn't end with destruction. The awesome Samvartaka fire leads to a new creation—the Krita, or Golden, Age:

> And when those terrible times will be over, the creation will begin anew . . . the Krita [Golden] age will begin again. And the clouds will commence to shower seasonably, and the stars and stellar conjunctions will become auspicious. And the planets, duly revolving in their orbits, will become exceedingly propitious. And all around, there will be prosperity and abundance and health and peace.[9]

In the Hindu prophecy, the Golden Age starts to restore the balance of nature and the Cosmos—creating greater prosperity, abundance, health and peace—before all the hard work is finally over. Then, Hinduism's own version of a messiah—namely, Kalki—comes on the scene, ready to finish the job. Kalki clearly has "Ascended" abilities, similar to what we can all do in our lucid dreams. He can manifest vehicles, weapons and warriors just by thinking of them.

> And commissioned by Time, a Brahmana of the name of Kalki will take his birth. And he will glorify Vishnu and possess great energy, great intelligence, and great prowess . . . vehicles and weapons, and warriors and arms, and coats of mail will be at his disposal as soon as he will think of them.[10]

According to Edgar Cayce's readings about this major change, the "Second Coming of Christ" is what happens to all of us as we go through this process: "To him, to her that is faithful, there shall be given a CROWN of light . . . ye become as rivers of light, as fountains of knowledge, as mountains of strength, as the pastures for the hungry, as the rest for the weary, as the strength for the weak."[11] Therefore, the wars and violent acts you are about to read, where corrupt people are murdered, are most likely part of the dream symbolism. Rather than literally involving people being killed, it may be a symbolic story of the journey we all make within ourselves, to purify the ego—that part of us that has been addicted to manipulation, power and control:

> And he will be the king of kings, and ever victorious with the strength of virtue. And he will restore order and peace in this world crowded with creatures and contradictory in its course . . . that Brahmana will exterminate all the mlecchas wherever those low and despicable persons may take refuge . . . when the Brahmanas will have exterminated the thieves and robbers, there will be prosperity everywhere (on earth) . . . when sin will thus have been rooted out and virtue will flourish on arrival of the Krita age, men will once more betake themselves to the practice of religious rites. . . .

And the Brahmanas will become good and honest, and the regenerate ones, devoted to ascetic austerities, will become Munis [silent meditators,] and the asylums of ascetics, which had before been filled with wretches, will once more be homes of men devoted to truth—and men in general will begin to honour and practise truth.

And all seeds, sown on earth, will grow, and, O monarch, every kind of crop will grow in every season. And men will devotedly practise charity and vows and observances . . . and the rulers of the earth will govern their kingdoms virtuously.[12]

If you read Helena Blavatsky's controversial work *The Secret Doctrine,* more information about this Hindu prophecy appears—complete with excerpts from the original text. We find out that there are "eight superhuman faculties" Kalki develops, associated with this prophecy—obviously far beyond what most of us have now:

As the "Satya-yuga" is always the first in the series of the four ages or Yugas, so the Kali ever comes the last. The Kali yuga reigns now supreme in India, and it seems to coincide with that of the Western age. Anyhow, it is curious to see how prophetic in almost all things was the writer of Vishnu Purana when foretelling to Maitreya some of the dark influences and sins of this Kali Yug. For after saying that the "barbarians" will be masters of the banks of the Indus [River], he adds:

"Thus, in the Kali age will decay constantly proceed, until the human race approaches its annihilation (pralaya). . . . When the close of the Kali age shall be nigh, a portion of that divine being which exists, of its own spiritual nature . . . shall descend on earth . . . (Kalki Avatar) endowed with the eight superhuman faculties. . . . He will reestablish righteousness on earth, and the minds of those who live at the end of Kali Yuga shall be awakened and become as pellucid [clear] as crystal.

"The men who are thus changed . . . shall be the seeds of human beings, and shall give birth to a race who shall follow the laws of the Krita age, the age of purity."[13]

Edgar Cayce went into detail about what he called the "fifth root race" in his own readings. John Van Auken discussed this prophecy in the March–April 2009 issue of the Association for Research and Enlightenment's *Venture Inward* magazine.

[Cayce's readings predicted] the shift to a new era and a new body type that he called the "fifth root race," indicating that there had been four previous ages and body types. The body change has been occurring in an evolving manner for some time, but perhaps, through mutation, there will be new bodies—ones that will be more accommodating to soulful consciousness. We may be content with our present bodies, but imagine incarnating again in a souped-up model that allows for more cosmic consciousness while incarnate. Sounds good, especially if it coincides with a new age when "Satan is bound" and "no evil distracts or temptations test the souls in the new earth."[14]

When Will the Golden Age Arrive?

When we go back to our excerpt from the Mahabharata in *The Secret Doctrine,* we come across a tantalizing clue: The ancient Hindu scriptures gave us a precise time window for when the Golden Age would arrive. They associated this with a rare conjunction of planets in the solar system, thus allowing us to calculate an exact date.

As it is said, "When the sun and moon and the lunar asterism Tishya and the planet Jupiter are in one mansion, the Krita (or Satya) age shall return."[15]

No calculation is presented in Blavatsky's book for when this may occur, but Geoff Stray presents an informed opinion in his book *Beyond 2012.*

> In *The Way to Shambhala,* [Edwin] Bernbaum says that the golden age will come when the Sun, Moon and Jupiter all meet in the same quadrant as the Tishya constellation (which is part of Cancer). The next time this happens will be on July 26, 2014, according to my astronomical software [Cyber-Sky]. . . .[16]

That's barely over a year and a half after December 21, 2012—the end of the Maya calendar. Until Graham Hancock peer-reviewed an early draft of this book, I was under the impression that most astronomers believed the shift from the Age of Pisces into the Age of Aquarius, in the Western system, also occurred around the year 2011 or 2012. According to Peter Lemesurier in *Great Pyramid Decoded,* the French Institut Géographique National fixed the Age of Aquarius as arriving in 2011.[17]

Obviously if there is a serious debate about the start time of the Age of Aquarius, we need to roll up our sleeves and dig for the answer. Most astronomers feel the Age of Aquarius begins whenever the sunrise moves into the constellation of Aquarius during the spring equinox—but no one can agree on when that is. When you go to NASA's Get a Straight Answer Web site, and ask David P. Stern when the Age of Aquarius begins, his straight answer is "I don't know."[18]

> The ancients defined constellations by their brightest stars, and drew no exact borders. Modern star charts have exact boundaries, usually straight lines like the boundaries of states in the western U.S., but I don't know when the spring equinox crossed the modern Pisces/Aquarius boundary.[19]

In modern times, the precession was rediscovered by Hipparchus, who began his work somewhere around the spring equinox of March 24, 146

B.C. That is an important date, as we will soon see. Shirley Burchill, an astronomy historian, suggested Hipparchus was working from much older records.

> Much of Hipparchus's work was only possible because he was able to consult the work of astronomers who had gone before. The ancient Babylonians had left records of their astronomical observations, methods and equipment. There is much evidence to show that Hipparchus used this information, and that [it] allowed him to make comparisons. Hipparchus's precise measurement of the equinoxes was, in fact, a mathematical interpretation of ancient Babylonian knowledge.[20]

David Andrew D'Zmura created a method to calculate when the shift into the Age of Aquarius would occur, partly by going back to the original data. He sought after and was ultimately awarded a U.S. Patent—number 676618—so his findings would not be stolen. In his patent, D'Zmura implies that Hipparchus was inspired to begin all his groundbreaking astronomy studies in 146 B.C. because he was tipped off. As we just read, Hipparchus had access to ancient Babylonian records. We already have seen the Babylonians displaying the pineal gland/pinecone/axis mundi/winged angel symbols in their sacred artwork. These records may very well have revealed that 146 B.C., or thereabouts, was the year we shifted into the Age of Pisces. If various traditions kept this knowledge secret all along, there would have been a great deal of interest in the coming of a new Age of the Zodiac. No one could be sure what might happen as this pivotal moment arrived. Everyone would be looking at the stars to try to understand the greater cycle that was driving these Ages—and Hipparchus's method for classifying the brightness of the stars in the night sky is still used today.[21]

D'Zmura calculated the average value for the precession between 150 B.C. and A.D. 2000, based on estimates of how fast the earth's wobble has been moving during this time, and came up with a number just slightly smaller than the traditional 2,160-year Age of the Zodiac:

some 2,158.1914 years. If we then add that to Hipparchus's start date of
146 B.C., we end up at seventy days after the beginning of the year 2012.

> This date of A.D. 2012 is accepted as significant to spiritu-
> alists, mystics and believers, many of whom prognosticate
> that the Messiah appears in this year.[22]

The Hindus, the Mayas and the Egyptian/Greek/Roman astrology
tradition all appear to converge on the same two-year period—from 2012
to 2014—as the window in which major changes are predicted to take
place. Hardly anyone is aware that these 2012 prophecies are truly a
worldwide phenomenon—appearing on either side of the Atlantic. An
ever-increasing body of data in myths and prophecies suggests that we
may undergo a phoenix-like transformation into a Fifth Root Race during this window of time—which may ultimately affect every person on
earth. It seems like an impossible, starry-eyed dream that something like
this could really happen to us—but the last thing I want to do is just
wait and see. I think it's even worse to just "trust the prophecies," and
not see if we can do any further research to clear things up.

Asclepius's Lament

Another excellent prophetic view of our future comes from an ancient
Egyptian document that cannot be any more recent than A.D. 400—
but is probably much older. It's known as "Asclepius's Lament," and is a
conversation that allegedly took place between Asclepius and Hermes—
thus classifying it as a Hermetic text. The very early Christians definitely
knew about it and quoted from it. G. R. S. Mead discussed the problems
with dating the Hermetic texts in 1906.

> It is impossible to base upon it any certain conclusions as
> to the date of the original or its precise worth in the history
> of religion. That, however, our Latin translation is an ancient
> one is proved by Augustine's verbal quotations from it. . . . It

was thus in existence about 400 A.D. at least. Tradition, however, has assigned to it a far higher antiquity. . . .[23]

The Cayce Readings repeatedly date the time of Hermes as being roughly twelve thousand years ago,[24] claiming he was the master architect of the Great Pyramid,[25] and also said he was a prior incarnation of Jesus.[26]

Mead's book has an older, harder-to-read translation of Asclepius's Lament.[27] Graham Hancock combined the clearest and most poetic aspects from Copenhaver's[28] and Scott's[29] modern translations, giving us a newer, friendlier version that appears, without credit, in various places online—as follows:[30]

There will come a time when it will have been in vain that Egyptians have honored the Godhead with heartfelt piety and service. . . . The gods will return from earth to heaven. . . . O Egypt, Egypt, of thy religion nothing will remain but an empty tale . . . only the stones will tell of thy piety.

And in that day men will be weary of life, and they will cease to think the universe worthy of reverent wonder and worship. And so religion, the greatest of all blessings . . . will be threatened with destruction; men will think it a burden and will come to scorn it. . . .

As for the soul, and the belief that it is immortal by nature, or may hope to attain to immortality, as I have taught you,—all this they will mock, and even persuade themselves that it is false . . . the gods will depart from mankind,—a grievous thing!—and only evil angels will remain, who will mingle with men, and drive the poor wretches into all manner of reckless crime, into wars, and robberies, and frauds, and all things hostile to the nature of the soul.

Then will the earth tremble, and the sea bear no ships; heaven will not support the stars in their orbits, all voices of the gods will be forced into silence; the fruits of the earth will rot; the soil will turn barren, and the very air will sicken with sullen stagnation; all things will be disordered and awry, all good will disappear.

But when all this has befallen, Asclepius, then God the Creator of all things . . . will call back to the right path those who have gone astray; he will cleanse the world of evil, washing it away with floods, burning it out with the fiercest fire, and expelling it with war and pestilence.

And thus he will bring back his world to its former aspect, so that the Cosmos will once more be deemed worthy of worship and wondering reverence. . . . Such is the new birth of the Cosmos; it is a making again of all things good, a holy and awe-inspiring restoration of all nature; and it is wrought inside the process of Time by the eternal Will of the Creator.

Again—the prophecy of floods, fires, war and pestilence has already come true, and we can and will prove that the earth's recent behavior is unprecedented in modern times. Notice that this prophecy again does not involve every living thing being destroyed. It points to a world in which the "gods" are no longer on earth—if such people ever did live here in the past. It also says the changes we're now going through pave the way for a "new birth of the Cosmos" that will create an "awe-inspiring restoration of all nature." Given all the other prophecies that associate the exact same set of circumstances with the 2012–2014 time window, this also seems to be a perfect fit. Another very curious clue in this passage is where Hermes says this transformation is "wrought inside the process of time." That's a very curious choice of words. What might he mean by the process of time, exactly? Could it have something to do with this Great Cycle? Time becomes much more interesting once we explore the new science concepts in Part Two.

I came across more and more of these mysterious Golden Age prophecies as my research went on—not just in Hancock's discussion of *Hamlet's Mill*, but in a variety of other sources. It was obvious to me that the ancients took this prediction very, very seriously. I realized that if these ancient prophecies were, in fact, talking about a real event, there had to be a physical process involved. It had to be something tangible, something measurable, and therefore something that could be studied scientifically. And clearly, the most important clue we're given in the worldwide ancient myths is "Study the precession of the equinoxes. Find out what it really means, and how it really works." As the years went by, I spared no expense of time or energy in that quest. One of the first major clues was apparently built into the Great Pyramid of Giza—which may forecast nothing less than a messianic event for humanity as we head into the Age of Aquarius. Once I understood the symbolism, the symbol on the back of the U.S. dollar bill became much more interesting. The founding fathers of America appear to have been very well aware of these archaic prophecies—and gave us a new and improved version of the same prophecies we see in Sumer, Babylon, India, Egypt, Greece and Rome. The American eagle is the new version of the Egyptian Bennu bird. The pyramid is the baetyl—a symbol of the awakened pineal gland. The founding fathers may have even started the United States to help usher these prophecies in. And once you understand the seemingly impossible miracles of the Great Pyramid's construction, it becomes much easier to see how this may have been considered as the ultimate, living proof that gods had once openly assisted humanity here on earth.

CHAPTER SEVEN

Shedding New Light on the Great Pyramid

Are we walking around in a hypnotic trance? Have we forgotten that we have lived before, and will live again? Are we connected to all the living things around us on a direct, conscious level? Is there a working third eye in the center of our brains? Are there techniques we can practice that will allow us to venture directly into the Source Field and perform seemingly impossible miracles? Can others go there with us at the same time, and experience the same things? Is the 25,920-year cycle just a wobble in the earth's axis? Did the ancients give us a working Source Field technology—pyramids—as a way of revealing that this Source Field can indeed be harnessed and directed for the benefit of all life on earth? Is the Great Pyramid ultimately our single best piece of surviving evidence to prove that our ancestors had very highly advanced technology? Does it also give us the tools to reconstruct their lost, ancient science?

The Great Pyramid is considered the largest stone building on earth, covering some thirteen acres at its base—the equivalent of seven Midtown city blocks in Manhattan—and it rises to the height of a forty-story building. Approximately 2.3 million limestone and granite blocks were used to build it, each of them weighing 2.5 to 70 tons apiece—for a total mass of about 6.3 million tons. No crane ever built in modern times is strong enough to lift stones this heavy—it would simply tumble over. The bedrock underneath the Great Pyramid was leveled out so perfectly that no corner of the pyramid's base is more than a half-inch higher or lower than the others.[1] Such precise leveling goes significantly beyond even the finest architectural standards of today.[2]

Strangely, the pyramid is also located at the exact center of the earth's landmass—the one true *axis mundi*. Its east-west axis sits precisely on the longest land parallel, covering the greatest amount of land and the least amount of water on earth—passing through Africa, Asia, and America along the way. The longest land meridian, crossing over Asia, Africa, Europe, and Antarctica, also passes right through the pyramid.[3] The likelihood of finding this "perfect location" by accident is 1 in 3 billion.[4] I didn't understand why this location was so important until years later, as we will see—but it has to do with the flow and positioning of natural energy fields from the earth that have remained unknown to mainstream scientists in our own modern times.

The sides of the pyramid line up so well with true rotational north that they only deviate by 3 minutes of arc in any one direction—less than 0.06 percent.[5] Another "coincidence" is that if you calculate the average height of land above sea level, with Miami as the low and the Himalayas as the high, you come out with 5,449 inches—which is the exact height of the Great Pyramid.[6]

To me, the most surprising fact of all was that when the Great Pyramid was first built, it was covered with twenty-one acres of gleaming, brightly polished white casing stones—a total of about 115,000 blocks of pure white limestone[7] averaging 100 inches, or 8.3 feet, in thickness. If you caught the glint of the sun's reflection off of these stones in the daytime, it would be blindingly bright—thus earning it the name Ta Khut, or "the Light." The reflections could apparently be seen from the mountains of Israel hundreds of miles away.[8] Despite the fact that some of these casing stones weighed sixteen tons, all six sides were carved to fit together so perfectly that the cracks between them were only one-fiftieth of an inch wide[9]—which is narrower than a human fingernail. Sir Flinders Petrie described this in the late 1800s as "the finest opticians' work on the scale of acres," comparing it to the precision used to grind lenses for a telescope. Richard C. Hoagland has pointed out that even the tiles on a NASA space shuttle do not fit together this closely. Even more surprisingly, these cracks are not empty—they are filled with a cement that is incredibly strong. There is no known way you could fit a mortar into cracks one-fiftieth of an inch wide, and evenly cover areas as large as five feet by seven feet wide in the vertical, with any known methods. And if you were foolhardy enough to smash the casing stones with a sledgehammer, you would find that the limestone itself breaks before the cement does.[10]

I'm well aware of how fantastic this must sound. It's one thing to see the pyramid sitting there as it is today—a giant mass of decaying stone blocks. It would be quite something else to witness it in its original form, looking like a gigantic, gleaming white sculpture in the desert—something totally unlike any other technological achievement we've ever seen on earth—whether from ancient times or in our modern world. Thankfully, many people witnessed these casing stones in their original form and documented their observations in writing over the centuries—and the history can be found in Peter Tompkins's *Secrets of the Great Pyramid.*[11]

According to Tompkins, limestone becomes harder and more polished with time and weather, unlike marble—think about the gorgeous stalactites and stalagmites of limestone you can find in underground caves. Therefore, the pyramid did not get progressively more dull-looking as the centuries rolled by after it was first built.[12] In approximately 440 B.C., Herodotus wrote that the pyramid's casing stones were highly polished—with joints so fine they could scarcely even be seen with the naked eye.[13] The thirteenth-century Arab historian Abd-al-Latif said that despite their polished appearance, these stones were inscribed with mysterious, unintelligible characters—enough to fill ten thousand pages. His colleagues assumed these writings were the graffiti of ancient tourists.[14] William of Baldensal visited the pyramid in the early 1300s and described these strange inscriptions as being all arranged in long, careful rows of strange symbols.[15] When the casing stones eventually were lost, so went any hope of documenting these mysterious writings for future codebreaking analysis and study.

Diodorus Siclus, who lived soon after the time of Christ, wrote that the casing stones were "complete and without the least decay."[16] The

Roman naturalist Pliny witnessed native boys running up the polished sides, to the delight of tourists. In about A.D. 24, Strabo visited Egypt, and said there was an entrance on the north face of the pyramid that was made of a hinged stone you could raise from the bottom up, but was otherwise indistinguishable from its surroundings when it lay flush.[17]

Inside the Great Pyramid there are three different chambers. The largest of these is known as the King's Chamber, and is the only part of the pyramid that is made of red granite, which is extremely hard. In the 1990s, Bernard Pietsch analyzed the twenty different stones on the floor of the King's Chamber and made startling discoveries. Strangely, although the stones are all either square or rectangular, hardly any of them are the same size—except when you have an identical pair side by side. These stones are arranged in a series of six different rows—and each row has a different width from any of the others. In *Anatomy of the King's Chamber,* Pietsch presents staggeringly complex and compelling evidence that a variety of measurements from Mercury, Venus, Earth, the Moon, Mars, Jupiter and Saturn—including their orbital periods—are encoded in the stones' dimensions.[18]

Within the King's Chamber there is a loose stone coffin carved out of an extremely hard chocolate-brown granite, estimated to weigh three tons. The external volume of the sarcophagus is exactly twice the internal volume. Thanks to the patterns of circular drill marks found inside, engineer Christopher Dunn calculated that the coffin was carved out by tubular drills that could cut through granite five hundred times faster than any technology we now have available.[19] [In chapter 13, I propose this is actually the result of a technology that can dramatically soften stone.] Skeptics believe this may have been done with diamond-tipped drill bits in Egypt, despite the impossibility of achieving the necessary speeds involved with any modern technology. Dunn points out that the strongest metal they had at the time was copper. The diamonds would have cut through the copper like butter before they ever even put a dent in the granite.[20]

The sarcophagus has grooves for a lid to be fitted in place, but no such lid has ever been found—as if it were never intended to be found. Many pyramid researchers, including Peter Lemesurier, interpret this open tomb as symbolizing a time when there will be no more death, i.e., the coming Golden Age. The coffin was empty—and there is no evidence it ever held a mummy. The granite sarcophagus also cannot fit through the Antechamber, meaning that it had to be built into the pyramid from the very beginning—totally in contrast with any known Egyptian burial practices.[21]

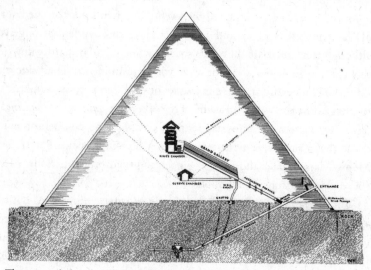

The internal chambers, passageways and airshafts of the Great Pyramid.

Although this was not discovered until much later, the north and south walls of both the King's Chamber and the Queen's Chamber also contained airshafts that went on an upward-sloping angle, all the way out to the surface of the pyramid. This supplied just enough oxygen to refresh the atmosphere inside each room. In the mid-1990s, Rudolf Gantenbrink sent a miniature robot some sixty-five meters up the shafts, and confirmed that in the King's Chamber, the south shaft points at the star Al Nitak, or Zeta Orionis. The north shaft points at Alpha Draconis, which used to be the pole star in the third millennium B.C.. The northern Queen's Chamber shaft is aimed at Beta Ursae Minoris, and the southern channel points to Sirius.[22] All these alignments date back to about 2500 B.C. That was the most recent time in which they all lined up.[23] According to ancient-civilizations researcher Joseph Jochmans, "As Bauval and Gilbert showed through computer calculations, the constellational alignments imprinted in the Air Passages for 2450 B.C.E. were also present earlier, in about 10,500 B.C.E., because of the Precession of the Equinoxes."[24] An Edgar Cayce reading from June 30, 1932, said that work on the Great Pyramid and the Sphinx began this very same year.[25]

In the thirteenth century, an Arab historian compared the pyramid to a gigantic female breast, noting the casing stones still looked perfect on the outside except for the original entrance carved by Caliph Al-Mamoun.[26] Disaster struck in the year 1356,[27] as the first of a series of earthquakes leveled significant areas of northern Egypt, collapsing entire city blocks to rubble. The pyramid was shaken so hard by these quakes that many of the casing stones broke off and tumbled into a giant mess. The people were desperate to rebuild—and used this fallen limestone from the pyramid as raw material to help build the new capital city El Kaherah, "The Victorious," as well as to rebuild Cairo. Apparently, the stones that hadn't already fallen off were then deliberately broken off, because the quality of the limestone was very pure and provided an excellent building material. According to the French Baron d'Anlgure, who visited this area of Egypt in 1396, "Certain masons demolished the course of great casing stones which covered [the pyramid,] and tumbled them into the valley."[28] Two bridges were built across the Nile specifically to help drag the stones across the river via camel trains, so as to build mosques and palaces in Cairo and El Kaherah.[29]

As the centuries rolled by, the legend of the once-great casing stones had faded into nothing more than a superstitious myth. However, Colonel Vyse conducted excavations in and around the pyramid beginning in 1836 that permanently eliminated the skeptics' arguments. Vyse found that the pyramid was surrounded by debris of limestone chunks and sand that had piled up around the base by as much as fifty feet. He cleared a patch in the center of the north façade, hoping to reach the base and bedrock of the pyramid. There he found two of the original casing stones—forever ending the scholarly argument about whether the

pyramid had ever been covered with a perfectly flat, polished white surface. The original blocks were still so finely carved that an exact measurement of the slope angle could be calculated.[30] According to Vyse, they
were perfect: "in a sloping plane as correct and true almost as modern
work by optical instrument makers. The joints were scarcely perceptible,
not wider than the thickness of silver paper."[31]

Vyse published his detailed measurements and notes in 1840, and his
assistant John Perring published his own book as well. This opened up a
whole new phase of study known as "Pyramidology."[32] John Taylor, a
gifted mathematician and amateur astronomer who worked as an editor
of the *London Observer* in the nineteenth century, was already in his fifties
when Vyse's data came in from Egypt. Taylor then began a rigorous
thirty-year investigation into all the measurements that had been reported
in and around the pyramid, looking for hidden mathematical and geometric formulas. Taylor found that if he measured the perimeter of the
base in inches, it came out to roughly 100 times 366—and if he divided
the perimeter by 25 inches, he got 366 once again. What's the big deal
about 366? It is suspiciously close to the exact length of an earth year—
365.2422 days.[33] Taylor found that by slightly changing the length of a
typical British inch, these figures could become exact reflections of the
earth year. Was this merely a cheap mathematical cheat, or was there any
worthwhile science behind it? That question was soon answered when a
highly fortunate "coincidence" struck at almost the exact same time.

Sir John Herschel, one of Britain's most highly regarded astronomers
at the turn of the nineteenth century, had very recently tried to invent a
new measuring unit to replace the existing British system. He wanted it
to be based on the exact dimensions of the earth. Without knowing
anything about Taylor's research, Herschel used the most accurate
dimensions of the earth available at the time to suggest that we should
be using inches that were very slightly longer than normal—by a mere
half the width of a human hair, or 1.00106 British inches. Herschel
blasted the French for basing their metric system on the curvature of the
earth, which can change, rather than using a line that went straight
through the earth's center, from pole to pole. A recent British Ordnance
Survey had fixed that pole-to-pole distance within the earth as 7898.78

miles, or 500,500,000 British inches. It would become exactly 500 million inches if the British inch were made just a slight bit longer. Herschel argued that the existing British inch should be officially lengthened to obtain this truly scientific measuring unit.

Fifty of these inches would then be exactly one ten-millionth of the earth's polar axis. Twenty-five of them would make a very useful cubit—which could replace the existing British yard and foot. Little did Herschel know that Taylor had already discovered these exact same units within the dimensions of the Great Pyramid.[34] When Taylor found out about this, he was thrilled. He now had compelling evidence that the builders of the pyramid must have known the true spherical dimensions of the planet, and built their whole measurement system off it. That again implies that the ancient Egyptians possessed a significantly more advanced technology than we normally give them credit for.[35] Lemesurier reported that in International Geophysical Year 1957, the earth's diameter from pole to pole was measured with flawless satellite precision—much more accurately than in Herschel's time. As a result, we now know that the pyramid inch is indeed one five-hundred-millionth of the earth's diameter at the poles—and this connection is so exact that the numbers check out down to multiple decimal points of accuracy.[36] This means the pyramid was indeed built to be a mathematically perfect reflection of the length of a year on earth around its perimeter. These precisely earth-scaled measurements appear again and again in obvious ways—both inside and outside the pyramid.

However, an even greater mystery is found when we measure the diagonals of the Great Pyramid—namely, the distance from one corner, over the top and down to the other corner. This distance comes out to 25,826.4 pyramid inches[37]—remarkably close to modern calculations of the true length of the precession of the equinoxes in years.

It definitely seems that the Great Pyramid's designers wanted us to use the Egyptian inch. By making the pyramid's diagonals add up to the precession of the equinoxes in Egyptian inches, we seem to have been given a message to pay attention to this great cycle. These same builders obviously knew the exact dimensions of the earth, and therefore may very well have traveled the world—seeding many different ancient myths in many

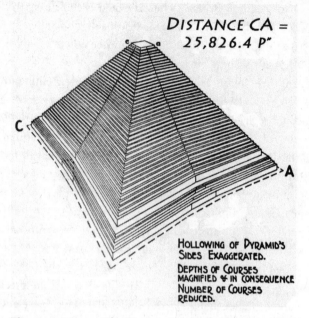

DISTANCE CA = 25,826.4 P"

C

A

HOLLOWING OF PYRAMID'S
SIDES EXAGGERATED.
DEPTHS OF COURSES
MAGNIFIED & IN CONSEQUENCE
NUMBER OF COURSES
REDUCED.

The exterior diagonals of the Great Pyramid add up to 25,826.4 Pyramid Inches—a figure remarkably close to modern estimates of the precession of the equinoxes.

different ancient cultures. As Santillana and Von Dechend revealed again and again in *Hamlet's Mill*, the hidden message in each of these ancient myths told us to look at the precession—or what many ancient cultures also called the Great Year. The Primitive Mountain, Benben stone, Shiva lingam, omphalos, baetyl and Ka'aba stone, not to mention the redundant worldwide pinecone symbolism of the Mayan, Egyptians, Hindus, Buddhists, Greeks and Romans, also suggests there was once a worldwide awareness that the end of the Great Year would somehow involve the awakening of the pineal gland. The Great Pyramid now appears to be yet another way in which our ancestors attempted to permanently preserve this message for future generations. The Vatican seems to know about it, as they put an open Egyptian-style sarcophagus directly behind their gigantic pinecone statue—which was flanked with Bennu/phoenix birds.

If the Great Pyramid does have a symbolic story to tell, another obvious part of the message would be that it was deliberately left unfinished on the outside. There is a flat, square area at the top where a pyramid-shaped capstone—another form of the baetyl stone—can be fitted. When we remember how well the Great Pyramid preserves the earth's exact measurements, it is no surprise that Peter Lemesurier, the author of *Great Pyramid Decoded,* suggested the flattened top meant the earth itself, like the Great Pyramid, is somehow unfinished. It could be that the folks who built the pyramid intended to return at some point—perhaps the end of the Great Year—to finish the job they started. The return of the capstone also transforms the pyramid from a six-sided object—with a base, four sides and a top—to a five-sided object. According to Lemesurier, in Egyptian numerology, six means "imperfection" and five means "Divine Initiation." Given that we see the exact length of an earth year in the perimeter, as well as the exact length of the precession in the diagonals, this suggests that the cycle of precession will ultimately remove the imperfections of humanity—by moving us through a Divine Initiation of some kind.

The Great Seal of the United States

I understand that some people might consider this entire interpretation of Great Pyramid prophecy to be numerology, and therefore lacking in any scientific credibility. However, no one can deny that this same symbolic message of a returning capstone was forever enshrined on the reverse side of the Great Seal of the United States. The strange symbol of a single eye inside a gleaming-white triangle, descending onto a thirteen-course pyramid, has appeared on every U.S. dollar bill in circulation since the 1930s. The Great Seal was first proposed on the very day the Declaration of Independence was signed—July 4, 1776. Thomas Jefferson commissioned a French West Indian portrait painter named Eugene Pierre du Simitiere to create the original design, which was then approved by Jefferson, Benjamin Franklin and John Adams.

Even in these earliest versions, the "Eye of Providence"—a single eye, gleaming with light—appears over the pyramid. The original phrase that

was written around the pyramid was "Deo Favente Perennis." *Deo* means
"God," as well as "the open sky" and something that is "charged with the
brightness of day." The word *favente* means "favor, befriend, support and
back up," and *perennis* means "continual, everlasting, perpetual, perennial
and eternal." So, a loose translation would be "God Supports [us] Eternally."
In Latin, the word *perennial* means "yearly," something that repeats every
year—so this could be another reference to the Great Year of precession:
"God Supports the Great Year." Some of the earliest American currency
featured the unfinished pyramid as the main symbol on the front—
although in this case the Eye of Providence did not appear at the top. As we
now know, the pyramid is also a baetyl—the symbol of the pineal gland in
many ancient cultures. Perhaps the founding fathers felt the inclusion of
this obviously Masonic symbol—the awakened pineal gland, or third eye,
inside a triangle—would be too controversial for the early American colo-
nists. In this case, the word *perennis* was written overhead, by itself.

By 1782, later revisions of the Great Seal changed the wording to what
we now see—with "Annuit Coeptis" on the top and "Novus Ordo Seclorum"

United States $50 bill from 1778 with 13-course pyramid and the word
Perennis—likely symbolizing the Great Year, or precession of the equinoxes.

on the bottom. These phrases make the message even clearer. The word *annuit* means "to favor or smile on," often by nodding approval—and the word *coeptis* means "undertaking," as well as "beginning, starting and commencing." When we include the Eye of Providence as a symbol of God, the phrase thus translates as "God has favored our beginnings." However, there's deeper symbolism in this phrase as well. The word *annuit* is related to other Latin words that mean "yearly"—and this is where we get the word *annual* from. One translation of the Latin word *annui* is a "yearly payment." So, *Annuit Coeptis* can also mean "The [Great] Year Begins." The payment we are expected to get from the Great Year appears to be written into the symbol itself—namely, the transformation of the earth, where the precessional cycle begins again.

This message is made much clearer when we delve into the mysterious roots of the phrase "Novus Ordo Seclorum," which was incorporated into the Great Seal of the United States in 1782 by Charles Thomson. The official record openly states that Thomson was inspired by line five of Virgil's Fourth Eclogue, which we will discuss shortly. The original Latin reads *Magnus ab integro seclorum nascitur ordo*, and it is interpreted to mean "and the majestic roll of circling centuries begins anew." This sounds very much like a description of the Great Cycle of precession—describing the "majestic roll of circling centuries" that now "begins anew," creating a Golden Age in the process.

The Great Roman Oracle

In my early years of intensive research, circa 1994, I found a direct quote from C. A. L. Totten, a 1st Lieutenant in the 4th artillery of the U.S. Army, who explained the deeper meaning of the Great Seal. This was published as a letter he wrote to Charles J. Folger, the secretary of the Treasury, on February 10, 1882:

> The All-Seeing Eye is one of the oldest hieroglyphics of the Deity. The triangle also is a cabalistic symbol of the most remote antiquity. . . . The descent of the mystic eye and

triangle in the form of a capstone to this mysterious monument [the Great Pyramid] of all times and nations, is to us
as a people most pregnant with significance. The motto,
Novus Ordo Seclorum, is a quotation from the 4th Eclogue
and was borrowed in turn by Virgil from the mystic Sibylline
records.[38]

Totten goes on to give the exact quote, which is stunning—but first,
let's explore the "mystic Sibylline records" in greater detail, so we understand the context. In the early days of the formation of Rome, the name
"sibyl" was derived from the Greek word *sibulla*, which meant a woman
who gives prophecies—also known as an oracle. The Oracle at Delphi
hosted the mysterious omphalos stone, a symbol of the pineal gland that
was also believed to be a direct telepathic conduit to the god Apollo.
There were ten famous sibyls throughout the ancient world, including
Persia, Libya, Delphi, Samos, Cimmeria, Erythraea, Tibur, Marpessus,
and Phrygia—but the most highly revered was the Sibyl of Cumae, who
lived in a cave near Naples.[39] Cumae was the first Greek colony founded
in Italy, in a volcanic region near Mount Vesuvius.[40] In 1932, the Sibyl of
Cumae's cave was discovered, dispelling rumors that she was only a
myth—and it had a 60-foot-high ceiling and a 375-foot-long passage
leading into it.[41] The Sibyl wrote her prophecies on oak leaves, which she
then left outside the cave, at any one of a hundred different entrances. If
no one came to pick them up when they arrived, they simply blew away
in the wind.

A 2001 *National Geographic* article suggested that the oracles' mystical abilities may have been the result of hallucinogenic gases such as
ethylene that naturally appear in the caves. Spring water near the site of
the Temple at Delphi tested positive for ethylene, which has a sweet smell
and creates a narcotic effect.[42] Apparently the Cumaean Sibyl would sit
on top of a tripod that was built directly over a grotto within the cave
that volcanic gases would rise through.[43] She also swallowed a few drops
of bay laurel juice before entering into the trance state where she received
the prophecies.[44] Virgil gave an intense description of the Sibyl of Cumae

at work in the *Aeneid*. Her behavior definitely suggests a powerful hypnotic influence had taken hold of her.

> She changes her features and the color of her countenance;
> her hair springs up erect, her bosom heaves and pants, her
> wild heart beats violently, the foam gathers on her lips, and
> her voice is terrible. . . . She paces to and fro in her cave and
> gesticulates as if she would expel the gods from her breast."[45]

During the time of the fiftieth annual Olympic Games and the
founding of the city of Rome, the Sibyl of Cumae approached King
Tarquin with nine books of her prophecies, claiming they contained the
entire future history of Rome.[46] Tarquin ruled from 534 to 510 B.C. This
wizened old woman asked the king for nine bags of gold as payment, and
he refused her exorbitant price. Right in front of King Tarquin she
burned the first three of the nine books, which at the time he didn't
think was a big deal. However, her fame and reputation as a prophetess
quickly grew, and when she later returned, she offered Tarquin the
remaining six books for the same price. Again he refused—and again she
burned the next three books right in front of him, making her seem all
the more crazy. Nonetheless, by the time she returned with the final
three books, she had become truly legendary for her accuracy. The king's
advisors urged him to accept her offer even though she still asked him
for nine bags of gold—and he finally accepted.

Regardless of what any skeptics may think in modern times about the
art of prophecy, the Sibylline Leaves were soon considered to be the
greatest treasure in all of Rome—precious beyond any and all other
government assets. They were renowned for their stunning accuracy,
which apparently included a prediction of the invasion of Hannibal and
his eventual defeat seven hundred years before it happened, as well as a
prediction of Constantine by name, eight hundred years before he was
born.[47] They were consulted in times of great national emergency, such
as earthquakes, floods, hurricanes, diseases and hardship.[48] Michelangelo
even included a depiction of the Sibyl of Cumae in his famous painting
of the ceiling of the Sistine Chapel.[49]

As the Sibyl of Cumae originally described to Tarquin, these books apparently did contain the future history of Rome—but the problem was that the prophecies were worded in cryptic language that was not always clear. In many cases, when Roman emperors attempted to use the mystery texts to avoid a major catastrophe, they ended up actually fulfilling the prophecy they had hoped to prevent. For this reason the books were considered to be potentially dangerous; by trying to use them to stop a disaster from happening, you might actually create the disaster. They were thus kept under high security in vaults within subterranean chambers in the Temple of Jupiter on the Capitoline Hill in Rome—accessible only to the high priests. The chambers and the temple were completed as of 500 B.C., specifically to store this treasure—which was only to be consulted in the most severe emergencies.

The Roman Senate considered the texts so valuable that ultimately an entire College of Priests was tasked to either track down or reenvision the first six lost volumes. They never succeeded in recovering the original words of the Sibyl. When Marcus Atilius authorized someone to copy the original three books, going against the official secrecy, he was punished by death—sewn into a sack and thrown into the Tiber River.[50] Virgil was finally allowed to copy some of the texts into his Eclogues as of A.D. 82,[51] and the temple of Jupiter then burned in A.D. 83, destroying most, if not all of the originals. General Flavius Stilicho burned the remaining copies in A.D. 405, believing them to be pagan and evil. Five years later, when Rome was invaded by the Visigoths, some felt this was Rome's punishment for having destroyed the prophetic texts.

Virgil's Fourth Eclogue is thus believed to be one of the last remaining transcripts of the original Sibylline texts. The fact that "Novus Ordo Seclorum" was directly adopted from these mystery texts, and was combined with the Great Pyramid in the design of the Great Seal of the United States as of 1782, makes the story of the founding fathers much more interesting. Peter Tompkins wrote about this in *Secrets of the Great Pyramid*.

> According to Manly P. Hall, an expert on Masonic lore,
> not only were many of the founders of the U.S. government
> Masons, but they received aid from a secret and august body

existing in Europe, which helped them to establish the United States for "a peculiar and particular purpose known only to the initiated few." The Great Seal, says Hall, was the signature of this exalted body, and the unfinished pyramid on its reverse side "is a trestleboard setting forth symbolically the task to the accomplishment of which the U.S. Government was dedicated from the day of its inception." The eagle was apparently intended to represent a phoenix, or symbol of the immortality of the human soul. Great currency has been given to the pyramid and phoenix symbols by placing them upon a one-dollar bill.[52]

It is fascinating to consider that the United States was founded for a secret purpose from the very beginning—which appears to be directly related to the end of the Great Year and the prophecies of a coming Golden Age. Based on the evidence we surveyed in chapter 3, the Great Seal now appears to be only the most recent version of this ancient symbol—which was featured prominently on Greek and Roman coins. The "secret and august body existing in Europe" appears to have originated in Sumer, Babylon and Egypt, and has hidden techniques that help awaken the pineal gland.

Let's return to Lieutenant Totten's letter, which described the exact content of the Sibylline text that "Novus Ordo Seclorum" comes from. When I first read this in 1994 I was shocked—and even more surprised that hardly anyone seemed to know about it. The Sibyl of Cumae broke up history into a series of "ages," and in this passage she refers to the coming of the last age in her story—which is referred to as the "Cumaean song." Here's the exact translation of the Sibylline mystery text as Totten wrote in 1882—and don't forget these are the exact words quoted, in shorthand, on the back of the U.S. dollar.

> The last age of Cumaen song now comes. (Novus Ordo Seclorum altered from Magnus Soeclorum ordo), A mighty order of ages is born anew. Both the prophetic Virgin and Saturnian kingdoms now return. Now a new progeny is let

down from the lofty heavens. Favor, chaste Lucina, the boy
soon to be born in whom the iron age shall come to an end,
and the golden one shall arise again in the whole earth.[53]

Let's review some of the astonishing elements of this passage: "The
last age . . . now comes. A mighty order of ages is born anew. . . . Now a
new progeny is let down from the lofty heavens." The word *progeny*
means "offspring"—so this may be describing some sort of transformation of the human species as we now know it, at the end of a great age.
What exactly might this new progeny be like? The answer may come in
the next passage: "The boy soon to be born in whom the iron age shall
come to an end, and the golden one shall arise again in the whole earth."
This implies a prophecy where humanity as a whole is transformed—not
just a single messianic figure. There is also a suggestion that other groups
will assist this process when we read the line, "Both the prophetic Virgin
and Saturnian kingdoms now return."

When we go on to read the rest of Virgil's Fourth Eclogue, from
other available translations, even more detail is given. Bear in mind that
in ancient Greek and Roman traditions, "heroes" are demigods—born
from one human parent and one parent who was a "god"—and this
unique genetic heritage apparently gave them abilities we would now
consider to be superhuman.

Under thy guidance, whatso tracks remain of our old
wickedness, once done away, shall free the earth from never-
ceasing fear. He shall receive the life of gods, and see heroes
with gods commingling, and himself be seen of them, and
with his father's worth reign o'er a world at peace. . . . Assume
thy greatness, for the time draws nigh, dear child of gods,
great progeny of Jove! See how it totters—the world's orbed
might, earth, and wide ocean, and the vault profound—all,
see, enraptured of the coming time![54]

From this passage, we see that the gods are indeed predicted to
return—and that humans on earth will "receive the life of gods"

themselves. This is the Great Seal of the United States—printed right on the dollar bill. Clearly we are expected in these prophecies to be seen as gods ourselves once this process is complete. These Sibylline prophecies therefore represent a bold prophecy of a coming Golden Age, in which "the Golden One shall arise again in the whole earth"—meaning everyone who is here. The founding fathers obviously realized that there was a relationship between these prophecies in the Sibylline records, the symbolism of the Great Pyramid, and the awakened pineal gland. Again, when we inspect the exterior of the Great Pyramid, there are 25,826.4 Pyramid inches of distance across the diagonals—just like the number of years in the precession. The capstone sits right on top of those same diagonal lines. So, when we put all these pieces together, it is obvious that the founding fathers of America clearly believed the return of the capstone on the pyramid symbolized the dawning of a new era in human history at the end of the Great Year. This would usher in the often-prophesied Golden Age that the ancient myths also discussed, complete with a transformation of humanity into a godlike state and the return of the original founding fathers. With the association between the capstone and the baetyl, we can clearly see how much they believed this prophecy was associated with the awakening of the pineal gland.

The Illuminati

There is abundant evidence—far outside the scope of this book—that the "secret and august body existing in Europe" is still in power today. We've already explored how the pineal gland symbolism is woven through Freemasonry, the Rosicrucians and other groups—including the Vatican. More and more people are beginning to suspect that there are some very dark things going on in world politics right now, and that our elected leaders may not really be the ones running the show. I've already discussed how some people who investigate the Source Field may be threatened, bought out, hurt or even killed. The Internet is absolutely flooded with articles and books you can read about all of this, and many of them are quite dreadful and filled with doom and fear. The original, positive prophecies of a Golden Age seem to have become contorted, over many thousands of years, into the perverted concept of a New World Order—in which an elite, multinational power group wishes to greatly reduce the earth's population and bring the people under the control of a worldwide dictatorship. In my opinion, perhaps the single most comprehensive source of written data on this subject is *New World Order: The Ancient Plan of Secret Societies* by William T. Still.[55] Many of the most provocative historical references on the Internet about the New World Order originated in Still's book from 1990. Still provides evidence that Sir Frances Bacon worked with this group to create plans for a "New Atlantis" that would usher in a universal democracy—a world free of war, crime and poverty. Bacon's vision apparently inspired the foundation of America and the principles of freedom in the U.S. Constitution. Bacon also believed human beings would regain mastery over forces of nature once this plan was fulfilled.

Let me be clear that I do not in any way support the politics, policies, treachery, lies and deceit of these world elites—which some people, including Still, now call the "Illuminati"—meaning the "illuminated ones." This illumination is apparently a metaphor of the awakened pineal gland—and these groups may believe their worldwide power and control are the result of arcane spiritual practices that make them feel superior to others, if not gods in their own right. Despite the horrors that are often attributed to these people, I also do not feel we should rush to condemn all those who have been involved with these groups—for if we do, we truly have not grown past Hitler's grotesque attitude toward the Jews in World War II. Hate begets hate. Every human being has a right to exist, and genocide is a crime against humanity—paving the way for the next group to become just as odious as those they opposed. According to several insiders I know personally, many innocent people are trapped in these groups—and would get out in a mass exodus if they could. However, the hate that has been whipped up on the Internet is so high these days that these people would genuinely fear for their lives if they actually were able to escape—and try to do sincere good for the world.

It clearly seems that the founding fathers of America were aware of these prophecies of a coming Golden Age, and of the transformation of humanity that was predicted to occur. The great world religions and the many secret traditions all appear to have originated from a common, worldwide source, which may have been humans who were well ahead of us in terms of biological and spiritual evolution—and were therefore seen as gods. Darkness, secrecy and the trappings of money and power may well have distorted the original intent of the message in various power groups—leading to a glaring difference between these secret, occult teachings and the positive, loving focus of many other religious and spiritual traditions that incorporated similar symbols and themes. I do feel that many people within these groups have been working for the good of humanity, but since they are forced to keep everything secret, the extraordinary malice and deceit of the few has now become a brush that tars and feathers the many—and this is a shame. Through good fortune in earlier years, and the publicity of my Web site and videos in more recent years, I have been able to meet several of the living inheritors of this tradition. I do believe that a change is occurring, where the members of these groups now realize they do not need to honor the negativity, narcissism and selfishness of some of their peers—and can step into a fuller understanding of what their ancient mission may really involve. I believe the secret lies in "coherence"—to restore this planet to the loving essence it originates from. This is no ancient cult teaching—this is the fruit of an active, ongoing scientific investigation. Negative, occult practices are a gross misunderstanding of the facts.

Although the founding fathers of America incorporated the pyramid into their design, we have no way of knowing how much they really knew about it. This philosophical tradition is obviously very old, and at one time was truly worldwide—before there was a terrible flood that may have nearly destroyed this civilization. The more time goes by since the original teachings were given, the more of a telephone game we have—and the message can become more and more confused and distorted. Obviously, these insider groups have not gone public with what they may know—and I feel the best thing we can do is fearlessly end the secrecy and set the truth free. Clearly, the Great Pyramid is a magnificent architectural marvel, and appears to be far beyond our current technological capabilities. Some people may have realized that and were inspired by it many hundreds, if not thousands, of years ago. Whether it was built by an advanced ancient civilization, extraterrestrial gods or both, the Great Pyramid may have been built to contain all the information we would need to understand the coming Golden Age—and perhaps even to help create that "New Earth" its individual architects may have forseen.

As we head into the next chapter, we will find out how Dr. Alexander Golod began building massive pyramids in Russia and the Ukraine, beginning in 1990. Many top Russian scientists did conduct research in them—and they were able to confirm many prior speculations about pyramid power and its mysterious effects. This has the potential to revolutionize our society in so many different ways that the implications are utterly mind-boggling. It's as if we've been given a massive inheritance that is worth more, in practical value, than all the money we have in the world—and it's been right there all along, just waiting until we were ready to rediscover it. The pyramid technology is indeed far more advanced than we ever realized, and has the power to completely transform our planet—as well as our own lives. The only thing holding us back was that our own science had not yet progressed to the point where we could identify and understand such a high technology.

CHAPTER EIGHT

"Pyramid Power"—Our Key to
the Golden Age?

The ancient prophecies do not speak of a worldwide extinction—they foretell a coming Golden Age. Even better, we have now found a significant number of technical details in the Great Pyramid's measurements—including the earth's exact size, the precise length of a year, the distance from the earth to the Sun, various planetary dimensions, star alignments, the precession of the equinoxes—suggesting its builders may have also been responsible for seeding the ancient world myths and prophetic religious teachings themselves. What if the pyramid structure itself was part of the Message we were supposed to inherit? Could it be a working technology—utilizing a science we have not yet rediscovered on a mainstream level?

The pyramid power movement of the 1970s has been laughed off by skeptics as a brief flash of gullible behavior on a mass scale. Much of the excitement originated in the story of a Frenchman named Antoine Bovis, who allegedly visited the Great Pyramid in the early twentieth century. According to the legends in many of the 1970s pyramid books, Bovis found a garbage can in the King's Chamber with corpses of cats and other small animals in it. Strangely, they did not smell bad, but appeared to have perfectly dried out and mummified—rather than having rotted away. If the Great Pyramid was indeed a tomb, then perhaps the Egyptians didn't need to work that hard to mummify the bodies of their beloved leaders—simply pop them in the Sarcophagus, give a little time for the magic to occur, pull them back out, and now the pyramid has done all the work.

History has not been kind to these beloved legends. In 1999, a former director of the Egyptian National Museum told a Danish skeptic there was never a garbage can in the King's Chamber that could have held the bodies of dead animals.[1] Furthermore, even though many authors went into great, loving detail about what Bovis felt, saw and smelled as he shuffled through this garbage can, the truth is that he never even left France, and the legend of his visit to the Great Pyramid was created by other authors who misinterpreted his work.[2] What did actually happen is that Bovis built a thirty-inch-tall wooden model of the Great Pyramid at his home in France, and claimed to have mummified a dead cat by leaving it in the King's Chamber position. According to this same Danish skeptic, Jens Laigaard, it may not all be a hoax.

> Thousands of people have tried leaving various foodstuffs inside a pyramid, and they've advanced numerous assertions that pyramid power can preserve fish, meat, eggs, vegetables, fruit and milk. Cut flowers, treated by the energy, will by all accounts keep their color and fragrance. Moreover, coffee, wine, liquor and tobacco are said to give off a more appetizing aroma after a turn in a pyramid.[3]

The skeptic's Web site that reprinted this Danish author's work revealed their true feelings in their endnotes, claiming Bovis "formed his pyramid ideas through armchair reasoning and occult experiments."[4]

Despite these skeptical dismissals, further research reveals that Karel Drbal, a radio engineer in Prague, successfully repeated Bovis's "armchair, occult experiments" in the 1950s with several different dead animals—preserving them quite nicely. Drbal concluded that "there is a relation between the shape of the space inside the pyramid and the physical, chemical and biological processes going on inside that space"[5]— though he wasn't sure why this was happening. Drbal was also the first to allegedly discover, in 1959, that dull razor blades would be sharpened if he placed them in a pyramid-shaped structure built out of cardboard.

Many East European countries had difficulty finding good razor blades during this time, so there was genuine interest in seeing if the pyramid trick really worked. The patent office in Prague refused to honor Drbal's request to protect his discovery unless their chief scientist could get the same results—and sure enough, he succeeded. Drbal was thus awarded Czechoslovakian patent number 91304 for the Cheops Pyramid Razor Blade Sharpener. In fact, this product was still being manufactured out of Styrofoam when Lyall Watson wrote about it in his excellent 1973 book *Supernature*.[6]

That's not all. In 2001, Russian scientist Dr. Volodymyr Krasnoholovets repeated Drbal's legendary razor-blade experiment and proved—with scanning-electron microscope photography—that the pyramid shape was able to change the molecular structure along the cutting edge of a razor blade.[7] Unlike what Drbal seemed to have discovered, a north-south alignment did not appear to make a fresh razor blade any sharper. However, an east-west position had a clear, measurable dulling effect on the blade—transforming its straight, flat surfaces into lumpy, bumpy, wavelike curves on a microscopic level.[8] This is obviously not supposed to happen in conventional science.

Lyall Watson, the author of *Supernature*, also repeated Bovis's original experiment with eggs, rump steak and dead mice, and found that "the ones in the pyramid preserved quite well, while those in the [shoe]box soon began to smell and had to be thrown out. I am forced to conclude that a cardboard replica of the Cheops pyramid is not just a random arrangement of pieces of paper, but does have special properties."[9] Without citing specific references, on the next page Watson shared additional, intriguing leads.

> A French firm once patented a special container for making yogurt, because that particular shape enhanced the action of the microorganism involved in the process. The brewers of a Czechoslovakian beer tried to change from round to angular barrels, but found that this resulted in a deterioration in the quality of their beer—despite the fact that the method of processing remained unchanged. A German researcher has

shown that mice with identical wounds heal more quickly if
they are kept in spherical cages. Architects in Canada report
a sudden improvement in schizophrenic patients living in
trapezoidal hospital wards.[10]

How could such spectacular-sounding discoveries possibly be true?

By this point, I can understand the skeptics' reaction. Very little of
this research has been done in the United States, and it also seems to
violate many of our cherished laws of physics. Hardly anyone in the
Western world is aware of the Russian investigations into the Source
Field that we will discuss later on—in which these strange anomalies
have elegant, new explanations. In this chapter, I ask you to be patient
with me as I explain to you all the different things pyramids can do—
because until you see the full extent of what we now know, any preliminary explanations will be incomplete and difficult to understand. Our
ancient ancestors were confident enough in the value of this technology
that they erected the most perfect structure in recorded human history
as a pyramid shape—not a big square box. Many other magnificent
pyramids appear throughout Egypt and South America—and new
research suggests there may also be pyramids in Bosnia,[11] Italy, Greece,
Slovenia, Russia and China,[12] among others, though most of them
(except for the ones in China) are covered with dirt, trees and other
vegetation—making them harder to spot. Some of them may also be
natural mountains that were sculpted into a pyramid shape. The Bosnian
Pyramid of the Sun would be over twice the size of the Great Pyramid,

and the geometric symmetry of this
unusual, mountainous area is very
compelling.

Why keep manipulating these
massive, multiton stone blocks again
and again, shape entire mountains

Aerial view of the Bosnian Pyramid of the
Sun—which is not yet acknowledged by
traditional archeologists as an intelligently
designed structure.

like pyramids, and/or build giant pyramid-shaped mounds of dirt, if there's no good reason for doing so? Why would so many different cultures independently get the same idea to build structures using techniques that may very well surpass our own level of technology? Once you start exploring the mysteries of what pyramids can actually do, this makes much more sense.

Pyramid Power Reboot

Regardless of the facts, the entire concept of pyramid power had collapsed into little more than an urban myth until 2001, when Dr. John DeSalvo's Giza Pyramid Research Association Web site first published the results of breathtaking new Russian pyramid studies for the Western world. The story begins in 1990, when Moscow scientist and defense engineer Dr. Alexander Golod began building large pyramids within Russia and the Ukraine. Seventeen pyramids had been constructed by 2001, in eight different sites within Russia and the Ukraine,[13] and by summer of 2010, more than fifty pyramids have been built worldwide, with the majority still in Russia and the Ukraine.[14]

Dr. Golod built each of his pyramids from an internal framework of PVC pipes covered with fiberglass sheets, forming smooth faces. They were all built to fit the Golden Section—the so-called phi ratio of 1 to 1.618— that appears so often in the growth patterns of living organisms, such as the spirals of seashells. This proportion makes Golod's structures steeper than the Great Pyramid, with a slope angle of about seventy degrees. The top stretches up to a distance about twice as high as the Great Pyramid goes, relative to the perimeter of its base—making Golod's pyramids look more like obelisks, church steeples or the baetyls on Greek and Roman coins.

Golod's largest pyramid soars at 144 feet (44 meters) in height, weighs more than 55 tons, took five years to complete, and cost him more than a million dollars to build.[15] It was finished in 1999, and used "nonconductive materials without a single metal element."[16] Golod found that any metal in the pyramid structure caused the seemingly magic effects to significantly decrease, if not disappear entirely—as if it had an absorbing effect upon whatever mysterious energy fields might be at work. This is one of the key design elements that could make a skeptic's attempts to replicate pyramid power fail. In the U.S. capital, the Washington Monument was built into an obelisk—perhaps another attempt to utilize such hidden technology by the United States government—but it has a great deal of metal in it, and therefore cannot be anywhere near as effective as Golod's pyramids.

Dr. John DeSalvo's Giza Pyramid Research Association Web site summarized Dr. Golod's results—along with those of his many professional colleagues.

> Many different experiments were done using these pyramids that include studies in medicine, ecology, agriculture, physics, and other areas. What is significant about this work is that it has been carried out by top scientists in Russia and Ukraine, and scientifically documents the changes that occur in these pyramids.[17]

As you can see, this was not occult or armchair science at all—it was being taken very seriously at the highest levels, and serious amounts of time and money were invested in these experiments. I was amazed when I read Dr. Volodymyr Krasnoholovets's summary of this research back in 2001.[18] Even though the English translation made it difficult to follow, I certainly understood the implications of what they had found—and this was a vast, multidisciplinary effort from many top minds of the former Soviet military-industrial complex. After the fall of the Iron Curtain, they still had their research labs and budgets, but didn't have to spend their time fighting wars. Dr. Golod's pyramids provided them with wonderful opportunities for scientific exploration. The only tragic part of the story was that no mainstream academic journal would publish their results, despite the meticulous care they took in using the strictest scientific protocols. The main reason for this seems to be that entrenched power groups would be heavily threatened by all the technological breakthroughs these discoveries would provide.

The Pyramid of Life Web site explains how much attention these pyramids have generated—on an international level.

> Hundreds of thousands of people including famous actors, singers, sculptors, majors and presidents have already been to the biggest Russian pyramid. This pyramid was built and is researched by scientists under Alexander Golod's supervision. Monks from Japan, Korea and Tibet got interested in the Russian pyramid; they consider it to be the ideal place, meaning the space inside and around it. Their ideas are confirmed by scientific researches made in institutes of the Russian Academy of Sciences. All the researches showed a positive influence on ecology and human health while visiting the pyramid, or using products, crystals, solutions and objects prepared there.[19]

Dr. Golod's research was taken seriously enough that crystals from his pyramids were flown on the Russian space station Mir for more than a year, and the experiment was later repeated on the International Space Station. The Pyramid of Life Web site says these studies have now been covered on "CNN, BBC, ABC, AP, *Boston Globe*, *The New York Times* and other international mass media."[20]

As I read about this research back in 2001 and absorbed the greater implications, I realized that pyramids were indeed the most stunningly advanced technology ever built on earth. They have been standing there all along, waiting to be inherited—but it was only in our ignorance that we did not recognize such an advanced technology when we saw it. Thankfully, multiple teams of accredited, mainstream Russian scientists did the work for us. Their results suggest that pyramid technology, and its offshoots, could save the world—and substantially improve our physical, mental and spiritual health along the way. In addition, these results tear the roof off everything we thought we knew about our own bodies, and about science in general. The more you learn about it, the more wonderful the implications become.

Imagine if you could take a simple drug that helps people fight viruses, and suddenly make it 3,000 percent more powerful. That's exactly what happened in one study from the Ivanovskii R & D Institute of Virology, within the Russian Academy of Medical Science. Professor Klimenko and Dr. Nosik were studying a naturally occurring virus-fighting compound in human beings called venoglobulin. When this drug was diluted into a concentration of fifty micrograms per milliliter and stored in a pyramid for a short time, apparently just a few days, it became approximately three times more effective at fighting viruses. Strangely, the drug worked just as well as they diluted it more and more—even though normally these ultra-weak concentrations, such as 0.00005 micrograms per milliliter, would have no effect whatsoever in the fight against viruses.[21]

If that isn't groundbreaking enough, the healing powers discovered by Professor A. G. Antonov and his associates, from the Russian R & D Institute of Pediatrics, Obstetrics and Gynecology, are seemingly miraculous. In their hospital ward, they routinely had to treat premature babies with grave medical problems, who were only given days to live. Since their colleagues knew the pyramid had a remarkable strengthening effect on medication, and the drug itself didn't even seem to be necessary, they tried something even more outrageous. Rather than using any known medicine, they took a simple placebo sample of 40 percent glucose in distilled water, and stored it in the pyramid. By administering only one milliliter of this solution to twenty different premature babies who were almost certainly going to die, every single one of them enjoyed a complete recovery.[22] The babies given ordinary glucose solution were just as likely to die as before.

Could the pyramid be somehow activating a natural healing chemical in the glucose, they wondered? The only way to find out for sure was to switch to ordinary water, and try the same experiment again—but a single milliliter of "pyramid water" worked just as well.

What happens if you put a diseased organism directly inside the pyramid? This was what a Russian Academy of Medical Science group headed by Dr. N. B. Egorova wanted to find out. Two groups of normal white laboratory mice were given strain 415 of the virus *S. typhimurium* (typhoid fever) in equal amounts over the course of one day. The only difference was that one group of mice was kept in the pyramid, and the other group was not. Amazingly, 60 percent of the mice in the pyramid survived smaller doses of the virus, whereas only 7 percent survived in the control group. Even in much larger doses of contamination, which would normally kill almost every single mouse, 30 percent of the pyramid mice still survived—while only 3 percent of those unlucky enough to be in the control group actually made it.[23]

Dr. Egorova also fed pyramid water to mice that had been given nasty carcinogens that would almost certainly give them massive cancerous tumors. The control group was given the same carcinogens, but they were given only ordinary water that had never been inside a pyramid. The mice drinking the pyramid water had significantly fewer tumors develop than the mice drinking the ordinary water.[24]

No dangerous or ill effects have ever been observed from these healing treatments. Golod's team found that the taller the pyramid was, the more powerful the effects became—but even the tallest one was still just a little more than a quarter the height of the Great Pyramid. It does cost money to build these pyramids, yes—but compared to the outrageous, spiraling costs of health care, and the struggle to find effective remedies everyone can afford, it's certainly worth investigating more. If it only takes one milliliter of water to save a baby from dying, think about how much healing water even one pyramid could create.

Quantum Effects

Miracle health cures are still only one piece of the puzzle. Remember the effects on the molecular structure of razor blades? Other strange quantum effects were discovered as well. For example, chunks of granite and crystal were scattered along the entire floor of Golod's tallest pyramid for months at a time. As we briefly see in some of the videos now online, a faint but visible whitening would occur along the tops of these rocks, which otherwise should have stayed reddish brown. These whitish areas did not appear on all the rocks—they formed a visible ring that was perfectly aligned with the central axis of the pyramid. Between the end of 1997 and the beginning of 1999, this result was duplicated forty times in the same pyramid, with different rocks each time. Each ring covered between fifty and three hundred rocks, with a total weight from twenty to two hundred kilograms. Golod's team also gathered evidence suggesting that when these rings formed most clearly, there were also fewer epidemics in the surrounding area.[25]

Dr. Golod also conducted studies of the air above the pyramid with a Russian instrument known as a "military locator," which is similar to radar. Using this device, a column of "unknown energy" was detected around the pyramid—some five hundred meters wide and two thousand meters tall. Unfortunately, Golod did not explain what this energy was, since the entire technology they used to detect it is still classified. They later found that there was an even larger circle of energy around the pyramid that was an astonishing three hundred kilometers wide. Golod's team calculated that if electrical energy were used to create such a massive disturbance in the atmosphere, you would need every single power plant in Russia running at full blast to do it. Furthermore, an ozone hole that was directly over the pyramid closed up only two months after they built it.[26]

Golod also built a series of pyramids over an oil well, and then compared the results with others that were nearby. It was discovered that the oil under the pyramids became 30 percent thinner, thus causing production to increase by 30 percent because the oil was so much easier to pump. The surrounding wells that did not have pyramids over them showed no change. Golod also found that the oil was much cleaner. Unwanted materials like gums, pyrobitumen, and paraffin all decreased substantially. The Gubkin Moscow Academy of Oil and Gas confirmed these results were fact, not fiction.[27]

In addition, Golod's team kept agricultural seeds in the pyramid for one to five days before they were planted. This was done with more than twenty different seed varieties, planted across tens of thousands of hectares. In every single case, the pyramid seeds experienced a 20 to 100 percent increase in crop production. These plants did not get sick, and were not affected by droughts. The same effects could be achieved by placing rocks that were stored inside the pyramid around the edges of the crops.[28]

Golod and his associates found that anything that was harmful to life would transform, for the better, if it was kept inside the pyramid. Poisons and other toxins would miraculously become far less destructive after even a short stay in the Pyramid of Life. Radioactive materials decayed faster than they were expected to. Dangerous pathogenic viruses and bacteria became much less harmful to living organisms after a stint in the pyramid. Even psychotropic drugs like LSD had less of an effect on people who were inside or within close range of the pyramid.[29] If we remember that some of our thoughts seem to occur directly within the Source Field, this antipsychotic effect starts to make more sense.

Ordinary placebo solutions like glucose in water now became effective remedies that could successfully treat alcoholism and drug addiction. All you have to do is keep them in the pyramid for a few days first. The cure could be administered either by an intravenous needle or through simply drinking the liquid.[30]

Ancient Technology

Now let's consider even more discoveries from some of the other, smaller pyramids Dr. Golod built in Russia and the Ukraine. In this case Dr. Yuri Bogdanov, from the Scientific and Technological Institute of Transcription, Translation and Replication, coordinated these studies.

In the Ramenskoe settlement of Moscow, a twelve-meter pyramid was able to make wheat grow 400 percent better than it had before. Radioactive carbon had a measurable reduction in its half-life. Salts displayed curious changes in their basic crystallization patterns. Concrete would set more strongly. Diamonds that were synthesized within the pyramid became harder and purer than normal. Other crystals experienced measurable changes, such as becoming clearer. I know this may all seem hard to believe right now, but as we go on, everything we are discussing will make much more sense. Bogdanov and his associates found that rabbits and white rats became 200 percent stronger in their endurance, and their white-blood-cell counts went up.[31] This discovery has obvious implications for professional sports. Such performance enhancements do not cause any of the damaging effects we see from the illegal use of steroids—in fact, those athletes would get healthier from the treatments. If the reality of this pyramid power were to spread, with national prestige and millions of dollars of endorsements at stake, what country wouldn't want their Olympic athletes enjoying the benefits of these effects—not to mention all the other professional sports teams fiercely competing around the world?

In the Arkhangelsk region of Russia, they had a serious problem with the water—and looked to Dr. Golod's pyramids as a potential solution. Strontium and heavy metals were contaminating their supply. The municipal administration ordered a series of pyramids to be built over the area, and within a short time they were pumping out clean water. It appears that this water has remained pure ever since. The same thing happened in the town of Krasnogorskoe near Moscow, where a single pyramid was able to clear up all the salt that had been polluting their water.[32]

The full extent of the power of this ancient technology didn't become clear until I read about what some of the other teams within the Russian National Academy of Sciences had discovered—where we see how the pyramids actually give us clear protection against catastrophic Earth Changes. Given the incredible damage that can be caused by hurricanes, tsunamis, earthquakes, volcanoes and the like, there is absolutely no reason why we shouldn't be exploring these possibilities on a worldwide, massive scale. And if a skeptic comes along and tries to tell you we shouldn't even try to use this technology, because it's "fringe pseudoscience," my obvious response would be, "How can we afford not to try it?" Do we dare to be so arrogant and overconfident in conventional science that we completely ignore the power of a cheap, easy-to-build technology that could save the earth?

Here's one powerful example of what we can do with pyramid technology. The Russian scientists compared how many earthquakes had occurred in their local areas before the pyramids were built with what they saw afterward in the same region. Amazingly, instead of getting one large and powerful quake, they found several hundred tiny earthquakes happening instead—which caused no damage whatsoever.[33] The pyramids were apparently bleeding off the charge of friction and geotectonic stress that would normally cause huge, catastrophic earthquakes to occur under the surface—obviously by a process that remains unknown to mainstream science.

A team from the All-Russian Electrotechnical Institute in Moscow found that if they took seven one-hundred-gram chunks of granite that had been stored in the pyramid and arranged them into a one meter circle, that area was 5,000 percent less likely to be struck by lightning. They were able to confirm this by putting the granite on a flat, metallic plane, with an electrode that would discharge one thousand, four hundred kilovolts of power overhead. Normally, when they turned on the juice for a short time, there was a good chance that the electrical current would "arc out" and form a lightning bolt—striking the metallic plate and creating a nasty burn mark that melted right through. Over the course of one hundred different discharges, the circle of pyramid granite proved to have a remarkable effect on protecting the inside area from lightning strikes—there were five times fewer eruptions, which again is 5,000 percent.[34]

Remember the five-hundred-meter-wide column of energy that formed around the pyramid, as well as the much larger three-hundred-kilometer circle—which would have taken all the energy from Russia's power plants to form? Apparently this enormous column doesn't just sit there doing nothing—it actively deflects storms and severe weather from the area around the pyramid.[35] Incredibly, incoming storms go around this whole area, not through it. Imagine what this technology could do for areas that were prone to being destroyed by hurricanes. The cost of building pyramids could be much, much less than the expense of rebuilding from inevitable hurricane damage.

Yet another series of observations further added mystery and intrigue to the puzzle. The three-hundred-kilometer column of energy just mentioned had appeared around a twenty-two-meter pyramid that was built on Seliger Lake. Several months later, the ozone hole that had been sitting over that area substantially improved. As time went on, new streams of water appeared in the surrounding countryside. A stork felt comfortable enough to set up a nest. And most amazingly, the fields became covered with flowers that shouldn't even exist—as they were supposedly extinct.[36] In short, the land was renewed, healed and transformed—suggesting that the life-giving energies harnessed by the pyramid had a significant effect upon everything around them.

The fact that all this data has been overlooked, and never even mentioned as a possibility after all these years, seems to be little more than criminal when you consider how many lives could have been saved in the process. And it also makes you wonder if other cultures in the past have built pyramids for very practical reasons—perhaps because they were in a race against time with climate change and possible catastrophes that could have wiped out their own civilization. That could explain why they had such a strong incentive to build massive pyramids.

New pyramids, or pyramid-shaped mountains, are being discovered that are not part of conventional archeology. One pair of alleged pyramids, or distinctly pyramid-shaped mountains in an otherwise flat plain, can be found in Nakhodka, one of the largest ports in the far east of Russia. Two large pyramid-shaped mountains there were named Brat, or "Brother," and Seska, or "Sister."

In the beginning of the twentieth century, the famous Russian traveler, historian and anthropologist Arseniev said these hills were holy places in ancient times—and many travelers from China and Korea went and visited them to pray there. The original Korean settlers said they were not natural formations—they had been built, a long, long time ago, and they did not know who was responsible. According to researcher Maxim Yakovenko, "Then and now, people say they feel happy and healthy on these hills, and I agree with them. The sides of those hills are oriented toward north, west, south and east, like the pyramids in Egypt." Tragically, in the 1960s the peak of Brat was blown off to harvest stones for building projects, reducing its height by 78.5 meters. Here's the surprising part: "After the destruction of Brat's peak (it's located 5 or 6 km. from the city), the climate in Nakhodka changed for some weeks. People told me that there had been very hard wind for some days after the detonations, and that it was raining."[37] Apparently the weather had been very calm prior to this point. This change is totally consistent with what Golod and his associates discovered about the effect of pyramids on our weather patterns. Even if Brat and Seska are only natural formations, it's still quite compelling that the weather changed so noticeably once Brat's structure was damaged.

The last study I read about from the Russian National Academy of Sciences, as we are about to see, really blew me away—as it shows how interconnected our consciousness may be with the world around us. If the pyramids can reduce earthquakes and severe weather, they probably can do the same for tornadoes, tsunamis and volcanic eruptions. Let's not forget that seven thousand people were able to reduce worldwide terrorism by 72 percent—just by meditating. If the Russian pyramids could create a similar effect on criminal behavior without any other human involvement, via meditation or otherwise, then we now have a powerful new connection worth exploring.

The Power of Consciousness

Could our consciousness somehow be responsible for strengthening, or even creating, earthquakes, hurricanes, severe weather and possibly volcanoes and tsunamis as well? Could this also mean that we have a cheap, easy way to help the earth through this critical transition period, so we don't have to simply hope and pray that someone or something else will rescue us? Would this also suggest that the earth is acting as a feedback mechanism for our own consciousness? Does our collective "dis-ease" appear as destructive Earth Changes? Are we getting a worldwide mirror for our own lack of love? Does the coming Golden Age represent a time where enough of us move into a positive, loving attitude that we can protect ourselves from further problems?

The Russian National Academy of Sciences confirmed that pyramid energy could reduce criminal behavior and increase feelings of love and peace. All they did was store granite and other crystalline structures in the pyramid and then set them up in and around certain jails in Russia, which held a total of about five thousand prisoners.[38] According to the Giza

Pyramid Research Association Web site's summary of these results, "In a few months most crimes almost disappeared, and behavior was much improved."[39] Nothing in the jails under study had changed except that this pyramid-charged granite had been built into their own surroundings.[40]

This last study with the prisoners is one of the most significant points—once you bring in the information we shared in the first five chapters about the Source Field. Somehow, feelings of love and peace, which are normally considered to be abstract emotional phenomena that are strictly psychological in nature, have a direct effect upon our surroundings. The pyramid energies create a measurable improvement in criminal behavior—just like the meditation effect of seven thousand people that we discussed earlier, which reduced worldwide terrorism by 72 percent. Armed with this knowledge, we can heal the earth. It's as if life itself has a yet-undiscovered energy field that supports its own existence, and it emanates directly from the earth—where it is then harnessed through these unique pyramid structures. Radiation can be quickly reduced, ozone holes closed up, earthquakes and severe weather reduced or even eliminated, water purified, crops improved, illness and disease dramatically lessened, buildings made far stronger and safer, and even crime, terrorism and mental illness greatly reduced—if not wiped out entirely. All these things we consider to be separate problems, well beyond the capacity of any one person to manage, can now be seen as part of an interconnected whole.

Once I sat back and absorbed the full implications of this new science, it became very clear why so many ancient cultures went to the enormous trouble of building gigantic pyramids, mounds, standing stones and other forms of megalithic architecture all over the world. It appears that natural, crystalline materials like limestone and granite are the most effective building supplies we could ever find—to build the best, strongest Source Field generators. The physics laws that make pyramid power a reality should also work on any planet that harbors intelligent life at any time, past, present or future—so it may well be that pyramids are very, very common throughout the Universe. It appears that we are only just now getting up to speed on the science behind them.

Energy Evolution

How does all this relate to 2012, and the prophecies of a Golden Age? Obviously, there are many mysteries in this new science that we have not tackled yet—and we have to go through them step by step to understand the blueprints for a Golden Age that we have seemingly been given. One of the most obvious areas we need to look into is our own biological makeup. These healing effects are so bizarre and fantastic that it seems we have overlooked some very, very basic aspects of the laws of physics—and of what it means to be a living organism. We are left with the inescapable conclusion that one of our most basic forms of nourishment must be energy of some kind. Furthermore, it would appear that we can receive this nourishment simply by being inside a pyramid, living near an object charged within a pyramid, or ingesting seemingly plain substances, such as pure water, that have been stored inside a pyramid.

As my research progressed, I found fantastic evidence to support this energetic connection with biological life. Best of all, this hidden force appeared to be the very source and creator of life itself—and could also spontaneously rewrite DNA to transform a given species into something entirely new and different. Think about the extinct plants that suddenly reappeared in the fields surrounding the pyramid near Seliger Lake. Where did they come from? Where did their genetic material come from? Could existing plants have been somehow rewritten, on the DNA level, to revert back to an older, more archaic species? And what about evolution? Is it possible that the DNA code is somehow written into the basic energy of the galaxy itself, so that we are actively being transformed into a whole new level of human evolution?

This could very well be the fulfillment of many ancient prophecies predicting the arrival of a Golden Age some time after 2012—a massive, energetically driven evolution of the human species as we now know it. I know it's obviously not something you're going to hear about in conventional science. You've probably been conditioned all your life to think such concepts are ridiculous. Before you laugh it off, I want you to join me in my investigation of the hard, scientific proof that such an evolution is indeed happening . . . and has actually been going on for quite some time.

CHAPTER NINE

The Source of the Source Field

A ncient human civilization may have been far more advanced than we normally believe. Our ancestors made an incredibly strong effort to get us to study the 25,920-year cycle known as the precession of the equinoxes, which was historically broken down into twelve 2,160-year Ages of the Zodiac. The Great Pyramid of Giza also appears to have been built to alert us to this 25,920-year cycle, when we measure the exact length of the diagonals in Pyramid inches. The craftsmanship of the Great Pyramid is well beyond our current technological capabilities, particularly when we consider the mirror-polished white limestone casing stones that once adorned the outside. And we now know the American founding fathers combined the symbolism of the return of the capstone with mysterious passages from the Sibylline prophecies that foretold a coming Golden Age. These prophecies strongly indicated that we would again comingle with the gods as the Great Year comes to an end, and in fact gain such supernatural abilities on our own—so that "the Golden One shall arise again in the whole earth."

If we want to take the Russian discoveries seriously, we would naturally assume that equally stunning effects on matter, energy, biology and consciousness should be achievable without any pyramids being involved. We've already explored the Source Field as a living, thinking form of consciousness—suggesting that we have to significantly broaden our ideas of what life really is. We share thoughts with all living things, and may well continue to experience awareness while our bodies are clinically brain dead. In this chapter we're going to begin exploring the biological aspects of the Source Field in much greater detail. In Part Two we'll move into the deeper mysteries of space and time that underlie the pyramid effects—and their influence on physical matter.

A wealth of little-known scientific data reveals the unique biological properties of the Source Field. A good place to start is with German scientist Hans Driesch in 1891. Driesch was examining the sea urchin, which is a unique organism in the sense that it has vegetative cells that look and behave exactly like plants do, as well as animal cells. In the earliest stages of development, the sea urchin embryo is nothing more than a hollow sphere. The vegetative cells are on the bottom half of the embryo, more or less, and the animal cells are on top. Once the embryo develops a little more, the vegetative cells roll inside and form a pocket, which becomes the gut—and the animal cells remain on the outside. In 1891, Driesch discovered that if he separated the very first two cells of a sea urchin embryo, each one produced a whole new embryo—rather than just growing into a deformed half-creature. At the time, this was considered quite a shocking and unexpected discovery. Furthermore, Driesch found he could cut the early, sphere-shaped embryo into as many as eight different pieces, and each of them would grow into a fully new embryo—even if the piece he cut out was from 100-percent vegetative cells, with no apparent animal characteristics whatsoever.[1]

Most people would think nothing of these observations in today's world. We automatically assume that each DNA molecule has all the building codes for an organism, so you can grow a whole new life-form out of a single cell. Bear in mind that this is one explanation, but it is not the only one . . . and it may not even be the right one. Driesch believed there was an overall guiding force that determined the growth of any one cell within an embryo.[2] The force contains information that gives each cell instructions on what it should do—depending on where that cell is located. The force is what tells a cell whether it should become a vegetable cell or an animal cell—in the case of the sea urchin.

Driesch published his key paper in 1912, and this inspired Alexander Gurwitsch, a Russian scientist, to continue this research. Gurwitsch

believed these energy fields were not only found within the embryo—
they governed and regulated the growth of fully adult life-forms as well.
Gurwitsch also believed that all organisms were being kept alive by this
"mitogenetic energy field," and that they both absorbed and radiated
these fields throughout their life cycle. Gurwitsch explored the radiant
aspect of these fields by using a growing onion. He assumed the majority
of life energy would shoot out from the top of a newly sprouting onion,
since that's where all the new leaves are growing. Gurwitsch thus aimed
the top of a sprouting onion at the side of another onion, without ever
actually letting them touch. Sure enough, those cells on the second
onion grew much faster than the rest—forming a noticeable bump where
the first onion was pointing. Interestingly, Gurwitsch also found that the
effect could be completely blocked by putting a piece of glass in the way,
which shields infrared and ultraviolet light. However, a piece of quartz
did not block the effect—and quartz allows infrared and ultraviolet to
pass through. So, we don't need pyramid power to get a sudden growth
spurt after all—just the life force of the onion itself is enough to have an
effect on other onion cells.

Gurwitsch published his key paper in 1926.[3] By this time, he had
conducted several other experiments that proved a very weak but measurable ultraviolet radiation was emanating from the tip of the onion,
creating his "mitogenetic effect."[4] Again, it appears that this ultraviolet
light is a signature of the Source Field, but is not the actual Source Field
itself—much like the ripple in the surface of a lake, from a stone you just
dropped in, is not the stone itself. Many Russian scientists replicated
Gurwitsch's classic experiment with positive results over the years,
though this intriguing research got washed away in the excited speculation that genes and DNA were responsible for all the codes that build
living organisms—and determine their growth.

Another early pioneer worth mentioning is neuro-anatomist Harold
S. Burr from Yale University. He discovered that even an unfertilized
salamander egg had an electrical energy field that was already shaped like
an adult salamander—showing a straight line of charge along the egg in
the direction it would eventually grow into an adult. In plant seedlings,
Burr found electrical fields that looked similar to the adult plant. Burr

found these electrical fields around many different life-forms. He noticed that the charge of these fields would change with growth, sleep patterns, the amount of light exposure, tissue regeneration, the presence of water, storms, the onset of cancer and even the cycles of the Moon.[5] Further-more, Dr. Robert Becker, an orthopedic surgeon, studied the human body's natural electrical fields and found that every person he studied had the strongest electrical charges on the Chinese acupuncture merid-ian points.[6] The ancient sciences apparently have much more truth to them than many of us have been led to believe.

The DNA Phantom Effect

Now I want to jump ahead in time to 1984, because this was the year our "addiction" to DNA was heavily challenged, if not defeated, by Dr. Peter Gariaev. Gariaev's discovery also gave us a compelling hint that Gur-witsch's mitogenetic radiation—the Source Field—may well be operat-ing through our DNA. Furthermore, Gariaev's discovery suggests that the complete genetic codes for an organism might not actually be found in the DNA molecule after all—at least not as their final location.

When Gariaev put a sample of DNA in a tiny quartz container, zapped it with a mild laser, and then observed it with sensitive equipment that could detect even single photons of light, he found that the DNA acted like a light sponge. Somehow, the DNA molecule absorbed all the photons of light in the area, and actually stored them in a corkscrew-shaped spiral.[7] This is very, very strange. The DNA apparently created a vortex of some sort that attracted the light, not unlike the idea of a black hole—but on a much, much smaller scale.

Few scientists would be willing to suggest that light could appear inside the pineal gland either—but Gariaev proved that the DNA mol-ecule is pulling in photons from somewhere, by some unknown process. Due to the difficulty of studying a living human brain, no comparable experiments like this have been done within the pineal gland—at least none that are openly available to the public. The only technology we have that could hold light in a spiral like Gariaev found in the DNA molecule

is a fiber-optic cable—but even then, fiber-optic cables don't hungrily draw in all the light from their surroundings.

We're not used to thinking of light as something that can actually be stored—it normally just zips along through space at a very nice speed. If

Dr. Peter Gariaev's DNA Phantom Effect proved that the DNA molecule captures and stores light. A mysterious force holds the light in the same place for up to 30 days after the DNA molecule itself has been removed from the area.

we could even capture it in one spot, we'd probably expect that it would just wear out—and lose its energy. Even in the case of photosynthesis, the only way a plant appears to be able to store light is by immediately converting its energy into green-colored chlorophyll. Now we're seeing light itself being used like a food supply that DNA can store away . . . not unlike a squirrel hiding acorns in a hollowed-out tree for winter. This triggers a bunch of new questions. What exactly is storing the light? How is it being stored? And why is it being stored? In order to answer those questions, we have to delve deeper into what Gariaev actually discovered—because this is just the beginning.

The real magic happened when Dr. Gariaev ended the experiment. He grabbed the quartz container with the DNA in it and moved it out of the way. Nothing more was supposed to happen. Nonetheless, to his utter amazement, even though everything was gone—the container, the DNA, you name it—the light continued spiraling along in the same space, as if the DNA were still there.

Whatever was holding that light in place, it did not need the DNA molecule at all. It was something else. Something invisible. Something powerful enough to store and control visible light within the shape of the DNA molecule itself. The only rational, scientific explanation is that there has to be an energy field that is paired up with the DNA molecule—as if DNA has an energetic "duplicate." This duplicate has the same shape as the physical molecule—but once we move the DNA, the duplicate still hangs around in the same spot the molecule was in before. It doesn't need the DNA molecule to be there in order for it to keep on doing its job—storing visible light. Some force, perhaps akin to gravity, is holding the photons in place.

The implications of this are mind-boggling. Obviously, in the case of a human body we have far more than one DNA molecule to consider—we have untold trillions of them, in a very highly structured arrangement. We have bone DNA, organ DNA, blood DNA, muscle DNA, tendon DNA, skin DNA, nervous-system DNA and brain DNA. So, just by a simple extension of Gariaev's experiment, it is very likely that our entire body must have an energetic duplicate. This fits in perfectly with what Driesch, Gurwitsch, Burr and Becker all theorized and observed—there is an information field that tells our cells what to do, and where to do it. Once we add Gariaev's discovery in, we find out that perhaps the most important thing the DNA molecule does is store light—both in our physical body and in our energetic duplicate body as well. Obviously, conventional science is significantly in need of an overhaul. There is a great deal of information about biological life that we simply do not know, or recognize, in the mainstream sense.

The DNA Phantom Effect is arguably one of the most significant scientific discoveries in modern history. It shows us that the DNA molecule has some bizarre relationship with quantum mechanics that our scientists have not yet discovered in the mainstream world. We now have proof that DNA is interfacing with an unseen, yet-undiscovered energy field that is not electromagnetic, but which obviously can control electromagnetic energy—in this case by storing photons, even when there is no physical molecule there to hold them in place.

And that's not all. When Gariaev blasted this Phantom with liquid nitrogen, which creates a sudden burst of great cold, the light spiral would disappear—but then it mysteriously returned after five to eight minutes.[8] This persistence of the DNA Phantom—our energetic duplicate—even in the face of seemingly certain destruction, is very strange. Even if you destroy the coherence in the area where the DNA Phantom had been, in this case by the sudden blast of cold, it will repair and restore that coherence once more. The surrounding light will again be organized into the unique spiraling pattern of the DNA that used to be there. Conventional science has nothing to offer us that can explain why this happens—but it does.

How long do you think this phantom could have lasted? Amazingly, the DNA Phantom remained visible for up to thirty days after it first appeared.[9] Gariaev could blast it with liquid nitrogen over and over again, during this entire time, but it just kept on coming back. As I'm sure you can see, this completely challenges everything in conventional biology—not to mention physics—but it works.

This information has been available for more than twenty-five years now, and the experiment was replicated in the United States by R. Pecora in 1990—but no one ever hears about it. Obviously, the DNA Phantom is not electromagnetic—there are all sorts of strange things about it that violate everything we know about electromagnetic energy. However, it does fit in very nicely with what we've been calling the Source Field. On a microbiological level, it appears that we have an energetic duplicate. Our DNA is somehow interfacing with an energy field that has remained largely unknown to Western scientists, and which leaves behind a phantom that can easily be measured. This means your duplicate is still doing its job capturing light for you, even when you're no longer there. If you're sitting in your chair right now, reading this book, and then get up and go somewhere else, your energetic duplicate is still spinning light into tiny little spirals, right where you were sitting—within each and every one of your untold trillions of DNA molecules—for at least thirty days after you leave your seat. Since the sizes involved are microscopic, you can't see any of this with your naked eye—but Gariaev was able to measure it in the laboratory. It's like a perfect hologram of your physical body—which is correct down to the tiniest cell.

Now think back to Dr. Ian Stevenson's studies we discussed in chapter 4. For more than forty years, Dr. Stevenson collected evidence for reincarnation from some three thousand children, and found that memories, personality quirks, talents and other attributes carried over from one apparent lifetime to another—including the ability to remember people's names and relationships—and there was a facial resemblance.[10] Dr. Jim Tucker went even further with this research, and used facial recognition software to confirm that these children had a forensic match with the people they remembered having been in their alleged past life.[11] Furthermore, let's not forget that lethal wounds from an allegedly prior lifetime often appeared as birthmarks in the "new" body. All of this can be explained if we assume that our energetic duplicate is not dying when our physical body ceases—it carries over from one alleged lifetime to another, and brings our memories along with it. Some of us are able to access these memories directly—particularly when we are children, before we are hypnotized into believing it is impossible by the compelling opinions of parents, teachers and other adults.

The Holographic Brain

If there is an energetic duplicate of your body in the Source Field, wouldn't that mean your entire brain has a holographic duplicate as well? Maybe so. This raises an even more controversial question. If all the DNA in your brain has an energetic duplicate, then could this holographic brain somehow be responsible for at least a part of how you are thinking and functioning? Is a part of your Mind working in a hidden, unseen parallel reality right now, as you read this book? Do you have a perfectly identical holographic brain that somehow interacts with your physical brain, using the DNA within every physical neuron almost like an antenna? These are intriguing questions. We've already given stunning new evidence to support the idea of an energetic mind in chapters 1, 2, 3, 4 and 5—but now it's time to look at some additional biological research.

In 1997, *The New York Times* reported that brain-damaged children actually improved their level of intelligence and physical coordination by having the entire hemisphere of their brain that was damaged—or should we call it the broken antenna—completely removed. If you lose half your brain, shouldn't you lose half of your memories, and half of your ability to function? Apparently not. This finding "astonishes even seasoned scientists," and according to Dr. Eileen P. G. Vining of Johns Hopkins University, who studied fifty-four different children who had the operation, "We are awed by the apparent retention of memory, and by the retention of the child's personality and sense of humor."[12] This kind of extreme operation is obviously not an easy thing to persuade any loving parents to do, but it works. Johns Hopkins published a newer version of the same study in 2003, now involving 111 children who had the operation between 1975 and 2001, and showed that 86 percent of them became either completely seizure free, or at least no longer needed to take medication. Dr. Eric Kossoff explained what a seemingly miraculous effect this procedure produced.

> It's clear now that the quality of life of children with chronic, severe seizures greatly improves following [the operation]. . . . In almost all cases, the children no longer depend on multiple medications, and post-operatively, most of the children are walking and running and living normal lives.[13]

In 1980, Roger Lewin published "Is Your Brain Really Necessary?" in the prestigious journal *Science*, discussing the work of Dr. John Lorber—arguably the world's top expert on a condition called hydrocephalus, or "water on the brain."[14] In these cases, cerebro-spinal fluid backs up into the skull and builds in pressure, with no way to drain out. In the most extreme cases, the skull can become almost entirely filled with fluid, leaving hardly any visible brain tissue at all. Many of these patients die or are severely disabled. Doctors now correct the problem with surgical shunts to drain the fluid, but in Lorber's time this was not being done.

Lorber studied a total of 253 hydrocephalus sufferers at the University of Sheffield in London. Of this group, nine of them only had 5 percent of their regular brain tissue left—which would appear to be an utter and complete tragedy. Nonetheless, four of these nine people had IQs that were greater than 100—and an additional two had IQs greater than 126. Six out of nine were fine—other than the fact that they were almost completely missing a brain as we now think of it.

Here's a direct quote from Lewin's paper about this astonishing phenomenon.

> "There's a young student at this university," says Lorber, "who has an IQ of 126, has gained a first-class honors degree in mathematics, and is socially completely normal. And yet the boy has virtually no brain." The student's physician at the university noticed that the youth had a slightly larger than normal head, and so referred him to Lorber, simply out of interest. "When we did a brain scan on him," Lorber recalls, "we saw that instead of the normal 4.5-centimeter thickness of brain tissue between the ventricles and the cortical surface, there was just a thin layer of mantle measuring a millimeter or so. His cranium is filled mainly with cerebrospinal fluid."[15]

Again, in case you didn't catch that, Lorber is saying the only brain tissue left was a one-millimeter-thick layer against the inside edge of the skull. According to Patrick Wall, a professor of anatomy at University College, London, this is nothing new.

> Scores of similar accounts litter the medical literature, and they go back a long way . . . but the important thing about Lorber is that he's done a long series of systematic scanning, rather than just dealing with anecdotes. He has gathered a remarkable set of data and he challenges, "How do we explain it?"[16]

After this controversial study emerged, there was naturally a tidal wave of criticism. Dr. Lorber acknowledged that it is difficult to interpret brain scans—and he published a much more thorough study in 1984. He found that in the case of the math student who had an IQ of 126, fully

44 percent of his entire brain volume had been lost—and the rest of his brain tissue was compressed down into a super-thin layer lining the inside of the skull.[17] Nonetheless, he was happily enjoying a significantly above-average IQ, and had no trouble thinking and remembering information. This shows just how far our concept of "thinking with the Source Field" can really go.

Luckily, no one has to suffer with this condition anymore, thanks to the surgical solution of installing shunts to drain the fluid. The same is not true for the animal population. Throughout Central Europe, many laboratory hamsters end up with hydrocephalus as a hereditary condition. In 2006, *Veterinary Pathology* journal published a study showing that even the hamsters with the most severe forms of hydrocephalus—again where their brains are almost completely nonexistent—still appear to be just fine. They do not show any strange behaviors or difficulties—and can act, think, remember, move their bodies and breed in all the normal ways.[18]

It is fascinating to explore the connection between Gariaev's DNA Phantom and the idea of a holographic brain that actually is doing some of the thinking for us. If Gariaev is right, and the DNA molecule really does capture and store light, then we should certainly assume that other scientists would have independently discovered the same thing.

DNA Stores, Transforms and Releases Coherent Light

One of my favorite parts of *The Field* by Lynne McTaggart is her discussion of the work of Fritz-Albert Popp, a theoretical biophysicist at the University of Marburg in Germany, who began making very similar discoveries starting in 1970.[19] Although Popp did not discover the DNA Phantom, his work ties in with Gariaev's findings very nicely—and also adds in additional breakthroughs. Popp started out by examining one of the most deadly carcinogens known to man, technically called benzo[a]-pyrene. When he zapped it with ultraviolet light, he found that it absorbed the light, but then sent it back out at a totally different frequency. A very similar chemical, benzo[e]pyrene, did not have this light-scrambling effect—and unlike its deadly cousin, it was totally harmless to living organisms.

Was this light-scrambling effect the missing key to understanding what causes cancer? After Popp studied thirty-seven other chemicals, some of which were carcinogens, he found that every single cancer-causing substance would rearrange ultraviolet light the same way. These deadly carcinogens consistently targeted the frequency of 380 nanometers. In fact, the only common link Popp could find between these various cancer-causing chemicals was that they all took in this 380-nanometer light and rearranged it to some other frequency. Obviously, this implies that 380-nanometer light is very important for our overall health and well-being—but if you never allow any sunlight to touch your skin without wearing sunscreen, you may not be getting very much of it, since sunscreen completely blocks ultraviolet light.

Popp then learned that many biological lab experiments have proven you can destroy 99 percent of a cell with ultraviolet light, but if you then give it a very weak pulse of the same wavelength, it almost completely recovers—in a single day. This is known as "photo repair," and no one really understands why it works. To Popp's amazement, the best photo-repair effects were already known to occur at 380 nanometers—even though none of these scientists knew anything about his discovery.[20]

Therefore, it appears that as the Source Field flows into our own measurable reality, its electromagnetic signature is the strongest at the 380-nanometer wavelength. The Source Field also has fluidlike properties—a very important point we will go into more detail about later on. This means you can create a rhythmic pulsation, or what most people would call a vibration, within the field itself and get much stronger effects. Think about how Roman soldiers had to change the speeds they were marching as they went over a bridge, in different groups. Otherwise, if they all marched at the same speed, the entire bridge would start shaking—and could even completely come apart. All those little vibrations kept on resonating, and pretty soon they would build up to much larger effects. The same thing applies to the Source Field—except that here it's a good thing.

So, in the photo-repair experiments, those weak pulses of 380-nanometer light apparently created a vibration in the Source Field that actually caused a much higher amount of healing, 380-nanometer energy to start flowing in. This, in turn, bathed the dead cells with a splash of rejuvenating, life-giving energy in a short period of time—and they enjoyed a remarkable healing effect.

Popp was hooked on the idea of finding out if the human body was indeed storing and giving off light. He challenged a student named Bernard Ruth to set up an experiment that could prove our bodies were giving off this light—in order for Ruth to finish out his Ph.D. dissertation. Ruth was a skeptic and thought the whole idea was ridiculous, so Popp challenged him to disprove the concept instead. Ruth then went to great lengths to design equipment that could count light—one photon at a time. His device is still considered one of the best light detectors out there. Ruth's equipment was ready for the first test in 1976, and they decided to start out with cucumber seeds. To their amazement, the seedlings were giving off photons—and these light pulses were significantly stronger than Popp had expected.[21] Ruth was skeptical, and felt it had to be due to the presence of chlorophyll—so they switched over to potatoes, which do not have chlorophyll or go through any photosynthesis. Nonetheless, the potatoes gave off even more light than the cucumber seeds. Furthermore, their light emissions were extremely coherent—meaning they were highly structured, just like a laser beam's.

Next, they tried hitting DNA with a chemical called ethidium bromide, which causes the molecule to unwind and die. Not surprisingly, the more Popp blasted DNA with this chemical, the more light burst out of it.[22] This led Popp to conclude that the ability to store and release light was a key aspect of how DNA works—just as Gariaev later discovered. Mainstream science still hasn't caught up with these breakthroughs yet, nor to how Gariaev proved that the energy field responsible for storing this light isn't electromagnetic—and doesn't even require DNA to be there for it to work.

As Popp's research went on, he found that all living things were continuously emitting photons—ranging from only a small number to many hundreds. Interestingly, rudimentary animals or plants give off significantly more light—some one hundred photons per square centimeter per second—than humans do, at only ten photons per second in the same-size area. This was high-frequency light, ranging between two hundred to eight hundred nanometers—well above the visible range. And again, it was coherent light—just like a laser beam.

Popp also discovered that if he shined light on living cells, they would first absorb it, and then release an intense burst of new light after a brief period of time. He called this "delayed luminescence." This is exactly what we would have expected to see after Gariaev's discovery that the DNA molecule stores light. Obviously, the DNA is doing something with the light—not just storing it indefinitely. This also fits in perfectly with Gurwitsch's observation of the energy emerging from the tip of an onion—including the fact that the effect could be blocked by shielding off ultraviolet light. In short, our DNA apparently stashes away light as if it were a direct source of energy and vitality. If the DNA gets too much light, it sends it back out—perhaps like an organism might excrete waste products it no longer needs. However, Popp believed that, unlike waste, these light emissions were serving a very useful purpose—they contained information. Specifically, these light pulses carried the codes to reestablish order and balance throughout the body.

Popp also found that we give off significantly more of these photons when we are going through stress, even though we are not taking in additional light. I consider this a very significant point. We know that many illnesses are enhanced or even caused by stress—and it could be that when we get stressed out or go through negative emotions, we're giving away some of our own vitality by shedding the light stored in our DNA, all throughout our cells. Why do our bodies end up doing this? It appears that these extra bursts of light contain the information our cells need to heal themselves—from all the damage we've been causing them through negative emotions.

Therefore, in order to get healthy again, we're going to have to charge our DNA back up—and get more light. This raises another interesting question. Obviously, the vast majority of our cells are not being exposed to outside light of any kind—other than the very top layer of our skin. So how exactly do we get more light? How does the light make its way through to the deepest, most internal parts of our bodies? Is all this light strictly coming from visible sources all around us? (Obviously, we don't die if we are kept in a totally dark room—but our DNA clearly seems to be using light all the time.) Indeed, could these photons be emanating directly out of the Source Field itself? And if the Source Field and its energy is fundamentally interconnected with consciousness, as the Russian pyramid research suggests, then could our minds and emotions be affecting how much light can get in—and where it gets in? Do we have to be open to the Source Field in order for its healing effects to move into our bodies? Could this explain the placebo effect, where simply believing we will be healed actually helps us get better? In short, is it possible that our attitude determines how well our DNA and our cells can absorb light?

DNA Measurably Responds to Human Consciousness

Dr. Glen Rein, a biochemist who graduated from the University of London, made stunning discoveries that reveal how DNA behaves in direct response to human consciousness. For starters, DNA unwinds when a cell is about to divide, or has been damaged (i.e., when it is dead), and it winds when it is working to repair and heal itself. The amount of winding or unwinding in DNA can be directly measured by how well it absorbs light at 260 nanometers. In these remarkable experiments, Dr. Rein started out by taking living DNA from a mix of human placentas, putting it in deionized water, and then storing the whole mixture inside a beaker. Then various people attempted to either wind or unwind the DNA—by nothing more than the power of their own thoughts, in heavy concentration. The control samples, where no one tried to do anything to them, changed by only 1.1 percent—but the treated samples changed by anywhere between 2 to 10 percent. This meant that our thoughts alone have, at the very least, a two-fold effect on the winding of human DNA.[23]

Even more interesting, the senders with the most coherent brain wave patterns had the strongest ability to change the structure of DNA. And on the flipside of the coin, "one individual who was particularly agitated (and had a very incoherent [brain wave pattern,]) produced an abnormal shift in the UV," or ultraviolet light, that the DNA was absorbing. The change occurred at a wavelength of 310 nanometers, which is close to Popp's magic value of 380 nanometers—that same frequency that can cause cancer when it is scrambled.[24] This angry person also caused the DNA to coil up tighter in its winding. Both of these are very unusual effects. According to Rein, this change in the 310-nanometer light could only mean that "an alteration in the physical/chemical structure of one or more of the bases in the DNA molecule has occurred."[25] That means our thoughts can actually create physical and chemical changes in the structure of the DNA molecule—as well as winding and unwinding it. This is the microbiological proof for the connection between angry thoughts and cancerous tissue growth that we've been waiting for—and the implications are just as profound for healing effects as well. Let's not forget how we can project significant bursts of photons into an electromagnetically shielded area when we are accurately remote-viewing that location, as we learned in chapter 4. Those photons may well have genetic information in them that can restructure others' DNA to restore health—such as the 380-nanometer light frequency.

In another case, when DNA was placed in front of people who were generating coherence in their brain wave patterns, but were not trying to change the DNA, there was no change in the winding or unwinding of the DNA sample. It was only when they wanted it to change that it actually did. This strongly suggests that the conscious intent of the people was causing these effects to occur. Dr. Lew Childre was able to wind or unwind DNA in the laboratory from a half a mile away. Valerie Sadyrin was able to wind DNA in Dr. Rein's California lab from his home in Moscow, thousands of miles away, during one thirty-minute period of time. According to Rein, the key quality of this energy that can generate coherence in the brain waves and directly affect DNA is love: "Although the techniques used by the different healers are quite varied, they all appear to require a heart focus."[26]

The implications of this are tremendous. The Source Field appears to be responsible for creating the DNA Phantom, and storing light in the

DNA molecule. It would appear that our thoughts change the DNA Phantom in Dr. Rein's experiments first, and only later do we see any changes in the physical DNA molecule. Best of all, we now know that the most important emotional quality of the Source Field is love. Dr. Rein proved that love has a direct, measurable effect on DNA—very likely through the same energetic process that creates the DNA Phantom.

Greater coherence, greater organization, greater structure and greater crystallization—all these effects show us that the energy fields, molecules and cells of our bodies are working in greater harmony and Unity. For the first time, this actually gives us a scientific definition of love. It is not strictly an abstract emotional and biological concept—like the chemicals fired off in the brain when we eat chocolate, or the genetic urge to reproduce. Love can now be seen as a basic principle of universal energy. The more coherence, the more structure, the more harmony we have, the more love there is. And as the Russian pyramid studies show, this also has a direct effect on the behavior of the earth—again suggesting we may all be living in a collective Lucid Dream, to some degree.

Now let's return to Dr. Fritz-Albert Popp, as some of his results are now being rediscovered by others. Popp found out that our bodies had a variety of different cycles—where the intensity of light would increase and decrease over time. This included biorhythms of 7, 14, 32, 80 and 270 days, which held true even after a year. He also found similarities by day and by night, and by the week and the month—suggesting our rhythms were somehow tapped into the movements of the earth as well. The basics of this phenomena were found again by Japanese scientists in a 2009 study. They were using extremely sensitive cameras that can detect single photons within very dark rooms—similar to the device Ruth developed for Popp's experiments. To their surprise, the Japanese scientists found our bodies were indeed glowing. The lowest intensity of light was at ten A.M., and the strongest point was at four P.M.—and it then dropped off gradually after that.[27] Another interesting discovery was that our faces glowed more than the rest of our bodies. The Japanese scientists firmly believe this light can help us understand the condition of a person's health—but they are seemingly not aware of all the other research that has already made great strides in these areas.

Dr. Fritz-Albert Popp found that cancer patients had lost their natural, cyclical human biorhythms. Furthermore, the light they were emitting was not anywhere near as coherent as a healthy person's.[28] It was as if the overall level of light stored in their bodies were significantly reduced. Multiple sclerosis seemed to be an exception to this rule of ill health, though. In this case, Popp found that people were absorbing too much light, and it appeared to be scrambling and confusing the cells' natural ability to function.

Popp wanted to find out whether the level of light stored in the body could indeed reveal how healthy the organism was—so he kept on doing more experiments. In one case, he found that free-range chicken eggs had significantly more coherent light than factory-raised eggs. When he examined various types of food, he found that the healthiest food consistently had the lowest and most coherent intensity of light.[29] That's an interesting point, as it truly suggests that it is quality, not quantity, that counts with this bioenergy system.

Popp made another significant breakthrough when he studied a common water flea known as *Daphnia*. To his amazement, he found that as one flea emitted light, other fleas reabsorbed it. They were drawing vitality directly from each other. This obviously implies that when we absorb too much light, the photons we give away are not waste products—they still contain all the vitality our bodies need. Sure enough, Popp found that small fish were also absorbing light from each other, sunflowers would position themselves to where the most number of photons could be absorbed, and bacteria would soak up light from their surroundings.[30] It is frankly quite amazing that this natural, biological system has eluded our mainstream scientific thought for so long—but once this knowledge spreads, the effects will be tremendously positive.

Popp then tested a variety of plant extracts to see if any of them could actually change the quality of light emissions from a human body—such as to potentially find a cure for the light-scrambling effects of cancer. Every substance he tried only seemed to make the problem worse, except for one: mistletoe. Indeed, one woman in Popp's care was able to completely cure her cancer through the use of mistletoe extract.[31]

Dr. Fritz-Albert Popp is not the only early pioneer whose work deserves a second look. Another classic breakthrough was Adamenko's "phantom leaf effect" from 1975. In this case, Adamenko was studying Kirlian photography. All you do is put a leaf or other living thing on an electrified Kirlian plate, and you then see a beautiful aura that appears around it as a fuzzy electrical current. To Adamenko's amazement, when he cut off the top of a living leaf and put it on the Kirlian plate, a phantom image of the missing piece would still appear for ten to fifteen seconds.[32] Many different groups have repeated this experiment around the world, and it was common to read about it in the 1970s pyramid power books.

Again, normal electromagnetic energy should not be able to do this—but the effect does fit in perfectly with our concept of a Source Field. Every living organism stores and releases photons inside its DNA, but you can remove the DNA, and the photons mysteriously still keep spiraling in that same area for up to thirty days. This is almost certainly what is causing the phantom leaf effect. It is therefore possible that if you left the leaf on the Kirlian plate for a longer period of time before you cut it, the phantom might also last longer—as that entire area has now built up a greater spiraling flow within the Source Field.

Genetic Restructuring and Healing

Just one year after the phantom leaf effect was discovered, Dr. Vlail Kaznacheyev made a very significant breakthrough that takes us even farther down the "rabbit hole." Kaznacheyev started out with two hermetically sealed cell cultures—and infected one of them with a disease. When he shined the light from the diseased cell culture into the healthy cell culture, the healthy cells mysteriously got infected with the disease.[33] Bear in mind that there was no possible way, through any known genetic process, that this could have happened. The only way this could have worked is if the DNA inside the healthy cells actually rearranged to form the DNA of the virus. The virus then cannibalized the cellular material around itself to form more viruses, as it normally would have done in its typical life cycle. We are seeing DNA and living tissue being rearranged by the genetic codes contained within coherent light.

Even more interestingly, when Kaznacheyev put a piece of glass in the way, the healthy cells did not get the disease. Glass, again, blocks infrared and ultraviolet light—so the genetic codes for the virus could not get through to the healthy cells. Of course, Gurwitsch used the same method to block the energy emerging from the tip of a growing onion. And if you put a pane of quartz in the way, in either Gurwitsch's or Kaznacheyev's experiments, the effect still works—and the key is that quartz allows infrared and ultraviolet to pass through.

How could a burst of coherent light completely transform the DNA molecule—and rearrange it from one life-form to another? Don't forget that we are constantly surrounded by electromagnetic waves that are bursting with information. We have cell-phone conversations, satellite television and high-speed Internet access going on all around us—uploading and downloading untold gigabytes of information. Laser light is very coherent—meaning there is a great deal of structure within it. This makes it ideally suited to carry information—just like we already do with other electromagnetic waves, but much more efficiently in this case. Just one pulse of light may well contain the entire genetic code to build an organism. And based on Kaznacheyev's landmark discovery, it appears that DNA is ready and waiting to be rearranged from one type of organism to another—if it receives the proper codes first. This will become much clearer, with multiple examples, as we go on.

After discovering the DNA Phantom Effect back in 1984, Dr. Peter Gariaev made additional discoveries in 2000 that have profound implications for human health. In this case, Gariaev started out by collecting seeds that had died of radiation poisoning from the Chernobyl nuclear disaster. Amazingly, by simply shining a non-burning laser light through healthy seeds of the same variety, and redirecting that light into the dead seeds, the radiated seeds miraculously recovered—and were completely healed. They could now grow into fully healthy adult plants.

This excited Gariaev greatly, so he decided to try a similar experiment on lab rats. In this case, he gave them a lethal dose of a toxin called alloxan. Typically, this toxin destroys the pancreas, an organ that creates insulin in the body to regulate blood sugar—and the rat dies within four to six days from Type 1 diabetes. Gariaev removed the pancreas and spleen from a healthy rat, shined a laser beam through it, and redirected that light into a rat that had been poisoned with alloxan. Amazingly, even though this experiment was repeated many times, involving three different research groups in 2000, 2001 and 2005, nearly 90 percent of all the rats who received this treatment experienced a full recovery. Their pancreas regrew, their blood sugar normalized, and within only twelve days, they were good as new.[34]

What's even more fantastic is that Gariaev was able to send the light from the healthy pancreas across a distance of twenty kilometers, using non-locality (no cables or wires required) and the healing effect still worked just as well.[35] As I'm sure you're starting to see, these healing results are equally as miraculous as what we saw from the Russian pyramids—and they are taking place without the use of pyramid technology. In 2005, Gariaev reported that "by the same means, we have significantly curbed the aging process in human cells, and even grown new adult human teeth in individuals who had lost them."[36] I contacted Dr. Gariaev to get more information. As some of his technical papers reveal, all of which are still in Russian at this time, this was an accident that happened while he was treating an elderly woman for diabetes. Specifically, he was trying to regrow a healthy new pancreas for her by energizing the blood of her ten-year-old grandson—and beaming in the proper healing frequencies. In Gariaev's model, a child's DNA still has the parents' and grandparents' energy signature in it—but in a healthier, younger configuration. This process involves the use of a specially modified, wide-spectrum red laser. Most of the details are still in Russian, but can be found at Gariaev's official Web site, wavegenetic.ru.

This woman only had one tooth left in the front of her mouth. After two weeks of treatment, she started experiencing pain and swelling in her jaw. Bumps appeared in her mouth and three new teeth cut through the skin—all of which were wisdom teeth in the back. This forced her dentist to completely redo both her top and bottom denture plates to account for the new growth. Gariaev also sent me an X-ray diagram of what happened, but did not have a "before" photograph available for comparison. Sadly, before Gariaev could repeat the experiment with others, Bauman's State University in Moscow declared it "pseudoscience," terminated the experiment and fired him. Some might consider this to be a fatal indictment of Gariaev's credibility as a scientist, but this is not uncommon. Many, if not most of the scientists who make discoveries like this end up being scorned, ridiculed, feared and attacked. So many different scientists have independently discovered the same things that it is very unlikely we are dealing with hoaxes or pseudoscience at all. Indeed, the evidence is clear that this is a medical revolution waiting to happen. Given the results of the pancreas study, a single organ donor could now regrow hundreds of organs for other human beings . . . and in rats, the entire process only took twelve days.

Another Russian scientist named Budakovski proved that we may not even need the donor organs at all. Budakovski started out by taking a holographic image of a healthy raspberry plant with a red laser. He then shined the hologram into a raspberry tumor, known as a "callus." Normally we consider tumors to be useless tissue that we should surgically remove and throw away—but the holographic light completely transformed the tumor back into a healthy raspberry plant.[37] This proves that once you have the energy signature you need—the information—you will get results. No living tissue is required to supply the original code— you just need the code itself, which can manifest in coherent light. In this case, the holographic image captured the wave information that told the tissue in the tumor how to regrow into a healthy plant.

One of the single most significant and revealing breakthroughs was discovered by Dr. A. B. Burlakov, another Russian scientist. Remember Popp's discovery that fleas, fish and other organisms are all absorbing light from each other? Burlakov put growing fish eggs next to each other, so light could pass between them—even though they were hermetically sealed. Here's the amazing part: if he put older, more mature eggs in front of younger eggs that were just getting started, the older eggs apparently sucked the life force out of the younger eggs. The older eggs grew stronger and faster, and the younger eggs withered, experienced deformities, and had significantly higher death rates. Burlakov noticed that mother fish were careful to never lay their eggs next to other fish eggs, and this seemed to explain why. On the other hand, if Burlakov put a slightly younger egg next to a slightly older egg, the younger egg would absorb life-giving energy from the older egg. Its growth and development would actually speed up until it was at the same level as the others.[38]

I spent years trying to find a scientific study featuring data like what Burlakov discovered, because so many other breakthroughs seemed to be leading us in this direction. Everyone has experienced being around people who are an energy drain, and some even call them psychic energy vampires—though that is an awfully harsh and disrespectful term.

It is easy to overreact once you are equipped with this knowledge, and accuse others of stealing your energy. However, this doesn't necessarily serve you well in the spiritual sense, because it reinforces the idea that your energy is a finite thing that can be taken from you. I believe the truth is that there is limitless energy in the Source Field—and if you do start to feel drained, you can replenish yourself by moving into a state of coherence. The loving space, coming from the heart, keeping your mind quiet and peaceful, all appear to actively rejuvenate your batteries in a very short time. A handy visualization that works for me is to think of our energetic duplicate, or aura, as being similar to a balloon filled with water. The size of the balloon can increase and decrease depending upon how much energy you have stored within you. We cannot directly measure the size or shape of this balloon with any instruments currently available, but with Burlakov's fish-egg study, we see the negative side of all this—where the strong can absorb Source Field energy directly out of the weak.

This may also be happening in pack animals that cluster around an alpha male for strength, guidance and protection. Popp found out that when we are under stress, we release a great deal of the light that is stored within our DNA. Some of it appears to be going to heal our cells, but perhaps that's not all it does. In Backster's experiments, the stress and death of living organisms sent out a wide-ranging signal that was available to plants, bacteria, eggs and other life-forms in the area. Nature may therefore have a built-in system where the herd automatically releases their energy when they are feeling stress and fear. Then, by looking up to their leader, their alpha male, they send their energy directly to him—just like in Dr. Glen Rein's study where the DNA samples did not get energized unless we wanted them to be. It could very well be that this is a natural survival mechanism where the herd sends their collective, combined Source Field energy to their leader, so he will be stronger, faster and more effective in battle to protect them. This may also explain why sports teams seem to consistently perform better in their home stadium rather than in their competitors' arenas. Granted, some of it is obviously caused by the fact that they know their own playing field better, and they are inspired by the sound of the crowd—but there may also be an energetic component as well that we just haven't acknowledged yet.

With Burlakov's discovery, we have solid evidence that this exchanging of energy is going on all the time. It is also interesting that healing effects occurred where the stronger eggs helped the weaker eggs—if they were fairly close in their level of development. It seems that if a mother fish lays some eggs, and some of them have minor birth defects that slightly slow down their rate of growth, Nature has a corrective mechanism that uses the energy from the other eggs to bring them up to speed. However, if the egg is significantly less developed than its neighbors, perhaps it's considered to be too far gone—and it's own life force is then absorbed for the benefit of the older, stronger eggs. Since Burlakov was also aware of Gurwitsch's work, he tried putting a piece of glass between the two sets of eggs—and once again, by shielding off infrared and ultraviolet light, the effect completely stopped. As expected, it worked perfectly if he used a piece of quartz instead.[39] Burlakov also found that by using different wavelengths of light and polarizing lenses, he could create freak abnormalities—such as multiple heads and multiple hearts. If he then reintroduced the normal wavelengths, these abnormalities disappeared—and the fish larvae would revert back to their usual pattern, showing no signs of ever having been mutants.[40] This creates significant trouble for the Darwinian model of evolution, which is all based on mutation—but let's not get ahead of ourselves.

According to Russian researcher Dr. Alex Kaivarainen, both bacteria and insects have been observed to experience remarkable healings by simply being close to other members of their own species who were healthy. Parsons and Heal poisoned bacteria with antibiotics in 2002, and found that they recovered if they were near other bacteria that were healthy. Agadjanian got the same results in 2003 with insects.[41] It certainly pays to have healthy friends. Think about how people who are dying tend to reach out with both hands to touch someone who comes up to speak with them. It may very well be that a two-handed touch enhances the absorption of the Source Field.

Is it possible that human beings can send energy to bacteria, plants, animals and other humans, and help improve their health in some way? This is exactly what Dr. Daniel Benor discovered after analyzing a total of 191 different controlled studies of spiritual healing. Amazingly, 64 percent of these studies showed statistically significant effects—including studies where the healing work was performed over substantial distances.[42] Let's not forget that 36 percent of the studies did not appear to show any healing effect—so what you usually see in the mainstream media is an article that discusses one of the experiments that failed, and then concludes that we have "scientific proof" these effects do not and cannot work. This is simply not the case.

Alexandra David-Neel visited Tibet in the 1920s, and wrote up her stunning observations in the 1931 classic *With Mystics and Magicians in Tibet*. Among many fascinating things she witnessed firsthand, some of which we will discuss later, the Tibetan monks explained to her that all of their mystical abilities came from being able to harness waves of energy—through meditation.

> The secret of the psychic training . . . consists in developing a power of concentration of mind greatly surpassing even that of men who are, by nature, the most gifted in this respect. Mystic masters affirm that by the means of such concentration of mind, waves of energy are produced which can be used in different ways. . . . That energy, they believe, is produced every time that a physical or mental action takes place.[43]

So, as we make our own thoughts more coherent, we may increase our ability to access the Source Field—and determine how and where it flows. This is a very important point, as it helps explain why so many ancient spiritual traditions place significant importance upon meditation. Let's again go back to our seven thousand people meditating, and reducing all terrorism in the world by 72 percent. It appears they are doing this by creating coherence in the Source Field. This in turn affects everyone else's minds directly, since we all share consciousness with each other in a measurable sense—and this is truly a fascinating new way of looking at ourselves and the world.

In Kaznacheyev's stunning discovery, healthy cells picked up the genetic code of a virus from diseased cells—through nothing more than the information structure of disease that he transmitted into them. This strongly suggests that DNA is not fixed in one configuration, but the code can actually be transformed from one life-form to another on a strictly energetic basis. This fascinating discovery opens the door to a whole new investigation of one of the greatest scientific mysteries of all: the evolution of species. Is this truly a random process, as most Darwinian scientists insist, or is something else going on? Believe me, I'm definitely not a creationist who thinks every word of the Bible is literally true, and that nothing on earth is over seven thousand years old. Nonetheless, it is ridiculous for the mainstream media to polarize the discussion between "science" on the one hand—a model that is more than one hundred years old, and fraught with problems we will soon explore—and "religion" on the other. The evidence we've already looked at suggests that the codes for life may exist in the Source Field itself. This information then flows into our own reality through ultraviolet light—not unlike how visual information may be flowing into the pineal gland through a stargate-like silver cord tethered to our energetic duplicate body. In the next chapter, we will explore new data on species evolution and find out if we have any proof of these radical new ideas.

CHAPTER TEN

Energetically Driven Evolution

The Great Pyramid appears to be one of many ways that our ancient ancestors gave us a prophecy of a coming Golden Age, which reaches a key turning point in and around the year 2012. The pyramid structure itself appears to be part of the message. When Russian scientists built pyramids out of PVC pipe and fiberglass, with no metal, they found a variety of remarkable effects. The scope of these discoveries is stunning—and it forces us to completely reexamine everything we think we know about science and physics. Cancer, rather than being some mysterious and awful problem, can now be traced back to a loss of coherence in the light we store in our bodies—as all carcinogens end up scrambling light at a 380-nanometer frequency. Within the pyramid, cancer-causing chemicals quickly become nontoxic—as if their molecular structure were rearranged in a way that supports life, rather than damaging it. Similarly, any geological and meteorological problems that threaten human life are remarkably reduced simply by building pyramids.

Once we begin looking for pyramid power–type effects on a scientific level, within biological systems, we find fantastic new discoveries. This includes the fact that we do appear to have the power to heal others with nothing more than our own thoughts, perhaps by visiting them directly with our energetic duplicate body and releasing photons containing healing codes—and ancient cultures were apparently well aware of this. We also found out that the DNA molecule leaves behind a phantom that absorbs light from its environment, almost like a miniature black hole, and holds it in place for up to thirty days—even once the molecule itself is taken away. This raises a very important question: Which came first—the DNA or the phantom? Is it possible that the phantom actually comes first?

Gariaev already proved that the DNA Phantom can absorb photons of light, and hold them in place. Could the DNA Phantom be strong enough to do the same thing with atoms and molecules? We do have some interesting clues. In 2008, Dr. Sergey Leikin put various types of DNA in ordinary salt water—with no proteins or material that could help them communicate with each other. Each type of DNA was tagged with a different fluorescent compound. Surprisingly, the DNA molecules that were identical to each other were then mysteriously drawn together—displaying a "telepathy-like quality." Specifically, matching DNA molecules were roughly twice as likely to gather together than molecules with different genetic sequences. Leikin believes this is merely caused by electrical charges, but the important point is that it works.[1] Further experiments may well prove that the Source Field is doing this—and assembles DNA out of tiny atoms and molecules that have not yet formed even basic amino acids.

In 2007, a team of scientists from Russia, Germany and Australia, led by Dr. V. N. Tsytovich, discovered that ordinary dust arranged into DNA-like structures when suspended in a plasma of charged particles—similar to the conditions we find in outer space. A computer model was built to reproduce this environment, and no order or structure was expected—but the dust naturally formed into corkscrew-shaped helical structures. These DNA-like structures were attracted to each other. They would divide and form two equal copies of the original, similar to the process of reproduction. They would change the structure of their neighbors simply by being nearby them. They also evolved into increasingly complex structures as the simulation continued. According to Tsytovich, "These complex, self-organized plasma structures exhibit all the necessary properties to qualify them as candidates for inorganic living matter . . . they are autonomous, they reproduce and they evolve."[2] Furthermore, in 2006, UCLA professor of astronomy Dr. Mark Morris announced the stunning discovery of a DNA-shaped double helix nebula near the center of our galaxy: "We see two intertwining strands wrapped around each other as in a DNA molecule. . . . Nobody has ever seen anything like that before in the cosmic realm. . . . What we see indicates a high degree of order."[3]

Just as this book was in final edits, in January 2011, a Nobel Prize–winning biologist announced that he had transferred a piece of bacterial DNA into a sealed test tube with nothing more than water inside. The water in the test tube rearranged into an exact duplicate of

NASA image of a nebula near the center of the Milky Way galaxy that is curiously similar to a DNA molecule in shape—first noticed by Dr. Mark Morris.

the DNA, which was floating in another sealed test tube next to it. In order for this to work, the original DNA sample needed to be greatly diluted, and a weak electromagnetic field of seven hertz had to be applied. After eighteen hours, some of the water molecules in the sealed tube transformed into perfect DNA molecules. John Dunn wrote about the implications of Dr. Luc Montagnier's discovery in Techworld.com.

What does all of this mean? It could be that the propagation of life is able to make use of the quantum nature of reality to project itself in subtle ways, as has been hinted at in previous experiments. Alternatively, it could be that life itself is a complex projection of these quantum phenomena and utterly depends on them in ways not yet understood because they are incredibly hard to detect. . . . Water might be a good medium in which DNA can copy itself using processes that hint at quantum entanglement and "teleportation" (our term).[4]

DNA may well be created by a quantum template that we can't even see or measure directly, but exists as a structure in the Source Field—and is written into the basic laws that govern matter and energy. Could this energetic structure gather photons, atoms and molecules together—to spiral life as we know it into existence? The answers may very well be staring us in the face, as Montagnier just discovered—but most scientists do not want to go there. Ever since the Reformation, there has been an unspoken deal between scientists and the Church—"You deal with the spirit and we'll deal with the facts, which of course is that life is an accident, and there is no higher purpose or intelligence to the Universe." Nonetheless, this is as much of a blind, religious belief as anything else. I personally believe in evidence. So let's see what we can find.

The Evolution of Life on Earth

No matter where we look on earth, we find bacteria. As reported in *Scientific American,* a wide variety of microorganisms were found in core samples taken from 500 meters below the Savannah River. Even at core samples from 1.7 miles below the earth's surface (2.8 kilometers), living bacteria are still being found. In normal topsoil you can find over one billion bacteria in a single gram of dirt, but even in rock samples from 400 meters down into the earth's crust, you can find anywhere between one hundred and ten million bacteria. Over nine thousand different types of microorganisms have been found in these subsurface areas, and some of them were found in temperatures as high as 167 degrees Fahrenheit (75 degrees C).[5]

You may also think that Darwinian evolution is scientific, but consider this—once you've got microbes, the vast majority of all the magic that needs to happen in order to create life has already taken place. You have DNA, protein synthesis, respiration, movement, awareness—as well as all the magical photon-capturing properties we've been exploring here. Our earth is only four billion years old, and it very likely started out as a molten rock. Things didn't cool down enough for oceans to form until 3.8 billion years ago, but even at this time, rock samples have been found that contain all the basic isotopes plants create from photosynthesis.[6] Even better, a primitive, yeastlike organism has also been found in 3.8 billion-year-old rocks.[7] That means that as soon as the earth had water, life essentially appeared instantaneously.

Once we reach 3.5 billion years ago, we find many more fossilized microbes in rocks that were not melted by volcanic activity. According to Dr. Johnjoe McFadden, "The world is just not big enough to evolve life if it relied entirely on chance. . . . These fossil microbes look like organisms alive today, and are likely to have been just as complex. Life may be improbable, but it was quick."[8] Just to prove how ridiculous the odds really are, an MIT biologist calculated how likely it is that even one protein with a hundred amino acids could form by random mutation—and it came out to one chance out of a number with sixty-five zeroes.[9]

A 2008 article in *Wired* magazine revealed new discoveries that bacteria can live in the earth's most inhospitable areas—including the smoldering heat inside volcanoes and nuclear reactors, and the freezing cold temperatures deep within the Antarctic ice. In fact, Antarctic bacteria were able to be thawed out and brought back to life after ten million years. The article also says that microbes can survive the shock of being launched into space, and amino acids—the precursors to all biological life—have been found in the dust from comet 81P/Wild 2.[10] Another recent study from the Imperial College of London found uracil and xanthine, the precursors to DNA, in fragments from a meteorite that crashed in Australia in 1969.[11] In January 2011, the Geological Society of America announced that living bacteria were found floating in fluid that was trapped inside salt crystals for 34,000 years. They were shrunken and small, and appeared to be in a hibernation-type state. It took them about two and a half months to wake up and begin reproducing normally. "We're not sure what's going on," Professor Tim Lowenstein said. "They need to be able to repair DNA, because DNA degrades with time."[12]

An even more stunning discovery was made by British astronomers Sir Fred Hoyle and Dr. Nalin Chandra Wickramasinghe, who explored the composition of galactic dust in the 1960s. More and more, the evidence suggested that the vast majority of dust throughout the entire galaxy—some 99.9 percent[13]—is actually freeze-dried bacteria. This discovery began when Hoyle and Wickramasinghe studied the infrared light from the dust in our galaxy, and concluded that these dust grains had to be 70 percent hollow on the inside. Bacteria have a hard outer cell wall and a softer interior. They were stunned when they found out that freeze-dried bacteria are also 70 percent hollow on the inside. By simply assuming that galactic dust grains were freeze-dried bacteria, they found a perfect fit to their observations.[14]

This led them to an utterly stunning conclusion: "Interstellar grains must surely be bacteria—albeit freeze-dried, perhaps mostly dead. At the very least this was a hypothesis that had to be explored." In a lecture from April 15, 1980, Hoyle spelled it all out.

> Microbiology may be said to have had its beginnings in the nineteen forties. A new world of the most astonishing complexity began then to be revealed. In retrospect I find it remarkable that microbiologists did not at once recognize that the world into which they had penetrated had of necessity to be of a cosmic order. I suspect that the cosmic quality of microbiology will seem as obvious to future generations as the Sun being the centre of our solar system seems obvious to the present generation.[15]

Some thirty years later, as I write this book, that predicted change in scientific thought has obviously still not arrived. Most scientists who even bother to write about interstellar bacteria still try to stick with the comfortable idea that they evolved by Darwinian mutation, freeze-dried in space, and then crashed to earth where they then seeded all life. It's a much greater step to realize that bacteria are everywhere, because that's what the Universe does—create life. If this is true, then how could we possibly have missed such a stunning discovery in the history of science?

In his noteworthy book *Sparks of Life,* Harvard professor James Strick revealed that there was an extensive conspiracy in the 1800s to suppress any scientific discoveries of microbes that appeared spontaneously, from nonliving material, rather than through allegedly "random Darwinian mutation."[16] Dr. Strick clarified his position at a 2003 conference held by the Wilhelm Reich institute, and it was written up and published online by Jack Flannel.[17] In the 1800s, the French Academy of Sciences offered prize money to any scientist who could conclusively prove that life was either spontaneous or random—and Louis Pasteur won the contest. When you see a carton of milk that says it is pasteurized, this means it was cooked to kill all the bacteria—and this process was named after Louis Pasteur. The problem is that Pasteur's competitors did get life-forms to grow out of nonliving environments—such as by using preparations of hay that had been totally sterilized in water. Pasteur simply refused to repeat these experiments. It's even more disappointing that Pasteur found life that spontaneously appeared in a small percentage of his own experiments, but he never even wrote about them—because he felt they had to be mistakes, and were not worth mentioning.[18]

The biogenesis side of the debate had evidence to support its conclusions going all the way back to 1837, with the little-known work of Andrew Crosse. At the time, electricity was a new and exciting phenomenon. Crosse wanted to try to grow crystals artificially, by zapping chemicals with a weak electrical current. Specifically, he mixed up a silicate of potash and hydrochloric acid, and then dropped a fist-size chunk of iron oxide rock into it. He then zapped the acid bath with a small battery, and hoped to find artificial silica crystals growing on the rock. Instead, he got something much, much weirder. After fourteen days, whitish specks started forming in the center of the electrified stone. Four days later, each speck was twice as large, and had six or eight tiny strands growing out from it. Each strand was longer than the speck itself.[19]

Crosse reported what happened next in a paper he wrote for the London Electrical Society in 1837.

> On the 26th day of the experiment, the objects assumed
> the form of perfect insects, standing erect on the bristles

which they were growing. Although I regarded this as most unusual, I attached no singular significance to it until two days later, the 28th day of the experiment, when the magnifying lens showed that these things were moving their legs. I must say now that I was quite astonished. After a few more days, they detached themselves from the stone and moved about through the caustic acid solution. In the course of a few weeks, more than a hundred of them made their appearance on the oxide of iron.[20]

The creatures appeared to be similar to the genus *Acari*, which is a form of mite: "Under a microscope I examined them, and found that the smaller ones had six legs, the larger ones had eight. Others who have examined them pronounced them to be of the genus acari, but some say they are an entirely new species." Crosse knew he would be attacked by his colleagues, so he carefully repeated the experiment by sterilizing all the ingredients with heat in a closed container before he ever started it—but the little critters still appeared the same way.

Other scientists repeated Crosse's experiment and got the same results, but according to the 1959 article by Frank Edwards that we pulled the above quotes from, they were too afraid to speak out about it.[21] This finally changed when the legendary Michael Faraday reported to the Royal Institution that he, too, had gotten these small creatures to grow under the same conditions.[22] He was not sure whether they were actually created spontaneously in the sterile solutions, or brought back to life by the electricity—but either result is a total challenge to mainstream science and biology as we now know it.

Another early pioneer we briefly mentioned in chapter 1 is Wilhelm Reich. His research into orgone energy, as he called it, was dismissed as a joke. Nonetheless, given everything we've been uncovering in this investigation, he appears to have been on the right track. Reich concluded that orgone fills all space in the Universe, does not have mass, penetrates matter, has a pulsating movement that can be measured, has a strong attraction to water, and is accumulated naturally in organisms by eating, breathing and taking it in through the skin. So far this all sounds very familiar. Reich created accumulators that concentrated this orgone energy, and found they remarkably increased the speed that wounds and burns would heal in laboratory mice. These treatments also decreased shock. Seeds grew into substantially larger and healthier plants when zapped by Reich's orgone accumulator.[23]

Reich also found evidence of spontaneous generation in sterile environments. He saw what he felt to be bluish points of light under the microscope, which appeared before the life-forms themselves were created—and he called these bursts of light "bions." This theory was widely ridiculed, and is still attacked by skeptics on the Internet today— criticizing Reich's protocols as scientifically unsound.[24] Nonetheless, Professor Ignacio Pacheco successfully replicated Reich's results in 2000—and the photographs of what grew in his test tube are quite stunning.[25] Pacheco heated ordinary sand from a nonpolluted beach to white-hot levels—namely, 1400° C. This destroys all known forms of biological life, other than the extremophile bacteria we spoke about earlier that appear in volcanoes and nuclear reactors. The sand was then cooled off in a sterile environment, poured into a sterile test tube with distilled water in it, and capped off. Each tube was then sterilized in an autoclave, two times in a row, with twenty-four hours between each sterilization. This process is used to destroy all known spores and vegetative cells. Pacheco then studied the particles floating at the top of the water under a microscope after each twenty-four-hour period following sterilization— and that's where the magic happened.

Amazingly, a variety of different structures appeared in the water that looked like complex living organisms—capable of growth and division. They were actively moving around in the solution, and Pacheco video-taped the results. Although Pacheco has not yet identified whether these structures have DNA in them, he feels "these bions can be considered living structures in almost every sense." Some of them look like simple microorganisms, but others were much more complex.

This included microscopic sea vegetables similar to Gorgonia. Some of Pacheco's most compelling photographs are of single leaves that broke

off from these plants when they were put on the microscopic slide. He also found soft-looking blobs which then started to grow a bright white spiraling shell of calcium around themselves—showing what appears to be the formation of an ordinary ocean shellfish at a very tiny level.

Dr. Ignacio Pacheco's photograph of a microscopic leaf-shaped object that formed in a sterile solution containing nothing but beach sand and distilled water.

The beginning spiral of the outer shell can be clearly seen, and it matches what we would expect to see perfectly—even though the soft inner body is still partially exposed.

My favorite photograph, as you can see on the next page, is of what looks like a critter with an obvious head, and a roughly spherical body that is covered with spikes for self-defense. Pacheco believes these are "transitional forms from the inorganic stage of organization to the organic and living condition of evolution."[26] Interestingly, if he did not sterilize the beach sand first, none of these little things would grow. It seems that the purity of the molecules was a very important element that allowed life to form. When we look at these little guys the obvious question is this: Where did their DNA come from?

The same question needs to be asked for all the bacteria we find in the most inhospitable places on earth—and indeed throughout all the dust in the galaxy. Pasteur may have made off with the prize money in the 1800s to support Darwin's model of evolution, but in the

Pacheco's photograph of what appears to be a shellfish beginning to form in a sterile solution containing only beach sand and distilled water.

process we've been robbed of a much greater truth—that life is indeed a product of intelligent design. You don't have to be a Bible thumper to see that—all you need is rational thinking in the face of all the evidence.

The Darwin Problem

Now let's talk about evolution. Although the official view is that Darwinian evolution is a proven fact, many scholars have concluded that it

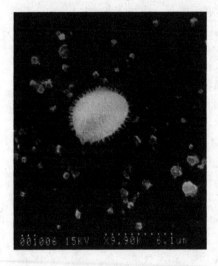

is simply impossible—and these are not creationists, but grounded scientific researchers with professional credentials. For example, Professor Louis Bonoure, Director of Research at the French National Center of Scientific Research, said, "Evolutionism is a fairy tale for

Pacheco's photograph of what appears to be a complex, multicellular organism, with a head and defensive spikes, formed out of a sterile solution of sand and water.

grown-ups. This theory has helped nothing in the progress of science. It is useless."[27] Wolfgang Smith, a mathematics professor from MIT and Oregon State University, made his position very clear.

> Today . . . the Darwinian theory of evolution stands under attack as never before. . . . A growing number of respectable scientists are defecting from the evolutionist camp. . . . For the most part, these "experts" have abandoned Darwinism, not on the basis of religious faith or biblical persuasions, but on strictly scientific grounds.[28]

Niles Eldredge, a paleontologist from the American Museum of Natural History, discussed the speed with which complex life suddenly appeared on earth.

> Beginning about six hundred million years ago . . . all over the world, at roughly the same time, thick sequences of rocks, barren of any easily detected fossils, are overlain by sediments containing a gorgeous array of shelly invertebrates: trilobites, brachiopods, mollusks. . . . Creationists have made much of this sudden development of a rich and varied fossil record where, just before, there was none. . . . [This] does pose a fascinating intellectual challenge.[29]

J. R. Norman, a zoologist from the British Museum of Natural History, said in 1975 that "the geological record has so far provided no evidence as to the origin of the fishes."[30] In 1960, W. E. Swinton, also from the British Museum of Natural History, said, "The [evolutionary] origin of birds is largely a matter of deduction. There is no fossil evidence of the stages through which the remarkable change from reptile to bird was achieved."[31] Professor Derek Ager, from the Imperial College of London's Department of Geology, wrote in 1976 that "it must be significant that nearly all the evolutionary stories I learned as a student . . . have now been 'debunked.' "[32]

The Darwinian crowd has naturally fought vigorously against this opposition, claiming there have been new advances—but in light of all the evidence we've been presenting, along with many other data points, the theory simply doesn't hold up very well. The fossil record consistently shows us one type of creature, which then upgrades into a new, improved, more evolved version over a very short period of time, geologically speaking. There are very few transitional fossils that could support Darwin's original theory. We don't see any examples of fish where the skeleton is half in and half out of the body—we have shellfish and bony fishes, with nothing in between. And that's just one of many curious examples. Even in the case of human evolution, there are significant and unsolvable problems. If you remember hearing about the search for a so-called missing link, a transitional species that can explain how human brain size suddenly doubled in a short time, bear in mind that it still hasn't been found. According to Lord Solly Zuckerman, Chief Scientific Advisor to the United Kingdom and a professor of anatomy at the University of Birmingham, "If man evolved from an apelike creature, he did so without leaving a trace of that evolution in the fossil record."[33]

If it's not Darwinian "random mutation" causing these changes to occur, then what is it? Two University of Chicago paleontologists, David Raup and James Sepkoski, may have found the answer. Together, they carefully assembled the largest collection of marine fossils ever accomplished—comprising an incredible 3,600 genera of ocean life. In 1982, they first published an article in the journal *Science* describing four mass extinctions they'd found in the fossil record, as well as a fifth one that was less significant.[34] As they continued to process this data, they faced a perplexing problem—patterns were increasingly appearing in the fossil record that shouldn't be there. Yet, the more research they did, and the harder they tried to get rid of it with the facts, the stronger the pattern became. In 1984, two years after they released their initial paper, they came clean—publishing their astonishing results, which still haven't had the effect on the scientific community that they should have. In short, new species were spontaneously appearing in short bursts in the fossil record—in a repeating cycle of approximately 26 million years.[35] This pattern extended back some 250 million years—out of a total of 542 million years of fossils they cataloged.

The story became even more interesting in 2005, when Dr. Richard A. Muller, a physics professor at University of California, Berkeley, and his graduate student Robert Rohde discovered another cycle of evolution in Raup's and Sepkoski's data. This time, it went all the way back to the beginning of the marine fossil record—some 542 million years ago. Muller and Rohde found that every 62 million years, more or less, all life on earth went through a relatively spontaneous upgrade—transforming the existing species into newer, more evolved forms.[36] In a *National Geographic* article that same year, Muller said, "I wish I knew what it all meant . . . I'm betting it will be astronomy, and he's betting it will be something inside of the earth."[37]

In a *Daily Galaxy* article originally from 2009, Muller seemed to be closer to winning the bet. As it turns out, astronomers have discovered that our solar system travels in a long, see-sawing wavelike motion, continually moving above and below the galactic plane as it goes along. One complete cycle of up-and-down movement takes approximately 64 million years—suspiciously close to the 62-million-year cycle discovered by Muller and Rohde. Obviously, such long-range astronomical calculations could be slightly incorrect, and the real figure for the galactic see-saw could actually be 62 million years. University of Kansas professors Adrian Mellott and Mikhail Medvedev believe this galactic cycle is the answer to the puzzle. The top half of our galaxy faces the Virgo cluster as we shoot through space, and Mellott and Medvedev believe this area should have an increased number of charged particles and cosmic rays— just like we see at the front end of our solar system from galactic dust. Their theory is that every time we rise out of the magnetic fields of the galactic plane and move into the northern area, we get a boost in cosmic-ray exposure. This radiation could then lead to more genetic mutations, and possibly create new species.[38]

That's certainly one possible explanation—but now that we are armed

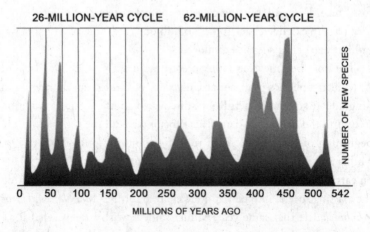

Adapted from Raup and Sepkoski, Rohde and Muller graphs by David Wilcock.

with our breakthrough research into the Source Field, there may well be other answers that move us even closer. This galactic see-saw theory also doesn't account for the roughly 26-million-year cycle that was originally discovered by Raup and Sepkoski. Something else has to be going on here. It does seem very likely that galactic energy fields will be responsible—and in Part Two, I'll present a new model that neatly explains everything, and gives us a solid, scientific way to map out these changes.

We've already seen how living bacteria and other species, complete with their DNA, could spontaneously emerge from seemingly nonliving matter. If DNA can be "created out of nowhere," and both Popp and Gariaev's research proves that DNA stores and releases light, then why couldn't DNA actually be reprogrammed and rewritten with the right light frequencies? Let's not forget that when Gariaev zapped a poisoned rat with the wave information from a healthy pancreas, its devastated pancreas regenerated in only twelve days. Budakovski found that the hologram of a healthy raspberry plant was all he needed to transform seemingly dead tumor tissue back into a perfectly normal new plant. What we're seeing is that coherent ultraviolet light can carry complex code that directly affects the structure and behavior of DNA—transforming diseased tissue back into full health. Are there any clues that the source code of DNA could indeed be like a jigsaw puzzle that has more than one correct solution, when given the right information? Surprisingly, the answer is yes.

DNA Is a Wave Structure That Can Be Rearranged

Many spiritually oriented people feel a great affinity with dolphins—and there appears to be much more to that story than most of us ever imagined. In 2000, NOAA scientist Dr. David Busbee discovered something truly astonishing.

> It became very obvious to us that every human chromosome had a corollary chromosome in the dolphin. . . . We've

found that the dolphin genome and the human genome basically are the same. It's just that there's a few chromosomal
rearrangements that have changed the way the genetic material is put together.[39]

This is quite amazing, as humans and dolphins certainly do not look
alike. Then, in 2004, the BBC News published the work of Dr. David
Haussler from the University of California, Santa Cruz, and his team.
When Haussler's team compared the DNA codes of human beings, rats
and mice, "they found—to their astonishment—that several great
stretches of DNA were identical across the three species." Chickens, dogs
and even fish also had almost identical DNA codes to human beings as
well—although sea squirt and fruit flies were less similar. Dr. Haussler
said, "It absolutely knocked me off my chair. . . . It's extraordinarily
exciting to think that there are these . . . elements that weren't noticed
by the scientific community before."[40]

If the DNA of humans, dolphins, rats, mice, chickens, dogs and fish
are all so similar, and the DNA molecule can absorb and release coherent
light, then we get tantalizingly close to the idea that all DNA is ultimately the product of a single wave, which undergoes relatively minor
modifications to produce different species.

If this is true, then could we change the wave by feeding it new
information—and actually rearrange one species into another, directly at
the DNA level? Indeed, if we think back to Dr. Alexander Golod's pyramid on Seliger Lake, this appears to have already happened. A variety of
seemingly extinct plants began growing in the land surrounding the pyramid. Do we have any other evidence that could verify such a fascinating
effect? The answer arrived in 1989, when a major chemical company
known as Ciba-Geigy patented a process that allowed them to cultivate
new and original forms of plants and animals. The process is deceptively
simple—they place seeds between two metal plates, and run a weak DC
current through them for three days as they germinate. When they
zapped an ordinary fern seed using this process, they were astonished to
find that it transformed into a formerly extinct species that had only ever
been found in fossils from coal deposits. The "extinct" fern had forty-one

chromosomes rather than the expected thirty-six. Furthermore, within four years, the original plants mutated into a wide variety of different strains of fern—some of which normally only grew in South Africa.[41]

When Ciba-Geigy tried the same technique with wheat, they were able to revert it back to a much older and stronger variety—from a time before it had been heavily over-bred. This wheat could be fully harvested after only four to eight weeks—and the norm is seven months. This, of course, has marvelous implications for impoverished areas where people suffer from starvation. When they tried it with tulips, they found thorns appearing on their stems—and this appeared to be an original trait that gardeners had long since bred away. The effect didn't just work on plant seeds either. When they tried the same experiments with trout eggs, they found that a much stronger and more disease-resistant trout was formed. Best of all, they tried out the process on 200-million-year-old spores that had been found in a salt deposit 140 meters deep in the ground. Even though nothing else had been able to revive these spores, simply zapping them with the electrostatic field brought them back to life—as if the 200 million years didn't even matter.[42]

Unfortunately, this was a chemical company—and a large part of their business depends on agricultural plants being weak and vulnerable, so they require chemical fertilizers. Once Ciba-Geigy realized that these plants could put them out of business, they quickly stopped pursuing this new technique. Thankfully, the original papers survived—so this information was not lost.[43]

Another weird discovery emerged in *National Geographic News* from 2009. Scientists from the University of Rennes in France drowned 120 different spiders, from three different species, in water. They probed the spiders every two hours until they appeared to be completely dead, which took twenty-four hours for the forest species and either twenty-eight or thirty-six hours for the two marsh species. Once the spiders had apparently died, the scientists left them out to dry, so they could be weighed. Amazingly, the spiders' legs began twitching and they came back to life—with the longest time interval being two hours for the marsh species that took thirty-six hours to die. Of course, the scientists assume this is the result of a coma rather than actual death, but it raises fascinating questions.[44] Life may be far more resilient than we normally give it credit for. Just like we saw in the 34,000-year-old bacteria that reanimated after two and a half months, or in Gariaev's dead seeds from Chernobyl, if you have genetic material that is already fairly close to being alive—even if it is technically dead—a little jump-start may be all you need to reanimate it. This is obviously a much easier and faster process for the Source Field to use, rather than creating life out of otherwise inanimate molecules.

Life-forms That Rewrite Their Own Genetic Code

If we want to understand this new concept of evolution even further, we must be aware that some species can rearrange their own DNA without the use of any outside electrostatic fields—such as we saw in the Ciba-Geigy experiments. As of April 2009, a Rockefeller University study revealed that a parasite known as *Trypanosoma brucei*, which creates African sleeping sickness, is able to spontaneously rearrange its own DNA so it cannot be defeated by the body's immune system. Amazingly, the parasite is able to dice up and rearrange both strands of its DNA, changing its outer coat so it can continue to avoid being detected. Though the scientists involved in this study suspected the parasite was doing this as early as 2007, they didn't find the proof until 2009. According to their press release, adapted for *Science Daily*, this "suggested a common mechanism by which parasites and humans rearrange their DNA. "It was unbelievable," Dr. Oliver Dreesen says. "One experiment after another and it just worked."[45]

These scientists were apparently unaware of a similar effect that was discovered by Dr. Robert Pruitt, a geneticist with Purdue University, in 2005. Pruitt and his associates were studying a mustardlike plant called *Arabidopsis*, which is commonly used in laboratory experiments. Specifically, they were exploring a mutation in one of the genes that made the flowers clump together in an odd, misshapen way. What they found was that even when the plants inherited this mutation from both of their parents, over a three-year period of study, fully 10 percent of them reverted back to normal. They rewrote their own DNA, and fixed the mutation. The startled scientists examined the plants' DNA and confirmed that it had been transformed back into its original, healthy form.[46] This is a spontaneous DNA rewrite to fix a mutation—and it deals another critical blow to the Darwinian model. If DNA has an underlying wave component that can correct mutations, Darwin may have just lost his job. According to Dr. Elliott Meyerowitz, a plant geneticist from the California Institute of Technology, Pruitt's finding "looks like a marvelous discovery."[47] I also like this study because it proves that no giant industrial company can ever create true "terminator seeds" that will always destroy themselves after a single generation. Nature always finds a way to repair the damage.

Another example of "marvelous" genetic repairs comes from Francis Hitching's 1982 book *The Neck of the Giraffe—Where Darwin Went Wrong.* Hitching reported on his experiments with the fruit fly, technically known as *Drosophila,* which is one of the most common living organisms studied in biology experiments. Even though various scientists have used radiation to try to dramatically speed up the rate of mutation, "Fruit flies refuse to become anything but fruit flies under any circumstances yet devised."[48] Even more interestingly, when Hitching took away all the genetic codes from both sets of parents that would build eyes for the fruit fly, they nonetheless regrew their eyes—in roughly five generations. According to Hitching, "Somehow the genetic code had a built-in repair mechanism that reestablished the missing genes."[49] Of course, that makes us ask a much deeper question: What is the "genetic code"?

More and more, we are seeing evidence of a guiding intelligence that can somehow modify the genetic code in ways that will benefit the organism. Are there other examples where organisms rewrite their own DNA to adapt to changes in their environment? Dr. John Cairns was one of the first to discover this sort of an effect in 1988. Cairns studied a type of bacteria that cannot digest lactose, and then put them in an environment where that's all there was. Of course, the vast majority of the bacteria starved and went into a suspended-animation state. However, after a day or two, several of his bacterial cells spontaneously evolved—rewriting their own DNA to digest lactose. And this was not a random event—if there wasn't any lactose in the area, the "adaptive mutation" did not happen.[50] Dr. Barry Hall continued this work with a study he published in 1990—and he found that if he deprived bacteria of certain key nutrients, such as the amino acids tryptophan and cysteine, some of their offspring ended up being able to synthesize these nutrients within their own bodies.[51] Whatever the bacteria needed to survive was provided for them—by the hidden laws of Nature. Hall also suspects that this same effect explains how dangerous bacteria are able to adapt to new antibiotics so quickly.[52]

In 2008, another study proved that organisms can quickly rearrange their own DNA to help them adapt to the challenges of their environment. Back in 1971, biologists moved five breeding pairs of Italian wall lizards from their barren island home in the South Adriatic Sea, where they survived on insects, to a neighboring island that was lush and tropical. Up until this point, these species had never existed on the neighboring island. When the biologists returned to the tropical island beginning in 2004, they were shocked to find that the descendants of these original parents had experienced substantial evolution in a short time.

As revealed in a *Daily Galaxy* article, "Striking differences in head size and shape, increased bite strength and the development of new structures in the lizard's digestive tracts were noted after only 36 years, which is an extremely short time scale," remarks Duncan Irschick, a professor of biology at the University of Massachusetts–Amherst."[53] Each of these changes was tailor-made to help the lizards eat plants. Thanks to a very rapid DNA rewrite, their digestive systems developed cecal valves—which were never before seen in this species. These organs create fermentation that breaks down plant material. Less than one percent of all lizard species in the world have this unique feature. Their heads became longer, wider and taller, which gave them a substantial increase in bite strength—so they could more easily chew through plant fibers. Interestingly, they also stopped defending their own territory, now that they were eating by browsing rather than hunting. According to Dr. Irschick, "Our data shows that evolution of novel structures [within an organism] can occur on extremely short time scales."[54]

Another classic study was performed by Rosemary and Peter Grant, who spent twenty years on an island in the Galapagos, studying and identifying every single individual bird there—beginning with four hundred when they first arrived, and surging to over a thousand during their stay. Throughout these twenty years, they continuously observed about twenty generations of finches. To their amazement, individual species made genetic changes in remarkably short periods of time. The majority of these improvements involved a change in the size and shape of their beaks. As one example, when the island went through a period of extended drought, seeds became tinier and harder to reach—so the birds evolved longer and sharper beaks to be able to eat them. The Grants also found that the birds had actually rewritten their own DNA to produce these changes. According to Jonathan Weiner, author of *The Beak of the Finch: A Story of Evolution in Our Time,* "Darwin . . . vastly underestimated the power of natural selection. Its action is neither rare nor slow. It leads to evolution daily and hourly, all around us, and we can watch."[55] In 2009, ornithologists announced another discovery of rapid evolution in forest birds. Soon after the forests were cut down, the birds' wingtips became pointier—but if the forests expanded, their wing tips became more round.[56]

In 2009, *National Geographic* reported that a never-before-seen "monster fish" had been found in the Congo River, which moves through several countries in Africa. Dr. Melanie Stiassny, a fish biologist at the American Museum of Natural History, said, "What we're seeing here is kind of evolution on steroids."[57]

When we go out into the oceans, we find that the "immortal jellyfish" can completely rewrite its own DNA in the presence of starvation, physical damage or other types of crisis. According to Maria Pia Miglietta, a Pennsylvania State University researcher, "instead of sure death, [the immortal jellyfish] transforms all of its existing cells into a younger state." The jellyfish convert their own tissues and genetic material back to their earliest stage of growth, and "the jellyfish's cells are often completely transformed in the process. Muscle cells can become nerve cells or even sperm or eggs." Another interesting fact was that every jellyfish of this species they found, worldwide, was genetically identical—even though the tropical jellyfish had only eight tentacles, whereas those in cooler waters could have as many as twenty-four. Drifting ocean currents could not explain how this species ended up appearing identically in so many different places around the world. Dr. Miglietta speculated that the jellyfish must be hitching rides on long-distance cargo ships.[58]

Energetic Evolution and Species Transformation

In 1997, another seemingly impossible genetic mystery was discovered in the oceans. In this case, Dr. Lingbao Chen and his associates found that fishes in the Antarctic and several species of northern cods had evolved nearly identical antifreeze proteins, even though there is abundant evidence from paleontology, paleoclimate research and the species' own physical appearance that they must have evolved separately. The conclusion was that these proteins had to have appeared through what they called convergent evolution, where this seemingly random process of Darwinian mutation is now doing the same exact thing—in two totally isolated environments.[59]

I was particularly amazed by a *National Geographic* news story that appeared on February 15, 2009. The International Census of Marine Life is making a focused effort to identify and assess all species in the ocean— past, present and potential future. In the process of assembling this vast body of data, the scientists found something astonishing—at least 235 different identical species have been discovered at the North and South Poles, and they do not exist anywhere else on earth. This includes swimming snails, whales, worms and crustaceans. There is simply no way that all these species could have been transported from one pole to the other—there are no shipping routes that go that way, and they could not survive a trip through warmer water. The scientists admitted that they were startled by this mystery.[60]

In 2002, Richard Pasichnyk released both volumes of *The Vital Vastness*—and I was particularly struck by his discussion of the so-called Lazarus Effect, which shows how species can spontaneously reappear after millions of years of extinction.

A striking example is the time when virtually no insect fossils can be found for most of the entire Cretaceous period. After the end of the Cretaceous and the demise of the dinosaur, insect fossils return in full force—along with a striking increase in flowering plants. . . . Are there times when conditions cause genetic material to revert to lost codes?[61]

A recently dead rodent with a long, fluffy tail called *Laonastes* was found for sale in a meat market in Laos. The only problem was that this creature had been extinct for 11 million years. This was reported in *Science* journal in 2006.[62] Mary Dawson of the Carnegie Museum of Natural History was quite surprised.

It is an amazing discovery. . . . It's the first time in the study of mammals that scientists have found a living fossil of a group that's thought to be extinct for roughly 11 million years. That's quite a gap. Previous mammals had a gap of only a few thousand to just over a million years.[63]

Another example concerns a strange-looking elephant called a gompothere. Its trunk and tusks point straight forward, and it also has two teeth that stick out from its lower jaw. They were believed to have gone extinct some 1.788 million years ago, but recently their fossils were found among ruins from early settlers of North America, known as the Clovis people. This was again referred to as the Lazarus Effect in action, and the Houston Museum of Natural Science Web site said, "This find has major implications."[64]

I also found an MSNBC article discussing French scientists who found a crustacean from the Glyphea group (genus Neoglyphea) some four hundred meters down in the Coral Sea, northwest of New Caledonia. Philippe Bouchet, a marine biologist, described it as "halfway between a shrimp and a mud lobster." The problem, again, is that according to the fossil record, this species has been extinct for 60 million years.[65] And in 2005, a UPI press release reported the discovery of a Wollemi pine tree within a small grove of trees in Australia. This tree can grow up to 120 feet high and has a three-foot-wide trunk. The problem is that this tree went extinct 200 million years ago—in the Jurassic period.[66] Security is so high that even the scientists who are working on the site are blindfolded before they are flown in. Specimens have been taken from this secret location and are being sold by auction to insure the survival of the species. As we see in the other cases, there are no examples of this tree anywhere in the fossil record from 200 million years ago until the present. According to UPI, "Sydney's Royal Botanic Gardens told the newspaper the discovery is 'the equivalent of finding a small dinosaur still alive.'"[67]

The Lazarus Effect may be caused by existing species rearranging into earlier versions on the DNA level, perhaps in the presence of unusual energetic stimulation—similar to what we saw in the Ciba-Geigy patent. Korean scientist Dr. Dzang Kangeng published a remarkable discovery in 1993 that demonstrates how this could happen. In this case, Kangeng found he could transfer the genetic code from one species into another through nothing more than an energy wave.[68] Kangeng placed a duck inside a five-sided, pentagon-shaped container, and covered it with a domed mirror roof. Each of the five sides of the container had a hole with a funnel mounted in it—and then each funnel had a pipe that fed into a neighboring room, where there was a pregnant mother hen. For five days, the duck was zapped with a high-frequency electrostatic generator. Amazingly, when the hen laid her eggs, what hatched out of them were not baby chicks—they were half-duck, half-chicken hybrids. Though they came from a chicken's body, they had the typical features of a duck—a flat beak, a longer neck and larger internal organs—such as the heart, liver, stomach and bowels. After one year, the hybrid birds weighed 70 percent more than a normal chicken.[69]

The experiment was repeated with a total of 500 eggs, of which 480 hatched and grew. Of these 480 chicks, 80 percent had a flat, duck-shaped head. Ninety percent had the eyes move to a position that was more like a duck's than a chicken's. And 25 percent had webbing appear between their toes, which chickens do not normally have.[70] These hybrids were able to breed with each other, and their own offspring continued to be half-duck, half-chicken hybrids rather than reverting to being ducks and/or chickens. Kangeng successfully applied for and was granted a patent for his invention as a "device for biological information-directed transfer," though it obviously is not in common use.[71] He was also able to zap peanuts and send their "wave information" into sunflower seeds, and this created hybrid plants that now looked, tasted and smelled similar to peanuts. Their production increased by 180 percent—and again the changes remained in place from one generation to another.[72]

Another little-known pioneer in this category is Italian scientist Pier Luigi Ighina, who worked as a student of Marconi—the revered inventor of radio, along with many other technologies. According to an article by Leonardo Vintini in *The Epoch Times,* a mainstream international newspaper, Ighina "harnessed the energy that passed between the earth and the sun," and used it to rejuvenate diseased cells. Another device he called Elios was allegedly able to purify any food he zapped with it. Given the effects we found in the Russian pyramid studies, this sounds quite familiar. In addition, Ighina apparently built practical, working technologies that accomplished the same stupendous feats as the Russian pyramids. One device apparently neutralized earthquakes. Another device he called the magnetic stroboscope looked like a "strange propeller"— and when he powered it up on a cloudy day, within a matter of minutes there would be a continually growing hole opening up in the clouds above his home, revealing blue skies. This must have been quite a sight to see: "Ighina admitted that the most satisfying component of his unusual invention was the innocent smiles of children as they watched the clouds retire, as if by magic."[73]

This next excerpt contains the most interesting part of Ighina's research as it relates to our discussion.

> After years of arduous lab work, Ighina discovered the most profound nature of matter—that atoms do not oscillate but vibrate. This revelation led to one of his more curious and brilliant inventions—the magnetic field oscillator. The scientist discovered that if he managed to change the vibratory state of a group of particles, the material itself could transform. What followed was a series of fantastic

experiments in which the field oscillator played a leading role. On one occasion, Ighina set up his apparatus before an apricot tree. He then altered the atomic vibration so that it gradually became the same as that of an apple tree. . . . After 16 days, he ascertained that the apricots had mutated, almost completely, into apples.[74]

This fits in very nicely with what Gariaev and Kangeng were both able to do—and the more we see the same discoveries appearing, the more likely it is that they are actually real. From here, Ighina's story gets even more interesting.

After this experience, Ighina ventured to investigate the reach of his invention on animals. He altered the vibrational state of the tail of a rat to change it, in four days, into the tail of a cat. Even though the rat died after such treatment (perhaps its body was incapable of enduring such a rapid molecular change), it prompted Ighina to try an experiment even more revelatory: Through studying the corresponding vibration of the healthy bone of a rabbit, he excited the atoms of another rabbit's fractured feet until they were healed in record time. In this way, Ighina understood that sick cells (including cancerous ones) of any individual were possible to cure through a simple, gradual alternation in their vibrational index, if this was correctly calculated.[75]

These are precisely the same results Gariaev and others have been able to independently achieve—not to mention what we saw in the Russian pyramid studies. This genetic information transfer may be happening all the time, without any technology—just by two organisms being in close proximity to each other over a prolonged period. Noted psychologist Robert Zajonc helped establish scientific proof that when people live with each other for long periods of time, say twenty-five years, they actually develop similar facial features. In this study, 110 participants were shown individual photographs of people in their first year of marriage and again after twenty-five years of marriage. The participants were able to match up the faces after twenty-five years much more easily than they did after a single year of marriage. This could not be explained by people all looking the same as they got older, or other predictable factors.[76]

Getting back to our laboratory DNA research, generating hybrid creatures is one thing—but is it possible to completely transform one species into another? Dr. Peter Gariaev sent a green nonburning laser through salamander eggs, and then redirected the beam into frog eggs. Amazingly, the frog eggs completely transformed into salamander eggs. Though these salamanders hatched from the genetic material of a frog, they lived normal lives—and could breed with other salamanders to produce healthy offspring.[77]

I heard about this breakthrough back in 2000—and it had a massive, life-changing effect on me. This was the direct proof I was looking for that evolution could be totally spontaneous—and requires nothing more than a rearranging of the DNA molecules within an existing species. As the years went by, I carefully collected other examples of the same phenomenon—and it is a great pleasure to finally put them all together while writing this book. Of course, I feel Gariaev's discovery has profound implications for all the ancient prophecies of a coming Golden Age—beginning around the year 2012.

Can we really be sure that we are at the pinnacle of human evolution? And how do we know the human design is only unique to the earth? If our solar system is dipping up and down through the galactic plane in 64-million-year intervals, and the fossil record is changing in 62-million-year intervals, then perhaps the galaxy actually contains the "source code" for all life. Our movement through the galaxy may be transforming all life on earth in regular cycles. Almost every grain of dust we see throughout the galaxy appears to be freeze-dried bacteria. This suggests that life is very, very abundant. Human life may well be a galactic design—naturally evolving on any planet that has the right conditions. Though we may find subtle differences in appearance from one planet to another, the overall look of these different species may be far, far less alien than we have been led to believe by manipulative, fear-oriented Hollywood propaganda. And best of all, we may be in line for another cosmic upgrade very soon. The proof that such sudden bursts of evolution can happen is already there in the fossil record—and we have direct proof of the mechanisms involved in Gariaev's frog-salamander study, and others just like it.

Dramatic Increases in the Speed of Evolution

If this is really what the 2012 prophecies are about, it seems unlikely that any sweeping genetic changes would occur within a single person's life span. There should be gradual changes that we can track over time. We can therefore look for clues in our own genetic heritage to see if there is any DNA evidence for our own evolution speeding up. This is precisely what was discovered by University of Madison–Wisconsin researcher Dr. John Hawks, and reported by the BBC News, *Daily Galaxy* and other mainstream media outlets. By studying various markers in human DNA, Hawks concluded that human evolution has been moving at a supercharged speed for the last forty thousand years. Even more stunningly, in the last five thousand years, human evolution is now moving one hundred times faster than any other moment in recorded history.[78] This timeframe only represents one hundred to two hundred generations. The other fascinating implication of this is that according to Hawks, a person from 3000 B.C. is more similar to a Neanderthal than they are to you and me—on a direct, measurable DNA level. Approximately 1,800 genes, or 7 percent of all human genetics, have experienced very recent evolution.[79]

Another sign that we are experiencing rapid evolution is the so-called Flynn Effect. In the 1980s, a New Zealand political scientist named James Flynn found that IQ scores were consistently going up. An IQ of 100 is supposed to be average, but people were scoring better and better on the tests—thus forcing psychologists to change the scoring systems. Since then, numerous studies have confirmed that we are seeing an average increase of over three IQ points per decade. This increase appears in every single intelligence test being used, delivered to virtually every type of group, across twenty different countries—including some that are not literate in the traditional sense. There is also evidence that the speed of the increases is now accelerating. Flynn examined one test called Raven's Progressive Matrices, which has been given for over a century. Shockingly, a person who scored in the best 10 percent a hundred years ago would now be among the weakest 5 percent. Furthermore, the number of people whose scores would now rank them at the "genius" level have increased by more than twenty times. These increases are not as likely to be seen on tests that emphasize culture or traditional school knowledge. Instead, the most dramatic increase is in tests that measure our ability to recognize abstract, nonverbal patterns. This should be leading to, as Flynn describes it, "a cultural renaissance too great to be overlooked."[80]

Humans are not the only ones who seem to be gaining intelligence. In 2008, *U.K. Times Online* revealed that naturalists were shocked to see orangutans swimming, which they never before have been observed doing—as well as using sticks to stun and capture fish, and in some cases even spearing them.[81] This is another area ripe for investigation and further discovery.

In 2009, *Wired* magazine revealed that the placebo effect has also become substantially more powerful in a short time. This is causing big trouble for the major pharmaceutical manufacturers, as in order for their drugs to pass clinical trials, they have to work better than placebos. From 2001 to 2006, 20 percent more products were cut after less-demanding Phase II clinical trials, and another 11 percent failed the more extensive Phase III trials. As one example, a startup stem-cell company called Osiris Therapeutics had to suspend trials for a Crohn's disease pill in March 2009, and said the reason was that their participants were getting an "unusually high" response to placebos. Just two days later, Eli Lilly had to abandon a new drug to treat schizophrenia when their volunteers showed a 200-percent increase in their response to the placebos.[82]

Existing drugs that are already on the market, like Prozac, are now also doing worse and worse when compared to placebos—to the point where they might not even get approved if they were applying for a new release. Two different comprehensive investigations into antidepressants found that there has been a remarkable increase in our responsiveness to placebos since the 1980s. One of these studies concluded that placebos have nearly doubled in their effectiveness during that time—across all these different trials. This is causing serious financial pain to the pharmaceutical industry, which had become more profitable than Big Oil—thanks to expensive, widespread drugs like Prozac. The "Big Pharma" companies say their drugs are not becoming weaker—instead, the placebo effect is getting stronger, and no one can figure out why.[83] This fits in perfectly with our notion that the Source Field itself is changing—pushing us toward a higher coherence, if you will, and rearranging our genetic code in favorable ways. The connection between our level of intelligence and the influx of the Source Field into our bodies now seems to be dramatically increasing in a relatively short time. The Source Field seems to appear in our DNA as virtual photons that are stored for usable energy.

Another sign of possible human evolution is that overall happiness levels, worldwide, have significantly increased between 1981 and 2007 in forty-five out of fifty-two countries, which included several developing countries—not just the West. Admittedly, the University of Michigan's Institute for Social Research, which conducted this study, felt this rise in happiness was due to economic growth, greater democracy and increased social tolerance.[84] Furthermore, in 2008, the *Journal of Happiness Studies* reported that happiness protects our bodies from becoming sick—to the point where a consistent lack of happiness is as toxic as cigarette smoking. This was the result of thirty different studies that were combined together and analyzed to find a single, overall effect.[85]

Another interesting study was conducted by two economists from the University of Pennsylvania—Betsey Stevenson and Justin Wolfers. They collected data every year from 1972 to 2006 with the University of Chicago General Social Survey, and in their findings, the overall level of happiness in America alone had not increased—but fewer people are reporting very high scores and fewer people are reporting lower scores. It's as if there were a normalizing factor at work in society. Stevenson said, "It's an interesting finding, because other research shows increasing gaps in income, consumption and leisure time."[86]

Is the 25,920-Year Precession a Genetic Evolution Cycle?

Many ancient myths suggest the 25,920-year precession of the equinoxes cycle will usher in a Golden Age. What happens if we examine our own historical record with this in mind? Is there any evidence that human evolution is following this 25,920-year cycle in some measurable way? And if so, how would we know what we were looking for, and where to find it? One obvious starting point would be to find out when the Neanderthals died out. That would be a time where humanity was rapidly evolving, and earlier species no longer survived. Sure enough, somewhere between 28,000 and 24,000 years ago, roughly speaking, the Neanderthals went extinct.[87]

Unless it all happened 24,000 years ago, which many scientists dispute, there is no climate shift event on earth that could help account for this change. Katerina Harvati, a paleoanthropologist from the Max Planck Institute for Evolutionary Anthropology, explained further.

> Our findings suggest that there was no single climatic event that caused the extinction of the Neanderthals. Only the controversial date of 24,000 radiocarbon years for their disappearance, if proven correct, coincides with a major environmental shift. Even in this case, however, the role of climate would have been indirect—by promoting competition with other human groups.[88]

This "major environmental shift" from 24,000 years ago was clarified in an article from the BBC. During that time, sea surface temperatures were the lowest they had been in the last 250,000 years—creating an Ice Age.[89]

If we go back another Great Year of 25,920 years into the past, we arrive at roughly fifty thousand years ago. This clearly corresponds with yet another sudden jump in human evolution. Humans did not use any tools more sophisticated than a crude stone blade until about fifty thousand years ago.[90] Suddenly, at this time, we began making musical instruments, needles and other sophisticated tools, as well as doing drawings.[91] According to anthropologist John Fleagle, we also see the carving of bone for religious reasons. Harpoons, arrowheads, beaded jewelry and other forms of ornamentation all appear as a "coherent package about fifty thousand years ago." Furthermore, "the first modern humans that left Africa between fifty thousand and forty thousand years ago seem to have had the full set."[92] Clear and undeniable religious art also appeared abruptly, fifty thousand years ago, for totally unknown reasons. Graves of human beings were marked with red ochre and oriented to a single star in the night sky. James Lewis continued on this theme in a 2007 article he wrote for *American Thinker.*

> All over the prehistoric world, physical symbols of power and devotion are laid in the ground, next to the honored dead; giant Neolithic stone works are found all over the Old World, like Stonehenge but spread far and wide; and even the utilitarian stone hand axes that did not change over hundreds of thousands of years, are suddenly refined into ritual shapes too fragile for any practical use. Something very profound happened to human nature fifty or seventy millennia ago, and it has all the earmarks of what we inadequately call religion.[93]

Interestingly, another significant change occurred in our biosphere during this same time that made the earth more comfortable for human life. As revealed by Professor Peter Ward in 2004, giant mammals experienced a mass extinction fifty thousand years ago on every continent except Africa.[94] Many of these giant mammals were dangerous to humans—so this appears to be another intelligent adaptation of the earth to be able to help our own evolution along.

If we go even farther back in time, two human skulls found in Africa were recently dated to be roughly 200,000 years old—and they are not from Neanderthals. University of Utah geologist Frank Brown said, "It pushes back the beginning of anatomically modern humans." Since culture, religious art and complex tool-making didn't appear until fifty thousand years ago, Brown said that this "would mean [we had] 150,000 years of Homo sapiens without cultural stuff."[95] Robert Roy Britt, writing for LiveScience, said, "The finding suggests our ancestors spent a long, long time wallowing in an uncultured era with no music, art or jewelry."[96]

Now we have an incredible case for mass, energetically directed evolution. Dr. John Hawks genetically proved that mass human evolution has been speeding up for the last forty thousand years, and began moving one hundred times faster in the last five thousand years. We have compelling evidence that the precession of the equinoxes has an effect upon these evolutionary bursts, as we see in the dying out of the Neanderthals roughly 25,000 years ago—and the sudden emergence of creativity and spiritual behavior in humans fifty thousand years ago. The trail of bread crumbs left by the wonders of the Great Pyramid have led us to a cornucopia of remarkable new healing technologies, and the potential to save the earth from the cataclysms that now seem to be threatening us. That technology, if you will, is coherence—it is the energy of love. This is no longer something that can be dismissed as a pseudoreligious burst of wishful thinking to be lambasted by skeptics—it is an active, working presence that we could call the Source Field. The next stop in our investigation will reveal the stunning proof that Time is a Source Field phenomenon as well—and can also be modified by various energetic processes. We will also explore compelling new evidence that some people considered everything in this book to be common knowledge—and left us all the blueprints to reconstruct their lost science. This includes the ability to create pyramids out of giant blocks of stone, as well as the understanding of how and why they work.

PART TWO

TIME AND SPACE

CHAPTER ELEVEN

It's About Time

The Source Field investigations give us hard scientific proof that nonelectromagnetic Universal Energy can affect how we think, how fast we heal, and even the structure and function of our own DNA. Existing species can be transformed into entirely new creatures by strictly energetic means. This appears to be already happening in our own human evolution, making the ancient prophecies of a coming Golden Age all the more interesting. The 25,920-year cycle is not just a number written into ancient myths and the dimensions of the Great Pyramid—it is a physical, measurable wobble in the earth itself. This suggests that the movements of the earth—and the other planets—may be directly affecting the behavior of our minds and bodies in time.

In order to find out if time can be measured, experienced and even driven by the energy we move through—even if it is not visible to the naked eye—we may have to throw away some of our deepest and most basic assumptions about what time really is. Once we do that, it may all very well make perfect sense . . . on a physical, mathematical and logical level.

Russian physicist Professor Simon Shnoll made truly civilization-changing discoveries by studying a "wide range of physical, chemical, and biological processes, from radioactive decay to the rates of biochemical reactions" for well over twenty years.[1] This may sound dreadfully boring, but it ultimately means Shnoll studied the behavior of every single atom and energy wave on earth, looking for any common patterns in how they were behaving—and when. What happens at the molecular level when you heat up water and turn it into steam? What happens when water freezes into ice? What happens when you mix two chemicals together? What happens when the cells in your body exchange information and nutrition with each other? What happens when radioactive isotopes slowly release energy? What happens to a burst of electricity as it flows through a conductor? These are very basic questions, and it's all about "how stuff works."

Most scientists expect that all physical, chemical, biological and radioactive processes will start small, steadily build up to a nice peak, and then glide nicely back down to zero—in a path that looks the same going down as it did going up. Any time the graph doesn't fit into a smooth bell curve like this, scientists are trained to throw the data away—by a simple process they call renormalization.

Professor Shnoll decided not to throw the data away. It's easy to understand why, because he found the graphs were not normal at all—they were very unusual. Sometimes these reactions would race up to maximum intensity, then plummet almost all the way back down to zero. Then, just as quickly, they would rush all the way back up to the peak again. They may even do this three times in a row over a short period of time. That's not a smooth flow at all. How can matter or energy even stay stable if it's actually doing this all the time?

Just go take a walk—and think about how many physical, chemical and biological reactions there are. Electricity is humming along through the power lines. Sunlight is striking the paint on everything around you and gradually bleaching it out. The leaves on the trees convert that sunlight into food. Running water dissolves salt crystals in the soil. Birds digest the seeds they peck off the ground. The dry glue from a postage stamp turns into a weird-tasting goo on your tongue as you walk up to your mailbox to drop in a letter. There are trillions of these various reactions going on—just within the area your eyes can see. Shnoll found that every single atom and energy wave around you is doing the same weird things at the same time—racing forward and backward in very specific patterns. These patterns are almost as unique as a fingerprint. We'll get back to why I said almost in a minute.

Did you have any idea that the untold trillions of atoms and energy pulses that are surrounding you right now are constantly rushing through this on-off, on-off behavior at the tiniest level? That they are not having nice, smooth, normal reactions, but instead are constantly jumping back and forth in fits and starts? You're not alone—hardly anyone knows about it, as Shnoll's research is still almost completely obscure in both scientific and spiritual circles—even though he published his findings in Russian scientific journals since at least 1985. Again, the most amazing part of the story is that everything around us works perfectly, despite the fact that the reactions themselves are switching on and off, on and off . . . all the time. Though this may seem like a gross leap in logic, it's almost as if energy waves and molecular reactions were behaving like they were made up of individual frames within a strip of film— flickering in and out of our reality all the time.

Perhaps the film only appears to be moving forward, creating the world we see all around us—but it's really just a collection of still frames. Either way, the "lucid dream," if that's what we're all really experiencing in some sense, is a very convincing illusion. Matter and energy move along just fine, regardless of how strangely they may be acting down at the quantum level. We never worry about whether our chair will suddenly dematerialize as we read this book.

All this is just the setup for the really good stuff. Let's say you mix two chemicals together, and chart out the unique zigzagging graph they make as they react. Now you have a friend in a lab, thousands of kilometers away, who graphs the flow of radioactive energy decay at the exact same time—and he sends his chart to you. Naturally we would expect that when you compare these two charts side by side, they would have absolutely nothing in common. If they did look the same, then that defeats everything we thought we knew about mainstream science . . . but in the process, we may just discover an even deeper layer of the Source Field investigations.

By the year 1985, Shnoll had discovered that any physical, chemical, biological or radioactive reactions do look the same, if you graph them out at the same time—even when they were measured in areas that were thousands of kilometers apart.[2] Since distance does not appear to pose any barrier to this effect, it appears to be a worldwide phenomenon. This would mean that every single atom, every single molecule and every burst of energy on earth is going through the exact same hiccups at the same time—at the very tiny, or quantum, level. This is obviously not the science we were taught to believe in school. These reactions are supposed to be separate and totally disconnected from each other—but they are not. Western quantum physicists do not appear to know about Shnoll's findings yet, though some of their discoveries lead us in this same direction.

So what are the hiccups that are happening in matter and energy? How could we possibly explain something like this? Professor Shnoll isn't sure, but he believes that "a global change of space-time structure" could be causing it.[3]

In the simplest possible terms, this means that time itself is speeding up and slowing down at the quantum level. And this is apparently happening all over the world, in the same way, at the same time. Space and time itself is doing this bizarre dance, on a level at least as massive as the entire earth—since we're all being affected by it. This creates distinctly measurable quantum effects—and yet somehow we continue to enjoy a nice, neat and linear experience of time.

Remember—no matter how weird the graphs look, everything works fine. This flickering does not appear to have any detrimental effect on how energy flows, or how chemicals react. In fact, thanks to Einstein's breakthrough discoveries, we know that if you could transport yourself down into the quantum level, and ride around in a tiny spaceship, your clock would appear to move along just fine—no matter how much time was rushing forward and backward all around you. The trick is that whatever happens to you will also happen to your clock—so within your own "frame of reference," you can't tell that anything is going on. The apparently smooth flow of time may well be little more than a psychological experience that keeps us from having severe mental disorientation. If these same quantum effects are somehow happening to us on a

large-scale level as well, and we just don't realize it yet, then from another
vantage point outside our own time flow, we would appear to be frozen
in place one minute and moving around really quickly the next.

Large-Scale Changes in the Flow of Time

As bizarre as this must sound, some people appear to have developed
technologies that use these principles on a scale much larger than the
quantum world. As reported in a 1977 issue of the *Vancouver Sun Times,*
Toronto inventor Sid Hurwich apparently discovered a way to change
the flow of time in a given "local" area—by a technological process.[4]
Given the remarkably weird effects that would occur when he used the
device, Hurwich realized his invention could have practical value—after
a rash of bank robberies in 1969.

Hurwich was friends with the police, and called a group of bank
security staff and officers over to his house one night to demonstrate his
new invention. The *Sun Times* article quoted the eyewitness testimony of
Inspector Bill Bolton.

> "All I can recall," says Bolton, "is that it was under the
> table—the device, whatever it was—and there was a bed-
> spread over the table. He froze my service revolver. You
> couldn't pull the trigger, you couldn't lift it up off the table
> and even on the table, you couldn't pull the trigger." Hurwich
> continues: "And then I said, 'Now take a look at your watches.'
> I remember one of them said, 'When did this happen?' and I
> said, 'The minute you walked through that door. You walked
> in there about 25 minutes ago. Now look at your watches.
> You're late about 25 minutes.' As the security officers filed out
> of his home, Hurwich's wife overheard one of them suggest
> that the army should be told about the device. "That was the
> first time it ever entered my mind for war or army purposes
> or anything like that," Hurwich says. He went back to work
> in his basement. When he felt the device was ready, he

contacted a brother living in Israel . . . Hurwich received a
visit shortly afterward from two high-ranking Israeli officers.
After a brief demonstration, they walked out with the working model, and every plan and design Hurwich had."[5]

Imagine the defense implications of a technology like this. The
December 1977 article also alleges that earlier that June, Hurwich was
given the "Protectors of the State of Israel [award] on behalf of the Zion-
ist Organization of Canada for a secret military device he had given
Israel seven years earlier."[6] To me, the most interesting part of the article
was this: "Hurwich insists his device is not really an invention. He says
he simply 'took one of the oldest BASIC principles of electricity and put
it to a different use.'[7] How is it possible that the police couldn't pull the
trigger on their revolvers—or even pick them up off the table? Again,
this forces us to think in an entirely new way, which most people would
consider to be pure science fiction. As crazy as this may sound, one explanation is that time was flowing so slowly in the world around them that
any attempt to move the weapon may have taken place within mere
microseconds of normal time. The pressure they put on the gun may
have seemed perfectly normal to them, but may not have lasted long
enough in conventional time to overcome the normal inertia that would
keep the weapon sitting on the table. In their own frame of reference,
everything appeared to be normal—but when they checked their
watches, they were in for quite a surprise. They may have had to push on
the gun for quite some time in order to get it to move at all, since conventional time had hardly changed in what they and their watches measured as twenty-five minutes.

It's All Relative

This, of course, naturally offends our rational mind. We automatically
take it for granted that linear time is nice and stable. We are conditioned
to believe there is no evidence that the rate of time could speed up or
slow down. We believe it is a scientific fact that time must move forward

at a constant speed. If you still think this is true, then you might want to check out Albert Einstein. According to *Discover* magazine, "The trouble with time started a century ago, when Einstein's special and general theories of relativity demolished the idea of time as a universal constant."[8]

What exactly does this mean? Einstein predicted that when you move through space, you're not simply moving through something that is empty and has no effect on you. Instead, as you move through space, you move through time as well. Ultimately, that means that time doesn't just happen on its own, as if by magic. Time is actually being powered by some form of energy, or what's called a fabric, that exists throughout all of space. The faster we move through space, the faster we move through time. This was actually proven by Hafele and Keating in October 1971. They flew four atomic clocks on commercial jet flights around the world, both east and west, and compared them to clocks at the U.S. Naval Observatory in Washington, D.C. The flying clocks were predicted to lose about 40 nanoseconds going east, and gain 275 nanoseconds going west. And believe it or not, it worked—within about 90 percent of what they expected.[9] Further experiments in 1976 proved it worked to within 99 percent of Einstein's original predictions.[10]

Would we experience any time at all if the earth were not moving? Maybe not. There are a variety of movements all happening at the same time that we have to think about. The earth rotates on its own axis and revolves around the Sun. There are longer-term cycles in the earth as well, including the 25,920-year precession. The Sun revolves around the center of the galaxy in about 250 million years, and the galaxy is also moving toward the so-called Great Attractor—a giant zone of gravitational pull in the constellation Virgo. All of these movements drive us through what Einstein called "space-time," and what I prefer to call the Source Field—the basic stuff the Universe is made of. Since we are moving along at a constant speed, more or less, our experience of time remains stable and consistent.

However, Einstein also concluded that once you begin traveling near the speed of light, you are now traveling through time much faster than everyone else back on earth. You could take a simple two-week trip away from the earth and back, at near–light speed, only to find out that five hundred years had gone by on earth while you were gone, let's say. If you could somehow beam a television signal back to the earth from inside your ship, then as soon as you started traveling near light speed, you would appear completely frozen to everyone who was watching you.

This is not speculation, crackpot science or foolishness—this is a commonly accepted fact within modern physics. Hurwich appears to have discovered a way to accelerate the flow of time like this in a local area. Of course, mainstream science would strongly disagree with these amazing new concepts I'm sharing with you. This started back in 1910, when Einstein rejected the idea that empty space actually had any actual energy in it, which most scientists of his day called "aether." Einstein's space-time was more of an abstract mathematical concept at that time; he didn't expect to see any actual energy appearing in space. This is still what almost all Western scientists believe—namely, that Einstein completely ruled out the idea that there is an aether of energy out there in empty space. A typical attitude is expressed in Robert Youngson's *Scientific Blunders:* "By 1930, younger physicists would smile in a supercilious fashion at any reference to the aether. All scientists now agree that, in the words of the American homespun philosopher: 'There ain't no such critter.'"[11]

All scientists now agree there is no aether in space? Then apparently Einstein is not a scientist. You see, by 1918, Einstein contradicted his earlier opinion.

> [Any] part of space without matter and without electromagnetic fields seems to be completely empty. . . . [But,] according to the general theory of relativity, even space that is empty in this sense has physical properties. This . . . can be easily understood by speaking about an ether, whose state varies continuously from point to point.[12]

In 1920, Einstein said it even more strongly.

> According to the general theory of relativity, space without ether is unthinkable; for in such space, not only would

there be no propagation of light, but also no . . . space-time intervals in the physical sense.[13]

What Einstein is saying here is that without some sort of aether in space, there could be no "time intervals" as we now know them. Our clocks would appear to be completely frozen—if their atoms could even hold together at all. Thus, in Einstein's own words, time is powered by an energy in space. And this energy is not all smooth and even wherever you go—it "varies continuously from point to point." The more space we move through, the more of this time energy we move through. And depending on how fast we go, the rate of time will speed up or slow down along the way. If we can accelerate the flow of this energy in a given local area, then we may well be able to create effects similar to those allegedly discovered by Sid Hurwich. Unfortunately, no additional information on Hurwich or his discoveries can be found. Most likely, he was either paid very well, ordered to keep his mouth shut, or permanently silenced.

Repeating Cycles of Time

If time is an energy in space that we move through, then how can we be so sure it only travels forward—into what we think of as the future? Einstein assumed that time is one-dimensional, meaning it can only move forward—in a single, straight line. That may have been his single biggest mistake. Is it possible that when the earth returns to the same orbital position it had been in before, relative to the Sun, that it could be returning to an area of time—a structured region within the Source Field—that has similar properties and influences as it had before?

That's exactly what Professor Shnoll discovered. Graph out any physical, chemical, biological or radioactive reaction and study the fingerprint you get from it. Now come back exactly one rotation of the earth—twenty-four hours—later . . . and your graph will be almost identical to the one you saw twenty-four hours before. Then check again one year later—and a very similar fingerprint again shows up.

This means that the forward-and-backward racing movement of time that Shnoll discovered is not random or haphazard. Though we don't yet know exactly why the graphs race forward and backward the way they do, we do know that the patterns repeat themselves according to the earth's basic cycles. In short, every molecule on earth, down at the quantum level, is somehow being directly affected by the earth's movement through space—in repeating patterns. If this is really true, then we have to rewrite almost every scientific law we now take for granted. We're already well on our way, thanks to our ancient inheritance—so I say let's go for it.

Professor Shnoll found these repeating patterns in the following intervals: "at approximately 24 hours, at 27.28 days [the Moon's orbit around the earth's relative to the center of the galaxy] . . . and at three time intervals close to a year: 364.4, 365.2 and 366.6 days."[14] The earth takes 365.2422 days to revolve around the Sun, and one of Shnoll's cycles was 365.2 days—so it's a very, very close fit.

Shnoll obviously didn't have enough data to witness these cycles unfolding over much longer periods of time—like the 25,920-year precession of the equinoxes. All he did was study the behavior of matter and energy, and found it was doing very strange things—and these patterns repeated in cycles. Further research is necessary to see if the movements of the other planets also create the same effects Shnoll discovered, but it seems very foolish to think it would only work with the earth and the Moon. The flow of time is likely getting pushed and pulled by the movements of the earth, the Moon and the planets in reliable, consistent ways that will repeat, nicely and neatly, from one orbital cycle to the next.

Once we bring in the evidence from chapters 9 and 10, we realize that time may have cyclical effects. Time appears to have structure in it, and that structure in turn influences the biological cycles discovered by Burr and Popp, as well as our conscious minds—as we're now seeing with the Flynn Effect and human evolution as we head toward the end of the 25,920-year cycle. These time cycles may not be arbitrary—some are directly related to the earth's movements through space. Now, thanks to the work of Professor Shnoll, we're seeing that this structure in time is actually affecting the basic behavior of physical matter.

Space and Time

Skeptics might say that Shnoll's discoveries are just "statistical noise," and have no real relevance to our large-scale world. Or, they may write it off as some interesting, little-known new effect in quantum physics. Maybe in another twenty-two years, enough scientists will believe Shnoll that his discovery is then taught in schools. Either way, any reputable scientist would expect that if all atoms, molecules and energy waves on earth were speeding up and slowing down, then we would need to see it happening to normal-size objects as well—speeding up or slowing down as they travel through space.

It is common knowledge that satellite probes we've sent out into deep space are doing just that—slowing down—even though they're not supposed to. Gravity should get weaker, not stronger, as we head out of the solar system. In 2001, David Whitehouse of BBC News reported that four different space probes were slowing down, including Pioneer 10 and Pioneer 11—which are on opposite ends of the solar system. This also included Galileo as it sped out to Jupiter, and Ulysses as it orbited the Sun. Dr. John Anderson from NASA's JPL said, "It is almost as if the probes were not behaving according to the known law of gravity. . . . We've been working on this problem for several years, and we have accounted for everything we could think of."[15]

The plot thickened in 2008, when the same NASA scientist added three more space probes to the puzzle—bringing it up to a total of seven. Galileo was again mentioned, but we also learned that the NEAR mission to the asteroid Eros, the Cassini mission to Saturn and the Rosetta mission to rendezvous with a comet all experienced changes in their traveling speed that could not be explained. In this case, as each of them flew past the earth in order to pick up speed for their trips into space, they would either slow down or speed up—depending on the direction they were traveling in. Dr. Anderson, now working as a retiree, said, "I am feeling both humble and perplexed by this. . . . There is something very strange going on with spacecraft motions. We have no convincing explanation for either the Pioneer anomaly or the flyby anomaly."[16]

As one example, NEAR came toward the earth at 20 degrees South latitude and flew away at 72 degrees South. This path caused it to fly 13 millimeters faster, per second, than it was supposed to. That might not seem like very much, but it was definitely real—the effect could be studied with extreme precision. NASA bounced radio waves off of the probe and could measure its speed with an accuracy of zero point one millimeters per second—so a 13-millimeter change was easy to spot.

Does this mean that space probes always speed up or slow down as they swing around the earth? Strangely not. The Messenger space probe made one pass that was symmetrical—coming in at about 31 degrees North latitude, and leaving at 32 degrees South. In that case, its speed hardly changed at all. Dr. Anderson found that the more a space probe angled away from the earth's equator as it passed by, the more its speed would change—and the more it made a nice, even path around the earth's equator like with Messenger, the less its speed changed. This led Dr. Anderson to conclude that the movement of the earth must somehow be responsible for causing these changes in how fast the space probes are traveling—but no one seems to know why this is happening.[17] This is not something you can explain with Einstein's theories of relativity as they now stand—but they are definitely a great start.

Even if this is nothing more than a mysterious gravitational effect, (although NASA said this is not explainable by any conventional means), it would still force us to rewrite the laws of physics. Then again, what if it has nothing to do with gravity? What if the flow of time itself is actually slowing down or speeding up?

In Einstein's model, time isn't expected to speed up or slow down in a given area of empty space, at least not by very much—it should essentially move at the same speed wherever you go, other than a black hole. It's really only how fast you travel through space that determines the rate of time. The Pioneer and Flyby anomalies are different from that—because they actually suggest that the rate of time can change in a given local area. And when we bring in Shnoll, we have stunning new evidence that this is happening all the time, and we just didn't know about it before. When our satellites speed up or slow down as they pass by the earth, we're only looking at a change of 13 millimeters per second—which is only one-millionth of their normal traveling speed—so it is a subtle effect that was easily missed for many years.

The rotation of the earth appears to be creating a ripple in the flow of time—almost like a lawn sprinkler spraying out time flow as the earth spins, caused by the movement of what we are calling the Source Field. What if the Sun's energy could also give a nice little push to the flow of time—not a huge amount, but more like the 13 millimeters per second we saw with our space probes? If true, this would be most likely visible when the Sun's energetic activity suddenly peaked. Based on the world-wide changes Shnoll observed, we may discover that every atom and every energy wave on earth would be affected by the Sun's behavior. And furthermore, since our brains are electrical systems, perhaps a sudden, unexpected hiccup in the flow of time would cause some disruptions in our brain wave patterns as well—which might make us feel uncomfortable, stressed out and overly emotional. If so, that might lead to outbreaks of war, violence and economic collapse.

Solar Cycles and Consciousness Effects

Enter A. L. Tchijevsky, a Russian scientist in the early twentieth century. Tchijevsky created an "Index of Mass Human Excitability" to study how chaotic and turbulent life on earth was in seventy-two different countries, for almost 2,500 years—from 500 B.C. to A.D. 1922. He looked for any obvious signals that people were really unhappy, such as wars, revolutions, riots, economic upsets, expeditions and migrations. He also ranked how severe these events were by how many people were involved. To his amazement, "Tchijevsky found that fully 80 percent of the most significant events occurred during the 5 years of maximum sunspot activity."[18] The sunspot cycle does not always run in an eleven-year interval—sometimes it comes sooner, sometimes later. Nonetheless, whenever solar activity was at its maximum, a whopping 80 percent of all the most negative events took place.

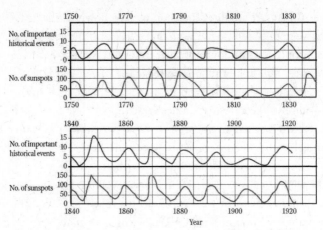

The Institute of HeartMath's reconstruction of Tchijevsky's discovery of a precise relationship between solar activity and civil unrest.

Sadly, Tchijevsky served thirty years in Soviet prisons for merely pointing out that the Russian Revolution of 1917 occurred during the height of the sunspot cycle. The Communists were adamant in their belief that there is no God. The last thing they wanted was to be accused of creating their revolution right when the Sun's activity was influencing them into doing it.

Now think back to what we learned in chapter 5. Seven thousand people were able to reduce worldwide terrorism by 72 percent, simply by meditating. They also reduced random acts of violence, deaths and hostilities between nations. With Shnoll, we discovered that the movement of our planet around the Sun affects every atom on earth in very measurable ways. Now with Tchijevsky, we see that solar activity has a direct effect on how we feel. As the Sun's activity increases, we feel an increasing sense of stress—and violence breaks out all over the world. As the Sun's activity decreases, we recover from the stress—and only 20 percent of the most negative events take place. This effect held true for the entire 2,500-year length of time that Tchijevsky studied.

If our model is correct, then we can assume that these changes in solar activity would also create changes in the flow of time. This, in turn, could interrupt the normally smooth flow of our brain wave patterns, causing us to feel uncomfortable without really knowing why. It would be very difficult for us to measure any changes in the flow of time with clocks based on earth, as they would also speed up or slow down at the same rate as the flow of time itself. However, we could check the speed of the earth's rotation, because the Sun is at a fixed position in the sky— so we have something stable, which is outside the earth, to compare it to.

Interplanetary Changes in the Flow of Time

In 1959, there was a huge solar storm—and the earth's rotation slowed down at the exact same time. This made the length of a typical day suddenly increase. Then an even greater storm occurred in August 1972— and according to John Gribbin and NASA scientist Stephen Plagemann in the prestigious journal *Nature*, "We have indeed found a discontinuous change in the length of day . . . immediately after that event."[19] The earth "hiccupped" in its orbit during a massive solar storm. Indeed, many scientists have found clear connections between solar activity and the length of the day.[20] In fact, there is a perfect relationship between the amount of solar activity and the speed of the earth's rotation throughout "much of the last forty years of the twentieth century"[21]—from 1960 onward. Bear in mind that 1950 was the first year that we had really good data to track the exact length of a day, and prior to 1920 the available data is even worse.[22] Solar activity also changes the speed that our atmosphere is traveling around the earth—though there is a delay between the solar activity and the resulting change in the overall speed of the atmosphere.[23] According to Djurovic in 1990, "The physical mechanism of these phenomena is still unknown."[24]

Another possible example of a change in the flow of time occurs when the planet Mercury starts moving backward, or retrograde, in its path through our night sky. Almost every astrologer will tell you from personal and professional experience that during this time, mechanical devices seem more likely to break down—perhaps because of disruptions in the flow of electricity—and people seem more likely to get into arguments with each other and have problems erupt. Even mainstream media outlets like *Wired* magazine[25] and CNet[26] have commented on this curious phenomenon, thanks to the brave journalism of Daniel Terdiman. Now that we know about Professor Shnoll's work, we can speculate about whether the flow of time itself gets disrupted when planets go into retrograde movement.

In August 2010, researchers from Stanford and Purdue universities added even more new data to the mix. These scientists were studying the decay rates of radioactive materials, just like Shnoll had done. As far as they knew, these rates were supposed to be constant and unchanging—but that's not what happened. Instead, they found some new variations on what Shnoll had already been tracking for years.

> Decay rates would slightly decrease during the summer and increase during the winter. Experimental error and environmental conditions have all been ruled out. . . . And there seems to be only one answer. As the earth is closer to the sun during the winter months in the Northern Hemisphere (our planet's orbit is slightly eccentric, or elongated), could the sun be influencing decay rates? In another moment of weirdness, Purdue nuclear engineer Jere Jenkins noticed an inexplicable drop in the decay rate of manganese-54 when he was testing it one night in 2006. It so happened that this drop occurred just over a day before a large flare erupted on the sun. . . . The sun link was made even stronger when Peter Sturrock, Stanford professor emeritus of applied physics, suggested that the Purdue scientists look for other recurring patterns in decay rates. As an expert of the inner workings of the sun, Sturrock had a hunch that solar neutrinos might hold the key to this mystery. Sure enough, the researchers noticed the decay rates vary repeatedly every 33 days—a period of time that matches the rotational period of the core of the sun.[27]

These changes in solar activity not only seem to alter the flow of time—they also accelerate the amount of negative events happening, or what Tchijevsky called "Human Excitability." Would it also have a similar effect on the strength of our intuitive and psychic abilities? Dr. James Spottiswoode studied twenty years' worth of solid, scientific research into "anomalous cognition," where ordinary people were tested to see how psychic they were. After exploring fifty-one different studies conducted from 1976 to 1996, which added up to a total of 2,879 different individual trials, he found that solar activity had a clear and measurable influence on our psychic ability.[28] In general, the more solar activity there was, the less effective we were in these "anomalous cognition" tests.

Now we have the strong suggestion that a burst of energy from the Sun can slow down time. The earth then rotates more slowly—though no one seems to understand why. This may also create stress in the human mind, by disrupting the electrical activity in our synapses—the level of coherence in our minds. This shock to the brain could lead to an increase in violence, war and unrest. When the Sun was calm, only 20 percent of these "Human Excitability" events took place—throughout the last 2,500 years. It may be that when the flow of time becomes smoother, the coherence increases. Our brain waves mellow out, and everyone gets along better with each other. This smoothing-out of our brain wave patterns may also help us go into deeper states of consciousness—thus increasing our performance on "anomalous cognition" tests.

Human Consciousness Changing the Flow of Time

If these cycles can push against us, and change the way we behave, then can we also push back? If high solar activity makes the flow of time more choppy, creating disruptions that slow down time, and low solar activity makes the flow of time smoother, then can we affect the flow of time as well? If everyone on earth was suddenly shocked by a negative event, would that cause a sudden flickering in the passage of time—disrupting coherence on a worldwide level? And if enough of us meditate, could we smooth out the flow of time—in a way that Shnoll would be able to concretely measure in his laboratory?

This brings us to Dr. Roger Nelson's work with the Global Consciousness Project. Beginning in 1979, Dr. Robert Jahn started the Princeton Engineering Anomalies Research laboratory to study "whether
sensitive electronic devices . . . might be affected by special states of
consciousness, including strong emotions and directed intention."[29]
Dr. Roger Nelson joined the team in 1980, and ultimately became the
main force behind this research. Early along, Jahn and Nelson decided
to see if the human mind could create any sort of measurable effect on
"a well-developed commercial source of electronic white noise."[30] Shnoll
was studying the flow of electricity as well, as one of his physical
reactions—so now we have two different groups looking at the same
thing.

Jahn and Nelson wanted to turn that electrical noise into numbers
they could graph out and measure. That way, if a person could actually
affect the flow of electricity in some way, they could prove it mathematically. They decided the best way to do this was to create a random-
number generator. This measures how smoothly electricity is flowing
through a circuit: Any hiccups in the flow of electricity will create regular patterns in the numbers it generates. Once we see a pattern, the numbers aren't as random anymore. Of course, in conventional science, time
isn't supposed to slow down and speed up as electricity moves along.
However, if time did start slowing down and speeding up within a random electrical circuit, then the numbers would indeed begin developing
patterns—which you could then measure and graph out. Shnoll was also
looking for these exact sorts of patterns in physical, chemical, biological
and radioactive reactions—but he never expected to find effects that
could be caused by the human mind.

Over the years, Dr. Nelson used three different kinds of random-
number generators that are either based on "thermal noise"—the natural
rise and fall of temperature within an electrical circuit—or "electron
tunneling," which is the flow of electrons through tiny pathways, such
as what we find in a computer chip. The circuits were carefully shielded
off so they could not be influenced by external electromagnetic fields or
temperature changes, and he also insured that the aging of the components could not be a factor either. According to Nelson, "Over more than

a decade, this basic experiment yielded an enormous database—with a bottom line indicating a small but significant effect of human intention on [these] random data sequences."[31]

To put it plainly, Nelson found that ordinary people like you and me, particularly in larger groups, could actually change the numbers that came out of the computers—and create "patterns in chaos."[32] As Nelson said in a 2008 paper,

> For example, we took the REG [Random Event Genera-
> tor], connected to a laptop or palmtop computer, to concerts,
> rituals, religious ceremonies, sporting events, board meetings,
> and various other events that might create a state of "group
> consciousness" . . . over several years we accumulated more
> than 100 datasets from "resonant" situations, and a smaller but
> substantial number of "mundane" locations [such as shopping
> centers, busy street corners and academic meetings]. . . . In a
> nutshell . . . the largest or most reliable effects seem to involve
> ritual, or some other influence that is designed to bring people
> to a shared state of mind.[33]

A Global Consciousness

In 1995, two different random-number generators, twelve miles apart, showed a measurable change during the exact time that millions of peo-ple were watching the Academy Awards on television.[34] Dr. Dean Radin found strong spikes at the most critical moments of the O. J. Simpson trial in 1997, across five different REGs in five separate locations—and this was one of the most highly watched events in television history.[35] During Princess Diana's funeral in 1998, twelve different REGs in the United States and Europe also showed "statistically significant depar-tures" from the normal levels "at the most critical or poignant times."[36]

In late 1997, they began building a worldwide network that could run twenty-four hours a day, seven days a week, to look for these patterns. All this data was transferred by the Internet to a central location at

Princeton University where it could be analyzed. By the year 2001, the Global Consciousness Project had expanded to the point where there were thirty-seven computers around the world generating these numbers, twenty-four hours a day, seven days a week. Right as 9/11 started happening, and the news began spreading across the world, they got results.

> We find that over a period of 3 months, one date is associated with a statistical anomaly: September 11, 2001. On this date, the time range appearing most often [among the 37 computers] is 6 AM—10 AM, peaking around 9:00—10:00 AM, and the location primarily the East Coast of the USA.[37]

Indeed, the closer the computers were to New York, the stronger the effect. A score this high would only occur about once in a million seconds by random chance alone, which is roughly a two-week period. According to Dr. Dean Radin in 2001, "These effects are the most strikingly persuasive evidence I've seen so far that mass-mind attention/intention affects the physical world—perhaps because this event has also been the most horrific."[38]

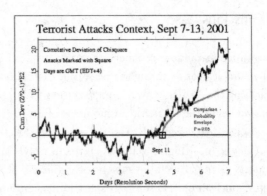

The Global Consciousness Project discovered that random-number generators display curious patterns of order that emerge during major, worldwide events.

Science is about prediction. You can't just sit there and wait for things to happen, and then analyze them afterward. In this case, when a major event is coming up in the world, you write down what you expect will happen in advance, and then see if your prediction comes true. As of 2008, Nelson reported that they had picked out "over 250 rigorously vetted, pre-specified events" ahead of time, so they could indeed predict whether something might happen—rather than just looking for "spikes in the data" like 9/11, and analyzing them afterward. These 250 events included "tragedies and celebrations, natural and human caused disasters, [and] planned and spontaneous gatherings of great numbers." In each of these 250 cases, a noticeable worldwide effect occurred—creating what they called "moments of global consciousness." The odds that all 250 of these events could have been caused by something other than our collective consciousness were calculated at ten million to one.[39]

Let's go back to September 11, 2001—the most striking effect they had ever observed at the time. If thirty-seven different computers all over the world recorded a noticeable change that peaked between nine and ten A.M., then that implies that every power line, every electrical circuit worldwide was experiencing a hiccup during this time—somehow caused by our global unrest. Now we're right back to Shnoll's effects again—except that this time, we are causing the same things to happen by our own collective consciousness.

If the combined power of our thoughts can create measurable effects in random-number generators all over the world, creating flickers in the flow of electricity, what about the earth's magnetic field? Geologist Gregg Braden revealed these effects in his book *Fractal Time*.

> In September 2001, two geosynchronous operational environmental satellites (GOES) orbiting the earth detected a rise in the magnetic field of the earth that forever changed the way scientists view our world and us. The GOES 8 and GOES 10 each showed a powerful spike of earth's magnetic field strength . . . that topped out at nearly 50 units (nano-Teslas) higher than any that had been typical for the same time previously. The time was 9:00 A.M. Eastern standard time;

15 minutes after the first plane hit the World Trade Center and about 15 minutes before the second impact. The correlation between the events and the readings was undeniable.[40]

On September 14, 2001, there was a worldwide prayer for peace that involved many beloved public figures, and was broadcast on all major television stations around the world. Millions and millions of people participated in this global meditation. Amazingly, during this exact time, the graphs showed a huge effect in the opposite direction from where they went in 9/11.

> On the 14th of September, there was a special emphasis on such collective spiritual moments, including major organized periods of silence in Europe and America. . . . The picture is compelling . . . the trend shows a marginally significant decrease . . . steadily opposite to the [usual] direction.[41]

This clearly implies that we can push the flow in both directions— either into more chaos and flickering in the case of a great tragedy, or greater coherence in the case of a worldwide prayer vigil for peace. When we are at peace, the randomness of the computer circuits becomes even more perfect—perhaps because the flow of electricity is much smoother and more coherent than usual. These effects are completely consistent with the Source Field data we've discovered in previous chapters, including the Russian pyramid studies.

When Obama won the 2008 presidential election, the electrical effects were at least as strong as 9/11—if not stronger: "The figure speaks for itself . . . it appears that the election shows at least as strong an effect as the terror attacks."[42] When Obama was inaugurated, millions of people focused their attention on thoughts of peace—and once again, the graphs decreased substantially, just like they did in the worldwide peace meditation of September 14, 2001.

> The result is graphically quite striking, with no trend for the first 4 hours of the period, then a very steady trend

showing smaller than expected network variance [i.e., network change] for about 12 hours. . . . [These decreases in] network variance [are] often associated with occasions that are meditative and celebratory.[43]

Dr. Nelson made formal predictions for seventeen different global meditations and found a "strong positive effect," saying that "overall, the odds against such a persistent departure from expectation are about 300 to 1."[44] Brian Williams later added in an additional thirty-nine global meditations to the original body of data they were studying, and although the effect was somewhat smaller, it was still there: "the result remains consistent with the hypothesis of a positive significant effect."[45]

My friend Dr. Claude Swanson, an MIT graduate and former applied-physics consultant for a variety of government, military and private corporations, summed it up very nicely in his excellent book *The Synchronized Universe.*

> Our Western culture has taught us that thoughts don't matter. If each one of us goes around each day carrying anger and resentment, the Western belief is that it has no direct effect on the world. As long as we refrain from overt violent actions, the present belief is that no harm will be done to others. But in view of the present evidence, this can no longer be maintained. We are truly tied to one another, and even our thoughts affect one another. James Twyman has led several worldwide synchronized group prayers for peace. Those prayers had measurable effects, and even altered the physics of the quantum background and the level of chaos worldwide for a time [as discovered in the Global Consciousness Project.] . . . He observes the following: ". . . conflict in the world is the result of conflict within us. We project that feeling into the world because we are not ready to accept that we are the cause, and therefore the solution, to that conflict. Thus wars have raged in the world since the beginning of time, because we are not ready to deal with the conflict where it really is—within us."[46]

CHAPTER TWELVE

The Gravity of the Source Field

I n life, afterlife and reincarnation, we have a continuing consciousness that is unified with the greater Mind of this Cosmos. Pyramid technology appears to have been built to concentrate this intelligent Source Field energy for biological, psychological and even spiritual healing. Thanks to the Global Consciousness Project, we now have compelling evidence that our own minds can also create a direct, measurable effect on how electricity flows throughout wires, components and computer chips all over the world. It appears that in moments of great tragedy, or times when many of us focus on the same event, our minds create worldwide hiccups in the flow of energy. Our thoughts do seem to create an energy that directly affects the behavior of others.

Einstein was ultimately looking for a unified field that he could build the entire Universe from—all space, all time, all matter, all energy, all life, and of course all of consciousness. In the famous "E equals mc squared" equation, you have Energy on one side and Matter on the other—which means that Matter must ultimately be made of Energy. Einstein hoped to prove that electromagnetic energy was the unified field—which would mean that the flow of time, as well as gravity, was an electromagnetic effect. He was never able to prove this was true—nor has anyone else since then. Einstein did, however, acknowledge that there had to be an energy in empty space that could make time speed up or slow down—depending on how fast you moved through it. Indeed, many scientists are looking for the unified field, and they have created a variety of different names for it: zero-point energy, virtual particles, quantum foam, dark matter, dark energy, and others. If anyone does solve the puzzle, the payoff is huge—as once you understand how to access the unified field, you could theoretically control gravity and time. The Source Field we've already talked about seems to fit these concepts perfectly—we just have to learn to think in an entirely new and unexpected way.

If there is a unified field—and most physicists are convinced there must be—it would automatically, by design, be responsible for creating all matter in the Universe. We're not just looking at an energy that drives the flow of time—we're looking at the Source of all space, time, matter, energy and life in the Universe. It does not appear that the Source Field created the Universe in a single, spontaneous Big Bang, in which all atoms then keep on running for infinity—with no new energy input. By design, the Source Field is actively responsible for keeping matter going—moment by moment.

Scientists normally assume that atoms and molecules will just keep on spinning and spinning forever, without ever running out of energy. Dr. Hal Puthoff[1] suggested they must be drawing off of an energy field in order to exist—just like a candle flame must burn oxygen and wax in order to stay lit. Since most single atoms are nice, round spheres, the Source Field will flow into atoms equally from all directions. The flow into the earth would obviously behave the same way. We would see a spherical current of Source Field energy flowing into it, moment by moment, to keep all the countless atoms and molecules that make up the earth humming along. The Source Field also needs to flow into all living creatures on earth. We now have seen very strong evidence that all life-forms on earth must continually absorb photons of light, and store them in their DNA in order to survive. The Source Field apparently creates these virtual photons when there is rotating, vortex movement within the field itself. For biological life, the most important frequency is 380 nanometers. If this frequency gets scrambled, our DNA can't absorb and store the light it needs—and we develop cancer.

It appears that gravity is actually caused by a massive current of energy flowing into the earth. The earth is obviously made of atoms, and my friend and colleague Dr. Nassim Haramein made a strong argument that atoms are gravity-powered. Haramein studied the energy fields and behaviors around a black hole, and found that they looked exactly the same as what we see around the nucleus of an atom. In Haramein's model, an atom is "a mini black hole, where protons are attracted to each other by gravitation rather than some mysterious, undefined 'strong force.'"[2] Another paper that convincingly argues that atoms are gravity-powered is *Central Oscillator and Space-Quanta Medium*.[3] Haramein has also concluded that space-time is fluidlike—which is a very important point, as we will see. In July 2010, a respected physicist concluded that gravity is "a side effect of something going on at deeper levels of reality" and "there is something more basic, from which gravity 'emerges'"—and this may explain mysteries such as "dark energy" and "dark matter."[4]

Obviously, if atoms are gravity powered, then every object will have the same flow going through it that the earth does—but on a much smaller scale. Objects on the earth's surface would then get caught up in the much greater river of energy that is flowing down into the earth. Gravity may therefore be pushing us down—not unlike mosquitoes being blown against a screen window by a gust of wind. Most people still talk about the pull of gravity, as if it were somehow reaching up from the ground and pulling us down. It seems to make much more sense to consider the idea that "gravity is a push"—as Walter Wright suggested in his 1979 book of the same title.[5] The specific details of Wright's model may not all be correct, but he does seem to be on the right track. Again, this would mean that Gravity is the Source Field. The Source Field is Gravity. These may well be two different names for the same thing—we just didn't understand what Gravity really was.

Pyramid Technology Explained

When we have a perfect sphere, the flow of the Source Field into that object would obviously be spherical. Now here is a significant question: How would the Source Field flow into the shape of a pyramid? Would it be equally as symmetrical? Obviously, if the object is not symmetrical, the flow will not be symmetrical either. The pyramid shape apparently acts like a funnel, and causes a vortex to form in the Source Field as it flows in—just like water swirling down the drain. This appears to be one of the single most important physics principles we have missed—but the ancients were seemingly well aware of it. Some people might think that each atom would act like an individual, separate unit—where the flow never spills over into its neighbors. Instead, the Source Field appears to be flowing through the entire object, with all of its atoms, as a single, large vortex. The shape of the object then determines how the fluidlike energy flows. Some shapes could create powerful currents just by sitting there—causing them to act like machines that run with no moving parts.

In 1995, Dr. Harold Aspden discovered a remarkable "swirling effect" inside a magnetic rotor—the central, rotating part of an engine. Aspden's experiment involved an eight-hundred-gram rotor that was spun up to a cruising speed of 3,250 revolutions per minute, from a dead stop. Normally it took three hundred joules of energy to get this to happen. However, if you run the rotor for five minutes or more and then bring it to a complete stop, it only takes thirty joules of energy to get it going again—if you do it within sixty seconds. It now takes ten times less energy to get the motor up to speed. The overall effect takes several minutes to wear off completely. This implies that once the spinning rotor comes to a complete stop, there is still some form of energy swirling around inside of it—which Dr. Aspden called "virtual inertia."

> The experimental evidence is that there is something spinning of an ethereal nature coextensive with the machine rotor . . . [it] can spin independently and take several minutes to decay, whereas the motor comes to rest in a few seconds. Two machines of different rotor size and composition reveal the phenomenon—and tests indicate variations with time of day, and compass orientation . . . this discovery was unexpected as it has crept in loud and clear in a project aimed at testing a motor principle totally unrelated to "vacuum spin."

It has appeared obtrusively and I do not yet know whether, in adapting to its presence, it can serve in improving machine performance or become detrimental.[6]

I propose that gravity is what pushes on the rotor to get it spinning again with ten times less energy. You create a flowing current in the Source Field and it will still be there for a while—it doesn't immediately disappear. The pyramid structure appears to operate on the same basic principles—a solid-state machine, with no moving parts, that creates a stable, ongoing vortex in the Source Field simply due to its shape. The flowing pyramid current doesn't seem to have any noticeable effect on the downward force of gravity, which is a much larger river of energy moving through the whole area—but the pyramid shape does create a dramatic increase in the coherence and structure of its surroundings, apparently by creating a measurable spin in the fluidlike flow of gravity. This, in turn, generates greater crystallization and organization within physical matter—and dramatically improves the health of biological life.

Of course, other shapes would create Source Field currents as well—such as cones and cylinders. Let's think back to Lyall Watson's quotes from his book *Supernature* that we shared earlier. A French firm patented a specially shaped container because it made better yogurt, claiming it somehow improved the microbial action. Czechoslovakian beer makers got better fermentation when they used round barrels instead of angular ones. A German researcher found that mice would heal faster in spherical cages. And Canadian architects discovered that schizophrenic patients showed a "sudden improvement" once they were relocated to a trapezoid-shaped hospital ward.[7] We are now concentrating and focusing the energy of Mind just like we might work with water or electricity—and the results are impressive.

Dr. Viktor Grebennikov made many breakthroughs with these same principles, studying what he called the Cavity Structural Effect. He initially discovered the effect from bee honeycombs. There was a noticeable tingling and burning sensation in his hand over certain types of honeycombs. He also noticed that when bees got lost on the way back to their hives late at night, they would start trying to ram themselves right through the brick wall of the building—as if they could feel the energy of their hive, which was directly on the other side of the wall. Grebennikov also speculated that bees were naturally attracted to the shape of flowers by this same effect. By simply creating a chair with honeycombs or a stack of egg cartons suspended over the top of it, he got noticeable healing effects—and was granted Russian patent number 2061509 for this invention.[8]

Einstein discovered that space and time were completely indivisible—two manifestations of the same underlying energy. This suggests that as the Source Field (gravity) flows into an atom, it drives the flow of time within the atom as well. The speed of time would then be determined by the speed of the motion inside the atom. As the flow inside the atom becomes more coherent, time begins moving faster inside of it as well. This is an extremely important concept—as it suggests that there could be much more variation in the flow of time from one local area to another than we ever imagined. Sid Hurwich may have independently discovered the Aspden effect—the swirling energy we just found inside a magnet—and found a way to drive that flow into a current, not unlike a propeller creating a powerful vortex in water. This appears to be how he created such a massive change in the flow of time within a local area. Pier Luigi Ighina may have discovered the same thing with his magnetic strobo-scope, shaped like a strange propeller, which was able to immediately open a hole in the clouds over his lab.

We already have a great start on a working model, but if this is really how things work, then we need to find more evidence. We need to invent some way to observe the flow of time in the laboratory—on a very sensi-tive mechanical level. (Precise digital clocks are built on the component level with a form of shielding that stops them from being able to detect these fluctuations easily—as we will discuss.) Once we find an appropri-ate system to detect the flow, we could potentially catch time in the act of speeding up and slowing down. We may even find ways to change that speed on our own, just like Sid Hurwich apparently discovered. This would obviously require innovative new designs that most scientists had never thought of. So what are the options?

Let's think back to the rotation of the earth on its axis. When the Sun gives off a burst of energy, the earth's rotation slows down. The rotation of the Sun's inner core changes the speed of radioactive decay rates. These effects may be caused by a change in the flow of time. What if we used a spinning gyroscope to give us a much smaller model of the earth's rotation in the laboratory? If we could change the flow of time in a small local area, wouldn't the speed of the gyroscope also change in that same spot?

This is exactly what Dr. Nikolai Kozyrev discovered in the 1950s.

Kozyrev's Stunning Breakthroughs

Kozyrev started out as a bright, gifted Russian scientist with a great future ahead of him. He was the first to propose that there may be ice on the moon we could use for water, so we could eventually live on bases up there. Tragedy struck when the fascist policies of Stalin condemned him and many other scientists to spend years in concentration camps. Stalin knew scientists were more apt to be freethinkers who would oppose his hard-line Communist policies. While suffering through the horrors of the concentration camp, Kozyrev worked out the concept of a changing flow of time—and he began conducting experiments to prove his ideas once he got free in the 1950s.

An incredible scientific revolution was triggered—leading to over ten thousand papers being published as of 1996.[9] More than half of these papers were written by Russian scientists, though others have explored these areas as well. This research has awesome implications, including a variety of usable new technologies. Since the flow of time can ultimately affect gravity, weather, electromagnetic devices and the human mind, any nation that knew how to control it would have a clear tactical advantage. Thus, the Soviet government kept much of this research classified for "national security." It wasn't until after the Soviet Union collapsed in 1991 that more of this groundbreaking information became available to the general public—ultimately thanks to the Internet—but most of the scientific community is still unaware of it. If it wasn't for this robust, largely classified scientific background, Dr. Alexander Golod would probably never have spent the money to build his pyramids.

The problem with keeping all this information secret is that this science contains many of the blueprints for a Golden Age. We've already seen how it can create miraculous healing effects—including completely regrowing human teeth, as well as dead or diseased organs. Ordinary water becomes a miracle cure that can save premature babies that would otherwise almost certainly die. Anything harmful to the human body becomes transformed into a nontoxic substance. Radioactivity is alleviated. Earthquakes, atmospheric disturbances and all other potential calamities are greatly reduced. Our overall level of intelligence and insight appears to increase—perhaps because the energy in our holographic brain is moving faster. This faster "vibrational speed" in the holographic brain may be causing our thoughts to move faster, making our overall IQ steadily increase. DNA can be seen like a jigsaw puzzle with more than one solution—so we can transform into a higher level of what it means to be human. And now, we're also finding out that we may even be able to control time.

So now we have a gyroscope in a laboratory. If we can change the flow of time in that local area, then perhaps the gyroscope will speed up or slow down. Here's the problem: The flow of time in the rest of our laboratory must not change. Otherwise, the clocks, the instruments, the energy fields and even our own bodies would all speed up or slow down at the same time the gyroscope did—and there would be no way for us to know that anything was happening. Einstein thought the flow of time could not change in a local area like a science lab—it was "locally invariant." However, Kozyrev's discoveries, along with the others we've already been discussing, throw that idea right out the window.

A spinning gyroscope has a slow, circular wobble called precession, just like the earth's. When the flow of time slows down or speeds up, a small but noticeable change will appear in the speed of a gyroscope's precession—if you set it up according to Kozyrev's instructions. These gyroscopes were electrically powered, so they would continue to run perfectly for long periods of time. That meant any hiccups we might see in the rotation were not the result of the gyroscope running out of energy and naturally slowing down.

The changes Dr. Anderson found in the speeds that various NASA probes traveled through space were very small—only about thirteen millimeters per second. Kozyrev's effects were also very small. According to

A. P. Levich, who wrote an incredible summary of Kozyrev's work that I will reference throughout this chapter, the amount of change in Kozyrev's gyroscopes, or other mechanical detectors, could be as little as ten to the minus six, or ten to the minus seven, of the overall amount of movement in the object.[10] This is comparable in size to the very small changes NASA found in the speed their space probes were traveling. Therefore, Kozyrev needed to develop extremely sensitive methods in order to detect changes in the flow of time.

Another mechanical detector that gave Kozyrev results was a beam balance, which is just a bar dangling horizontally on a string, or filament, so it remains perfectly level from left to right. Kozyrev found it was important that the beam weighed much more on one side than the other—in fact ten times as much—as this made it much more sensitive to tiny little movements. However, the real "secret ingredient" was to vibrate the hook the beam was hanging from at a high speed. Once you did this, the beam would move very suddenly and noticeably—even from touching it with the most delicate puff of air. For this very reason, you had to keep it sealed under a glass dome, and suck all the air out of the inside. That way you could guarantee that air would not cause it to move. You then let the beam come to a perfect state of rest, so it doesn't appear to move at all. However, when there is a flicker in the flow of time, the vibrating speed of the hook at the top will make a subtle but delicate change. The beam is so precariously balanced that this little change in vibrational speed actually causes it to move—noticeably.

Kozyrev found a variety of things that would cause a change in the flow of time, as we will discuss in a minute. However, the greatest surprise of his life came when he was reading Goethe's classic *Faust,* in which the hero is approached by the devil, Mephistopheles, and offered the greatest riches of the world in exchange for his immortal soul. Don't forget that Kozyrev went through grinding hunger, poverty and hard labor in the concentration camp. It's easy to see how many temptations he must have felt to steal food, shoes, clothing, blankets or soap, or to find a way to avoid working. Thus, the story had a very personal feeling. He sat there reading the book in his lab, near the balance-beam detector. As the story reached its climax, he had a sudden emotional surge. Right at that very same moment, the beam suddenly turned and pointed at him.

This was when he first realized that he had not merely discovered the flow of time. It was not just an energy that flowed in and out of physical matter. It was the energy of Mind as well. The Source Field. With this discovery, Kozyrev could now prove that our thoughts were not locked away privately in our own brains—they created measurable signals that his detectors could pick up. Many more tests confirmed that this effect was real—and in the Global Consciousness Project, we find that when enough people think the same way, it creates a worldwide effect we can measure electronically. Kozyrev's discovery fits perfectly with everything we discovered in the early chapters—from Backster, Braud and so on. We do appear to be sharing the same Mind—at least to some degree. That energy is all around us—and it actually has fluidlike flow patterns.

Some people might attack Kozyrev's work and say that it had to be caused by magnetic fields, or static electricity. He prevented this by also placing his detectors inside a Faraday cage, which screens out all electromagnetic fields. Keeping his detectors in a vacuum under glass insured that air couldn't move them either. If his detector started moving, he was now observing the flow of time directly—a ripple in the Source Field.

Another effective mechanical detector Kozyrev developed was a swinging pendulum, which was also electrically powered like the gyroscope. Once again, if he vibrated the hook it was hanging on, the pendulum responded to the time flow much more noticeably—just like we saw with the balance beam and the gyroscope. In this case, the actual direction of the pendulum's swing would change. Of course, he also had to keep it sealed in a vacuum and shielded from electromagnetic fields.

Creating and Absorbing Time

So now what? We have three different choices of detectors, but now we have to figure out what we can do to speed up or slow down the flow of time. Kozyrev found that "ice melting, liquid evaporation, dissolution of substances in water and even plant withering" would speed up the flow of time, or create time, as Kozyrev called it. Furthermore, "the contrary processes, such as cooling of bodies and water freezing, [will] absorb time," thus causing the flow of time to slow down in a tiny but measurable way.[11]

This gives even more proof for the idea that the flow of time is actually responsible for building and maintaining physical matter. When matter starts breaking apart—when a piece of ice melts, a liquid evaporates, a substance dissolves in water or a plant dies—it gives off some of the energy stored within it. We already saw Dr. Fritz-Albert Popp strike living DNA with a chemical that made it unwind and die, and in the process it released a burst of photons. I also suggested that the photons were not the only energy we should be looking at; currents in the Source Field are also being released at the same time, causing effects Kozyrev could measure in the laboratory.

This is such a central point that it does require more explanation. When matter breaks down, the tight little circuits of coherent energy that have been spinning along on the quantum level suddenly burst free. This creates a ripple—a sudden release of energy and movement—in the Source Field. Then, as Kozyrev discovered, time speeds up in that immediate area as all that energy flows out. On the other hand, when the Source Field is spiraling into an area to increase coherence, making matter more organized, time slows down in the surrounding, outside region. The flow in that outside area now behaves like the outer edge of a whirlpool—where the water moves more slowly than it normally would if the vortex wasn't there. In the case of Burlakov's fish-egg experiment, where older fish eggs seemed to be sucking the life force out of the younger ones, we can now see that there is no cruelty involved by the hand of Nature. The older eggs are simply absorbing more Source Field energy than the weaker eggs, by their nature—creating a stronger, faster vortex. This naturally draws energy away from the slower, weaker vortex of energy flowing into the younger eggs.

As Kozyrev discovered, this temporary slowdown in the flow of time starts happening when an object cools down (thus making its quantum movement less chaotic and more coherent, which in turn draws in more Source Field energy), water freezes (causing more coherent crystals to form), a life form such as a plant grows (increasing the coherence as new cells are formed), or crystals form out of a liquid solution. So again, any time we're seeing crystallization and growth, these processes absorb energy from the Source Field—and time moves more slowly in the surrounding area. This is obviously a whole new way of thinking about things. It's strange to think of a decrease in heat as actually drawing an increase in the flow of the Source Field, since we're used to thinking of an increase in heat as an increase in energy. In this case, there appears to be an inverse relationship between the level of heat and the amount of Source Field flow—or at least the amount of coherence we find in the Source Field. Heat destroys coherence by increasing the amount of random, chaotic movement at the quantum level.

Here are some of the things Kozyrev found that could change the flow of time in his laboratory, one way or the other—creating measurable ripples in the Source Field, much like waves moving through a body of water:

- the bending, breaking or deforming of a physical object
- shooting a burst of air at an object
- operating an hourglass filled with sand
- friction
- burning
- any object or surface absorbing light
- heating or cooling an object
- phase transitions in substances (frozen to liquid, liquid to vapor, etc.)
- dissolving and mixing substances
- running electrical current through a wire
- the actions of an observer, such as a movement of the head
- the fading death of plants
- sudden changes in human consciousness

In one case, simply lifting a ten-kilogram weight up and down would create a ripple in the flow of time—a wave—that could be measured two to three meters away. This is just like what we would see if we were raising and lowering the weight underwater—there would be ripples we could then measure at a distance. Some time after I first read about this in 1999, I realized that this meant the Source Field, which exists all throughout space and time, must behave like a fluid—and this became the key to solving the mysteries of sacred geometry, as we will soon see—not to mention the pyramids.

Kozyrev found that these ripples could travel right through solid brick walls as if they weren't even there.[12] This has led most Russian scientists to conclude that the flow of time has a much closer relationship with gravity than it does electromagnetism—as I said before. Electromagnetic energy can be shielded—but the force of gravity holds you down equally as well inside a brick building, or a lead-lined cage, as it does outside.

Nonmechanical Detectors

So far, we've only studied the mechanical detectors Kozyrev developed. He also found other nonmechanical ways to study the flow of time as well—meaning these were methods that did not use any moving parts as we would normally think of them. The simplest of these detectors was heat.

Every atom is filled with a constant frenzy of whirling movement, which scientists call spin. When an object heats up, there is an increasing amount of chaotic, unpredictable movement in the atom—which eventually causes it to give off a glowing red, yellow or white light. Heat creates random, unpredictable, chaotic movements that disrupt the free flow of the Source Field at the quantum level—reducing coherence. On the other hand, when an object cools down, there is less resistance to the quantum flow, and it will move faster and more smoothly. This explains why superconductors need to be kept at super-cool temperatures. The lack of heat creates a lack of movement that would interrupt the flow of electrical current. Kozyrev thus realized he could measure changes in time with an ordinary mercury thermometer—kept in an environment where the temperature was otherwise being held constant.

Kozyrev also found that his experiments worked best in the first half of the winter. In the summer, the heat in the surrounding area seemed to have a scrambling effect on the overall flow of time—and this made it difficult or even impossible for any of his experiments to work properly. The increase in heat reduced the coherence in the Source Field.

Kozyrev also found that the flow of electricity could be affected by changes in the flow of time—and this was the same effect that the Global Consciousness Project was apparently detecting. Professor Simon Shnoll also used electrical current as one of his tools to detect changes in the flow of time. Kozyrev found that tungsten metal was extremely responsive to the flow of time. Tungsten's electrical conductivity could be permanently changed if you zapped it with a strong enough time flow. Another time flow detector was a quartz crystal. When you see the word *quartz* on a watch, that means there is a crystal inside of it with electricity running through it. The flow of electricity causes the quartz crystal to resonate at a speed that is steady enough to keep solid time. The crystal in a watch is shielded from Source Field influence, on a component level, by methods we will discuss below. For that reason, we normally do not see any changes in how a quartz watch keeps time—and the scientists who built them that way probably never realized what they were actually doing. However, if you blast a nonshielded quartz crystal with a strong enough time flow, its vibrating speed will change— and Kozyrev could measure this in the laboratory. Again, this change can be permanent—showing that the molecular structure has actually changed.

Yet another interesting nonmechanical detector of the time flow was the thickness or viscosity of water. When the flow of time slows down in water, there is less coherence. Random movements interrupt the water's ability to flow. As a result, the water becomes thicker, or more viscous, meaning it will not flow as quickly or easily. When the flow of time speeds up in water, coherence increases—and it flows faster. This can easily be measured. Chemical reactions also speed up and slow down, just like we saw in Shnoll's research. And lastly, Kozyrev found that living things such as bacteria and plants will grow faster or slower depending upon how fast the flow of time is moving through them—and their own local area. This should sound very familiar by now. Kozyrev was another early pioneer who discovered that our own health could be directly affected by the flow of time as it moves through our cells.

Spiraling Currents of Time

Kozyrev also found that the flow of time does not push through space in a straight line—it spins, or twists, as it moves along: "time possesses not only energy but also a rotation . . . which it can transmit to a system."[13] This means the flow will manifest as a rotating movement once you see it affecting a gyroscope, beam balance, pendulum or any other system— just like what we saw in Dr. Aspden's experiment with the magnetic rotor. A scientific word for "spinning" or "twisting" is *torsion*. For this reason, many Russian scientists call these "waves of time" torsion fields. I prefer to use the term Source Field, because I feel it gives us a much better sense of how this energy is ultimately responsible for creating everything in the Universe. Nonetheless, this twist in gravity is where we find all the magic of the Source Field in our model.

Some molecules, such as sugar, are considered right-handed, meaning that their molecules predominantly spiral together in a clockwise fashion. Others, such as turpentine or salt, are left-handed, where the molecules are mostly counterclockwise. Kozyrev found that right-handed molecules absorb the flow of time and slow it down. Similarly, left-handed molecules strengthen the flow of time—and speed it up. As Kozyrev and others discovered, the more this Source Field energy flows into your body, the healthier you will be—so if you eat too many sweets, you are causing the Source Field to be absorbed by the sugar, rather than by your DNA—which needs to store light to maintain itself. A great way to test how well you're doing is by checking your pH balance, which can be done with little strips of paper you hold in your mouth for a few minutes. Sugars, saturated fats, meats, dairy, sweet fruits, white flour, prepackaged foods, alcohol and drugs all bring you closer to the acid side of the scale, and healthy, natural foods like fresh organic vegetables, nuts, seeds, and less-sweet fruits bring you closer to the alkaline side. You do need both sides, to some degree. Although Kozyrev found that salt strengthens the flow of time, too much is very bad, because of its effect on your blood pressure—and the work your body has to do to clean it out of your bloodstream. In some rare cases, people can become too alkaline—but in general it's very, very hard to overdose on fresh vegetables. Either way, it's all about balance.

So, the flow of time can actually speed up in left-handed molecules and slow down in right-handed molecules. These same principles led Kozyrev to discover that common polyethylene film, like PVC plastic, could actually shield the spinning currents in the Source Field. Aluminum is also a very effective shield. This makes it a very bad idea to live inside an aluminum trailer, as you are shielding off the very fields that will keep you healthy. They will still get in, but the spin is disrupted. The amount of coherence within those spaces will be lower. Gravity will still push you down, but the level of spin, or torsion, within it will be reduced—and in our model, the genetic information in the Source Field is hidden in these spiraling forces. Aluminum is used in electronics at the component level due to its extremely light weight—and many components are also then coated in plastic. Therefore, digital watches and highly accurate laboratory clocks are not likely to respond to changes in the flow of time in a noticeable way. However, in 1993 Dr. Bruce DePalma found that the Accutron watch, which runs on a metallic tuning fork, does speed up and slow down in the presence of these fields.[14]

In 2001, Dr. Hartmut Müller[15] used the spin fields within gravity to make a telephone call from the Toezler Medientage building in Germany to Saint Petersburg in Russia. No electromagnetic fields were ever used to make this call— just as Backster's plants, bacteria, insects, animals and human cells could "talk" to each other while they were in shielded rooms. You can call from deep inside a concrete parking garage, at the bottom of the ocean or halfway across the galaxy, and you will always get a perfect real-time signal. Müller's discovery also does not create "electromagnetic smog" that can cause cancer, headaches and other problems,[16] and this technology could be easily adapted for wireless Internet access—using the same systems preferred by biological life.

Astrophysical Observations

Some scientists who have studied Kozyrev's material are willing to consider that something significant is going on, but they're not comfortable
with the idea that these effects are actually caused by the flow of time.
This brings us to one of the most fascinating areas Kozyrev studied—
namely astronomy. Kozyrev believed that "stars are machines" that get
their energy from the time flow—and he found very compelling evidence to prove it. As Levich wrote in 1996, most of Kozyrev's experiments in the later years of his life were "dedicated to direct detection . . .
of non-electromagnetic [energy] flows from planets, stars, galaxies, stellar clusters and nebulae."[17]

What exactly does this mean? Beginning in the mid-1950s, Kozyrev
designed a special type of telescope that had one of his time flow detectors located right at the focal point. As strange as this sounds, he could
put a metal plate in front of the telescope—blocking out all visible light
and all electromagnetic radiation—but the time-flow detector still
picked up a measurable signal when he aimed the telescope at a star, or
any other celestial object. This could not be possible unless he was detecting an energy that was not electromagnetic—and had nothing to do
with visible light.

The light from a star can take many millions of years to reach us—
and in the meantime, the real position of the star has actually drifted
somewhere else. So when we look at the night sky, we are looking at the
past. Kozyrev found that if he aimed his telescope at the true position of
a star, which could be estimated through various means, the signal was
much stronger.[18] This suggested that the waves within the Source Field
traveled much, much faster than the speed of light—effectively instantaneously.

And if that isn't already confusing enough, Kozyrev could then look
at where the star would likely end up in the future, and he detected
energy coming from that position as well. I know—it sounds totally
crazy, but when you get new data that is strange, that doesn't mean we

throw it away. Instead, we try to understand what the heck is going on, and explain the data. Obviously, as I'm sure you can see, the comfortable, old-fashioned notion of linear time simply can't hold up in light of this new evidence, if Kozyrev is actually right.

Indeed, the strongest energy from a star or celestial object came from its true position—defeating Einstein's belief that no energy field could ever travel faster than the speed of light. A star's energy then got steadily weaker when you moved toward its position in the past, and weaker when you moved the telescope toward its position in the future. The overall change of intensity would graph out the same way in both directions.[19] It's as if the star were spread out in time, like a wave—and you could detect its position in the past, present and future all at once, just by observing the Source Field instead of the electromagnetic light waves. The closer you were to the star's current position, the more of its energy you could detect.

Time Must Be Three-Dimensional

This is a very significant discovery, as it shows that the Source Field is not confined to linear time. As mind-boggling as it must seem, everything is all there at once. The past, present and future positions of the star all give off measurable energy, and only the strength of the energy changes—in time. This may explain how Dr. Hartmut Müller's cell-phone technology created phone calls that were instantaneous, regardless of the distance involved. We take it for granted that the past is forever behind us and the future cannot be known, but in Kozyrev's science, the future actually casts a shadow into the past—which we can see and measure with relatively simple technology. Time could not behave like this if it was only one-dimensional. In some very real sense, time must be three-dimensional in order for this effect to work—and we will explore that idea in the next chapter.

Doesn't this all sound familiar, though? Remote viewers rigorously demonstrated their ability to see events in the future before they actually happened. Dr. Daryl J. Bem, an emeritus professor at Cornell University, got a study published in *The Journal of Personality and Social Psychology* that rigorously demonstrated the ability of ordinary people to predict the future. Many people have experienced prophetic events in their own lives, but often write them off as coincidence. Remember our discussion about the energetic duplicate that you leave behind in your chair every time you get up? Remember how some part of you is still sitting there in the chair, capturing light into photons, for up to thirty days? Kozyrev's astonishing observations finally help us explain the DNA Phantom Effect. Once DNA has been kept in a certain area for a period of time, its energy will still be there when the physical molecules are moved away. Gravity provides the force to hold the photons in place—on the quantum level. Gariaev did not detect any effect from the future position of DNA, but this may simply require new experiments with these concepts in mind. We definitely see a phantom effect happening in stars, thanks to Kozyrev's work.

Kozyrev didn't live to see how his observations of the nonlocal behavior of stars may have extended into our own DNA—but as we remember, he did find that his own thoughts could generate a time flow that the detectors would pick up. Given all the wavelike effects Kozyrev discovered, it is clear that the energy of our DNA Phantom and energetic duplicate is rippling into our surroundings—it is not just stuck within our own bodies, even from one moment to the next as we are sitting still. In fact, it may very well be that all the thoughts we have are rippling through the entire Source Field in some way—instantaneously. Brain waves may be much more than just electrical signals—they apparently create currents that we constantly release into our surroundings. This was rigorously demonstrated in the first five chapters—and our pineal gland may well be the most important part of the brain for sending and receiving these thoughts. Obviously, the closer we are to the source of the thoughts, the stronger the signal will be. In the Global Consciousness Project, the closer any one computer was to New York during 9/11, the stronger the effects became. Our thoughts are not confined to our own brains and bodies— they have measurable effects on our environment.

Kozyrev realized that stars are sending energy through the Universe at instantaneous speeds. He then had a remarkable insight—this instantaneous energy exchange could explain the often-overlooked problem of binary stars in conventional astronomy. A surprising number of stars we see in the night sky show up in pairs. You have two stars sitting right next to each other with similar size, brightness and light emissions. It is as if they were talking to each other—there is an energetic connection between them that allows them to synchronize. From where we look, they seem so close to each other that ordinary electromagnetic fields could explain this effect. However, according to Kozyrev, the speed of light is actually much too slow to account for this communication—the actual distances involved are far too great. In 1966, at a meeting of the International Astronomical Union, Kozyrev proposed that binary stars were caused by two stars energetically harmonizing with each other through the flow of time—at speeds much faster than light.[20]

So again, Kozyrev discovered that there was energy emerging from the past, present and future positions of a star. We have also seen our own DNA leaving behind a measurable energetic blueprint from where it had been in the past. Even when the DNA is no longer there, our DNA Phantom can still capture and store photons of light—it has very real, measurable energetic effects. Now that we are armed with all this knowledge, we have a practical model for how solar, planetary and other astronomical cycles, perhaps including the 25,920-year precession, may be affecting us. As earth traces its orbit around the Sun, it will leave a measurable energy behind in its position from the past. Once we come back around to the same position again, a year later, that energy is still there. That means if the energy has measurable effects on how we think and feel, those consciousness effects will also return once more. This may also be happening as earth's axis changes position while it drifts through the precession.

With Kozyrev's discoveries under our belt, we now have definite, provable signs of action at a distance, as Einstein called it. The position of every planet, moon, asteroid and comet in our solar system now has the potential to affect all the others in measurable ways—just as Shnoll's discoveries strongly implied. Energy appears to be exchanged instantaneously as these celestial objects dance around—pushing and pulling on the flow of time. Our own solar system appears to be moving into an area of greater coherence—which is creating a short-term, rapid evolution of human DNA and consciousness, as we've discussed. The Maya calendar end-date, the expected arrival date for the Age of Aquarius and the exact time window for the coming Golden Age in Hindu scriptures all highlight the same, small window of time—circa 2012—as a key watermark for when these changes will occur. Humans gained a massive burst of intelligence fifty thousand years ago, and the Neanderthals phased out of the evolutionary cycle some twenty-five thousand years ago—right on schedule with the end of each Great Year. Our DNA has been evolving one hundred times faster in the last five thousand years than in all human history. More and more, it seems that our ancient ancestors knew what they were talking about.

How Much Can We Change the Flow of Time?

The strangest and most amazing part of Kozyrev's work was in finding out that our own minds can actually change the flow of time. This also appears to be what the Global Consciousness Project discovered. If the human mind really can make the flow of time speed up or slow down, then what about highly gifted people? Could they possibly do things that were much more extraordinary and dramatic than what Kozyrev has discovered?

In his book *China's Super Psychics,* Paul Dong wrote about children who are "Extra High Functioning," or EHF. In 1992, China held an official meeting for U.S. oil executives at the Tianjin City Human Body Science Institute. This was considered a high honor for the visiting dignitaries, as they were permitted to witness something that very few Westerners have ever been allowed to see. A young girl named Yao Zheng was seated in front of a series of flower buds that were days or even weeks away from opening. The dignitaries watched her in good lighting, from several different angles. After she prayed for about fifteen minutes, she was able to speed up time within the buds—and they suddenly bloomed in front of everyone's own eyes. Another child sitting next to her was able to teleport pills out of a sealed glass bottle, without ever opening it, and never brought any part of her body closer than one or two feet away from the bottle.

Paul Dong revealed just how far this phenomenon really can go.

> There are many people with the ability to open flowers in China, and Yao Zheng is only one example. Of course, there are others whose powers are stronger. On the evening of April 1, 1994, in the Beijing Signal Corps auditorium, Colonel Fu Songshan was able to open all of the flower buds in the hands of an audience of over a thousand people within thirty minutes. . . . However, Fu Songshan is not the top man. There is one mysterious woman who, facing thousands upon thousands of flower buds, can make them all bloom instantly by saying, "I want you all to open," and waving her hand."[21]

In *The Synchronized Universe,* Dr. Claude Swanson discusses experiments in China in which a tiny, battery-powered radio transmitter was allegedly teleported from the pocket of one individual, through a wall and into a sealed container held by another person. The transmitter broadcast a steady frequency of electromagnetic signals, allowing for a precise measurement of time to be calculated. These impressive feats were witnessed by Hartwig Hausdorf and discussed in his 1998 book *The Chinese Roswell.*

> As the teleportation occurred, the frequency of the transmitter . . . slowed down and actually stopped for a brief moment during the transmission, then gradually returned to the original frequency. This suggests that time itself may have been affected by the teleportation, since frequency is a measure of time. This behavior is reminiscent of what happens in quantum mechanics. If an elementary particle, such as an electron, stops in space, its frequency becomes very low and its position becomes spread out over a large area. This is a

consequence of the Uncertainty Principle. If this is [what
happened in] the Chinese experiment, it suggests that the
teleportation process involves a quantumlike delocalization of
the object.[22]

Swanson also mentions Tara Bey, an Indian yogi who could slow time
to almost a standstill within his own body. His helpers actually covered
his eyes, ears, nose and mouth with wax to prevent insects from entering
his body—and if he was going to do it for weeks or more, he instructed
his helpers to seal his entire body in wax. That's right—he never even
drew a single breath. The yogi explained to Paul Brunton how it works.

> People, when confronted with the phenomena which I can
> produce, think it either some kind of conjuring, or else some-
> thing entirely supernatural. In both cases they are wrong.
> They do not seem to grasp the fact that these things are per-
> fectly scientific, obeying the laws of nature herself. It is true
> that I am using psychic laws which are little understood—but
> nevertheless, they are laws. Nothing that I do is arbitrary,
> supernatural, or against such laws.[23]

The ancient prophecies of a Golden Age suggest that spectacular abilities like this will not remain in the hands of a small number of extremely
talented people—they will become commonplace. And if human beings
can create such remarkable changes in the flow of time, then we should
ultimately be able to accomplish the same feats with technology—just as
Sid Hurwich apparently discovered. Indeed, Kozyrev's work may well be
just the very beginning of a whole new world that we will soon have at
our fingertips.

CHAPTER THIRTEEN

What's the Matter—Dematerialization, Teleportation and Time Travel

D r. Nikolai Kozyrev's most astonishing discovery was that stars give off measurable energy—from their past, present and future positions. The energy is the strongest in the current, actual position of the star, and decreases in a smooth, even curve as you look at either its past or its future position. We do also know there is a very similar effect occurring in quantum physics—though only a handful of scientists seem to understand what is actually going on. Every quantum physicist knows you can look at a subatomic particle and measure it as if it were perfectly solid and stable—but then when you use other measuring techniques, the particle turns into a wave—and it becomes nonlocal. This seems to defy our intuition completely, and has led to the so-called Uncertainty Principle—which is a fancy way of saying, "We just don't know what the heck is going on down at the quantum level. Nothing seems to exist in any stable, rational, logical way down there. It's not a particle, it's not a wave—it's something we can never understand. It's both at the same time."

Since Einstein proved that space and time are interconnected, particles are not merely spreading out in space when they turn into waves—they are also nonlocal in time.[1] That means some of the particle now appears in the past, some of it is still there in the present, and some of it has moved into the future. As mind-boggling as this must sound, "wave-particle duality" has been observed in protons, neutrons, electrons and even entire atoms[2]—and that's all there is down there. This means everything in the quantum realm pops in and out of existence all the time. We do have all the evidence we need to understand this, but we're just not used to thinking this way. Conventional scientists cannot explain what is going on, and therefore have concluded that the mystery will never be solved. We simply live in a universe of uncertainty. Thankfully, this is not true. There is an answer, as we will see—it just hasn't gotten very popular yet.

If this idea of entire atoms dematerializing isn't strange enough, the mystery got even greater in 1999, thanks to Dr. Olaf Nairz and his colleagues. Nairz and his crew were able to transform a soccer-ball-shaped cluster of 60 carbon molecules—known as a fullerene or buckyball—directly into a wave. (This hollow, geometric sphere of carbon atoms was first devised by Buckminster Fuller, so it was named after him.) Bear in mind that buckyballs are solid objects. They can even be used to store other materials inside of them. Each buckyball has a mass of 720 atomic units, built from 60 different carbon atoms that are tightly bound together. And yet, by simply bumping the buckyball against a wall with a series of tiny slits in it, Nairz was able to transform it into a wave—and it popped through more than one slit at the same time.[3]

If you and I had this ability, a locked door would never be able to stop us. All we'd have to do is run toward it at top speed and collide with it. As soon as we hit the door, instead of having a terribly painful injury, we'd pop into a wave. Then, as a wave, we would slip through the cracks along one or more of the four sides of the door—only to immediately pop back into our normal, solid physical form on the other side. That's what these little geometric objects are doing.

This experiment is ridiculously simple, and its full implications have definitely not yet become a part of our common knowledge—even though it was published in the prestigious journal *Nature*.[4] Then in 2001, this same group discovered they did not need to slam the buckyballs against a wall—all they needed was laser light, which is coherent light, to transform these solid objects into waves.[5] This was published in *Physics Review Letters,* a respected science journal.[6]

Faced with these paradoxes, some scientists have already started to "think the unthinkable." What if these particles are not actually doing something that is seemingly impossible? What if they are simply flip-flopping in and out of a reality where they have some room to stretch out and relax, because time is not linear? Tim Folger discussed a similar concept in a *Discover* magazine article from 2007.

> Some four decades ago, the renowned physicist John Wheeler, then at Princeton, and the late Bryce DeWitt, then at the University of North Carolina, developed an extraordinary equation that provides a possible framework for unifying relativity and quantum mechanics. But the Wheeler-DeWitt equation has always been controversial. . . . "One finds that time just disappears from the Wheeler-DeWitt equation," says Carlo Rovelli, a physicist at the University of the Mediterranean in Marseilles, France. . . . "It may be that the best way to think about quantum reality is to give up the notion of time—that the fundamental description of the universe must be timeless."[7]

Ever since relativity and quantum mechanics emerged, dealing with the very large and the very small, scientists have struggled to unify them. Einstein's dream was that ultimately everything would be made from the unified field—meaning there are no protons, no neutrons, no electrons—just rotations of the Field itself. The problem, of course, is that these weird time-bending properties of quantum mechanics don't seem to allow us to build a working model like that. However, according to *Discover*, we may be able to solve all these problems by changing how we think about time.

> A sizable minority of physicists, Rovelli included, believe that any successful merger of the two great masterpieces of twentieth-century physics will inevitably describe a universe in which, ultimately, there is no time. . . . [Even better,] all the laws—whether Newton's, Einstein's, or the quirky quantum rules—would work equally well if time ran backward.[8]

Therefore, these radical new concepts about the nature of time cannot be shot down by skeptics who use science as a weapon—they are already on the verge of being accepted as scientific facts. We don't need time to be linear in order to explain the laws of physics. It is unfortunate that Kozyrev's research is not commonly known outside of Russian scientific circles, as it provides dramatic new evidence to help us understand that when the particle turns into a wave, it's still a particle. Only now, it's a particle in time.

Dewey Larson and Three-Dimensional Time

In our own reality, time keeps moving forward at a steady rate—barring a few little hiccups and glitches. That's why Einstein assumed it was only one-dimensional. However, if we want to solve the biggest scientific mysteries, all we have to do is allow time to have three dimensions. The idea of anything in nature being one-dimensional is nothing more than a mathematical concept—not unlike the idea that the earth could be flat. Dr. Dewey Larson built a very successful model of our Universe, beginning in the 1950s, by assuming time has three dimensions—but mainstream scientists wouldn't accept it. Nonetheless, Larson was able to solve many of the greatest quantum physics problems, as well as many perplexing issues in astronomy, with this model. Larson concluded there was a three-dimensional Time Region, or what I and others now like to call time-space—which is constantly interacting with our own three dimensions of space-time. Larson's other big concept was that the entire Universe is formed by nothing more than motion—and what's moving, in my opinion, is the Source Field. Gravity, electromagnetic energy, and all the other forces normally associated with quantum mechanics are just different ways of talking about the same thing. The entire Universe is built from nothing more than fluidlike, swirling vortexes within the Source Field. Einstein's greatest dream—of a Unified Field—was correct.

Here's a more technical way of saying the same thing from K. Nehru, a scientist developing Larson's theory.

Larson asserts that the atom is without parts, that it is a unit of compound motion—[with] motion being the basic constituent of the physical universe. This means that both the nucleus and the so-called orbital electrons are non-existent. Secondly, he argues that there is no electrical force either, involved in the atomic structure. This, therefore, leaves gravitation and the space-time progression as the only two motions (forces) that operate inside the Time Region. . . .[9]

Based on all the available evidence, gravitation and the "space-time progression" are the exact same thing—which is ultimately what Larson is saying by concluding that "All is Motion." It's a very mind-expanding concept to consider that gravity is powering physical matter. That's all there is. Nothing else. Just a flowing vortex within a mysterious force we usually call gravity. Without the flow of gravity doing its work, there would be no matter—at least not anything that was visible in our own space-time.

According to Nehru, this same theory, which Larson calls the Reciprocal System, also does an excellent job of clarifying astrophysics observations.

Besides other things, the concept of coordinate [three-dimensional] time in the Reciprocal System explains and derives the characteristics of supernovae, the white dwarfs, the pulsars, the quasars, the compact X-ray sources and the cosmic rays—without taking recourse to concepts like degenerate matter, the curvature of space-time, etc. . . . All [Einstein's] so-called Relativistic effects come out, in the Reciprocal System, of the existence of this additional time component.[10]

Better yet, Larson predicted the existence of quasars in 1959, even though they weren't officially discovered until 1963 by Maarten Schmidt.[11]

A computer programmer named Dave Ashley[12] read Larson's books after hearing me talk about them in my videos, and then was brave enough to start a discussion on the James Randi skeptics' forum about it.

[Larson's physics] makes obsolete the last 100 years or so of conventional wisdom as regards the physics of everything. As such it is not acceptable to the mainstream scientific communities. It can't get accepted into peer-reviewed journals because it essentially is debunking all of current theory. . . . [Larson's model] makes a huge number of accurate predictions about atoms, chemicals, spacing between atoms in compounds, and such. The numbers add up. . . . If [Larson] is right, a whole lot of professors and graduate students are out of a job. There goes the gravy train of government grants. If the underlying physics is really much simpler, it won't take years of painstaking study to "get it." It could be taught in high school. So there is a very strong vested interest in maintaining the status quo.[13]

Space and Time Are Exact Opposites of Each Other

Larson named his theory the Reciprocal System because he felt that space and time were in a perfectly opposite relationship to each other . . . a reciprocal relationship. Though most people believe space and time couldn't be more different, Larson said that's only because we've been conditioned to think that way. Instead, Larson now invites us to envision a parallel reality, all around us, which is just like the space we now see—in almost every way. This parallel reality would have solid objects and livable areas just like our own—made from the same atoms and molecules we see all around us. Our scientists would normally think these atoms exist only as waves in this stage of their existence. Remember—a wave over here is a solid particle over there.

We might even enter this parallel reality and walk around in it by certain means we will soon discuss. The only difference is that from our perspective, this parallel reality would all exist in a higher dimension—or more correctly, three parallel dimensions. Theoretically, we are surrounded by this parallel reality—by time-space—right now. It's where the energetic duplicate of our physical body and brain would be found. It's very likely where we go in dreams, out-of-body experiences, remote-viewing sessions or the so-called afterlife. And the main way we can measure this parallel reality is by tracking its effects on the flow of time.

One of the most mind-expanding concepts Larson raises is that the space we see around us, the Known Universe, isn't strictly real at all. The parallel reality of time-space isn't actually real either. The only thing that does genuinely exist is the three real dimensions that they both are a part of. Within these three real dimensions, energy constantly flows between the two realities so they can both continue to exist. (Technically, Larson would call this motion, not energy, but I believe we are still talking about the same thing.)

Simply put, all the energy that makes space in our reality is the same energy that powers time in the parallel reality. And all the energy that makes space in the parallel reality is the energy that powers time in our reality. Although this seems totally impossible to visualize at first, the reason why it works is that this flowing exchange between space and time is constantly happening within every single atom and molecule of our visible Universe. That means both of these realities are stable locations we can visit—and they are totally interconnected with each other. Neither of these two realities can exist separately. They are intimately and totally dependent upon each other for their own survival. It is utterly impossible to separate them. We can watch atoms and molecules winking into and out of this parallel reality all the time—but up until now we have had no idea what we're really seeing. This also means the space we see is actually an illusion and every point is ultimately the center of the universe.

A Parallel Reality—in Time

Again, theoretically this means everything you see around you has an energetic duplicate—not just your own body. In this parallel reality, your room would still look like your room. More precisely, your room would at least be the most obvious area you would see, because your room would be the closest point in time to the moment you entered into this parallel reality. You might also see dimmer, ghostlike images where your house didn't exist yet—because there was another building there. Or there was no building at all—just an open field. Under the right circumstances, you may even be able to see back into prehistoric times, where there were dinosaurs around. Or perhaps you see glorious hints of a crystal city that might be there in the future. Nonetheless, these would be like shadows or phantoms in most cases—and may be far too weak to even be visible.

Another strange outcome of this theory is that simply walking around in this parallel reality will have an effect much like fast-forwarding or rewinding a videotape, in terms of what you actually see. How can you know whether you will walk into the future or stroll into the past? You have to stretch your imagination even more to get the answer, but this does seem to be how the Universe really works.

If you stay perfectly still when you go into this parallel reality, you won't travel in time. It's only when you start moving around that you either go into the future or the past. Let's be clear that even though you could walk around and explore things, no one here in our reality would be able to see you. Larson said that from our normal perspective on earth, you would be stuck in space. From a quantum physics perspective, you would appear to have turned into a wave. If anyone could see you at all, you might look like the typical description of a ghost. Even though you are free to move around in this parallel universe, and you certainly can, all you're actually doing is moving around in time. "Only motion in time can take place in the time region."[14] That means moving from one location to another in this parallel reality is actually time travel.

Time Travel Explained

However, saying you are totally stuck in space isn't strictly correct either. The evidence we will investigate in later chapters tells us that if you pop in at one point, walk to another location and pop back out, you will indeed teleport between those two locations here on earth. Even better, if you walked far enough in the parallel reality, you would have noticeably time-traveled when you return. This is called a time slip, and we will review solid evidence that vortexes naturally appear on earth that can cause this to happen. Such vortex experiences are often misrepresented as "UFO abductions" with "missing time." Skeptics have thrown a wealth of scientific data in the garbage because they just can't stretch their imagination far enough to recognize the truth. As we will see, even a decent walk in time-space won't typically buy you more than five days of travel through time—at least under typical circumstances. The distance you travel over there by walking doesn't really add up to a whole lot of time.

How do you know which way you're going, in time, if all you're doing is walking around? Here's the secret: If you go ahead of where the earth was when you got there, you will go into the future. If you go behind where the earth was, you will go into the past. The trick, of course, is that the earth is rotating on its axis and revolving around the Sun. The Sun in turn is revolving around the galaxy, and the galaxy is drifting toward the Virgo cluster. Thankfully, the laws of the Universe don't leave us stranded out in our absolute position in space when we move into time-space. Even as we move forward and backward in time, we stay with the earth. The earth rotates from west to east—so that means if you head east, you will start seeing the future, and if you head west, you will start seeing the past. (If you want to get really technical about it, you could say that you will see more of the future, or more of the past, since time is all spread out.)

Gravity is also pushing you down, and that's powering time as well. The flow of gravity is the flow of time—just like gravity is the flow that makes matter. Therefore, if you go up in time-space, you will move into the past—before the moment of time gravity had pushed you into when you started. If you go down, you will move into the future—after the moment of time gravity had pushed you into. The amount of time you shift through in these cases may not be very much, but in certain circumstances the effects can be measured precisely.

The National Airlines 727 "Time Slip"

A plane obviously heads down on the way into an airport. What if it then hits a relatively small vortex into time-space? In 1974, Charles Berlitz wrote a tantalizing three-paragraph summary of an event just like this in his classic book *The Bermuda Triangle.* In this account, Berlitz says the plane was approaching from the northeast, meaning it would be traveling southwest—but as we will see, Martin Caidin interviewed many more eyewitnesses and said the plane was coming in west of Miami International, meaning it was traveling east—making it even more likely to be heading into the future if it did hit such a vortex.

> An incident involving time lapse occurred at the Miami airport about five years ago, which has never been satisfactorily explained. It concerned a National Airlines 727 passenger plane which, on approach to landing from the northeast, and being tracked on radar by the Air Control Center, suddenly disappeared from the radar screen for about ten minutes and then reappeared. The plane landed without incident, and the pilot and crew evinced some surprise over the expressed concern of the ground crew since, as far as the crew was concerned, nothing unusual had happened. By way of an explanation, one of the Air Control staff said to one of the pilots, "Man, for ten minutes you just did not exist." It was at this point that the crew checked their watches and the various time indicators in the plane, and discovered that they were uniformly ten minutes slow according to real time. This was especially remarkable, as the plane had made a routine time check twenty minutes before the incident, and at that time there was no time discrepancy.[15]

There seems to be much missing from this story, if it is really true. You have an entire plane full of people who spontaneously popped ten minutes into the future. If they were at 8:50 P.M. when they went in, they were still at 8:50 P.M. when they came back out—even though everyone else's watch now said 9:00 P.M.. Thankfully, a pilot and researcher named Martin Caidin did a much more thorough investigation of this incident, and reported his results in his 1991 book *Ghosts of the Air.* Caidin didn't just read books about it.

I spoke to some of the people involved. Airline captains, friends of mine who aided in research, officials of the Federal Aviation Administration, a literal host of investigators, all pooled their information to bring it together before I put this down on paper.[16]

Caidin writes that the 727 was coming in for a landing at Miami with all their equipment working just fine. The pilots followed the air traffic controllers' instructions and turned the plane when they were asked to—heading in on the invisible corridors they were assigned. Then, without warning, their blip on the radar disappeared. Of course, this could be caused by electrical failures, radar glitches, or a crew member switching off the transponder system—but it also meant the 727 could have crashed into "the swampy ground far to the west of Miami International."

Now, by necessity, there was a real panic.

Immediately the alarms sounded. The reactions are automatic. The word goes out from Miami Approach and Departure, and the tower, for all aircraft in that sector to "look for a Seven Two Seven that's gone off the scope." Pilots strain to see any signs; a reflection of sunlight from metal, a flashing strobe, bright flames, rising smoke—anything.

Nothing. She was gone.

Miami Approach hit the alarm signals to the coast guard and other rescue forces. Choppers bolted from the ground and raced to the last-known position of the National 727.

Nothing.

Then, precisely ten minutes after the radar blip vanished from the set scopes in Miami Approach, the blip reappeared before the astonished eyes of the people now crowded around that radar position.

Reappearance was strange enough. But this was ten minutes after the 727 had disappeared, and now it had reappeared in exactly the same position it held in flight when it vanished—both on radar and in flight. [It may have moved slightly, but only enough to cause a ten-minute time slip.]

The 727 pilot continued talking with Miami Approach, and then Miami Tower, in an absolutely calm voice. Nothing unusual could be discerned from his tone or his words. The still-astounded radar operator worked the 727 in closer, and then handed off the airliner to the tower for final landing instructions. The 727 slid in, flaps extended and gear down, and made an absolutely normal landing.

The airliner was directed to park in an area separate from the terminal gate. When it stopped and the doors opened, federal investigators and officials of National couldn't get into that jetliner fast enough. The crew regarded with some astonishment of their own this unexpected and unexplained flurry of activity and barrage of questions. Then they were told what had happened. "You disappeared from the scope on your descent. For ten minutes there was no radar picture of you people. When you came back on the scope, your position was exactly where it had been. Not only that, but several airliners flew through the space you had occupied in those ten minutes. What happened up there?"

The crew—and the passengers who were questioned—were in a different situation. Something incredible had happened to them, and they didn't know the first thing about it. "Nothing happened," the captain insisted. "Nothing out of the ordinary, that is. We were on approach, and we came in, and we got tower, and we landed. Period."

"No break in communications?"

"None."[17]

Caidin goes on to say that one of the flight crew checked his watch, compared it with everyone else's in the flight crew, and then checked it against all the other clocks throughout the aircraft. Every one of their own clocks told the same time—but they were all ten minutes behind.

The Bermuda Triangle was a classic book I read at the beginning of my quest, but it took me years to understand and explain what actually happened. Since this is a very technical discussion, I deliberately have not presented all the evidence for how Larson solved the mysteries of quantum mechanics and astrophysics. If you really want to roll up your sleeves and get the specifics, there is a tremendous amount of written material available to read, and it's all been posted for free online. My colleague Dr. Bruce Peret, who runs the RS Theory Web site,[18] his associate Dr. K. Nehru and others in the International Society for Unified Science are actively developing the model past the point Larson started with. Eric Julien independently rediscovered some of the same concepts, as well as others that are not in Larson's model, in *The Science of Extraterrestrials,* which is also very technical and has gained the appreciation of respected Russian scientists.[19]

Mass Decreases as We Reach the Speed of Light

Here's the burning question that immediately pops into my mind: "If time-space really exists, then how do we get there?" Once we have that answer, we may very well be able to dematerialize, teleport and travel in time—which would certainly make for a very interesting and fun-filled Golden Age. The first big clue I found for how we could directly enter into time-space came from Dr. Vladimir Ginzburg.

In his books and technical papers, Ginzburg reveals another mistake Einstein made in the Theory of Relativity. (In my opinion, Einstein did a great job—we just need to fix up a few things.) As you may already know, conventional relativity theory says nothing can travel faster than the speed of light. Einstein's equations suggested that as you approach the speed of light, you gain mass. You can never actually reach the speed of light, because theoretically at the speed of light you are now as massive as the entire Universe. Ginzburg, however, made a revolutionary discovery: You could turn that same relativity equation upside down. In the process, everything still works—you don't violate any laws of physics, but there is one major difference: As you approach the speed of light, you lose mass instead of gaining it. This means that once you reach light speed, you have no mass left—at least not in space-time. This simple change to one Einstein equation has absolutely stunning implications for human civilization.

Here's how Ginzburg explains it on his Web site.

> You may not be prepared to abandon immediately the century-old relativistic equations. But once you are ready to do so, you will discover many amazing things: Only when a particle is at rest, it may be considered as pure matter. As soon as the particle begins to move, its gravitational mass and electrical charge will start to decrease . . . so a part of [that] matter will be converted into a field. When the particle velocity V becomes equal to the ultimate spiral field velocity C [the speed of light], its gravitational mass and electric charge become equal to zero. At this point, matter will be completely converted into a "pure" field.[20]

Now we're onto something. If we can push the whirling movement inside an atom past the speed of light, then we've just popped that atom over into time-space. It wasn't until very recently that I realized there was an even more important concept hiding behind this: The motion inside the atom is already going at the speed of light, or very close to it—so it doesn't take much to finish the job. Right then, years and years of weird little scientific facts I had been collecting in my mind all came together—and I had one of the finest Eureka moments of my entire life.

Just a Little Push

Physical matter is always right on the edge between these two realities. All we need to do is give it a little push to get it over the boundary—and flip it into time-space. This is how our buckyballs were able to turn into a wave just by slamming against a wall. Protons, neutrons, electrons and atoms in the quantum realm are flip-flopping all the time. You can't necessarily see the atoms disappear out of a solid object when they flip into waves, but once I realized this is what they were doing, it became clear that others had observed and measured it happening.

For example, Dr. Nikolai Kozyrev found that simply smashing an object against a hard surface would cause its weight to decrease. In one case, he smashed a ball bearing against a lead plate, and weighed it before and after the collision. In another case, he dropped a piece of lead against a stone basement floor. Some of the atoms popped over into time-space just from being bumped—and the objects weighed less. Even better, "These experiments showed that the weight defect does not disappear immediately after a collision, but decreases gradually—with relaxation times of about 15-20 minutes."[21] That means that the missing weight slowly comes back as those atoms quiet back down. They don't immediately return to light or sub-light speeds—there is a fifteen to twenty-minute delay involved. This again suggests we are dealing with a fluidlike flow between our two "parallel realities" of space-time and time-space.

Smashing the objects with violence wasn't necessary either. In another experiment, Kozyrev found that simply shaking a weight up and down thirty times by hand was enough to cause its weight to go down.[22] The strangest part of all was that the weight did not all come back in a nice, smooth curve—it came back in sudden little quantized jumps over time. Each time the weight suddenly changed, its newest increase in mass was proportional to the others. Each weight change was also proportional to the total amount of mass that disappeared in the first place.

If this is confusing, the easiest way I can explain it is by using a hypothetical example. If you smash a weight and it loses a hundred milligrams, let's say, it might initially gain back ten milligrams. Then you wait . . . but nothing happens. Then, suddenly, it gets ten milligrams heavier. Then nothing happens for a while. Then ten more milligrams appear. This keeps on happening over the course of fifteen to twenty minutes. According to Kozyrev, "We succeeded in obtaining fivefold and even tenfold effects." He also found out that this so-called effect quantization actually "takes place in almost all the experiments."[23] So again, we are looking at a basic property of physical matter. As the atoms pop back in from time-space, they don't do so in a nice, smooth, even fashion—it's as if there were layers within each atom. Each layer only pops in once it has slowed back down enough to cross over the light-speed boundary. That means individual atoms could be both in and out of our reality at the same time, depending on which layer you're looking at. This will make much more sense once we discuss the layers of geometry you will find within each atom—but that comes later.

So again, the basic idea is that by smashing, bumping or even just shaking an object, some of its atoms pop over into time-space and its weight goes down. This also explains Dr. Bruce DePalma's mysterious Spinning Ball Experiment. DePalma was working for Polaroid in photographic sciences, and lectured part time at MIT. One of his students wanted to see if there was a difference between the effect of gravity on a rotating object and a nonrotating object. DePalma designed an experiment to help find the answer. Two one-inch-wide ball bearings were given a "precisely measured thrust" that should normally cause them to rise and fall in exactly the same arc. The only difference between the two was that DePalma used a hand router to get one of them spinning at 18,000 revolutions per minute, or 300 revolutions per second, first—so this is obviously a very fast spin. He then launched them off in the dark, and photographed the results with a sixty-cycle strobe light. The results were explained on the official Bruce DePalma Web site.

> Repeating this numerous times, and analyzing the parallel trajectories of the ball bearings as documented photographically, . . . the rotating ball . . . went to a higher point in its trajectory, fell faster, and hit the bottom of its trajectory before the non-rotating ball bearing.[24]

Since the spinning ball traveled higher, that obviously meant it had become lighter. And since it plunged faster than ordinary gravity should allow, that also suggested it was then moving slightly faster in time as well. DePalma didn't know exactly what was causing the ball to fly higher—but once I figured it out, many other pieces fit together. Nairz saw the same thing when he slammed a buckyball against the wall, and

Kozyrev saw it by smashing ball bearings and vigorously shaking weights. Then when we add in Ginzburg, we now have a theoretical framework: as soon as a particle begins to move, part of it will transform into pure Field.

DePalma found that you didn't even need to shoot the balls through the air—simply dropping two ball bearings straight down, from a height of only six feet, "repeatedly demonstrated a small but significant and clearly perceptible effect" if one of them was rotating at a fast speed.[25] DePalma got his results published in the *British Scientific Research Association Journal* in 1976. He also explained it to Dr. Edward Purcell, one of Harvard's top experimental physicists. Dr. Purcell definitely realized what the implications of this really were: "According to DePalma, Purcell, after contemplating the experiment for several minutes, remarked, 'This will change everything.'"[26] In his 1977 paper on the Spinning Ball Experiment, DePalma revealed he had the same basic idea as Kozyrev.

"Time as a manifestation of a much deeper and basic force is what we have a concern for here. The point of connection I want to make is the inertia of objects relates to the time energy flowing through them."[27] Sounds familiar.

So far, all we've done is create a small effect that you need special laboratory equipment to even notice. That's not very exciting. How do we get the really good stuff to happen on a larger scale? In order to find the answer, we have to go back and take another look at gravity. Remember that in Larson's model, gravity is all there is. Atoms and molecules are nothing more than vortexes within an energy field we call gravity.

CHAPTER FOURTEEN

The Gravity—and Levity—of the Situation

Protons, neutrons, electrons, whole atoms and even clusters of sixty or more atoms called buckyballs have all been found to pop in and out of a wavelike state, where they no longer appear to exist. With the help of Larson's new physics model, we now see that these particles are popping into a parallel reality called time-space, where time is three-dimensional. Dr. Vladimir Ginzburg turned a classic Einstein equation upside down and found that atoms and molecules lose mass as they are accelerated to the speed of light and beyond. Then we discovered that by simply smashing or shaking an object, as in Kozyrev's experiments, or rapidly rotating an object, as in DePalma's Spinning Ball Experiment, we can apparently accelerate the internal movement in an atom past light speed—and measurably reduce its weight. Kozyrev also found that it took about fifteen to twenty minutes for the missing mass to return, and it did so in sudden jumps—rather than a smooth, gradual change as we might expect. In this new science, gravity and time are interconnected. Ultimately, all atoms are vortexes of motion within an energy most people call gravity, and which we are calling the Source Field.

Let's look at a whirlpool in a stream of water for a minute. Does any of that water actually disappear when it goes into the whirlpool? What happens to the water after it shoots through the vortex? Does it shift into some parallel reality, never to return? Of course not. The water is obviously still there in the stream, and it keeps right on flowing along. How does this apply to the earth? Simply put, the energy flowing into the earth must also flow back out of the earth. Gravity, as a downward force, must also have an upward force—and my favorite name for gravity's counterpart is levity. The Source Field, or gravity, rushes into our planet to create all the atoms and molecules on earth simultaneously—but it still has to keep moving. Once this same flow of energy streams back out of our planet, it has now lost some of its momentum—so it would be traveling a little more slowly than it went in. Once you understand this, you will see there may be an upward-pushing force from the earth that is in a constant tug-of-war with the downward-pushing force—and the downward force only wins by a very small amount. If we did not have the upward-pushing force to balance everything out, we would very likely be instantaneously crushed flat by the pressure of gravity.

Atoms and molecules are nothing more than vortexes within gravity. In Larson's model, there are only three real dimensions—and in this absolute reality, space and time are one and the same. You then have two parallel realities where the space in one reality creates the time in the other reality, and vice versa. There is a constant, flowing exchange between these two realities going on within every atom. When an atom pops over into time-space, its spinning momentum is transferred over into the fluidlike energy within the parallel reality—and it is no longer affected by gravity in our own space-time. Gravity now moves right through that area without pushing on the atom anymore. However, if the atom (or vortex in time-space) starts losing its speed and momentum, gravity pulls it back over into space-time. The full transition can take fifteen to twenty minutes in a larger object with many atoms, as we saw in Kozyrev's experiments. Interestingly, the renowned mathematician and physicist Roger Penrose said in a 1997 issue of *Scientific American* that gravity triggers the transition between a particle and a wave at the quantum level.[1] Dr. Hal Puthoff calculated that there was a direct relationship between gravity and the trembling motion within all particles the Germans dubbed *Zitterbewegung.*[2]

Back in 1982, Princeton scientists had discovered that electrons become fluidlike when kept at super-cold temperatures and zapped with the world's most powerful magnet. This fits very nicely with our model.

> The electrons . . . seemed to "cooperate" and work together to form what scientists call a "quantum fluid," an extremely rare situation where electrons act identically, in lockstep, more like soup than as individually spinning units.[3]

Levity Creates Thrust

And here's my favorite part of all. Theoretically, an atom in space-time gets pushed on by gravity—but once an atom pops over into time-space, it gets pushed on by levity. This means that within our reality, that atom now has thrust . . . as long as it is still bound together with other atoms that have not yet popped over. Therefore, if you want to get an object to levitate, you would need to bring its molecules to a point where they are half in and half out of our own three-dimensional reality of space-time. That way, the levity force can then balance out against gravity—not unlike how you can float perfectly still underwater by controlling how much air you hold in your lungs. If you push an object too far over into time-space, it will dematerialize. Then the same force that was causing it to rise up in our reality will now make it fall down in the parallel reality. Gravity takes over—but in a totally parallel reality. This may work in a manner similar to a Möbius loop as you pass between realities.

Nature uses these principles all the time. The DNA molecule stores photons of light, and it appears that this same flip-flopping at the light-speed boundary is what allows DNA to easily exchange energy and information between space-time and time-space—between our physical body and our energetic duplicate. In the remaining part of this chapter, we will explore gravity-shielding effects occurring in air vortexes (tornado levitation), water vortexes (trout rising through vertical waterfalls), plant fibers (the secret ingredient involved in sap flow) and insect wings (to keep certain large insects airborne and prevent collisions with other insects)—not to mention the flow of electromagnetic energy, once properly understood. And that's not all.

Tornado Anomalies Explained

Let's start with tornadoes. The conventional explanation is that the levitation inside a tornado is caused by air suction—and that certainly should account for some of what we're seeing. However, once you add in other curious effects that have been documented, even on government NOAA Web sites, we can no longer be so sure that this is the only cause of the levitation—or even the main cause of it. There are many cases of people, animals, objects, even entire homes ending up inside a whirling tornado and transported large distances without being damaged[4]—where the fiercely rotating air should have torn them to pieces. Many matter-blending effects have been documented as well. The first time I read about this was in a technical paper by Dr. Alexei Dmitriev. The story that jumped out at me the most was of a clover leaf that had been found pushed into a stucco wall, during a tornado—as if the wall had become soft and spongy.[5] At the time, this was a mystery to me—but now it all makes sense. Another good example was of an Oklahoma tornado in 1942 that tore one of the wheels off of a car, while leaving the rest of the car undamaged.[6] I realized that if the lug nuts on the wheels had become soft and liquidlike, the levity force could then pull the tire off the car and lift it into the air quite easily.

Dmitriev's paper also presents evidence of complete dematerialization cases, where the matter is then blended together with other objects once it pops back over into space-time. An old, charred wooden board that was brittle and porous went through a wooden house wall without breaking—and an inch-and-a-half-thick gate frame was punctured by a piece of wood.[7] I realized if these stories were true, there should be many more examples. I later found an official NOAA government Web site that collected eyewitness reports from a tornado outbreak in Grand Rapids, Michigan, on April 3, 1956. NOAA said that "in the interest of historical accuracy, these statements have not been edited for content, but are presented as they were submitted to the National Weather Service." The reports included a living room window that was embedded with sand, but did not break. A farm machine had several leaky holes in the oil pan from pieces of straw that had shot through. Straw was found embedded into the brick wall of a house. A three-inch twig blended into a wall without breaking or cracking the twig or the wall. Blades of grass were driven into tree trunks, and a cow became embedded in a tree.[8]

In her WeatherBug blog, Stephanie Blozy alluded to stories of a coat hanger blended into a wooden board, and wood splinters stuck into a brick, though no direct references were given. In the comments section, Russell L. DeGarmo claimed he saw a two-by-four driven through both the front and back walls of a two-story brick home, where the entry hole was smaller than the size of the plank. His parents had driven him to see this odd event in Pennsylvania in the early 1940s. Another commenter claimed to have seen a banana embedded halfway into a telephone pole. And Jim Mims claimed that NASA's Marshall Space Flight Center in Huntsville, Alabama, has a display of a section of telephone pole with a drinking straw embedded into it.[9] Stephanie was brave enough to offer an opinion about what causes these events, which now seems fairly accurate.

> Another theory based on quantum physics states that the piece of straw is electrically charged super fast as it spins in the center of the tornado, allowing it to exist on a "higher energy density." When it flies out of the tornado and comes in contact with something of a lower energy density, it passes through that object like a ghost—until the energy levels are equal, and the straw is frozen in the object.[10]

Of course, numerous commenters attacked her for even stating this as a potential explanation.

In *Freaks of the Storm*, climatologist Dr. Randy Cerveny shared additional examples. A Minnesota tornado "split open a tree, jammed in an automobile, and clamped the tree shut again" in 1919.[11] A tornado in India from 1838 caused a long stalk of bamboo to be completely embedded through a five-foot-thick wall with bricks on both sides.[12] In 1896, a tornado in St. Louis, Missouri, drove a two-by-four plank of pine wood through solid iron, five eighths of an inch thick, on the Eads Bridge—and there is an excellent picture of it in the book from NOAA.[13]

This tree branch was pushed through the thick metal of an iron bridge during the massive St. Louis tornado of 1896.

In Mount Carmel, Illinois, a tornado in 1877 drove a brick through the outer wall of a house, the interior wood, the plaster wall, twenty-seven more feet between two rooms, and lodged it into a rear wall, without ever breaking any corners off the brick.[14] In 1951, a bean was blended halfway into a fresh chicken egg—without ever cracking the shell—in Scottsbluff, Nebraska. Cerveny found a photograph of this peculiar incident, though there is not enough detail to really see what the egg looks like up close.[15]

Washburn University has a Web site discussing the June 8, 1966, tornado in Topeka, Kansas. This includes a report from Jan Griffin that describes how when her car was dug out from the wreckage two days later, items from her bathroom had somehow appeared in the trunk—though she obviously did not put them there, and apparently saw no sign of the trunk ever having opened.[16] Another Web site features a photograph of glass pieces that had been embedded into an aluminum pipe—in a tornado on the Isle of Wight on June 19, 1985.[17] In 2004, the

Boonshoft Museum of Discovery displayed "bizarre artifacts that historical societies like to keep under wraps" in Dayton, Ohio, as reported in an AP press release. This exhibit included a gas meter that had been speared by a stick of wood in the Xenia tornado from 1974.[18]

This wooden board was driven through a vertical wooden post during the infamous Tristate tornado of 1925.

In some cases, strange orbs are seen. The NOAA Web site reported eerie yellow-colored "giant puffballs" in one tornado. Fred Schmidt reported seeing what looked like greenish "glassy marbles on a plate glass window" that were being "pushed across the sky." There was no rain, thunder or lightning as he saw this. He also reported what now appears to be a classic case where he was popped over into time-space—thus causing all the normal sounds within space-time to disappear.

> The quietness was eerie. There were no birds singing, which there usually were. In fact there were no sounds from any animals at all. . . . I also [later] saw what appeared to be a straw embedded in a telephone pole about halfway in, just as perfect as could be.[19]

Natural Antigravity in Water, Trees and Insects

A simple case of rotating air is enough to cause effects that fit our model
nicely. What about rotating water? Let's not forget that in our new
model, gravity has spin currents in it—because it is caused by a fluidlike
energy. If these spin currents get strong enough—by rotating vortex
motion within the Source Field—they can create their own gravitational
force. They seem to work in a sideways direction, creating rotating
currents—such as tornadoes, hurricanes, ocean currents, and mantle
currents below the continental plates—but in some cases this force can
directly counteract the normal downward push of gravity. As Olof Alexandersson described in the classic *Living Water,* Viktor Schauberger
allegedly discovered a gravity-shielding effect in nature by studying how
trout could jump straight up, through high waterfalls, with seemingly
very little effort.[20] For decades, he observed that the fish would first
"dance in a wild spinning movement" and then "float motionlessly
upward" through the waterfall, even at unusually large heights. Even
more surprisingly, on a late winter night with bright moonlight, he witnessed this same effect happening with egg-shaped rocks. He was looking into a mountain pool, within a rushing stream, when an egg-shaped
stone almost as big as a human head started doing a spinning dance just
like the trout would do. It then rose to the surface of the water—and a
circle of ice quickly formed around it. (Such bizarre and sudden changes
in temperature are also consistent with matter popping into time-space.
Remember—we might think that a gateway into time-space would
increase temperature, but Kozyrev actually proved it makes things
colder.) Eventually, Schauberger saw several egg-shaped stones all do the
same thing in sequence. He analyzed them and found that besides the
egg shape, they all contained metals.[21]

How do giant trees actually pull sap all the way up their trunks?
Physicist Dr. Orvin E. Wagner, who worked at Oak Ridge National
Laboratory, taught physics at California State Polytechnic University and
conducted research in condensed matter physics at Lockheed Research

Laboratory in Palo Alto, California, researched this subject. He did biophysics research since 1966 that led him to discover a wave effect in plants as of 1988, wherein he began devoting himself full-time to studying these mysteries.[22] In 1992 and 1994, he published papers in mainstream journals outlining his discovery that plants and trees are using a gravity-shielding effect to create sap flow.[23] Although some of the flow could be caused by suction from the evaporation in the leaves, that cannot account for everything Wagner observed. It appears that the branches of trees create a vortex effect not unlike what we see in the pyramids. They may create a rotating spin current of gravitational force that is sufficient to push the sap up the tree.

Wagner cut small holes into the xylem tissue of trees and used tiny accelerometers to confirm that gravity was not as strong inside those areas. Tiny hanging weights recorded a decrease of up to 22 percent of the force of gravity inside vertical holes of slightly leaning trees. He also found similar forces in a hole within a horizontal root—creating thrust in the direction the root was pointing. Wagner believes that "inside the plant tissue itself, likely the forces are much larger." He also found consistent evidence that plant branches tend to grow at angles that are always multiples of five degrees, suggesting they are somehow harnessing a spiraling, geometric wave component that naturally exists within gravity.

Wagner also claims to have demonstrated the existence of these waves by simply rotating glass tubes filled with particles of dust. The waves appeared in how the particles arranged themselves. Wagner has an interesting theory of how all this works.

> A growing plant stem acts like a tuned wave guide. . . . A stem growing at a certain angle to the gravitational field adjusts its cell sizes, internodal spacings and other structures to conform to the [geometric] wavelengths associated with that particular angle.[24]

Dr. Viktor Grebennikov was an entomologist (insect scientist) who discovered the Cavity Structural Effect, as we previously discussed—but this also led to a realization that certain insects appear to be naturally using gravity-shielding technology as well.

I was examining the chitin shells of insects under my microscope in the summer of 1988 along with their pinnate antennae, the fish-scale microstructure of butterfly wings, iridescent colors, and other inventions of nature. I became interested in an amazingly rhythmical microstructure of one large insect [wing casing]. . . . It was an extremely well-ordered composition, as though stamped out by factory equipment according to special blueprints and calculations. As I saw it, the intricate sponginess was clearly unnecessary either for the strength of the part, or for its decoration. I have never observed anything like this unusual micro-ornament either in nature, in technology, or in art. Because its structure is three-dimensional, I have been unable to capture it in a drawing so far, or a photograph. . . . Was it perhaps a wave emitter using "my" multiple cavity structures effect? That truly lucky summer, there were very many insects of this species, and I would capture them at night. . . .

I placed the small, concave chitin plate on the microscope stage in order to again examine its strangely star-shaped cells under strong magnification. I again admired this masterpiece jewel work of nature. I was about to place a second identical plate with the same unusual cell structure on its underside, almost purposelessly on top of the first one. But then. The little plate came loose from my tweezers, hung suspended above the other plate on the microscope stage for a few seconds, then turned a few degrees clockwise and slid to the right, then turned counterclockwise and swung—and only then it abruptly fell on the desk.

You can imagine what I felt at that moment. When I came to my senses, I tied a few panels together with a wire and it wasn't an easy thing to do. I succeeded only when I positioned them vertically. What I got was a multi-layered chitin block and I placed it on the desk. Even a relatively large object, such as a thumbtack, would not fall on it. Something pushed it up and aside. When I attached the tack on top of the "block," I witnessed incredible, impossible things. The tack would disappear from sight for a few moments. That was when I realized that this was no "beacon," but something entirely different.

And I became again so excited that all the objects around me became foggy and shaky. I managed to pull myself together with huge effort in a couple of hours, and I continued working. This is how it all started. Of course, much still remains to be understood, verified, and tested.[25]

These results are spectacular to a conventional mind-set, leading most to conclude Dr. Grebennikov must be lying—but already we are seeing an effect consistent with our model. When he put the tack in the direct center of the vortex current created by the insect's wing casing, the tack's atoms all popped over into time-space and it seemingly disappeared. In a 2005 issue of *New Energy Technologies,* we find out that although Grebennikov never disclosed the exact genus and species of the insect he discovered this effect with, he does make multiple mentions in his book about the remarkable properties of the wing cases for scarabaeus, bronze poplar borer and particularly Cetonia. There are five species of bronze poplar borer that have an unusual honeycomb pattern on the inside of their wing cases, similar to his description.[26]

So if you really love Mother Nature, you just might learn something. Some folks here on earth have apparently been aware of these dueling gravitational forces for thousands and thousands of years—and the techniques to overcome normal downward gravitational flow by understanding how to speed up the spiraling motion within the Source Field—to create currents that push in a different direction. This appears to be the great secret of how the Pyramids were built. However, we still haven't really answered our deeper question: How do we pop enough atoms over into time-space to actually make an object levitate? Once again, an old friend comes to the rescue: coherence. We need to bring the frequency inside the atom to a point that is faster than light speed—so it then pops over into time-space. This can be done by creating a harmonic pulsation in the Source Field—in gravity. So, if we want the magic to happen, all we have to do is start vibrating an object, or a given area, with the right frequencies. Then, by creating coherence in that area, some of the atoms will start popping over the light-speed boundary—where they then get pushed on by what we call levity.

Tibetan Acoustic Levitation

This might sound complicated, but the actual techniques are easy once you know what you're doing—and hardly any technology is required to create the coherence. The most intriguing example I've ever discovered is called Tibetan Acoustic Levitation, and this is another piece of weird science that I struggled for years to understand. This comes to us from Henry Kjellson, a Swedish aircraft designer, who described the whole story to a journalist who then published it in a German magazine. A truly groundbreaking New Zealand researcher named Bruce Cathie then wrote a detailed analysis of it in David Hatcher Childress's *Anti-Gravity and the World Grid*.

Henry Kjellson was a close friend and colleague of a medical doctor, also from Sweden, who chose to be identified only as Dr. Jarl. According to Kjellson, Dr. Jarl befriended a young Tibetan student while he studied at Oxford. When Dr. Jarl was later paid to visit Egypt by a scientific society in England, his Tibetan friend found out—and sent a messenger to find him. The message was very good. Dr. Jarl's friend had become a trusted member of the monastery, and now a high Tibetan lama said he wanted to meet Dr. Jarl—urgently. Apparently Dr. Jarl then got permission to stay in Tibet for a fairly long time, take notes, and report back on what he found. While he was there, Dr. Jarl got to see a variety of things that few Westerners had ever been allowed to witness before. The greatest secret of all, according to Swedish engineer Olaf Alexanderson, was that "a vibrating and condensed sound field can nullify the power of gravitation." Other experts on Tibet, including Linaver, Spalding and Hue, had heard about the Tibetans using sound to levitate gigantic stones, and Dr. Jarl had also heard about these legends—but he was the first Westerner to witness it.

Dr. Jarl was led into a sloping meadow that was surrounded by high cliffs to the northwest. One of the cliffs had a ledge that led into a cave, some 250 meters above the ground. The Tibetans were in the process of building a wall out of huge stone blocks up on this ledge—but there was no way to get there, except by climbing straight up on a rope. About 250 meters away from the cliff, there was a polished rock slab that had a bowl-shaped area carved out of the middle of it. The slab was a meter wide and the bowl area was fifteen centimeters deep. Then, a team of yak oxen hauled a giant stone block into the bowl. The stone was incredibly huge—it was a full meter high, and a meter and a half long.

Here's the weird part. A perfect quarter-circle arc (90 degrees) was set up with thirteen drums and six trumpets all aiming at the stone. All the drums were made of three-millimeter-thick sheet iron, and instead of any type of animal skin for a head, there was metal on the end that the monks beat with leather clubs. The other end was left open. The six trumpets were all quite long—3.12 meters to be exact—with 0.3-meter openings. The monks carefully measured the distance from the stone to this quarter-circle of instruments, and it came out to 63 meters. Eight of the thirteen drums were exactly the same size as the stone—a meter wide and a meter and a half long. Four of the drums were smaller in size, but were exactly one third the volume of the larger drum, at 0.7 meters wide and one meter long. One additional drum was the smallest, at 0.2 meters wide and 0.3 meters long—again in perfect harmonic proportion. You could fit 41 of the small drums into the medium drum, in volume, and 125 into the larger drum.[27]

All the instruments were fixed on mounts that allowed you to precisely aim them. And finally, you needed another key ingredient to make it work—a total of nearly two hundred monks who lined up in rows, about eight or ten deep, behind each of the nineteen instruments. Most people wouldn't think the monks could add any measurable energy to the mix, but with what we now know about the Source Field, all that has changed. It seemed that the instruments were tools that helped focus and concentrate the energy that was being consciously generated by the monks. (This is also why the experiment might not work if the people lining up behind each instrument were not properly trained in generating coherence within themselves, through meditation.)

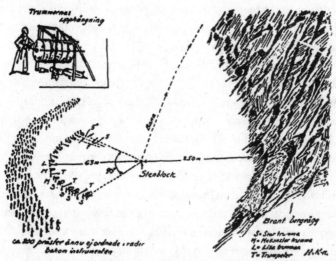

Swedish aircraft designer Henry Kjellson's sketch of Tibetan Acoustic Levitation—where 200 monks with drums and trumpets somehow levitated massive stones.

Now, let's hear directly from Bruce Cathie about what happened next.

When the stone was in position, the monk behind the small drum gave a signal to start the concert. The small drum had a very sharp sound, and could be heard even with the other instruments making a terrible din. All the monks were singing and chanting a prayer, slowly increasing the tempo of this unbelievable noise. During the first four minutes nothing happened; then as the speed of the drumming, and the noise, increased, the big stone block started to rock and sway, and suddenly it took off into the air with an increasing speed in the direction of the platform in front of the cave hole 250 meters high. After three minutes of ascent, it landed on the platform.[28]

Incredible. We're watching a gigantic stone, as big as some of the ones used to build the Great Pyramid, making a long, slow, lumbering three-minute trip up through the air in a 500-meter arc. Obviously, the power of the drums, trumpets and chanting is nowhere near enough to cause an object to levitate by any conventional means—but if they were creating the right coherence in the block, they could resonate atoms inside the rock over the light-speed boundary. They then enter into time-space, and provide thrust as they get pushed on by the levity force. If you touched the rock during this time, it would have almost certainly become spongy, since as many as half of the molecules are no longer in our reality. This appears to be how the gigantic stone blocks in Peru, at Sacsayhuaman, were able to be fitted together with cracks so tight you can't even fit a razor blade between them. The rocks become soft and malleable, like clay, as their builders popped more and more of the atoms into time-space. As we already saw in the tornado anomalies, there are many examples of solid materials becoming soft and spongy when they become coherent.

Some of the stones split from the intensity, and the monks moved them away. Nonetheless, they were able to keep the production line going and transport a total of five or six blocks an hour with this method. Now here's the incredible part. Dr. Jarl thought he was either being hyp-notized or going through some sort of mass psychosis, so he actually set up a movie camera and filmed the whole process—two different times. When he played the films back later on, they showed exactly the same thing he had witnessed. Dr. Jarl was astonished, and obviously felt this discovery would shake the very foundations of the world as we know it—maybe even literally. When the scientific society that had been spon-soring Dr. Jarl heard about these films, disaster struck. They swooped in and confiscated the originals, declaring them classified—which Dr. Jarl felt was "hard to explain, or understand." They tried to appease him by saying the films would be released in the year 1990—but this obviously never happened.

Building a Craft You Can Fly In

This form of levitation still seems to be a cumbersome process, and may require a level of consciousness that most of us do not now possess. What if we build something where the propulsion system is inside a craft we can actually fly in? Let's go back to Dr. Viktor Schauberger, who found levitation effects occurring with trout and rocks in water. He built structures with the same egg shape he saw in the rocks, and built special turbines that rotated water at a high speed inside them—creating the same vortex shapes he had carefully observed in nature. There is a great wealth of reading material on how he succeeded in building a working gravity-shielding craft by using this process.[29]

Researchers such as Nick Cook and Joseph Farrell have written about how this and other technologies came into the hands of Nazi Germany—though there is clear evidence that Schauberger resisted cooperating with them, and only ended up participating because of dire threats to him and his family. In Nick Cook's *The Hunt for Zero Point,* he explains that the Nazi code word for this gravity-shielding project was Chronos—which means "time." As our model predicts, the Nazis apparently found that a movement through space creates a movement through time.

> If you generate a torsion field of sufficient magnitude, the theory says you can bend the . . . space around [Schauberger's] generator. The more torsion you generate, the more space you perturb. . . . When you bend space, you also bend time.

Later, Cook goes into more detail.

> If a whirling torsion field, with or without an electromagnetic component, was binding with gravity to produce a levitational effect—an antigravity effect—it wasn't doing so in the four dimensions of this world, but somewhere else. It explained why the Germans had attempted to use a torsion

field to act upon the fourth dimension of time. Time, like gravity, the theorists said, was simply another variable stemming from the hyperspace.[30]

Dr. Viktor Grebennikov, who discovered a gravity-shielding effect in insect wings, was also able to use this discovery to build a working craft that was big enough for him to fly in. He organized multiple wing cases together on layers that could open and close like Venetian blinds, designed to spread open like an oriental fan. The lifting power of the wings would dramatically increase when you crossed them over the tops of each other, and this mechanical system allowed him to control that process. When they were all stacked on top of each other, he achieved plenty of vertical lift. He then built this mechanism into a small, rectangular wooden box: "I chose a rectangular design because it is easier to fold and once folded, it may resemble a suitcase, or a painter's case, and it can be therefore disguised and not arouse any suspicions. I have naturally chosen a painter's case."[31] He would ride it standing up, like a scooter. The vertical thrust was controlled by a bicycle brake caliper that could open and close the fanlike layers of wing cases. His forward speed was controlled by a second brake caliper that determined the tilt angle of the wings. He steered by leaning his body, and belted himself to the metal pole that held the handlebars for the bicycle calipers. Grebennikov's account of what actually happened when he used this device fits with our model so perfectly well that this seems very unlikely to be a hoax.

First of all, since he popped over into time-space, once he reached a certain height he looked more like a wave to viewers on the ground.

> [When in flight,] I can't be seen from the ground—and not just because of the distance. I cast almost no shadow even in a very low flight. Yet, as I found out later, people sometimes see something where I am in the sky. I appear to them either as a light sphere, a disk, or something like a slanted cloud with sharp edges, which moves strangely according to them, not exactly the way a real cloud would.[32]

He also experienced time distortions, such as the inability to close his camera shutter: "I could see but couldn't take photographs. . . . My camera shutter wouldn't close, and both rolls of film I had with me, one in the camera and the other in my pocket, got light-struck."[33] This reminds me of Sid Hurwich's device—where his experience of time became so much faster than the time flow in Grebennikov's camera that his pressure on the button did not last long enough to actually open the shutter. If he were patient enough, it might work, but he'd probably have to wait awhile.

Best of all, he found out that by simply traveling through space using gravity shielding, he also automatically traveled through time.

> By the way, besides the camera, I have experienced sometimes trouble with my watch and possibly also with the calendar. While descending onto a familiar glade, I would occasionally find it slightly "out of season," with about a two-week deviation. . . . Thus, it may be possible to fly not just in space but also, or so it seems, in time. I cannot make the latter claim with a 100 percent guarantee, except perhaps that in flight, particularly at its beginning, a watch runs erratically, now too slow and then too fast. But, the watch is at its accurate time and speed at the end of the excursions. Nevertheless, this is one of the reasons why I stay away from people during my journeys. If time manipulation is involved alongside the manipulation of gravitation, I might, perhaps, accidentally disrupt cause-and-effect of relations and someone might get hurt. This is where my fears were coming from.[34]

Grebennikov also tried to bring insects back, only to have them disappear from the tube. However, in one case, a captured adult insect reverted to a living chrysalis stage when he brought it back—showing an undeniable time-travel effect.

> Insects captured "there" disappear from my test tubes, boxes and other receptacles. They disappear mostly without a trace. Once I had a test tube crushed to tiny bits in my pocket, another

time there was an oval hole in the tube glass with brown [edges], as though [it was] chitin-colored. . . . I did feel a kind of burning or an electric shock inside my pocket on many occasions, perhaps at the moment of my prisoner's disappearance. I found the captured insect in my test tube only once, but it wasn't the adult ichneumon with white rings on its feelers, but its chrysalis, i.e., its earlier stage. It was alive and it moved its belly when touched but, much to my dismay, it has died a week later.[35]

Before he takes off, he is in our space-time. When he lands, he fully returns to space-time once more—only now he has traveled in time. When he tried to bring insects back, they often didn't make it—but in the case of the ichneumon, he actually saw the adult body revert to its larval stage in the tube.

According to the *New Energy Technologies* article, Dr. Grebennikov sent a patent application to Russia with Professor V. Zolotarev for this stunning invention. He got nothing but resistance from the scientific community. A Russian newspaper published a prerelease of Grebennikov's book about his invention in 1992, complete with a photograph allegedly showing him levitating about two or three feet off the ground on his platform.[36]

Dr. Viktor Grebennikov allegedly levitating on a device he built. Insect wing casings, which apparently could shield gravity, were used as a power source.

There are also a variety of close-up photographs of the platform itself. A Russian magazine, *Technika Molodezhi,* also published the photographs—and mentioned that he had publicly demonstrated the device at the Siberian Research Institute of Agriculture and Agricultural Chemistry. His book was originally going to be five hundred pages, with four hundred color images, and the original newspaper article said he would give all the precise details of exactly how to build his device. He was then told by his publishers and editor that it was forbidden to publish this information—clearly suggesting they were warned by the Russian government not to release the data for matters of "national security." Two photos of Grebennikov in flight were left in the book since they had already leaked—but the page count dropped to just over three hundred, and he had to rewrite the entire manuscript.[37]

Gordon Novel, who claims to have had access to classified technologies, also reported the connection between gravity shielding and time travel in an interview with Kerry Cassidy of Project Camelot.

> A UFO is probably very much like the cars back in "Back to the Future," a flying time machine. They're capable of going backwards and forwards in time. . . . To negate gravity, you've got to negate time. So time is the power . . . of the bird. . . . We don't believe [its power] comes from space or zero point. We believe it comes from time, purely and simply, and that energy and time are the same thing.[38]

Tesla Technology

Nikola Tesla also allegedly developed a working gravity-shielding technology—and he may have even had some help. Sidney Kirkpatrick was the first person allowed full access to the Cayce archives, including all the original names—and that's how we now know that Nikola Tesla and Thomas Edison both had professional interaction with Edgar Cayce from 1905 to 1907.[39] This almost certainly meant Tesla had at least one reading. Later, a series of Cayce readings were done that went into extreme technical detail with an inventor who was working on a gravity-shielding prototype called the No-Fuel Motor. Specifically, in reading 195-54, question 13, Cayce's source says that gravity is the result of two forces—one going down and one going back up. It also explains that this is a fairly crude way to explain it, because there is an ongoing amount of circular, spiraling vortex movement occurring in both directions as well.[40] Unfortunately, two separate fires at Cayce's photography studio destroyed all the records from Cayce's early years, including any readings he may have done for Tesla. Additional correspondence between Tesla, Thomas Edison and Cayce was "also later destroyed by a well-meaning but short-sighted volunteer at the Edgar Cayce archive in Virginia Beach."[41]

Regardless of whether Tesla had any help from Cayce, just four years after they began corresponding with each other, Tesla made some provocative statements in an interview with *The New York Herald*.

> The flying machine of the future—my flying machine—will be heavier than air, but it will not be an aeroplane. It will have no wings. . . . Yet it will be able to move at will through the air in any direction with perfect safety, [and at] higher speeds than have yet been reached. . . . It can remain absolutely stationary in the air, even in a wind, for great lengths of time. . . . Its lifting power will not depend upon any such delicate devices as the bird has to employ, but upon positive mechanical action."

When asked by the *Herald* journalist to clarify what he meant by "mechanical action," Tesla said:

> "Through gyroscopic action of my engine—assisted by some devices I am not yet prepared to talk about. . . . My airship will have neither gas bag, wings nor propellers."[42]

In *Lost Science*, Gerry Vassilatos gives testimony from alleged eyewitnesses to Tesla actually using this technology.

Tesla was seen standing on a platform, surrounded by a purplish corona, some thirty feet above the ground. The contrivance had a small coil [on top], and was entirely covered underneath with a smooth surface of sheet copper. The platform was perhaps two feet in total depth, being crammed with components. Tesla strode over to the platform, stood before a control panel, and whisked aloft in a crown of white sparks. The excessive sparks subsided with increased distance from the ground, often arcing to metal fencing. Tesla went out of his way to avoid the numerous metallic ranch fencing beneath his aerial course. . . . It was said that Tesla often delighted in soaring through the night air for hours each night.[43]

Ralph Ring, Otis Carr and Tesla's "Utron"

In August 2006, Project Camelot interviewed Ralph Ring, a seventy-one-year-old technician who worked with Otis T. Carr—inventor of the Otis elevator system—in the late 1950s and early 1960s. Carr had studied under Nikola Tesla, and was allegedly given the secret to his gravity-shielding technology. Carr finished developing a working saucer-shaped craft in 1947, and built a number of them—but initially it did not generate any official interest. In 2006, Ralph Ring finally came forward with an impressive barrage of technical documents, including detailed blueprints, from Carr's OTC Enterprises company.

Major Wayne Aho, a former Army Combat Intelligence Officer during World War II, announced that he would take the craft to the moon on December 7, 1959, that the trip would take 5 hours, and that he would remain in orbit for 7 days before returning. The 45 diameter craft he was to use weighed 30 tons, and "was powered by the Utron engine."[44]

The Utron engine was obviously Tesla's invention—and there was a key emphasis placed on the fact that it was round from the top-down

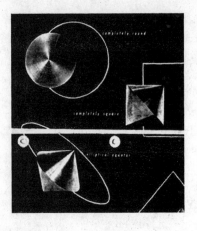

Otis Carr's promotional illustration of a gravity-shielding turbine originally invented by Nikola Tesla. Otis Carr was also the inventor of the elevator.

view and a perfect square from the side view. This caused it to be shaped like a top—or two cones connected base to base. Ring did not gain any financial benefits from coming forward, and had clear and extensive documentation, including photographs of Carr with the device, and detailed technical blueprints he obviously would not have spent money faking. When you read what Ring actually says, the case becomes very compelling.

First of all, we see solid metal becoming flexible—in this case like Jell-O.

> When recalling the heady events of the late 1950s working day and night with Carr, Ring again and again stressed that the key was working with nature. "Resonance," he would emphasize repeatedly. "You have to work with nature, not against her." He described how when the model disks were powered up and reached a particular rotational speed, . . . "the metal turned to Jell-O. You could push your finger right into it. It ceased to be solid. It turned into another form of matter, which was as if it was not entirely here in this reality. . . . It was uncanny, one of the weirdest sensations I've ever felt."[45]

The craft also traveled through time while also traveling through space.

> Did the craft fly? "Fly is not the right word. It traversed distance. It seemed to take no time. I was with two other engineers when we piloted the forty-five-foot craft about ten miles. I thought it hadn't moved—I thought it had failed. I was

completely astonished when we realized that we had returned with samples of rocks and plants from our destination. It was a dramatic success. It was more like a kind of teleportation. What's more, time was distorted somehow. We felt we were in the craft about fifteen or twenty minutes. We were told afterwards that we'd been carefully timed as having been in the craft no longer than three or four minutes.[46]

Perhaps even more interesting is the direct, conscious interaction that took place with the Source Field in this process.

The Utron was the key to it all. Carr said it accumulated energy because of its shape, and focused it, and also responded to our conscious intentions. When we operated the machine, we didn't work any controls. We went into a kind of meditative state, and all three of us focused our intentions on the effect we wanted to achieve. It sounds ridiculous, I know. But that's what we did, and that's what worked. Carr had tapped into some principle which is not understood, in which consciousness melds with engineering to create an effect. You can't write that into equations. I have no idea how he knew it would work. But it did.[47]

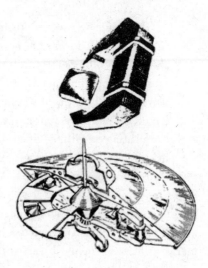

Carr told everyone to stuff their pockets with rocks, clumps of dirt and grass from their destination. Otherwise, when they returned, they wouldn't have any conscious memory of going anywhere, and would think the whole thing was a failure—not unlike Backster's roommate

Otis Carr's illustration of how the Tesla turbines fit into the saucer-shaped gravity-shielding craft he developed.

waking up from hypnosis and thinking nothing had happened. Sure enough, when Ring came back from the trip, he remembered nothing—but his pockets were stuffed with grass. He was absolutely stunned—and only later remembered the trip, as if waking up from a dream. When he asked Carr how it worked, this is what he said.

> Your brain is there to operate your body. You're in a vessel here. It's an illusionary vessel that people don't realize, because we're creating it in microseconds. From one second to the other, these shutters are opening and shutting, creating all this reality you see around you, but it doesn't really exist. It's all spirit. It's all energy, but we're creating it. . . . People don't realize that Man in a sense created time. Time doesn't exist, in essence. It does when we create it, and we have a beginning and an end to something. We call that time. But in a greater reality, there is no time.[48]

The "shutters opening and closing" sounds just like the fluctuations in physical, chemical, biological and radioactive reactions that Shnoll discovered are happening all over the world.

Unfortunately, agents working within classified projects swooped in on Carr in 1961, and they wouldn't take no for an answer.

> They came over with all their bells and whistles and said, "You're shuttin' down right now." And we asked them why, and they said, "Because of your threat to overthrow the monetary system of the United States of America." That was their ploy. . . . "And we're confiscating everything." They went into the offices and they went into the lab, and they started just confiscating everything. Then they debriefed us and told us, in essence, "You guys are wrong. You're attempting to overthrow the monetary system."[49]

This secrecy has gone on for quite some time—a "Cosmic Watergate," as Dr. Stanton Friedman referred to it in an article that circulated through mainstream media while I was writing this book.[50] This may be an outgrowth of the same secrecy the founding fathers kept around the meaning of the Great Seal of the United States—putting a message out there for those who would bother to find it, but never explaining it in any direct, open way. I hope it has become clear by now that there is an obvious, uniform system of principles behind these technologies. Once we fix the mistakes we've made in science, we can explain all the observations—and realize how these same forces already appear in nature. Right for now, no one has made a definite breakthrough with a technology like this that has gone mainstream—though similar discoveries were made by Thomas Townsend Brown (the Biefield-Brown effect), Professor John Searl (the Searl Levity Disc) and others. Brown decided to cooperate with the security apparatus and his work became classified, whereas Searl fought against it and was ruined—but their results are also consistent with everything we've been discussing here. Two Russian scientists, Roschin and Godin, independently rebuilt Searl's technology and got a very strong lift, though their device had to be bolted to the laboratory table for safety.[51] Searl and his associates have recently released videos online showing his unique turbine in action, which skeptics previously attacked him about and had said was impossible.[52] Searl's team is allegedly working to develop a fully operational prototype of their device, as is Ralph Ring.

Do It Yourself—with Lung-Gom

At the time I write this book, none of us have open access to these technologies—but perhaps this shift into the Golden Age represents a time where we won't need them. Is it possible to generate enough coherence that you could actually levitate your own body—without any technology at all? The Tibetans appear to have inherited the secrets to this amazing trick as well. The technique is called lung-gom, and it was witnessed by Alexandra David-Neel and written up in her 1931 classic *With Mystics and Magicians in Tibet*.[53] In this case, the monks are able to go into a deep trance state where they can run along in huge leaps at a remarkably fast speed—using their bodies in a way that completely defies gravity as we now understand it.

Lung-gom may have originally been used to travel vast distances much more quickly than walking or riding a yak. Each time one of their feet hits the ground, they launch off again in another huge leap. Though this may be an exaggeration from one too many movies, each leap may lead to them traveling as much as thirty feet high and one hundred feet forward, if not more. David-Neel had heard stories about this practice, but finally one day she witnessed it happening, at a distance, through binoculars. Her Tibetan traveling partners could see the image of the monk with their naked eye, and confirmed that it was, indeed, a *lung-gom-pa*—a monk skilled in this fascinating art.

She wanted to go to the man, witness it up close and ask him questions, but she was sternly warned.

> Your Reverence will not stop the lama, nor speak to him. This would certainly kill him. These lamas when traveling must not break their meditation. The god who is in them escapes if they cease to repeat the ngags [mantras], and when thus leaving them before the proper time, he shakes them so hard that they die.[54]

To me, this sounds like a mythical legend that was created to explain something we now can understand scientifically. Based on these new laws of physics we are now rediscovering, we can assume that in order for the monk to accomplish the practice of lung-gom, he would have to be able to bring roughly half the atoms and molecules in his body into time-space. He would then be half-in, half-out. How exactly did they learn this practice? Does this require some sort of "pineal gland awakening" process? That may be part of it. David-Neel explained that in order to train for this ability, you must first spend several years practicing various types of breathing exercises. Eventually, your teacher gives you a mantra that you repeat in a rhythmic fashion. Your breathing and your footsteps all have to keep time with the syllables of the mantra while you do the practice.

To me, there is a remarkable amount of data in this report that is consistent with what we have been learning so far—which David-Neel obviously had no idea about at the time. Heat disrupts the coherence in the Source Field—and during the hottest times of day, lung-gom doesn't work very well. Also, the shape of an area determines the structure of the Source Field, just like the pyramid effect—so uneven ground, narrow valleys and trees all create influences that can disrupt the path of a lung-gom-pa, whereas flat land and wide desert spaces make it much easier. And lastly, your normal state of mind shifts into a deep trance, where most of your awareness is no longer here in space-time. Your pineal gland is probably quite active, as most of your awareness has now transferred over into your astral body or energetic duplicate in time-space, as Gariaev and others have shown in the DNA Phantom. Interestingly, David-Neel also reports that if the monks did this practice too often, they could become stuck in a halfway point—and then actually have to weigh themselves down with chains in order to be able to stay on the ground.

Although there are many well-documented cases of human levitation that could not have been faked, including Christian saints, yogis and the exceptional abilities of Daniel Dunglas Hume in the 1800s, witnessed by scientists, scholars, governmental figures and other luminaries,[55] one story of levitation, in Dr. Claude Swanson's *The Synchronized Universe*, stood out to me. This involves Peter Sugleris, a young Greek boy in the 1980s who could move objects, bend spoons and other metal utensils without even touching them—as witnessed by many people. These spoon-bending feats can now be explained by the atoms flipping over into time-space, so the material actually starts to be bendable. And yes— Sugleris was also able to levitate. In 1986, his wife photographed him as he hovered eighteen inches off the kitchen floor and stayed up there for forty-seven seconds. The exertion appeared on his face as a frightening grimace, and he broke out in a cold sweat and was exhausted afterward. It took him ten or fifteen seconds to regain normal consciousness. In order to do it, he "required immense concentration and a purification vegetarian diet for several weeks before the event."[56]

CHAPTER FIFTEEN

Geometry Class Just Got Much More Interesting

O ur quest to recover the lost secrets of the ancients appears to be nearly complete. Our biggest discovery has been that the three dimensions of space we see all around us—as the real world—is only half of the picture. The other half is a parallel reality, in which all the rules are basically the same—but space over there is time over here, and vice versa. These two realities are intimately and totally dependent upon each other for survival—their swirling movements blend together within every atom. Nature was never told that gravity shielding was impossible—it seemingly happens all the time in tornadoes, waterfalls, the stems of plants and trees, and certain insects' wing cases. Gravity appears to have much more structure in it than merely being a tug-of-war between the downward-pushing gravity force and the upward-pushing levity force. There are spiraling motions within gravity as well, which push in other directions besides strictly down. In order to cancel out gravity, achieve coherence and enter into time-space, we have to know how to create the proper vortex currents in the Source Field—so we can levitate, teleport and travel in time, which may be a key part of the predicted Golden Age. Geometry appears to be the key to creating the vortex currents we need to achieve these stunning results.

Geometric Vortex Points

It is entirely possible that certain areas on earth could have greater coherence than other areas—thus making levitation, teleportation and time travel much easier in those spots. Gravity may take on a spiraling, sideways push in these areas—creating circular or oval-shaped flow patterns in air, water, magnetic fields or the mantle. Ivan T. Sanderson was searching for just such vortex points in the 1960s with his Society for Investigation of the Unexplained. Charles Berlitz actually made extensive use of Sanderson's library when he wrote *The Bermuda Triangle* in 1974. From 1945 to 1975, fully 67 different ships and boats, and 192 aircraft of all different types, disappeared in the Bermuda Triangle. As a result of these events, 1,700 different people vanished. These incidents do not include many other disappearances that were later given conventional explanations.[1] In 2004, Gian Quasar revealed that in the preceding twenty-five years, 75 aircraft and hundreds of pleasure yachts vanished in the Bermuda Triangle without a trace—and on the cover of his book, he indicates that more than 1,075 people disappeared as a result.[2]

The Bermuda Triangle was only one of a series of locations Sanderson had found where strange things were happening. By the late 1960s, Sanderson had clearly determined that there were ten areas on earth, approximately equidistant, where ships and planes kept disappearing, strange phenomena were seen in the sea and in the air, and/or equipment malfunctioned.[3]

Five of these areas were on the same northern tropical latitude, and each one was 72 degrees of longitude apart from the next. Five others had the same basic layout in the southern hemisphere, but they were all shifted 20 degrees to the east of the ones in the north. Almost all of Sanderson's network television appearances in the early 1970s discussed these vortex points, which created a great deal of mystery and intrigue. Well over one thousand people had disappeared in the Bermuda Triangle alone, though Sanderson said there was nothing triangular about it. As a result of his popularity, military and commercial pilots began supplying him with even more interesting data. The pilots said that in these same ten spots, or immediately near them, they were experiencing time anomalies—arriving at their destinations either "much too early" or "much too late." This could be confirmed with their own instruments as well as ground records.[4]

The Dick Cavett Show was extremely popular on ABC in the late 1960s and early 1970s. Arthur Godfrey was a frequent guest—a seasoned pilot who enjoyed thirty years as a television personality, often representing the view of the biggest aviation companies. A debate was set for March 16, 1971, between Godfrey and Sanderson about these ten vortex points. Although they were old friends, in two earlier appearances Godfrey skeptically dismissed Sanderson's idea as "a lot of bloody nonsense," or something to that effect. Nonetheless, when Sanderson brought out the globe with the points clearly marked, and laid out all the evidence, Godfrey was blown away. He'd had three different experiences, in those same areas, that directly confirmed what Sanderson was saying.

In one case, Godfrey lost all radio and instrument contact for an hour and a half while flying through the Devil's Sea, south of Japan, with only four hours of gas to go—and he was clearly terrified. He also said that when pilots head straight down the East Coast over the ocean, which is faster than sticking close to the land, they have to keep a very watchful eye on their instruments. Other pilots had already said the same thing, including Bob Durant on Barry Farber's radio show. When Dick Cavett finally asked Godfrey, flat out, if this phenomenon warranted proper scientific investigation, he looked straight into the camera, and with total, deadpan seriousness, simply said yes.[5]

This triggered a wave of new interest from scientists and engineers. One of them pointed out that the North and South Poles should also be included, as they fit the same geometric relationships very nicely. Sanderson published a diagram of these twelve "vile vortices," as he called them, in the April 1971 issue of *Pursuit*, his journal. He then got a huge new burst of publicity when his classic article "The Twelve Devil's Graveyards Around the World" appeared in a 1972 issue of *Saga* magazine. This triggered a scientific investigation by three Soviet researchers—Nikolai Goncharov, Vyacheslav Morozov and Valery Makarov—who

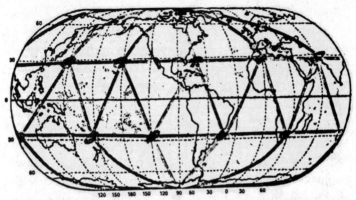

Ivan T. Sanderson discovered that most ship and plane disappearances occurred in twelve equidistant locations around the world, forming this geometric pattern.

published a paper about it in the USSR Academy of Sciences' popular journal *Khimiya i Zhizn,* or *Chemistry and Life.* Their paper came out in 1973, and was titled "Is the Earth a Large Crystal?" These three guys represented an interesting mix of talent—Goncharov was a historian, Morozov was a construction engineer and Makarov was an electronics specialist. Together, they realized that Sanderson's twelve vortexes created an icosahedron when you connected the dots in three-dimensional space. This, again, is a roughly spherical geometric object that has twenty sides, each of which is a perfect equilateral triangle. They felt this was an energetic crystal structure of some kind that existed within the earth.[6] They referred to it as a "matrix of cosmic energy."[7]

The icosahedron, discovered in earth's vortex points by Sanderson, can be geometrically inverted to form a dodecahedron, as we see here.

They also knew that when you turn the icosahedron inside out, you get its geometric opposite, called the dodecahedron—a twelve-sided object that looks like a soccer ball, where each of the twelve faces is a five-sided pentagon. They drew all the lines for where these geometries appeared over the surface of the earth, based on Sanderson's twelve original points, and found a wealth of hidden treasures.

Many of the greatest earthquake-prone seismic fracture lines were directly on this grid. Undersea volcanic mountain ridges often lined up perfectly with the grid, including the Mid-Atlantic Ridge—as well as above-ground mountain ranges.[8] All of these effects could be the result of natural spin currents in the mantle, where this sideways force of gravity pushes the molten material into cyclical flow patterns. The highest and lowest atmospheric pressure zones also appeared in some of the areas where any three lines crossed—of which there were a total of sixty-two places. Again, this could be caused by gravitational force affecting the behavior of the atmosphere—via spiraling currents not yet acknowledged in mainstream science. These vortex areas formed the center points for major ocean currents and whirlpools as well—showing the gravitational effects upon the flow patterns of water. The areas of highest and lowest geomagnetic gauss strength fit neatly within this geometry.[9] Significant concentrations of ores and petroleum also appeared in these

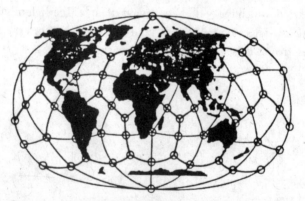

Once the dodecahedron was added to Sanderson's original discovery, Russian scientists discovered that over 3,300 different ancient sites were built on this grid.

areas. Animals naturally followed these paths in their migrations. Unique wildlife appeared in these areas—and anomalies in the gravitational field.[10]

Best of all, advanced prehistoric cultures and ancient civilizations also showed up in these spots. In fact, fully 3,300 different sacred complexes and ancient monuments, often built out of massive stones, appeared on this grid. This included the Great Pyramid in Egypt, the ruins of Great Zimbabwe in central Africa, Stonehenge and Avebury in England, the pyramids of China in the Xian province, the Kunoonda stone circle complex in Australia, the ruins of Nan Madol at Pohnpei, the mysterious stone heads of Easter Island, Machu Picchu in Peru, the pyramids of the Sun and Moon at Teotihuacan in Mexico, the Four Corners area of the Hopi in the American Southwest including Sedona, Arizona, and many more.[11] This is very compelling evidence that the ancients built their gigantic stone monuments in the places where it was the easiest and also the most coherent, thereby making it much easier to shield gravity—and also get much more powerful healing effects as well. It may even have been possible to use these points for time travel if you knew when the right planetary alignments would occur.

William Becker and Bethe Hagens further refined and enhanced the work of the Russian scientists, drawing lines that connected more of the geometric points together—and created what may be the most advanced visualization of the Global Grid yet. In their classic work *The Planetary Grid: A New Synthesis,* two different grid-related aircraft cases were given, where sudden and unpredictable course changes occurred without the pilots' control that fit the structure of the grid lines.[12] The first involved KAL 007, out of Anchorage, Alaska, on September 1, 1983. The second was KAL 902, heading from Paris to Anchorage on April 20, 1978. Both these flights occurred during significant holidays in two different cultures: KAL 007 happened during a major Hindu feast for Vishnu, and KAL 902 took place during Good Friday/Passover.[13] It is possible that certain ancient holidays were chosen for a reason—the earth's alignment, as we move through the seasons, may have given atoms and molecules on earth a little extra kick to get over the light-speed boundary on these special days. Obviously, much more research is needed to confirm this speculation—and some holidays do not appear on the same day from one year to the next—but it's an interesting possibility.

Ley Lines And Beyond

In the twentieth century, Sir Alfred Watkins found that a huge number of architectural sites, from all different historical periods, appeared throughout England on straight-lined paths called ley lines. One in particular cut almost horizontally across southern England.

I was delighted to find a BBC article in 2005 that soberly discussed these mysteries.

> "[Ley lines are] alignments and patterns of powerful, invisible earth energy said to connect various sacred sites, such as churches, temples, stone circles, megaliths, holy wells, burial sites, and other locations of spiritual or magical importance." *(Harper's Encyclopaedia of Mystical and Paranormal Experience)* . . . It is true that more "paranormal" activity is evidenced in these areas [including hauntings] . . . effects of this type of energy are said to be similar to those of static electricity: feelings of "tingling" on the skin and hairs standing on end. . . . A phenomenon often reported during investigations is that of technical equipment behaving erratically. . . . Major prehistoric structures of higher importance can frequently be found to occupy locations where two or more leys intersect with each other.[14]

At the end of this article, there is a disclaimer saying it is "user-generated content" that does not represent the views of BBC Gloucestershire—just so there is no confusion. All of the effects they mentioned are a perfect match with what we've been learning about the Source Field.

I was also greatly inspired by an article from Joseph Jochmans entitled "Earth: A Crystal Planet?," which appeared in a 1996 issue of *Atlantis Rising,* and features some of the points I've already mentioned above. Jochmans revealed that many ancient cultures around the world had a unique focus on these ancient, straight lines. The Irish called them fairy paths. The Germans called them holy lines. The Greeks referred to them as the Sacred Roads of Hermes. The ancient Egyptians called them the Pathways of Min. The Chinese called them *lung mei,* or dragon currents—and believed that placing stones, trees, temples, houses and pagodas along these lines would directly help the earth, as part of the ancient practice of Feng-shui. The earth was treated in much the same way as the body would be healed—through the acupuncture lines. The idea of the *axis mundi* also fits in very nicely. If you have a major energy vortex in a particular land, that obviously would become the focal point for everyone—if enough people knew about it and could make use of its benefits.

The Australian Aborigines called them dream paths—and would do seasonal walkabouts along these lines to reenergize the life force in those regions. They would map out the dream lines on boards called Turingas, and could locate game animals and predict the approach of storms by meditating on the lines. Ancient Polynesians called them *te lapa,* or "lines of light," and could apparently see them as visible, luminous lines in the ocean that they used for navigation. The residents of Easter Island and Hawaii called them aka threads, and built the stone heads and sacred Ahu platforms in Hawaii to harness the *mane,* or "life power," from these lines. The Incas organized their entire civilization along ceque lines, building wacas or sacred centers along the way—all of which converged at the Pyramid of the Sun in Cuzco.

The Maya built raised white roadways called Sacbes that followed the lines with perfect straightness, going right through the swamps, to connect their pyramid complexes together. Medicine wheels and kiva circles in western North America are also found in straight-line arrangements, and the Mound Builders in the Midwest and East Coast regions of what is now the United States also left their structures in curious alignments—again seemingly to harness the powers of this grid, and the coherence it produces. Jochmans also said that Native American shamans often speak of healing energies from the earth they call Orenda, Manitou and other such names. Interestingly, Jochmans also claimed that the Hopi elders said the earth was like the back of a spotted fawn. As the fawn gets older, the spots change positions—and new points appear.[15]

Geometric Expansion of Earth

A NOAA scientist named Dr. Athelstan Spilhaus published a paper in 1976 proving the Hopi may have been absolutely right. Spilhaus, who passed away in 1998, was a highly decorated scientist, a genius inventor and the author of a syndicated comic strip. He developed the "bathythermograph," a device for submarine detection that was vital in helping crush Hitler in World War II.[16] Spilhaus also was the inventor and research director of the top-secret Project MOGUL weather balloon project, which was officially said (in 1994) to have been what really crashed at Roswell.[17] Therefore, Spilhaus's credibility is essential to the alleged UFO cover-up.

The story begins with Dr. Hanshou Liu, of NASA's Goddard Space Flight Center, who was the first to discover that when the original supercontinent Pangaea broke up 220 million years ago, it did so along equidistant lines—forming the edges of a pyramid-shaped geometry called a tetrahedron. In this case, you have a pyramid shape with an equilateral triangle on the bottom, and three more equilateral triangles making the sides.

In a discussion with Spilhaus, who was highly talented at creating unique map projections, they realized that the continents, volcanic ridges and seismic fault lines then moved into a shape that was a combination of a cube and an octahedron. An octahedron looks like two Egyptian pyramids base to base, where each face is again an equilateral triangle. From this phase, the earth again shifted—into the exact same pattern that was rediscovered by Sanderson in 1971 and the Russians in 1973. Spilhaus then created a special map projection where he took a single point in the Pacific Ocean and stretched it out into a great circle, so that everything on earth was inside this circle. From that perspective, the geometry became very, very obvious—covering the vast majority of all seismic and volcanic ridges with astonishing precision.

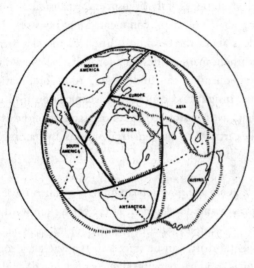

Earth's continents, mountain ranges and undersea volcanic ridges later expanded into this icosa-dodeca geometry. A single point in the Pacific Ocean was widened to form the edge of the entire circle in this map projection by Spilhaus.

I personally contacted Dr. Hanshou Liu in June 2004 to see if this remarkable scientific story was true—and he gave me permission to publish the following statement.

Dear Mr. Wilcock: Dr. Athelstan Spilhaus visited me at NASA Goddard Space Flight Center in 1976, and asked for reprints of my three papers: Deformation and Instability of Underthrusting Lithospheric Plates, Dynamical Model for the Detachment of Descending Lithosphere, and On the Breakup of Tectonic Plates by Polar Wandering. . . . In 1976, I pointed out such a [geometric] pattern to Dr. Spilhaus in my office from my work. He was heartened to see that the breakup [of the earth] occurred along equidistant points and lines which formed a geometric solid known as a tetrahedron. . . . We had [also] discussed the possible cuboctahedron and icosadodecahedron stages of the lithospheric expansion. Before Dr. Spilhaus left my office, he commented [on] my work: "Now, your ideas about the breakup of the tectonic plates can be stated without mathematics, in a form that people without a scientific education can understand. Your combination of boldness, insight and courage has enabled you to produce ideas that have transformed our understanding of the dynamics of the earth." As a mathematical physicist by training, I felt that I was honored.[18]

Obviously, geometry now appears to have a much more significant role in the growth and development of the earth than we thought. The conventionally accepted model of plate tectonics, or what used to be called continental drift, can be traced all the way back to Dr. Alfred Wegener in 1912—and has remained largely unchanged for almost a century.[19] However, both Karl W. Luckert, professor emeritus of the University of Southern Minnesota,[20] and James Maxlow[21 22] have demonstrated clear scientific cases that the earth has been expanding from within since at least 220 million years ago—when the mega-continent Pangaea first separated. Maxlow simply subtracted each stage of expansion that the seafloor went through, worldwide, from the overall volume of the earth's surface. The results are quite striking, as it appears that all the continents fit perfectly together if you shrink the earth down to 55 to 60 percent of its current size. Maxlow's work is being taken seriously in certain scientific circles—for example, it was discussed in a 2007 issue of the *New Concepts in Global Tectonics* newsletter.[23] Maxlow and Luckert are just two of many scientists now promoting such models.[24]

Very few scientists have wanted to touch the Earth Expansion Theory, because it suggests that a massive amount of new matter is being generated within the earth itself. Yet, at the same time, most of them have no problem supporting the Big Bang theory—where allegedly all the matter

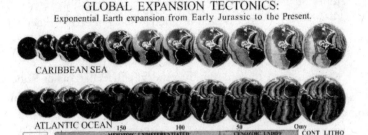

GLOBAL EXPANSION TECTONICS:
Exponential Earth expansion from Early Jurassic to the Present.

Dr. James Maxlow's model of the earth's expansion. Undersea volcanic ridges generate new crust as earth increases in size.

in the Universe was created in a single, gigantic explosion . . . out of nothing. Maxlow, Luckert and others have conclusively shown that the plate tectonics model is loaded with problems. If we allow the earth to be expanding from within, by a process of continuous matter creation, we have a much more perfect fit with the real-world data that is available. This, of course, means that matter can be spontaneously generated from the Source Field. And best of all, we see that the earth has been expanding through geometric phases along the way.

Earth's Crystal Core

So far, this geometry has appeared as either hidden energy patterns or outlines along the surface of the earth, which we can measure by the location of seismic fault lines, mountain ranges and undersea volcanic ridges— all of which could be caused by gravitational stress currents. What about a real, honest-to-God crystal in the earth that is shaped like this? On the Pittsburgh Supercomputing Center Web site, a division of Carnegie Mellon/University of Pittsburgh, I found the following revealing quote.

There's a giant crystal buried deep within the earth, at the very center, more than three thousand miles down. It may sound like the latest fantasy adventure game or a new Indiana

Jones movie, but it happens to be what scientists discovered in 1995 with a sophisticated computer model of earth's inner core.[25]

I was delighted to discover that indeed, the Glatzmaier-Roberts model[26] of the earth's core had a very clear geometric shape—which some scientists called a "hexagonal" pattern.[27]

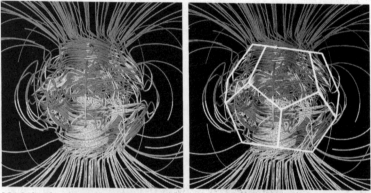

NASA's Glatzmaier-Roberts model revealed a geometric "crystal" pattern in the earth's core that fits perfectly into a dodecahedron, as illustrated on the right.

However, if you pop in a dodecahedron and then tilt it slightly (about 10 degrees), it fits perfectly. No other geometry we have been discussing matches this well. We can also clearly see a spiraling, fluidlike vortex moving through the center of the geometry as well. One study has concluded that some of the earth's inner core is behaving like a liquid, despite its geometric structure . . . exactly as we might expect, given the fluidlike qualities of the Source Field.[28] The American Geophysical Union has openly stated that the angular tilt of the geometric core is not aligned with the earth's rotation.[29] As reported in another mainstream study, "even more surprisingly, [the core] is rotating faster than the rest of the earth."[30] We'll come back to that point later. Scientists even have admitted that current models cannot fully explain this "crystal" in the center of the earth. As reported in Physics Today Online, "The [geometric] alignment [of the earth's core] may not result from a single force, such as that due to the electromagnetic stresses, but a combination of forces present in the inner core."[31]

I struggled for years to understand what could be causing all this geometry to appear so obviously in the actual structure and behavior of the earth—not to mention the "tetrahedral geometry" Richard C. Hoagland pointed out on the Sun (sunspot patterns that do not go above 19.5 degrees north or south), Mars (the Olympus Mons shield volcano, three times higher than Mount Everest, at 19.5), Venus (two volcanoes at roughly 19.5), earth (the Hawaiian Islands at 19.5), Jupiter (the Great Red Spot at 19.5) and Neptune (the Great Dark Spot at 19.5).[32] [33] Straight lines aren't supposed to appear in nature—at least not in any conventional mind-set. It took quite some time for me to figure out that gravity was actually responsible for creating these cyclones in the atmosphere and/or volcanic upwellings in the mantle.

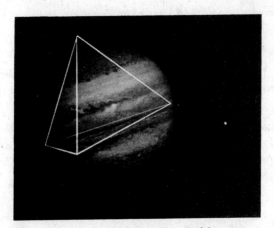

The swirling winds of Jupiter's Great Red Spot appear to be driven by gravitational forces that naturally circulate in the shape of a tetrahedron. On solid planets, the mantle surges up to form volcanoes at these same vortex points.

Geometry Naturally Occurs in a Vibrating Fluid

I was greatly relieved when I found the work of Dr. Hans Jenny (pro-nounced "yenny"), who found that this geometry appears quite naturally in a fluid—by simply vibrating it. Almost immediately, I realized this was the big piece I had been missing, and I was thrilled.

In his Cymatics research,[34] Dr. Jenny took ordinary water and filled it with tiny, free-floating particles known as colloids. These particles will not sink because they are so small—they are in suspension. When Dr. Jenny then vibrated the water at different frequencies, the particles imme-diately assembled themselves into clear and beautiful three-dimensional geometries. Each pattern stayed nice and still, maintaining the same shape—but there was a great deal of rotational movement within the shape itself. The particles were always on the move. Long, curving loops were also seen emerging from each point of the geometry, showing a constant particle flow from one area to another—and a curving pattern to contrast with the straight lines in the geometry itself. As long as he didn't change the shape of the fluid, the same geometric pattern would again reappear each time he played a certain frequency of sound. Thus, you could have the same fluid, with the same particles, show a number of different geometric patterns. Every time you played a certain frequency, the same geometry would return—almost as if by magic.

Higher-frequency sounds created more complex geometry, and vice versa. Furthermore, when Dr. Jenny vibrated a larger area of water, instead of just seeing one shape emerge, he got multiple copies of the same pattern—all lined up in nice, neat, organized rows. These patterns seemed to resemble a group of atoms forming a larger structure. Was this the big secret to how all of physical matter really formed? It certainly looked that way. It appears that as the frequency of the energy streaming into the earth increases, the complexity of the geometry that is structuring the continents, fault lines and volcanic ridges increases as well—moving from tetrahedron, to cuboctahedron, to our current pattern.

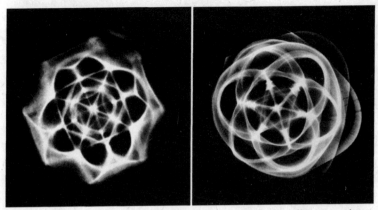

Dr. Hans Jenny found that particles floating in a liquid naturally arranged into different geometric patterns depending on the frequency of vibration he introduced.

By 1996, I had already realized that geometry must be the big secret to understanding energy, matter, the mechanisms responsible for biological life, and even consciousness—although I didn't find the proof in Jenny's work until later on. If we want to find out exactly what coherence looks like in a fluid, we look no further than these five basic Platonic solids—the tetrahedron, cube, octahedron, icosahedron and dodecahedron. Mathematicians already know these shapes have more symmetry, as in more coherence, than any others. Simply put, each of them will fit perfectly in a sphere, and each point is equidistant from its neighbors. Each side of the geometry has the same shape, and every internal angle will also be the same.

Quantum Geometry: The Big Secret

Physicists were always looking for the missing link that could unify the very large with the very small. Now that there were clear and obvious geometric patterns in the earth, it seemed very likely that if we are truly dealing with a unified field model, the patterns we see on a larger scale would also appear in quantum mechanics. Atoms, rather than being a bunch of seemingly solid particles whirling around a nucleus, could now be reimagined as geometric patterns of flow—within the fluidlike energy of the Source Field. When you increase the frequency of vibration, the geometry becomes more complex. Once we understand how this principle really works, it might also lead to the transmutation of elements—such as the classic alchemist's dream of turning lead into gold.

Where do we start, then? In Larson's model, if we're looking for geometry within the atom, all we have to do is study the nucleus—as he feels the nucleus is the atom: "In *The Case against the Nuclear Atom,* Larson . . . points out that, in fact, the 'size' of the nucleus . . . is rather the size of the atom itself."[35] Larson's model did not have geometry in it—but Nehru also admits they haven't worked all the kinks out yet.

> It is certain that there is a lot more to be done toward enlarging the application of the Reciprocal System to the intrinsic structure of the atom. Perhaps it is time to break new ground in the exploration of the mechanics of the Time Region. . . . Breaking new ground involves some fresh thinking, and leaving no stone unturned.[36]

The first scientist I found who had a working quantum physics model, based entirely on geometry, was Rod Johnson—who posted intriguing concepts on Richard C. Hoagland's discussion forum back in 1996. In the ensuing years, I have interviewed him extensively and published the results on my Web site, Divine Cosmos—and unfortunately he passed away in 2010. I was stunned at how many mysteries of quantum mechanics he could explain with geometry—including Planck's Constant, the Fine Structure Constant, the ratio between the weak force and the strong force, the structure of the photon, and others.[37] Without ever knowing about Larson's model, Johnson independently developed a similar concept. In Johnson's model, there was indeed a parallel reality that is constantly intersecting with our own in every atom, at the tiniest level. Every atom had one geometry in our reality, and an opposite, inverse geometry in the parallel reality. The two geometries then counter-rotated inside of each other. Each stage of this process carried you through the different elements. Clearly, Johnson had a great model, although he didn't have enough specifics to resolve the entire Periodic Table yet—but he felt all the answers could be found in James Carter's theory of circlons.[38]

Later on I found Dr. Robert Moon, who could explain everything in the Periodic Table with geometry. He was one of the key scientists involved in the Manhattan Project, which developed the world's first controlled thermonuclear fission reaction. He was the second scientist ever to build a cyclotron in the 1930s, and significantly improved the first—which had been built by E. O. Lawrence. In the Manhattan Project, Dr. Moon solved critical problems to make the first atomic pile possible, and built the first scanning X-ray microscope after World War II. From 1974 until his death in 1989, he was a key collaborator with Lyndon H. LaRouche, Jr.[39] A variety of articles on his new quantum physics model can be found at LaRouche's 21st Century Science and Technology Web site.[40]

In 1986, Dr. Moon finally realized that geometry was the key to understanding quantum physics—and it was a geometry in time as well as in space. That means that when you move through space, or time, you must move through geometry. You can't just move in a nice, smooth, even curve—you have to pop through one quantity of space, or one quantity of time, before you can go to the next one. The scientific word for this kind of movement is that it would be *quantized*. Dr. Moon outlined his concept that space and time are quantized in a lecture from 1987.

> One interpretation . . . [is] that we have two kinds of time, and [laughs] the secret is that we should have quantization of time for this quantum potential to work. . . . In other words, you have both the quantization of space . . . [and] time. . . . That just struck like a bolt of lightning. Then, the next thing that struck was: Well, if space is going to be quantized, it should be quantized with the highest degree of symmetry.

And so that immediately said, well, those are the Platonic solids. And [laughs], so I was pondering over that until the Sun came up. . . . It seemed very obvious how these solids should fit.[41]

The Platonic solids, of course, are all the same geometries we've been discussing here—the tetrahedron, cube, octahedron, icosahedron and dodecahedron. The details are quite technical, but here's the gist of what Dr. Moon found: The same geometric shapes we see in the expansion of the earth also appear within the nucleus of the atom. Furthermore, in Moon's model, more than one geometric form can nest within the nucleus at the same time—each one inside the next. This geometry actually determines how many protons our scientists will find in any one atom. The trick is to count the number of points on each of the so-called Platonic solids. There are eight points on a cube, six on an octahedron, twelve on an icosahedron and twenty on a dodecahedron, for a total of forty-six. In Moon's model, that's the first half of the naturally occurring elements in the Periodic Table. Moon knew there are a total of ninety-two elements that appear in nature, or two times forty-six—so he believed that every atom with an atomic weight of forty-seven or higher was a combination of two nests of geometry connected side by side, growing increasingly unstable along the way.[42]

You may have noticed Dr. Moon did not include the tetrahedron in this grouping. He feels that since the geometric opposite of the tetrahedron is still a tetrahedron, it plays a different role. Indeed, in Rod Johnson's model as well as Buckminster Fuller's earlier model, a photon appears as two tetrahedrons back-to-back—and we have the solid data to prove it in Planck's Constant.[43]

Anyway, some very cool things happen when you use Moon's model. The first completed shell in the nucleus is the cube, with eight protons. This corresponds to oxygen, which is highly stable—and makes up 62.55 percent of all the atoms in the earth's crust. It is also interesting that oxygen is one of the single most important elements to sustain life. The second completed shell is the octahedron, with fourteen protons—and now you have silicon, which comes in at 21.22 percent. Although we are considered carbon-based life-forms, silicon is also very important for biological life—and seems to be the key ingredient in the spontaneous generation experiments, such as Dr. Ignacio Pacheco's work with the silicon in beach sand.

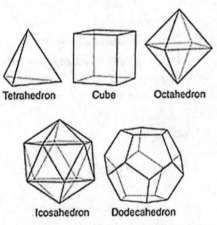

Dr. Robert Moon discovered that the protons of atoms naturally assemble into the Platonic solids, as seen here. Each proton corresponds to a vertex of the geometry.

So, between these first two shells alone—oxygen with a cubical nucleus and silicon with an octahedron-shaped nucleus—you have 84 percent of all the atoms in the earth's crust. Then, when you move up to complete the next shape, the icosahedron, you now have twenty-six protons. This is the iron atom, which is the best metal we have for creating naturally occurring magnetic fields. This hidden geometric symmetry may very well be responsible for iron's magnetic properties—by acting as a conduit for the Source Field, as we will discuss. Of all the atoms in the earth's crust, 1.20 percent are iron, but they add up to 5 percent of the total weight. Then, the dodecahedron fills up at forty-six protons, and you now have palladium—which is an unusually symmetrical atom that was used in all the cold fusion experiments. And in case you think cold fusion was all just a waste of time, don't forget that Dr. Eugene Mallove resigned from his position as the chief editor of MIT's technical newsletter when he allegedly discovered they were falsifying their own data on cold fusion—as if to say there was no effect.[44]

According to a paper by Laurence Hecht, Moon's model satisfies all sorts of quantum puzzles—including the processes of fission and fusion, the mystery period of fourteen for the rare earth elements, the exact number of elements in each row of the Periodic Table, and Maria Goeppert-Mayer's Magic Numbers, in which the properties of the nucleus tend to suddenly change at certain numbers that curiously reappear—whether you're looking at protons, neutrons or the mass number.[45] Hecht has continued developing and refining Moon's model ever since Moon's death in 1989.[46]

Microclusters and Quasi-Crystals

I was even more impressed when I found out that atoms naturally gather together into these exact same geometric patterns when they are set loose, one at a time, in a given area. These are called microclusters, and they are completely baffling to mainstream scientists. The microcrystals floating in the pineal gland may be similar—albeit larger. A 1989 issue of *Scientific American* revealed that microclusters do not have characteristics like liquids or gases.

> They belong instead to a new phase of matter, the microcluster. . . . They pose questions that lie at the heart of solid-state physics and chemistry. . . . How might the atoms reconfigure if freed from the influence of the matter that surrounds them?[47]

I then found the college textbook *Microcluster Physics* by Satoru Sugano and Hiroyasu Koizumi, which revealed even more—including compelling images of the geometry.[48]

Microclusters can be anywhere between ten to a thousand atoms. The strangest thing about them is that the electrons appear to orbit the center of the cluster, rather than the center of each individual atom. Of course, this weird behavior suggests there are no electrons. Instead, what scientists actually see is geometrically arranged electron clouds, which appear to be where the fluidlike flow of the Source Field enters into the atom. Once some of this stored energy is released from the atom, it turns into a photon—which then looks like a particle. Microclusters are also called "monatomic elements" or "ORMUS elements" in various sources—elegantly summarized in Lawrence Gardner's *Lost Secrets of the Sacred Ark*.[49] Microclusters appear to display gravitational anomalies, including levitation, under certain circumstances—as well as superconductivity. Ancient peoples believed that ingesting microcluster gold would awaken their pineal glands—and the Egyptians even stored it in cone-shaped cakes.[50]

Yet another tantalizing clue that atoms are geometric patterns within a fluidlike energy flow is the phenomenon of quasi-crystals. In this case, you have crystals that look just like the Platonic solids we've been discussing, including the dodecahedron—along with other forms. They are created by supercooling certain combinations of molten metals at a very fast speed—apparently capturing the molecules while they are flip-flopping between space-time and time-space, and freezing them into a half-in, half-out crystal pattern. The problem is that these crystals destroy all the known rules of crystal formation—they should not be able to exist, because you cannot build perfect five-sided crystals out of atoms that are made of particles.[51]

According to Edgar Fouche, who claims to have worked at the semi-mythical Groom Lake/Area 51, quasi-crystals were found in wreckage recovered from the Roswell crash and eight other similar incidents. They were found to be extremely strong, extremely heat-resistant, and would not conduct electricity—even though the metals within them normally did. Fouche also said they were found to be very useful.

> I've discovered that the classified research has shown that quasi-crystals are promising candidates for high energy storage materials, metal matrix components, thermal barriers,

exotic coatings, infrared sensors, high power laser applications and electro-magnetics. Some high strength alloys and surgical tools are already on the market.[52]

Here, he's obviously referring to Kevlar and Teflon, which some insiders say were "reverse-engineered" from crashed extraterrestrial craft. Fouche also said these crystals were baffling to the scientists working in these projects.

> The lattice of hydrogen quasi-crystals, and another material not named, formed the basis for the plasma shield propulsion of the Roswell craft, and was an integral part of the biochemically engineered vehicle. A myriad of advanced crystallography undreamed of by scientists were discovered by the scientists and engineers who evaluated, analyzed and attempted to reverse-engineer the technology presented with the Roswell vehicle, and eight more vehicles which have crashed since then. Arguably after 35 years of secret research on the Roswell hardware, those who had recovered these technologies still had hundreds if not thousands of unanswered questions about what they had found—and it was deemed "safe" to quietly introduce "quasi-crystals" to the non-initiated scientific world.[53]

Obviously, with our new quantum mechanics model in place, we are now much closer to understanding how these crystals may have formed—and it seems that our visitors know much more about this science than we do.

Rocks with Naturally Occurring Quasi-Crystals

In *Lost Science* by Gerry Vassilatos, I found the intriguing suggestion that certain rocks may have naturally occurring quasi-crystals in them. Apparently Dr. Charles Brush, an American physical chemist who studied gravity in the Victorian era, found certain rocks known as Lintz Basalts, which actually fell more slowly than other materials—by a tiny but measurable amount. As he studied them further, he also found they had an unusual amount of "excess heat." While this would obviously sound crazy to most people, it makes perfect sense when we remember that if you have the right coherence—which we now know means the right geometry—you can indeed get a gravity-shielding effect and may also be able to pull in energy directly from time-space.[54]

Dr. Thomas Townsend Brown got samples of these rocks and found that they would spontaneously give off surprisingly high voltages. Just putting wires on the rocks could give you several millivolts—and if you sliced them up into multiple pieces, you could get a full volt of free energy when you put them all together. Brown also found that the rock batteries would get stronger at six P.M., and weaker again at seven A.M.—showing that the light and heat of the Sun had a de-cohering effect on the energy they were pulling in. They also worked better at higher elevations, possibly thanks to a pyramid effect from mountains. Other inventors, such as Hodowanec, independently duplicated and verified these same results.[55]

According to Vassilatos, certain researchers traveled to the Andes and got up to 1.8-volt surges from a single rock. The more graphite was in the rocks, the more voltage they put out. Best of all, Brown found that they gave off two different electrical signals. One was steady, but the other would fluctuate with solar activity and the positions and configurations between the Sun and the Moon. He also found that distant pulses of gravity in space caused small electrical bursts in the rocks. Other rocks that were rich in silica also produced these charges. Brown was able to spot pulsar activity and supernovas long before they were announced by radio astronomers, as well as solar flares—even though the rocks were shielded from radioactivity, heat and light.[56]

In the same book, Vassilatos reveals the work of Dr. Thomas Henry Moray, another suppressed scientist who apparently found an even more powerful rock with the same properties. Moray only referred to it as the "Swedish Stone," and did not say where exactly it came from. It was a soft, silvery white material he found in two different areas—one from a rock outcropping in crystalline form, and another from a smooth white powder he scraped off of a railroad car. When he tried to use the crystal as a piezoelectric detector for radio waves, the signal came out with such power that it destroyed his headphones. Even a very large loudspeaker would blast at an extremely high volume whenever he tuned in to a given radio station. Moray was able to use this material to create an extremely powerful free energy device—and even his first prototype, which only used a wristwatch-size piece of "Swedish Stone," could simultaneously run a 100-watt light bulb and a 655-watt electric heater. The deeper he drove his grounding rods into the ground, the brighter the light became. In 1925, he demonstrated this technology to the Salt Lake City General Electric Company, as well as several qualified witnesses from Brigham Young University. They tried everything they could to prove it was a fraud, and were allowed to disassemble the entire setup—but they could find nothing. Later, Moray developed prototypes that could pump out fifty kilowatts of energy—enough to power a small factory all day, every day, without ever running out or needing to pay for energy.

Moray began trying to secure a patent in 1931, but was continually refused. And in 1939, the Rural Electrification Association sent a "scientific expert" along with others for a meeting with Moray. It turned out they were carrying guns and intended to kill him—but Moray had his own firearm and shot back, driving them off. As a result, Moray replaced all the windows on his car with bulletproof glass, and felt he had to constantly carry a revolver. He was never bothered again, but his breakthrough technology also never saw the light of day.

Later, he found that the Swedish Stone was doing other strange things. For example, he found that by using a standard radio receiver, he was tuning in the sounds of people's conversations and other day-to-day activities at long distances away—even though there were no microphones in those areas. He was able to travel to the exact sources of the sounds and confirm that he was picking them up. He also found that significant healing effects occurred from these stones as well. Then, by 1961, Moray found he could direct the energy fields his devices generated to grow micro-crystals (sound familiar?) of gold, silver and platinum—from otherwise worthless soil that came from where these elements were mined. Soil that initially only had 0.18 ounces of gold per ton could be used to produce as much as 100 ounces of gold and 225 ounces of silver. He had achieved the alchemist's dream of transmutation—in this case by starting with tiny crystals of gold, silver or platinum that were already in the soil, and causing them to grow much, much larger—like seeds. Through similar techniques, he was able to manufacture lead that was impossible to melt below 2,000 degrees Fahrenheit, and copper that was extremely strong and heat-resistant—which he used as bearings in high-speed motors. Another alloy he developed could be heated to 12,000 degrees Fahrenheit without melting.[57] According to Vassilatos, Moray attempted to synthesize more of the Swedish Stone on his own, and submitted it to a comprehensive microanalytical profile. From these results, we now know the main ingredient was ultra-pure Germanium, which does contain a small, relatively harmless amount of radioactivity that can easily be shielded.

Arthur L. Adams, a retired electrical engineer, found a smooth, silvery gray material in Wales in the 1950s that also created extraordinary amounts of power on its own. When a special battery made from slices of these stones was dipped in water, the power became far more substantial—and when the stones were taken out, the water continued to produce electrical power for hours . . . not unlike the DNA Phantom Effect.[58] British authorities seized all Adams's research papers and materials, claiming this was being done for "future social distribution." That time obviously has not yet arrived.

Genetic Geometry

Amino acids fit together to make proteins. These rules are complex—and scientists really don't understand why certain amino acids fit together and others do not. Dr. Mark White analyzed these relationships and found that everything makes sense if you map out the amino acids over the surface of a dodecahedron.[59]

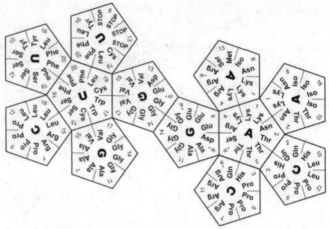

Dr. Mark White discovered that all the perplexing relationships of how nucleotides fit together in the genetic code can be solved by mapping them on a dodecahedron.

What is the ideal form of a DNA molecule? *It is a double helix.* What is the ideal form of the double helix? *It is a dodecahedron.* What is the ideal form of the genetic code? It is also a dodecahedron. As important as the double helix was toward understanding DNA, the dodecahedron is equally important toward understanding the genetic code. Perhaps more so.[60]

The same geometric laws seem to appear in quantum mechanics, planetary geodynamics and life itself—thanks to the fact that the Source Field is fluidlike, and geometry naturally appears when a fluid is pulsated. Pyramids and other funnel-shaped structures harness this flow and generate coherence in a given area, creating increasingly refined geometric patterns—and thus healing biological life, improving our mental health, regularizing the flow of currents in the mantle, the oceans, the atmosphere and the ionosphere to protect us from cataclysms, and improving the hardness and purity of crystalline structures. This science may also pave the way for a wealth of free energy technologies that could permanently end our crippling dependence on oil—and usher in a new era of peace, freedom and prosperity that we may never have dreamed possible before.

CHAPTER SIXTEEN

The Maya Calendar and the Gateway to Intelligent Infinity

Every astronomer owes Johannes Kepler a debt of gratitude for working out the basic laws of planetary motion. Sadly, they've all abandoned his greater vision: namely that the spacing of planetary orbits in our solar system could be precisely defined by the Platonic solids. Where did he get this idea from? Was it strictly an original thought, or had he been "tipped off" by the mystery schools? Just as I was finishing this book, I found solid proof, from a true master of geometry, that Kepler was right. The orbits of the planets do indeed hold the same three-dimensional geometric relationships that we see in the earth's grid, in DNA and protein synthesis, and all throughout quantum mechanics—namely, the Platonic solids.

I was taught in school that Kepler's concept of interplanetary geometry was a hilarious wrong turn in science, and certainly had never been proven. Years later, I came to feel he might have been right—but I didn't have the proof. Then, by a seemingly "random chance," I "just so happened" to "stumble over" what I was looking for. A friend handed me a book and said, "You might want to read this." And the best part was the title: *A Little Book of Coincidence,* by John Martineau.[1] Within minutes, I realized I'd been handed the final key I needed to unlock the mysteries of the ancients.

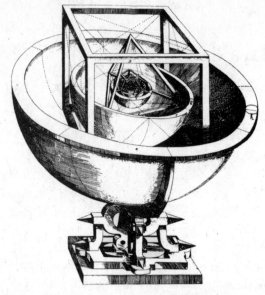

Johannes Kepler worked out the basic laws of planetary motion. He also believed the planets were spaced
apart by geometric relationships, as he illustrated here.

Geometric Forces in Planetary Orbits

I already knew there were impressive harmonic relationships in the orbits
of the planets. I wrote about them extensively in all three of my earlier
scientific books, which you can go back to my Web site and read for all the
details. I also saw some compelling suggestions of a hidden geometry in
the planetary orbits when I read *Time Stands Still* by Keith Critchlow, now
considered rare and hard to find. (My copy cost me 150 dollars.) Critchlow's
book also features stunning images of Platonic solids carved into Neolithic
stone spheres that were dug up, by the hundreds, all throughout Scotland.
Martineau's book had the final piece I was looking for: Geometry is the
key to unlock the mysteries of the solar system. The planets are apparently
being held in place and driven through their orbits by the same geometric

forces that very likely create atoms and molecules—as well as the global grid. This, of course, makes it much more interesting to chart planetary alignments. We can now reimagine these alignments as moments when the gears in a giant, invisible clock line up with geometric precision. However, instead of flat, circular wheels with teeth on them, these gears are the Platonic solids. And when they line up, we may have the key to stargate travel, far beyond the reach of our solar system—and perhaps across much larger chunks of time than just a few days here and there.

In November 2010, Prince Charles released his new book *Harmony: A New Way of Looking at Our World*—in which he uses Martineau's groundbreaking research to argue that the Universe displays evidence of a "grammar of harmony."

> I was captivated when I came across the work of a young geometer called John Martineau while he was studying at my School of Traditional Arts some years ago. He decided to make a close study of how the orbits of the planets relate to each other and how the patterns that can be drawn from them fit so precisely with things made down here on earth. He found many rather beautiful relationships. . . . This is all pretty remarkable evidence that there is a mysterious unity [in] the patterns found throughout the whole of creation. From the smallest of molecules to the biggest of the planetary "particles" revolving around the Sun, everything depends for its stability upon an incredibly simple, very elegant geometric patterning—the grammar of harmony.[2]

Kepler's vision of the planets is first discussed on page 12 of Martineau's book.

> Looking for a geometric or musical solution to the orbits, Kepler observed that six heliocentric planets meant five intervals. The famous geometric solution he tried was to fit the five Platonic solids between their spheres.[3]

On page 14, things get much more interesting: "Kepler . . . particularly noticed that the ratios between planets' extreme angular velocities were all harmonic intervals." Then, Martineau begins delivering the goods.

> Two nested pentagons define Mercury's orbital shell (99.4%), the empty space between Mercury and Venus (99.2%), Earth's and Mars's relative mean orbits (99.7%), and the space between Mars and Ceres (99.8%). Three nested pentagons define the space between Venus and Mars (99.6%) or Ceres' and Jupiter's mean orbits (99.6%). A hidden pattern?[4]

Absolutely yes. The five-sided pentagon is found in both the dodecahedron, with its five-sided faces, and the icosahedron, with groups of five triangles sharing common points—so we're definitely on to something.

On page 20, Martineau makes the intriguing suggestion that even though the planetary orbits are elliptical, we can still study the basic proportions that hold them in place as if they were spherical. This is probably because their naturally spherical energy fields are being squeezed by the pressure and momentum of their movement through clouds of gas and dust in the galaxy.

I was stunned to see that if you draw one circle for the average orbit of Mercury, and put three of these circles together to make a triangle, then when you draw a circle around them, you get the orbit of Venus—within 99.9 percent. Of course, since these are actually spheres, it's not a triangle at all—it's our classic three-sided tetrahedron, the simplest of all the Platonic solids.

Then, on page 24, Martineau produces a remarkable geometric diagram of the relationship between Earth, Venus and the Sun. Every eight Earth years, or thirteen Venusian years, they line up to form the next corner of a perfect pentagon—with 99.9 percent precision. Even better, when we work in the nearest and farthest points Venus reaches during this eight-year dance, another pentagon is formed that is even larger—and in perfect proportion to the others. This very likely is the result of Platonic geometries within spheres of energy that are precisely structuring

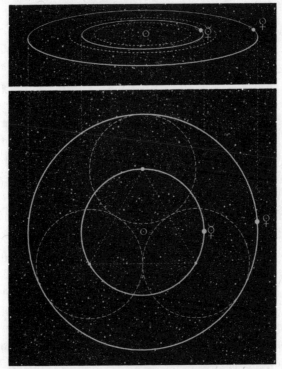

John Martineau illustrates a perfect triangular relationship
between the orbits of Mercury and Venus. This triangle
forms a tetrahedron in three dimensions.

where the planets travel—again, in this case, thanks to the dodecahedron and icosahedron with their five-sided symmetry.

On page 32, we find out that there is geometric precision between
earth and the Moon—thanks to the work of Robin Heath. There are
between twelve and thirteen full moons in a year. If we then draw a
circle (again, a sphere) with a diameter of thirteen units, and inscribe
a perfect, five-sided star inside it, each arm of the star will measure
12.364 units. This is the exact number of full moons in a year—to a
99.95-percent level of accuracy. This again suggests there is a sphere
of force between earth and the Moon—where the Moon's movements
are being precisely driven by the rotating vortex currents of gravity

within the dodecahedron geometry, which is all based on five-fold symmetry.

I was amazed when I saw pages 34 and 35, as Martineau shows that the relationships between the spacing of Venus, Earth and Mars are all perfectly defined by the icosahedron and dodecahedron. In this case, Martineau directly names and illustrates these two geometries. Mars is obviously the farthest away of these three planets, and if you make that orbit into a perfect sphere, you can then put the sphere of Venus's orbit inside of it. The distance between the sphere of Venus and the sphere of Mars is precisely defined by the dodecahedron—with 99.98-percent perfection. Then, if you flip this same dodecahedron inside out to get the icosahedron, you can fit a larger sphere inside of it—and that happens to be the exact distance of Earth's orbit, within 99.9-percent accuracy. If the details seem confusing, you can go read the book and get into all the specifics—but these are very clear geometric relationships between the planets, just like the geometry we see in quantum mechanics and the global grid.

The magic continues to happen as we go farther out. When we draw a circle for the orbit of Mars, we can then put it in the middle of a group of four larger circles that touch each other perfectly. Each of these four larger circles is precisely the size of Jupiter's average orbit, with 99.98-percent perfection. This obviously forms a square, which becomes a cube—so there appears to be a hidden, cubical energy field between these two planets, determining the exact distance and timing of their orbits from each other. Martineau also shows a beautiful cubical relationship between Jupiter's two largest moons, Ganymede and Callisto—and also reveals a perfect cubical relationship (within 99.9 percent) by comparing the orbit of Earth and Mars.

One of the biggest dead giveaways that there is geometry in the solar system is in the Trojans, which are clusters of asteroids that orbit in front of and behind Jupiter in the same loop. One cluster is always precisely sixty degrees ahead of Jupiter, and the other cluster is always sixty degrees behind Jupiter. There has never been a compelling scientific explanation of why this is happening. Obviously, this sixty-degree spacing allows you to start drawing geometric patterns if you represent Jupiter's orbit as a perfect sphere. I was stunned to see that if you take the sphere of Jupiter's orbit and nest three cubes, three octahedrons or any other combination of these two shapes together, one inside the other, you get a sphere in the center that is exactly the size of earth's orbit—with 99.8 percent perfection.

Then, Jupiter and Saturn have a very close five-to-two relationship between their orbital periods. They make a conjunction every twenty years, but each conjunction appears at a new point within the great circle of their shared orbits. If you plot out six of these conjunctions within that shared circle and connect the dots, you get a perfect Star of David. This is the geometry of the star tetrahedron or merkabah—where you have one tetrahedron pointing up and another one pointing down, blended together. Again, the Platonic solids are working their magic.

Lastly, on pages 48 and 49, we find another triangle, or tetrahedron, in the relationship between the orbit of Uranus and Saturn. I was also intrigued that the radius of Saturn's orbit is equal to the circumference of Mars's orbit, to 99.9-percent accuracy—and the circumference of Saturn's orbit is the same as the diameter of Neptune's orbit. Just so Pluto doesn't feel left out, we discover on page 50 that "Neptune's orbital period is twice that of Uranus, and Uranus's is two-thirds that of Pluto." That means our entire solar system is being governed by a series of absolutely perfect geometric relationships, many of which can be directly associated with the Platonic solids. As Prince Charles said, "This may, of course, all be a coincidence, but such is their precision it does begin to challenge the popular notion that we live in an accidental universe. . . ."[5]

I was absolutely stunned. I had felt for fifteen years that this must be the answer, but other books I'd read on sacred geometry seemed to suggest that Kepler's dream was ultimately a failure. Now I realized they simply hadn't worked hard enough to see the truth—but John Martineau had done his homework and figured everything out. I did already know that galaxies gathered into massive superclusters, and those superclusters mysteriously arrange into gigantic, diamond-shaped octahedrons.[6] The octahedrons form a matrix—repeating over and over again across vast distances.[7][8][9]

The background dust and gas at the farthest reaches of the Universe also clusters into the shape of an octahedron.[10] Further analysis revealed a dodecahedron pattern in the dust as well.[11] These laws truly do extend throughout the entire Universe, at all levels of size.

If you're scratching your head at this point and wondering why I even bothered to mention all this, let me make myself clear. We've already seen evidence that Sanderson's twelve main vortex points create direct gateways into time-space. A huge number of ships and planes have seen strange lights appear in the sea or in the sky, had bizarre equipment malfunctions, spontaneously moved forward or backward in time, warped through space from one place to another, or simply dematerial-ized entirely—making a complete crossover into time-space. The key, as the ancients obviously knew, is in the geometry. Or, as the old saying goes, "X marks the spot."

Conjunctions Become Stargate Portals

I now had the proof that these same three-dimensional geometric rela-tionships existed in the planetary orbits. This meant planetary conjunc-tions were much more interesting than just dates on a calendar. During these alignments, gigantic interplanetary geometry is lining up as well—creating greater coherence here on earth as all that energy multiplies. The more of an alignment you have between these hidden geometric energy patterns in the solar system, the more coherence you have—and the more likely you are to be able to directly travel through time-space.

The ancients may have been very aware that at certain times, a par-ticular geometric node on earth would come into alignment with other geometry in the solar system—and this is when the magic happens. Then, if you've built a pyramid, or even a stone circle, you can generate even more coherence—as we saw with the Russian pyramid experiments. (Don't forget that when the Russians charged rocks in the pyramid, and then arranged them around a growing crop, they got much more coher-ence in the area inside the rocks. So if you charged up the rocks that made Stonehenge, you now would get the same effect. And even if you didn't charge them up first, simply arranging them in a circle should be enough to harness and concentrate the earth's energy—by creating a circular vortex pattern.) I've also heard from insider sources that these alignments are the secret to alchemy. Lead will turn into gold in certain methods, but you have to know when to do it. Only when the earth and solar system produces the proper coherence will this ancient science of *Al-Kemit*—literally "the Science of Egypt"—actually work.

A New View of the Maya Calendar

The Maya were obviously a pyramid-building culture, or at least inherited all their traditions from a pyramid-building culture. I do not believe that human sacrifice had anything to do with the original founding of the Maya civilization—this represented the end result of a long period of decay, moving ever-increasingly farther away from where it once started. It may well be that the ancient founders of the Maya civilization were, in fact, aware that you could levitate large stone blocks, teleport through space, and even travel through time when the geometry of the earth lined up with the geometry of the solar system. It is very likely that one of the main reasons they built the pyramids was to have a coherence generator—so that when these special alignments opened up, they could harness them. Obviously, if this were true, they would be very interested in tracking the orbits of the planets—with great precision.

I've seen many, many skeptics stridently attack the Maya calendar as if it were a bunch of meaningless nonsense. And even when people write about it in a favorable way, suggesting that the end date of 2012 is truly a significant event, hardly anyone actually crunches the numbers within the calendar to see if they mean something. More specifically, why were the Maya counting all these different cycles that mesh together with each other so perfectly? Why not just count earth days, lunar months and earth years, and leave it at that? I suspected that if I actually did the homework, I might find that the Maya were counting these cycles for a reason—and I struck gold.

The Maya, and many other indigenous Mesoamerican cultures, gave every day a name—for a total of twenty days. This twenty-day period was called a *veintena* in many pre-Columbian Mesoamerican cultures. It was also referred to as a *winal* in the Maya calendar, as well as in the Zapotec and Mixtec cultures. It seemed to serve the same basic function as a month does in our own calendar system. Eighteen winals of twenty days each were counted up to get 360 days, or a *tun*. Then an additional five "nameless days," called *nemontemi* in many cultures and *wayeb* in the Maya calendar, were added in to get our typical 365-day earth year— so you had eighteen twenty-day months in a year, plus the five nameless days added in.[12] This whole system of counting the earth year was collectively known as the *Haab*. Interestingly, the nameless days were considered to be a dangerous time, where the boundaries between the mortal realm and the underworld dissolved. Allegedly, rambunctious spirits could get through during this time and cause disasters to occur.[13] This might be the result of a thinning of the veil between space-time and time-space—given a more supernatural explanation. It is also interesting that if the 360 days represent a perfect sphere—a harmonic geometry— then perhaps those five days are where we lose symmetry . . . and the coherence is broken.

The twenty-day cycle was considered to be an astrology system, where each of these days had a particular character or quality to it. Their counting system also went one through twenty—unlike our own, which only goes one through ten. And despite their meticulous tracking of the Haab, or solar year, they also followed other cycles at the same time. Even though they counted twenty days as the veintena or winal, they also gave each day a number, which they called the *trecena* cycle. Strangely, these numbers only count up to thirteen—and then on the fourteenth day you start on the number one again. That means that the twenty-day and thirteen-day cycles don't line up until 260 days—or thirteen times twenty. This 260-day cycle was known as the *tzolkin*— and it is considered the oldest and most important timing system throughout all Mesoamerican regions, appearing earlier than the very first Maya inscriptions that ever featured it.[14]

Decoding the 260-Day Tzolkin Cycle

It took years of detective work for me to track down the answer of why the ancients were so interested in these cycles—and I only found the answer late in 2009, while I was putting the research together for this book. Professor Robert Peden, from Deakin University's School of Sciences in Australia, crunched the numbers and wrote up his discoveries in 1981—but never published the results. It didn't actually appear online until 2004—but it answered all my questions beautifully.[15] In short, the tzolkin is nothing less than the ultimate cycle that links all the planetary orbits, and their geometry, together with one single common denominator—or at the very least Venus, earth, the Moon, Mars and Jupiter. Furthermore, it is the only cycle that is under a hundred years in length that can do this—with an accuracy better than one day in one hundred years.

If this sounds confusing, let me explain how it works. Take fifty-nine tzolkin cycles and add them up. This is almost exactly the same length of time as forty earth years, with 99.6 percent precision. Forty-six tzolkins equals 405 lunar months, at 99.7 percent accuracy. Sixty-one Venus years is 137 tzolkins, with 99.2 percent precision. Three tzolkins give you one Mars year—at 97.2 percent accuracy. And lastly, 135 tzolkins add up to eighty-eight Jupiter years—with 99.7 percent perfection. I was really blown away when I saw this—and hardly anyone who writes and lectures about the Maya calendar knows about it. In regards to this counting system, Peden quotes Coe in 1966.

> How such a period of time ever came into being remains an enigma, but the use to which it was put is clear. Every single day had its own omens and associations, and the inexorable march of the twenty days acted as a kind of fortune-telling machine, guiding the destinies of the Maya and all peoples of Mexico.[16]

Peden explains this further in his own words.

> Two hundred sixty was more accurate than 360 days in tracking the moon. [It] was able to satisfactorily track Venus and Mars. [It] is the best choice to track Jupiter and is the only choice that can simultaneously track all five cycles . . . these factual astronomical derivations are ipso facto sufficient to demonstrate the astronomical base for the Mesoamerican calendrical system.[17]

The Twenty-Year Katun Cycle

The next cycle the Maya tracked was called the *katun,* made up of twenty 360-day tuns, for a total of 7,200 days. This is a little less than twenty years in length—and only fifty-four days less than a Jupiter-Saturn conjunction. One of the first books I read about ancient mysteries was *Our Ancestors Came from Outer Space* by Maurice Chatelain[18]—and he found that the Jupiter-Saturn conjunction also tied in with a variety of cycles in our solar system. He felt that the correct katun should be 7,254 days, to match the Jupiter-Saturn conjunction perfectly, which I do not think is true—but it doesn't appear to be an accident that they are so close. There is a definite resonance there. When you consider that earth's orbit is only a little over five days away from being a perfect 360 days per year, the precession of the equinoxes is a little less than the ideal harmonic value of 25,920 years, and the Jupiter-Saturn conjunction is only fifty-four days away from being a perfect 7,200 earth days, this may all be the result of a catastrophic planetary explosion in what is now the Asteroid Belt—as Dr. Tom Van Flandren has compellingly argued.[19] The solar system would still be harmonic in the aftermath of such an event, but perhaps not as perfect as it once was. It may be that all these cycles are ultimately being driven by galactic energy fields, as we will see—and the solar system may have fallen a bit out of sync with the galaxy . . . at least for now.

Here's what Chatelain had to say about this cycle.

For the Mayas the katun of 7,254 days was not only a measure of time but also an astronomical unit to express the synodic periods of revolution of planets—or the count of days needed for each planet to be realigned with the Sun and Earth. For example, 5 katuns were equal to 313 revolutions of Mercury, 13 katuns were equal to 121 revolutions of Mars, or 27 katuns were equal to 7 returns of Halley's comet.[20]

Notice that Mercury was not present in Peden's analysis, and Mars was the weakest of the cycle connections—but here Chatelain found very nice alignments. It's important to point out that Chatelain was director of communications for NASA's Apollo program, and very familiar with complex calculations like this. I should also mention that at least three different insiders I spoke to—each of whom made a compelling case that he had worked in classified top-secret projects—told me earth has a natural twenty-year cycle that forms a direct conduit between different periods of time.

The Four-Hundred-Year Baktun Cycle

Next we take twenty katuns of 7,200 days to get the *baktun*, which weighs in at 144,000 days—or 394.3 years. In *Beyond 2012*, Geoff Stray pointed out that this is very close to the time it takes earth's inner core to make one complete rotation. Let's not forget that earth's core appears to be a dodecahedron, based on the most accurate modeling we now have available. In modern times, it wasn't until 1996 that we found out the core is rotating slightly faster than the rest of earth—and takes about four hundred years to complete one cycle.[21] Specifically, Drs. Xiaodong Song and Paul G. Richards, from Lamont-Doherty, the earth sciences division of Columbia University, discovered there was a nearly vertical line in earth's core—where seismic waves moved faster through this area than anywhere else. The line was tilted about ten degrees off of earth's rotational axis—which led them to conclude earth's core was actually on a slightly different axis than the exterior. After studying thirty-eight earthquakes between 1967 and 1995, as well as other seismic data, Columbia made its official press release.

> Dr. Song and Dr. Richards calculated that over a year, the inner core rotates about one longitudinal degree more than the Earth's mantle and crust. The inner core makes a complete revolution inside the Earth in about 400 years.[22]

Could this be what the Maya calendar was tracking? Think about it—the core is a dodecahedron. It's three-quarters the size of the Moon, and is almost thirteen times denser than water—meaning it has 30 percent more mass than the Moon.[23] When we think about how much of an effect the Moon has on our oceans, creating the tides, it's clear that the core exerts a powerful force. And since the core is a perfect dodecahedron, that means it may also be creating its own time portals. "Natural stargates" may be more likely to occur when geometric vortex points on earth's surface line up with this geometry in the core. If it takes four hundred years for this geometry to make a full circuit inside earth, then every day within that four-hundred-year cycle will be different in terms of the alignments. That may be why the Maya used the baktun as their largest cycle—other than the full calendar itself. It is a compelling idea—but if it's really true, then I would also expect this four-hundred-year cycle should be doing something else that we can measure. Then we could make an even greater case for why the ancients would be so interested in tracking this cycle. I found a study by Takesi Yukutake, from 1971, that clearly spelled it out.

> Periods of Earth warming and cooling occur in cycles. This is well understood, as is the fact that small-scale cycles of about 40 years exist within larger-scale cycles of 400 years, which in turn exist inside still larger scale cycles of twenty thousand years, and so on.[24]

The small-scale cycles of forty years are, of course, exactly two katuns in length—again forming a very nice fit with the Maya calendar cycles.

And even in 1971, Yukutake was aware that not only was there a four-hundred-year warming and cooling cycle on earth, there were also small changes in the rotational speed of earth's core that took about four hundred years to cycle through. (This was rigorously proven in 1996, as we said, but obviously there had been some leading evidence well before then.) In general terms, the Medieval Warm Period ran from 1000 to 1400, the Little Ice Age ran from 1400 to 1900, but the up-trend began in 1800—right in tune with the cycle. That also means we are now at the exact halfway point. It's been two hundred years since earth began warming up again. That should also mean the temperatures will start going down again, since we're about to pass the top of the wave—and we may already be seeing that happening.

I found even more supporting evidence when I read the work of Finnish scientist Timo Niroma, who explores the idea that solar activity is, in some way, directly related to planetary cycles. For example, Jupiter has an 11.86-year cycle, and the generally accepted average value for the sunspot cycle is 11.1 years.[25] Naroma often uses "the Elatina data"—meaning he tracks the year-to-year variations in the amount of radiation we find in a 680-million-year-old rock sample from Elatina, South Australia, in 1982. There are 9.4 meters of laminations that span a total of nineteen thousand years of time.[26] It isn't until we head into the fifth large Web page of his analysis that we find multiple references to a two-hundred-year sunspot cycle that has been found in Elatina and other sources. The solar activity is believed to be responsible for the cyclical changes in earth's temperature.

> The historical data seem to show that the 200-year oscillation has been there at least since A.D. 200. The even centuries seem to be have been cold, odd ones warm—not to the accuracy of a year, but in the average anyway.[27]

Naroma quotes at least five different scientific studies that found a two-hundred-year cycle in the amount of solar radiation reaching earth. One thing we do have to keep in mind is that this may not actually be a solar cycle. It is possible that the rotation of earth's geometric core determines how much solar radiation, or how little, can actually get through earth's protective shield at any one time. The geometric relationships of the core may be causing the solar radiation levels and the overall temperature levels on earth to rise and fall in an obvious two-hundred-year pattern of change—perhaps by changing the permeability of the magnetosphere.

It is utterly fascinating to realize that the Maya appear to have been tracking this exact same earth cycle for thousands of years. I don't think they'd be very interested in long-term warming and cooling cycles, if that's all it was. However, if this system also controls when the time portals open, then that cycle becomes much more interesting. Let's not forget that in this new physics model, there are multiple geometries that we have to look at—and they all nest together. So earth's core is only one of the geometries we have to look at. There could very well be others, appearing in the different spherical layers within earth, that would be even more difficult for our scientists to detect at this point. Each of them would probably have a different rotational period. There may, however, be a way to locate them—by studying their effects.

The "Temporary Local Risk" Factor

Is there any additional proof that the Maya calendar may have been used to track time portals? There certainly appears to be. Two German scientists, Graznya Fosar and Franz Bludorf, made a stunning discovery in 1998. They found what appears to be a vertical line in the earth's energy fields, which rotates along at 1.86 degrees of longitude per day—for a total of about 194 days. Two of these cycles add up to 388 days. The reason why this line is so important is that if you happen to be in the wrong place on earth when it crosses over you (or the right place, depending on what you're trying to do), a portal into time-space apparently opens.

Fosar and Bludorf first found out about this cycle by noticing that four different aircraft incidents occurred in the same basic area. The infamous TWA 800 crash happened over the ocean, south of Long Island,

on July 17, 1996. Several eyewitnesses, including a National Guard heli-
copter crew, reported seeing a bright object fly toward the jet and collide
with it—where it then exploded in midair, killing everyone. Conspiracy
theories were concocted that it was a missile or projectile, but it may
actually have been a spherical portal of energy released by the earth—as
we will discuss. On August 9, 1997, Swissair 127 nearly collided with
another unidentified bright object in the same area—off of Long Island.
There were 388 days between TWA 800 and Swissair 127.

Fosar and Bludorf had already been tracking two other airline incidents that both happened near Peggy's Cove, off the east coast of
Canada—not too far northeast of Long Island. Swissair 111 detected
smoke in the cabin, tried to make an emergency landing but crashed,
killing all 229 people aboard on September 2, 1998. Only five days later,
BALAIR 188 experienced smoke in the kitchen and had to make an
emergency landing—and this incident happened just a short distance
east of the Swissair 111 event less than a week before. It was these two
events, happening in the same area in such a short time, that first convinced Fosar and Bludorf that something might be going on. Then they
noticed the 388-day interval between TWA 800 and Swissair 127—and
were even more surprised to discover that there were 389 days between
Swissair 111 and Swissair 127.

From this beginning, they were able to calculate that a straight, vertical line of invisible energy may be slowly crawling across the northern
hemisphere at 1.86 degrees of longitude per day—for a 194-day cycle. By
tracking this line, and calculating exactly where it was at any one time,
they found fully nine different airplane crashes that were directly correlated with its position. They called this the Temporary Local Risk
factor, or TLR. They admitted they did not know what was actually
causing this.[28]

I was surprised that Fosar and Bludorf didn't crunch the numbers any
further—but I was also delighted, because it gave me the opportunity to
rediscover things that we haven't known about for a long, long time. I
believe that with further analysis, we will discover a spherical layer
within the earth that is slowly rotating in a 194-day orbit—and it will

have a geometric structure, such as the dodecahedron, that we can track to know when these portals will open. There may even be ways to make these Source Field currents visible—as the ancients appeared to possess.

If our model is correct, then the TLR cycle should also be a perfect subdivision of the earth's own orbit. As soon as I did the numbers, I found that in 17 earth years (of 365.2422 days), there were 16 cycles of 388 days—and 32 cycles of 194 days. A 17-to-16 cycle ratio definitely looks like a long-term geometric relationship between the orbit of the TLR cycle and the rotation of the earth. But what about the Maya calendar? It didn't take long for me to find an even greater surprise. The baktun in the Maya calendar is 144,000 days long—and there are almost exactly 742 TLR cycles in that same period of time. It becomes exact if you round up the TLR cycle to just over 194.07 days, which is probably a more accurate measurement of the cycle. This also meant there were 37.1 of these Temporary Local Risk cycles in every 20-year katun, and 371 of them within ten katuns—or roughly 200 years.

The greater implications are that this is one of a series of geometric energy patterns, nested inside the earth, that combine together at various times and create powerful effects—including portals into time-space. This cycle has direct effects on physical matter, precisely lines up with the earth's orbit after seventeen years, and fits perfectly into the Maya calendar. It was identified by studying equipment malfunctions and strange aerial phenomena. This also suggests the Maya may have been tracking time portals with their calendar, at least in the early days— given that the giant dodecahedron inside the earth completes a full rotation every time the Maya calendar reaches the end of a baktun.

I think this is just the beginning of what we can discover once we really begin doing our homework. We do not yet know the exact geometric pattern that is causing these effects to occur, but that is obviously an important quest to pursue. Given the potential dangers involved with random accidents, it is important that this knowledge not be covered up or suppressed. Innocent lives can be saved by tracking the TLR cycle, learning more about it, and rerouting flight pathways around potential trouble spots—particularly when it fires up a vortex point on the grid.

Investigating the Maya Calendar Cycle of 5,125 Years

The last Maya calendar cycle we need to look at is the length of the calendar itself. In order to obtain this number, you take thirteen baktuns, for a total of 1,872,000 days—or approximately 5,125 years. Five Maya calendar cycles add up to approximately 25,627 years—which is remarkably close to the precession of the equinoxes or Great Year. As of 2000, the International Astronomical Union fixed the precession at 25,771.5 years[29]—slightly over 144 years longer than five cycles of the Maya calendar. That is certainly interesting, but does it mean anything? I believe it is definitely important—but we'll get to that. Is there anything interesting and measurable that is directly related to the 5,125-year cycle?

Lonnie Thompson, a glaciologist from Ohio State University, found that there was a significant climate change on earth, not unlike the one we're now having, about 5,200 years ago. He determined this number from "the mountains of data drawn by analyzing countless ice cores, and a meticulous review of sometimes obscure historic records." The press release sums it up nicely.

> A professor of geological sciences at Ohio State and a researcher with the Byrd Polar Research Center, Thompson points to markers in numerous records suggesting that the climate was altered suddenly some 5,200 years ago, with severe impacts.[30]

The press release also strongly implies that this is a cycle, since the title includes the line, "Evidence suggests that history could repeat itself." We're obviously seeing climate change events happening now that are very similar to the ones that happened 5,200 years ago. Thompson believes this was caused by solar activity.

> Evidence shows that around 5,200 years ago, solar output first dropped precipitously and then surged over a short

period. It is this huge solar energy oscillation that Thompson believes may have triggered the climate change he sees in all those records . . . "Any prudent person would agree that we don't yet understand the complexities with the climate system and, since we don't, we should be extremely cautious in how much we tweak the system," [Thompson] said. "The evidence is clear that a major climate change is under way."[31]

I find it very interesting that the amount of solar radiation first made a huge drop and then had a massive surge in such a short time. If the Maya calendar is tracking a natural, long-term earth cycle, then perhaps what was changing was the permeability of the earth's own energy fields, such as the Van Allen belts—rather than the Sun. I already suggested the same idea for why we see a 400-year cycle in solar radiation on earth, which seems to correspond perfectly to the baktun in the Maya calendar and the rotation of the earth's core. Now, Dr. Thompson has discovered that a massive, worldwide climate change event occurred only about 75 years away from when the Maya calendar/"Long Count" cycle began. The entire cycle itself appears to be the exact same length as the Maya calendar. This is extremely interesting—but such a connection would never even be imagined by a mainstream scientist. If he even dared to make such a suggestion, he could suffer ridicule at the very least, and financial and career ruin at the worst. I haven't seen any other scholar who writes or lectures about the Maya calendar ever point out this correlation, but it is a very strong argument that this ancient system is not just "a bunch of nonsense"—it actually is tracking very real changes in our solar system. Furthermore, if Thompson's figure is correct, and the actual value is closer to 5,200 years, then five of the climate-change cycles he discovered will add up to exactly 26,000 years—which is only 80 years more than the ideal cycle of 25,920 years.

We may well be rediscovering the hidden mechanism behind this wobble in the earth's axis that was so interesting to the ancients. It may be that this sudden drop in solar activity, followed by the massive surge, has direct energetic effects upon our consciousness and even biological evolution—as we've argued earlier. Is this something that is strictly a product of cycles within the earth, or is there yet another pattern that we can definitely identify with the Sun? Maurice Cotterell may have found the answer.

Maurice Cotterell's Sunspot Cycle

Maurice Cotterell noticed that the Sun rotates faster at the equator—at a rate of about twenty-six days—than the thirty-seven days it takes to rotate at the poles. He crunched these numbers in a supercomputer and found that we need 18,139 years for those two cycles to line up. He thus discovered a long-term solar cycle that no one else had found in modern times. As he shows in his classic book *The Mayan Prophecies,* co-authored with Adrian Gilbert, there is very compelling evidence that the Maya were almost certainly aware of this same long-term cycle in the Sun— and tracked it with extreme precision. I wrote about this in detail in my first free online book, *The Shift of the Ages.*[32] Since 18,139 years is quite a long time, I was immediately drawn to investigate that number—and see if it had any connection with the precession of the equinoxes. If so, it could show that the precession was part of a greater cycle happening throughout the entire solar system, possibly being driven by the Sun itself—or maybe even by the galaxy working through the Sun.

Was there a connection between the precession and Cotterell's solar cycle? I found the answer by considering the importance of the number fifty-two—as it appears over and over again in the Maya system. It's twice the number twenty-six, and of course there are 260 days in the tzolkin cycle. Furthermore, it takes exactly fifty-two years for the tzolkin and the 365-day Haab to line up. This fifty-two-year cycle was called a Calendar Round,[33] and the Maya considered its ending to be a period of chaos and unrest. They would wait in anticipation to see if the gods would grant them another fifty-two years to live each time it came along.[34] When you're deal-ing with cycles, you get harmonics. One example is that you can add extra zeroes to a particular cycle and it will still have the same underlying vibra-tional quality—so fifty-two Calendar Round years can harmonize with 5,200 years. This, again, is the exact cycle Lonnie Thompson discovered for when the last major climate change happened on earth—and it's also very close to the length of the Maya calendar Long Count of 5,125 years.

What does this have to do with Cotterell's cycle? Just add up four of them, at 18,139 years each—and you get 72,556 years. Then, if you add on another 5,200 years at that point, you get 77,756 years—which is almost exactly three cycles of 25,920 years. (It comes out to three cycles of 25,918.6 years—just 1.4 years away from being absolutely perfect.) The 5,200-year cycle is the approximate length of the Maya calendar and shows up as a cycle of massive climate change in the earth. The number fifty-two appears repeatedly in the Maya counting systems—and the Maya systems synchronize very nicely with the harmonics of the solar system. This 5,200-year unit of time may be a shift cycle for an even larger system, which only lines up in even longer periods of time. Such a large-scale cycle may well be driven by the galaxy itself. The precession of the equinoxes, far from being a random wobble in the earth's orbit, may be part of a Great Clock throughout the entire solar system—powered by geometric energy fields.

Tracking the Portals

The Maya seemed to be very interested in tracking these cycles. The TLR cycle caused weird electrical problems, making planes either explode, crash-land or have major equipment malfunctions. In at least two different cases, bright points of light were seen during these events—and that may be our first clue about what a vortex between these "parallel realities" of space-time and time-space will actually look like. The Maya may have been levitating stones to build their countless numbers of pyramids by creating coherence—like we saw in the fascinating case of Tibetan Acoustic Levitation. Perhaps the Maya also had to wait for the right alignments between the geometry of the Sun, the planets, and earth's own internal energy patterns for this process to work the best.

If the TLR effect moves along by 1.86 degrees of longitude per day, that comes out to about 128.4 miles of drift every twenty-four hours, or about 5.3 miles per hour—if we use earth's circumference from pole to pole as a guide. If we then say the overall vortex itself is about twenty miles wide (and this is completely arbitrary—I haven't figured out the actual size at this point), that means you'd only have about four hours where you could potentially open a gateway into time-space and actually travel in time. It may be that if you wanted to practice this science, you would have to time it precisely—as your people could get stuck out there if they didn't return within those same four hours.

Then again, if you simply return at the exact same spot you left, then no time would have elapsed. It's only if you return at a different location that you will either pop into the future or slide back into the past—depending on where you go. Furthermore, if you had a large group of people gathered around the pyramid for a ceremony, to help contribute their own energy, the effect might be even more powerful—and you may have even greater success in actually getting a portal to open. Remember, this is a science of coherence—causing a greater amount of crystallization and spin to appear in the Source Field—and our own thoughts have a direct effect on that process.

Evidence of "Natural Stargates" Through Space

In 2008, NASA announced that about every eight minutes, a portal forms between the Sun and earth that allows solar particles to flow through. Each magnetic portal, or "flux transfer event," is as wide as earth—and scientists did not believe they even existed until recently. Dr. David Sibeck of Goddard Space Flight Center explained the mysterious new discovery.

> We used to think the connection [between the earth and the Sun] was permanent and that solar wind could trickle into the near-earth environment anytime the wind was active. . . . We were wrong. The connections are not steady at all. They are often brief, bursty and very dynamic. . . . Ten years ago I was pretty sure they didn't exist, but now the evidence is incontrovertible.[35]

In 2008, scientists from the Oak Ridge National Laboratory ran a computer simulation that found "numerous . . . streams of dark matter within the halo of the Milky Way, and more substructure appears within each subhalo. . . . Every substructure has its own sub-substructure, and so on."[36] These "streams of dark matter" could represent the visible energetic signatures of natural stargate portals that pass between stars. Also in 2008, scientists in Switzerland, France and the United States found unexpected plasma flow between neighboring objects in the galaxy using X-ray satellite imagery. They found this phenomenon quite by accident, as PhysOrg explained.

> Researchers have recently discovered the phenomenon of funneling hot plasma. Flowing plasma may funnel from one region to another through empty space, connecting otherwise isolated clouds and clusters throughout the galaxy. . . . [The scientists found] a million-degree plasma flowing from the [Orion] nebula into the adjacent interstellar medium, and then into the neighboring superbubble Eridanus.[37]

We now have very good evidence that this system really works. There is excellent science to support the idea of a global grid. This same geometry likely appears in quantum mechanics, the genetic code, the solar system, the distribution of galaxies at the largest level, and the gas and dust at the far reaches of the Universe. As we head into the next chapter, we will explore some of the most fascinating information of all—where we go face-to-face with natural vortex events, and find out what they look like and what they do.

CHAPTER SEVENTEEN

Time Slips, Time Warps and Vortex Phenomena

The Source Field is the master key—a fluidlike energy that ultimately creates space, time, matter, energy, biology and consciousness. The ancients appeared to know vastly more about the Source Field than we ever gave them credit for. They built stone structures that may well have created enough coherence to harness "natural stargates" that appear in the earth—when the geometry inside the earth aligns with the geometry in the solar system. When I found out that the TLR cycle nested in perfectly with the baktun, I really knew I was on to something. The Maya may very well have been tracking cycles they could use to open portals—for travel through time and space. The flowing geometric currents discovered by Hans Jenny could be truly galaxy-wide—and lead to traversable wormholes, or stargates, where all you have to do is go in one side and the current will naturally carry you out to the other side—which may be quite some distance away.

If all this is true, and this system really works, then there should be a variety of examples where these portals into time-space naturally and spontaneously appear on earth—causing mysterious disappearances, time displacements and other anomalies. What would one of these portals look like? Since the Source Field is fluidlike, we can expect that a vortex within the Field will appear as a spherical bubble. The surrounding pressure of the Source Field would push in equally on it from all sides, just like the atmosphere pushes on a soap bubble. Furthermore, since matter is being transformed into a wave function inside this vortex, including the atmosphere, we would no longer see solid objects—we would see photons of light in a foggy and misty sphere. Witness reports confirm this foggy sphere could be gray, white, yellow, green, red or even other colors. It would also shield gravity—much like a tornado, or the vortexes Schauberger discovered in water that caused levitation effects to occur. Anything or anyone that goes inside such a vortex could then pop over into time-space—and if you didn't know what you were doing, you might not come back. Living or nonliving matter that gets captured into this vortex would disappear from our reality and move over into the parallel reality, at least temporarily. These vortexes could theoretically travel in any direction—there is no reason to assume they would remain stationary, since these geometries have flowing currents moving through them all the time.

Some vortexes may start on the surface of the earth, capture materials or living organisms in them, and then rise. Once they reach a certain height, they may lose the momentum that keeps their internal vortex activity moving faster than the speed of light. Then, the material inside of them pops back over into space-time—and everything inside of them suddenly falls—seemingly out of thin air. Let's say one of these vortexes first appeared inside a lake filled with fish. The fish would temporarily pop over into time-space, get captured inside the gravitational force created within this sphere of energy, levitate into the air, pop back into space-time, return in what may be an entirely different time, and fall out of the sky.

Falling Out of Time

Before we get to fish falls, our first example involves rocks. This event contains many obvious signs of the effects from time-space—although it is considered a classic poltergeist case.[1] W. G. Grotten-Dieck awoke one night in September 1903 to the sight of black stones, no bigger than three-quarters of an inch, warping directly through his roof and ceiling as they fell in a smooth, even curve—in "slow motion." They landed on

the floor near his pillow. In a 1906 letter to the British Society for Psychical Research, he explained some of the strange things that happened.

> I . . . tried to catch the stones while they were falling
> through the air toward me, but I could never catch them. . . .
> It seemed to me that they changed their direction in the air
> as soon as I tried to get hold of them.[2]

This indicates the stones still had a levity effect, and were being
repelled by matter in space-time—such as his own body. They also were
very likely not fully materialized yet—explaining why he was never able
to catch one of them. They may have moved right through his hand like
it wasn't even there.

To me, the most interesting part was that the stones appeared to be
falling slower than they should have been—but according to Grotten-
Dieck, "The sound they made in falling down on the floor was also
abnormal, because considering their slow motion, the bang was much too
loud."[3] It would appear that time was moving more slowly within the
stones themselves, and their own immediate area. Everything outside
that area was still moving at the normal time—and the stones still had
the same amount of inertia. So, once the sound of the stones hitting the
floor moved out of the region where time was passing more slowly, it sped
back up and sounded perfectly normal—because Grotten-Dieck was not
standing within that slower zone of time himself. He also found the
stones were warmer than usual when he picked them up—which is
another frequently reported element of poltergeist cases. This effect seems
to be due to the stress they experienced in popping back over to space-
time, causing them to lose coherence.

On October 16, 1997, a "Civil War–type" cannonball blasted through
Leonard and Kathy Mickelson's mobile home in House Springs, Missouri, going through a window and two walls. The police investigated
the idea that someone was using a Civil War reenactment cannon, and
that may be all it was—but this seems like a pretty strange crime, not to
mention expensive . . . and one that could be easily traced to the perpe-
trator. Can you honestly imagine some guy setting up a Civil War

cannon and firing it at someone's home in the middle of a trailer park? Okay, maybe if there was enough alcohol involved—but it certainly doesn't seem very likely. There is at least a possibility that this was caused by a portal into time-space that had opened up in a Civil War battlefield, allowing a much longer duration to be traversed.[4] Just like in the cases of hauntings where someone's murder seems to keep being replayed for people who stay in the house, it could be that the deaths and trauma on the battlefield created a strong-enough disturbance in the Source Field to open up a portal—literally a rift in time.

Fish Falls

The most classic example of a vortex capturing various items, levitating and then dropping them is the many cases of live fish falling from the air. The phenomenon is real, though unexplained—and was even written up in the prestigious *Natural History* magazine in 1921 with complete seriousness.[5] There are many, many documented examples of this phenomenon, but the case that jumped out at me the most occurred near Calcutta in 1839. In this case, a single variety of fish, about three inches in length, fell in a perfectly straight line within a greater rain shower. The line was "not more than a cubit in breadth"—and this is compelling evidence that the fish were falling directly out of a single vortex in the sky. The author points out the staggering number of documented cases from all over the world, by people who were unaware of the phenomenon—and he ultimately makes a bold conclusion.

> To proclaim disbelief in the phenomenon of rains of fishes, to refuse credence to accounts so widespread in time and space, so thoroughly corroborative, would in the mind of the writer be indicative of an inability properly to evaluate evidence.[6]

Now, that's *Natural History* magazine—not the *National Enquirer*. "I don't buy it," the skeptic says. "None of this stuff happens anymore. People were crazy back then. That's all it is." In March 2010 the UPI published an article describing how hundreds of small white fish known as spangled perch, many of which were still alive, fell over a remote Australian desert town for two days. The nearest river was 326 miles away—and similar phenomena occurred in the same town in 1974 and 2004.[7]

OOPARTS

Fish falls and other such Fortean events may well be caused by a vortex that captures matter, rises into the air, potentially moves into a different time, and then collapses back into space-time—thereby dropping its contents. What about a vortex that captures items from the surface and then sinks down into the earth while it is in time-space, passing right through the earth's crust as if it weren't even there? As one potential example, there is a great body of data on Out of Place Artifacts, or OOPARTS, that have been found in deep layers of rock—much earlier than any intelligent human habitations would be expected on earth. The most scientifically rigorous collection of this data is in *Forbidden Archeology* by Michael Cremo and Richard Thompson.[8]

One collection of possible OOPART examples includes an ornately carved candlestick holder in rocks estimated to be 100,000 years old, though the picture is believed to be a hoax, a metal medallion with carved figures and a strange form of writing from 100,000-year-old rock, a copper hook and a ring from a 150,000-year-old sand layer, a curious mechanical object resembling a spark plug in 500,000-year-old rock, a perfect modern nail in a piece of million-year-old quartz, a nail found in rock estimated to be 75,000 to 100,000 years old in Peru from 1572, a nail found in British sandstone estimated to be at least 40 million years old, a two-inch metal screw in 21-million-year-old feldspar found in a Nevada mine, a cast-iron cube found in 60-million-year-old brown coal that was studied in scientific journals in 1886, a gold chain in 300-million-year-old Pennsylvanian coal, an iron pot in coal from 300 to 325 million years ago, an ornately carved brass bell found in West Virginia coal, and stone spheres found in California rock estimated to be billions of years old.[9]

"Toad in the Hole"

An even more interesting phenomenon involves cases where living frogs or toads are found embedded in rocks, lumps of coal, or within the trunks of large trees. Over 210 cases of this have been documented in Europe, the United States, Canada, Africa, New Zealand and the West Indies—dating from the late fifteenth century to the early 1980s. In many cases, multiple witnesses independently reported what they saw.[10] The famous surgeon Ambroise Paré ordered workmen to break up two large stones at his vineyard in 1575, and a large living toad was found inside one of them—with no visible opening to the outside. The miner said this was not the first time he had found toads as well as other types of animals inside stone.

In 1686, Professor Robert Plot described three different cases of "Toad in the Hole." In one case, a large limestone block had been recently placed as a stepping-stone to help people cross a stream. Croaking sounds were heard inside the stone, and after a long discussion, they decided to break it open—and a living toad came out. Plot also reported a case where the very top stone in the spire of a church tower had fallen and broken open. A living toad was found inside the stone, and it died quickly after it was exposed to the air—which Plot said was a common occurrence for these unfortunate creatures. Another live toad was found in the stone wall of France's Le Raincy castle in September 1770, which created a new wave of interest in the phenomenon. M. Jean Guéttard, from the French National Academy of Sciences, said this was one of the most baffling mysteries in all of natural history, and urged his colleagues to spare no expense in solving the problem—which was known and documented for more than two hundred years.[11] The reason why this is less likely to be seen in today's world may simply be that we usually crush any stones we quarry. With the advent of pourable concrete and lightweight, sturdy building materials, we usually do not quarry stone blocks directly out of the earth.

In June 1851, French miners were digging a well near Blois, and split open a large flint stone with a pickaxe. A large, living toad jumped out of a hole in the stone. The stone had a perfect impression of the toad's body in it, and a team of experts from the French Academy of Sciences were perplexed by how well it fit. They concluded they could not find any evidence of fraud, and the toad had apparently been alive and well in the rock for some time.

Another strange detail from many of these cases is that the toads' mouths often seem to be covered with a thick membrane, their skin is unusually dark, and there is a mysterious bright shining glow from their eyes.[12] A living toad was found in a block of magnesium limestone in Hartlepool, England, on April 7, 1865. Again, the cavity fit the toad's body perfectly—and the *Hartlepool Free Press* reported that "the toad's eyes shone with unusual brilliancy." The toad was extremely pale when it was first found—with a color very similar to the surrounding stone— but it soon darkened to an olive-brown color.[13] Its mouth was sealed shut, forcing it to breathe through its nostrils with a loud barking sound—and it also seemed to be a more prehistoric creature as well. As reported by the *Hartlepool Free Press*, "The claws of its fore feet are turned inward, and its hind ones are of extraordinary length and unlike the present English toad."[14]

In another case, an inch-and-a-quarter-long lizard was found by a stonemason named David Virture. It was brownish yellow in color with "bright sparkling projecting eyes." Although it seemed dead at first, it showed signs of life after about five minutes. It was found in rock that was twenty-two feet underground, and the rock cavity had again formed perfectly around the lizard's body. Even though the stone was very hard, about half an inch of the area around the lizard was soft and sandy—and had become the same color as the lizard. There were no cracks or fissures that could have allowed it to get in. This was written up in an 1821 edition of *Tilloch's Philosophical Magazine*.[15]

A British soldier found a large toad and a nine-inch-long lizard side-by-side in stone that was being quarried in Algeria—to make roads and refill bomb craters during World War II. Both were alive, and the rock was twenty feet below the top of the quarry. An 1890 issue of *Scientific American* reported that "many well-authenticated stories of the finding of live toads and frogs in solid rock are on record."[16] Like we saw in the tornado cases, it could well be that some of the material within their bodies has blended with the stone, causing the change in color—but somehow this effect does not cause instant death. The glowing eyes may well be caused by some of their bodies not fully collapsing back into space-time, thus appearing bright—as a part of them still exists as a wave. This light may be the most visible in parts of the body that are watery by nature—such as the eyes.

This living frog was found inside a giant boulder from a Swedish sandstone quarry, more than 10 feet below the surface, by Johan Gråberg and his men in 1733.

Why haven't other living animals been found inside rocks? My guess is that this is because amphibians and some reptiles can indeed go into a state of hibernation—and survive for long periods of time without food, air or water. When the "Toad in the Hole" story became popular in the 1700s, many amateur English naturalists tried burying live toads in flowerpots sealed with plaster or mortar—and they were still alive once freed. Zoologist Edward Jesse kept a toad buried for twenty years in a flowerpot, and it jumped out vigorously when the pot was opened.[17] In 1825, a professor of geology at Oxford named Dr. William Buckland set up a series of rigorous experiments to prove or disprove whether toads could in fact survive within rocks. After one year of burial, toads in a sandstone block had died, as well as small toads within a solid limestone block. However, toads that had been buried in a porous limestone block were still alive—and two of them had even gained weight. He then reburied them in the same block and checked them periodically during a second year. Each time he looked in on them they were awake, but increasingly emaciated—and finally they all died.[18] This led Buckland and other scientists to conclude that toads could not survive in rocks for an extended period of time, and thus the whole phenomenon was written off as a hoax.

It could be that once these amphibians have passed into a vortex, they move into a state of suspended animation as long as they stay still—neither fully in space-time nor in time-space, and therefore outside of time as we now think of it. Then, once the rock is disturbed, such as by quarrying, it "collapses the wave function"—as a quantum physicist might say. Then the unfortunate creature pops fully over into space-time. At this point, most animals would probably die of asphyxiation almost immediately—but toads and lizards seem to be durable enough to survive for some time once this has happened, possibly even for years.

The Russian Science of Vacuum Domains

Dr. Alexei Dmitriev has conducted detailed investigations of naturally occurring vortex phenomena that have many of the qualities we've been discussing—including the gravity-shielding capabilities. He believes tornadoes are one of a variety of examples of these types of vortexes in action, which he calls vacuum domains. Other examples include ball lightning, "natural self-luminous objects," poltergeists, a curious phenomenon known as "small comets" or "atmospheric holes," glowing forms associated with earthquakes and volcanoes, "sprites" and "elves" in the upper atmosphere, and kimberlite pipes in the earth's crust, which I will explain. Dmitriev cites the ongoing increase of tornado and other related activities throughout the twentieth century as evidence that the overall amount of these vortexes entering into our solar system, and thereby the earth, has gone up dramatically.[19]

In Dmitriev's model, which is partly based on the physics work of Terletskiy, these vortexes are directly transforming "gravi-spin" energy (gravitation and the spin force within it) into electromagnetic energy—which appears as photons emerging from these spherical areas. Obviously, if we could create such events on a reliable basis, we'd be able to permanently free ourselves from the need to pay for energy—or damage the environment to power our civilization. Gravity would supply us with more energy than we could ever possibly need. This may very well be happening already in natural materials such as the "Swedish Stone" discovered by T. Henry Moray—thanks to its quasi-crystal properties.

The properties of these vortexes include the ability to penetrate matter, the emission and absorption of light and other electromagnetic radiation, the disruption of electrical systems leading to breakdowns, strong magnetic fields, significant increases or decreases in the weight of objects, the rotation of air and dust inside them, explosions which often do not change their size or shape, a spherical outline, and a very substantial increase in the number of reported sightings during years of high solar activity. Dmitriev also claims that "almost all" earthquakes and volcanic eruptions feature these luminous forms at some point before, after and/or during the events.

Historical and contemporary poltergeist episodes also occurred during sudden increases in geomagnetic activity.[20] This data implies that poltergeist events are not random, but can be clearly traced back to energetic vortexes rising out of the earth. Sudden increases in earth's magnetic field strength, possibly triggered by surges in solar activity, appear with the creation of vacuum domains, or portals into time-space, in the core—which then rise to the surface through certain areas. A 1992 article in the *Society for Psychical Research* journal revealed Guy Lambert's discovery that poltergeist sightings clustered around the course of a river—and when it rained there were many more reports. Anne Arnold Silk plotted "large numbers of reported cases of sightings of ghostly figures, balls of light and suchlike" and found that they all clustered very strongly around geological fault lines. Furthermore, sightings of anomalous lights occurred at the ends of these lines as well.[21]

The explosions occur when there is a collapse inside the object—and since Dmitriev believes these vortexes are being created by the Sun and then flow into the earth, he feels these collapses release "captured solar energy." These explosions can occur in the atmosphere, the water or the earth's crust. Such explosions in the earth may be the real cause of volcanic eruptions and earthquakes—and in our Source Field model, the lack of coherence on the surface of the earth creates imbalances in the Field, which create a low-pressure zone. Our own state of consciousness, on a collective level, is directly responsible for creating this lack of coherence. Once we have a low-pressure zone, it may draw a large vortex of energy out of the earth's core, which then rises and eventually explodes inside the earth as it collapses back down into space-time—causing an earthquake or volcanic eruption. In other cases, these vortexes rise all the way up into the atmosphere—creating hurricanes, tornadoes, severe weather systems or "poltergeists." Dmitriev has also gathered compelling evidence that tornadoes are much more likely to form over areas with geological faults, such as seismically active regions.

Kimberlite Pipes

Dmitriev also believes these explosions inside the earth's crust are responsible for creating kimberlite pipes. These are elongated tube-shaped formations that were named after where they were originally discovered—in Kimberley, South Africa. The fun starts when an explosion is seismically detected in the earth, normally associated with volcanic activity. A narrow, dome-shaped ring then appears on the surface, barely detectable—but once you dig down to where the tube is found, it is filled with diamonds.[22] Conventional geologists believe diamonds only form at depths below 150 kilometers in the earth, and can take many millions of years to crystallize. Their theory is that strong volcanic activity then lifts the diamonds to the surface after they are formed, and deposits them in the kimberlite pipes within a mixture of magma and transported rock. The theory also states that the explosive force from deep within the earth shoots dissolved gas, magma, rock and diamonds through the mantle at a very rapid speed, which can reach several hundred kilometers per hour—and the rapid expansion of the gas cools the whole area so the diamonds are not disturbed. Typically kimberlite pipes form in several clusters simultaneously, and can be tens of kilometers apart from each other.[23]

This is the prevailing model, and it may well be correct—but Dmitriev believes these diamond-laced pipes are the result of the "intrusion, movement and explosion of a vacuum domain in the earth's crust." Dmitriev points out the strange fact that the neighboring rocks do not seem to be affected by these "self-localized" explosions.[24] Another interesting possibility that Dmitriev may not have considered is that the flow of time may be dramatically accelerated within these explosions, causing crystals that normally should form over millions of years to develop in very short periods of time—at least by our standards. Dmitriev also alleges to have found "vigorous relations" between the origin, existence and disappearance of these vortexes and the "energetic discontinuities in the lithosphere and ionosphere"—namely, the crust and the charged particles in our upper atmosphere.[25]

The Consciousness Connection

Interestingly, Dmitriev also suggests a direct connection between the appearance of these vortexes and the overall level of human consciousness in a given area. His classic 1997 paper "Planetophysical State of the Earth and Life" had a tremendous impact on me when I found it in December 2000. One of his central statements has become a major theme in this book.

> There are reasons favoring, or pointing to, the fact that a growth in the ethical, or spiritual quality, of humanity would decrease the number and intensity of complex catastrophes.[26]

I would absolutely agree—and the Russian pyramid studies certainly give valuable evidence that this may indeed be true. Dmitriev made his opinion very clear—but no one in the mainstream is listening.

> It has become vitally important that a world chart be prepared, setting forth the favorable, and the catastrophic, regions on earth—taking into account the quality of the geologic-geophysical environment, the variety and intensity of cosmic influences, and the real level of spiritual-ethical development of the people occupying those areas.[27]

In light of the 2012 prophecies we've inherited, other quotes from Dmitriev are even more interesting.

> The multitude of such [vortex] phenomena, which is rich in its quality and variety, is already growing quickly. Hundreds of thousands of these natural self-luminous formations are exerting an increasing influence upon earth's geophysical fields and biosphere. We suggest that the presence of these formations is the mainstream precedent to the transformation of earth; an earth which becomes more and more subject to the transitional physical processes which exist within the borderland between the physical vacuum [i.e., time-space] and our material world.[28]

Time Storms

Dmitriev's model has almost everything we've been looking for—except that I have not yet found a paper from him that associates these luminous, spherical vortexes with any time-related anomalies. However, in her vast, encyclopedic and wonderful book *Time Storms,* veteran paranormal researcher Jenny Randles independently validates everything in Dmitriev's model.[29] The main difference is that she is reporting what happens to people who enter into these vortexes—and cites a truly staggering number of different, documented cases where time slips, typically of up to five days, occur.

I was thrilled to find this book, because it was a prodigious research effort that tied together many cases—some of which had been written off as "UFO abductions" with missing time. There is far too much data in her book to cover it all here, but she has definitely broken new ground in identifying many common elements of "time slip" cases that other researchers had not noticed. These include glowing mist, spherical vortexes on the move, strong tingling sensations in the people near them, and in some cases, aching in the joints and/or painful skin rashes after exposure—as well as longer-term nausea, muscle pains and significant loss of motor coordination, where people cannot even grab a door handle and open it properly. Some people also emerge from these experiences covered in water—even though there was no visible water in the area they left from. So yes—it probably rains in time-space just like it does here sometimes.

Other characteristics include the powering-down of running cars and their batteries, strange increases in heat—as in the case of the falling rocks—and a very curious series of changes in human consciousness Randles calls the "Oz Factor." Typically this involves an eerie silence, as if the entire world has stopped. One witness said it felt as if her mind had been "sucked out." Others report numbness, heaviness, a sense of being caught in slow motion, and very real time distortions.

Time Distortions

In one case from Kent, U.K., in 1966, a witness named David reported a variety of these effects all at once. As he reached a bridge over a stream, in a wooded area near his girlfriend's house, he saw a group of teenage boys running in terror from something that seemed to be chasing them. David then felt everything become very quiet, as if his ears had become closed off. There was numbness and a strange depression, accompanied with a sense of heaviness and moving his head in slow motion. His girlfriend felt giddy, and the voices of the teenagers now sounded like they were coming through an echo. A white mist then swirled around them, and time seemed to slow down. When David tried to move his body, it seemed to "take forever"—and his cigarette smoke spiraled upward far too slowly. Sounds traveled too slowly and seemed hollow. His girlfriend clung to him in hysterics, and the teenage motorcycle gang now appeared to be moving in slow motion. The heaviness eventually left, causing their ears to pop—like in an airplane that was landing. Even though the whole process seemed to take hours, his cigarette had not burned down any farther when it finally stopped.[30] Obviously, it would seem that the ancients learned how to manage and control these experiences—so as not to have such unpleasant effects. However, if you can't create coherence within your own mind, body and energetic duplicate, then you may have a bit of a rough ride.

Gravity Shielding/Levitation Effects

In chapter 7, Randles then goes on to report that many of these cases also feature gravity-shielding effects—as we've already discussed in cases like Tibetan Acoustic Levitation, tornado anomalies, fish falls, alleged technological breakthroughs that have been suppressed, and Dmitriev's scientific model of vacuum domains. On pages 51–52, there is a case of hay levitating out of a field. It condenses into a lens shape, then hovers at 150 feet—where it begins moving across the sky slowly, easily mistakable as a "flying saucer" by this point. As it passed over the heads of the crowd, the witness reported feeling a soft pressure on his shoulders—and some of the children felt tingling sensations. Eventually the cloud thinned out and separated into pieces that looked like a spiral galaxy. Much of the hay fell at this point and was dropped on a golf course, while the rest drifted away in a "strange cloud." This occurred on June 15, 1988, in Marple Ridge, Peak District, U.K., and a variety of strange events have been reported in this area—including a car that mysteriously lost electrical power and stopped running in 1968, and many local legends of strange glowing lights—including blue glows that caused tingling sensations.[31]

In a 1971 event in Cuers, France, a man's car was levitated fifteen feet off the road inside an orange glow, after the engine failed and the radio filled with static. Once he realized he was levitating and became astonished, the glow disappeared and his car smashed to the road—causing heavy damage. He also found that he somehow had jumped three hours forward in time. (This may have been caused by the car drifting east while it was levitating.) The event happened at about one thirty A.M., and it should have been no later than three A.M. when the tow truck brought him home—but it was actually six A.M. when he arrived.[32] Beginning on page 70, Randles reports a case from the Isle of Mull, U.K., in 1987, where a mist "appeared out of nowhere" and attached itself to a car. It caused a heavy feeling of downward pressure and a vibrating sensation, which made it feel like the car was moving sideways and upward. The fog was now too thick to see through, though it had a swirling movement within it. When the mist disappeared, they found their car trunk had popped open, even though it had been locked—and all of its contents were now scattered across the road. Randles says this is a frequently recurring theme in many cases. As I have said before in our tornado discussion, this could be caused by a temporary softening of the metal in the lock that opened the trunk—followed by gravity-shielding effects that emptied out its contents.[33]

In another example, Peter Williamson experienced an event like this on July 28, 1974, in Somerset, U.K. A heavy electrical storm moved through and caused their dog to cower under a tree. As Peter went to rescue the dog, there was a huge flash—and as far as everyone else was concerned, Peter had vanished. Police explained away the disappearance as simply a lightning flash. Peter was found three days later in a nearby locked garden at eight A.M.—and there was no way he could have gotten in, as the gardener had the only key. He spent several days recovering in a hospital, and began having dreams where he remembered standing in an unfamiliar garden—covered in water. In his dreams, he wandered around in a daze and was eventually found and taken to a hospital. He could remember the names of a doctor, a sister and various nurses, as well as the name of the ward—though he did not know any of these details in his waking life. He began suspecting the dreams might be real, because they were long and mundane.

He noticed that the hospital would sometimes "shimmer" around him in these memories, and furniture appeared where it hadn't been before—only to have the ward then snap back to its usual state. All of this fits with the idea that this took place in time-space, not space-time. He also noticed that when he tried to speak, his voice sounded like it was in "slow motion." As he improved, he was allowed to walk the grounds, and he began to feel normal again as he walked down a lane outside. This was the last of his memories before waking up in the garden. A researcher named Colin Parsons stayed with the family for three days, and was able to confirm that a nearby cottage infirmary had a ward with that name—as well as the doctor and the sister with the same names. However, the doctor did not recognize Peter—and there were no records of him having stayed there.[34]

Three Astonishing Cases

Three cases jumped out at me when I read *Time Stories*. In the first example, a videotape from Florida was submitted anonymously to a TV station in 1996. Several investigators explored this case, including psychiatrist John Carpenter, physical scientist Ted Phillips, criminologist Dr. William Schneid and Dan Ahrens, a computer analysis expert—most of whom worked for the Mutual UFO Network (MUFON). They all felt this was a genuine video recording of something that really happened, and could not have been a hoax. The tape was from the security camera footage of a small factory in Florida, showing multiple camera feeds all together. In one frame, at 11:16 P.M., a worker walks toward the rear gate, apparently to look at something. A fuzzy white glow arrives in the area where the man is standing, while electromagnetic interference briefly disrupts the picture.

The glow lasts a few seconds, and when it goes away, the cameras are all working normally but the man has disappeared. When the film was analyzed one frame at a time, the man is seen to vanish almost instantly. The glow came back at 1:06 A.M., after a search for the man had found nothing. The factory lights all went out, and the man was again seen within the light—in only a fraction of a second. He was now in distress, on all fours, and began throwing up. The security guard rushed out to help him, but he could remember nothing of what happened—he had lost those two hours. He went home in shock, said he was too sick to work the next day, and never returned to the factory.[35]

The second case is very intriguing. A man named Bernard, from the north of England, reported a bizarre incident that occurred in Pennines, U.K., on a hill east of Manchester in the summer of 1942, while he was a child. Later on, he was concerned about reporting this case, as he was happily married and had risen to a prominent level in his work as a nurse. He described his experience to several psychologists at work, but no one could explain what had happened to him. On that day in 1942, he and a female friend felt a sudden, overwhelming sense of calm and quiet on the hill. They felt like their minds were drifting off. They sat by a tree and enjoyed the strange sense of deep relaxation. Gradually, they began hearing two voices, and when they sat up to see what was going on, two men were now standing over them—discussing their observations as if they did not expect the children to be able to hear them. One man said, "Here they are." The other man held some sort of device in his hand, and kept reading off numbers from it. The men were discussing time as if it were a landscape that you could navigate through—and they occasionally paused to say something positive about the children.

The two men were entirely human-looking and were wearing unusual, bright suits that looked synthetic—totally out of place for wartime Britain. Eventually the two men started talking to the children directly, and described events that were going to happen in their lives as if they had already happened. When Bernard asked them who they were and where they were from, one of them smiled, looked up at the sky and said, "From a long way away." They also told the children not to say anything, as it was a secret. When the children then went to the foot of the hill, they were greeted by a farmer who asked them who they were. When they told him their names, he said they should rush home as soon as possible. Once they arrived, their relatives had gathered and were very worried about them. The children felt like the experience had only lasted two hours, when in fact they had been gone for more than a day. Although they said they had been on the hill the whole time, it had been thoroughly searched and no one could find them.[36]

The third and final case I want to discuss from *Time Storms* opens up a whole new area of investigation. It concerns an area on the M56 motorway in the U.K., between Dodleston and Altrincham, known as Helsby Hill—a quartz-rich outcropping of sandstone. A remarkable number of unusual events have occurred in this area—including green glows, curtains of light, poltergeists, missing time, car blackouts with spontaneous travel through time and space, an odd white powder scattered on the ground after a white glow and high-pitched humming noise filled the area, as well as the disappearance of a one-hour block of time—and there were also six other cases of glowing lights with similar distortions of time and space. A woman who was driving on the slip road off the M56 between Preston Brook and Daresbury lost six hours of time in March 1988 after seeing a glow overhead.

Three months later, Randles discovered that at the exact same time this six-hour time slip happened, two TV reporters, Steve Winstanley and Fred Talbot, were filming a local news story about canal barges when they heard a strange noise. Then, to their amazement, two tin cans rose up off the boat, hovered for a short time and then fell into the water. They were actually passing under the very same vortex where the other time slip case had just occurred. The owner of the land, Bill Whitlow, described many cases of people hearing strange noises in the canal, which created the legend that it was haunted. Then, in August 1990, a crop circle appeared on Whitlow's land within a hundred yards of where the previous event had occurred two years earlier. Witnesses heard a high-pitched wailing noise on the night the circle appeared—and Randles photographed it before Whitlow harvested the crop. Then, while she stood there taking photographs, a car lost control on the road. The driver claimed he was pulled across the road toward the field—even though he could not see the crop circle. Police could find nothing wrong with his car, even though he felt it was from a flat tire—and no evidence of dangerous driving. Sadly, Randles's parents had parked their brand-new car off the side of the road, and this stray car slammed into them—causing serious injury to Randles's mother, who had to be cut free from the wreckage. Other events occurred in this same area since this time.[37]

Crop Circles and Mystical Beings

That brings us to the mystery of crop circles, which have been reported since at least A.D. 815—when Agobard, the Archbishop of Lyons, in France, had to issue a formal decree prohibiting the locals from taking crops out of circles that had formed in the fields. The locals wanted to use them for fertility rituals—probably because of the exceptional energetic effects they felt from them. The farmers were clearly upset by this loss. The interesting part about this story is that Agobard never denied the circles existed—he only went after the townspeople because they were removing all the crops inside of them. In his book *Dimensions,* Jacques Vallée draws from a ninth-century French text that gives further detail behind this story.

Supposedly, three men and a woman were witnessed emerging from "aerial ships" that were powered by beings called sylphs, who showed them many great wonders. They were told the human-looking beings came from "Magonia." The fearful locals turned on them and felt they were now evil magicians. The witnesses were about to be burned alive when Agobard saved their lives by denying that sylphs existed—as well as the idea that anyone could be a magician. Agobard's written notes from the event reveal the same level of sarcasm we would come to expect from skeptics 1,200 years later.

> We have seen and heard many men plunged in such great stupidity, sunk in such depths of folly, as to believe that there is a certain region, which they call Magonia, whence ships sail in the clouds—in order to carry back to that region those fruits of the earth which are destroyed by hail and tempests. . . .[38]

In Richard Thompson's epic research work *Alien Identities: Ancient Insights into Modern UFO Phenomena,* we hear about the traditional European legends of fairy rings, which appear to be crop circles.[39] In these legends, however, these are not merely interesting patterns in the crops—they also feature direct portals into time-space. In one traditional Celtic story, a hero named Ossian was enticed into a mystical land by a beautiful fairy princess. He married her and spent three hundred years living in the mystical land of Tir na nog. When he eventually felt like he wanted to return to Ireland, he traveled back on the same horse—and his wife warned him not to ever set foot on the ground. All of his friends had long since passed away once he came back, and the country seemed quite different. He eventually had an incident that caused him to get off of his horse and touch the ground, and he immediately turned into a blind and feeble old man.[40]

In another case from the early 1800s, two farm workers named Rhys and Llewellyn were walking home in the Vale of Neath, Wales. Rhys heard strange music along the way and decided to stay back and explore it, but Llewellyn couldn't hear anything. Rhys never returned, and Llewellyn was thrown in jail on suspicion of murder after an investigation. Two weeks later, a man familiar with fairy legends felt there might be an explanation. He advised them to return to the area where Rhys was last seen, and look for a fairy ring. Indeed, Llewellyn found such a circle in the grass—and when his foot touched the circle, he could hear the music of harps. As each man in the party put his foot on Llewellyn's, they were all able to hear the music—and they saw a variety of short but otherwise human-looking people dancing in a circle. Rhys was dancing with these little people at his normal height, and Llewellyn pulled him out. Rhys then said he'd only been in there for five minutes—but when he found out how long he had apparently been missing, he went into a depression, took on an illness and soon passed away.[41]

Thompson went into detail about this parallel reality in Celtic lore.

The otherworld of the Celts has various names, such as Avalon, Tir na nog (Land of Youth), and Plain of Delight. Examination of the stories makes it clear that this realm would have to exist in a higher dimension. To reach it, one must go to the right place in three-dimensional space, and then one must travel in a mystical fashion that we do not understand.[42]

France, Germany, Ireland, Scotland, Wales, England, Scandinavia and the Philippines all have legends of "fairy rings"—crop circles that marked portals into parallel realities inhabited by small humans with mystical abilities.

At least not until now.

Thompson also notes that the harvest of grain was often associated with fairies—and pulls a quote from Robert Rickard, who says, "Throughout the range of Indo-European cultures, the fairies were given their tithes of corn and milk at harvesting, over which they presided."[43] This raises the possibility that some people actually live in this parallel reality of time-space as their normal existence, rather than here in space-time—and may well have their own traditions and customs. Over time, these reports have become mythologized, and the stories get stranger and stranger—but there may well be a seed of truth in them.

Time-Traveling Dinosaurs

Could these time portals occasionally create a bridge that spans millions of years of time—and allow living creatures to pass through? Maybe so. We already discussed the Lazarus Effect, in which extinct species suddenly reappear in the fossil record—sometimes after millions of years. This may be the result of a DNA-wave effect that rearranges existing organ-isms into earlier forms, or creates life out of inanimate matter—but it may also be the result of portals that allow these creatures to pass directly from one time to another.

There have been many reports of lake monsters that have long necks, long tails and flippers instead of legs. The anatomical details of these sightings are almost identical to fossil records of the plesiosaurus. The most popular example is the Loch Ness Monster, a legend that originated in the seventh century with Saint Columba. There are many eyewitness reports—some estimate over three thousand just since 1933.[44] In 2010, *The Times* in the U.K. published an article asserting that William Fraser, one of Scotland's most senior police officers, considered the existence of Nessie to be "beyond doubt" in the 1930s.[45] George Spicer and his wife saw a dinosaur-type creature cross the road in front of their car on July 22, 1933. It was about twenty-five feet long, with a long neck that was a little thicker than an elephant's trunk. They did not see any lower limbs. It lurched across the road toward the loch some twenty meters away.[46] Intriguing photographic and video evidence has been extensively scruti-nized.[47] Loch Ness is also situated directly above a major geological fault line known as The Great Glen[48]—and we have already seen poltergeist cases and vortex activity associated with seismically active regions.

In 1993, Professor P. LeBlond of the University of British Columbia reported on many different sightings of "Caddy"—short for Cadborosaurus—off the coast of British Columbia, going as far south as Oregon. A whale allegedly swallowed a three-meter juvenile Caddy and the remains were found in its stomach. This story was covered in *Science Frontiers* and *New Scientist*.[49] In 2010, Russian fishermen demanded an investigation into a creature that looked identical to descriptions of the Loch Ness Monster, but kept appearing in a remote Siberian lake—which is one of the largest in all of Russia. This hungry monster has apparently been responsible for nineteen deaths from 2007 to 2010 alone.[50] In February 2011, *The Daily Mail* reported eight sightings in the past five years of a long, hump-backed creature known as "Bownessie" in the U.K.'s Lake Windermere—and revealed new photographic evidence.[51]

There are many documented sightings and/or local eyewitness reports of Mokele-Mbembe in the Congo—a four-legged dinosaur-type creature, similar to a brontosaurus but much smaller, known as a sauropod.[52] Most of the sightings occur in the Likouala Swamp, which has been officially declared 80 percent unexplored, and is mostly inhabited by indigenous pygmies. Similar sightings have been reported in other nations near the Congo, including Equatorial Guinea, Central African Republic, Gabon and Cameroon.[53] Similar or identical creatures have also been spotted in Papua New Guinea, above Australia.[54][55] Nine people saw a dinosaur-type creature on Umbungi Island in West New Britain.[56] One of the main vortex points on the global grid is in this same area—directly below Papua New Guinea. In 1993, *China Today* reported that more than one thousand people saw a dinosaur-like monster around Sayram Lake in Xinjang.[57] And in Canada, a young Inuit Eskimo working with scientists from Memorial University in Newfoundland found a fresh bone on Bylot Island that was identified as belonging to part of the lower jaw of a duck-bill dinosaur.[58] The Geological Society of America and *The Journal of Pale-ontology* both reported on fresh bones found in Alaska that were identified, twenty years later, as belonging to horned dinosaurs, duckbill dinosaurs, and small carnivorous dinosaurs.[59]

Marco Polo's own written records from his expeditions in China in the late 1200s reveal that the royal house kept living dragons in captivity for special ceremonies, and dragons were also hunted for meat and medicine in the province of Karazan. Polo reported seeing these menacing creatures himself.[60] Herodotus, a Greek historian, and Josephus, a Jewish historian, both describe flying reptiles in ancient Egypt and Arabia. Many ancient legends, including Greek, Roman and Egyptian mythology, describe heroes killing these creatures.

> Dinosaur-like creatures are featured on Babylonian landmarks, Roman mosaics, Asian pottery and royal robes, Egyptian burial shrouds and government seals, Peruvian burial stones and tapestries, Mayan sculptures, Aboriginal and Native American petroglyphs (carved rock drawings), and many other pieces of ceremonial art throughout ancient cultures.[61]

Dragons appear in literature from England, Ireland, Denmark, Norway, Scandinavia, Germany, Greece, Rome, Egypt and Babylon, as well as in American Indian legends, including the Cree, Algonquin, Onandaga, Ojibway, Huron, Chinook, Shoshone and Alaskan Eskimoes.[62] Another interesting lead is that maps from as recent as the 1600s feature drawings of dragon-like monsters in unknown regions.[63]

There are a surprisingly large number of credible eyewitness sightings of what appear to be pterodactyls or pterosaurs in modern times.[64][65][66] Traditional Native American legends of the Thunderbird bear remarkable similarity to modern pterosaur sightings as well. Forensic videographer Jonathan Whitcomb concluded that at least 1,400 Americans have seen what appear to be living pterosaurs between the early 1980s and the end of 2008. Whitcomb interviewed witnesses from nineteen different states across America. The statistical average estimate of the wingspan was eight to ten feet, but 27 percent of the estimates were over eighteen feet—much too large to be any form of bird in today's world.[67] Whitcomb also conducted extensive investigations of pterosaur sightings in Papua New Guinea, where they are called Ropens, and published the results on numerous Web sites as well as his book *Searching for Ropens*.[68]

Witnesses such as David Woetzel reported seeing a Ropen that had a reddish orange glow when it first appeared—and others have confirmed sightings of such a "bioluminescent glow." In 2007, Whitcomb issued a press release claiming that Paul Nation captured two pterosaurs on video in 2006, for fourteen seconds. Further analysis of the videotape revealed two tiny spots that were indeed glowing and slowly flickering. Cliff Paiva, a missile defense physicist working in Southern California, could not find any common explanation for what the footage showed.[69] This slowly moving reddish orange glow could be easily interpreted by ancient cultures as fire—and this may very well be the root cause of the fire-breathing dragon legends. Apparently, as these creatures first appear in our reality out of time-space, they haven't fully solidified yet—and their bodies glow because they still partially exist in a wave state.

The Egyptians may have seen pterosaurs as well—and created their legends of the Bennu bird of fire, or phoenix, from these events. The Was staff is a very popular Egyptian symbol of power and authority—held by

Many Egyptian gods carried the Was staff, symbolizing power and guidance through the afterlife. The head on the Was staff bears remarkable similarity to a pterosaur—and may have been modeled from actual sightings.

the gods and featured in hundreds of examples of ancient Egyptian art. The head at the top of each Was staff is nearly identical to a pterosaur in its shape and structure, and it cannot be associated with any other known living creature due to the unique spike that projects from the back of the head.[70]

In 1993, Russian scientists found remains of dwarf mammoths that had been alive only 3,700 years ago on Wrangel Island, off the coast of Siberia.[71] That same year, British explorer Colonel John Blashford-Snell photographed what appeared to be living mammoths, or stegodons, believed to be extinct, taken in an isolated valley in Nepal—as reported in the United Kingdom's *The Mail on Sunday*.[72] Admiral William Byrd fueled the hollow-earth theory when he reported seeing green pastures and mastodons as he flew over the South Pole in the 1930s—but this may have been an example of him peering through a vortex into the past, as the South Pole is one of Sanderson's twelve main vortices.

The Ta Prohm temple in Cambodia was finished and dedicated in 1186—and many people believe there is a perfect image of a stegosaurus carved into the exterior of the temple. This is but one of a variety of illustrations of living creatures that are framed in the same circular design—but all the other creatures are very conventional by comparison. The most comprehensive analysis of this enigmatic formation was written by a creationist, but nonetheless raises interesting points—including the fact that the original patina from 1186 can still be seen in the cracks, even though the exterior of the temple was slightly polished more recently.[73]

This carving appears on the outside wall of the Ta Prohm temple in Cambodia, dedicated in 1186. Other similar carvings depict conventional animals, such as birds, fish, buffalo, monkeys, deer and lizards—but this looks like a stegosaurus.

Lastly, on March 21, 1922, the *Boston Transcript* revealed that "During a heavy snowstorm in the Alps recently, thousands of exotic insects resembling spiders, caterpillars, and huge ants fell on the slopes and quickly died. Local naturalists are unable to explain the phenomenon."[74]

CHAPTER EIGHTEEN

The Galactic Clock Strikes the Hour

We've now seen geometry in the quantum realm, in biology, in the earth and in the solar system—as well as on the very large levels of superclusters and the background gas and dust at the farthest reaches of the Universe. What about geometry within the galaxy itself? By simple logic, the geometric laws we see at work in the solar system should extend well beyond just one star and its planets. If the galaxy also has geometric force fields, we could potentially cross millions of years in an instant—once we know how to access them. Many scientists estimate that the galaxy takes about 250 million years to complete one rotation.[1] If life appeared on earth roughly 3.5 billion years ago, as our micro-fossil records of bacteria suggest,[2] then the entire history of life on earth only appeared during the last fourteen galactic rotations.[3] That makes it seem much faster than we usually would think. The earth itself didn't exist prior to 4.54 billion years ago,[4] which is just over eighteen rotations into the past. Even the origin of the Universe, estimated at no more than 13.9 billion years ago,[5] is only about fifty-five rotations away. If all life on earth is only fourteen galactic years old, it becomes much easier to imagine how all these rotations could blend together in time-space—forming one giant repeating cycle. Each time you're at the same place in the galaxy you were at before, the same energetic conditions might again prevail.

Let's think back for a minute to the evolution cycle discovered by Muller and Rohde. Every 62 million years, we see massive bursts of evolution appear on earth—and this is directly correlated with an up-and-down motion of our solar system through the galaxy, which is believed to take 64 million years to complete. Richard C. Hoagland was the first to point out to me, in private conversation, that if you set the rotation of the galaxy at roughly 250 million years, you find exactly four of these 62-million year cycles in one galactic rotation. Four equidistant points in a circle form a square—so we may very well be looking at an octahedron in the galaxy (or a cube) that is actually driving evolution on earth. This was a stunning development. Our solar system's up-and-down movement through the galactic plane could be the direct result of the gravitational flow around each corner of the geometry, since Hans Jenny showed there is a constant, flowing movement in, around and through these geometric vortexes when they appear in a fluid. So as we head toward one corner, we're on an upswing—and then when we pass that corner, we shift into another current, and get pulled into a downswing.

What about other geometry in the galaxy? Remember that Sanderson's icosahedron on earth created ten vortex points that were near the Tropic of Cancer and the Tropic of Capricorn—all evenly spaced apart. If you divide the galaxy's 250-million-year orbit into ten equal parts, you have 25 million years each—which is reasonably close to the 26-million-year cycle Raup and Sepkoski originally discovered. In fact, if the level of solar radiation increased in a measurable way once this new sphere of geometry kicked in, that could increase the amount of radiation being stored in the fossil record—and thus make it look more like 26 million years had gone by each time, when it was really closer to 25 million.

Soon afterward, I realized that the double tetrahedron has six equidistant points along the equator, just like the Star of David in two dimensions, but there are six more equidistant points in the interior. This means you get a total of twelve equidistant points along the equator, within one sphere of energy. This now potentially explained the basis of the Moon's twelve orbital cycles for every earth year, as well as the deeper meaning of the twelve signs and houses in the Zodiac. Furthermore, the twelve Ages of the Zodiac could represent a larger double-tetrahedron geometry that takes us 25,920 years to move through. We may now have a geometric basis for why the number twelve appears so repeatedly in these cycles.

We know that based on the behavior of these unseen energy fields, both the galactic octahedron and the galactic icosahedron should also have spheres of energy that surround them and travel along with them. And we also know that a more complex geometry would be vibrating at a higher frequency, just like Liu and Spilhaus observed in the growth of the earth. Therefore, it would appear that during the 62-million-year cycle, a lower-frequency sphere of galactic energy was moving through the solar system. This sphere would have the geometry of an octahedron or cube in time. Each sphere appears to be rippling away from the center of the galaxy at a slow, even speed. Once the galactic octahedron passed us by, we came under the influence of the galactic icosahedron—though the shadows of the octahedron still are tugging on us a bit, as Muller and Rohde discovered.

A higher-frequency sphere of energy then flooded into our solar system—and this may have created enough of an increase in solar radiation that it made the fossil record appear to have a 26-million-year cycle rather than a 25-million-year pattern. Carbon dating is based on a smooth, unchanging flow of solar radiation in order to produce the results we see. The new 25-million-year cycle started appearing in the fossil record some 250 million years ago—meaning we've now had ten cycles, or one complete revolution of the galaxy, since it started. Since we've now completed a full circle, that may very well mean that we're now moving into the next big bubble of energy—with an even higher level of coherence. Also, let's not forget that the original solid crust of the earth began breaking up along equidistant points that formed a tetrahedron by about 220 million years ago—perhaps showing the gradual, long-term earth effects that kicked in once this new sphere of energy arrived. The grid may very well be shifting into a new configuration at this time—which could explain why honeybees and other migratory animals are getting increasingly lost and confused.

Galactic Energy Spheres Outside the Milky Way

If this is truly a universal, harmonic system we're dealing with, then these expanding spheres should be detectable in other galaxies. We remember that the Source Field often flows into our space-time through nonvisible electromagnetic frequencies, such as ultraviolet. So, we could look for changes in the electromagnetic spectrum of galaxies—in rippling, circular, concentric layers like an onion. And that is exactly what we find. This amazing story was covered in an April 1993 issue of *Discover* magazine.[6]

Hypothetical illustration of zones of microwave energy in the Milky Way, based on Dr. William Tifft's discoveries of these patterns in many other galaxies.

Dr. William Tifft was studying redshift, which is electromagnetic radiation from space—outside the visible spectrum in the microwave range. Normally, astronomers assume these frequencies indicate how far away something is. Tifft's discoveries seriously challenged that preciously guarded model, because he found that redshift did not stay the same in one galaxy—it was separated into concentric layers. The frequency grew increasingly higher as you moved toward the center—and it always changed by the same amount. Again, he used the word *quantized* to describe these separate layers. The *Discover* article compared this galactic phenomenon to the "energy states of an atom"—and let's not forget that Kozyrev also discovered a quantized change in the weight of an object after he bumped some of its atoms over into time-space. The atoms seemed to be popping back in through layers of geometry that would reappear, one at a time, over fifteen to twenty minutes.

Best of all, Tifft found that these spheres of energy were on the move, just as we would expect, based on the fossil record.

> More recently Tifft has also claimed to have evidence, from observing the same galaxies over a period of ten years, that their redshifts change over time. We may be seeing some form of galactic evolution taking place before our very eyes, he says.[7]

Despite the fact that this is considered rogue astronomy, because it slaughters the sacred cow of redshift, a variety of credible investigations have concluded that the quantized-redshift effect is genuine. One 2006 study detected one of Tifft's redshift values at a 95 percent confidence level.[8] A 2007 study reviewed the history of all these investigations from the 1970s up until the time they published, and concluded that the effect really could be genuine.[9] In 2003, Bell and Comeau found the same quantized layers of energy, like concentric spheres within an onion, in fully ninety-one different galaxies.[10] A different study from the *Journal of Astrophysics and Astronomy* in 1997 examined over 250 different galaxies, and found these same layers of energy in every single one of them. The effect was so obvious that it could be "easily seen by eye" in maps of the frequencies, and they said the confidence levels were "extremely high."[11]

Independent Proof—from Dr. Harold Aspden

Dr. Harold Aspden has created an incredible, encyclopedic body of work on his Energy Science Web site. Since the 1960s, he has explored the idea that all matter is created from an aether—and he concluded that it has different levels of density, or thickness. These discoveries were generated by a reshuffling of the Maxwell equations, which are still used in calculations to design and construct electrical equipment. Maxwell's equations automatically assume there is an aether—and because it works, no one questions it. Aspden was the first to find out that he could rearrange these equations, all in logical ways, and conclude that this aether had to have different levels of density. These equations also revealed what the exact electromagnetic frequencies would be when these layers of aether flowed into our own reality. Aspden was utterly shocked to discover that the numbers he had generated theoretically, in these equations, were identical to the actual frequencies Tifft had measured in his spherical, concentric layers—or "space domains"—which have been seen in over 250 different galaxies.[12]

> The conclusion one reaches from this remarkable result is that galaxies can, so far as the different space domain origins of their primary radiation sources are concerned, lock into slightly different sets of fundamental physical constants. . . . The author recognized the need to accept the existence of such "space domains" even within our local galactic system in Chapter 16 of his 1972 book. . . . Such domains have bearing on geological events, such as geomagnetic field reversals occurring as the solar system transits through boundaries separating adjacent space domains.[13]

This is direct confirmation of what I expected—namely, that we can prove there are layers of energy in the galaxy that can completely transform the earth and solar system as they sweep through, causing

measurable changes. Geomagnetic pole reversals are not what we're looking for—it's the effects on life that seem to be jumping out at us, since
many evolutionary events did not involve any cataclysmic activity.

Tau Space

Tifft himself also theorized about what was creating these strange
effects—and given everything we've been discussing, the results are
astonishing. Tifft has obviously never read Dewey Larson's physics, but
he came up with the exact same thing to explain what he was seeing: "In
summary, we have examined a model based upon two coexisting 3-D
spaces, one of time, one of space."[14] I was thrilled when I realized Tifft
had independently discovered this on his own. Let's read a little more.

> Quantum physics resides in tau-space and conventional
> dynamics operates in sigma-space. Although there as yet exists
> no formal mathematical framework linking these spaces [at
> least none Tifft was aware of at the time], there is a wealth of
> empirical consistency with observations. This includes proper-
> ties ranging from the masses and forces at the fundamental
> particle level, through redshift quantization, to cosmological
> effects on the largest scale. Time as a 3-dimensional quantity
> appears to be a promising subject for investigation.[15]

The word *tau* means "time"—so Tifft is almost using the exact same
language as the term *time-space*, only with the Greek letter for time
instead. In this same paper, he says, "At a given cosmic radius in tau
space, a galaxy occupies a specific temporal state. It must change that
temporal state in discrete steps."[16] I was amazed at how well all of this fit
together. The model is extremely elegant. When we combine Tifft and
Aspden's conclusions, we know that at least at some point, we could enter
into a new space domain of tau space, where matter and energy as we
know it "locks into a slightly different set of fundamental physical constants," and "changes its temporal state" in a "discrete step." Neither of

these great scientists seem to be aware of how well their model extends to explain the 26- and 62-million-year cycles that were found in the fossil record—showing that these changes in the flow of time also affect biological life as well as the "fundamental physical constants" of matter and energy.

Changes in the Solar System

We've almost got a perfect model at this point. The last thing we need to find out is whether our solar system is already going through a change in its temporal state where we indeed enter into a new space domain that will lock in a slightly different set of fundamental physical constants. In simple terms, if we're at the boundary of one of these domains right now, complete with all the coherence-increasing, DNA-evolving properties that come along with it, we should expect to see measurable changes in the Sun and planets. This would provide "smoking gun" proof that the ancient prophecies were indeed correct. As Dmitriev already suggested, these changes would be the direct result of an increasing flow of time through the solar system—or as he put it, an increase in the number of vacuum domains, or vortexes into time-space, coming in. And, lo and behold, once we begin seeking evidence for interplanetary climate change, we find many solid data points from reputable NASA and ESA scientists.

The Sun

Since at least the late 1970s, the Sun's overall radiation emissions have increased by 0.5 percent per decade.[17] Between 1901 and 2000, the Sun's magnetic field increased in size and strength by 230 percent.[18] As of 1999, high increases in the amount of helium and heavier charged particles coming out of the Sun were observed.[19] One NASA scientist said in 2003 that the Sun was "more active than in living memory."[20] A mainstream geophysical team recently proved that the Sun has been more active since the 1940s than in the previous 1,150 years combined.[21] The new brightening all started in the last 150 years.[22] As of November 2004, this same group proved that the Sun is more energetic than it has been in at least eight thousand years.[23]

Then in 2006, NASA announced that the Sun's "great conveyor belt," a massive circulating current of hot plasma, had slowed down from a normal walking speed of 1.0 meters per second to 0.75 meters per second in the north—and only 0.25 meters per second in the south.[24] Prior to recent times, the speed had stayed consistent since the nineteenth century, and it took about forty years—two katuns—to complete a circuit. This may be a sign that the "flow of time" within the Sun is changing, as we discussed earlier. In 2008, NASA said this was a "substantial . . . historic and important" change—"the sun's surface flows have slowed dramatically."[25] In 2009, NASA reported that "this is the quietest sun we've seen in almost a century" due to the surprising lack of sunspots and flares on the surface.[26][27] BBC News admitted that astronomers were baffled by this—particularly because, as Dr. Mike Lockwood explained, the Sun's overall activity peaked in about 1985 and has been on a noticeable downtrend since then, even as overall global temperatures have risen: "If the Sun's dimming were to have a cooling effect, we'd have seen it by now."[28] At the same time, scientists also fear there might be a massive new peak of solar activity that could potentially fry electronics on earth—and gave a surprisingly familiar-sounding target date of September 2012 for when this may happen.[29] A LiveScience article in 2007 seriously considered the social anthropologist Dr. Benny Peiser's suggestion that the Sun could be responsible for measurable "global warming" on Mars, Jupiter, Neptune's moon Triton and Pluto, as well as the earth.[30] Surprisingly, this is one of very few mainstream media articles to have ever made this obvious connection—but the data in Peiser's analysis is only a small part of the story.

Mercury

Despite supposedly high surface temperatures, Mercury seems to have ice in its polar regions.[31] It also has an unexpectedly dense core and strong magnetic field. Scientists would like to know how these anomalies are possible.[32] In 2008, Mercury was found to have "several signatures indicating significant pressure within the magnetosphere" that it didn't have in the 1970s.[33] By 2009, it had gotten much more intense—the Messenger probe was now seeing "magnetic twisters," and the scientists were surprised at how strongly it changed.[34] These tornadoes were ten times as strong as any ever seen on earth.[35]

Venus

The amount of sulfur in Venus's atmosphere decreased dramatically between 1978 and 1983.[36] Venus's overall night-side brightness increased by a whopping 2,500 percent between 1975 and 2001.[37] Scientists cannot explain this sudden change in brightness, though it suggests that the oxygen content of Venus's atmosphere may have substantially increased.[38] [39] A tail of charged plasma trailing behind Venus was measured to be 60,000 percent longer in 1997 than in the late 1970s.[40] Both the northern and southern hemispheres of Venus dramatically brightened in January 2007, and a strange, unusual and mysterious bright spot appeared in July 2009.[41] Regarding this sudden new bright spot, Dr. Sanjay Lamaye said, "It's fair to say something unusual happened on Venus. Unfortunately, we don't know what happened."[42]

Mars

Between the mid-1970s and 1995, Mars developed clouds, had an overall reduction in atmospheric dust content, and revealed a "surprise . . . abundance" of ozone in its atmosphere.[43] The Mars Surveyor probe was damaged in 1997 by an unexpected 200 percent increase in the density of Mars's atmosphere.[44] In 1999, a hurricane appeared on Mars for the first time in more than twenty years, and was 300 percent larger than any previously seen.[45] The biggest global dust storm in "several decades" engulfed the entire planet very rapidly in 2001, "something quite unheard of in previous experience."[46]

Interestingly, this storm peaked directly before 9/11—suggesting the possibility, however remote, that the massive stress everyone felt on earth from that event actually reflected back through time-space and had profound energetic effects upon our nearest neighboring planet. In 2001,

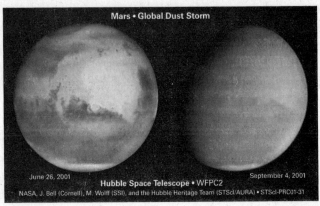

The atmosphere of Mars erupted into an unprecedented global dust storm between July and September 2001, shocking NASA scientists.

mainstream media announced global warming on Mars, including dramatic year-to-year losses of snow at the south pole and rapid erosion of ice features at the south pole.[47] NASA described this as "recent global climate change" in 2003. In 2005, European astronomers noticed a glow on the night side of Mars for the first time.[48]

Jupiter and Its Moons

Hot plasma was observed in Jupiter's magnetic field in 1979, though it was not visible in 1974.[49] Jupiter's atmosphere was discovered by NASA scientists to be hundreds of degrees hotter than anticipated.[50] The amount of heavy elements (such as oxygen) in Jupiter's atmosphere decreased by a stunning 10 percent between 1979 and 1995, which is equivalent to twenty earth-masses of oxygen "embarrassingly" disappearing in sixteen years.[51][52] Radiation emissions from Jupiter increased by about 25 percent between 1973 and 1995.[53] In April 2004, a major new study announced the surprise merging of three different oval formations in Jupiter's atmosphere, two of which were quite large. Without these vortexes in place, heat would not be released as efficiently and Jupiter might experience substantial global warming within the following ten years—a whopping temperature increase of 18 degrees Fahrenheit, or 10°C.[54] The same scientist also notes that the Great Red Spot has changed from its traditional red to "something more like salmon," and that this color change may be due to an overall increase in temperature.[55] These changes are theorized to be part of a seventy-year cycle, which is believed to have started when the three largest ovals first appeared in 1939.

In 2006, the three ovals that had merged together in 2004 were now becoming a huge storm rivaling the Great Red Spot, further indicating a "global change" in Jupiter's climate.[56] In 2008, two massive new storms emerged in Jupiter's atmosphere that were hotter than any ever observed before. NASA announced that this was part of a "dramatic, planet-wide disturbance on Jupiter that is ongoing. The cause of the disturbance has yet to be explained."[57] In order to properly model this "global upheaval" in computer simulations, NASA scientists had to increase the water vapor in Jupiter's atmosphere to "very high levels—about three hundred times that measured by the Galileo spacecraft . . . in 1995."[58]

In 1995, Jupiter's moon Io had a huge, bright, two-hundred-mile-wide feature show up in only sixteen months, which was a "more dramatic change than any seen in the previous fifteen years."[59] Io's ionosphere became 1,000 percent higher between 1973 and 1996.[60] Io's entire surface became over 200 percent hotter between 1979 and 1998.[61] New colors were seen in Io's aurorae in 1998.[62] Yet additional new colors were discovered in 2001.[63] A doughnut-shaped tube of glowing plasma energy fills the entire path of Io's orbit of Jupiter. Scientists think this tube is caused by charged particles spewing from Io's volcanoes. The charged particles in this tube became 50 percent denser between 1979 and 1995.[64] The overall density of the tube increased by 200 percent between 1979 and 1995.[65] A ribbon-like cold portion separated out and significantly brightened between 1999 and 2000.[66]

Confounding the mainstream models, another "surprisingly dense" plasma tube was discovered in 2003, this time sharing the orbit of the moon Europa. In this case there are no volcanoes to account for where the charged particles are coming from.[67] As of about 2003, Europa's aurora was observed to be substantially brighter than it was expected to be in a

1998 model.[68] The third large moon, Ganymede, has an aurora that became over 200 percent brighter between 1979 and the mid-1990s.[69] This increase in brightness is believed to be caused by a 1,000 percent increase in the density of Ganymede's atmosphere since 1979.[70] Ganymede also has its own magnetic field, in defiance of all conventional expectations.[71] The fourth large moon, Callisto, was recently observed to have an aurora that is fully 100,000 percent higher in intensity than Jupiter's own magnetic field in that area.[72] A third plasma tube, bigger than Io's tube and the one in Europa's orbit, was discovered in 1998. In defiance of all mainstream thought, it rotates in the opposite direction of Jupiter itself.[73] Counter-rotating fields are a basic aspect of the flowing interaction between the spin fields of space-time and time-space, as I have described in my other books on the Divine Cosmos Web site. Similarly, in 2007, Italian scientists discovered that our entire galaxy has two different halos, composed of different types of stars, which are counter-rotating inside of each other. Our Sun is part of one flattened halo of stars traveling at about twenty kilometers per second. A spherical halo of stars with a different chemical composition is counter-rotating at seventy kilometers per second.[74]

Saturn

Saturn's own tube-shaped cloud of plasma energy became 1,000 percent denser than expected between 1981 and 1993.[75] Bright aurorae were seen at Saturn's poles for the first time in 1995.[76] In 2008, NASA announced a "bright aurora" at Saturn's north pole, which "covers an enormous area. . . . Our current ideas . . . predict that this region should be empty, so finding such a bright aurora here is a fantastic surprise."[77] Clouds at Saturn's equator slowed down by 58.2 percent between 1980 and 1996[78]— again suggesting a reduction in the "flow of time" similar to what we are seeing in the Sun. "Massive" emissions of X-rays from Saturn's equatorial region were detected for the first time in 2004.[79] Such changes suggest that a fundamental shift has occurred within Saturn. In addition, curious dark areas named "spoke" formations were first observed in Saturn's rings in 1980, and were seen to rotate faster than the rings themselves.[80] By December of 2003, scientists working with the Cassini probe—the first probe to return to Saturn since the Voyager missions in 1980–1981—were already getting excited about seeing the spoke formations in the rings again.[81] However, by February, 2004, the scientists acknowledged that the spokes were no longer visible.[82] A "gigantic storm" with lightning bolts a thousand times stronger than any seen on Earth was announced in 2006.[83]

Saturn's moon Titan appears to have had a 10–15 percent increase in the size of its atmosphere between 1980 and 2004.[84] However, if NASA's more conservative, published estimates of Titan's former atmosphere size at 250 kilometers are correct,[85] then Titan's atmosphere may have actually expanded by as much as 200 percent in its overall height. Fast-moving, bright clouds have now been seen in Titan's southern hemisphere, which are inexplicable in mainstream models.[86] Ozone atoms, again a sign of ionized plasma, were detected on Saturn's moons Dione and Rhea in 1997.[87] A "severe storm" was seen for the first time near Titan's equator in April 2008, blatantly contradicting NASA's models and leaving scientists feeling puzzled.[88]

Uranus

Though Uranus "appeared as featureless as a cue ball" in 1986,[89] remarkably bright clouds began to appear as of at least 1996. By 1998, Hubble had discovered nearly as many clouds in a short time as had ever before been observed in the entire history of Uranus.[90] By 1999, NASA articles were referring to Uranus as being "hit" by "huge storms," making it "a dynamic world with the brightest clouds in the outer solar system."[91][92] The head NASA scientist referred to these increasingly bright and active clouds as "really big, big changes" on Uranus. In October 2000, a NASA briefing admits that "long-term ground-based observations [of Uranus are showing] seasonal brightness changes whose origins are not well understood."[93]

In November 2004, Uranus again made headlines: thirty distinct, large clouds were now visible—more than the entire amount of clouds ever counted prior to 2000—and these clouds were brighter than ever before.[94] According to one NASA scientist from Berkeley, "We have never seen such vigorous . . . activity in the southern hemisphere before. . . . Penetration of these clouds' activity to higher altitudes is unprecedented."[95] Additionally, carbon monoxide gas was detected in Uranus's atmosphere for the first time in December 2003, and the scientists feel that this gas comes from dust flowing throughout the solar system.[96] "Dramatic changes" in Uranus's rings were announced in 2007, including brightness increases, a potentially new ring and a cloud of dust particles pervading the entire ring system.[97]

Neptune

By June 1994, Neptune's Great Dark Spot, a circular feature in the southern hemisphere like the Great Red Spot on Jupiter, had disappeared. By March or April 1995, it had reappeared in the northern hemisphere. NASA said that this new spot was a "near-mirror image of the first spot previously imaged by Voyager 2." This also led NASA scientists to say that "Neptune has changed radically since 1989."[98] Two years later, NASA wrote of "a looming mystery": The newly migrated spot "appears to be trapped at a fixed latitude" in its new position in the northern hemisphere.[99] This appears to have been caused by a perfect geometric shift in

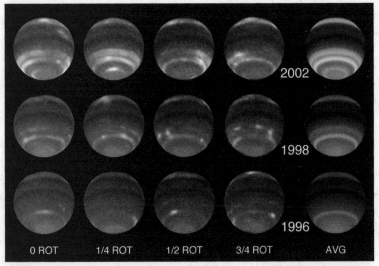

Between 1996 and 2002, Neptune's brightness increased by 40 percent in the near-infrared range. The images on the far right are composites.

the grid, as the new northern latitude was the same as the southern. By 1996, less than a year after the "hyperdimensional pole shift," Dr. Lawrence Sromovsky noticed an increase in Neptune's overall brightness—which continued dramatically increasing through to 2002. Blue light became 3.2 percent brighter, red light 5.6 percent brighter and near-infrared light intensified by a whopping 40 percent. Some areas of latitude became fully 100 percent brighter.[100]

The physics to explain such a change in brightness are just not there in the conventional models, since Neptune "seems to run on almost no energy."[101] Neptune's south pole was found to be 18 degrees warmer than the rest of the planet in 2007.[102]

Neptune's moon, Triton, experienced a "very large" 5 percent temperature increase between 1989 and 1998. This is comparable with earth's atmosphere heating up by twenty-two degrees Fahrenheit in only nine years.[103] It is believed that Triton's atmospheric pressure has "at least doubled in bulk since the time of the Voyager encounter (in 1989)."[104]

Pluto

Even though Pluto has been drifting away from the Sun since 1989, its atmospheric pressure increased by 300 percent between 1989 and 2002, causing a noticeable rise in surface temperatures. Again, this is attributed to "seasonal change."[105] According to one leading NASA scientist, "The changes observed in Pluto's atmosphere are much more severe [than in Triton's]. . . . We just don't know what is causing these effects."[106] "These changes are not subtle."[107] Indeed, the idea of "seasonal changes" being responsible for such a "severe" increase is said to be "counterintuitive."[108] The NASA team acknowledges this unexpected "global warming" of Pluto, but says that it is "likely not connected with that of the Earth" since the "Sun's output is much too steady."[109] The scientists suggest "some longer-term change, analogous to long-term climatic changes on Earth" could be responsible for the massive global warming of Pluto.[110] The Associated Press revealed in February 2010 that Pluto's colors did not change between 1954 and 2000, but then the red levels became 20 to 30 percent stronger by 2002.[111] In addition, "Nitrogen ice [is] shifting in size and density in surprising ways."[112]

Earth Changes Not Related to Industrial Pollution

Some Earth Changes cannot be attributed to human industrial pollution. According to NASA scientists, "Activity in [earth's] two known Van Allen radiation belts grew so intense in May, 1998, that a new belt was created . . . generating excitement and awe in the scientific community."[113] This new belt contains mostly ionized nitrogen, neon, and oxygen particles, which are new and unexpected since the inner Van Allen radiation belt itself consists mostly of protons.[114] The original source of the atoms is believed to be the local interstellar medium; i.e., the gas, dust and energy between the stars.[115] In February 1996, NASA's "Tethered Satellite" experiment hoped to harness 3,500 volts of electricity from space, using a super-strong cable to stretch a satellite out away from the space shuttle and hold it there while the cable gathered energy. However, the satellite appeared to have encountered vastly more energy in the earth's upper atmosphere than NASA had expected. First, it encountered a variety of mysterious problems; its "computer and two of its four gyroscopes had stopped working. In addition, both thrusters mysteriously had opened and spewed out nitrogen gas."[116] These problems caused the experiment to be delayed— and are totally consistent with the observed electrical effects of what appears to be a vortex into time-space. When the satellite was finally deployed, the supposedly foolproof tether actually broke, sending the satellite reeling off into space—and NASA was unwilling to speculate as to the cause of the break,[117] or whether the earlier computer/gyroscope/thruster problems were related to the break itself.[118] Astronauts did describe that the tether's "outer coating of nylon and Teflon looked charred and melted."[119] Thus there appears to have been vastly more energy in earth's upper atmosphere than earlier measurements had shown.

As of the mid-to-late 1990s, fully 5,060 percent more ozone was being detected in earth's middle atmosphere than was expected, even though pollution is expected to reduce ozone, not increase it.[120] This area is above where the "ozone holes" are located. There are also more hydroxyl (OH) molecules appearing in earth's upper atmosphere than conventional scientists can explain.[121] Furthermore, "strong emissions from atomic neon, argon and xenon" were seen in earth's aurora, apparently for the first time, in 2001.[122] Overall, earth has been losing 3 percent of its sunlight per decade since the 1950s. There has been a 10 percent decrease in sunlight reaching earth's surface in the last thirty years, and 15 percent over the last fifty years, showing that the effect is accelerating.[123] This suggests that the atmosphere itself has become noticeably denser. Most scientists would expect the earth to cool down as a result of a thicker atmosphere, not warm up, so this "shocking" finding "went against all scientific thinking" and was "ignored" as a result. "The first reaction has always been that the effect is much too big, I don't believe it and if it's true then why has nobody reported it before."[124]

NASA announced in 2009 that over the last twenty-five years, noctilucent clouds in earth's upper atmosphere are becoming more and more frequent, migrating down from the poles, and shining brighter than ever before.[125] This cannot be attributed to a change in temperature, and atmospheric scientist Dr. Vincent Wickwar said, "I suspect, as many of us feel, that it is global change, but I fear we don't understand it. . . . It's not as simple as a temperature change."[126]

The oceans of the world have warmed significantly since the late 1940s, and interestingly, slightly less than half of the increase in heat content is occurring below three hundred meters (roughly nine hundred feet).[127] These rapid, unpredictable changes in temperature were previously thought impossible, since sunlight cannot penetrate to these depths.[128] These subsurface temperature changes can predict the behavior of surface weather several months later.[129 130 131] There are temperature anomalies in the deepest levels of the Pacific Ocean that exhibit a slow, clockwise circulating movement,[132] and these deep temperature anomalies are neatly correlated with variations in solar energy output. This has allowed for the creation of a successful model to predict El Niño and La Niña events in advance.[133]

Earthquake activity also appears to have increased. A worldwide database system for reliably cataloging earthquakes was established by the United States Geological Service as of January 1, 1973.[134] According to the USGS, 98 percent of earthquakes are less than a magnitude 3 on the richter scale[135] and "earthquakes greater than about magnitude 3 usually can be felt by people near the source area,"[136] and thus are easily detectable.

For this same reason it is unlikely that improvements in the technology or number of detection stations would cause a significant increase in the actual number of earthquakes that are reported above 3.0. Nonetheless, in 1973 there were 4,517 earthquakes above 3.0 on the Richter scale worldwide, and by 2003 there were 17,443. This represents a total of a 386 percent increase in earthquake activity above 3.0 between 1973 and 2003.[137]

Despite this significant, steadily increasing trend in earthquake activity, there is the obligatory USGS Web page that attempts to blame this on increases in the number of detection stations.[138] However, a careful read reveals that this "disclaimer" document only discusses earthquakes larger than 7.0, creating a more easily manipulated dataset of less than twenty events per year. If you have an eye for the politics, you can see how the USGS did not actually admit nor deny an overall increasing trend in earthquakes—all they truly said is that "earthquakes of magnitude 7.0 or greater have remained fairly constant." (This is actually good, because it means that the most damaging earthquakes are not increasing in frequency.) Furthermore, an increase in our ability to locate earthquakes is only offered as "a partial explanation" for the public's frequent perception that earthquake activity is on the rise.[139]

Prior to 1998, earth was gradually getting narrower at the equator and longer at the poles. However, from 1998 onward, this trend has reversed itself—earth is bulging out at the equator and contracting in at the poles. Estimates of the weight loss caused by melting icecaps and glaciers are far too small to account for the magnitude of the effect.[140] Anomalies in earth's magnetic field suggest that a magnetic pole shift is already under way, and the models have no clear way of predicting exactly how soon this will complete itself.[141][142] Interestingly, in March 2004, a hurricane was detected for the first time in the earth's southern hemisphere.[143]

Global Warming

The effects of "climate change" have become so obvious that the U.N. World Meteorological Association feels that the world must be made aware of these changes immediately, as "the increase in temperature in the twentieth century is likely to have been the largest in any century during the past 1,000 years."[144] In addition, the 1990s are likely to have been the warmest decade of the last 1,000 years.[145] The amount of water vapor in the atmosphere of the northern hemisphere has increased in the last 25 years.[146] The average thickness of summer Arctic Sea ice has decreased by 40 percent in the last 30 years.[147] The average lake or river in the northern hemisphere will now have about two less weeks of ice cover per year than one hundred years ago.[148] Since 1966, the overall snow cover in the northern hemisphere has decreased by about 10 percent.[149] Glaciers in the Argentina/Chile region are melting fully 200 percent faster in 2003 than in 1975.[150] Even NASA has admitted that "the (Antarctic) peninsula has warmed 2 to 3 degrees Celsius (3.6 to 5.4 degrees Fahrenheit) over the past 50 years, causing rapid thinning, enhanced melting and rapid disintegration of its ice shelves."[151] Lastly, "since 1950, according to one estimate, some 600,000 plant and animal species have disappeared, and currently nearly 40,000 more are threatened. This is the fastest rate of extinction since the dinosaurs disappeared."[152] Forty percent of all known species on earth are now at risk of extinction. Somewhere between 2.7 and 270 species disappear every day. The most conservative estimate is that the current rate of extinction is one hundred times greater than the background rate, but Harvard biologist Edward O. Wilson has calculated that the true rate may be as high as ten thousand times above the background level. Wilson predicts that half of all plant and animal species will be extinct by 2100.[153]

The Local Interstellar Medium

Now, thanks to our study of the fossil record, combined with Tifft's and Aspden's models, it may be that all of the changes we have listed are caused by the solar system moving into a more highly charged area of energy in the galaxy. This appears to be directly affecting the behavior of our planets and their moons—showing an overall energetic increase as matter itself goes through a change of state, and the flow of time speeds up at the quantum level. If we are indeed moving into such a new zone in the galaxy, then we would expect to see an increase in the amount of dust and energized particles in our local interstellar medium—which is the area of the galaxy immediately surrounding our Sun's magnetic field. Dr. Don Shemansky, a NASA scientist, reveals that NASA has had a "persistent, pernicious bias" against anyone trying to do research on possible changes in the local interstellar medium.[154] Does NASA know something that they would like to keep a secret from the public? Have they been quietly documenting this interplanetary climate change, and putting the pieces together? Have they decided that humanity is too immature to handle the big picture? It is certainly possible.

However, some of these studies have made it through the cracks. In 1993, a NASA probe detected ionized helium and extreme ultraviolet radiation in the local interstellar medium for the first time. This led astronomers to realize that "the hot, ionized gas of the local interstellar medium extends much farther than previously thought."[155] In 2000 ESA/NASA reported steady increases in the density and temperature of helium in the outer areas of the Sun's magnetic field. One scientist said, "It's not yet clear that the source of the helium is [from the local] interstellar [medium]. But we've done everything we can to remove sources within the [Sun's own magnetic field] and the density's still going up. . . ."[156] He goes on to say, "A continued elevation would raise interesting questions about what's going on immediately outside our Sun's sphere of influence."

By 2003, the Ulysses probe measured dust in the interstellar medium at a "factor of 4 to 5 larger" (i.e., 400–500 percent more dust) than what had previously been seen in ground-based observations, leading NASA/JPL to suggest that there may be "an enhancement of interstellar dust in the local interstellar medium."[157] As of August 2003, an ESA/NASA experiment called DUST, launched with the Ulysses satellite in 1990, discovered that 300 percent more galactic dust streamed into the solar system between 2000 and 2003 than occurred throughout all of the 1990s.[158] In 2009, NASA made a startling announcement about these ongoing changes in the "Local Fluff" outside our solar system.

> The solar system is passing through an interstellar cloud that physics says should not exist. . . . Using data from Voyager, we have discovered a strong magnetic field just outside the solar system . . . [it] is much more strongly magnetized than anyone had previously suspected—between 4 and 5 microgauss.[159]

NASA scientist Richard Mewaldt announced that "in 2009, [galactic] cosmic ray intensities [from outside the solar system] have increased 19 percent beyond anything we've seen in the past fifty years. . . . The increase is significant."[160] In 2008, NASA announced that the Sun's magnetic field, which extends well beyond Pluto's orbit, had shrunk by 25 percent in the last decade and was now at its lowest level since the beginning of the space race fifty years ago.[161]

NASA scientists were baffled by this, but if we are moving into a zone of higher pressure in the local interstellar medium, this could obviously compress the Sun's magnetic field. Lastly, although scientists think it is "purely coincidental," not part of any natural law, all the energy and dust clouds in the local interstellar medium are expanding outwardly . . . away from the center of the galaxy: "For an observer at the Sun, the interstellar wind seems to flow [out] from the central part of the galaxy (the Sagittarius area)."[162]

This incoming energy does appear to have bioactive properties. In 2007, scientists from Arizona State University announced that salmonella bacteria became 300 percent stronger after being flown in NASA's space shuttle *Atlantis*. Fully 167 different genes changed—making it three times more likely to cause disease.[163] In 2008, it was announced that the Chinese were growing fruits and vegetables that were massive in size, such as twenty-one-pound tomatoes—simply by flying the seeds through space first.[164] Dr. James Spottiswoode found that the earth's alignment with the galaxy could create up to a 450 percent increase in psychic accuracy each day—within one hour of 13:30 local sidereal time—and the effect held true over twenty years' worth of trials.[165]

The Darwinian model of evolution has been proven incorrect at every turn. What the fossil record shows is sudden, spontaneous changes from one form to another, like simple shellfish with external skeletons into complex bony fish with internal skeletons. No transitional fossils have been found for this and many other similar examples, like the transition from finned to limbed creatures. Furthermore, Drs. David Raup and John Sepkoski have discovered that these mass evolution events occur, like clockwork, every 26 million years in the fossil record—while Muller and Rohde found a 62-million-year cycle. This appears to be caused by geometric forces in the galaxy, as we said. How could the simple presence of a higher frequency of galactic energy affect DNA? As we said in chapter 10, Dr. Peter Gariaev was able to completely transform a frog embryo into a salamander embryo, causing a complete, fast-processing mutation, without conventional gene splicing of any kind . . . using nothing more than a laser beam. In Gariaev's experiment, all that was required to transform DNA was a sufficient source of energy—in this case a laser light. Now, in our entire solar system, a similarly great source of energy appears to be streaming in from the galaxy's own natural energy fields. It may be actively transforming earth, the sun, the planets and their moons. Since we are living on the earth, we might also be feeling the effects of this transformation—through a transformation of consciousness as well as biology and physical matter. Dr. John Hawks revealed genetic proof that human evolution is now moving 100 times faster than it was five thousand years ago, with fully 7 percent of our genetic material having transformed during this time—and the rate is continually accelerating.[166]

The Nineveh Constant

I've saved the best for last. Maurice Chatelain, the director of communications for NASA's Apollo program while working for North American, a major defense and aerospace contractor, published some incredible cycle research in his classic book *Our Ancestors Came from Outer Space*. What do you get when you mix together 240 cycles of the 25,920-year precession? And who might have known about it? Chatelain studied the Sumerian clay tablets, which were apparently written in 700 B.C., and described events that took place three thousand years before they were imprinted. The Sumerian tablets were first translated in 1872 by George Smith, a young English Assyriologist. Chatelain explained how he found a tremendous new cycle on these same tablets.

> Among the tablets translated by Smith was a certain quantity that contained nothing but numbers, fantastically huge numbers, apparently derived from very complicated calculations. . . . The translation into our decimal system was finally published a few years ago, and one number stood out. It consisted of fifteen digits: 195,955,200,000,000. . . . Many specialists in different countries tried to find out what this fantastic number could have meant three thousand years ago to the Assyrians, who were not known to be great mathematicians or astronomers. It seemed that [Assyrian king] Assurbanipal must have found this number somewhere, probably in Egypt, or Chaldea, or even in Persia.

> I personally discovered the existence of the number in 1955, when I had just arrived in California. . . . Then in 1963 in Paris, when I was told about the calendar of the Mayas, who also calculated with enormously high numbers, I remembered this number from Nineveh, and began suspecting that it could somehow prove there was a tie between the Assyrian and the Maya civilizations. At that time I made some calculations, which showed that the Nineveh number could also be expressed as 70 multiplied seven times by 60. Then one day I remembered that the Sumerians . . . used calculations based on multiples of sixty, more than three thousand years ago. We still do not know for sure who the Sumerians were and where they came from, but we have found out that they were truly great astronomers who knew the revolution periods of all the planets of the solar system, including Uranus and Neptune. They were the ones who divided the day of 86,400 seconds into 24 hours of 60 minutes with 60 seconds each.

> Immediately, the realization came to me that the number

of Nineveh represented the value of a very, very long period of time . . . expressed in seconds. It did not take long to calculate that the number of Nineveh with its fifteen digits was equal to [exactly] 2,268 million days of 86,400 seconds each. That was a good start, but did not answer the main question—what did this huge time span of more than 6 million years [about 6.2 million, to be exact] stand for?[167]

Did you catch that? The Sumerian cycle is 6.2 million years long. Ten of those cycles are 62 million years long—which is exactly the length of time Muller and Rohde discovered as a cycle of sudden species evolution in the fossil record. Now we may be seeing yet additional information suggesting that the ancients knew about these cycles—even on a galactic level. I was truly astonished when I first realized how this Sumerian cycle fit in with the evolution we see within the fossil record. It really does demonstrate how knowledgeable our ancient ancestors were—and how much of a story there is behind the 2012 prophecies.

Let's continue with Chatelain, as this isn't even half of what he discovered with this cycle.

[This 6.2-million-year cycle] was certainly longer than the age of man on earth. Then the thought flashed in my mind that the clever Sumerians were familiar with, among other things astronomical, the precession of the equinoxes.[168]

When I first read this part in 1993, I didn't understand what the precession was, and I found it all highly frustrating. But now I know. And it is very exciting.

This movement [of the precession] has a cycle of about 26,000 years, or 9.450 million days of 86,400 seconds each. When I divided the Nineveh number by the cycle of the precession of the equinoxes, also called the Big Year, I had the greatest surprise of my life. The sacred number of Nineveh divided exactly into 240 Big Years of 9.450 million days each.

The Sumerians—an ancient culture—were tracking a cycle that is a direct subdivision of the 62-million-year cycle in the fossil record. This 62-million-year cycle also shows up as a galactic octahedron, or cube, that our solar system see-saws through as we travel along. Better yet, this same Sumerian cycle—one-tenth of the 62-million-year fossil cycle—can directly subdivide into the precession of the equinoxes by a factor of 240. Knock off the zero and you have twenty-four, which is two times twelve—and we've already seen how prevalent twelve-sided geometry is. We may now have a unified model that directly links the precession to the 62-million-year evolution cycle.

How did the Sumerians figure this out? And let's not forget that this number was expressed not in years, not in months, not in weeks, not in days, not in hours, not in minutes, but in seconds. The complexity is astonishing, and yet it all fits together. And that's just the beginning of all the goodies that are hiding in this cycle.

The Great Constant of the Solar System

Chatelain had done enough research to know that the ancients were after a holy grail of their own—the true Master Number that all other cycles, including every orbit of every planet, were being driven by.

> Then came my conclusion that this enormous number of Nineveh could very well be the long-lost magic number called the "Great Constant of the solar system," the number that alchemists, astrologers, and astronomers had been looking for for a very long time, while their ancestors were familiar with it more than 3,000 years ago. . . .[169]

Now he sets up the rules for how this Great Constant works.

> If the number of Nineveh really was the Great Constant of the solar system, it had to be an exact multiple of any revolution or conjunction period of any planet, comet, or satellite

of the solar system. It took some time to do this work and lots of numbers, but just as I had thought and expected, every period of revolution or conjunction of all the solar system bodies calculated by the Constant of Nineveh corresponded exactly, down to several decimal points, with the values given in the modern tables of United States astronomers—and nearly so with the French tables, which give slightly different numbers for the planets Uranus, Neptune and Pluto.

I have not been able to find even a single period of revolution or conjunction of a solar system planet or satellite that would not be an exact fraction, down to the fourth decimal point, of the Great Constant of the solar system. For me that is a sufficient proof that the Nineveh Constant is a true solar constant, and has full validity today—as it had when it was calculated many thousands of years ago.[170]

Even Pluto, way out at the far edge of the solar system, moving so slowly, fits this cycle perfectly with only a very small tweak.

The sidereal year of Pluto has been estimated by American astronomers to be 90,727 solar days. But sometimes, as in the case of the comet Kohoutek in 1975, astronomers too make some mistakes. Since its discovery, Pluto has made only about one fifth of its voyage around the sun, so a slight mistake in observations is possible. A negligible error of only seven days in the calculated long year of Pluto would be perfectly excusable. So let's suppose that the true year of Pluto is, in reality, 90,720 solar days. Now the Constant of Nineveh represents exactly 25,000 revolutions of Pluto—and this can be no more a coincidence than the fact that it also represents exactly 240 cycles of precession of the equinoxes.[171]

Tying It All Together

Pluto goes through 25,000 cycles every time this 6.2-million-year Nineveh Constant happens. Four of these Nineveh cycles add up to 24.8 million years, which seems close to Raup and Sepkoski's 25-to-26-million-year cycle in the fossil record. Forty of these Nineveh cycles harmonize with the 250-million-year orbit of the galaxy, if the exact value is 248 million years. It really does seem that everything fits. The Maya calendar may have used the 260-day tzolkin as a much smaller version of this master cycle to serve a similar purpose. Elsewhere in the same book, Chatelain gives stunning proof that the ancient Maya civilization also had a number that allows us to calculate the Great Constant of the solar system.[172] The Maya calendar cycles have therefore been clearly correlated with geometric phenomena that begin at the quantum level, extend through into the behavior of the earth and the rotation of its dodecahedron-shaped core, move on through the relationships of the solar system, and now appear to extend through the entire galaxy. These geometries create coherence, and since they are structures in time, they may allow for seemingly enormous blocks of time to be traversed instantaneously—and allows dinosaurs to appear in the present-day earth. This also suggests that when we finally move into a new sphere of galactic energy, many more portals of time will open up to us. The transformations in the solar system, as well as the enigmas of rapidly increasing human evolution, suggest that major changes are under way.

Were the American founding fathers quoting an accurate prophecy when they referred us to the Sibylline mystery texts from Virgil's Fourth Eclogue—predicting a Golden Age in which "heroes and gods comingle" and we all gain these supernatural abilities, so that "the Golden One shall arise again in the whole earth?" Are we being led through a galactic evolution, and have not yet seen the full extent of who and what we will become? I will now share a bit more of the ancient traditions with you and let you decide for yourself.

CHAPTER NINETEEN

Not Just a Golden Age

Throughout this book, we've been trying to discover whether the 2012 prophecies of a Golden Age are genuine—and we've come up with a very clear case for DNA and consciousness evolution, as well as the possibility that some sort of dimensional shift may be going on as well. So let's finish our quest to understand the legends of a Golden Age. If we want to know how the tradition got started in Western culture, we need to go back to the oldest literature in the Western world that described it—the classical literature of Greek and Roman times—and search for clues to reveal the even more archaic roots of these Golden Age prophecies.

In 1952, H. C. Baldry wrote "Who Invented the Golden Age?" for the *Classical Quarterly* journal—a truly heavy-duty piece of scholarship, showing complete fluency in multiple languages, often without even offering any translations. You have to be a major scholar to get through this paper without the help of a translator, including the ability to read the Greek alphabet and language. Amid all this intellectual chest-thumping, Baldry gives a remarkably thorough analysis of how the idea of a Golden Age came into being.

> There are many passages in ancient literature which depict
> an imaginary existence different from the hardships of real
> life—an existence blessed with Nature's bounty, untroubled

by strife or want. Naturally this happy state is always placed somewhere or sometime outside normal human experience, whether off the map in some remote quarter of the world, or in Elysium after death, or in the dim future or the distant past. Such an imaginary time of bliss in the past or the future has become known as the golden age. . . .

[We know that] (i) the picture of a happy existence remote from ordinary life . . . came from sources earlier than any extant classical literature; (ii) this traditional picture was normally known in antiquity before the Roman Empire as the age of Kronos [Time] or Saturnus; [and] (iii) gold and the use of gold had no place in the traditional picture. . . . When first mentioned in [Hesiod's] *Works and Days* (42-46) it is not explained, but briefly alluded to as the state which men would now enjoy if the gods had not hidden the means of life from them. . . .[1]

Hesiod is believed to have lived around 800 B.C.—and this is a particularly fascinating quote. It implies that we, as humans, once lived in a state that was far better than what we experience now. Baldry's research is implying that during the Golden Age—the age of Time—we experience a state of being that has now been "hidden from us" by the gods. Bear in mind that since this is a mythological retelling of ancient information, in this case the gods may represent nothing more than natural cycles of earth, Sun and galaxy that affect our state of being and our level of evolution.

References in later literature show an even greater variety of belief about the time and place of the happier life—a variety which cannot be traced back to Hesiod or any other single source, but suggests an old and widespread tradition handled at different times and places, and by different authors, in many different ways. . . . Further confirmation may be sought in the various parallels contained in Eastern literature, notably the Indo-Iranian myth in which Yima of the [Zoroastrian] Avesta and Yama of the [Hindu] Vedas must have had their common source—the story of a past age of happiness

under a ruler who, when it ended, became lord of a Paradise
inhabited by the souls of the blessed. . . . [2]

The Golden Age represented a "Paradise inhabited by the souls of the
blessed." Baldry mentions a common source that we can trace all the
Golden Age prophecies back to—namely the primordial "Indo-Iranian
myth" which gave rise to both Zoroastrianism and Hinduism. Both
religions appear to be talking about the same hero-king, the name
slightly changed depending on which religion you look at. His name was
Yima in Zoroastrianism and Yama in the Vedas.

Zoroastrianism

We've already gotten a good look at the Hindu legends of the Golden
Age in Part One, but we haven't explored Zoroastrianism at all. The
Traditional Zoroastrianism Web site features an extremely comprehensive collection of research articles on the subject, and in "History of the
Ancient Aryans" by Porus Homi Havewala,[3] we find out more about this
primordial Indo-Iranian civilization that later (probably much later)
splintered off into Zoroastrianism and Hinduism:

> All the ancient Zoroastrian scriptures speak of an earlier
> homeland from where our people came, the lost "Airyane
> Vaejahi" or seedland of the Aryans. From this homeland, the
> Indo-Europeans or Aryans moved to upper India, Iran, Rus-
> sia and the nations of Europe such as Greece, Italy, Germany,
> France, Scandinavia, England, Scotland and Ireland. . . . The
> "Vendidad" is one of the ancient scriptures of the Zoroastri-
> ans. . . . In the first "Fargad" or chapter, the Golden Age of
> the ancient Aryans is outlined with their greatest king, "Yima
> Kshaeta" (Yam Raj in the Indian Vedas), who banished old
> age and death.
>
> Then, the ice age broke on the ancient home, and the Ary-
> ans were forced to migrate southward, to the southeast and

the southwest. Mr. Bal Gangadhar Tilak, a great Brahmin (Indian Aryan) scholar of India in the last century, studied the Vedas and the Vendidad to find an ancient homeland of the Aryans. The Vedas are scriptures written by the Indo-Europeans or Aryans after they migrated to India. From the descriptions of the weather patterns mentioned in the Vedas, Tilak concluded that the ancient home must be in the Arctic regions, i.e., above present Russia. The Aryans migrated from the ancient home to Iran, and from there to India and Greece and Europe. Tilak also said that the most ancient historical scripture was the Iranian Vendidad, which actually describes the ancient homeland of the Aryans. . . .[4]

The great nineteenth-century Indian scholar Bal Gangadhar Tilak concluded that the Zoroastrian Vendidad was the "most ancient historical scripture" in the world. The name Zoroaster is actually a Greek pronunciation of "Zarathushtra," so both names refer to the same man. Zarathushtra allegedly made contact with Ahura Mazda, the Zoroastrian equivalent of God—but according to the Vendidad, this was only a more recent reconnection.

> Zarathushtra asked Ahura Mazda: "O Ahura Mazda, righteous Creator of the corporeal world, who was the first person to whom You taught these teachings?" Then spoke Ahura Mazda: "YIMA the splendid, who watched over his subjects, O righteous Zarathushtra. I first did teach the Aryan religion to him, prior to you.[5]

The author then describes the prior Golden Age in which "there be neither cold wind nor hot wind (neither extreme winter or summer), [and] there be no sickness nor death," in which people are "undying and unwanting, and gloriously happy." We then have a very interesting statement about time: "In the first 1,000 years of his rule, Yima the splendid enjoined righteous order on his Aryan subjects. He controlled invisible time itself, making it so much large in size so as to praise and spread the righteous law."⁶ It is very interesting to speculate on what was meant by controlling "invisible time itself." Given what we now know, this carries much more potential impact than most people may realize. Graham Hancock points out similar statements from Egyptian texts in his introduction to this book—that life is maintained by the "progress and movement of time"—and these words now sound very cutting-edge.

As the Vendidad continues, we have what appears to be a very clear description of the coming of the last major Ice Age.

> That glorious age of the Aryans did not last for ever, O Zarathushtra. It was time for the evil one's attack. I Who am Ahura Mazda spoke then to Yima Kshaeta: "O splendid Yima, toward the sacred Aryan land will rush evil as a severe fatal winter; evil will rush as thick snow flakes falling in increased depth. From the three directions will wild and ferocious animals attack, arriving from the most dreadful sites. Before this winter, any snow that fell would melt and convey the water away. Now the snow will not melt (but will form the Polar ice cap) . . . Now, there will be no footprints discernible at all on the packed sheets of hard ice that will form."⁷

Hence, the ancient Aryan civilization appears to have originated in what is now the frozen wasteland of northern Russia—prior to the coming of the last great Ice Age. Given all the work of Graham Hancock and others, we can safely associate this with the time of the purported civilization of Atlantis.

Boyce and Grenet's Pioneering Research

As soon as I read this, I wanted to know as much about the ancient prophecies inherited by Zoroaster as I could. This may be as close as we can get, in our own historical record, to the original teachings about what 2012 and the Golden Age really means. This brings us to Mary Boyce and Frantz Grenet's epic scholarly work from 1991, *A History of Zoroastrianism, Volume*

Three: Zoroastrianism Under Macedonian and Roman Rule.[8] In it, considered among scholars to be the defining standard of all research into Zoroastrianism, we find out that some of the literary, archeological and
numismatic (coin) evidence used to paint the picture of Zoroastrianism
has only recently come to light. What I find interesting about this book is
that the original Zoroastrian concepts about the end of the age do not have
the apocalyptic quality that many other prophecies do.

Zoroaster did not espouse the idea of human beings levitating up into
the heavens and disappearing.

> [Zoroaster's] future expectations were fixed upon this
> loved and familiar earth. It is on it, restored to its original
> perfection, that the kingdom of Ahura Mazda is to come; and
> the blessed are to live here eternally in his presence, solid flesh
> on solid ground. . . . It was an end of history that he foretold,
> not an end of the world.[9]

On page 382, we get more detail about how this transition into the
Golden Age is expected to take place. Namely, we see a "progressive weaken-
ing" of evil thanks to the hard work of many people in exposing the truth.

> Prophecies of woes and iniquities in the last age are alien
> to orthodox Zoroastrianism, for Zoroaster's fundamental
> message was that the triumph of goodness would come when
> evil had been progressively weakened through the concerted
> efforts of the just. . . . [H]uman virtues, such as justice, faith,
> liberality, joyfulness, will then be increasing throughout the
> world, and vices such as tyranny, enmity, heresy and injustice
> will dwindle away. . . .[10]

Zoroaster "perceived the salvation of the world as dependent both on
cosmic striving and on the sum of individual human choices; and these
two conjoined aspects of his teachings—emphasis on individual respon-
sibility and concern for the whole cosmos—made his doctrines strikingly
relevant to the conditions and problems of the Hellenistic age."[11]

Of course, the Hellenistic age inherited these teachings, as did all other religions. That's one of the points that Boyce and Grenet make so effectively. Everything traces back to the original seed of information and insight—and it appears that Zoroaster is the farthest back in time, and therefore the closest to the original essence of it.

Very interesting context about the true nature of evil was revealed on page 443: "Zoroastrianism taught that Ahura Mazda's rule over earth in the beginning had been deliberately brief, since he wished for the invasion of his Adversary, the Evil Spirit, so that he might defeat and annihilate him."[12] This, of course, suggests that the real purpose of the negative forces are simply to help us evolve in consciousness; but they were never intended to win—and never can win. They can only adapt to the basic nature of the Universe itself, which is loving kindness.

Fraso-Kererti

On pages 427–428, we find out that time itself is expected to change—by basically ceasing to exist as we now know it—once the Golden Age has arrived. This passage also speaks of a "Great Judgment," which could obviously be disturbing to many people—and this may already represent how the original teachings were starting to get watered down and altered. Based on many other prophetic sources I have encountered, it appears that all this judgment really means is that we will be given a choice of whether we wish to continue reincarnating, and learning the same lessons, or move into a state where we can pass through space-time and time-space with equal effectiveness—basically in an Ascended form. If we don't decide to take the "Great Invitation," we're not punished—we live our lives, pass away when it is normal and right, and continue moving through the growth opportunities that future lives in a physical body can give us.

This passage is taken out of 2 Enoch in the old Zoroastrian scriptures.

Before everything was, before all creation came to pass, the Lord established the Aion of Creation. Thereafter He created all His creation, the visible and the invisible. After all

that He created man in His image. . . . Then for the sake of
man, the Lord caused the Aion to come forth, and divided it
into times and hours. . . . When all the creation that was created by the Lord will come to an end, and every man will go
to the Great Judgment of the Lord, then the times will perish:
there will not be any more years, or months or days, the hours
will not be counted anymore, but the Aion will be one. And
all the righteous that will escape the Great Judgment of the
Lord will join the great Aion, and at the same time the Aion
will join the righteous, and they will be eternal. . . .[13]

This all sounds very much like a blending together of space-time and
time-space—so we can function in both worlds at the same time. Boyce
and Grenet give valuable context from other sources about the same
thing on pages 444–445.

In another passage (I Corinthians 7:29, 31) Paul, believing
that "the appointed time has grown very short," declared that
"the form of this world is passing away." Some centuries later
Augustine . . . saw this change of the world's "form." . . . The
cosmos, too, is to pass out of time into eternity, [and] is to
share, according to its capacity, in the eternity of the immutable Truth. . . . In the final consummation of all things, therefore, time will be no more; all will be eternal—God, man, the
world." This teaching, found by Augustine in Paul, has been
characterized as remarkable; but it is in fact what had been
taught by Zoroaster, and believed by his followers down the
ages.[14]

On pages 365–366, we hear about how we will have a "future body"
that is a "return to perfection."

Among Zoroaster's eschatological ideas was his teaching
about the "future body," that at the Last Day the bones of the
dead will be clothed again in flesh and reanimated by the soul

> (which has been existing apart, in heaven, hell or limbo,
> according to the individual judgment passed on it at
> death). . . . According to him, each created thing, animate or
> inanimate, possesses its own indwelling force or spirit; and
> Ahura Mazda created these spirits first and then clothed them
> in material forms . . . at the end of time there will be a return
> to that perfection, with the blessed entering into the kingdom
> of Ahura Mazda in the ideal form of a just soul clad in an
> unblemished body, made immortal and undecaying.[15]

Bear in mind this is not talking about a single Messianic figure—this is saying that "the blessed" will achieve this feat. This could be many different people.

Boyce and Grenet carefully trace how the difficulties of Roman and Macedonian rule affected Zoroastrian prophecies as well—causing later writers to adopt much more of a doom-and-gloom approach, which then seeded into all other Western religions. Nonetheless, what we see in the oldest, least-disturbed accounts is of a world that is transformed—in which time as we know it has come to an end, but not in a cataclysmic fashion. Evil is exposed and dwindles away, and humanity on earth appears to have transformed into an "unblemished body, made immortal and undecaying."

The Golden Race

Getting back to the intense, multilingual scholarship of Baldry on the Roman writings about the Golden Age, he concludes that the Roman poets mistranslated the words *saecula* and *aetas* as both meaning "age"— but in fact, *saecula* may mean either "race" or "age," and *aetas* should be translated as "race."

Now it all comes together. Everyone thinks the classical prophecies are talking about a Golden Age—and that's definitely a part of it—but that's also a mistranslation. The Zoroastrian prophecy of immortality in an ideal and unblemished body made its way into Greek thought as a

Golden Race—but this was then mistranslated by the Romans into the idea of a Golden Age—without necessarily describing what would happen to us once we get there. The last word in "Novus Ordo Seclorum" is derived from *saecula* as well—so this directly relates to the Sibylline prophecies, giving them even greater context—as well as the Great Seal of the United States.

It is extremely important to mention that this Golden Race is not some weird and sick Hitlerian vision of a bunch of blond-haired, blue-eyed wunderkinder, or Nietzschean overmen, that everyone else must die off in order to make room for. Just like the Cayce Readings said about the "Fifth Root Race," this Golden Race may well be everyone on earth, within a finite period of time—not just a particular nationality or skin color. As we just learned, Zoroaster called it the "Future Body." Let's pick up with Baldry again to learn more about this so-called Golden Race:

> Gold played no part in the generally accepted picture of those whom Hesiod called the golden race. . . . These Greek authors, like Hesiod, all refer to a golden race. It is only in Latin poetry that this is sometimes replaced by a golden age. . . . Gold, far from having a place in the traditional picture, was seen as one of the causes of degeneration from that happy state. . . . It was Roman writers who made the transition from a golden race to a golden age, and from them the concept was handed down into more modern literature.[16]

This really blew my mind. The coming of the Age of Aquarius, surrounding the year 2012, is the repetition of a cycle that has already occurred before—a cycle in which everyone on earth apparently had mystical abilities much greater than what most of us now possess, leading them to have perpetual bounty and a life "untroubled by strife or want . . . a Paradise inhabited by the souls of the blessed." The pursuit of gold was seen as "one of the causes of degeneration from that happy state." Unfortunately, our current scientific models are woefully insufficient to explain how something like this could be possible—but that doesn't mean it couldn't actually happen.

Apotheosis in 2012

The Sibylline prophecies speak of a coming Golden Age in the Zoroastrian tradition, and clearly state that this will be a time where "the Golden One shall arise again in the whole earth"—meaning everyone who is here. Intriguingly, there are thirteen courses on the pyramid in the Great Seal of the United States, and the year 1776 is inscribed at the bottom. During the time the Spanish conquerors came to Mesoamerica, the natives were using a thirteen-katun system to count time that they called *U Kahlay Katunob,* which adds up to about 256 years.[17] A katun is 7,200 days, or less than 20 years. The time of the founding of the United States occurred as the Maya calendar shifted to a new katun, and this may have been intentional.

The pyramid in the Great Seal of the United States may reveal a time-encoded prophecy that 13 Maya katuns of 19.7 years would pass, beginning in the 1756 to 1776 cycle, before the Golden Age was believed to begin in 2012.

If you add 256 years to 1776, you get 2032—but if you count the first course of the pyramid on the Seal as 1754 to 1776, then the top course of the pyramid would end in 2012—as Raymond Mardyks originally suggested and other authors then co-opted. The Eye would then appear in the final twenty-year katun between 2012 and 2032, as the pineal gland opens. The phoenix symbolism, as we now know, is directly associated with the ability to travel through time-space—and it also refers to the transformation of the earth.

Furthermore, in the very top of the U.S. Capitol dome in Washington, D.C., on the inside, there is a painting called *The Apotheosis of Washington*, where he is portrayed on a rainbow—indicating he has transformed himself into a divine state, which is also known as Apotheosis.[18]

The Apotheosis of Washington appears in the domed ceiling of the U.S. Capitol. This is a cropping of the original image from the Architect of the Capitol.

This image is surrounded by a ring of seventy-two five-pointed stars. William Henry and Dr. Mark Gray point out that this adds up to a total of 360 star points, and if we multiply the number of star points by the

number of stars, we get 25,920—again suggesting the American founding fathers were well aware of the precession, and the prophecies of what
it might do for humanity.[19] Every other star in this ring has a pinecone
pointing at it from the outside.

Apotheosis means "Man becomes God." Washington is portrayed as living among
the gods and goddesses of antiquity and sealed on a rainbow—which may indicate a belief he had reached an "Ascended" state called the Rainbow Body.

The Capitol dome may also be intended to resemble the shape of the
pineal gland, similar to the Masonic symbol of the beehive—where
"only the bees inside are aware of the inner activities of the lodge/hive."[20]
   If you look farther down within the Capitol dome, you see a frieze
along the inside wall that shows the moment Cortès conquered the
Aztecs. The Aztec calendar—which ends in 2012—is clearly pictured
behind Montezuma, and we also see the image of a serpent curled around
a jar of fire, which may again symbolize the pineal gland.[21]

This frieze also appears in the Capitol dome. It depicts Cortès's initial meeting with Montezuma. The Aztec calendar is prominently pictured—and it ends in 2012.

Regardless of the lies and corruption now so obviously displayed by various world governments, I do feel there is an underlying positive tradition they inherited. The meanings may have long since been lost, or confused with other, more recent teachings, but it does seem that America was secretly founded to help fulfill these ancient prophecies. In no way do I believe the elites are going to be able to create a new world order in which everyone will go along with some sort of world dictatorship. The very essence of the science and prophecies we've detailed in this book show that the change we are going through is woven directly into our DNA. No government can stage-manage or control this process. The United States may have been intended to help pave the way for this transformation, such as by creating a system of laws that encourage freedom of the press, freedom of religion and freedom from tyranny—but ultimately it is the galaxy, the Sun and earth itself that are directing this evolutionary process, as well as various relatives we appear to have.

The Rainbow Body

Could humanity be prepared to move into a "light body" of some kind, as the mystical prophecies of Zoroaster, the founding fathers of America and others seem to have suggested? William Henry and Dr. Mark Gray reveal the widespread prevalence of light-body references in numerous ancient traditions—where the human body is transfigured into a new form.

In Sufism it is called "the most sacred body" and the "supracelestial body." Taoists call it "the diamond body," and those who have attained it are called "the immortals" and "the cloudwalkers." Yogic schools and Tantrics call it "the divine body." In Kriya yoga it is called "the body of bliss." In Vedanta it is called "the superconductive body." The ancient Egyptians called it "the luminous body or being" *(akh)* or the *karast.* This conception evolved into Gnosticism, where it is called "the radiant body." In the Mithraic liturgy it was called "the perfect body.". . . In the Hermetic Corpus, it is called "the immortal body." In the alchemical tradition, the Emerald Tablet calls it "the golden body."[22]

Tibetan Buddhism has ongoing reports of the "Rainbow Body" to this very day—in which people transform their physical bodies into a new, rainbow-colored energetic form after many years of practice. In many cases, they would complete this process of transformation by meditating in a cave. When they come out, and are ready to graduate to this next level of their own evolution, they will often push their hand or foot directly into the stone. They can now easily flip the stone molecules into time-space, and leave an impression behind—and some of these handprints and footprints have been photographed and published online.[23] There are fully 160,000 documented cases of the Rainbow Body in Tibet and India alone.

Kathok monastery in eastern Kham in Sichuan Province, China, has records indicating that over 100,000 within the Kathok lineage achieved this state since its founding in the twelfth century, while nearby Dzogchen monastery had 60,000 lineage holders reach such a state since the monastery

This is one of many depictions of the Rainbow Body from Tibet. More than 160,000 documented cases of the Rainbow Body have occurred in Tibet and India alone.

was established in the seventeenth century. Both monasteries are of the Nyingma Sect.[24]

I first heard about this when I read *Dream Yoga and the Practice of Natural Light* by Namkhai Norbu Rinpoche. Here's a particularly good description of the process.

> Body of Light: Tibetan, ja-lus. Also known as the "rainbow body." Certain realized beings . . . achieve the transformation of their ordinary bodies into a Body of Light. . . . In this process the physical body dissolves into its natural state, which is that of Clear Light. As the elements of the body are purified, they transform from their gross manifestation (body, flesh,

bone, etc.) into their pure essence as the five colors: blue, green, white, red and golden yellow. As the body dissolves into these five colors a rainbow is formed, and all that remains of the physical body are fingernails and hair. Twentieth-century practitioners of Dzogchen who have attained the Body of Light include the teachers and family members of Namkhai Norbu Rinpoche—for example, his uncle Urgyen Danzin (Togden), his two teachers Changchub Dorje and Ayu Khandro, and Changchub Dorje's master, Nyala Pema Dendul.[25]

As reported in 2002, David Steindl-Rast, a Benedictine monk, proposed a scientific investigation of the Rainbow Body phenomenon with the Institute of Noetic Sciences—and got an enthusiastic approval. Steindl-Rast explains the effect it would have if this phenomenon were studied and widely acknowledged as genuine.

> If we can establish as an anthropological fact that what is described in the resurrection of Jesus has not only happened to others, but is happening today, it would put our view of human potential in a completely different light.[26]

Steindl-Rast then contacted Father Francis Tiso, an ordained Catholic priest who frequently visited Tibet, and encouraged him to explore recent cases of Rainbow Body and document his findings. Tiso explored the case of Khenpo A-chos, a Gelugpa monk from Kham, Tibet, who died in 1998. Tiso located the village where he died, and recorded multiple interviews with eyewitnesses to Khenpo A-chos's death. The witnesses said Khenpo A-chos had a warm, spiritual nature that touched everyone he met.

> This was a very interesting man, aside from the way he died. . . . Everyone mentioned his faithfulness to his vows, his purity of life, and how he often spoke of the importance of

cultivating compassion. He had the ability to teach even the roughest and toughest of types how to be a little gentler, a little more mindful. To be in the man's presence changed people.[27]

The witnesses reported a rainbow appearing over Khenpo A-chos's hut a few days before he died, and that "dozens of rainbows" appeared in the sky afterward. He was not sick and nothing appeared to be wrong with him—he simply chanted a mantra.

> According to the eyewitnesses, after his breath stopped his flesh became kind of pinkish. One person said it turned brilliant white. All said it started to shine. Lama A-chos suggested wrapping his friend's body in a yellow robe, the type all Gelug monks wear. As the days passed, they maintained they could see, through the robe, that his bones and his body were shrinking. They also heard beautiful, mysterious music coming from the sky, and they smelled perfume. After seven days, they removed the yellow cloth, and no body remained. Lama Norta and a few other individuals claimed that after his death Khenpo A-chos appeared to them in visions and dreams . . . Lama A-chos told Tiso that it takes sixty years of intensive practice to achieve the rainbow body. "Whether it always takes that long, I don't know," acknowledges Tiso, "but we would like to be able to incorporate, in a respectful way, some of these practices into our own Western philosophical and religious traditions." . . . To our knowledge, says Tiso, the bodies of most Christian saints did not disappear or shrink after their deaths. . . . However, he adds, bodily ascensions are mentioned in the Bible and other traditional texts for Enoch, Mary, Elijah, and possibly Moses. And there are numerous stories of saints materializing after their death, similar to the widespread phenomenon known as the "light-body."[28]

Divine Synthesis

Given all that we have learned, how can we analyze and hope to understand such an incredible series of prophecies scientifically? Clearly there is a wealth of evidence suggesting that the ancients were absolutely convinced that major events would be heading our way as we go through the shift into the Age of Aquarius. We've seen proof that the Maya calendar corresponds to real cycles in the solar system that may well be driven by the galaxy—cycles that are now causing us to experience interplanetary climate change as we head into the Age of Aquarius. We've seen many ancient prophecies describing the coming of a Golden Age, where humans would again be as gods. This obviously shows us much more is at work than just a major catastrophe, as so many 2012 scholars have concluded. In fact, I firmly believe these disaster prophecies are a misunderstanding, and we're already seeing the worst of the Earth Changes right now. We appear to be in safe hands—guided through an evolutionary process by forces much greater than most of us could ever comprehend.

All these ancient traditions suggest that humanity is undergoing some type of evolutionary event. The Tibetan Rainbow Body observations give strong support to Biblical prophecies suggesting that we may transform into some sort of energetic body—the Perfected Body. Hence the American founding fathers and others often called themselves the "Perfectibilists."

Obviously there is no way to know if we will transform into a light body of some sort—but we do now know we are going through a rapid phase of evolution, on a direct, biological level. Our civilization has grown by leaps and bounds within the last few hundred years, and it appears that greater forces are at work—forces that the ancients may have known much more about than we do now. One thing is for certain: The old models of a human body as a random genetic accident that only showed up on earth by Darwinian mutations must be thrown out. In fact, we have suffered under a variety of illusions about who and what we are that have kept us trapped in a prison of materialistic thought. Our bodies grow out of, and are nurtured by, a hidden energy field unknown to the Western mainstream scientific community. This field ultimately unifies all of our thoughts together as One—in directly measurable, provable ways. With this knowledge come powerful new tools that help us evolve as conscious beings. We gain remarkable new methods to heal ourselves and expand our own evolution in a remarkably short time. We have clearly shown how the ancient stone relics of a lost Golden Age point toward the elaborate, technological use of these energy fields. The year 2012 may represent a time when we begin to collectively rediscover this lost science—and start using it to heal ourselves and our planet.

There are certain intriguing Bible quotes I'd like to share with you—as with everything else we've shared as context, they become quite interesting to consider. These quotes may have been inspired by the same tradition of Fraso-kererti that was inherited from the Zoroastrian scriptures—and was widely believed to be an accurate prophecy.

The First Adam was made a living soul, and the last Adam a quickening spirit. —I Corinthians 15:45

The first man is of the earth, the second man is the Lord from heaven. —I Corinthians 15:47

We shall bear the image of the heavenly. . . . I show you a mystery, we shall all be changed in the twinkling of an eye . . . the corruptible must put on incorruption, and the mortal must put on immortality. —I Corinthians 15:49–53

We look for new heavens and a new earth, wherein dwelleth righteousness. —2 Peter 3:13

Behold, I create new heavens and a new earth: The former world shall not be remembered, nor even come into mind. —Isaiah 65:17

As the new heavens and the new earth, which I will make, shall remain before me, so shall your seed and your name remain.   —Isaiah 66:22

There shall be signs in the sun, and in the moon, and in the stars [planets?]; and upon the earth the distress of nations, with perplexity; the sea and the waves roaring; Men's hearts failing them for fear, and for looking after those things which are coming on the earth: for the powers of heaven shall be shaken.

And then shall they see the Son of man coming in a cloud with power and great glory. And when these things begin to come to pass, then look up, and lift up your heads; for your redemption draweth nigh.   —Luke 21:25–28

CHAPTER TWENTY

Disclosure

I do believe a formal, open disclosure of the ET/UFO phenomenon is an essential aspect of our movement into a Golden Age. I have tried to avoid relying on UFO-related accounts in this book, but I do feel there is undeniable evidence that we were visited by human-looking extraterrestrials in ancient times—and that these visits have continued through to this very day. No discussion of the Source Field is complete without an examination of UFOs and their influence on technology, ancient peoples, and the 2012 prophecies.

In 2009, Dr. Alan Boss of the Carnegie Institution of Science speculated that there could be one hundred billion earthlike planets in our Milky Way galaxy alone. This estimate is based on the widespread prevalence of extra-solar planets that have been discovered, leading him to assume there could be an average of one earthlike planet per star. He also believed they are probably inhabited—at least by microbial life-forms.[1] During this same time frame, scientists from the University at Edinburgh ran a computer simulation where they constructed a synthetic galaxy with billions of stars and planets. From this data, which included extinction events, they concluded that "at least 361 intelligent civilizations have emerged in the Milky Way since its creation, and as many as 38,000 may have formed."[2]

In December 2009, *Discover* magazine published a "controversial study" of a series of archeological findings that began in the autumn of

1913—in a South African town called Boskop. Two farmers dug up hominid skull fragments that seemed "unusual." Eventually, S. H. Haughton, a formally trained paleontologist, concluded that the Boskop skull contained a brain that was potentially 25 percent larger than our own—or more.

> Boskop has a face that takes up only about one-fifth of his cranium size, closer to the proportions of a child. Examination of individual bones confirmed that the nose, cheeks, and jaw were all childlike. . . . Boskop's brain size is about 30 percent larger than our own—that is, a 1,750-cc brain to our average of 1,350 cc. And that leads to an increase in the prefrontal cortex of a staggering 53 percent.[3]

The prefrontal cortex is where we process our highest cognitive functions—and, it is suspected, our intuition.

> With their perhaps astonishing insights, they may have become a species of dreamers with an internal mental life literally beyond anything we can imagine. . . . In a classroom with 35 big-headed, baby-faced Boskop kids, you would likely encounter five or six with IQ scores at the upper range of what has ever been recorded in human history. They died and we lived, and we can't answer the question why. Why didn't they outthink the smaller-brained hominids like ourselves and spread across the planet? Perhaps they didn't want to. . . . [Nonetheless,] anthropologists report that Boskop features still occasionally pop up in living populations of Bushmen, raising the possibility that the last of the race may have walked the dusty Transvaal in the not-too-distant past.[4]

It's one thing to dismiss people as "crazy" if they think they've encountered beings like this in a spaceship. It's quite another when we find archeological evidence that people like this lived and died here, and

Discover magazine took it seriously enough to publish the article. Were the Boskops dangerous villains? Just the opposite, according to those they lived with.

> Just about 100 miles from the original Boskop discovery site, further excavations were once carried out by Frederick FitzSimons. He knew what he had discovered and was eagerly seeking more of these skulls. At his new dig site, FitzSimons came across a remarkable piece of construction. The site had been at one time a communal living center, perhaps tens of thousands of years ago. There were many collected rocks, left-over bones, and some casually interred skeletons of normal-looking humans. But to one side of the site, in a clearing, was a single, carefully constructed tomb, built for a single occupant—perhaps the tomb of a leader or of a revered wise man. His remains had been positioned to face the rising sun. In repose, he appeared unremarkable in every regard . . . except for a giant skull.[5]

Dr. Steven Greer has worked tirelessly to gather together more than 560 witnesses who directly worked in classified programs where UFOs and ETs were dealt with directly. *Disclosure* is the term Greer and others use to describe a hypothetical moment in which the governments around the world openly reveal their secret archives of UFO knowledge—including any retrieved technology—or may even give us a direct introduction to ETs themselves. We are getting closer and closer to achieving real transparency, and governments have been increasingly sharing their formerly classified materials about these encounters. They kept them hidden for years because they apparently feared it would trigger a worldwide epidemic of terror—but with the coming of the Golden Age, I believe the public response will be one of awe and acceptance, not chaos and panic. All we need is a congressional subpoena; Dr. Greer's witnesses are prepared to testify to exactly what they know in open, public hearings in Congress. I was fortunate enough to attend Greer's "Closed Executive

Summary Briefing" for members of Congress and VIPs that took place on May 10, 2001—and the mood in the room was electric. The witness who stood out the most was Sergeant Clifford Stone, who allegedly worked on crash-retrieval projects. He was so traumatized by the things he had witnessed in the line of duty that he burst into tears and almost could not finish his presentation. Among many other intriguing data points, Stone revealed that he had a field manual describing fifty-seven different varieties of extraterrestrial intelligent life now visiting the earth. Every one of these fifty-seven varieties was human in appearance, with only superficial differences from the way we look here on earth—if any.

Other members of Dr. Greer's entourage reported direct ET interventions that powered down nuclear missile installations, or actively disabled missiles that were in flight—rendering them completely nonradioactive once they crashed to the earth. These and additional witnesses came forward in a major public conference at the National Press Club on September 27, 2010,[6] and were given generous coverage in the mainstream media.[7] The military-industrial complex has been forced to see these power-downs as hostile acts, but another equally valid viewpoint is to see that we are being protected from a nuclear holocaust by our long-lost relatives. These visitors may well account for the many reports of angels and gods in a variety of ancient cultures—and we may now be on the threshold of a true Family Reunion.

The Circlemakers

On October 20, 2009, the U.K. *Telegraph* reported a story where a police officer saw three men, each with blond hair and over six feet tall, taking instrument readings near a crop circle. The officer heard a hissing sound similar to static electricity, and this crackling noise seemed to run through the entire field—while also causing the crop to gently move. He shouted at the three men but they did not seem to be able to hear his voice. However, when he entered the field, they all looked at him and began running.

> They ran faster than any man I have ever seen. I'm no
> slouch but they were moving so fast. I looked away for a sec-
> ond and when I looked back they were gone.[8]

A similar case was disclosed on March 22, 2009, after the British government officially released many of its UFO files. On November 20, 1989, an anonymous woman called R.A.F. Wattisham in Suffolk to report a strange experience she had while walking her dog. She saw a man wearing a light brown one-piece garment, similar to a flying suit, who had a "Scandinavian-type accent." He asked her if she had heard anything about large, flattened circles appearing in wheat fields. During the course of a ten-minute conversation, the man told her he was from another planet that was similar to the earth, and there were others like him who had traveled to earth and were making these formations. These visitors were here for a friendly purpose, but "they were told not to have contact with humans for fear that they would be considered a threat."[9] Apparently he never said who told them not to contact us. The woman was "completely terrified"—and as she ran home, she heard a "loud buzzing noise" behind her, and saw a large spherical object, glowing with orange-white light, rise straight up from behind some trees. The R.A.F. operator said the woman spoke for about an hour—and had no doubt that she was reporting a genuine experience.[10]

The Crop Circle Connector Web site has an archive of every formation that has occurred in England since 1978, and many others around the world as well. For a nominal fee, you can explore this vast resource— and you will be stunned at the number of formations that reveal three-dimensional geometric patterns like the ones we've been discussing. Although some formations are undoubtedly hoaxes, I do feel the Circle-makers are giving us a variety of symbolic messages in these formations that can help us transition into a Golden Age. For me, perhaps the single most compelling crop formation appeared on July 15, 2008, at Avebury Manor in Wiltshire. This pattern appeared directly next to the northwest portion of an elaborate series of standing stones, not unlike Stonehenge, that are found in this same area. What we see is a clear, unambiguous illustration of our solar system—with a large, flattened circle in the middle for the sun, surrounded by a series of circular rings representing planetary orbits. In each of these rings, a smaller circle gives an exact position for each planet. Andreas Müller and Red Collie both independently analyzed this pattern, using astronomy software, and concluded that the alignment depicted a particular day in our future: December 21, 2012.[11]

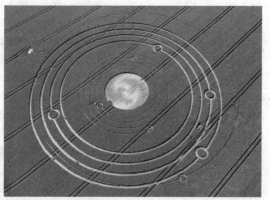

This crop circle appeared on July 15, 2008, next to the Avebury stone megaliths. It is an exact diagram of the alignment of the planets on December 21, 2012.

Of course, there is no way to ever know for certain whether a particular formation is real or not. High-quality hoaxes are routinely being done. However, it is quite unlikely that the crop circles described by Agobard, some 1,200 years ago, were also done by hoaxers. Nor do I think hoaxers were responsible for the crop formations Robert Plot diligently recorded in the 1600s. I went to England in August 2010 to witness this phenomenon myself, and walked through four different formations. The part I found the most intriguing was that each of the formations was written into a hillside—and you could not see the entire formation from any one spot on the ground due to the shape of the land. The patterns were designed to be seen from the air—it appeared that the geometry on the ground had been slightly stretched to make it look right from the sky in some cases. On the ground it was very difficult to tell what any of these formations actually looked like—and the real ones appear overnight.

This fractal Julia Set crop formation appeared next to Stonehenge on July 7, 1996, in broad daylight. Witnesses reveal it had to have formed in fifteen minutes or less.

In July 1996, a complex Julia Set pattern appeared in broad daylight, between five thirty and six fifteen P.M., directly next to Stonehenge—and was made of 151 circles. Flies have been found stuck to the crops as if their wings had been melted. Radiation levels 76 percent above normal have been observed, only to mysteriously disappear soon afterward. The growth nodes on the crop stems often appear to be elongated, consistent with the effects of microwaving, and their cells reveal microscopic pit-holes—suggesting they were flash-heated in a microsecond. Some plants also have a thin layer of carbon covering them. Ninety percent of crop circles are formed over aquifers, suggesting a technology may be pulling water out of the ground to keep the crops from burning. Electrical equipment often fails inside the formations and magnetic compasses pick up unusual readings. The rate of time has been observed to change slightly within a crop circle in two different sets of experiments.[12]

I also highly recommend *Crop Circles: A Beginner's Guide* by Hugh Manistre,[13] and "Crop Circles and their Message" by David Pratt, which has a variety of great photographs in addition to many unique data points.[14] In part one of Pratt's article we discover that the soil under crop circles is much looser and dryer than usual, has an increase in crystallization, and features unusual microscopic spheres of pure iron. In young crops where the seeds are still forming, the seeds are stunted and do not germinate well, if at all—whereas "in mature plants with fully formed seeds, seeds often exhibit a massive increase in vigour and a growth rate up to five times that of control seeds."[15] In part two, Pratt reveals that there are many reports of balls, discs or columns of light that have been seen over the areas where crop circles then appeared. Several dozen people have heard a high-pitched trilling noise before crop circles occurred. Approximately seventy people have witnessed crop circles forming right in front of their eyes. They report that the whole process is very rapid, taking between ten and twenty seconds—and in some, but not all cases, there appears to be a visible whirlwind in the atmosphere as it happens.

One evening in July 1981, Ray Barnes witnessed a wave or line moving through the heads of a cereal crop in Wiltshire. After travelling across the field in an arc, the line dropped to the ground and radially described a 75-foot circle in a clockwise direction in a single sweep in about four seconds, accompanied by a hissing noise. The crop went down as neatly as if it had been cut by a giant flan cutter, and the plants showed absolutely no spring-back.[16]

Getting back to our 2012 crop circle that appeared on July 15, 2008, the farmer at Avebury was not pleased—and tried to destroy it by driving three lines through it with his tractor. The Circlemakers then returned, and made a series of modifications—including a second circle that was as big as the solar system diagram had been, positioned directly next to the original. This second circle was completely hollow on the inside, but it was surrounded by a series of strange, small illustrations.

On July 22, 2008, this formation was heavily enhanced after the farmer drove three lines through the original pattern. The size of the sun was dramatically increased.

At a conference I spoke at in 2009, Dr. Beverly Rubik pointed out that these little symbols all looked like various types of cell organelles. The large circle could therefore represent a cell membrane—but now there was nothing inside of it. Although no one can be sure of its intended meaning, this symbolism may suggest that some sort of fundamental transformation of biological life might begin to occur after December 21, 2012—akin to the Tibetan legends of the Rainbow Body. What I found even more interesting was that the Circlemakers also widened the diameter of the Sun in the solar system glyph—all the way out to the orbit of

Venus. This implies that December 21, 2012 may represent the tipping point for this profound energetic change that is already occurring in the solar system.

In this image we clearly see the circular trench dug into the ground surrounding the Avebury megaliths— directly above our definitive 2012 crop formation.

Crop circles may also be used as reference points for time travel within the Source Field. They often appear right near the ancient vortex points and monuments, which may serve as portals for travel through time-space to this very day. By keeping a comprehensive log of what formations were positioned, and when, you could quickly scan through a large databank of different points in time. Once you see the formation you are looking for, you can then enter into that point in time. This may dramatically simplify the process of identifying a particular window of time you wish to visit.

Reverse-Engineering the Pineal Gland

Project Looking Glass was a program that allegedly involved our ancient ancestors reverse-engineering the pineal gland and developing it into a working technology on a larger scale. The idea was to stand in front of this massive machine that acts as a psychic amplifier—projecting your thoughts into a giant yellowish bubble with a fish-eye-lens distortion around the edges. This would allow you to detect potential future events before they arrive—but there are always various probabilities and time-lines of what may happen. I have spoken to a variety of insiders who claim to have worked in classified research projects, and Project Looking Glass is one of the most common things you hear them talk about. Robert Lucien Howe claimed to have gained access to classified documents in his government work for the U.K., and gave a description of this device, which you can read online. I do not agree with everything he says in his written posts, but some of his words do fit in very nicely with what others have told me. In order to understand what he is telling us, it is important to mention that the insiders apparently call our energetic duplicate the transient body, and our access to the Source Field is called transience. In other posts, Howe said the pineal gland was called a transiator within these programs.

> People all have a transiator sensor that tries to make our future better and looks for things that threaten us and warns us . . . it is what we use to protect ourselves from entropy so we can live much longer. A human with no transiator at all might only live 5 or 10 years. Sadly, most of this is in the past because human transiators can never have more than about 5–10 watts (and often only milliwatts) while some machines

have achieved tens of kilowatts. We can still win here sometimes because 5 milliwatts can win against 5 kilowatts because
of the complex rules that transience follows. . . .

The machine is actually a time accelerator. It works by
creating a change of momentum or energy of matter inside a
Schrodinger box. The box is actually very simple to make. Its
heart is a very strong EM shield. It is electrically shielded.
Inside is a special box full of warm water at body temperature
35 degrees Celsius. It is non-conducting and non-metallic and
should have a magnetic field of-or-near zero. Finally it should
have little or no sound vibration, and the machine must generally not move in any way.

Extraneous pulsations of any kind will tend to stop the
machine working. The shape of the machine decides what it
does in the same way that shape decides the function of ordinary machines. The heart of the machine, though, is that it
must survive into the Future. If someone breaks it in the
Future, it will stop working now. They also work better the older
they are, though this was apparently omitted from the CIA's
version.[17]

What Howe is calling a box has usually been described to me as a
barrel, shaped like the pineal gland, that is filled with water. This barrel
is apparently surrounded by three rings that rotate around the barrel and
create the electromagnetic shielding effect.

As various insiders described this to me in private conversations, and
even produced illustrations of approximately what it looked like, I was
quite surprised to realize that the movie *Contact* featured a very similar
set of rotating rings. Carl Sagan may well have been tipped off about
Looking Glass, but he never told Jim Hart there was any truth to the
story. According to these various testimonies, once the shielding is fully
activated, the water inside the barrel creates a direct gateway into time-
space. One form of this technology is "Looking Glass," as we've been
describing it, where you only get to look at these locations from afar.
Another version of this technology is code-named "the Ark"—and this

Multiple insider witnesses have revealed the existence of Project Looking Glass—a gigantic machine, built by the ancients, that reverse-engineered the pineal gland to create a means of peering through time and space.

forms an actual stargate you can physically travel through and use to teleport from one space and time to another. Again, the whole secret to this technology is the shielded, electrified barrel of water in the center. It is fascinating to consider that the pineal gland may be able to create a stargate that is powerful enough to teleport the human body through space and time—if it becomes large enough for the entire body to fit through.

As Howe goes on explaining this, he discusses many physics concepts that sound very similar to what we've been talking about in this book. Apparently the light-speed frequency in an atom is called the Crescendo point. Ordinary matter is apparently referred to here as tardon matter, as it exists in a state where it is actively retarded from going over light speed. The insiders' theory also states that matter is in a quantum superposition where it keeps popping over the light-speed boundary, or Crescendo point. Once it crosses that point, Howe refers to it as being in "the super-light part of its superposition."

Such machines can be very dangerous because they can emit enormous quantities of radiation and energy without warning. This is because the space inside the machine can reach 90 percent of crescendo. "Crescendo theory" says that all tardon matter is trying to spontaneously jump to light-speed in a special kind of superposition. Matter is at "crescendo" when it has enough energy to reach lightspeed, [and] the super-light part of its superposition has lower or equal energy than its tardon state.

There are 2 routes for matter to reach crescendo: zero energy or total energy. The zero energy state works by touching energy that is already moving at the speed of light. One of the most difficult parts of crescendo theory to grasp is that matter can be transient (at the speed of light) while not moving (this is not a contradiction) because crescendo matter can deform space completely on the atomic scale.

The theory is part of a greater theory called "common atom" that gives space a finite strength against bending. On small scales, space is smaller and so has less energy. At atomic scales, it becomes deformed completely. Each atom is a tiny massed singularity with its own independent internal time space. An atom's universe only lives for a few seconds. But this doesn't matter because its time is static compared to ours, thanks to space-time curvature.

The same theory allows photons to co-exist as real particles and waves, and greatly simplifies Quantum Mechanics and Relativity by allowing all the different theories to co-exist together. The graviton particle turns out to be physical matter itself.

If you can decode the above, you have the bare bones of about 80–90 percent of all the military censorship ever done to physics.[18]

The graviton particle turns out to be physical matter itself. Photons coexist as real particles and waves. Space can be bent and curl in on itself to form an atom—and the interior of an atom is moving at a much different time rate than the area outside of it. When you accelerate atoms past lightspeed, you reach crescendo and they pop into a parallel reality. All of these concepts should sound very familiar by now, even though the wording may be a little different. The implications are stunning, because it means that the pineal gland may very well function as a literal stargate once it is fully activated—based on these same principles—and as this stargate widens to the size of our entire body, we appear to be glowing with light. This may well be why the ancients created so many different myths, symbols and metaphors to get us investigating this subject. Each of us already has this pineal gland technology installed in our own bodies—and the ancient gods who visited many different cultures, worldwide, seemed very keen on teaching us how to switch it on and help create the Golden Age. Though certain negative groups have co-opted these concepts, the vast majority of spiritual traditions emphasize that the nature of the Universe is love—and our research into the Source Field provides strong evidence that this is true.

ET Contact in Modern-Day India

The *India Daily* Web site has a section called "Technology"—and well over 50 percent of the articles in this section appear to be leaked from divisions of the Indian government itself. There appears to be a very strong effort toward disclosure being made in these reports—unlike anything else I've ever seen in the world. Naturally, since most of the writers are anonymous, and at this point they cannot prove their sources, most people could easily dismiss them. However, the level of technical detail in these articles—and how well it ties in with what we've been discussing in this book—is nothing short of astonishing.

One article from April 29, 2006, revealed that India was originally contacted by extraterrestrials after conducting its first nuclear test in the early 1970s—and the ETs showed up again when India performed new tests on May 11 and 13, 1998.[19] India's version of NASA is the Indian Space Research Organization, or ISRO. In 2008, *India Daily* revealed that ISRO chairman G. Madhavan Nair is "in charge of the very secret mission of keeping ISRO UFO files secret, coordinated by the secretly driven U.N. efforts."[20] The article goes on to say that U.N. officials are very concerned that India may not keep these secrets much longer. Some areas within the ISRO are kept classified—but according to *India Daily*, not everyone is staying quiet.

> One [scientist] who works inside this closed area said India is just starting to receive reverse-engineered technologies from extraterrestrial UFOs controlled by U.N. Security Council efforts. In exchange, India must keep quiet about what it has learnt about UFOs through its space missions.[21]

The article goes on to say that the BJP party is known for making decisions that surprise the U.N.—and disclosure may be another example.

> Against all odds and threatening from the United States and other countries, the BJP-led Indian government went ahead with the tests of multiple nuclear bombs. This time it will reveal how the world was kept in secret about the UFOs for the last one hundred years through a well-organized international forum of secrecy. But there is one catch. India will forfeit its chance to become the sixth member of the U.N. Security Council (UNSC) if it goes ahead with telling the truth about UFOs. BJP most likely will reveal the truth and then fight for India's spot in the UNSC.[22]

In 2004, *India Daily* announced that defense research scientists and engineers in Pune, the top city for this work in India, have been told they cannot tell the world what they know from these classified projects until 2012.

> If you carefully keep your ears on these whispers you will realize India has tested something no one wants to talk about.

It is a breakthrough in conventional physics and traditional mechanical and aeronautical engineering . . . If the whispers are right, India may be changing the world forever. But why the magic year 2012? Why does everything have to be kept secret till then?[23]

India has already entered the space race—and in 2008, *India Daily* reported that they are already aware of ET bases on the moon.

India may surprise the world. The surprise may come any time. The country must reveal the existence of the underground infrastructure of UFO bases.[24]

A report from July 4, 2005, revealed what these alleged extraterrestrials have apparently been telling the Indian government and military—and by now it should sound very familiar.

Once we are in one of the parallel universes, we can view time and space the same way we can differentiate length, height and width. The time travelers from future human and alien civilizations visit us using UFOs through the network of wormholes. . . . Traveling through the wormholes is fascinating. One can plan and program time and space separately. Then you apply the entry and exit points of the wormhole to match the time and space reference points. One has to perform the time and space reference point calculations using higher dimensions (in a parallel universe) . . . Adjusting the entry and exit points of the wormholes can be comparatively easy once performed from a higher dimension in a parallel universe. It can be an extremely difficult numerical analysis problem if we try to do it in our physical universe.[25]

The idea that time can be viewed "the same way we can differentiate length, height and width" is exactly what we've been saying throughout Part Two of this book. The degree of technical detail in many of these

India Daily articles is startling, and goes well beyond the space we have in this book to properly describe. One article says that portals can be formed by bombarding the ionosphere with very high intensities of energy.[26]

> Unless the wormholes are specially processed and manipulated, the physical entity loses all physical attributes at the core. . . . Through the parallel universe, though, the entity can traverse time and space instantaneously. Then comes the real challenge where the aliens really are way ahead of our civilization—they know how to transform back to physical entities in another wormhole, leading back to our physical universe . . . According to some researchers, the transformation from physical to parallel universe entities happens automatically once the wormhole is programmed to carry an entity out to a parallel universe.
>
> Programming a wormhole is not easy. It can be programmed from the parallel universe easily, but from this side it will be a classical challenge in terms of numerical analysis. However, advancement in computational algorithms and processing powers will allow us to solve the complex equations and program the wormholes.[27]

An article from October 7, 2006, said that time can be detached from space, creating a holding zone in hyperspace that can later be attached to another point in time. "The detachment of space and time is achieved through the use of gravitational radiation manipulation."[28] Other articles indicate that there are many parallel realities in time-space—and as paradoxical as this may seem, we can actually coexist in many different locations at once.[29] "Do we coexist as a separate entity when we dream? No, say experts; the same entity coexists in multiple time dimensions. This is also true when we think about someone and mentally will them to get something done."[30]

How Do We Travel into the Parallel Universe?

On July 9, 2005, the *India Daily* Technology Team said the key to making this stargate travel possible is the creation of negative mass. This appears to be exactly the same concept as what we've been discussing here—namely, that mass converts to negative mass as its internal movement is accelerated past the speed of light.

> Once the negative mass is created, all the puzzles of time travel, bending space and time, movement in and out of a parallel universe—all can be instantaneously solved. As you enter [a] black hole, if you can accelerate the process of making your mass negative you can easily pass through. . . . The onboard computers [on a spaceship] are able to control the mass factor from positive to negative and so on just like airplanes balance weight during takeoff, flight and landing. Once mass of the entity can be manipulated, the travel through wormholes will be easy. This will not only enable us to travel to different time dimensions but also into parallel universes and beyond.[31]

With this technology, we apparently will be able to see any potentially negative events in the future before they arrive, and take precautionary steps to change the outcome.[32]

> Also if a civilization can see the future and is able to change the future by replacing the time axis, they will reach immortality in the terrestrial sense. That is exactly what the advanced aliens have achieved. And that is exactly what we will achieve in the next few hundred years.[33]

On July 22, 2005, further information was given regarding the idea of three-dimensional time—and it sounds very familiar.

What really happens in the parallel universe [is that] the
lack of time as a dimension . . . makes living through that
environment very different from the physical universe. . . .
Like we can walk around in the physical universe from point
A to point B, in the parallel universe, it is possible to walk
from one time to the next time.[34]

On July 23, 2005, the concept of parallel universes was further
described.

The super space of higher dimensions defies all known
laws of physics that hold true in the physical universe. It is a
universe in which time does not exist as a dimension. It is a universe in which you can create parallel time dimensions. The
physical objects collapse into multi-entity objects. . . . We
belong to multiple parallel universes right at this moment. . . .
While the physical body is in the physical universe . . . we
communicate with [ourselves] from the parallel universe, and
guide the brain to do work and live our lives. Once we die,
we continue to live, except we withdraw from the physical
universe since the body is not usable. We continue to live in
the parallel universes.[35]

On July 26, 2005, the *India Daily* Technology Team made a statement that is precisely identical to the science I independently worked out
for this book. I was stunned when I saw this connection.

. . . [W]hat happens to the photon if [the] time dimension
is not only moving at the speed of light, but is actually made
to accelerate further? . . . [T]he net result is that an entity can
fall back from the physical universe and merge into the parallel universe. That is fascinating. Because that is what happens
to advanced civilizations that know how to live an immortal
life in the parallel universe, and once in a while hover around

the physical universe. Some scientists now believe that after death, the electromagnetic spatial source of energy, or the soul, just moves through a tunnel of decelerating time to end up at the white light—which represents the entry to the parallel universe.

According to researchers in this field, an advanced civilization can achieve immortality by being able to access the physical and parallel universe anytime. Most probably that is what happens when we are born and when we die. But the technology of accelerating time or decelerating time will allow us within the physical universe to access and move in and out of the parallel universe.[36]

On July 27th, the *India Daily* Technology Team discussed this science in terms of biology—and again sounded very similar to what we have been discussing.

Two-thirds of our brain is not under our control. It is guided by the entities in the parallel universe. We communicate using mind-generated signals commonly known as telepathy with many other entities, and even with ourselves in higher spatial dimensions of the parallel universe. . . . We do traverse the parallel universes with our mind all the time without physically leaving the physical universe. That part of the brain is not even under our control. It therefore seems that we are connected genetically to some advanced life-forms that can traverse from the physical to the parallel universe all the time.[37]

Other articles say many extraterrestrials are visiting us from the M15 Star Cluster, which is the densest part of our local universe—and has many black holes, providing extraterrestrial civilizations with a giant transfer station. These extraterrestrials are apparently preparing to reveal themselves to earth in 2012.[38] An August 10, 2005, article said that "many of the UFOs that are reported are actually time-reversing phenomena initiated by our own future generation hundreds of years later. They can come and visit us, observe us, but they cannot change any event."[39]

Preparing for the "Galactic Family Reunion"

One report in 2006 revealed that UFOs and extraterrestrial civilizations will be announced to humanity in December 2012—and "the general consensus is to make the world slowly ready for it."[40] An article from December 29, 2006, said that world governments have been hiding the truth of UFOs and ETs for decades, but secret preparations are being made to reveal the truth in 2012. It also says that "Brazil, India and China are taking the lead in this matter," and that the world will secretly use the help of extraterrestrials to avoid any potential disasters that may occur due to this transition.[41] On May 12, 2005, *India Today* said we will be visited by representatives from all eighty-eight constellations in the night sky as of December 2012. At this time, we will "finally understand the actual process of evolution, the process of bending time and space, the fact that gravity is a wave and not a force," and much more.[42]

Another article, from January 4, 2007, reveals what is expected to happen when this "galactic alignment" reaches its peak in December 2012.

> Galactic alignment changes the world. The civilizations get reincarnation. The earth gets rejuvenated. It is a function of [the] gravity wave. The gravity wave in higher dimensions is programmed to create this galactic alignment for earth to have reincarnation.
>
> The major galactic alignment happened before. Some believe the dinosaurs disappeared millions of years back during a major galactic alignment. The Vedic literature talks about galactic alignment. Atlantis was lost during a galactic alignment. Interestingly, ancient literature also hints at formal extraterrestrial visitation during and after galactic alignment. About one hundred years before the galactic alignment,

advanced extraterrestrial civilizations start visiting the earth. Interestingly, modern UFO sightings were first recorded in 1911 in Germany. The extraterrestrials create the environment for their formal visitation. This may be no different. We might see in 2012 or after that time the extraterrestrial civilizations—the type IV advanced aliens responsible for the big bang. The science, history, philosophy and all aspects of human life may change that day as we watch with astonishment."[43]

In total, these disclosures from *India Daily's* "Technology" section are so numerous, specific and ongoing that I feel it is highly likely that they are indeed telling us the truth. And this data corroborates what certain witnesses who worked for the military-industrial complex in the United States and elsewhere have said.

The Testimony of "Mr. X"

This brings us to the words of "Mr. X," the very first witness interviewed by Project Camelot. He died suddenly of a massive stroke as he was getting ready to come forward, reveal his identity and tell much more of what he learned in classified projects. Nonetheless, we do have his written testimony of the top-secret documents he read, which revealed the messages that had been given to our world leaders as early as the 1950s. Jerry Pippin directly interviewed this witness, and wrote about what he heard.

... [T]he ETs have said they will conduct a mass landing all over the world on December 21st or 22nd, 2012, whether our leaders like it or not. Apparently our media will be used (or some similar worldwide method—more likely to be telepathic) to convey this information to the whole world—it will be something everyone will know. People will be given a choice as to whether they want to evolve spiritually and travel with the ETs or not:

"Mr. X: We'll be given choices. Q: And the choice is what? Mr. X.: [Whether or not] we want to learn where they came from, and to learn to evolve more spiritually—so we, too, can go throughout the universe and make life."[44]

It's easy to overlook the impact of what "Mr. X" really means when he says we will have the choice to "evolve more spiritually." A transcript of their interview reveals even more details. I have no idea if this will actually happen, but it is certainly interesting to speculate.

There will be a mass of information released that will shatter most of our core beliefs. Some will panic because their belief system will be shattered. Some will be angry because they have been lied to for so long. Some will think that the end of the world is here. Most will be confused at best about religious issues, since the truth will be told and that truth will shatter ALL religious beliefs. We will learn the true history of man through the ETs and the powers that be. It is inevitable. If the world stays on the track it is on—and I see no reason for it to change—we will have to be shown the truth. And if those who run the world do not do it, the ETs will.[45]

As the old saying goes, "the truth will set you free." I have handpicked the very best data from thirty years of dedicated research to put this book together for that very reason—and with this knowledge we have the tools to create the Golden Age. We can create limitless, clean, nonpolluting free energy. We can create spectacular new healing technologies. We can conquer gravity, space and time, and move effortlessly throughout the galaxy. We may well experience a worldwide awakening of the pineal gland, giving us dramatic new intuitive abilities—possibly even enabling us to move into a light-body state. If the Zoroastrian legend of Fraso-kererti is indeed true, then Time as we know it may change in some fundamental way—giving us the ability to enter into nonlocal, nonlinear time—the realm of time-space—much more easily.

I feel that we are being given an invitation to use the knowledge this book contains, along with many other sources of positive, uplifting and inspiring information. The Golden Age is a participatory event, not something we sit back and wait for. The technologies I have shared with you are real. They can be developed. And they can transform our society into a level that we would normally only think of as science fiction. We are not helpless against Earth Changes and shadowy quasipolitical world powers. Our own minds are in symbiosis with one another, and with the earth, in a way we do not currently understand on any mass level. Our human relatives appear to have been responsible for planting the seeds of every major world religion—and their messages about the importance of loving and respecting others have reached everyone on earth. The energy of the Universe is provably loving in nature—and this makes it very likely that all the events now happening on earth and throughout our solar system, despite how ominous they may appear to so many people, do have a positive purpose—to help inspire a mass, collective human evolution and awakening. The love we create in our own lives may even extend all the way through into a complete evolution of what it means to be human. We tend to adore complexity, and mental puzzles, but in this case the truth may be very simple: The earth is a school for spiritual learning, and we are all students. Graduation day is upon us—and we get our diploma by proving, to ourselves and everyone else on a higher level, that we don't need to keep repeating the same lessons anymore— lifetime after lifetime—and creating a mass dream of hell. If we are indeed on the threshold of such a radical shift in the nature of what it means to be alive and conscious, then soon we will experience this majestic transformation in the Now. It will happen, in real time—as a living, breathing, vividly wonderful experience. We may indeed come to realize that the world has been like a vast illusion—a lucid dream where everything we create keeps reflecting back to us—and we finally recognize that we have never truly been awake before.

The facts are on the table. The Source Field is a reality. We all want to make this world a better place, and we now have a new set of tools to help us do it. We are not victims and we are definitely not alone. The Universe itself may well be a conscious superbeing, encouraging us to make a quantum leap in our own understanding of who and what we are—and giving us the solar-system-wide galactic energy boost we need to get there. Thousands of years' worth of prophecies, from every major culture around the world, were given to help us understand what is actually happening—and rebuild the science we need to finish the job. We create the Golden Age ourselves—beginning in our own lives—and the rewards are almost beyond imagination. By moving through the self-hatred and fear to reach that hard-earned place of acceptance and forgiveness—of both self and others—we heal the world:

I love you. I am sorry. Please forgive me. Thank you.

Acknowledgments

In January 1996, I began reading The Law of One, a series of five books that were allegedly transmitted telepathically by very advanced extraterrestrials. These ETs claimed to have helped build the Great Pyramid, originally for positive purposes, but were forced to withdraw from the earth when it became contorted for negative uses. They also said the main reason they made this contact in modern times was to apologize for what they had done, and give us this new gift in the hopes of improving the desperate situation they had inadvertently created. A surprisingly large number of the points I have made in this book appear in the Law of One series, most of which came through in 1981. They reveal that the mind is indeed infinite, but nonetheless has a singular identity at a vast cosmic level—which they call the One Infinite Creator. We are told that we are all perfect, holographic reflections of the One Infinite Creator; that we reincarnate to work on spiritual lessons, and will eventually return to our original identity; that the "25,000-year cycle" creates biological and spiritual evolution in sudden jumps, and that the cycle will be complete in the approximate neighborhood of 2011 to 2013—ushering in a quantum transformation of space, time, matter, energy, biology and consciousness that is already well under way. The Law of One series also describes the global grid, goes into great detail about the physics of space-time and time-space, discusses levels of spiritual evolution that are based on the rainbow color spectrum, suggests that the galaxy is an intelligent superbeing that has designed the human form to appear on millions of inhabited planets, and says that we do have the potential to evolve into an entirely new level of being as we go through this transformation.[1] The benevolent group they refer to as "The Confederation of Planets in Service of the One Infinite Creator" has apparently been assisting the earth throughout its entire evolution—and is particularly focused on helping us move through this transition smoothly and safely. This material formed the basis of much of my work, and many specific details were given that could later be explored and verified scientifically. Every credible insider I know has given me stunning confirmations of specific details in the Law of One series, though not one of them ever read it. I have had many fascinating personal experiences that have led me to believe this material is indeed accurate and truthful—and I therefore consider it to be quite different from most other allegedly channeled teachings, which seem to invariably contradict each other, and often do not line up with the science I disclose in this book.

Another notable exception to the rule is the Seth books, brought through by Jane Roberts and Robert Butts—particularly the earlier volumes. The concluding chapters of *The Seth Material* feature a long dissertation on what Seth calls consciousness units—and this data fits in very nicely with everything I've presented in this book.

I hope you have found this investigation into the Source Field as fascinating and as informative as I have in writing it. This book is the most significant effort I have made so far to help the process of disclosure along—so these advanced technologies and sciences do not seem so impossible to believe anymore. I feel there is no reason to fear these changes that are now happening. We are moving through a process that may well be intelligently scripted—to promote our own evolution. We have the power to increase our own coherence by learning to be more loving, accepting and forgiving of others—for in forgiveness of others, there is forgiveness of self.

I do wish to thank the many heroes and pioneers whose work allowed this book to be possible—and so many others who are working in these same areas. Without your stunning efforts of magnificent genius, we would never be aware of our true potential. I wish to thank my mother, father and brother, my beautiful female life partner, and the many people who have shared their lives with me over the years in various ways—and have given me love and guidance. I also want to thank Brian Tart, Graham Hancock, Jim Hart, the staff at Dutton and so many others who have helped me fully realize this work. I also wish to thank those who are outside of time, and gave me such extensive support in the research and development of these ideas and the writing of this book—including ongoing dream feedback, critiques and new breakthrough ideas, not to mention an incredible number of remarkably accurate future prophecies—both personal and planetary. I hope we will get to meet in person, or the energetic equivalent thereof, some time soon—as I find the concept of a "Galactic Family Reunion" to be highly inspiring.

Notes

Introduction

1 Walter Scott (ed.), *Hermetica: The Ancient Greek and Latin Writings which Contain Religious or Philosophic Teachings ascribed to Hermes Trismegistus, vol.1* New York: Shambala, 1985 p. 327.
2 Ibid., p. 351.
3 Ibid., p. 351.
4 Ibid., p. 355.
5 Ibid., p. 425.
6 Ibid., p. 387.
7 Ibid., pp. 387–389.

Preface

1 Wilcock, David. *The 2012 Enigma* (documentary). DivineCosmos.com, March 10, 2008. http://video.google.com/videoplay?docid=-4951448613711060908# (accessed December 2010).
2 Wilcock, David. Divine Cosmos Web site. http://www.divinecosmos.com.
3 Akimov, A. E. and Shipov, G. I. "Torsion Fields and their Experimental Manifestations." Proceedings of International Conference: New Ideas in Natural Science, 1996. http://www.eskimo.com/~billb/freenrg/tors/tors.html (accessed December 2010).

Chapter One

1 Backster, Cleve. *Primary Perception: Biocommunication with Plants, Living Foods and Human Cells.* Anza, CA: White Rose Millennium Press, 2003. http://www.primaryperception.com.
2 Ibid., p. 12.
3 Ibid., p. 12.
4 Ibid., p. 14.
5 Sherman, Harold. *How to Make ESP Work for You.* DeVorss & Co., 1964. http://www.haroldsherman.com (accessed December 2010).
6 Ibid., pp. 165–166.

7   Talbot, Michael. *The Holographic Universe.* New York: HarperCollins, 1991, p. 141.

8   Backster, Cleve. Op cit., p. 17.

9   Ibid., p. 18.

10 Ibid., p. 22.

11 Ibid., p. 23.

12 Ibid., pp. 23–24.

13 Ibid., p. 24.

14 Ibid., p. 25.

15 Ibid., p. 25.

16 Ibid., p. 31.

17 Ibid., p. 32.

18 Ibid., p. 34.

19 Ibid., p. 48.

20 Ibid., p. 51.

21 Ibid., p. 52.

22 Ibid., pp. 54–55.

23 Ibid., p. 55.

24 Ibid., p. 57.

25 Ibid., p. 59.

26 Ibid., p. 59.

27 Ibid., p. 73.

28 Ibid., pp. 76–77.

29 Ibid., p. 79.

30 Ibid., pp. 40–41.

31 Ibid., pp. 110–111.

32 Ibid., p. 127.

33 Ibid., p. 127.

34 Ibid., pp. 127–128.

35 Backster, Cleve. Personal communication, 2006.

36 Bailey, Patrick G. and Grotz, Toby. "A Critical Review of the Available Information Regarding Claims of Zero-Point Energy, Free-Energy, and Over-Unity Experiments and Devices." Institute for New Energy, Proceedings of the 28th IECEC, April 3, 1997. http://padrak.com/ine/INE21.html (accessed December 2010).

37 Aftergood, Steven. "Invention Secrecy Still Going Strong." *Federation of American Scientists,* October 21, 2010. http://www.fas.org/blog/secrecy/2010/10/invention_secrecy_2010.html (accessed January 2011).

38 O'Leary, Brian; Wilcock, David; Deacon, Henry and Ryan, Bill. "Brian O'Leary and Henry Deacon at Zurich Transcript." Project Camelot, July 12, 2009. http://projectcamelot.org/lang/en/Zurich_Conference_Brian_O_Leary_12_July_2009_en.html.

39 Mallove, Eugene. (1999) "MIT and Cold Fusion: A Special Report." *Infinite Energy Magazine,* 24. http://www.infinite-energy.com/images/pdfs/mitcfreport.pdf (accessed December 2010).

40 *Infinite Energy: The Magazine of New Energy Science and Technology.* http://www.infinite-energy.com/.

41 Wilcock, David. "Historic Wilcock/Art Bell/Hoagland Show!" Divine Cosmos, June 21, 2008. http://divinecosmos.com/index.php?option=com_content&task=view&id=391&Itemid=70.

42 Ibid.

Chapter Two

1   Hermans, H. G. M. *Memories of a Maverick.* Chapter 9. The Netherlands: Pi Publishing, 1998. http://www.uri-geller.com/books/maverick/maver.htm.

2   Rueckert, Carla; Elkins, Don and McCarty, Jim. *The Law of One, Book I: The Ra Material.* Atglen, Pennsylvania: Whitford Press, 1984.

3   Hermans, H. G. M. *Memories of a Maverick.* op. cit.

4   Ibid.

5   Ibid.

6   Quinones, Sam. "Looking for Doctor Grinberg." *New Age Journal,* July/August 1997. http://www.sustainedaction.org/Explorations/professor_jacobo_grinberg.htm (accessed December 2010).

7   Grinberg-Zylberbaum, Jacobo. (1994) "Brain to Brain Interactions and the Interpretation of Reality." Universidad Nacional Autonoma de Mexico and Instituto Nacional Para el Estudio de la Conciencia, Project: D6APA UNAM IN 500693 and IN 503693. http://www.start.gr/user/symposia/zylber4.htm (accessed December 2010).

8   Grinberg-Zylberbaum, Jacobo, and Ramos, J. "Patterns of interhemisphere correlations during human communication." *International Journal of Neuroscience,* 1987; 36: 41–53; Grinberg-Zylberbaum, J. et al., "Human Communication and the electrophysiological activity of the brain." *Subtle Energies,* 1992; 3(3): 25–43.

9   Grinberg-Zylberbaum, Jacobo. "The Einstein-Podolsky-Rosen Paradox in the Brain; The Transferred Potential." *Physics Essays* 7,(4), 1994.

10 Jacobo Grinberg-Zylberbaum Facebook page. http://www.facebook.com/group.php?gid=25113472687 (accessed December 2010).

11 Quinones, Sam. *Looking for Doctor Grinberg. New Age Journal,* July/August 1997. http://www.sustainedaction.org/Explorations/professor_jacobo_grinberg.htm (accessed December 2010).

12 Tart, Charles. "Physiological Correlates of Psi Cognition." *International Journal of Parapsychology,* 1963; 5; 375–86.

13 McTaggart, Lynne. *The Field: The Quest for the Secret Force of the Universe.* New York: HarperCollins, 2002; pp. 126–127.

14 Institute of Transpersonal Psychology. *William Braud's Faculty Profile.* http://www.itp.edu/academics/faculty/braud.php (accessed December 2010).

15 Institute of Transpersonal Psychology. *William Braud: Publications.* http://www.itp.edu/academics/faculty/braud/publications.php (accessed December 2010).

16 Braud, W. and Schlitz, M. J. "Consciousness interactions with remote biological systems: anomalous intentionality effects." *Subtle Energies,* 1991; 2(1): 1–46.

17 Schlitz, M. and LaBerge, S. "Autonomic detection of remote observation: two conceptual replications." In Bierman (ed), Proceedings of Presented Papers: 465–78.

18 Braud, W., et al.: "Further Studies of autonomic detection of remote staring: replication, new control procedures and personality correlates." *Journal of Parapsychology,* 1993; 57: 391–409.

19 Sheldrake, Rupert. *Papers on the Sense of Being Stared At.* Sheldrake.org. http://www.sheldrake.org/Articles&Papers/papers/staring/index.html (accessed December 2010).

20 Braud, W. and Schlitz, M. *Psychokinetic influence on electrodermal activity. Journal of Parapsychology,* 1983; 47(2): 95–119.

21 Braud, W., et al.: "Attention focusing facilitated through remote mental interaction." *Journal of the American Society for Psychical Research,* 1995; 89(2): 103–15.

22 Braud, W. G. "Blocking/shielding psychic functioning through psychological and psychic techniques: a report of three preliminary studies." In White, R. and Solfvin, I. (eds), *Research in Parapsychology,* 1984 Metuchen, NJ: Scarecrow Press, 1985, pp. 42–44.

23   Braud, W. G., "Implications and applications of laboratory psi findings." *European Journal of Parapsychology*, 1990–91; 8: 57–65.

24   Braud, W., et al. "Further studies of the bio-PK effect: feedback, blocking, generality/specificity." In White, R. and Solfvin, I. (eds), *Research in Parapsychology*: 45–48.

25   Andrews, Sperry. *Educating for Peace through Planetary Consciousness: The Human Connection Project*. Human Connection Institute. http://www.connectioninstitute.org/PDF/HCP_Fund_Proposal.pdf (accessed December 2010).

26   Andrews, Sperry. *Educating for Peace through Planetary Consciousness: The Human Connection Project*. Human Connection Institute. http://www.connectioninstitute.org/PDF/HCP_Fund_Proposal.pdf (accessed December 2010).

27   Schlitz, M. J., Honorton, C. "ESP and creativity in an exceptional population." Proceedings of Presented Papers: 33rd Annual Parapsychological Association Convention; Washington, D.C.; 1990. In Andrews, Sperry (ed). *Educating for Peace through Planetary Consciousness: The Human Connection Project*. Human Connection Institute. http://www.connectioninstitute.org/PDF/HCP_Fund_Proposal.pdf (accessed December 2010).

28   Jahn, R. G., Dunne, B. J. *Margins of Reality: The Role of Consciousness in the Physical World*. New York: Harcourt Brace Jovanovich, 1987.

29   Bisaha, J. J., Dunne, B. J. "Multiple subject and long-distance precognitive remote viewing of geographical locations." In: Tart C., Puthoff, H. E., Targ, R., eds. *Mind at Large*. New York: Praeger, 1979: 107–124.

30   Kenny, Robert. (2004) *What Can Science Tell Us About Collective Consciousness?* Collective Wisdom Initiative. http://www.collectivewisdominitiative.org/papers/kenny_science.htm (accessed December 2010).

31   Henderson, Mark. "Theories of telepathy and afterlife cause uproar at top science forum." *The Sunday Times*, September 6, 2006. http://www.timesonline.co.uk/article/0,2-2344804,00.html (accessed December 2010).

32   Carey, Benedict. "Journal's Paper on ESP Expected to Prompt Outrage." *The New York Times*, January 5, 2011. http://www.nytimes.com/2011/01/06/science/06esp.html?_r=2&hp (accessed January 2011).

33   Ibid.

Chapter Three

1   Johnston, Laurance. "The Seat of the Soul." *Parapalegia News*, August 2009. http://www.healingtherapies.info/PinealGland1.htm (accessed December 2010).

2   Mabie, Curtis P. and Wallace, Betty M. (1974) "Optical, physical and chemical properties of pineal gland calcifications." *Calcified Tissue International*. 16, 59–71.

3   Wilcock, David. *The 2012 Enigma* (documentary). DivineCosmos.com, March 10, 2008. http://video.google.com/videoplay?docid=-4951448613711060908# (accessed December 2010).

4   Bay, David and Sexton, Rebecca. "Pagans Love Pine Cones and Use Them in Their Art." *The Cutting Edge*. http://cuttingedge.org/articles/RC125.htm (accessed December 2010).

5   Wilcock, David. *The 2012 Enigma*, Op. cit.

6   Palmgren, Henrik. "Biscione—Italian Serpent Symbolism Strikingly Similar to Quetzalcoatl in Mayan Mythology." *Red Ice Creations*. http://www.redicecreations.com/winterwonderland/serpentman.html (accessed December 2010).

7   Komaroff, Katherine. *Sky Gods: The Sun and Moon in Art and Myth* New York: Universe Books, 1974, p. 52. In *Amazing Discoveries. Serpent and Dragon Symbols*. http://amazingdiscoveries.org/albums.html?action=album&aid=542635335220957278 5 (accessed December 2010).

8   Olson, Kerry. *Temple of Quetzalcoatl (Plumed Serpent) at Teotihuacan*. Webshots American Greetings. http://travel.webshots.com/photo/1075984150033121848BHPuxi (accessed December 2010).

9   Thorsander, Glen. (2008) *The Tree of Life Omphalos and Baetyl Stone*. FirstLegend.info. http://firstlegend.info/3rivers/thetreeofomphalos.html (accessed December 2010).

10   Ryewolf. (2003) "The Legend and History of the Bennu Bird and the Phoenix." *The White Goddess*. http://web.archive.org/web/20041119225528/http://www.thewhitegoddess.co.uk/articles/pheonix.asp?SID=Egypt (accessed December 2010).

11   Thorsander, Glen. (2008) *The Tree of Life Omphalos and Baetyl Stone*, Op. cit.

12   Ryewolf. (2003) "The Legend and History of the Benu Bird and the Phoenix," Op. cit.

13   Ibid.

14   Ibid.

15   Ibid.

16   Thorsander, Glen. (2008) *The Tree of Life Omphalos and Baetyl Stone*, Op. cit.

17   Ibid.

18   Palmer, Abram Smythe. (1899) "Jacob at Bethel: The Vision—the Stone—the Anointing." In Lexic.us, *Literary Usage of Baetyls*. http://www.lexic.us/definition-of/baetyls (accessed December 2010).

19   Thorsander, Glen. (2008) *The Tree of Life Omphalos and Baetyl Stone*., Op. cit.

20   Ibid.

21   Papafava, Francesco, ed. *Guide to the Vatican Museums and City*. Vatican City: Tipografia Vaticana., 1986. In Peterson, Darren (ed), *Vatican Museum—Court of the Pigna. Tour of Italy for the Financially Challenged*. http://touritaly.org/tours/vaticanmuseum/Vatican06.htm (accessed December 2010).

22   Holy Bible. Matthew 6:22. King James Version.

23   Thorsander, Glen. (2008) *The Tree of Life Omphalos and Baetyl Stone*, Op. cit.

24   Blavatsky, Helena. "Ancient Landmarks: The Pythagorean Science of Numbers." *Theosophy*, 27, 7, May 1939, pp. 301–306. http://www.blavatsky.net/magazine/theosophy/ww/additional/ancientlandmarks/PythagScienceOfNumbers.html (accessed December 2010).

25   Hall, Manly Palmer. (1928) *The Secret Teachings of All Ages*. The Philosophical Research Society Press.

26   Hall, Manly Palmer. *The Occult Anatomy of Man*. Los Angeles: Hall Pub. Co; 2nd ed. (1924), pp. 10–12.

27   Hall, Manly Palmer. (1928) *The Secret Teachings of All Ages*. The Philosophical Research Society Press, page facing XCVII. In (ed) Kundalini Research Foundation, *The Philosopher's Stone*. http://www.kundaliniresearch.org/philosophers_stone.html (accessed December 2010).

28   Steiner, Rudolf and Barton, Matthew. (2010) *The Mysteries of the Holy Grail: From Arthur and Parzival to Modern Initiation*. Rudolf Steiner Press, p. 147. http://books.google.com/books?id=EeIPM90Gx70C&pg=PA171&lpg=PA171 (accessed December 2010).

29   Ibid., p. 158.

30   Hall, Manly Palmer. *The Orphic Egg: From Bryant's An Analysis of Ancient Mythology*. Philosophical Research Society. http://www.prs.org/gallery-classic.htm (accessed December 2010).

31   Hall, Manly Palmer. (1928) *The Secret Teachings of All Ages*., Op. cit.

32   Lokhorst, Gert-Jan. *Descartes and the Pineal Gland*. Stanford Encyclopedia of Philosophy, April 25, 2005, revised November 5, 2008. http://plato.stanford.edu/entries/pineal-gland/ (accessed December 2010).

33   EdgarCayce.org. *True Health Physical-Mental-Spiritual: The Pineal*. October 2002.
     http://web.archive.org/web/20080319233929/http://www.edgarcayce.org/th/tharchiv/
     research/pineal.html (accessed December 2010).

34   Cox, Richard. *The Mind's Eye. USC Health & Medicine*, Winter 1995. In Craft, Cheryl
     M. (ed.)., EyesightResearch.org. http://www.eyesightresearch.org/old/Mind%27s_Eye
     .htm (accessed December 2010).

35   Ibid.

36   Miller, Julie Ann. "Eye to (third) eye; scientists are taking advantage of unexpected simi-
     larities between the eye's retina and the brain's pineal gland." *Science News*, November 9,
     1985. http://www.highbeam.com/doc/1G1-4016492.html (accessed December 2010).

37   NIH/National Institute of Child Health and Human Development "Pineal Gland
     Evolved to Improve Vision, According to New Theory," *ScienceDaily*. August 19, 2004.
     http://www.sciencedaily.com/releases/2004/08/040817082213.htm (accessed December
     2010).

38   Wiechmann, A. F. *Melatonin: parallels in pineal gland and retina*. Exp Eye Res. June 1986;
     42(6):507–27. http://www.ncbi.nlm.nih.gov/pubmed/3013666 (accessed December 2010).

39   Lolley, R. N., C. M. Craft, and R. H. Lee. "Photoreceptors of the retina and pinealocytes
     of the pineal gland share common components of signal transduction. *Neurochem Res*,
     17(1): 81, 1992. http://www.springerlink.com/content/uj3433344j061353/.

40   Max, M., et al. "Light-dependent activation of rod transducin by pineal opsin." *Journal
     of Biological Chem*istry, 273(41): 26820, 1998. http://www.ncbi.nlm.nih.gov/
     pubmed/9756926 (accessed December 2010).

41   Baconnier, S. S., Lang, B., et al. (2002) "Calcite microcrystals in the pineal gland of the
     human brain: first physical and chemical studies." *Bioelectromagnetics* 23(7): 488–95.

42   Field, Simon Quellen. *Science Toys You Can Make With Your Kids*. Chapter 4: Radio.
     Sci-Toys.com. http://sci-toys.com/scitoys/scitoys/radio/homemade_radio.html (accessed
     December 2010).

43   Harvey, E. Newton. *The Nature of Animal Light*. (Triboluminescence and Piezolumines-
     cence.) Project Gutenberg, November 26, 2010. http://www.gutenberg.org/
     files/34450/34450.txt (accessed December 2010).

44   Bamfield, Peter. (2001) *Chromic Phenomena: The Technological Applications of Colour
     Chemistry*. The Royal Society of Chemistry, Cambridge, U.K., p. 69. http://www.scribd
     .com/doc/23581956/Chromic-Phenomena-Bamfield-2001 (accessed December 2010).

45   Johnston, Laurance. "The Seat of the Soul." *Parapalegia News*, August 2009. http://www
     .healingtherapies.info/PinealGland1.htm (accessed December 2010).

46   Hanna, John. *Erowid Character Vaults: Nick Sand Extended Biography*. Erowid.org.
     November 5, 2009. http://www.erowid.org/culture/characters/sand_nick/sand_nick_
     biography1.shtml (accessed December 2010).

47   Baconnier, S. S., Lang, B., et al. (2002) "Calcite microcrystals in the pineal gland of the
     human brain: first physical and chemical studies." *Bioelectromagnetics* 23(7): 488–95.

48   Baconnier, Simon, Lang, B., et al. (2002) "New Crystal in the Pineal Gland: Characteriza-
     tion and Potential Role in Electromechano Transduction." *Experimental Toxicology* http://
     www.ursi.org/Proceedings/ProcGA02/papers/p2236.pdf (accessed December 2010).

49   Johnston, Laurance. "The Pineal Gland, Melatonin & Spinal-Cord Dysfunction." *Para-
     palegia News*, August 2009. http://www.healingtherapies.info/PinealGland1.htm
     (accessed December 2010).

50   Luke, J. (1997) *The Effect of Fluoride on the Physiology of the Pineal Gland*. Ph.D. Thesis.
     University of Surrey, Guildford. In Fluoride Action Network. Health Effects: Fluoride &
     the Pineal Gland. http://www.fluoridealert.org/health/pineal/ (accessed December 2010).

51 Bob, P. and Fedor-Freybergh, P. (2008) *Melatonin, consciousness, and traumatic stress.* *Journal of Pineal Research,* 44: 341–347. http://onlinelibrary.wiley.com/doi/10.1111/j.1600-079X.2007.00540.x/full (accessed December 2010).

52 Groenendijk, Charly. (2001) *The Serotonergic System, the Pineal Gland & Side-Effects of Serotonin Acting Anti-Depressants. Antidepressants Facts.* October 9, 2001 (updated March 11, 2003) http://www.antidepressantsfacts.com/pinealstory.htm (accessed December 2010).

53 Ibid.

54 Ibid.

55 Price, Weston A. *Nutrition and Physical Degeneration.* La Mesa, CA: Price Pottenger Nutrition, 8th Edition, 1998.

Chapter Four

1 Kelly, Kevin and Steven Johnson, "Where Ideas Come From." *Wired,* September 27, 2010. http://www.wired.com/magazine/2010/09/mf_kellyjohnson/ (accessed December 2010).

2 Gladwell, Malcolm. "In the Air: Who Says Big Ideas Are Rare?" *The New Yorker,* May 12, 2008. http://www.newyorker.com/reporting/2008/05/12/080512fa_fact_gladwell?currentPage=all (accessed December 2010).

3 Laszlo, E. (1995) *The interconnected universe: Conceptual foundations of transdisciplinary unified theory.* River Edge, NJ: World Scientific, pp. 133–135.

4 Sheldrake, R. *ThePresence of the Past: Morphic Resonance and the Habits of Nature.* New York: Times Books., 1988.

5 Pearsall, Paul, Schwartz, Gary and Russek, Linda. *Organ Transplants and Cellular Memories.* In *Nexus Magazine,* April–May 2005, pp. 27–32, 76. http://www.paulpearsall.com/info/press/3.html (accessed December 2010).

6 Ibid.

7 The Co-Intelligence Institute. *Morphogenetic Fields.* 2003–2008. http://www.co-intelligence.org/P-morphogeneticfields.html (accessed December 2010).

8 The Co-Intelligence Institute. *More on Morphogenetic Fields.* 2003-2008. http://www.co-intelligence.org/P-moreonmorphgnicflds.html (accessed December 2010).

9 Combs, Allan, Holland, Mark and Robertson, Robin. *Synchronicity: Through the Eyes of Science, Myth, and the Trickster.* New York: Da Capo Press, 2000, pp. 27–28. http://books.google.com/books?id=ONXhD2NZtJgC&pg=PA27&lpg=PA27 (accessed December 2010).

10 Stafford, Tom. "Waking Life Crossword Experiment," *Mind Hacks,* January 16, 2007. http://mindhacks.com/2007/01/16/waking-life-crossword-experiment/ (accessed December 2010).

11 Sheldrake, Rupert. In Ted Dace (ed) *Re: Dawkins etc.* Journal of Memetics discussion list, September 11, 2001. http://web.archive.org/web/20070302014159/http://cfpm.org/~majordom/memetics/2000/6425.html (Accessed December 2010).

12 Swann, Ingo. *The Ingo Swann 1973 Remote Viewing Probe of the Planet Jupiter.* Remoteviewed.com, December 12, 1995. http://www.remoteviewed.com/remote_viewing_jupiter.htm (Accessed December 2010).

13 Morehouse, David, *Psychic Warrior: The True Story of the CIA's Paranormal Espionage Programme.* New York: St. Martin's Press, 1996. http://davidmorehouse.com/ (accessed December 2010).

14 Joe McMoneagle's books include *Mind Trek* (1997), *The Ultimate Time Machine* with Charles T. Tart (1998), *Remote Viewing Secrets: A Handbook* (2000), *The Stargate Chronicles* (2002), and *Memoirs of a Psychic Spy* with Edwin C. May and L. Robert Castorr (2006). http://www.mceagle.com/ (accessed December 2010).

15 McMoneagle, Nancy. *Remote Viewing in Japan*. McEagle.com. http://www.mceagle
    .com/remote-viewing/Japan2.html (accessed December 2010).

16 Radin, D. *The Conscious Universe: The scientific truth of psychic phenomena*. New York:
    HarperCollins, 1997, p. 105. www.boundaryinstitute.org/ or www.psiresearch.org.
    (accessed December 2010).

17 McTaggart, Lynne. *The Field: The quest for the secret force of the universe*. New York:
    HarperCollins, 2002, p. 160.

18 Utts, J. (1996) "An assessment of the evidence for psychic functioning," *Journal of Scientific Exploration*, 10, pp. 3–30.

19 Putoff, H. & Targ, R. (1976, pp. 329–353) "A perceptual channel for information transfer
    over kilometer distances: historical perspective and recent research," *Proceedings of the
    IEEE*, 64 (3). Cited in McTaggart, Lynne, *The Field*, Op. cit.

20 Jahn, R. G., Dunne, B. J. *Margins of Reality: The Role of Consciousness in the Physical
    World*. New York: Harcourt Brace Jovanovich, 1987.

21 Bisaha, J. J., Dunne, B. J. "Multiple subject and long-distance precognitive remote viewing of geographical locations." In: Tart, C., Puthoff, H. E., Targ, R., eds. *Mind at Large*,
    New York: Praeger, 1979: pp. 107–124.

22 Osis, K., and McCormick, D. (1980) "Kinetic Effects at the Ostensible Location of an
    Out-of-Body Projection during Perceptual Testing," *Journal of the American Society for
    Psychical Research*, 74, pp. 319–329.

23 PRC, Chinese Academy of Sciences, High Energy Institute, Special Physics Research
    Team. "Exceptional Human Body Radiation," *PSI Research*, June 1982, pp. 16–25,

24 Yonjie, Zhao and Hongzhang, Xu. "EHBF Radiation: Special Features of the Time
    Response," Institute of High Energy Physics, Beijing, People's Republic of China, *PSI
    Research*, December 1982.

25 Hubbard, G., Scott, May, E. C., and Puthoff, H. E. (1986) *Possible Production of Photons
    During a Remote Viewing Task: Preliminary Results*. SRI International, in D. H. Weiner
    and D. I. Radin (eds.) *Research in Parapsychology*. Metuchen, NJ: Scarecrow Press, 1985,
    pp. 66–70.

26 MacDougall, Duncan, M.D. "Hypothesis Concerning Soul Substance Together with
    Experimental Evidence of the Existence of Such Substance." *American Medicine*, April 1907;
    also in *Journal of the American Society for Psychical Research*, Vol. 1 (1907), pp. 237–244.

27 Carrington, Hereward. *Laboratory Investigations into Psychic Phenomena*. Philadelphia:
    David McKay company, ca 1940.

28 Williams, Kevin. (2007) *The NDE and the Silver Cord*. Near-Death.com. http://www
    .near-death.com/experiences/research12.html (accessed December 2010).

29 Holy Bible. Ecclesiastes 12:6. New International Version. http://www.biblegateway.com/
    passage/?search=Eccl.%2012:6-7&version=NIV (accessed December 2010).

30 University of Southampton, "World's Largest-ever Study of Near-Death Experiences."
    ScienceDaily. September 10, 2008. http://www.sciencedaily.com/releases/
    2008/09/080910090829.htm.

31 Van Lommel, Pim. "About the Continuity of Our Consciousness." In (ed) *Brain Death and
    Disorders of Consciousness*. Machado, C. and Shewmon, D. A., eds. New York, Boston, Dordrecht, London, Moscow: Kluwer Academic/Plenum Publishers; "Advances in Experimental
    Medicine and Biology," *Adv Exp Med Biol*. 2004; 550: 115-132. http://www.iands.org/research/
    important_studies/dr._pim_van_lommel_m.d._continuity_of_consciousness_3.html
    (accessed December 2010).

32 "Near Death Experiences & the Afterlife." (2010) *Scientific evidence for survival of consciousness after death*. http://www.near-death.com/evidence.html (accessed December 2010).

33 Ibid.

34 Newton, Michael. (2000) *Destiny of Souls: New Case Studies of Life Between Lives.* St. Paul, MN: Llewellyn Publications, pp. xi–xii. http://www.spiritualregression.org/ (accessed December 2010).

35 Newton, Michael. (1994) *Journey of Souls: Case Studies of Life Between Lives.* Llewellyn Publications, 1st Edition. http://www.spiritualregression.org/ (accessed December 2010).

36 Newton, Michael. (2000) Op cit., pp. 5–8.

37 Backman, Linda. (2009) *Bringing Your Soul to Light: Healing Through Past Lives and the Time Between.* Llewellyn Publications. http://www.bringingyoursoultolight.com (accessed December 2010).

38 Stevenson, Ian. *Twenty Cases Suggestive of Reincarnation: Second Edition, Revised and Enlarged.* University of Virginia Press, October 1, 1980.

39 Penman, Danny. "'I died in Jerusalem in 1276,' says doctor who underwent hypnosis to reveal a former life," Daily Mail Online, April 25, 2008. http://www.dailymail.co.uk/pages/live/articles/news/news.html?in_article_id=562154&in_page_id=1770.

40 Tucker, Jim. *Life Before Life: Children's Memories of Previous Lives.* New York: St. Martin's Press, April 1, 2008.

Chapter Five

1   LaBerge, Stephen. *Lucid Dreaming: The Power of Being Awake and Aware in Your Dreams.* New York: Ballantine Books, 1986. http://www.lucidity.com/ (accessed December 2010).

2   LaBerge, Stephen and Rheingold, Howard. *Exploring the World of Lucid Dreaming.* New York: Ballantine Books, 1990. http://www.lucidity.com/ (accessed December 2010).

3   Ullman, Montague; Krippner, Stanley and Vaughan, Alan. (1973) *Dream Telepathy: Experiments in Nocturnal Extrasensory Perception.* Hampton Roads Publishing, 2003. http://www.siivola.org/monte/ (accessed December 2010).

4   LaBerge, Stephen. *Lucid Dreaming,* Op cit.

5   Waggoner, Robert. *Lucid Dreaming: Gateway to the Inner Self.* Needham, MA: Moment Point Press, October 1, 2008. http://www.lucidadvice.com/ (accessed December 2010).

6   LaBerge, Stephen. *Lucid Dreaming,* Op. cit.

7   Brooke, Chris. *Czech speedway rider knocked out in crash wakes up speaking perfect English.* Daily Mail, September 14, 2007. http://www.dailymail.co.uk/news/article-481651/Czech-speedway-rider-knocked-crash-wakes-speaking-perfect-English.html.

8   "Croatian Teenager Wakes from Coma Speaking Perfect German," *Telegraph.* April 12, 2010. http://www.telegraph.co.uk/news/worldnews/europe/croatia/7583971/Croatian-teenager-wakes-from-coma-speaking-fluent-German.html.

9   Leaman, Bob. *Armageddon: Doomsday in Our Lifetime?* Chapter 4. Australia: Greenhouse Publications, 1986. http://www.dreamscape.com/morgana/phoebe.htm.

10 LaBerge, Stephen. *Lucid Dreaming,* Op. cit.

11 Ibid., pp. 12–13.

12 *Journal of Offender Rehabilitation* 36, 2003, 1/2/3/4, pp. 283–302. http://proposal.permanentpeace.org/research/index.html.

13 *Social Indicators Research* 47: 153–201, 1999. http://proposal.permanentpeace.org/research/index.html.

14 Ibid.

15 Orme-Johnson, D., "The science of world peace: Research shows meditation is effective," *The International Journal of Healing and Caring On-Line, 3* (3), September 1993, p. 2.

16 St. John of the Cross. *The Collected Works of St. John of the Cross*. Washington, D.C.: ICS Publications, 1979, in Aron, Elaine and Aron, Arthur, eds., *The Maharishi Effect: A Revolution Through Meditation*. Walpole, NH: Stillpoint Publishing, 1986.

17 Wolters, C., ed. *The Cloud of Unknowing and Other Works*. New York: Penguin, 1978, in Aron, Elaine and Aron, Arthur, *The Maharishi Effect*, Op. cit.

18 Van Auken, John. *Soul Life: Destiny, Fate & Karma*. Association for Research and Enlightenment, 2002. http://www.edgarcayce.org/ps2/soul_life_destiny_fate_karma.html.

19 Edgar Cayce Reading 3976-28, June 20, 1943. http://www.edgarcayce.org/are/edgarcayce.aspx?id=2473/.

20 Edgar Cayce Reading 3976-27, June 19, 1942. http://www.edgarcayce.org/are/edgarcayce.aspx?id=2473/.

21 Edgar Cayce Reading 3976-8, January 15, 1932. http://www.edgarcayce.org/are/edgarcayce.aspx?id=2473/.

22 Len, Ihalekala Hew. IZI LLC/Ho'oponopono. http://www.hooponoponotheamericas.org/

23 Vitale, Joe and Len, Ihalekala Hew. *Zero Limits*. New York: Wiley, 2007. http://www.zerolimits.info/.

24 Ibid.

25 Ibid.

26 Len, Ihalekala Hew. IZI LLC/Ho'oponopono, Op. cit.

27 Commentary on Vitale, Joe, *I'm Sorry, I Love You*. http://www.wanttoknow.info/070701imsorryiloveyoujoevitale.

28 Ostling, Richard N., "Researcher tabulates world's believers.," *Salt Lake Tribune*, May 19, 2001. http://www.adherents.com/misc/WCE.html.

29 Edgar Cayce Reading 281-16, March 13, 1933. http://www.edgarcayce.org/ps2/mysticism_interpretating_revelation.html.

30 Ibid.

Chapter Six

1 Flem-Ath, Rand and Flem-Ath, Rose. *When the Sky Fell*. New York: St. Martin's Press, 1995, p. 33.

2 Wilson, Colin. *From Atlantis to the Sphinx: Recovering the Lost Wisdom of the Ancient World*. New York: Fromm International, 1996, pp. 278–279.

3 Bulfinch, Thomas. *Bulfinch's Mythology: The Age of Fable, or Stories of Gods and Heroes*. Chapter XL. 1855. http://www.sacred-texts.com/cla/bulf/bulf39.htm (accessed December 2010).

4 StateMaster Encyclopedia. Great Year. http://www.statemaster.com/encyclopedia/Great-year.

5 Ibid.

6 Ibid.

7 Ibid.

8 Mahabharata, Book 3: *Vana Parva: Markandeya-Samasya Parva:* Section CLXXXVII. http://www.sacred-texts.com/hin/m03/m03187.htm.

9 Mahabharata, Book 3: *Vana Parva: Markandeya-Samasya Parva:* Section CLXXXIX and CLXL. http://www.sacred-texts.com/hin/m03/m03189.htm and http://www.sacred-texts.com/hin/m03/m03190.htm.

10 Ibid.

11 Edgar Cayce Reading 281-28, October 26, 1936. http://www.edgarcayce.org/ps2/mysticism_interpretating_revelation.html.

12 Blavatsky, H. P. *The Secret Doctrine*, Vol. 1, Book 2, p. 378. http://www.sacred-texts.com/the/sd/sd1-2-07.htm.

13 Ibid.

14 Van Auken, John. *Ancient Mysteries Update: Pyramid Prophecy. Venture Inward*, March-April 2009. http://www.edgarcayce.org/are/pdf/membership/VentureInwardMarApr2009.pdf.

15 Blavatsky, H. P. *The Secret Doctrine*, Vol. 1, Book 2, p. 378. http://www.sacred-texts.com/the/sd/sd1-2-07.htm.

16 Stray, Geoff. *Beyond 2012: Catastrophe or Awakening?* p. 54. Rochester, Vermont: Bear and Company, 2009, http://www.diagnosis2012.co.uk.

17 Lemesurier, Peter. *The Great Pyramid Decoded.* Boston, MA: Element Books, 1977.

18 Stern, David P. *Get a Straight Answer.* NASA Goddard Space Flight Center. http://www-istp.gsfc.nasa.gov/stargaze/StarFAQ21.htm#q374.

19 Ibid.

20 Burchill, Shirley. *History of Science and Technology: Hipparchus (c. 190–c. 120 B.C.)* The Open Door http://www.saburchill.com/HOS/astronomy/006.html.

21 Ibid.

22 D'Zmura, David Andrew. *U.S. Patent 676618—Method of determining zodiac signs.* Issued on August 17, 2004. http://www.patentstorm.us/patents/6776618/description.html.

23 Mead, G. R. S. *Thrice-Greatest Hermes, Vol. 2.* 1906. http://www.sacred-texts.com/gno/th2/th252.htm.

24 Edgar Cayce Readings. *Edgar Cayce Great Pyramid and Sphinx Reading from 1932.* Cayce .com. http://www.cayce.com/pyramid.htm.

25 Ibid.

26 Sanderfur, Glen. *Lives of the Master: The Rest of the Jesus Story.* Virginia Beach, VA: A.R.E. Press, 1988. http://www.edgarcaycebooks.org/livesofmaster.html.

27 Mead, G. R. S. *Thrice-Greatest Hermes,* Op. cit.

28 Copenhaver, Brian P. *Hermetica: The Greek Corpus Hermeticum and the Latin Asclepius in a New English Translation, with Notes and Introduction.* Cambridge University Press, 1995, pp. 81–83.

29 Scott, Walter. *Hermetica, Vol. 1: The Ancient Greek and Latin Writings Which Contain Religious or Philosophic Teachings Ascribed to Hermes Trismestigus.* New York: Shambhala, 2001.

30 Prophecies of the Future. *Future Prophecies Revealed: A Remarkable Collection of Obscure Millennial Prophecies. Hermes Trismestigus (circa 1st century CE).* http://futurerevealed .com/future/texts-date-1.htm.

Chapter Seven

1 Gray, Martin. *Giza Pyramids.* World-Mysteries.com, 2003. http://www.world-mysteries .com/gw_mgray5.htm.

2 Ibid.

3 Lemesurier, Peter. *The Great Pyramid Decoded.* Rockport, MA: Element Books, 1977, p. 8.

4 Zajac, John. "The Great Pyramid: A Dreamland Report." *After Dark Newsletter,* February 1995. http://www.europa.com/~edge/pyramid.html.

5 Gray, Martin. *Giza Pyramid,.* Op. cit.

6 Zajac, John. *The Great Pyramid: A Dreamland Report.* Op. cit.

7 Gray, Martin. *Giza Pyramids,* Op cit.

8 Ibid.

9 Lemesurier, Peter. *The Great Pyramid Decoded,* Op cit.

10 Tompkins, Peter. *Secrets of the Great Pyramid.* New York: Harper and Row, 1971, 1978.

11 Ibid.

12 Ibid., p. 1.

13 Ibid., p. 2.

14 Ibid.

15 Gray, Martin. *Giza Pyramids,* Op cit.

16 Tompkins, Peter. *Secrets of the Great Pyramid.* Op cit., p. 3.

17 Ibid.

18 Pietsch, Bernard. *The Well-Tempered Solar System: Anatomy of the King's Chamber.* 2000. http://sonic.net/bernard/kings-chamber.html.

19 Christopher Dunn, *The Giza Power Plant: Technologies of Ancient Egypt.* Santa Fe, NM: Bear & Company, 1998. http://www.gizapower.com.

20 Ibid.

21 Gray, Martin. *Giza Pyramids.* Op cit.

22 Lemesurier, Peter. *Gods of the Dawn.* London: Thorsons/HarperCollins, 1999, p. 84.

23 Ibid., p. 85.

24 Jochmans, Joseph. *The Great Pyramid—How Old is it Really?* Forgotten Ages Research, 2009. http://www.forgottenagesresearch.com/mystery-monuments-series/The-Great-PyramidHow-Old-is-It-Really.htm (accessed May 2010.)

25 Cayce, Edgar. Reading 5748-5. Association for Research and Enlightenment, June 30, 1932. http://arescott.tripod.com/EConWB.html.

26 Tompkins, Peter. *Secrets of the Great Pyramid.* Op cit., p. 17.

27 Gray, Martin. *Giza Pyramids.* Op cit.

28 Tompkins, Peter. *Secrets of the Great Pyramid.* Op cit., p. 18.

29 Ibid., p. 17.

30 Ibid., p. 67.

31 Ibid., p. 68.

32 Ibid., p. 69.

33 Ibid., p. 72.

34 Ibid., p. 73.

35 Ibid., p. 74.

36 Lemesurier, Peter. *The Great Pyramid Decoded.* Op cit., p. 309.

37 Ibid.

38 Spenser, Robert Keith. *The Cult of the All-Seeing Eye.* California: Christian Book Club of America, April 1964.

39 Monaghan, Patricia. *The New Book of Goddesses and Heroines.* St. Paul, MN: Llewellyn, 1997. http://www.hranajanto.com/goddessgallery/sibyl.html.

40 Fish Eaters. *The Sybils (Sybils).* http://www.fisheaters.com/sibyls.html (accessed May 2010).

41 Ibid.

42 Roach, John. "Delphic Oracle's Lips May Have Been Loosened by Gas Vapors," *National Geographic News,* August 14, 2001. http://news.nationalgeographic.com/news/2001/08/0814_delphioracle.html.

43 Fish Eaters. *The Sybils (Sybils).* Op cit.

44 Morgana's Observatory. *The Cumaean Sibyl—Ancient Rome's Great Priestess and Prophet.* 2006. http://www.dreamscape.com/morgana/desdemo2.htm.

45 Ibid.

46 Wikipedia. *Cumaean Sibyl.* http://en.wikipedia.org/wiki/Cumaean_Sibyl.

47 "Royal76." *December 21, 2012. . . . The End . . . or just another beginning.* Above Top Secret Forum, May 22, 2007. http://www.abovetopsecret.com/forum/thread283740/pg1

48 Friedman, Amy and Gilliland, Jillian. *The Fire of Wisdom (an ancient Roman tale).* Tell Me a Story, UExpress.com, August 25, 2002. http://www.uexpress.com/tellmeastory/index.html?uc_full_date=20020825.

49   The Ion. *Sibylline Oracles: Judgment of the Tenth Generation.* Hearth Productions, January 21, 1997.

50   Lorre, Norma Goodrich. *Priestesses.* Perennial, November 1990. http://www.dreamscape.com/morgana/desdemo2.htm.

51   Mayor, Joseph B.; Fowler, W. Warde and Conway, R. S. *Virgil's Messianic Eclogue: Its Meaning, Occasion and Sources.* London: John Murray, Albemarle Street, 1907. http://www.questia.com/PM.qst?a=o&d=24306203.

52   Tompkins, *Secrets of the Great Pyramid,* Op cit., p. 38.

53   Spenser, Robert Keith. *The Cult of the All-Seeing Eye.* California: Christian Book Club of America, April 1964.

54   Fish Eaters. *The Eclogues by Virgil (37 B.C.).* http://www.fisheaters.com/sibyls8.html (accessed May 2010).

55   Still, William T. *New World Order: The Ancient Plan of Secret Societies.* Lafayette, LA: Huntington House, 1990.

Chapter Eight

1   Laigaard, Jens. "excerpt from Chapter Eight of *Pyramideenergien—kritisk undersøgelse* (1999)." Translation by Daniel Loxton and Jens Laigaard. *Skeptic.com.* http://www.skeptic.com/junior_skeptic/issue23/translation_Laigaard.html (accessed May 2010).

2   Ibid.

3   Ibid.

4   Ibid.

5   Ostrander, S. and Schroeder, L. *Psychic Discoveries Behind the Iron Curtain.* Englewood Cliffs, NJ: Prentice-Hall, 1971.

6   Watson, Lyall. *Supernature.* Doubleday/Bantam Books, New York, 1973, p. 88.

7   Krasnoholovets, Volodymyr. *On the Way to Disclosing the Mysterious Power of the Great Pyramid.* Giza Pyramid Research Association, January 24, 2001. http://www.gizapyramid.com/DrV-article.htm (accessed May 2010).

8   Ibid.

9   Watson, Lyall. *Supernature.* Op cit., p. 89.

10   Ibid., p. 90.

11   Osmanagic, Semir. *Bosnian Pyramid.* http://www.bosnianpyramid.com/ (accessed May 2010).

12   Lukacs, Gabriela. *World Pyramids Project.* http://www.world-pyramids.com (accessed May 2010).

13   Krasnoholovets, Volodymyr. *On the Way to Disclosing the Mysterious Power of the Great Pyramid.* Giza Pyramid Research Association, January 24, 2001. http://www.gizapyramid.com/DrV-article.htm (accessed May 2010).

14   Gorouvein, Edward. *Golden Section Pyramids.* Pyramid of Life. http://www.pyramidoflife.com/eng/golden_section.html (accessed May 2010).

15   DeSalvo, John. *Russian Pyramid Research: Introduction.* Giza Pyramid Research Association. http://www.gizapyramid.com/russian/introduction.htm (accessed May 2010).

16   Gorouvein, Edward. *Golden Section Pyramids.* Pyramid of Life. http://www.pyramidoflife.com/eng/golden_section.html (accessed May 2010).

17   DeSalvo, John. *Russian Pyramid Research: Introduction.* Op cit.

18   Krasnoholovets, Volodymyr. *On the Way to Disclosing the Mysterious Power of the Great Pyramid.* Op cit.

19   Gorouvein, Edward. *Golden Section Pyramids.* Op cit.

20   Ibid.

21 Krasnoholovets, Volodymyr. *On the Way to Disclosing the Mysterious Power of the Great Pyramid.* Op cit.

22 Ibid.

23 Ibid.

24 Ibid.

25 Ibid.

26 Ibid.

27 Ibid.

28 Ibid.

29 Ibid.

30 Ibid.

31 Ibid.

32 Ibid.

33 Ibid.

34 Gorouvein, Edward. *Tests and Experiments.* Pyramid of Life. http://www.pyramidoflife .com/eng/tests_experiments.html#3 (accessed May 2010).

35 Krasnoholovets, Volodymyr. *On the Way to Disclosing the Mysterious Power of the Great Pyramid.* Op cit.

36 Gorouvein, Edward. *Tests and Experiments.* Op cit.

37 Yakovenko, Maxim. *Nakhodka, the city of prehistoric times.* World Pyramids. http://www .world-pyramids.com/nakhodka.html (accessed May 2010).

38 DeSalvo, John. Press Release: "International Partnership for Pyramid Research." Giza Pyramid Research Association. http://www.gizapyramid.com/russian/press-release.htm (accessed May 2010).

39 Ibid.

40 Dr. DeSalvo had previously misunderstood the translation from Russian into English and seemingly assumed that the word for granite, which was similar to "salt and pepper," meant that the prisoners had been fed salt and pepper from the pyramids.

Chapter Nine

1 Beloussov, Lev V. "Biofield as Engendered and Currently Perceived in Embryology. In Savva, Savely (ed.), *Life and Mind: In Search of the Physical Basis.* Victoria, BC, Canada: Trafford Publishing, Victoria, 2006.

2 Driesch, Hans. (1921) *Philosophie des Organischen.* Engelmann, Leipzig.

3 Gurwitsch, A.G., *Das Problem der Zellteilung* (The Problem of Cell Division), 1926.

4 Lillge, Wolfgang, M.D., "Vernadsky's Method: Biophysics and the Life Processes," *21st Century Science & Technology Magazine,* Summer 2001. http://www.21stcenturysciencetech .com/articles/summ01/Biophysics/Biophysics.html.

5 McTaggart, Lynne. *The Field: The Quest for the Secret Force of the Universe.* New York: HarperCollins, New York, 2002, p. 48.

6 Ibid., p. 55.

7 Gariaev, P. P., Friedman, M. J., and Leonova-Gariaeva, E. A. "Crisis in Life Sciences: The Wave Genetics Response." Emergent Mind, 2007. http://www.emergentmind.org/ gariaev06.htm.

8 Ibid.

9 Ibid.

10 Stevenson, Ian. *Twenty Cases Suggestive of Reincarnation: Second Edition, Revised and Enlarged.* Charlottesville, VA: University of Virginia Press, 1980.

11 Tucker, Jim. *Life Before Life: Children's Memories of Previous Lives*. New York: St. Martin's, 2008.

12 Zuger, Abigail. "Removal of Half the Brain Improves Young Epileptics' Lives," *New York Times,* August 19, 1997. http://www.nytimes.com/yr/mo/day/news/national/sci-brain-damage.html.

13 Johns Hopkins Medical Institutions. "Study Confirms Benefits of Hemispherectomy Surgery," *ScienceDaily,* October 16, 2003. http://www.sciencedaily.com/releases/2003/10/031015030730.htm (accessed May 2010).

14 Lewin, Roger. "Is Your Brain Really Necessary?" *Science*, Dec. 12, 1980, pp. 1232–1234.

15 Ibid.

16 Ibid.

17 Lorber, J. *The family history of 'simple' congenital hydrocephalus. An epidemiological study based on 270 probands*. Z Kinderchir 1984; 39(2): 94–95.

18 Edwards J. F., Gebhardt-Henrich S., Fischer K., Hauzenberger A., Konar M., Steiger A. "Hereditary hydrocephalus in laboratory-reared golden hamsters (Mesocricetus auratus)." *Vet Pathol.* July 2006; 43(4): 523–9.

19 McTaggart, Lynne. *The Field: The Quest for the Secret Force of the Universe,* Op cit.

20 Ibid., p. 40.

21 Ibid., p. 42.

22 Ibid., p. 44.

23 Rein, Glen. *Effect of Conscious Intention on Human DNA*. Denver, CO: Proceeds of the International Forum on New Science, October 1996. http://www.item-bioenergy.com/infocenter/ConsciousIntentiononDNA.pdf (accessed June 2010.

24 Ibid.

25 Rein, Glen and McCraty, Rollin. *Local and Non-Local Effects of Coherent Heart Frequencies on Conformational Changes of DNA*. Institute of HeartMath/Proc. Joint USPA/IAPR Psychotronics Conference, Milwaukee, Wisconsin, 1993. (Accessed June 2010.) http://appreciativeinquiry.case.edu/uploads/HeartMath%20article.pdf.

26 Rein, Glen. *Effect of Conscious Intention on Human DNA*. Denver, CO: Proceeds of the International Forum on New Science, October 1996. http://www.item-bioenergy.com/infocenter/ConsciousIntentiononDNA.pdf (accessed June 2010).

27 Choi, Charles Q. "Strange! Humans Glow in Visible Light," *LiveScience,* July 22, 2009. http://www.livescience.com/health/090722-body-glow.html (accessed May 2010).

28 McTaggart, Lynne. *The Field: The Quest for the Secret Force of the Universe*. Op cit. p. 50.

29 Ibid., p. 52.

30 Ibid., p. 53.

31 Ibid., p. 54.

32 Gariaev, Peter P., Friedman, M. J., and Leonova-Gariaeva, E. A. *Crisis in Life Sciences: The Wave Genetics Response*. Russian National Academy of Sciences/Emergent Mind. http://www.emergentmind.org/gariaev06.htm.

33 Kaznacheyev, Vlail P., et al. "Distant intercellular interactions in a system of two tissue cultures," *Psychoenergetic Systems,* March 1976, pp. 141–42.

34 Gariaev, Peter P., Friedman, M. J., and Leonova-Gariaeva, E.A. *Crisis in Life Sciences: The Wave Genetics Response*. Russian National Academy of Sciences/Emergent Mind. http://www.emergentmind.org/gariaev06.htm.

35 Ibid.

36 Gariaev, Peter P. "An Open Letter from Dr. Peter Gariaev, the Father of "Wave-Genetics." *DNA Monthly,* September 2005. http://potentiation.net/DNAmonthly/September05.html (accessed May 2010).

37   Ibid.

38   Lillge, Wolfgang, M.D., "Vernadsky's Method: Biophysics and the Life Processes," *21st Century Science & Technology Magazine,* Summer 2001. http://www.21stcenturysciencetech .com/articles/summo1/Biophysics/Biophysics.html.

39   Ibid.

40   Ibid.

41   Kaivarainen, Alex. *New Hierarchic Theory of Water and its Role in Biosystems. Bivacuum Mediated Time Effects, Electromagnetic, Gravitational & Mental Interactions.* Institute for Time Nature Explorations. http://www.chronos.msu.ru/EREPORTS/kaivarainen_new .pdf (accessed May 2010).

42   Benor, Daniel: *Spiritual Healing: A Unifying Influence in Complementary/Alternative Therapies.* Wholistic Healing Research, January 4, 2005. http://www.wholistichealing research.com/spiritualhealingaunifyinginfluence.html.

43   David-Neel, Alexandra. *With Mystics and Magicians in Tibet.* Chapter VIII. London: Penguin Books, 1931. http://www.scribd.com/doc/21029489/With-Mystics-and-Magicians-in-Tibet.

Chapter Ten

1   Choi, Charles Q. "DNA Molecules Display Telepathy-Like Quality." *LiveScience,* January 24, 2008. http://www.livescience.com/health/080124-dna-telepathy.html (accessed May 2010).

2   Institute of Physics, "Physicists Discover Inorganic Dust with Lifelike Qualities," *ScienceDaily* (August 15, 2007) http://www.sciencedaily.com/releases/2007/08/070814150630 .htm (accessed December 2010).

3   Melville, Kate. "DNA Shaped Nebula Observed at Center of Milky Way," *Scienceagogo*, March 16, 2006. http://www.scienceagogo.com/news/20060216005544data_trunc_sys .shtml (accessed December 2010).

4   Dunn, John E. "DNA Molecules Can 'Teleport,' Nobel Winner Says," Techworld.com, January 16, 2011. http://www.pcworld.com/article/216767/dna_molecules_can_teleport_ nobel_winner_says.html (accessed January 2011).

5   Fredrickson, James K. and Onstott, Tullis C. "Microbes Deep Inside the Earth," *Scientific American*, October 1996. http://web.archive.org/web/20011216021826/www.sciam .com/1096issue/1096onstott.html (accessed May 2010).

6   McFadden, J. J. and Al-Khalili (1999). "A quantum mechanical model of adaptive mutations," *Biosystems* 50: 203–211.

7   Milton, Richard. *Shattering the Myths of Darwinism.* Rochester, VT: Park Street Press, 2000. http://web.archive.org/web/20040402182842/http://www.newsgateway.ca/ darwin.htm (accessed May 2010).

8   McFadden, J. J. and Al-Khalili (1999). *A quantum mechanical model of adaptive mutations.* Op cit.

9   Milton, Richard. *Shattering the Myths of Darwinism.* Op cit.

10   Keim, Brandon. "Howard Hughes' Nightmare: Space May Be Filled with Germs," *Wired*, August 6, 2008. http://www.wired.com/science/space/news/2008/08/galactic_ panspermia.

11   Gruener, Wolfgang. "We may be extraterrestrials after all," *TG Daily*, June 13, 2008. http://www.tgdaily.com/trendwatch-features/37940-we-may-be-extraterrestrials-after-all.

12   Mustain, Andrea. "34,000-Year-Old Organisms Found Buried Alive!" *LiveScience,* January 13, 2011. http://www.livescience.com/strangenews/ancient-bacteria-organisms-found-buried-alive-110112.html (accessed January 2011).

13 Hoyle, F. (1988), "Is the Universe Fundamentally Biological?" in F. Bertola, et al. (eds), *New Ideas in Astronomy.* New York: Cambridge University Press, pp. 5–8.

14 Suburban Emergency Management Project. *Interstellar Dust Grains as Freeze-Dried Bacterial Cells: Hoyle and Wickramasinghe's Fantastic Journey.* Biot Report #455, August 22, 2007. http://www.semp.us/publications/biot_reader.php?BiotID=455 (accessed May 2010).

15 Ibid.

16 Strick, James. *Sparks of Life: Darwinism and the Victorian Debates Over Spontaneous Generation.* Cambridge, MA: Harvard University Press, 2002.

17 Flannel, Jack. *The Bionous Nature of the Cancer Biopathy.* Report on Orgonon conference. 2003. http://www.jackflannel.org/orgonon_2003.html.

18 Ibid.

19 Crosse, A. *The American Journal of Science & Arts* 35: 125-137, January 1839. http://www.rexresearch.com/crosse/crosse.htm.

20 Edwards, Frank. "Spark of Life," from Stranger than Science, 1959. http://www.cheniere.org/misc/sparkoflife.htm.

21 Ibid.

22 Ibid.

23 "What Is Orgone Energy & What Is an Orgone Energy Accumulator?" Orgonics http://www.orgonics.com/whatisor.htm (accessed May 2010).

24 Wilcox, Roger M., "A Skeptical Scrutiny of the Works and Theories of Wilhelm Reich as related to SAPA Bions." February 23, 2009. http://pw1.netcom.com/~rogermw2/Reich/sapa.html (accessed May 2010).

25 Pacheco, Ignacio. "Ultrastructural and light microscopy analysis of SAPA bions formation and growth in vitro." Orgone.org, January 31, 2000. http://web.archive.org/web/20051108193642/http://www.orgone.org/articles/ax2001ignao1a.htm (accessed May 2010).

26 Ibid.

27 Bounoure, Louis. The Advocate, March 8, 1984, p. 17. In Luckert, Karl W. (ed.) *Quotations on Evolution as a Theory.* 2001. http://web.archive.org/web/20011126101316/http://www.geocities.com/Area51/Rampart/4871/images/quotes.html.

28 Smith, Wolfgang. *Teilhardism and the New Religion: A Thorough Analysis of the Teachings of de Chardin.* Tan Books & Publishers, 1998, pp. 1–2. In Luckert, Karl W. (ed.) *Quotations on Evolution as a Theory.* 2001. http://web.archive.org/web/20011126101316/http://www.geocities.com/Area51/Rampart/4871/images/quotes.html.

29 Eldredge, Niles. *The Monkey Business: A Scientist Looks at Creationism.* New York: Washington Square Press, 1982, p. 44. In Luckert, Karl W. (ed.) *Quotations on Evolution as a Theory.* 2001. http://web.archive.org/web/20011126101316/http://www.geocities.com/Area51/Rampart/4871/images/quotes.html.

30 Norman, J.R. "Classification and Pedigrees: Fossils. A History of Fishes," Dr. P.H. Greenwood (editor). British Museum of Natural History, 1975, p. 343. In Luckert, Karl W. (ed.) *Quotations on Evolution as a Theory.* 2001. http://web.archive.org/web/20011126101316/http://www.geocities.com/Area51/Rampart/4871/images/quotes.html.

31 Swinton, W. E. *Biology and Comparative Physiology of Birds.* A. J. Marshall (ed.), Vol. 1, New York: Academic Press, 1960, p. 1. In Luckert, Karl W. (ed.) *Quotations on Evolution as a Theory.* 2001. http://web.archive.org/web/20011126101316/http://www.geocities.com/Area51/Rampart/4871/images/quotes.html.

32 Ager, Derek. *The Nature of the Fossil Record.* Proc. Geological Assoc., Vol. 87, 1976, p. 132. In Luckert, Karl W. (ed.) *Quotations on Evolution as a Theory.* 2001. http://web.archive

.org/web/20011126101316/http://www.geocities.com/Area51/Rampart/4871/images/
quotes.html.

33   Zuckerman, Lord Solly. *Beyond the Ivory Tower*. New York: Taplinger Publishing Company, 1970, p. 64. In Luckert, Karl W. (ed.) *Quotations on Evolution as a Theory*. 2001. http://web.archive.org/web/20011126101316/http://www.geocities.com/Area51/Rampart/4871/images/quotes.html.

34   Raup, David M. and Sepkoski, J. John Jr. "Mass Extinctions in the Marine Fossil Record," *Science* March 19, 1982, pp. 1501–1503. http://www.sciencemag.org/cgi/content/abstract/215/4539/1501.

35   Raup, David M. and Sepkoski, J. John Jr. "Periodicity of extinctions in the geologic past." Proc. Natl. Acad. Sci. USA, Vol. 81, pp. 801–805, February 1984. http://www.pnas.org/content/81/3/801.full.pdf.

36   Rohde, Robert A. & Muller, Richard A. "Cycles in fossil diversity," *Nature*, March 10, 2005. http://muller.lbl.gov/papers/Rohde-Muller-Nature.pdf.

37   Roach, Joan. "Mystery Undersea Evolution Cycle Discovered," *National Geographic News*, March 9, 2005. http://news.nationalgeographic.com/news/2005/03/0309_050309_extinctions.html.

38   Kazan, Casey. "Is There a Milky Way Galaxy/Earth Biodiversity Link? Experts Say 'Yes.'" *Daily Galaxy*, May 15, 2009. http://www.dailygalaxy.com/my_weblog/2009/05/hubbles-secret.html (accessed May 2010).

39   Evans, Mark. "Human genes are helping Texas A & M veterinarians unlock the genetic code of dolphins." NOAA Oceanographic and Atmospheric Research, 2000. http://web.archive.org/web/20030421105717/www.oar.noaa.gov/spotlite/archive/spot_texas.html (accessed May 2010).

40   Kettlewell, Julianna. "'Junk' throws up precious secret." BBC News Online, May 12, 2004. http://news.bbc.co.uk/2/hi/science/nature/3703935.stm.

41   Fosar, Grazyna and Bludorf, Franz. "The Living Internet (Part 2)." April 2002. http://web.archive.org/web/20030701194920/http://www.baerbelmohr.de/english/magazin/beitraege/hyper2.htm (accessed May 2010).

42   Ibid.

43   Ibid.

44   Choi, Charles Q. "Spider 'Resurrections' Take Scientists by Surprise". *National Geographic News*, April 24, 2009. http://news.nationalgeographic.com/news/2009/04/090424-spider-resurrection-coma-drowning.html (accessed May 2010).

45   Rockefeller University. "Parasite Breaks Its Own DNA to Avoid Detection." *ScienceDaily*, April 19, 2009. http://www.sciencedaily.com/releases/2009/04/090415141210.htm (accessed May 2010).

46   Wade, Nicholas. "Startling Scientists, Plant Fixes its Flawed Gene." *New York Times*, March 23, 2005. http://www.nytimes.com/2005/03/23/science/23gene.html.

47   Ibid.

48   Hitching, Francis. *The Neck of the Giraffe—Where Darwin Went Wrong*. Boston: Ticknor & Fields, 1982, pp. 56–57.

49   Hitching, Francis. *The Neck of the Giraffe—Where Darwin Went Wrong*. Op cit., p. 55.

50   McFadden, Johnjoe. *Quantum Evolution: Outline 2*. http://www.surrey.ac.uk/qe/Outline.htm (accessed May 2010).

51   Milton, Richard. *Shattering the Myths of Darwinism*. Rochester, VT: Park Street Press, 2000. http://web.archive.org/web/20040402182842/http://www.newsgateway.ca/darwin.htm (accessed May 2010).

52   McFadden, Johnjoe. *Quantum Evolution: Outline 2*. Op cit.

53 Sato, Rebecca, University of Massachusetts, "'Hyper-Speed' Evolution Possible? Recent Research Says 'Yes.'" *Daily Galaxy,* April 21, 2008. http://www.dailygalaxy.com/my_weblog/2008/04/scientists-disc.html (accessed May 2010).

54 Ibid.

55 Amazon.com Reviews on Jonathan Weiner. *The Beak of the Finch: A Story of Evolution in Our Time.* http://www.amazon.com/gp/product/product-description/067973337X/ref=dp_proddesc_0?ie=UTF8&n=283155&s=books (accessed May 2010.)

56 Milius, Susan. "Rapid Evolution May Be Reshaping Forest Birds' Wings." *Science News,* September 12, 2009. http://www.sciencenews.org/view/generic/id/46471/title/Rapid_evolution_may_be_reshaping_forest_birds%E2%80%99_wings (accessed July 2010).

57 Eichenseher, Tasha. "Goliath Tiger Fish: 'Evolution on Steroids' in Congo." *National Geographic News,* February 13, 2009. http://news.nationalgeographic.com/news/2009/02/photogalleries/monster-fish-congo-missions/index.html (accessed May 2010).

58 Than, Ker. "'Immortal' Jellyfish Swarm World's Oceans." *National Geographic News,* January 29, 2009. http://news.nationalgeographic.com/news/2009/01/090130-immortal-jellyfish-swarm.html (accessed May 2010).

59 Chen, Lingbao, et al. "Convergent evolution of antifreeze glycoproteins in Antarctic notothenoid fish and Arctic cod." Proc. Natl. Acad. Sci. USA, Vol. 94, pp. 3817–3822, April 1997. http://www.life.illinois.edu/ccheng/Chen%20et%20al-PNAS97b.pdf.

60 National Geographic Society. *PHOTOS: Odd, Identical Species Found at Both Poles.* February 15, 2009. http://news.nationalgeographic.com/news/2009/02/photogalleries/marine-census-deep-sea/ (accessed May 2010.)

61 Pasichnyk, Richard Michael. *The Vital Vastness, Volume 1: Our Living Earth,* p. 360. iUniverse/Writers Showcase, 2002. http://www.livingcosmos.com.

62 Dawson, Mary R., Marivaux, Laurent, Li, Chuan-kui, Beard, K. Christopher, and Metais, Gregoire. "Laonastes and the 'Lazarus Effect' in Recent Mammals," *Science,* March 10, 2006, pp. 1456–1458, http://www.sciencemag.org/cgi/content/abstract/311/5766/1456.

63 Carey, Bjorn. "Back From The Dead: Living Fossil Identified." LiveScience, March 9, 2006. http://www.livescience.com/animals/060309_living_fossil.html (accessed June 2010).

64 Van Tuerenhout, Dirk. "Of gompotheres, early American Indians, the Lazarus effect and the end of the world." Houston Museum of Natural Science Website, December 17, 2009. http://blog.hmns.org/?p=5922 (accessed June 2010).

65 Associated Press. "'Living fossil' found in Coral Sea." MSNBC Technology & Science, May 19, 2006. http://www.msnbc.msn.com/id/12875772/GT1/8199/.

66 United Press International. "A Jurassic tree grows in Australia." PhysOrg, October 17, 2005. http://www.physorg.com/news7303.html.

67 Ibid.

68 Dzang Kangeng Yu. V., "Bioelectromagnetic fields as a material carrier of biogenetic information." Aura-Z. 1993, N3, pp. 42–54.

69 Gariaev, Peter P., Tertishny, George G.,. and Leonova, Katherine A. "The Wave, Probabilistic and Linguistic Representations of Cancer and HIV." *Journal of Non-Locality and Remote Mental Interactions,* Vol. 1, No. 2. http://www.emergentmind.org/gariaevI2.htm (accessed May 2010).

70 Brekhman, Grigori. "Wave mechanisms of memory and information exchange between mother and her unborn child (Conception)." International Society of Prenatal and Perinatal Psychology and Medicine 2005. http://www.isppm.de/Congress_HD_2005/Brekhman_Grigori-Wave_mechanisms_of_memory.pdf (accessed May 2010.)

71   Dzang Kangeng Yu. V., "A method of changing biological object's hereditary signs and a device for biological information directed transfer. Application N3434801, invention priority as of 30.12.1981, registered 13.10.1992."

72   Gariaev, Peter P, Tertishny, George G and Leonova, Katherine A. *The Wave, Probabilistic and Linguistic Representations of Cancer and HIV.* Op cit.

73   Vintini, Leonardo. "The Strange Inventions of Pier L. Ighina," *The Epoch Times,* September 25-October 1, 2008, p. B6. http://epoch-archive.com/a1/en/us/bos/2008/09-Sep/25/B6.pdf (accessed June 2010).

74   Ibid.

75   Ibid.

76   Zajonc, R. B., Adelmann, P. K., Murphy, S. T., and Niedenthal, P. M., "Convergence in the physical appearance of spouses. Motivation and Emotion," 11(4), (1987), 335–346. http://www.spring.org.uk/2007/07/facial-similarity-between-couples.php.

77   Baerbel-Mohr. *DNA.* (Summary of the book *Vernetze Intelligenz* by von Grazyna Fosar and Franz Bludorf.) http://web.archive.org/web/20030407171420/http://home.planet.nl/~holtj019/GB/DNA.html.

78   Lever, Anna Marie. "Human evolution is 'speeding up.'" BBC News, December 11, 2007. http://news.bbc.co.uk/2/hi/science/nature/7132794.stm.

79   Kazan, Casey and Hill, Josh. "Is the Human Species in Evolution's Fast Lane?" *Daily Galaxy,* April 17, 2008. http://www.dailygalaxy.com/my_weblog/2008/04/is-the-human-sp.html.

80   Heylighen, F. "Increasing intelligence: the Flynn effect." Principia Cybernetica, August 22, 2000. http://pespmc1.vub.ac.be/FLYNNEFF.html.

81   Smith, Lewis. "Swimming orang-utans' spearfishing exploits amaze the wildlife experts." U.K. Times Online, April 28, 2008. http://www.timesonline.co.uk/tol/news/environment/article3828123.ece.

82   Silberman, Steve. "Placebos Are Getting More Effective. Drugmakers Are Desperate To Know Why." *Wired,* August 24, 2009. http://www.wired.com/medtech/drugs/magazine/17-09/ff_placebo_effect.

83   Ibid.

84   "Despite Frustrations, Americans are Pretty Darned Happy." ScienceDaily, July 1, 2008. http://www.sciencedaily.com/releases/2008/06/080630130129.htm.

85   "Happiness Lengthens Life." ScienceDaily, August 5, 2008. http://www.sciencedaily.com/releases/2008/08/080805075614.htm.

86   "'Happiness Gap' in U.S. Narrows." ScienceDaily, January 28, 2009. http://www.sciencedaily.com/releases/2009/01/090126121352.htm.

87   Jenkins, Simon. "New evidence on the role of climate in Neanderthal extinction." *EurekAlert,* September 12, 2007. http://www.eurekalert.org/pub_releases/2007-09/uol-neo091107.php.

88   Ibid.

89   Rincon, Paul. "Did Climate Kill Off the Neanderthals?" BBC News, February 13, 2009. http://news.bbc.co.uk/2/hi/science/nature/7873373.stm.

90   LiveScience Staff. Humans Ate Fish 40,000 Years Ago." LiveScience, July 7, 2009. http://www.livescience.com/history/090707-fish-human-diet.html.

91   Britt, Robert Roy. "Oldest Human Skulls Suggest Low-Brow Culture." LiveScience, February 16, 2005. http://www.livescience.com/health/050216_oldest_humans.html.

92   Ibid.

93   Lewis, James. "On Religion, Hitchens Is Not So Great." American Thinker, July 15, 2007. http://www.americanthinker.com/2007/07/on_religion_hitchens_is_not_so_1.html.

94 Ward, Peter. "The Father of All Mass Extinctions." Society for the Conservation of Biology/Conservation Magazine, 5, 3, 2004. http://www.conservationmagazine.org/articles/v5n3/the-father-of-all-mass-extinctions/.

95 Britt, Robert Roy. "Oldest Human Skulls Suggest Low-Brow Culture." LiveScience, February 16, 2005. http://www.livescience.com/health/050216_oldest_humans.html.

96 Ibid.

Chapter Eleven

1   Tennenbaum, Jonathan. "Russian Discovery Challenges Existence of 'Absolute Time.'" *21st Century Science and Technology Magazine,* Summer 2000. http://www.21stcenturysciencetech.com/articles/time.html.

2   S. E., Namiot V. A., Khohklov N. B., Sharapov M. P., Udaltsovan B., Dansky A. S., Sungurov A. Yu., Kolombet V. A., Kulevatsky D. P., Temnov A. V., Kreslavskaya N. B. and Agulova L. P. (1985). Discrete Amplitude Spectra (Histograms) of Macroscopic Fluctuations in Processes of Different Nature. Preprint IBF AN SSSR. Pushchino. 39 pp. (in Russian). In Levich, A. P. (ed.) *A Substantial Interpretation of N. A. Kozyrev's Conception of Time.* Singapore, New Jersey, London, Hong Kong: World Scientific, 1996, pp. 1–42. http://www.chronos.msu.ru/EREPORTS/levich2.pdf.

3   Tennenbaum, Jonathan. "Russian Discovery Challenges Existence of 'Absolute Time.'" *21st Century Science and Technology Magazine,* Summer 2000. http://www.21stcenturysciencetech.com/articles/time.html.

4   Jones, David. "Israel's Secret Weapon? A Toronto inventor may hold the key to Entebbe." *Vancouver Sun Times, Weekend Magazine,* Dec. 17, 1977, p. 17. http://www.rexresearch.com/hurwich/hurwich.htm.

5   Ibid.

6   Ibid.

7   Ibid.

8   Folger, Tim. "Newsflash: Time May Not Exist." *Discover Magazine,* June 12, 2007. http://discovermagazine.com/2007/jun/in-no-time.

9   Hafele, J. C. and Keating, Richard E. "Around-the-World Atomic Clocks: Predicted Relativistic Time Gains." *Science,* July 14, 1972, pp. 166–168. http://www.sciencemag.org/cgi/content/abstract/177/4044/166/.

10 Rindler, Wolfgang. *Essential Relativity: Special, General, and Cosmological.* New York: Springer-Verlag, 1979, p. 45.

11 Youngson, Robert. *Scientific Blunders: A brief history of how wrong scientists can sometimes be.* London: Constable & Robinson Publishing, 1998. http://www2b.abc.net.au/science/k2/stn/archives/archive53/newposts/415/topic415745.shtm.

12 Einstein, Albert. *Dialog über Einwande gegen die Relativitätstheorie.* Die Naturwissenschaften, 6 (1918) 697–702, in Kostro, Ludwik (ed,), *Albert Einstein's New Ether and his General Relativity.* Proceedings of the Conference of Applied Differential Geometry—General Relativity and the Workshop on Global Analysis, Differential Geometry and Lie Algebras, 2001, 78–86. http://www.mathem.pub.ro/proc/bsgp-10/0KOSTRO.PDF.

13 Einstein, Albert. *Aether und Relativitätstheorie,* Berlin: Verlag von J. Springer, 1920, in Kostro, Ludwik (ed.), *Albert Einstein's New Ether and his General Relativity.* Proceedings of the Conference of Applied Differential Geometry—General Relativity and the Workshop on Global Analysis, Differential Geometry and Lie Algebras, 2001, 78–86. http://www.mathem.pub.ro/proc/bsgp-10/0KOSTRO.PDF.

14 Tennenbaum, Jonathan. "Russian Discovery Challenges Existence of 'Absolute Time.'" Op cit.

15   Whitehouse, David. "Mystery force tugs distant probes." BBC News, May 15, 2001.
      http://news.bbc.co.uk/2/hi/science/nature/1332368.stm.

16   Choi, Charles Q. "NASA Baffled by Unexplained Force Acting on Space Probes."
      SPACE.com, March 3, 2008. http://www.space.com/scienceastronomy/080229-
      spacecraft-anomaly.html.

17   Ibid.

18   Moore, Carol. "Sunspot cycles and activist strategy." Carolmoore.net, February 2010.
      http://www.carolmoore.net/articles/sunspot-cycle.html.

19   Gribbin, John and Plagemann, Stephen. "Discontinuous Change in Earth's Spin Rate
      following Great Solar Storm of August 1972." *Nature,* May 4, 1973. http://www.nature
      .com/nature/journal/v243/n5401/abs/243026a0.html.

20   Mazzarella, A. and Palumbo, A. "Earth's Rotation and Solar Activity." Geophysical
      Journal International 97:1, 169-171. http://www3.interscience.wiley.com/journal/
      119443769/abstract.

21   R. Abarca del Rio, et al. "Solar Activity and Earth Rotation Variability." *Journal of Geo-
      dynamics* 36, 2003, pp. 423–443. http://www.cgd.ucar.edu/cas/adai/papers/Abarca_
      delRio_etal_JGeodyn03.pdf.

22   Ibid.

23   Ibid.

24   Djurovic, D. "Solar Activity And Relationships Between Astronomy And The Geosci-
      ences." Belgrade, Yugoslavia: Publications of the Department of Astronomy—Beograd,
      no. 18, 1990. http://elib.mi.sanu.ac.rs/files/journals/pda/18/broj18_clanak2.pdf.

25   Terdiman, Daniel. "Uh-Oh, Mercury's in Retrograde." *Wired,* September 15, 2003.
      http://www.wired.com/culture/lifestyle/news/2003/09/60424.

26   Terdiman, Daniel. "Tech problems due to Mercury in retrograde?" CNet News Blog,
      June 28, 2007. http://news.cnet.com/8301-10784_3-9737163-7.html.

27   O'Neill, Ian. "Is the Sun Emitting a Mystery Particle?" *Discovery News,* August 25, 2010.
      http://news.discovery.com/space/is-the-sun-emitting-a-mystery-particle.html (accessed
      December 2010).

28   Spottiswoode, S., and James, P. "Anomalous Cognition Effect Size: Dependence on
      Sidereal Time and Solar Wind Parameters." Palo Alto, CA: Cognitive Sciences Labora-
      tory. http://www.jsasoc.com/docs/PA-GMF.pdf.

29   Nelson, Roger. "GCP Background." Institute of Noetic Sciences. http://noosphere
      .princeton.edu/science2.html.

30   Ibid.

31   Ibid.

32   Nelson, R. D., Bradish, J., Dobyns, Y. H., Dunne, B. J., and Jahn, R. G . . . "Field REG
      Anomalies in Group Situations." *Journal of Scientific Exploration,* 10:111-42.(1996)

33   Nelson, Roger. "Consciousness and Psi: Can Consciousness Be Real?" Utrecht II: Chart-
      ing the Future of Parapsychology, October 2008, Utrecht, The Netherlands, in Global
      Consciousness Project, July 29, 2008. http://noosphere.princeton.edu/papers/pdf/
      consciousness.real.pdf.

34   Radin, Dean I., Rebman, Jannine M., and Cross, Maikwe P., "Anomalous Organization
      of Random Events by Group Consciousness: Two Exploratory Experiments." *Journal of
      Scientific Exploration,* 10, 1 (1996) pp. 143–168.

35   Nelson, Roger. *Consciousness and Psi: Can Consciousness Be Real?* Op cit.

36   Ibid.

37   Radin, Dean. "Global Consciousness Project Analysis for September 11, 2001." Institute
      of Noetic Sciences, 2001. http://noosphere.princeton.edu/dean/wtc0921.html.

38   Radin, Dean. "Terrorist Disaster, September 11, 2001: Exploratory Analysis." Institute of
     Noetic Sciences, 2001. http://noosphere.princeton.edu/exploratory.analysis.html.
39   Ibid.
40   Braden, Gregg. *Fractal Time: The Secret of 2012 and a New World Age.* Carlsbad, CA: Hay
     House Publishers, 2009, p. 193.
41   Radin, Dean. "Formal Analysis, September 11, 2001." Institute of Noetic Sciences, 2001.
     http://noosphere.princeton.edu/911formal.html.
42   Nelson, Roger. "Barack Obama Elected President." Institute of Noetic Sciences, 2008.
     http://noosphere.princeton.edu/obama.elected.html.
43   Nelson, Roger. "Barack Obama Inaugurated as President." Institute of Noetic Sciences.
     http://noosphere.princeton.edu/obama.inauguration.html.
44   Nelson, Roger. "Global Harmony." Global Consciousness Project. http://noosphere
     .princeton.edu/groupmedit.html.
45   Williams, Brian. "GCP Technical Note: Global Harmony Revisited." Global Conscious-
     ness Project, 2004. http://noosphere.princeton.edu/williams/GCPGlobalHarmonyBW
     .pdf.
46   Swanson, Claude V. *The Synchronized Universe: New Science of the Paranormal.* Tucson,
     AZ: Poseidia Press, 2003, p. 102.

Chapter Twelve

1   Puthoff, Hal. Institute for Advanced Studies. Austin, Texas. http://www.earthtech.org/
     iasa/index.html.
2   Haramein, Nassim. "Haramein Paper Wins Award!" The Resonance Project. http://
     theresonanceproject.org/best_paper_award.html (accessed June 2010).
3   Crane, Oliver, Lehner, J. M., and Monstein, C. "Central Oscillator and Space-Quanta
     Medium." June 2000. http://www.rqm.ch, http://www.rexresearch.com/monstein/
     monstein.htm (accessed June 2010).
4   Overbye, Dennis. "A Scientist Takes On Gravity." *New York Times,* July 12, 2010. http://
     www.nytimes.com/2010/07/13/science/13gravity.html?_r=2 (accessed December 2010).
5   Wright, Walter. *Gravity Is a Push.* New York: Carlton Press, 1979.
6   Aspden, Harold. "Discovery of Virtual Inertia." *New Energy News,* 2, pp. 1–2. (1995).
     http://www.aspden.org/papers/bib/1995f.htm (accessed December 2010).
7   Watson, Lyall. *Supernature.* New York: Doubleday/Bantam Books, 1973, p. 90.
8   Grebennikov, Viktor. "Cavity Structural Effect and Insect Antigravity." Rex Research,
     November 2001. http://www.rexresearch.com/grebenn/grebenn.htm (accessed June
     2010).
9   Akimov, A. E. and Shipov, G. I. "Torsion Fields and their Experimental Manifestations."
     Proceedings of International Conference: New Ideas in Natural Science. 1996. http://
     www.amasci.com/freenrg/tors/tors.html.
10   Levich, A. P. "A Substantial Interpretation of N. A. Kozyrev's Conception of Time."
     Singapore, New Jersey, London, Hong Kong: *World Scientific,* 1996, pp. 1–42. http://
     www.chronos.msu.ru/EREPORTS/levich2.pdf.
11   Kozyrev, Nikolai. "Possibility of Experimental Study of Properties of Time." September
     1967. http://www.astro.puc.cl/~rparra/tools/PAPERS/kozyrev1971.pdf.
12   Ibid.
13   Ibid.
14   DePalma, Bruce. "On the Nature of Electrical Induction." July 28, 1993. http://depalma
     .pair.com/Absurdity/Absurdity09/NatureOfElectricalInduction.html (accessed June
     2010).

15   Müller, Hartmut. Global Scaling Theory. http://globalscalingtheory.com/ (accessed May 2010).

16   Baerbel-Mohr. "The free of charge bio-mobile phone." May 6, 2001. http://web.archive .org/web/20021018142034/http://baerbelmohr.de/english/magazin/beitraege/20010506_ bio_mobile.htm (accessed May 2010).

17   Levich, A. P. A Substantial Interpretation of N. A. Kozyrev's Conception of Time. Op cit.

18   Kozyrev, N. A. (1977). "Astronomical observations using the physical properties of time." In *Vspykhivayushchiye Zvezdy* (Flaring Stars). Yerevan, pp. 209–227. See also: Kozyrev N. A. (1991). *Selected Works*. Leningrad, pp. 363–383. From: Levich, A. P., A *Substantial Interpretation of N. A. Kozyrev's Conception of Time*. Singapore, New Jersey, London, Hong Kong: World Scientific, 1996, pp. 1–42. http://www.chronos.msu.ru/EREPORTS/ levich2.pdf.

19   Nachalov, Yu. V. *Theoretical Basis of Experimental Phenomena*. http://www.amasci.com/ freenrg/tors/tors3.html.

20   Kozyrev, Nikolai. "Possibility of Experimental Study of Properties of Time. Op cit.

21   Dong, Paul and Raffill, Thomas E. *China's Super Psychics*. New York: Marlowe and Company, 1997.

22   Swanson, Claude V. *The Synchronized Universe: New Science of the Paranormal*. Tucson, AZ: Poseidia Press, 2003, pp. 116–117.

23   Ibid., p. 204.

Chapter Thirteen

1   Saetang, David. "Great Scott! Scientists Claim Time Travel is Possible." *PCWorld*, January 18, 2011. http://www.pcworld.com/article/216946/great_scott_scientists_claim_ time_travel_is_possible.html?tk=mod_rel (accessed January 2011).

2   Nairz, Olaf; Zeilinger, Anton, and Arndt, Markus. "Quantum interference experiments with large molecules." American Association of Physics Teachers, October 30, 2002. http://hexagon.physics.wisc.edu/teaching/2010s%20ph531%20quantum%20mechanics/ interesting%20papers/zeilinger%20large%20molecule%20interference%20ajp%202003 .pdf (accessed June 2010).

3   Markus Arndt, Olaf Nairz, Julian Voss-Andreae, Claudia Keller, Gerbrand van der Zouw and Anton Zeilinger. "Wave-particle duality of C60." *Nature* 401, October 14, 1999. pp. 680-682.

4   Ibid.

5   Olaf Nairz, Björn Brezger, Markus Arndt, and Anton Zeilinger. "Diffraction of the Fullerenes C60 and C70 by a standing light wave." October, 2001. http://www.univie .ac.at/qfp/research/matterwave/stehwelle/standinglightwave.html (accessed June 2010).

6   Olaf Nairz, Björn Brezger, Markus Arndt, and Anton Zeilinger, Diffraction of Complex Molecules by Structures Made of Light, *Physical Review Letters* 87, 160401 (2001).

7   Folger, Tim. "Newsflash: Time May Not Exist." *Discover Magazine*, June 12, 2007. http:// discovermagazine.com/2007/jun/in-no-time.

8   Ibid.

9   Nehru, K. "Quantum Mechanics' as the Mechanics of the Time Region." *Reciprocity*, Spring 1995, pp. 1–9; revised February 1998. http://library.rstheory.org/articles/KVK/ QuantumMechanics.html (accessed June 2010).

10   Nehru, K. "Precession of the Planetary Perihelia Due to Co-ordinate Time." Reciprocal System Theory Library, March 16, 2009. http://library.rstheory.org/articles/KVK/ PrecPlanetPeri.html (accessed June 2010).

11   Peret, Bruce. "Frequently Asked Questions—Reciprocal Theory." http://rstheory.org/
     faq/9 (accessed June 2010).

12   Ashley, Dave. "Dave Ashley's House o' Horrors." April 29, 1998. http://www.xdr.com/
     dash/ (accessed June 2010).

13   Ashley, Dave. "Law of One Material and Dewey B Larson's Physics." James Randi Edu-
     cational Foundation, January 30, 2008. http://forums.randi.org/showthread.php
     ?t=105001 (accessed June 2010).

14   Peret, Bruce. *Frequently Asked Questions—Reciprocal Theory.* Op cit.

15   Berlitz, Charles. *The Bermuda Triangle.* New York: Avon Books, 1974, pp. 124–125.

16   Caidin, Martin. *Ghosts of the Air.* Lakeview, MN: Galde Press/Barnes and Noble, 2007,
     original edition 1991, p. 223.

17   Ibid., pp. 223–226.

18   Peret, Bruce. RS Theory Website. International Society for Unified Science. http://rstheory
     .org (accessed June 2010).

19   Julien, Eric. *The Science of Extraterrestrials.* Fort Oglethorpe, GA: Allies Publishing,
     October 10, 2006.

20   Ginzburg, Vladimir B. "About the Paper." Spiral Field Theory Website, 2000. http://
     web.archive.org/web/20010217014501/http://www.helicola.com/about.html.

21   Levich, A. P. "A Substantial Interpretation of N. A. Kozyrev's Conception of Time."
     Singapore, New Jersey, London, Hong Kong: World Scientific, 1996, pp. 17–18. http://
     www.chronos.msu.ru/EREPORTS/levich2.pdf.

22   Ibid.

23   Ibid., p. 32.

24   "Spinning Ball Experiment." Bruce DePalma website. 2010. http://www.brucedepalma
     .com/n-machine/spinning-ball-experiment/ (accessed June 2010).

25   Ibid.

26   Ibid.

27   DePalma, Bruce. "Understanding the Dropping of the Spinning Ball Experiment."
     Simularity Institute, May 3, 1977. http://depalma.pair.com/SpinningBall%28
     Understanding%29.html (accessed June 2010).

Chapter Fourteen

1   Yam, Philip. "Bringing Schrödinger's Cat to Life." *Scientific American,* June 1997, p. 124.

2   McTaggart, Lynne. *The Field: The Quest for the Secret Force of the Universe.* New York:
     HarperCollins, 2002, p. 28.

3   MacPherson, Kitta. "Princeton scientists discover exotic quantum states of matter."
     News at Princeton, April 24, 2008. http://www.princeton.edu/main/news/archive/
     S20/90/55G21/index.xml?section=topstories (accessed December 2010).

4   Dmitriev, A. N., Dyatlov, V. L., and Merculov, V. I. "Electrogravidynamic Concept of
     Tornadoes." The Millennium Group. http://www.tmgnow.com/repository/planetary/
     tornado.html (accessed June 2010).

5   Ibid.

6   Cerveny, Randy. *Freaks of the Storm—From Flying Cows to Stealing Thunder, The World's
     Strangest True Weather Stories.* New York: Thunder's Mouth Press, 2006, p. 31.

7   Dmitriev, A. N., Dyatlov, V. L., and Merculov, V. I. *Electrogravidynamic Concept of
     Tornadoes.* Op cit.

8   National Weather Service. "Grand Rapids, MI: The April 3, 1956 Tornado Outbreak."
     NOAA, May 20, 2010. http://www.crh.noaa.gov/grr/science/19560403/vriesland_
     trufant/eyewitness/ (accessed June 2010).

9   Blozy, Stephanie. "Can a Tornado Drive a Piece of Straw Into a Tree?" WeatherBug, July 2005. http://web.archive.org/web/20060523120043/http://blog.weatherbug.com/Stephanie/index.php?/stephanie/comments/can_a_tornado_drive_a_piece_of_straw_into_a_tree/ (accessed June 2010).

10 Ibid.

11 Cerveny, Randy. *Freaks of the Storm*, Op. cit., p. 30.

12 Ibid., p. 33.

13 Ibid., pp. 35, 44.

14 Ibid., p. 35.

15 Ibid., pp. 36–37.

16 Washburn University/KTWU. Stories of the '66 Topeka Tornado—Personal Topeka Tornado Stories. http://ktwu.washburn.edu/productions/tornado/stories.htm (accessed June 2010).

17 San, Vee and Pean, Yoke. "Pictures of Things from the Sky." Oracle ThinkQuest Education Foundation. http://library.thinkquest.org/C004978F/arrivals_pics.htm (accessed June 2010).

18 Hannah, James. "Odd items populate museum exhibit." *The Beacon Journal,* June 20, 2004. http://web.archive.org/web/20041031125254/http://www.ohio.com/mld/beaconjournal/news/state/8973306.htm (accessed June 2010).

19 National Weather Service. *Grand Rapids, MI: The April 3, 1956 Tornado Outbreak.* Op cit.

20 Alexandersson, Olof. *Living Water: Viktor Schauberger and the Secrets of Natural Energy.* Houston, TX: Newleaf, 1982, 1990, 2002, p. 22.

21 Ibid., p. 23.

22 Wagner, Orvin E. "Dr. Ed Wagner.." Wagner Research Laboratory, July 2007. http://home.budget.net/~oedphd/Edbio.html (accessed June 2010).

23 Wagner, Orvin E. "A Basis for a Unified Theory for Plant Growth and Development." *Physiological Chemistry and Physics and Med. NMR* (1999) 31:109-129. http://home.budget.net/~oedphd/plants/unified.html (accessed June 2010).

24 Ibid.

25 Grebennikov, Viktor. "Cavity Structural Effect and Insect Antigravity." Rex Research, November 2001. http://www.rexresearch.com/grebenn/grebenn.htm (accessed June 2010).

26 "An anti-gravity platform of V. S. Grebbenikov." New Energy Technologies 3(22): 58–74 (2005). http://www.rexresearch.com/grebenn2/greb2.htm (accessed June 2010).

27 Davidson, Dan. "Free Energy, Gravity and the Aether." KeelyNet, October 18, 1997. http://www.keelynet.com/davidson/npap1.htm (accessed June 2010).

28 Cathie, Bruce. "Acoustic Levitation of Stones." In Childress, David Hatcher (ed.), *Anti-Gravity and the World Grid.* Kempton, IL: Adventures Unlimited Press, 1987, 1995, pp. 211–216.

29 Alexandersson, Olof. *Living Water: Viktor Schauberger and the Secrets of Natural Energy.* Houston, TX: Newleaf, 1982, 1990, 2002.

30 Cook, Nick. *The Hunt for Zero Point: Inside the Classified World of Antigravity Technology.* New York: Broadway Books, 2002, pp. 228–229, 234.

31 Grebennikov, Viktor. *Cavity Structural Effect and Insect Antigravity.* Op cit.

32 Ibid.

33 Ibid.

34 Ibid.

35 Ibid.

36 Ibid.

37 "An anti-gravity platform of V. S. Grebbenikov." Op cit.

38 Cassidy, Kerry; Novel, Gordon and Ryan, Bill. "Renegade: Gordon Novel on Camera." Project Camelot, Los Angeles, December 2006. http://projectcamelot.org/lang/en/gordon_novel_interview_transcript_en.html (accessed June 2010).

39 Kirkpatrick, Sidney. *Edgar Cayce: An American Prophet*. New York: Riverhead Books, 2000, pp. 123–124.

40 Cayce, Edgar. Reading 195-54. Association for Research and Enlightenment, January 13, 1929. http://all-ez.com/nofuel2.htm (accessed June 2010).

41 Kirkpatrick, Sidney. *Edgar Cayce: An American Prophet*. Op cit., pp. 123–124.

42 "Tesla's New Monarch of Machines." New York Herald. October 15, 1911. http://www.tfcbooks.com/tesla/1911-10-15.htm.

43 Vassilatos, Gerry. *Lost Science*. Bayside, CA: Borderland Sciences Research Foundation, 1997, 1999. http://www.hbci.com/~wenonah/history/brown.htm (accessed June 2010).

44 Cassidy, Kerry; Ring, Ralph, and Ryan, Bill. "Aquamarine Dreams: Ralph Ring and Otis T. Carr." Project Camelot, Las Vegas, August 2006. http://projectcamelot.org/ralph_ring.html (accessed June 2010).

45 Ibid.

46 Ibid.

47 Ibid.

48 Cassidy, Kerry; Ring, Ralph and Ryan, Bill. "Ralph Ring Interview Transcript." Project Camelot, Las Vegas, August 2006. http://projectcamelot.org/lang/en/ralph_ring_interview_transcript_en.html (accessed June 2010).

49 Ibid.

50 Spiegel, Lee. "Nuclear Physicist Describes Vast UFO Cover-Up." AOL News, June 7, 2010. http://www.aolnews.com/weird-news/article/stanton-friedman-a-scientist-searches-for-the-truth-of-ufos/19503350 (accessed June 2010).

51 Roschin, V. and Godin, S. "Magneto-Gravitational Converter. (Searl Effect Generator)" Summary/List of Technical Papers. Rex Research. http://www.rexresearch.com/roschin/roschin.htm (accessed June 2010).

52 Moore, Terry. "SEG Voltage Controlled Demonstration." YouTube, March 26, 2007. http://www.youtube.com/watch?v=z8qvSNkiB9M (accessed June 2010).

53 David-Neel, Alexandra. *With Mystics and Magicians in Tibet*. Chapter VI: Psychic Sports. London" Penguin Books, 1931. http://www.scribd.com/doc/21029489/With-Mystics-and-Magicians-in-Tibet.

54 Ibid.

55 Swanson, Claude V. *The Synchronized Universe: New Science of the Paranormal*. Tucson, AZ: Poseidia Press, 2003, pp. 105–111.

56 Ibid., p. 108.

Chapter Fifteen

1 Caidin, Martin. *Ghosts of the Air*. Lakeview, MN: Galde Press/Barnes and Noble, 1991, 2007, p. 206.

2 Quasar, Gian J. *Into the Bermuda Triangle*. New York: International Marine/McGraw Hill, 2004, p. 1.

3 Grigonis, Richard. *Ivan T. Sanderson*. Chapter 13: Downfall. Richard Grigonis/Society for the Investigation of the Unexplained, 2009, 2010. http://www.richardgrigonis.com/Ch13%20Downfall.html (accessed June 2010).

4 Ibid.

5 Ibid.

6 Ibid.

7   Paranormal Encyclopedia. "Vile Vortices." http://www.paranormal-encyclopedia.com/v/ vile-vortices/ (accessed June 2010).

8   Grigonis, Richard. *Ivan T. Sanderson Op cit.*

9   Jochmans, Joseph. "Earth: A Crystal Planet?" *Atlantis Rising,* Spring 1996. http://web .archive.org/web/19990128233845/http://atlantisrising.com/issue7/ar7cryspi.html (accessed June 2010).

10 Ibid.

11 Ibid.

12 Becker, William and Hagens, Beth. "The Planetary Grid: A New Synthesis." *Pursuit Journal of the Society for the Investigation of the Unexplained,* Vol. 17, No. 4 (1984). http:// missionignition.net/bethe/planetary_grid.php.

13 Ibid.

14 Wood, Dave; Piper, Anne, and Nunn, Cindy. "Gloucestershire's ley lines." BBC Gloucestershire History, June 29, 2005. http://www.bbc.co.uk/gloucestershire/content/articles/ 2005/06/29/ley_lines_feature.shtml (accessed June 2010).

15 Jochmans, Joseph. "Earth: A Crystal Planet?" Op cit.

16 "Athelstan Frederick Spilhaus: Lieutenant Colonel, United States Army. American Memory obituary. Died March 30, 1998." Arlington National Cemetery, http://www .arlingtoncemetery.net/spilhaus.htm (accessed June 2010).

17 Manbreaker, Crag. "Glossary of Physical Oceanography: Sn-Sz, Spilhaus, Athelstan (1912–1998)." UNESCO, August 17, 2001. http://web.archive.org/web/20030916211451/ http://ioc.unesco.org/oceanteacher/resourcekit/M3/Data/Measurements/Parameters/ Glossaries/ocean/node36.html (accessed June 2010).

18 Ibid.

19 University of California Museum of Paleontology. "Plate Tectonics: The Rocky History of an Idea." University of California at Berkeley, August 22, 1997. http://www.ucmp .berkeley.edu/geology/techist.html (accessed June 2010).

20 Luckert, Carl W. Plate Expansion Tectonics. http://www.triplehood.com/expa.htm (accessed June 2010).

21 Maxlow, James. "Quantification of an Archean to Recent Earth Expansion Process Using Global Geological and Geophysical Data Sets." Curtin University of Technology Ph.D. Thesis, 2001. http://espace.library.curtin.edu.au/R?func=dbin-jump-full&local_ base=gen01-era02&object_id=9645 (accessed June 2010).

22 Maxlow, James. Global Expansion Tectonics. November 1999. http://web.archive.org/ web/20080801082348/http://www.geocities.com/CapeCanaveral/Launchpad/6520/ (accessed June 2010).

23 Ollier, Cliff. "Exceptional Planets and Moons, and Theories of the Expanding Earth." *New Concepts in Global Tectonics Newsletter,* December 2007. http://www.ncgt.org/ newsletter.php?action=download&id=52.

24 Roehl, Perry O. "A Commentary. Let's Cut to the Chase: Plate Tectonics Versus Expansion of the Planet." *Society of Independent Professional Earth Scientists/SIPES Quarterly,* February, 2006. http://www.sipes.org/Newsletters/NewsltrFeb06.pdf (accessed June 2010).

25 Schneider, Michael. "Crystal at the Center of the Earth: Anisotropy of Earth's Inner Core." Projects in Scientific Computing, Pittsburgh Supercomputing Center, 1996. http://www.psc.edu/science/Cohen_Stix/cohen_stix.html (accessed June 2010).

26 Glatzmaier, Gary A., Coe, Robert S., Hongre, Lionel, and Roberts, Paul H. "The role of the earth's mantle in controlling the frequency of geomagnetic reversals." *Nature,* October 28, 1999, pp. 885–890. http://www.es.ucsc.edu/~rcoe/eart110c/Glatzmaieretal_ SimRev_Nature99.pdf (accessed June 2010).

27   Buffett, Bruce A. "Earth's Core and the Geodynamo." *Science,* June 16, 2000, pp. 2007–
      2012. http://www.sciencemag.org/cgi/content/abstract/288/5473/2007 (accessed June
      2010).

28   Singh, S. C., Taylor, M. A. J., Montagner, J. P. "On the Presence of Liquid in Earth's
      Inner Core." *Science,* pp. 2471–2474. http://bullard.esc.cam.ac.uk/~taylor/Abstracts/
      SCIENCE_Published_InnerCore.pdf (accessed June 2010).

29   U.S. Geological Survey. "Inner Core." U.S. National Report to IUGG, 1991–1994. *Rev.
      Geophys.* Vol. 33, Suppl., © 1995 American Geophysical Union (accessed June 2010).
      http://web.archive.org/web/20071009130628/http://www.agu.org/revgeophys/trompo1/
      node2.html.

30   Jacobs, J. A. "The Earth's inner core." *Nature* 172 (1953), pp. 297–298. http://www.nature
      .com/nature/journal/v172/n4372/pdf/172297a0.pdf (accessed June 2010).

31   Levi, Barbara Goss. "Understanding Why Sound Waves Travel Faster along earth's Axis
      in the Inner Core." Physics Today Online, Search & Discovery, November 2001, p. 17.
      http://web.archive.org/web/20050213235821/http://www.physicstoday.org/pt/vol-54/
      iss-11/p17.html (accessed June 2010).

32   Hoagland, Richard C. *The Monuments of Mars: A City on the Edge of Forever.* Berkeley:
      North Atlantic Books, 1992.

33   Hoagland, Richard C. and Torun, Erol O. "The 'Message of Cydonia': First Communi-
      cation from an Extraterrestrial Civilization?" *The Enterprise Mission,* 1989. http://www
      .enterprisemission.com/message.htm (accessed January 2011).

34   Jenny, Hans. "Cymatics—A Study of Wave Phenomena." MACROmedia. (accessed June
      2010.) McTaggart, Lynne. *The Field: The Quest for the Secret Force of the Universe.* New
      York: HarperCollins, 2002.

35   Nehru, K. "The Wave Mechanics in the Light of the Reciprocal System." Reciprocal
      System Library, August 19, 2008. http://library.rstheory.org/articles/KVK/Wave
      Mechanics.html.

36   Ibid.

37   Wilcock, David. *The Divine Cosmos—Convergence Volume Three.* Chapter 4: The Sequen-
      tial Perspective. http://divinecosmos.com/index.php?option=com_content&task=view&
      id=98&Itemid=36 (accessed June 2010).

38   Carter, James. Absolute Motion Institute. http://www.circlon-theory.com/HTML/
      about.html (accessed June 2010).

39   Hecht, Lawrence. "Who Was Robert J. Moon?" 21st Century Science and Technology.
      http://www.21stcenturysciencetech.com/articles/drmoon.html (accessed June 2010).

40   Hecht, Lawrence. "The Moon Model of the Nucleus." 21st Century Science and Technol-
      ogy. http://www.21stcenturysciencetech.com/moonsubpg.html (accessed June 2010).

41   Moon, Robert J. "Robert J. Moon on How He Conceived His Nuclear Model." Tran-
      script of a Presentation in Leesburg, VA, September 4, 1987. *21st Century Science and
      Technology,* Fall 2004, pp. 8–20. http://www.21stcenturysciencetech.com/Articles%20
      2005/moon_F04.pdf (accessed June 2010).

42   Hecht, Laurence. "Advances in Developing the Moon Nuclear Model." 21st Century
      Science and Technology, 2004. http://www.21stcenturysciencetech.com/articles/moon_
      nuc.html.

43   Wilcock, David. *The Divine Cosmos—Convergence Volume Three.* Chapter 4: The Sequen-
      tial Perspective. Op cit.

44   Mallove, Eugene. "MIT and Cold Fusion: A Special Report." Infinite Energy 24, 1999.
      http://www.infinite-energy.com/images/pdfs/mitcfreport.pdf (accessed June 2010).

45   Hecht, Laurence. "Advances in Developing the Moon Nuclear Model." Op cit.

46   Hecht, Laurence. "The Geometric Basis for the Periodicity of the Elements." *21st Century Science and Technology*, May–June 1988, p. 18. http://www.21stcenturysciencetech.com/Articles%202004/Spring2004/Periodicity.pdf (accessed June 2010).

47   Duncan, Michael A. and Rouvray, Dennis H. "Microclusters." *Scientific American*, 261(6), 1989, pp. 110–115. http://www.subtleenergies.com/ormus/research/research.htm.

48   Sugano, Satoru and Koizumi, Hiroyasu. *Microcluster Physics: Second Edition*. Berlin, Heidelberg, New York: Springer-Verlag, 1998.

49   Gardner, Lawrence. "Ormus Products & M-State Elements." Graal.co.uk. http://graal.co.uk/whitepowdergold.php (accessed December 2010).

50   Ibid.

51   Ibid.

52   Fouche, Edgar. "Secret Government Technology." 2000. http://web.archive.org/web/20001202132200/http://www.fouchemedia.com/arap/speech.htm (accessed June 2010).

53   Ibid.

54   Vassilatos, Gerry. *Lost Science*. Bayside, CA: Borderland Sciences Research Foundation, 1997, 1999. http://www.hbci.com/~wenonah/history/brown.htm (accessed June 2010).

55   Ibid.

56   Ibid.

57   Ibid.

58   Ibid.

59   White, Mark. "Introducing: The Perfect Code Theory." Rafiki Incorporated Website. http://www.codefun.com/Genetic.htm (accessed December 2010).

60   Ibid.

Chapter Sixteen

1   Martineau, John. *A Little Book of Coincidence*. New York: Wooden Books/Walker & Company, 1995, 2001, 2002.

2   "Prince Charles Explores 'Mysterious Unity' of the Universe in New Book." *The Huffington Post*. November 24, 2010. http://www.huffingtonpost.com/2010/11/24/prince-charles-harmony_n_786565.html (accessed December 2010).

3   Martineau, John. *A Little Book of Coincidence*. Op cit., p. 12.

4   Ibid., p. 14.

5   "Prince Charles Explores 'Mysterious Unity' of the Universe in New Book." Op cit.

6   Wilcock, David. "The 'Matrix' Is a Reality." *Divine Cosmos*, April 10, 2003. http://divinecosmos.com/index.php/component/content/49?task=view (accessed December 2010).

7   Battaner, E. and Florido, E. "The rotation curve of spiral galaxies and its cosmological implications." *Fund. Cosmic Phys.* 21 (2000) 1–154. http://nedwww.ipac.caltech.edu/level5/March01/Battaner/node48.html (accessed December 2010).

8   Battaner, E. The fractal octahedron network of the large scale structure. *Astronomy and Astrophysics*, 334 No. 3 (1998), pp. 770–771. http://arxiv.org/pdf/astro-ph/9801276 (accessed December 2010).

9   Haramein, Nassim. "A Scaling Law for Organized Matter in the Universe." American Physical Society, October 4-6, 2001. http://adsabs.harvard.edu/abs/2001APS..TSF.AB006H (accessed December 2010).

10   Whitehouse, David. "Map Reveals Strange Cosmos." BBC News Online, March 3, 2003. http://news.bbc.co.uk/2/hi/science/nature/2814947.stm (accessed December 2010).

11   Dumé, Belle. "Is the Universe a Dodecahedron?" PhysicsWorld.com, October 8, 2003. http://physicsworld.com/cws/article/news/18368 (accessed December 2010).

12 "Veintena." Wikipedia. http://en.wikipedia.org/wiki/Veintena (accessed June 2010).

13 "Mayan Calendar." Wikipedia. http://en.wikipedia.org/wiki/Mayan_calendar (accessed June 2010).

14 Miller, Mary and Taube, Karl. *The Gods and Symbols of Ancient Mexico and the Maya: An Illustrated Dictionary of Mesoamerican Religion.* London: Thames & Hudson, (1993). pp. 48–50.

15 Peden, Robert. *The Mayan Calendar: Why 260 Days?* 1981, updated May 24 and June 15, 2004. Robert Pendon Website http://www.spiderorchid.com/mesoamerica/mesoamerica.htm (accessed June 2010).

16 Ibid.

17 Ibid.

18 Chatelain, Maurice. (1977). *Our Ancestors Came from Outer Space.* New York: Dell Books 1977.

19 Van Flandren, Thomas. (2000). *The Exploded Planet Hypothesis 2000.* Meta Research Website. http://www.metaresearch.org/solar%20system/eph/eph2000.asp (accessed December 2010).

20 Ibid.

21 "Core Spins Faster Than Earth, Scientists Find." National Science Foundation. Press Release 96-038, July 17, 1996. http://www.nsf.gov/news/news_summ.jsp?cntn_id=101771&org=NSF.

22 "Core Spins Faster Than Earth, Lamont Scientists Find." Lamont-Doherty Earth Observatory, 2005. http://www.columbia.edu/cu/record/archives/vol22/vol22_iss1/Core_Spin.html (accessed June 2010).

23 Ibid.

24 Yukutake, Takesi. "Effect on the Change in the Geomagnetic Dipole Moment on the Rate of the Earth's Rotation." In Melchior, Paul J and Yumi, Shigeru (eds.), *Rotation of the earth: International Astronomical Union Symposium no. 48,* Morioka, Japan, May 9–15, 1971, p. 229.

25 Niroma, Tino. "One Possible Explanation for the Cyclicity in the Sun: Sunspot cycles and supercycles, and their tentative causes. June–December 1998. http://personal.inet.fi/tiede/tilmari/sunspots.html (accessed June 2010).

26 Ibid. http://personal.inet.fi/tiede/tilmari/sunspot4.html#bassuper (accessed June 2010).

27 Ibid. http://personal.inet.fi/tiede/tilmari/sunspot5.html (accessed June 2010).

28 Fosar, Graznya and Bludorf, Franz. "The TLR Factor: Mysterious temporal and local patterns in aircraft crashes." http://www.fosar-bludorf.com/archiv/tlr_eng.htm (accessed June 2010).

29 N. Capitaine, et al. "Expressions for IAU 2000 precession quantities." Astronomy & Astrophysics 412, (2003), 567–586. http://www.aanda.org/articles/aa/abs/2003/48/aa4068/aa4068.html.

30 Holland, Earle. "Major Climate Change Occurred 5,200 Years Ago: Evidence Suggests that History Could Repeat Itself." *Ohio State University Research News,* December 15, 2004. http://researchnews.osu.edu/archive/5200event.htm (accessed June 2010).

31 Ibid.

32 Wilcock, David. (2000) *The Shift of the Ages—Convergence Volume One.* Chapter 16: Maurice Cotterell and the Great Solar Cycle. http://divinecosmos.com/index.php/start-here/books-free-online/18-the-shift-of-the-ages/72-the-shift-of-the-ages-chapter-16-maurice-cotterell-and-the-great-sunspot-cycle (accessed December 2010).

33 "Calendar Round." Wikipedia. http://en.wikipedia.org/wiki/Calendar_Round (accessed June 2010).

34 "Mayan Calendar." Wikipedia. http://en.wikipedia.org/wiki/Mayan_calendar (accessed June 2010).

35 "Magnetic Portals Connect Sun and Earth." Science@NASA (November 2,2008). *ScienceDaily.* http://www.sciencedaily.com/releases/2008/11/081101093713.htm (accessed December 2010).

36 "Clumps And Streams of Dark Matter May Lie In Inner Regions of Milky Way." University of California—Santa Cruz (August 7, 2008). *ScienceDaily.* http://www.sciencedaily.com/releases/2008/08/080806140124.htm (accessed December 2010).

37 Zyga, Lisa. "Million-Degree Plasma May Flow throughout the Galaxy." PhysOrg.com, February 7, 2008. http://www.physorg.com/news121602545.html (accessed December 2010).

Chapter Seventeen

1 Laursen, Chris. "Rock the House." Sue St. Clair and Matthew Didier's Paranormal Blog, June 20, 2007. http://seminars.torontoghosts.org/blog/index.php/2007/06/20/weird_wednesday_with_chris_laursen_29 (accessed June 2010).

2 Ibid.

3 Ibid.

4 Walsh, Dave. Blather.com, October 8, 1998. http://www.blather.net/blather/1998/10/super_sargasso_surfin.html.

5 Gudger, E. W. "Rains of Fishes." *Natural History,* November-December 1921. http://web.archive.org/web/20040423135240/http://www.naturalhistorymag.com/editors_pick/1921_11-12_pick.html.

6 Ibid.

7 UPI. "Fish rain on Australian town." March 1, 2010. http://www.upi.com/Odd_News/2010/03/01/Fish-rain-on-Australian-town/UPI-83001267492501/.

8 Cremo, Michael A. and Thompson, Richard L. *Forbidden Archeology.* Los Angeles, CA: Bhaktivedanta Book Publishing, 1998. http://www.forbiddenarcheology.com/anomalous.htm.

9 Twietmeyer, Ted. "How Solid Matter Can Pass Through Rock." Rense.com, June 19, 2005. http://www.rense.com/general66/solid.htm.

10 Bondeson, Jan. "Toad in the Hole." *Fortean Times,* June 2007. http://www.forteantimes.com/features/articles/477/toad_in_the_hole.html.

11 Ibid.

12 Ibid.

13 Krystek, Lee. "Entombed Animals." The Museum of Unnatural Mystery. http://www.unmuseum.org/entombed.htm (accessed June 2010).

14 Ibid.

15 Ibid.

16 Ibid.

17 Bondeson, Jan. "Toad in the Hole." Op cit.

18 Ibid.

19 Dmitriev, A. N., Dyatlov, V. L., Tetenov, A. V. "Planetophysical Function of Vacuum Domains." The Millennium Group. http://www.tmgnow.com/repository/planetary/pfvd.html.

20 Gearhart, L. and Persinger, M. A. (1986) Geophysical variables and behavior: XXXIII (accessed June 2010). "Onsets of historical and contemporary poltergeist episodes occurred with sudden increases in geomagnetic activity." *Perceptual and Motor Skills* 62 (2), pp. 463–466.

21 Ruffles, Tom. "Fields and Consciousness." *Society for Psychical Research,* Winter 1992. http://www.spr.ac.uk/main/page/online-library.

22   Kundt, Wolfgang. "The Search for the Evasive 1908 Meteorite Continues." Tunguska 2001 Conference Report. http://lists.topica.com/lists/tunguska/read/message.html?mid =801582031&sort=d&start=25 (accessed June 2010).

23   Natural Resources Canada. "The Atlas of Canada: Location of Kimberlites." March 11, 2009. http://atlas.nrcan.gc.ca/site/english/maps/economic/diamondexploration/ locationofkimberlites/1.

24   Dmitriev, A. N., Dyatlov, V L., Litasov, K. D. "Physical Model of Kimberlite Pipe Formation: New Constraints from Theory of Non-Homogenous Physical Vacuum." Extended Abstract of the 7th International Kimberlite Conference, Cape Town, South Africa, 1998, pp. 196–198. http://www.tmgnow.com/repository/planetary/kimberlite.html.

25   Dmitriev, A. N., Dyatlov, V. L., Tetenov, A. V. "Planetophysical Function of Vacuum Domains." Op cit.

26   Dmitriev, Alexei N. "Planetophysical State of the Earth and Life." IICA Transactions, Volume 4, 1997. http://www.tmgnow.com/repository/global/planetophysical.html (accessed June 2010).

27   Ibid.

28   Ibid.

29   Randles, Jenny. *Time Storms: Amazing Evidence for Time Warps, Space Rifts and Time Travel.* New York: Piaktus/Berkley, 2001, 2002.

30   Ibid., pp. 49–50.

31   Ibid., pp. 51–53.

32   Ibid., pp. 54–55.

33   Ibid., pp. 70–71.

34   Ibid., pp. 77–78.

35   Ibid., pp. 167–168.

36   Ibid., pp. 172–174.

37   Ibid., pp. 188–191.

38   Vallee, Jacques. *Dimensions: A Casebook of Alien Contact.* Chicago: Contemporary Books, 1988, p. 84.

39   Thompson, Richard. *Alien Identities: Ancient Insights into Modern UFO Phenomena.* Alachua, FL: Govardhan Hill, Inc., 1993, Revised Second Edition 1995.

40   Ibid., p. 282.

41   Ibid., pp. 282–283.

42   Ibid., p. 283.

43   Ibid., p. 289.

44   Essortment. *The Loch Ness Monster of Scotland.* http://www.essortment.com/loch-ness-monster-scotland-33544.html (accessed January 2011).

45   Malvern, Jack. "Archives reveal belief in Loch Ness Monster." *The Times,* April 27, 2010. http://www.timesonline.co.uk/tol/news/uk/scotland/article7109019.ece (accessed June 2010).

46   Dinsdale, Tim. (1961) *Loch Ness Monster.* p. 42. In Wikipedia. *Loch Ness Monster.* http:// en.wikipedia.org/wiki/Loch_Ness_Monster (accessed June 2010).

47   Bauer, Henry H. "The Case for the Loch Ness Monster: The Scientific Evidence." *Journal of Scientific Exploration,* 16(2): pp. 225–246 (2002). http://henryhbauer.homestead .com/16.2_bauer.pdf (accessed January 2011).

48   Mystical Blaze Website. "The Loch Ness Monster." http://www.mysticalblaze.com/ MonstersNessie.htm (accessed January 2011).

49   "Is Caddy a mammal?" *Science Frontiers,* May–June 1993, p. 2; Park, Penny, "Beast from the Deep Puzzles Zoologists." *New Scientist,* January 23, p. 16.

50   "Russian fishermen demand an investigation into killer Nesski's 19 lake deaths in three years."
     Daily Mail, July 12, 2010. http://www.dailymail.co.uk/news/worldnews/article-1293955/
     Russian-fishermen-demand-investigation-killer-Nesski.html (accessed December 2010).

51   Collins, Nick. "New photo of 'English Nessie' hailed as best yet." *Daily Mail,* February
     18, 2011. http://www.telegraph.co.uk/news/newstopics/howaboutthat/8332535/New-
     photo-of-English-Nessie-hailed-as-best-yet.html (accessed February 2011).

52   Petsev, Nik. "Mokele-Mbembe." Cryptozoology.com, 2002. http://www.cryptozoology
     .com/cryptids/mokele.php (accessed June 2010).

53   Unknown Explorers. "Mokele-Mbembe." 2006. http://www.unknownexplorers.com/
     mokelembembe.php (accessed June 2010).

54   Irwin, Brian. "Theropod and Sauropod Dinosaurs Sighted in PNG?" Creation Ministries
     International. http://creation.com/theropod-and-sauropod-dinosaurs-sighted-in-png
     (accessed June 2010).

55   *The Independent* (Papua New Guinea.) December 30, 1999, p. 6. In Creation Ministries
     International. "A Living Dinosaur?" Creation 23 (1): p. 56, December 2000. http://
     creation.com/a-living-dinosaur (accessed June 2010).

56   Irwin, Brian. "Theropod and Sauropod Dinosaurs Sighted in PNG?" Op cit.

57   Lai Kuan and Jian Qun, "Dinosaurs: Alive and Well and Living in Northwest China?,"
     China Today, February 1993, p. 59, In Doolan, Robert (ed.) "Are dinosaurs alive today?
     Where Jurassic Park Went Wrong." Creation 15 (4): pp. 12-15, September 1993. http://
     www.answersingenesis.org/creation/v15/i4/dinosaurs.asp.

58   Ibid.

59   Davies, Kyle L. "Duckbill Dinosaurs (Hadrosauridae, Ornithischia) from the North
     Slope of Alaska," *Journal of Paleontology,* Vol. 61 No. 1, pp. 198–200.

60   All About Creation. *Marco Polo in China FAQ.* (Accessed June 2010.) http://www
     .allaboutcreation.org/marco-polo-in-china-faq.htm.

61   All About Creation. "Dragon History." http://www.allaboutcreation.org/dragon-history
     .htm (accessed June 2010).

62   All About Creation. "Dragon History 3." http://www.allaboutcreation.org/dragon-
     history-3.htm (accessed June 2010).

63   All About Creation. "Dragon History 4." http://www.allaboutcreation.org/dragon-
     history-4.htm (accessed June 2010).

64   All About Creation. "Dinosaur Sightings." http://www.allaboutcreation.org/dinosaur-
     sightings-faq.htm (accessed June 2010).

65   Conger, Joe. "Sightings of mysterious bird continue in San Antonio." MySanAntonio
     .com, July 28, 2007. http://web.archive.org/web/20071011031437rn_1/www.mysanantonio
     .com/news/metro/stories/MYSA072707.mysterybird.KENS.ba5c450e.html (accessed
     June 2010).

66   Ibid.

67   Whitcomb, Jonathan. "Apparent Living Pterosaurs Seen by 1400 Americans, According
     to Author Jonathan Whitcomb." 24-7 Press Release, Long Beach, CA, August 19, 2009.
     http://www.24-7pressrelease.com/press-release/apparent-living-pterosaurs-seen-by-1400-
     americans-according-to-author-jonathan-whitcomb-112924.php.

68   Whitcomb, Jonathan. "Searching for Ropens: Nonfiction book on living pterosaurs in
     Papua New Guinea." http://www.searchingforropens.com/ (accessed June 2010).

69   Whitcomb, Jonathan. "Author Jonathan Whitcomb Reports Glowing Creatures Video-
     taped in Papua New Guinea." Long Beach, CA/Eworldwire, February 7, 2007. http://
     www.eworldwire.com/pressreleases/16421.

70 Parker, Chris. "Pteranodon on a Stick: Egyptian 'Was' Scepter Creature No Mystery Without Darwinian History." S8int.com, September 28, 2009. http://s8int.com/WordPress/?p=1433.

71 "Reassessing the marvellous mammoths." *The Age* (Melbourne), March 29, 1993.

72 "The elephant that time forgot." *The Mail on Sunday,* May 23, 1993.

73 "Dinosaurs in ancient Cambodia temple." The Interactive Bible. http://www.bible.ca/tracks/tracks-cambodia.htm (accessed January 2011).

74 Fort, Charles. (1925) *New Lands.* Part II, pp. 535. http://www.sacred-texts.com/fort/land/land38.htm (accessed January 2011).

Chapter Eighteen

1 Smith, Eugene. "Gene Smith's Astronomy Tutorial: The Structure of the Milky Way." University of California, San Diego Center for Astrophysics & Space Sciences. April 28, 1999. http://casswww.ucsd.edu/public/tutorial/MW.html.

2 Speer, B. R. "Introduction to the Archaean—3.8 to 2.5 billion years ago." Berkeley UCMP, March 9, 1997. http://www.ucmp.berkeley.edu/precambrian/archaean.html.

3 Charity, Mitchell N. "Geologic Time Scale—as 18 Rotations." http://www.vendian.org/mncharity/dir3/geologic_time_galactic/.

4 Dalrymple, G. B. *The Age of the Earth.* Palo Alto, CA: Stanford University Press, 1991.

5 "The Big Bang." Wikipedia. http://en.wikipedia.org/wiki/The_Big_Bang.

6 Sobel, Dava. "Man Stops Universe, Maybe." *Discover Magazine,* April 1993. http://discovermagazine.com/1993/apr/manstopsuniverse206.

7 Ibid.

8 Godlowski, W., Bajan, K., and Flin, P. "Weak redshift discretization in the Local Group of galaxies?" *Astronomische Nachrichten,* January 16, 2006, pp. 103–113.,http://www3.interscience.wiley.com/journal/112234726/abstract?CRETRY=1&SRETRY=0.

9 Bajan, K., Flin, P., Godlowski, W. and Pervushin, V. N. "On the investigations of galaxy redshift periodicity." *Physics of Particles and Nuclei Letters,* February 2007. http://www.springerlink.com/content/qt7454133824p423/.

10 Bell, M. B. and Comeau, S. P. "Further Evidence for Quantized Intrinsic Redshifts in Galaxies: Is the Great Attractor a Myth?" May 7, 2003. http://arxiv.org/abs/astro-ph/0305112.

11 Napier, W. M. and Guthrie, B. N. G. "Quantized redshifts: A status report." *Journal of Astrophysics and Astronomy,* December 1997. http://www.springerlink.com/content/qk27v4wx16412245/.

12 Aspden, Harold. "Tutorial Note 10: Tifft's Discovery." Energy Science, 1997. http://web.archive.org/web/20041126005134/http://www.energyscience.org.uk/tu/tu10.htm.

13 Ibid.

14 Tifft, W. G. "Three-Dimensional Quantized Time in Cosmology." SASTPC.Org, January 1996. http://articles.adsabs.harvard.edu/cgi-bin/nph-iarticle_query?db_key=AST&bibcode=1996Ap%26SS.244..187T&letter=.&classic=YES&defaultprint=YES&whole_paper=YES&page=187&epage=187&send=Send+PDF&filetype=.pdf.

15 Ibid.

16 Ibid.

17 "NASA Study Finds Increasing Solar Trend that can Change Climate." NASA Goddard Space Flight Center, March 20, 2003. http://www.gsfc.nasa.gov/topstory/2003/0313irradiance.html.

18 Suplee, Curt. "Sun Studies May Shed Light on Global Warming." *Washington Post,* October 9, 2000, p. A13. http://www.washingtonpost.com/wp-dyn/articles/A35885-2000Oct8.html.

19 Bartlett, Kristina. "ACEing the sun." American Geophysical Union/Geotimes News Notes, April 1999. http://www.geotimes.org/apr99/newsnotes.html.

20 Whitehouse, David Ph.D. "What is Happening to the Sun?" BBC News Online, November 4, 2003. http://news.bbc.co.uk/2/hi/science/nature/3238961.stm.

21 Hogan, Jenny. "Sun More Active than for a Millennium." *New Scientist*, November 2, 2003. http://www.newscientist.com/article/dn4321-sun-more-active-than-for-a-millennium.html

22 Leidig, Michael and Nikkah, Roya. "The truth about global warming: it's the Sun that's to blame." *The Telegraph*, July 18, 2004. http://www.telegraph.co.uk/science/science-news/3325679/The-truth-about-global-warming-its-the-Sun-thats-to-blame.html.

23 Solanki, et al. "Carbon-14 Tree Ring Study." Max Planck Institute, November 2004. http://www.mpg.de/495993/pressRelease20041028.

24 Phillips, Tony. "Long Range Solar Forecast." Science@NASA, May 10, 2006. http://science.nasa.gov/science-news/science-at-nasa/2006/10may_longrange/ (accessed December 2010).

25 *Changes in the Sun's Surface to Bring Next Climate Change.* NASA Space and Science Research Center. Press Release SSRC-1-2008. January 2, 2008. http://web.archive.org/web/20080106054533/http://www.spaceandscience.net/id16.html.

26 Phillips, Tony. "Deep Solar Minimum." Science@NASA, April 1, 2009. http://science.nasa.gov/science-news/science-at-nasa/2009/01apr_deepsolarminimum/ (accessed December 2010).

27 Spinney, Laura. "The sun's cooling down—so what does that mean for us?" *The Guardian*, April 23, 2009. http://www.guardian.co.uk/science/2009/apr/23/sun-cooling-down-space-climate (accessed December 2010).

28 Ghosh, Pallab. "'Quiet Sun' baffling astronomers." BBC News, April 21, 2009. http://news.bbc.co.uk/2/hi/science/nature/8008473.stm (accessed December 2010).

29 Hanlon, Michael. "Meltdown! A solar superstorm could send us back into the dark ages—and one is due in just THREE years." Mail Online, April 19, 2009. http://www.dailymail.co.uk/sciencetech/article-1171951/Meltdown-A-solar-superstorm-send-dark-ages—just-THREE-years.html (accessed December 2010).

30 Than, Ker. "Sun Blamed for Warming of Earth and Other Worlds." LiveScience, March 12, 2007. http://www.livescience.com/environment/070312_solarsys_warming.html (accessed December 2010).

31 Jong, Diana. "Mysteries of Mercury: New Search for Heat and Ice." Space.com, December 31, 2002. http://web.archive.org/web/20090523002302/http://www.space.com/scienceastronomy/mysteries_mercury_021231.html.

32 Ibid.

33 Campbell, Paulette. "NASA Spacecraft Streams Back Surprises from Mercury." NASA, April 29, 2008. http://www.nasa.gov/mission_pages/messenger/multimedia/jan_media_conf.html (accessed June 2010).

34 Bates, Claire. "Mysterious Mercury: Probe reveals magnetic twisters and mammoth crater on hottest planet." Mail Online, May 5, 2009. http://www.dailymail.co.uk/sciencetech/article-1176069/Mysterious-Mercury-Probe-reveals-magnetic-twisters-mammoth-crater-hottest-planet.html (accessed June 2010).

35 Grossman, Lisa. "This Just In: Mercury More Exciting than Mars." Wired Science, April 30, 2009. http://www.wired.com/wiredscience/2009/04/messengermercury/ (accessed December 2010).

36 Bullock, Mark, et al. "New Climate Modeling of Venus May Hold Clues to Earth's Future." University of Colorado at Boulder News, February 18, 1999. http://www.colorado.edu/news/r/ce03b3e37c81e0d2649470f69ec1056a.html.

37 Resnick, Alice. "SRI International Makes First Observation of Atomic Oxygen Emission in the Night Airglow of Venus." SRI International, January 18, 2001. http://www.sri .com/news/releases/01-18-01.html.

38 "Night-time on Venus." Physics Web. January 18, 2001. http://www.physicsweb.org/ article/news/5/1/10.

39 Perew, Mark. "Evidence of Atomic Oxygen Challenges Understanding of Venus." Universe Today, January 19, 2001: http://www.universetoday.com/html/articles/2001-0119a .html.

40 Hecht, Jeff. "Planet's Tail of the Unexpected." New Scientist, May 31, 1997. http://web .archive.org/web/19970605230452/http://www.newscientist.com/ns/970531/nvenus.html (also see http://www.holoscience.com/news/balloon.html).

41 Courtland, Rachel. "Mysterious bright spot found on Venus." New Scientist, July 29, 2009. http://www.newscientist.com/article/dn17534-mysterious-bright-spot-found-on-venus.html (accessed December 2010).

42 Ibid.

43 Savage, Don, et al. "Hubble Monitors Weather on Neighboring Planets." HubbleSite News Center, March 21, 1995, no. 16. http://hubblesite.org/newscenter/archive/releases/ 1995/16/text.

44 Wheaton, Bill. "JPL and NASA News." November 1997. http://www.wwheaton.com/ waw/canopus/canopus_9711.html.

45 Villard, Ray, et al. "Colossal Cyclone Swirls Near Martian North Pole." HubbleSite News Center, May 19, 1999, no. 22. http://hubblesite.org/newscenter/archive/releases/ 1999/22/.

46 Savage, Don, Hardin, Mary, Villard, Ray, Neal, Nancy. "Scientists Track 'Perfect Storm' on Mars." HubbleSite NewsCenter, October 11, 2001, no. 31. http://hubblesite .org/newscenter/archive/releases/2001/31/text/.

47 Britt, Robert Roy. "Mars Ski Report: Snow Is Hard, Dense and Disappearing." Space .com, Dec. 6, 2001. http://web.archive.org/web/20100820112631/http://www.space.com/ scienceastronomy/solarsystem/mars_snow_011206-1.html.

48 Mullen, Leslie. "Night-side glow detected at Mars." Astrobiology Magazine/SPACE .com, January 31, 2005. http://www.space.com/737-night-side-glow-detected-mars .html.

49 NASA/JPL. "Voyager Science at Jupiter: Magnetosphere." Jet Propulsion Laboratory, California Institute of Technology. http://voyager.jpl.nasa.gov/science/jupiter_magneto sphere.html.

50 Bagenal, Fran, et al. "Jupiter: The Planet, Satellites and Magnetosphere, Chapter 1: Introduction." 2004. http://dosxx.colorado.edu/JUPITER/PDFS/Ch1.pdf.

51 Ibid.

52 Guillot, Tristan, et al. "Jupiter: The Planet, Satellites and Magnetosphere, Chapter 3: The Interior of Jupiter." 2004. http://dosxx.colorado.edu/JUPITER/PDFS/Ch3.pdf.

53 Bolton, Scott J.. et al. "Jupiter: The Planet, Satellites and Magnetosphere, Chapter 27: Jupiter's Inner Radiation Belts." 2004. http://dosxx.colorado.edu/JUPITER/PDFS/ Ch27.pdf.

54 Yang, Sarah. "Researcher predicts global climate change on Jupiter as giant planet's spots disappear." UC Berkeley Press Release, April 21, 2004. http://www.berkeley.edu/news/ media/releases/2004/04/21_jupiter.shtml.

55 Britt, Robert Roy. "Jupiter's spots disappear amid major climate change." USA TODAY/ Tech/Space.com, April 22, 2004. http://www.usatoday.com/tech/news/2004-04-22-jupiter-spots-going_x.htm.

56 Goudarzi, Sara. "New Storm on Jupiter Hints at Climate Change." Space.com, May 4, 2006. http://www.space.com/scienceastronomy/060504_red_jr.html (accessed December 2010).

57 Shiga, David. "Jupiter's raging thunderstorms a sign of 'global upheaval.'" *New Scientist,* January 23, 2008. http://space.newscientist.com/article/dn13217-jupiters-raging-thunderstorms-a-sign-of-global-upheaval.html (accessed December 2010).

58 Ibid.

59 Spencer, J. (Lowell Observatory) and NASA. "Hubble Discovers Bright New Spot on Io." Hubble News Center, October 10, 1995, No. 37. http://hubblesite.org/newscenter/newsdesk/archive/releases/1995/37/.

60 Murrill, Mary Beth and Isabell, Douglas. "High-Altitude Ionosphere Found at Io by Galileo Spacecraft." NASA/Goddard Space Flight Center, Release 96-216, October 23, 1996. http://nssdc.gsfc.nasa.gov/planetary/text/gal_io_ionosphere.txt.

61 Morton, Carol. "Scientists find solar system's hottest surfaces on Jupiter's moon Io." NASA/The Brown University News Bureau, July 2, 1998. http://www.brown.edu/Administration/News_Bureau/1998-99/98-001.html.

62 "PIA01637: Io's Aurorae." NASA/JPL Planetary Photojournal, October 13, 1998. http://photojournal.jpl.nasa.gov/catalog/PIA01637.

63 Porco, Carolyn, et al. "Cassini Imaging of Jupiter's Atmosphere, Satellites, and Rings." *Science,* 299 (5612) 1541–1547, March 7, 2003. http://www.sciencemag.org/content/299/5612/1541/suppl/DC1.

64 Russell, C T., et al., "Io's Interaction with the Jovian Magnetosphere." *Eos, Transactions, American Geophysical Union,* Vol. 78, No. 9 (1997), pp. 93, 100. http://www-ssc.igpp.ucla.edu/personnel/russell/papers/Io_Jovian/.

65 Saur, Joachim, et al. "Jupiter: The Planet, Satellites and Magnetosphere, Chapter 22: Plasma Interaction of Io with its Plasma Torus." http://dosxx.colorado.edu/JUPITER/PDFS/Ch22.pdf.

66 Schneider, N. M., et al. "Substantial Io Torus Variability 1998-2000." NASA Planetary Astronomy Program, DPS 2001 meeting, November 2001. http://aas.org/archives/BAAS/v33n3/dps2001/513.htm?q=publications/baas/v33n3/dps2001/513.htm.

67 Buckley, Michael, et al. "Johns Hopkins Applied Physics Lab Researchers Discover Massive Gas Cloud Around Jupiter." JHU Applied Physics Laboratory, February 27, 2003. http://www.jhuapl.edu/newscenter/pressreleases/2003/030227.asp.

68 McGrath, Melissa, et al. "Jupiter: The Planet, Satellites and Magnetosphere, Chapter 19: Satellite Atmospheres." 2004. http://dosxx.colorado.edu/JUPITER/PDFS/Ch19.pdf.

69 Ibid.

70 Ibid.

71 Stenger, Richard. "New revelations, riddles about solar system's most intriguing satellites." CNN.com/Space, August 23, 2000. http://archives.cnn.com/2000/TECH/space/08/23/moons.of.mystery/index.html.

72 McGrath, Melissa, et al. "Jupiter: The Planet, Satellites and Magnetosphere, Chapter 19: Satellite Atmospheres." Op cit.

73 Platt, Jane. "New Class of Dust Ring Discovered Around Jupiter." NASA/JPL Press Release, April 3, 1998. http://www.jpl.nasa.gov/releases/98/glring.html.

74 Merali, Zeeya. "Milky Way's two stellar halos have opposing spins." NewScientist.com, December 12, 2007. http://space.newscientist.com/article/dn13043-milky-ways-two-stellar-halos-have-opposing-spins.html (accessed December 2010).

75 Sittler, Ed, et al. "Pickup Ions at Dione and Enceladus: Cassini Plasma Spectrometer Simulations." NASA/Goddard Space Flight Center/Journal of Geophysical Research, Vol. 109: January 20, 2004. http://caps.space.swri.edu/caps/publications/Sittler.pdf.

76 Trauger, J. T., et al. "Hubble Provides the First Images of Saturn's Aurorae." HubbleSite NewsCenter, October 10, 1995, no. 39. http://hubblesite.org/newscenter/newsdesk/archive/releases/1995/39/—see also http://hubblesite.org/newscenter/newsdesk/archive/releases/1998/05/.

77 "Mysterious glowing aurora over Saturn confounds scientists." Mail Online, November 13, 2008. http://www.dailymail.co.uk/sciencetech/article-1085354/Mysterious-glowing-aurora-Saturn-confounds-scientists.html (accessed December 2010).

78 Hill, Mary Ann. "Saturn's Equatorial Winds Decreasing: Spanish-American Team's Findings Raise Question About Planet's Atmosphere." Wellesley College News Release, June 4, 2003. http://www.wellesley.edu/PublicAffairs/Releases/2003/060403.html.

79 Roy, Steve and Watzke, Megan. "X-rays from Saturn pose puzzles." NASA/Marshall Space Flight Center News Release #04-031, March 8, 2004. http://www.nasa.gov/centers/marshall/multimedia/photos/2004/photos04-031.html.

80 "Overview: Saturn." NASA Solar System Exploration. http://solarsystem.nasa.gov/planets/profile.cfm?Object=Saturn&Display=OverviewLong.

81 Finn, Heidi. "Saturn Details Become Visible to Cassini Spacecraft." NASA GISS Research News, December 5, 2003. http://ciclops.lpl.arizona.edu/PR/2003L05/NR2003L05A.html.

82 Porco, Carolyn. "Approach to Saturn Begins." Cassini Imaging Central Laboratory for Observations News Release. February 27, 2004. http://www.ciclops.org/index/54/Approach_to_Saturn_Begins.

83 Associated Press. "Scientists Studying Saturn Lightning Storm." February 15, 2006. http://web.archive.org/web/20060217224253/http://apnews.myway.com/article/20060215/D8FPC9K8B.html (accessed December 2010).

84 Harvard-Smithsonian Center for Astrophysics. "Titan Casts Revealing Shadow." Chandra X-Ray Observatory Photo Album Web site of NASA/SAO. April 5, 2004. http://chandra.harvard.edu/photo/2004/titan/.

85 "A dense, hazy atmosphere at least 400 kilometers (250 miles) thick obscures the surface [of Titan.]" In Woodfill, Jerry. The Satellites of Saturn: Titan. NASA JSC Space Educator's Handbook, Last Updated February 11, 2000. http://web.archive.org/web/20060827091938/http://vesuvius.jsc.nasa.gov/er/seh/satsaturn.html.

86 Brown, Michael E., et al. "Direct detection of variable tropospheric clouds near Titan's south pole." Nature, December 2002. http://www.gps.caltech.edu/~mbrown/papers/ps/titan.pdf.

87 Sittler, Ed, et al. "Pickup Ions at Dione and Enceladus: Cassini Plasma Spectrometer Simulations." NASA/Goddard Space Flight Center/Journal of Geophysical Research, Vol. 109: January 20, 2004. http://caps.space.swri.edu/caps/publications/Sittler.pdf.

88 Moskowitz, Clara. "Tropical Storm Spotted on Saturn's Moon Titan." LiveScience, August 12, 2009. http://www.livescience.com/space/090812-titan-clouds.html (accessed December 2010).

89 NASA/Karkoschka, Erich, et al. "Huge Spring Storms Rouse Uranus from Winter Hibernation." HubbleSite NewsCenter, March 29, 1999, no. 11. http://hubblesite.org/newscenter/archive/releases/1999/11/text/.

90 Karkoschka, Erich, et al. "Hubble Finds Many Bright Clouds on Uranus." HubbleSite NewsCenter, October 14, 1998, no. 35. http://hubblesite.org/newscenter/archive/releases/1998/35/.

91 NASA/Karkoschka, Erich, et al. Huge Spring Storms Rouse Uranus from Winter Hibernation. Op cit.

92 NASA. "Huge Storms Hit the Planet Uranus." Science@NASA Web site, March 29, 1999. http://science.nasa.gov/science-news/science-at-nasa/1999/ast29mar99_1/.

93 McLachlan, Sean. "UA scientists look closely at Uranus." University of Arizona Daily Wildcat, March 30, 1999. http://wc.arizona.edu/papers/92/123/01_3_m.html.

94 "1.29 Completed WF/PC-2 8634 (Atmospheric Variability on Uranus and Neptune)." Period Covered: 09/29/00-10/02/00. Hubble Space Telescope Daily Report #2719. http://www.stsci.edu/ftp/observing/status_reports/old_reports_00/hst_status_10_02_00.

95 Sromovsky, Lawrence A., et al., Press Release, University of Wisconsin, Madison, November 2004. http://www.news.wisc.edu/10402.html.

96 de Pater, et al., Press Release, UC Berkeley, November 2004. http://www.berkeley.edu/news/media/releases/2004/11/10_uranus.shtml.

97 Encrenaz, T., et al. "First detection of CO in Uranus." Observatoire de Paris Press Release, SpaceRef.com, December 17, 2003. http://www.spaceref.com/news/viewpr.html?pid=13226.

98 Perlman, David. "Rare edge-on glimpse of Uranus' rings reveals graphic changes." San Francisco Chronicle, August 24, 2007. http://www.sfgate.com/cgi-bin/article.cgi?f=/c/a/2007/08/24/MNS5RNAVQ.DTL&type=science (accessed December 2010).

99 Savage, Don, et al. "Hubble Discovers New Dark Spot on Neptune." HubbleSite News-Center, April 19, 1995. http://hubblesite.org/newscenter/newsdesk/archive/releases/1995/21/text/.

100 Sromovsky, Lawrence, et al., University of Wisconsin-Madison. "Hubble Provides a Moving Look at Neptune's Stormy Disposition." ScienceDaily Magazine, October 15, 1998. http://www.sciencedaily.com/releases/1998/10/981014075103.htm.

101 Sromovsky, Lawrence A., et al. "Neptune's Increased Brightness Provides Evidence for Seasons." University of Wisconsin-Madison Space Science and Engineering Center, April 22, 2002. http://www.ssec.wisc.edu/media/Neptune2003.htm.

102 Associated Press. "Scientists: Cold Neptune has a warm spot." CNN.com, September 21, 2007. http://web.archive.org/web/20071005070400/http://www.cnn.com/2007/TECH/space/09/21/neptune.ap/index.html (accessed December 2010).

103 Halber, Deborah. "MIT researcher finds evidence of global warming on Neptune's largest moon." MIT News, June 24, 1998. http://web.mit.edu/newsoffice/1998/triton.html.

104 Savage, Don, Weaver, Donna, and Halber, Deborah. "Hubble Space Telescope Helps Find Evidence that Neptune's Largest Moon Is Warming Up." HubbleSite NewsCenter, June 24, 1998, no. 23. http://hubblesite.org/newscenter/newsdesk/archive/releases/1998/23/text/.

105 Britt, Robert Roy. "Puzzling Seasons and Signs of Wind Found on Pluto." Space.com, 2003. http://web.archive.org/web/20090629054158/http://www.space.com/scienceastronomy/pluto_seasons_030709.html.

106 Halber, Deborah. "Pluto is undergoing global warming, researchers find." MIT News, October 9. 2002. http://web.mit.edu/newsoffice/2002/pluto.html.

107 Britt, Robert Roy. "Global Warming on Pluto Puzzles Scientists." Space.com, October 9, 2002. http://www.space.com/scienceastronomy/pluto_warming_021009.html (accessed December 2010).

108 Halber, Deborah. "Pluto's Atmosphere is Expanding, Researchers Say." Massachusetts Institute of Technology Spaceflight Now News Release, July 9, 2003. http://www.spaceflightnow.com/news/n0307/09pluto/.

109 Halber, Deborah. "Pluto is undergoing global warming, researchers find." Op. cit.

110 Britt, Robert Roy. "Puzzling Seasons and Signs of Wind Found on Pluto." Op. cit.

111 Associated Press. "Hubble sees Pluto changing color, ice sheet cover." February 4, 2010. http://current.com/news/92072563_hubble-sees-pluto-changing-color-ice-sheet-cover.htm (accessed December 2010).

112 Ibid.

113 Baker, Daniel, et al. "Radiation Belts Around Earth Adversely Affecting Satellites." American Geophysical Union/University of Colorado at Boulder News, December 7, 1998. http://www.scienceblog.com/community/older/1998/C/199802852.html.

114 Schewe, Phillip F. and Stein, Ben. "Physics News Update." The American Institute of Physics Bulletin of Physics News, May 27, 1993. http://www.aip.org/enews/physnews /1993/split/pnu130-1.htm.

115 "Explorers: Searching the Universe Forty Years Later." NASA Goddard Space Flight Center. October 1998: FS-1998(10)-018-GSFC. http://www.nasa.gov/centers/goddard/ pdf/106420main_explorers.pdf.

116 "Wayward satellite can be seen from Earth: CNN Interviews Columbia Astronauts." CNN Interactive/Technology News Service, February 27, 1996. http://web.archive.org/ web/20080614225040/http://www.cnn.com/TECH/9602/shuttle/02-27/index.html.

117 "Shuttle Astronauts Lament Loss of Satellite." CNN Interactive/Technology News, February 27, 1996. http://www.cnn.com/TECH/9602/shuttle/02-26/crew_reax/index.html.

118 "Wayward satellite can be seen from Earth: CNN Interviews Columbia Astronauts." Op. cit.

119 "Failed satellite experiment a devastating blow: A probe into the Columbia mission is under way." CNN Interactive/Technology News Service, February 26, 1996. http://web .archive.org/web/20080614224953/http://www.cnn.com/TECH/9602/shuttle/02-26/ index.html.

120 Day, Charles. "New Measurements of Hydroxyl in the Middle Atmosphere Confound Chemical Models." Physics Today Online, Vol. 53, No. 11, p. 17, 2001. http://web.archive .org/web/20071030074008/http://www.aip.org/pt/vol-53/iss-11/p17.html.

121 Ibid.

122 Osterbrock, Don, et al. "Telescope Studies of Terrestrial and Planetary Nightglows." SRI International, July 23, 2001. http://www-mpl.sri.com/projects/pyu02424.html.

123 Adam, David. "Goodbye Sunshine." *Guardian Unlimited*, December 18, 2003. http:// www.guardian.co.uk/science/2003/dec/18/science.research1.

124 Ibid.

125 Madrigal, Alexis. "Mysterious, Glowing Clouds Appear Across America's Night Skies." Wired Science, July 16, 2009. http://www.wired.com/wiredscience/2009/07/nightclouds/ (accessed December 2010).

126 Ibid.

127 UNEP/WMO Intergovernmental Panel on Climate Change. Climate Change 2001: Working Group I: The Scientific Basis. Chapter 2: Observed Climate Variability and Change, Executive Summary. UNEP/WMO/IPCC, 2001. http://www.grida.no/ climate/ipcc_tar/wg1/049.htm.

128 Levitus, Sydney. "Temporal variability of the temperature-salinity structure of the world ocean." NOAA/NWS, The 10th Symposium on Global Climate Change Studies. Rutgers University. http://marine.rutgers.edu/cool/education/Sydney.htm.

129 Piola, A. R., Mestas Nunez, A. M., and Enfield, D. B. "South Atlantic Ocean Temperature Variability: Vertical Structure and Associated Climate Fluctuations." International Association for the Physical Sciences of the Oceans, IC02-49 Oral. http://web.archive.org/ web/20060925034528/http://www.olympus.net/IAPSO/abstracts/IC-02/IC02-49.htm.

130 National Academy of Sciences. "El Niño and La Niña: Tracing the Dance of Ocean and Atmosphere." March, 2000. http://web.archive.org/web/20050516054542/http://iceage .umeqs.maine.edu/pdfs/PDFelnino2.pdf.

131 National Weather Service. "Weekly ENSO Update." NOAA/NWS Climate Prediction Center. http://www.cpc.ncep.noaa.gov/products/precip/CWlink/MJO/enso.shtml.

132   Zhang, Rong-Hua and Levitus, Sydney. "Structure and Cycle of Decadal Variability of
      Upper-Ocean Temperature in the North Pacific." *NOAA/AMS Journal of Climate,* Sep-
      tember 9, 1996, pp. 710–727. http://journals.ametsoc.org/doi/abs/10.1175/1520-
      0442%281997%29010%3C0710%3ASACODV%3E2.0.CO%3B2.

133   Landscheidt, Theodor. "Solar Activity Controls El Niño and La Niña." Scrhoeter Insti-
      tute for Research in Cycles of Solar Activity, Nova Scotia, Canada. http://web.archive
      .org/web/20011116200002/http://www.vision.net.au/~daly/sun-enso/sun-enso.htm.

134   USGS Earthquake Hazards Program. "Global Earthquake Search." U.S. Geological Sur-
      vey National Earthquake Information Center, July 10, 2003. http://web.archive.org/
      web/20030628162258/http://neic.usgs.gov/neis/epic/epic_global.html.

135   Baxter, Stefanie J. "Earthquake Basics." USGS/Delaware Geological Survey, Special Pub-
      lication no. 23, University of Delaware, 2000. http://www.dgs.udel.edu/sites/dgs.udel
      .edu/files/publications/sp23.pdf.

136   Watson, Kathie. "Volcanic and Seismic Hazards on the Island of Hawaii: Earthquake
      Hazards." U. S. Geological Survey, July 18, 1997. http://pubs.usgs.gov/gip/hazards/earth
      quakes.html.

137   These figures were derived from the USGS/NEIC (PDE) 1973–Present database on the
      USGS Web site referenced below. Each year from 1973 to 2003 was individually searched
      in this database with the dates January 1 to December 31, with a magnitude range of
      3.0–10. The results were downloaded in comma-delimited spreadsheet format and
      imported into Microsoft Excel 2003, where the exact number of line entries (one per
      quake) could be automatically counted for each year. The link to replicate this study,
      when we conducted it in summer 2003, is as follows: USGS Earthquake Hazards Pro-
      gram. "Global Earthquake Search." U.S. Geological Survey National Earthquake Infor-
      mation Center, July 10, 2003. http://web.archive.org/web/20030628162258/http://neic
      .usgs.gov/neis/epic/epic_global.html.

138   USGS Earthquake Hazards Program. "Are Earthquakes Really on the Increase?" U.S.
      Geological Survey National Earthquake Information Center, June 18, 2003. http://web
      .archive.org/web/20051214124438/http://neic.usgs.gov/neis/general/increase_in_earth-
      quakes.html.

139   Ibid.

140   Chandler, Lynn. "Satellites Reveal a Mystery of Large Change in Earth's Gravity Field."
      NASA/Goddard Space Flight Center, August 1, 2002. http://www.gsfc.nasa.gov/
      topstory/20020801gravityfield.html.

141   Jones, Nicola. "Anomalies hint at magnetic pole flip." *New Scientist,* April 10, 2002.
      http://www.newscientist.com/article/dn2152-anomalies-hint-at-magnetic-pole-flip.html.

142   Whitehouse, David. "Is the Earth preparing to flip?" BBC News Online World Edition,
      March 27, 2003. http://news.bbc.co.uk/2/hi/science/nature/2889127.stm.

143   Radowitz, Bernd. "Powerful Storm Hits Southern Brazil Coast." AP News, March 27,
      2004. http://www.highbeam.com/doc/1P1-92767036.html.

144   "Reaping the Whirlwind: Extreme weather prompts unprecedented global warming
      alert." *The Independent.* July 3, 2003. http://www.independent.co.uk/environment/
      reaping-the-whirlwind-585577.html.

145   UNEP/WMO Intergovernmental Panel on Climate Change. Climate Change 2001:
      Working Group I: The Scientific Basis. Chapter 2: Observed Climate Variability and
      Change, Executive Summary. UNEP/WMO/IPCC, 2001. http://www.grida.no/
      climate/ipcc_tar/wg1/049.htm.

146   Ibid.

147   Ibid.

148   Ibid.

149   Ibid.

150   Press Association. "Warming doubles glacier melt." Guardian Unlimited, October 17, 2003. http://www.guardian.co.uk/science/2003/oct/17/sciencenews.theguardianlifesupplement.

151   Buis, Alan. "NASA Study Finds Rapid Changes in Earth's Polar Ice Sheets." NASA/JPL, August 30, 2002. http://www.jpl.nasa.gov/releases/2002/release_2002_168.html.

152   Hinrichsen, Don. "Hopkins Report: Time Running Out for the Environment." Population Reports Press Release, Johns Hopkins University/Bloomberg School of Public Health Information and Knowledge for Optimal Health Project, January 5, 2001. http://info.k4health.org/pr/press/010501.shtml.

153   Whitty, Julia. "Animal Extinction—the greatest threat to mankind." *The Independent*, April 30, 2007. http://news.independent.co.uk/environment/article2494659.ece (accessed December 2010).

154   Shemansky, D. E., Ph.D. Curriculum Vitae. University of Southern California http://ame-www.usc.edu/bio/dons/ds_biosk.html.

155   Cleggett-Haleim, Paula and Exler, Randee. "New Discoveries by NASA's EUV Explorer Presented." NASA Science Blog, Release 93-105, June 7, 1993. http://www.scienceblog.com/community/older/archives/D/archnas1848.html.

156   ESA. "Third day brings bonanza of new results." European Space Agency Science and Technology, October 5, 2000, last updated June 10, 2003. http://sci.esa.int/science-e/www/object/index.cfm?fobjectid=24680.

157   NASA/JPL. "6. Theme 4: The Interstellar Medium." NASA/JPL/Ulysses, 2003. http://web.archive.org/web/20060107084150/http://ulysses.jpl.nasa.gov/5UlsThemes3-4.pdf.

158   Clark, Stuart. "Galactic Dust Storm Enters Solar System." *New Scientist*, August 5, 2003. http://www.newscientist.com/article/dn4021-galactic-dust-storm-enters-solar-system.html.

159   Phillips, Tony. "Voyager Makes an Interstellar Discovery." Science@NASA, December 23, 2009. http://science.nasa.gov/headlines/y2009/23dec_voyager.htm (accessed December 2010).

160   Cooney, Michael. "NASA watching 'perfect storm' of galactic cosmic rays." Network World, October 1, 2009. http://www.computerworld.com/s/article/9138769/NASA_watching_perfect_storm_of_galactic_cosmic_rays?taxonomyId=17 (accessed December 2010),

161   Gray, Richard. "Sun's Protective Bubble Is Shrinking." *The Telegraph*, October 18, 2008. http://www.telegraph.co.uk/news/worldnews/northamerica/usa/3222476/Suns-protective-bubble-is-shrinking.html (accessed December 2010).

162   Lallement, Rosine. "The interaction of the heliosphere with the interstellar medium." In *The Century of Space Science*, Ch. 50, pgs. 1191–1216. 2001. http://www.springer.com/?SWGID-4-102-45-132575-0.

163   "Trip to outer space makes nasty bacteria nastier." CBC News September 24, 2007. http://www.cbc.ca/technology/story/2007/09/24/spacebug.html?ref=rss (accessed December 2010).

164   Derbyshire, David. "Anyone for rocket salad? How the Chinese are now growing mega veg from seeds they sent into space." Mail Online, May 12, 2008. http://www.dailymail.co.uk/pages/live/articles/news/worldnews.html?in_article_id=565766&in_page_id=1811 (accessed December 2010).

165   Spottiswoode, S.J.P. (1997a) Apparent association between anomalous cognition experiments and local sidereal time. *Journal of Scientific Exploration* 11 (2), summer. pp. 109–122. http://www.jsasoc.com/docs/JSE-LST.pdf.

166   Kazan, Casey and Hill, Josh. "Is the Human Species in Evolution's Fast Lane?" *Daily Galaxy*, April 17, 2008. (Adapted from a University of Wisconsin press release.). http://www.dailygalaxy.com/my_weblog/2008/04/is-the-human-sp.html.

167   Chatelain, Maurice. *Our Ancestors Came from Outer Space*. New York: Dell, 1977.

168   Ibid., pp. 26–28.

169   Ibid., p. 28.

170   Ibid., pp. 28–29.

171   Ibid., p. 37.

172   Ibid., p. 49.

Chapter Nineteen

1   Baldry, H. C. "Who Invented the Golden Age?" *The Classical Quarterly*, (Jan.–Apr. 1952), pp. 83–92. http://www.jstor.org/stable/636861.

2   Ibid.

3   Havewala, Porus Homi. "History of the Ancient Aryans: Outlined in Zoroastrian Scriptures." Traditional Zoroastrianism, 1995. http://tenets.zoroastrianism.com/histar33.html.

4   Ibid.

5   Ibid.

6   Ibid.

7   Ibid.

8   Boyce, Mary and Grenet, Frantz. *A History of Zoroastrianism. Volume Three: Zoroastrianism Under Macedonian and Roman Rule*. Leiden, Netherlands: E. J. Brill, 1991. http://books.google.com/books?id=MWiMV6llZesC.

9   Ibid. p. 366.

10   Ibid., p. 382.

11   Ibid., p. 400.

12   Ibid., p. 443.

13   Ibid., p. 428.

14   Ibid., pp. 444–445.

15   Ibid., pp. 365–366.

16   Baldry, H. C. "Who Invented the Golden Age?" Op. cit.

17   Finley, Michael J. "U Kahlay Katunob—The Maya short count and katun prophecy." Maya Astronomy, February 2004. http://web.archive.org/web/20040305155540/http://members.shaw.ca/mjfinley/katun.html (accessed December 2010).

18   Henry, William and Gray, Mark. *Freedom's Gate: The Lost Symbols in the U.S. Capitol*. Hendersonville, TN: Scala Dei, 2009. http://www.williamhenry.net (accessed December 2010).

19   Ibid., p. 222.

20   Ibid., p. 119.

21   Ibid., pp. 143–147.

22   Ibid., p. 25.

23   Foulou.com. http://www.folou.com/thread-88064-1-1.html (accessed May 2010).

24   Zhaxki Zhuoma.net. "Rainbow Body." http://www.zhaxizhuoma.net/SEVEN_JEWELS/HOLY%20EVENTS/RAINBOW%20BODY/RBindex.html (accessed May 2010).

25   Norbu, Namkhai. *Dream Yoga and the Practice of Natural Light*. p. 67. Ithaca, NY: Snow Lion Productions, 1992.

26   Holland, Gail. "The Rainbow Body." *Institute of Noetic Sciences Review*, March–May 2002. http://www.snowlionpub.com/pages/N59_9.html.

27   Ibid.

28   Ibid.

Chapter Twenty

1   "Galaxy has 'billions of Earths.'" BBC News, February 15, 2009. http://news.bbc.co.uk/2/
    hi/science/nature/7891132.stm (accessed December 2010).

2   Pawlowski, A. "Galaxy may be full of Earths, alien life." CNN, February 25, 2009.
    http://www.cnn.com/2009/TECH/space/02/25/galaxy.planets.kepler/index.html
    (accessed December 2009).

3   Lynch, Gary and Granger, Richard. "What Happened to the Hominids Who May Have
    Been Smarter Than Us?" *Discover Magazine,* December 28, 2009. http://discovermagazine
    .com/2009/the-brain-2/28-what-happened-to-hominids-who-were-smarter-than-us.

4   Ibid.

5   Ibid.

6   "Witness Testimony-UFO's at Nuclear Weapons Bases." National Press Club. September
    27, 2010. http://press.org/events/witness-testimony-ufos-nuclear-weapons-bases (accessed
    January 2010).

7   "Ex-Air Force Personnel: UFOs Deactivated Nukes." CBS News. September 28, 2010.
    http://www.cbsnews.com/stories/2010/09/28/national/main6907702.shtml (accessed
    January 2010).

8   Jamieson, Alastair. "UFO alert: police officer sees aliens at crop circle." *The Telegraph,*
    October 20, 2009. http://www.telegraph.co.uk/news/newstopics/howaboutthat/
    ufo/6394256/UFO-alert-police-officer-sees-aliens-at-crop-circle.html (accessed Decem-
    ber 2010).

9   Knapton, Sarah. "Dog walker met UFO 'alien' with Scandinavian accent." *The Tele-
    graph,* March 22, 2009. http://www.telegraph.co.uk/news/newstopics/howaboutthat/
    5031587/Dog-walker-met-UFO-alien-with-Scandinavian-accent.html (accessed December
    2009).

10 Ibid.

11 "Crop Circle at Avebury Manor (2), nr Avebury, Wiltshire." Crop Circle Connector, July
    15, 2008. http://www.cropcirclearchives.com/archives/2008/aveburymanor/avebury
    manor2008a.html (accessed December 2010).

12 Stray, Geoff. "Crop Circle Anomalies." Diagnosis 2012. http://mmmgroup.altervista
    .org/e-ancrops.html (accessed December 2010).

13 Manistre, Hugh. "Crop Circles: A Beginner's Guide." Scribd.com., 1997. http://www
    .scribd.com/doc/211243/Crop-circles (accessed December 2010).

14 Pratt, David. "Crop Circles and their Message." Part One. June 2005. http://web.archive
    .org/web/20071116163223/http://ourworld.compuserve.com/homepages/dp5/cropcirc1
    .htm (accessed December 2010).

15 Ibid.

16 Pratt, David. "Crop Circles and their Message." Part Two. June 2005. http://web.archive
    .org/web/20071117174652/ourworld.compuserve.com/homepages/dp5/cropcirc2.htm
    (accessed December 2010).

17 Howe, Robert Lucien. "The Science Behind Project Looking Glass." End Secrecy discus-
    sion forum, May 23, 2002. http://www.stealthskater.com/Documents/LookingGlass_2
    .pdf (accessed December 2010).

18 Ibid.

19 India Daily Technology Team. "In 1998 near the nuclear testing site when Indian Air
    Force encountered hovering extraterrestrial UFOs." *India Daily,* April 29, 2006. http://
    www.indiadaily.com/editorial/8306.asp (accessed December 2010).

20 Staff Reporter from Bangalore. "The secret UFO files inside Indian Space Research
    Organization—when will India reveal the existence of UFOs or become the member of

the US Security Council?" *India Daily*, May 26, 2008. http://www.indiadaily.com/editorial/19513.asp.

21 Ibid.

22 Ibid.

23 Singhal, Juhi. "A secret project in India's Defense Research Organization that can change the world as we know it—anti-gravity lifters tested in Himalayas?" *India Daily*, December 4, 2004. http://www.indiadaily.com/editorial/12-04e-04.asp (accessed December 2010).

24 India Daily Technology Team. "Will India reveal the existence of the UFO bases in the moon? *India Daily*, October 25, 2008. http://www.indiadaily.com/editorial/20219.asp.

25 India Daily Technology Team. "Not all UFOs are extraterrestrials—some are time travelers from future human civilization using the same network of wormholes." *India Daily*, July 4, 2005. http://www.indiadaily.com/editorial/3439.asp.

26 India Daily Technology Team. "Achieving technical capabilities of alien UFOs—creating artificial wormholes in ionosphere to traverse into the parallel universe." *India Daily*, July 8, 2005. http://www.indiadaily.com/editorial/3499.asp.

27 Ibid.

28 India Daily Technology Team. "Detaching 3D space from time is the techniques extraterrestrial UFOs use for stealth, propagation and communication." *India Daily*, October 7, 2006. http://www.indiadaily.com/editorial/13657.asp (accessed December 2010).

29 India Daily Technology Team. "Time is multidimensional—a new concept from Extraterrestrial UFOs allows coexistence of one entity in many different time dimensions." *India Daily*, July 9, 2005. http://www.indiadaily.com/editorial/3509.asp (accessed December 2010).

30 Ibid.

31 India Daily Technology Team. "Creation of "negative" mass is the key to success for advanced alien and future human civilizations." *India Daily*, July 9, 2005. http://www.indiadaily.com/editorial/3510.asp (accessed December 2010).

32 India Daily Technology Team. "Using multidimensional time dimensions to change the future." *India Daily*, July 13, 2005. http://www.indiadaily.com/editorial/3568.asp (accessed December 2010).

33 Ibid.

34 India Daily Technology Team. "The concept of negative time—common in the parallel universes and fascinating to live through." *India Daily*, July 22, 2005. http://www.indiadaily.com/editorial/3726.asp (accessed December 2010).

35 India Daily Technology Team. "The parallel universe exists within us—it is closer to you than you can ever imagine." *India Daily*, July 23, 2005. http://www.indiadaily.com/editorial/3728.asp (accessed December 2010).

36 India Daily Technology Team. "Advanced alien civilizations are capable of traveling from physical to parallel universes by artificially accelerating the time dimension." *India Daily*, July 26, 2005. http://www.indiadaily.com/editorial/3780.asp (accessed December 2010).

37 India Daily Technology Team. "The fact that our mind can traverse the spatial dimensions of the parallel universe shows we are genetically connected to the aliens." *India Daily*, July 27, 2005. http://www.indiadaily.com/editorial/3818.asp (accessed December 2010).

38 India Daily Technology Team. "2012—official revealing visit from M15 Globular Star Cluster." *India Daily*, July 29, 2005. http://www.indiadaily.com/editorial/3835.asp (accessed December 2010).

39   India Daily Technology Team. "Halting and reversing time—reverse engineered tech-
      nologies from extraterrestrial UFOs." *India Daily,* August 10, 2005. http://www.indiadaily
      .com/editorial/4041.asp (accessed December 2010).

40   India Daily Technology Team. "International Space Agencies getting ready for accepting
      the inevitable—UFOs and Extraterrestrial civilizations exist." *India Daily,* April 12,
      2006. http://www.indiadaily.com/editorial/7976.asp (accessed December 2010).

41   Sen, Mihir. "December 21, 2012, the world will change forever as major Governments are
      forced to confess the existence of advanced extraterrestrial UFOs. *India Daily,* December
      29, 2006. http://www.indiadaily.com/editorial/14929.asp (accessed December 2010).

42   Staff Reporter. "An orderly visit of Extraterrestrial Federation in 2012 representing 88 star
      constellations—the world is getting ready for the most spectacular event." *India Daily,*
      May 12, 2005. http://www.indiadaily.com/editorial/2656.asp. (accessed December 2010).

43   India Daily Technology Team. "Galactic alignment and formal extraterrestrial
      visitation—the history tells us they will expose their existence in December 2012 or
      after." *India Daily,* January 4, 2007. http://www.indiadaily.com/editorial/15022.asp
      (accessed December 2010).

44   Pippin, Jerry. "Jerry Pippin Interviews Mr. X." http://www.jerrypippin.com/UFO_
      Files_mr_x.htm (accessed June 2010).

45   Ibid.

Acknowledgments

1   Elkins, Don; Rueckert, Carla and McCarty, Jim. *The Law of One Study Guide.* Compiled
      by Bob Childers, Ph.D. and David Wilcock. The Divine Cosmos. http://divinecosmos
      .com/index.php/start-here/books-free-online/23-the-law-of-one-study-guide (accessed
      January 2011).

Index

plants
consumption of, 23–24
effect of pyramids on, 152, 155, 198
extinction rates for, 407
and flow of time, 252–53, 255
gravity-shielding effect used by, 289–90
and light, 161
and local interstellar energy, 409
mind-reading abilities of, 14–20, *15*, 68
restoration of extinct species of, 152, 155, 198–99
transformation of, 208
wave effect in, 290
plasma structures, 184–85
plate tectonics theory, 320
Plato, 51–52
Platonic solids
coherence of, 325
and Moon's model, 328–29, *329*
Neolithic carvings of, 338
and planetary orbits, 337, 340–41, 343
Pliny, 121
Plot, Robert, 366, 442
Pluto, 343, 403, 414, 415
politics, global, 135
pollution, 404–6
poltergeists, 369, 370–71
polyethylene film, 257
polygraphy, 13–21
Polynesians' "lines of light," 317
Popp, Fritz-Albert, 167–68, 173–75, 179, 197, 228, 252
portals
appearance of, 361–62
crop circles and fairy rings as, 380–82, *382*
and dinosaurs, 382–87
effect of coherence on, 359
effect of traumatic events on, 364
and geomagnetic activity, 370
gravity shielding in, 362
Mayan's tracking of, 352, 354, 358–59, 361
between stars, 360
and sub-surface rotating spherical layer of Earth, 353–54
between the Sun and Earth, 359
and Temporary Local Risk factor, 352–54
prayers, 24, 241
precession of the equinoxes, 101–5, *104*
and ancient civilizations, 117, 157

centrality of, 117, 126
and Cotterell's solar cycle, 357–58
and Great Pyramid, 125, *126*
and Great Seal of the United States, 129
Hipparchus's rediscovery of, 112–14
and human evolution, 213, 215
and imperfections of humanity, 127
and Nineveh Constant, 412
symbolized on U.S. currency, *128*
Presence of the Past, The (Sheldrake), 70
Price, Weston, 65–66
Primitive Mountain, 43, 104, 126
Princeton Engineering Anomalies Research laboratory, 236–41
Project Camelot, 301, 303, 459
Project Looking Glass, 447–48, *449*
Pruitt, Robert, 200
psychic abilities, 27–29, 235, 409
pterosaurs, 385–86
Puharich, Andrija, 28–30
Purcell, Edward, 281
Pure Consciousness, 93
Pushkin, V. N., 20
Puthoff, Hal, 20–21, 243, 283
PVC plastic, 257
pyramids, 139–56
advanced technology of, 145
and baetyl, 104, 117, 128
capstones of, 44, 127, 135, 157
and coherence, 246, 344, 345
on coins, *46*, 104
energy around, 148, 151, 155
and geological/meteorological events, 151, 152–53, 183
and geometric vortex points, 315
Golod's construction of, 138, 143–45, 248
healing properties of, 146–47, 148, 155, 242
legends of, 139–40
of Mayan culture, 358
preservation properties of, 139–40, 141–42
pyramid power movement, 139–40
pyramid-shaped mountains, 152–53
research on powers of, 143–47
and Roman empire, 105
Russian investigations of, 141–46, 149–53, 157, 183, 240, 344
shape of, 244–45, *246*
and spiraling gravity currents, 292

About the Author

DAVID WILCOCK is a professional author, lecturer, filmmaker, musician and researcher of ancient civilizations, consciousness science, and new paradigms of matter and energy. He has fastidiously documented and analyzed his dreams every morning since September 1993. David graduated with a B.A. in psychology from the State University of New York at New Paltz in 1995, followed by two years of postgraduate jobs in mental health–related fields. He began posting research articles on the Internet in 1996, wrote his first full online book investigating the Source Field in 1998, and launched his own Web site, DivineCosmos.com, beginning in 1999. David worked as a full-time intuitive consultant, for a total of five hundred paid clients, beginning in 1998—and retired from this practice in 2005 to move to Los Angeles and work as the executive producer and cowriter of *Convergence: The Movie*—partnering up with *Contact* screenwriter Jim Hart in 2009.

David is also the subject and coauthor of the international bestseller *The Reincarnation of Edgar Cayce?*, which explores the remarkable facial, astrological and character similarities between these two men—and also examines the numerous connections between David's work, the Law of One series, and the Cayce Readings. David is also the lead vocalist on Wanderer Awakening, a "metaphysical musical" based on the ageless wisdom of all spiritual traditions—cowritten with nine-time Grammy-winning musician and composer Larry Seyer. David has appeared in seven episodes of History Channel's *Ancient Aliens* series, a National Geographic special on Atlantis released in May/June 2011, and other television programs still in development as of this writing. David's documentary film *The 2012 Enigma* was the number one most-viewed video on Google.com for December 1, 2008—and its stunning popularity and content provided the initial inspiration for David to write this book.